St. Paul Convent
Fr. M. J. Bresnahan.

D1269995

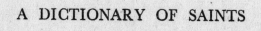

A DICTIONARY OF SAINTS

A DICTIONARY OF SAINTS

*Being also an Index to the Revised Edition
of Alban Butler's 'Lives of the Saints'*

Compiled by
DONALD ATTWATER

P. J. KENEDY AND SONS
NEW YORK

First Printed, 1938
Second Impression, 1942

MADE AND PRINTED IN GREAT BRITAIN

PREFACE

THIS book is, as the title page says, both an index to the revised edition of Alban Butler's *Lives of the Saints* (edited, as regards the first six volumes by Father Herbert Thurston, S.J., and as regards the last six by Father Thurston and the present writer) and a catalogue with brief particulars of the principal saints and *beati* venerated throughout the ages in the Catholic Church.

The heading of each entry consists of the name of the saint, description, date of commemoration, and volume and page reference to Butler's *Lives*.

Name. The names are indexed so far as possible in the form most usual in England, failing that, generally in the Latin form. The Latin form of a name is also often given in italics at the end of the notice, and has usually been taken from the Roman Martyrology. There is an occasional alteration of the form of a name from that used in Butler's *Lives* when this was necessary for uniformity in the index. Certain groups of martyrs are indexed under the name of the place where they suffered, including several groups of the English martyrs. A few saints have been added that were omitted from the revised Butler's *Lives*, and for them, of course, there is no index reference.

Description. This is given as *bishop, martyr, virgin, apostle, doctor, abbot*, according to the liturgical office of the saint or the Roman Martyrology, and does not necessarily agree with the historical fact or probability. When there is no description the saint was either a *confessor* or *holy woman* according to sex.

Date of commemoration. This usually agrees with the date of entry in Butler's *Lives* and is, according to circumstances, the date (or principal date) on which the saint's feast is or was observed, or the date given in the Roman Martyrology or other kalendar, or the date of death.

Order of names. When there are several saints of the same name the order is as follows, according to the most common usage in referring to them : the name alone (if more than one, in order of date) ; the name alone with a partner ; the name followed by surname, in alphabetical order of the surnames ; the name followed by an epithet to which it is joined by a preposition, in the alphabetical order of the epithets ; when there is a large number of names (*e.g.*, John) epithets of place are grouped together after the others. For example :

> John, St. July 21.
> John, St, ap. December 27.
> John and Peter.
> John Colombini.
> John Fisher.
> John the Almoner.

John of the Cross.
John of Beverley.
John of Parma.

Abbreviations.   b. = born.
d. = died.
c. = *circa*, about.
cd. = canonized.
bd. = beatified.
c.c. = ancient cultus confirmed by the Holy See.
h.d.q. = hanged, drawn, and quartered.
ab. = abbot.
ap. = apostle.
bp. = bishop.
doct. = doctor of the Church.
evang. = evangelist.
mart. = martyr.
virg. = virgin.

The asterisk (*) indicates that the saint's name figures in the Roman Martyrology.

The dagger (†) indicates that the saint concerned is commemorated liturgically in the general kalendar of the Western Church (the so-called universal kalendar).

It is perhaps necessary to remark that some of the greatest of the saints venerated in the Church have never been canonized, as the expression is now understood, since for centuries there was no formal process of canonization. The first solemn canonization at Rome is said to have been of St Ulric of Augsburg by Pope John XV in 993, and the present Roman process has been in full operation only since the time of Pope Urban VIII (d. 1644). Another point I may refer to in terms in which I wrote of it in the November volume of Butler's *Lives*, under the feast of All Saints. It is sometimes objected against the ideal of holiness held up by the Church before all men indiscriminately that it is incompatible with that secular life in which the overwhelming majority of men and women are, and are meant to be, engaged. And in support of this objection it is alleged that more clergy and members of religious orders of both sexes become saints than do lay people, more relatively and perhaps absolutely. This is not known to be so, and is impossible of proof. If it be a question of *canonized* and *beatified* saints, then it is true that there are far more religious than lay people, and also far more bishops than priests and men than women. But canonization and beatification are exterior marks, "certificates," if the expression may be allowed, with which the Church honours certain individuals, a selection from among those many holy ones who contribute to her sanctity. And in the making of that selection some purely natural factors necessarily come into play. A religious order has the means and the motive for forwarding the "cause" of an individual who in other circumstances would have never been heard of outside his own circle; the episcopal office brings its holder into greater prominence, lends of itself a weight to his name, and carries with it the means and influence to prosecute his cause; and men, as opposed to women, have by their very sex greater opportunities of notable achievement and of the fame of their virtues becoming widespread in the world. But even so a modification is taking place. Among those saints or candidates for canonization in our own day whose cause, where it has been introduced, was or is the interest of so many diverse people that it could almost be said to be proposed by the Church herself, and not by a particular country, order, or diocese, a greater variety of " states of life " is exhibited : a pope, Pius X, and a country parson, St John Vianney ; St Teresa of Lisieux, a simple nun ; Frederick Ozanam, Contardo Ferrini, Ludovico Necchi, Matt Talbot, laymen ; Blessed Anna Maria Taigi was the wife of an obscure man-servant, but her public recognition is probably due, under God, to the interest of the Trinitarian Order, of which she was a tertiary. As Alban Butler reminds us, there is but one Gospel, one Sacrifice, one Redeemer, one Heaven, and one way to Heaven : it has been traced out by Jesus Christ, and the rule of salvation laid down by Him is invariable and the same for all.

D.A.

A DICTIONARY OF SAINTS

*The heading of each entry gives the name and description of the Saint, the
date of commemoration, and the volume and page reference for a fuller account
in the twelve volumes of Alban Butler's* Lives of the Saints, *edited by Fr.
Herbert Thurston, S.J., and Donald Attwater. The abbreviations and
order are explained on p.* vi *of the Preface.*

ABBO, ST, ab. and mart. November 13.   Nov., p. 161
    Before becoming abbot of Fleury Abbo was for two years
director of the monastery school at Ramsey in Huntingdonshire.
He was among the most conspicuous monks of his time, and
favoured the reform of Cluny. While trying to restore discipline in a
Gascon monastery he was killed in a brawl between two parties whom he
sought to reconcile, in 1004.

ABBO. *See also* Goericus.

†*ABDON and **SENNEN, SS,** marts. July 30.   JULY, p. 415
    They were Persians who were martyred at Rome, probably in the per-
secution of Diocletian. Their feast was already known in 354.

*ABERCIUS, ST, bp. October 22.   OCT., p. 299
    He was bishop of Hieropolis during the second half of the second century
and knowledge of his existence and of his visit to Rome at the age of
seventy-two is due to the epitaph written by himself ; the authenticity of
this epitaph was confirmed archæologically by Sir W. M. Ramsay in 1882.

*ABIBUS, ST, mart. November 15.   Nov., p. 186
    He was a deacon at Edessa, martyred by burning in 322, and buried
with his friends, SS Gurias and Samonas.

ABRAHAM, ST, bp. February 14.   FEB., p. 217
    A hermit in Syria who forwarded the conversion of a village in the
Lebanon by borrowing money to pay its taxes. He was made bishop of
Harran in Mesopotamia. d. *c.* 422.

*ABRAHAM KIDUNAIA, ST. March 16.   MAR., p. 275
    A hermit in the desert near Edessa, who had fled from his wealthy home
and the marriage arranged for him. He was much sought after for spiritual
guidance. Eventually he was ordained priest and converted the heathen
town of Beth-Kiduna after he had received much ill-treatment at the hands
of its inhabitants. He was a friend of St Ephraem. d. *c.* 366. The story
of his niece Mary, which is associated with the life of St Abraham, is
probably spurious.

ABRAHAM OF KRATIA, ST, bp. December 6.   DEC., p. 90
    He was b. at Emesa in Syria in 474, and while very young became abbot

of a monastery at Kratia in Bithynia ; later he was made bishop in the same place. Twice he ran away from his offices in search of quiet ; the second time he found a refuge in a Palestinian monastery, where he d. *c.* 558.

*ABUNDIUS, BD, bp. April 2. APR., p. 22

A Greek priest who became bishop of Como ; he was an able theologian and preacher, and was Pope St Leo's legate to the Council of Constantinople in 450. d. *c.* 468.

*ABUNDIUS, etc., **SS,** marts. September 16. SEPT., p. 204

Their legendary *acta* state that Abundius was a Roman priest, Abundantius a deacon, and Marcian a senator whose son, John, was raised from the dead by Abundius. They were all martyred *c.* 303.

ACACIUS, ST, mart. May 8. MAY, p. 97

He was a Cappadocian centurion, stationed in Thrace, who was beheaded for the faith of Christ at Byzantium in 303 or 305.

ACCA, ST., bp. October 20. OCT., p. 276

Acca was a disciple of St Wilfrid and succeeded him in the see of Hexham, where his activity was very varied. St Bede refers to him as being " great in the sight of God and man." d. 742.

ACHATIUS, ST, bp. March 31. MAR., p. 453

A bishop in hither Asia who is said so to have impressed the emperor Decius by his defence of Christianity that he was suffered to profess his religion in peace. d. *c.* 251.

*ACISCLUS and **VICTORIA, SS,** marts. November 17. NOV., p. 216

These martyrs were put to death, probably at Cordova, in the imperial persecutions, but even the approximate year is not known.

ADALBALD D'OSTREVANT, ST, mart. February 2. FEB., p. 40

Son or grandson of St Gertrude of Hamage, and attached to the court of Dagobert I. He married a Gascon girl called Rictrudis, with whom he lived in great holiness and happiness. But some of her relatives did not approve of the match, and so long as sixteen years after, in 652, ambushed Adalbald and killed him. Rictrudis is also venerated as a saint (May 12). *Adebaldus.*

*ADALBERT, ST, bp. and mart. April 23. APR., p. 269

B. in Bohemia in 956 and educated by St Adalbert of Magdeburg. He was elected bishop of Prague in 983, but his holiness seemed to make no impression on his flock and he retired for five years to Rome, where he became a Benedictine. Twice he attempted to return to his diocese, but each time was unable to do anything with the turbulent people there. He went to preach the gospel with more success among the heathen of Poland and Prussia ; but he met with opposition there as well and was martyred by Prussians near Danzig in 997. St Adalbert (Voitech) is greatly venerated in Yugoslavia. *Adelbertus.*

ADALBERT, ST, bp. June 20. JUNE, p. 254

Adalbert was sent from Trier as a missionary to Russia in 961, but all his companions were slain, and he returned to become abbot of Weissenburg, where he did much to encourage learning. In 968 he was nominated first archbishop of Magdeburg ; in this office he laboured unceasingly for the conversion of the Wends. d. 981.

*ADALBERT OF EGMONT, ST. June 25. JUNE, p. 336

He was a Northumbrian who was a monk in Ireland and then one of the deacons of St Willibrord in Friesland. His gentleness, patience, and humility made a deep impression around Egmont, where he laboured and d. *c.* 740 (?).

ADAM. *See* Adamnan.

ADAM, BD. December 22. DEC., p. 222

This Cistercian monk of Loccum in Saxony lived early in the thirteenth century : nothing is known of him except that he said he had been twice miraculously cured of sickness.

ADAMNAN, ST, ab. September 23. SEPT., p. 297

Adamnan (Eunan, " Adam "), fifth abbot of Iona, is best remembered for his Life of St Columba, one of the most important ancient hagiographical documents in existence. He spent a good many years propagating the celebration of Easter on its right date in Ireland and other Celtic centres, but he was not successful in imposing it in his own monastery. d. 704. The feast of St Adamnan is observed in the diocese of Argyll and the Isles, and a commemoration is made of him throughout Ireland (he was b. at Drumhome in county Donegal), but the Eunan of Raphoe was probably a different person. *Adamnanus.*

ADAMNAN OF COLDINGHAM, ST. December 2. DEC., p. 28

He was an Irish monk at Coldingham, near Berwick, who lived a life of great austerity in expiation of a youthful sin. He foretold the destruction of his monastery because of its irregularities. d. *c.* 680.

*ADAUCUS, ST, mart. February 7. FEB., p. 103

Adaucus was a distinguished Roman, a magistrate and imperial finance minister, who was put to death for the Faith in 303 while still holding the latter office. With him are connected a number of Phrygian Christians whose town was burnt over their heads and them with it.

ADDAI and MARI, SS, bps. August 5. AUG., p. 62

They are venerated as the evangelizers of East Syria and Persia, where they are known as the Holy Apostles. St Addai (Thaddeus) was probably a missionary in Edessa, before the end of the second century ; of St Mari nothing certain is known.

ADELA, ST. December 24. DEC., p. 234

She was the sister of St Irmina. When she became a widow she established and ruled a convent at Pfalzel, near Trier. d. *c.* 730.

ADELAIDE, ST, virg. February 5. FEB., p. 85

Abbess of Bellich, near Bonn, and then of a convent at Cologne. d. 1015. *Adelheidis.*

ADELAIDE, ST, virg. June 15. JUNE, p. 189

A young Cistercian nun of Brussels whose simple life, written down by a contemporary, has survived. In early life she contracted leprosy and had to be segregated from her community; she bore her affliction with ever-increasing patience, and was strengthened by ecstasies and visions. d. 1250. c.c. 1907.

ADELAIDE, ST. December 16. DEC., p. 184

On the death of her husband, Lothaire of Italy, she was treated with great brutality by Berengarius of Ivrea, but was rescued by the emperor Otto the Great, who married her. After his death in 973 she was badly treated by her son Otto II, and later by her daughter-in-law, who was regent for Otto III. Adelaide herself succeeded to this position, but she was then too old to cope with it. She was peace-loving and generous, and took as her counsellors St Adalbert of Magdeburg and SS Majolus and Odilo of Cluny. d. 999.

ADELARD, ST, ab. January 2.   JAN., p. 38
    Otherwise *Adalhard*, b. 753. Grandson of Charles Martel. Became a monk and abbot of Corbie. Forced by Charlemagne to take part in public life, and persecuted for political reasons. Founded the abbey of New Corbie. d. 827. *Adelardus.*

ADELELMUS, ST, ab. January 30.   JAN., p. 386
    Benedictine abbot of Chaise Dieu and then of Burgos. d. *c.* 1095.

*ADO, BD, bp. December 16.   DEC., p. 182
    He became archbishop of Vienne in 859 and was an altogether admirable prelate, but he is best remembered as the compiler of a martyrology which bears his name ; this and other writings of his were responsible for the perpetuation of a number of baseless and misleading statements. d. 875.

ADOLPH, ST, bp. February 14.   FEB., p. 223
    Little is known of him except that he was bishop of Osnabrück and d. June 30, 1224. *Adulphus.*

ADOLPH, ST, bp. June 17.   JUNE, p. 220
    He was the brother of St Botolph and is said to have been a missionary bishop in Friesland. He was buried with his brother at Ikenhoe. *Adulphus.*

ADRIAN, ST, mart. March 4.   MAR., p. 51
    During one of their numerous descents upon the coast of Scotland the Danes murdered St Adrian and his fellow missionary monks on the isle of May in the Firth of Forth, *c.* 875. His identity and earlier history are uncertain. *Hadrianus.*

*ADRIAN, ST, mart. August 26.   AUG., p. 318
    Nothing is known of this Adrian, whom it is difficult to disentangle from other martyrs of the same name.

*ADRIAN III, ST, pope. July 8.   JULY, p. 95
    He became pope in 884 but there is nothing in the little that is known of his brief pontificate (he d. 885) to account for his ancient cultus in the diocese of Modena, which was confirmed in 1892.

*ADRIAN and EUBULUS, SS, marts. March 5.   MAR., p. 57
    Martyred at Cæsarea in Palestine when they came to visit the Christians in prison there in 308.

†*ADRIAN and NATALIA, SS, marts. September 8.   SEPT., p. 84
    Adrian is said to have been a pagan officer at the imperial court at Nicomedia. He was imprisoned for identifying himself with the persecuted Christians, and his wife Natalia tended him and his fellow prisoners. After the execution of Adrian in *c.* 304 Natalia gathered up his relics and fled to Argyropolis, where she died in peace but is reckoned amongst the martyrs. There was formerly a very considerable cultus of this St Adrian, who was reckoned a patron of soldiers and butchers.

ADRIAN FORTESCUE, BD, mart. July 9.   JULY, p. 120
    Sir Adrian Fortescue, knight of the Bath and of Malta, tertiary of the Order of Preachers, was b. in 1476. He married (1) Anne Stonor of Stonor, (2) Anne Rede of Boarstall, and had five children. He led the life of a gentleman of his time. In 1539 he was attainted by Parliament, with Cardinal Pole and others, for " treasons and sedition " against King Henry VIII, and was beheaded on Tower Hill. His feast is kept by the

knights of the military order of Malta and in the diocese of Birmingham. bd. 1895.

ADRIAN OF CANTERBURY, ST, ab. January 9. JAN., p. 125
An African, abbot of Nerida near Naples. Sent by Pope St Vitalian to England with St Theodore of Tarsus. Became abbot of SS Peter and Paul's at Canterbury, where he d. 710.

AEDH MAC BRICC, ST, bp. November 10. Nov., p. 115
He was a disciple of St Illathan at Rathlihen in Offaly, and is said to have founded churches at Rathugh and other places in his native Meath. Many miracles are recorded of St Aedh. Sixth century. *Aidus.*

ÆGIDIUS. *See* Giles.

AELRED, ST, ab. January 12. JAN., p. 154
B. in north of England in 1109. Master of the household of King David of Scotland. Became a Cistercian monk at Rievaulx in 1133 ; abbot of Revesby in Lincolnshire, then of Rievaulx. Author of several treatises, *e.g.* "On Spiritual Friendship", "The Mirror of Charity", and biographies of saints. Sternly austere, yet notably gentle with his monks, of whom he dismissed not one in seventeen years. In spite of ill health made several long journeys, including, it seems, to Citeaux. d. 1167. His feast is kept on March 3 in the dioceses of Hexham, Liverpool, Middlesbrough, and Nottingham. *Aelredus.*

*AEMILIANA, ST, virg. January 5. JAN., p. 78
An aunt of St Gregory the Great. d. *c.* 590.

AENGUS, ST, bp. March 11. MAR., p. 194
Aengus or Oengus is generally distinguished as "the Culdee" ; he was a very famous holy man but no early account of him is extant and he is not commemorated liturgically in any Irish diocese. He is said to have been first a monk at Clonenagh and then at Tallacht Hill, where he composed the famous metrical hymn to the saints called the *Félire* or *Festilogium.* He returned to Clonenagh, where he was made abbot and bishop, and d. between 819 and 830.

*AFRA, ST, mart. August 5. AUG., p. 65
Afra was a martyr who suffered at Augsburg and was venerated there from early times. She was probably a victim of the persecution of Diocletian, *c.* 304, but the story of her being a converted harlot from Cyprus is worthless.

*AFRA OF BRESCIA, ST, mart. May 24. MAY, p. 290
A local martyr of Brescia of whom nothing is known. Her name is connected with the legend of SS Faustinus and Jovita.

*AGABUS, ST. February 13. FEB., p. 196
Agabus is the prophet referred to in the 11th and 21st chapters of the Acts of the Apostles. He is mentioned in the Roman Martyrology and in some Eastern kalendars.

*AGAPE, ST, virg. and mart. February 15. FEB., p. 228
She is specially honoured at Terni in Umbria as a martyr and contemporary of the bishop St Valentine. Nothing certain is known about her and she has probably been confused with other martyrs of the same name.

*AGAPE, etc., SS, marts. April 3. APR., p. 33
Agape, Chionia, and Irene were three sisters at Salonika during the persecution of Diocletian. With three other women and a man they were charged with refusing to eat meat sacrificed to false gods ; Agape and

Chionia were sentenced to be burnt alive ; Irene, who had been detected also in concealing Christian sacred books, was exposed in a brothel and put to death later ; 304.

†*AGAPITUS, ST, mart. August 18. AUG., p. 199

He was a boy of fifteen at Palestrina who, upon refusing to deny Christ, was beaten, imprisoned and beheaded in 274.

*AGAPITUS I. ST, pope. April 22 APR., p. 257

Agapitus was pope for only eleven months, dying in 536. This short time was spent in contending with various heresies. His memory was greatly honoured by St Gregory the Great.

†*AGATHA, ST, virg. and mart. February 5. FEB., p. 80

There is good evidence for the early veneration of St Agatha, but nothing can be confidently affirmed about her history except that she was martyred in Sicily c. 251. Traditionally her breasts were cut off and she was represented in art bearing them on a platter ; later these were mistaken for loaves, whence arose the custom of blessing bread on a dish on St Agatha's feast. She is the patroness of bell-founders.

AGATHANGELUS, ST, mart. *See* Clement of Ancyra.

AGATHANGELO and **CASSIAN, BB,** marts. August 7. AUG., p. 87

Agathangelo of Vendôme and Cassian of Nantes were Capuchin friars who were sent to Egypt in 1633 to work for the reconciliaticn of the dissident Coptic Christians. Their mission was so handicapped by the ill-behaviour of the European Catholics there that they went on into Ethiopia, where there were many more Christians outside Catholic unity. Stirred up by a German Protestant, King Fasilidas had them arrested and hung, by the cords of their Franciscan habits, in 1638. bd. 1905.

*AGATHO, ST, pope. January 10. JAN., p. 133

A Sicilian Greek who became pope in 679. Sent legates to the sixth œcumenical council (Constantinople III), with a letter condemning the monothelite heresy. He restored St Wilfrid to the see of York. d. 681.

*AGATHO, ST, mart. December 7. DEC., p. 104

He is the same as St Besas, the soldier who suffered with SS Julian and Cronian (February 27).

*AGATHOPUS and **THEODULUS, SS,** marts. April 4. APR., p. 48

Martyred by drowning at Salonika for refusing to give up the sacred books, in 303.

AGAUNUM, THE MARTYRS OF. *See* Theban Legion.

*AGERICUS, ST, bp. December 1. DEC., p. 3

In French, *Airy*. He was bishop of Verdun and enjoyed the friendship of St Gregory of Tours and St Venantius Fortunatus. d. 591.

AGILBERT, ST, bp. October 11. OCT., p. 152

He was a Frank who studied in Ireland and came as a missionary to England, where he was made bishop of the West Saxons and was a leader of the " Roman party " at the Synod of Whitby. When King Coinwalch got tired of having a French bishop, and divided the Wessex diocese, St Agilbert resigned and went home, where he became bishop of Paris in 668. d. c. 685. *Agilbertus*.

AGNELLUS OF PISA, BD. March 13. MAR., p. 241

He was appointed by St Francis himself to establish the Friars Minor in England and landed at Dover in 1224 with eight companions, four of whom were English. Agnellus himself founded the Canterbury friary and then went to London to take charge of the house founded on Cornhill by Friar Richard Ingworth. He then established the friary at Oxford, with a school for which he engaged Grosseteste as teacher and which became very famous. Agnellus gained the friendship of King Henry III and in 1233 negotiated with the insurgent Earl Marshal. d. at Oxford 1236. c.c. 1892.

†*AGNES, ST, virg. mart. January 21. JAN., p. 250

A Roman maiden who was martyred in the year 304 or 305 and buried beside the Via Nomentana, where a basilica was built in her honour before 354 ; Pope St Damasus wrote an epitaph for her. Her name occurs in the canon of the Mass and as a special patroness of chastity she is one of the most popular of saints. But little reliance can be placed on the details of the story of her martyrdom as it has come down to us : it alleges that she was unharmed in a brothel whither she was sent to break down her constancy to Christ, and put to death (by stabbing ?) at a tender age. Her age, about 13 years, has been confirmed by the examination of her skull at Rome in 1903. On her feast every year two white lambs are solemnly blessed in her church, from whose wool are made the *pallia*, which the pope confers on all archbishops of the Western church as a token of jurisdiction.

AGNES OF ASSISI, ST, virg. November 16. Nov., p. 203

She was the sister of St Clare and was first abbess of the Poor Clare convent of Monticelli at Florence, which became only less famous than San Damiano itself. d. 1253.

AGNES OF BOHEMIA, BD, virg. March 2. MAR., p. 24

Agnes was the daughter of King Premysl Ottokar I of Bohemia and niece of Andreas II of Hungary, and until she was twenty-eight or so her life was a series of sojourns in convents and betrothals to various royal suitors. She accepted none of them, but with the help of Pope Gregory IX became a Poor Clare, founding a convent at Prague to which St Clare sent five of her nuns. Bd Agnes was a religious here for forty-six years, and there are extant four affectionate letters written to her from Assisi by St Clare. d. 1282. c.c. by Pope Pius IX.

*AGNES OF MONTEPULCIANO, ST, virg. April 20. APR., p. 235

B. 1268. At a very youthful age she was abbess of a convent at Procena and afterwards returned to Montepulciano to take charge of a new house of Preacheresses. A number of very remarkable visions and other supernatural manifestations are narrated of St Agnes, who also had gifts of healing and prophecy. d. 1317. cd. 1726.

*AGRECIUS, ST, bp. January 13. JAN., p. 161

A bishop of Trier, who was at the Council of Arles in 314 and died c. 333. According to a quite unreliable document he had been patriarch of Antioch and brought our Lord's seamless robe (" The Holy Coat ") to Trier, together with other unlikely relics.

*AGRICOLA, ST, bp. March 17. MAR., p. 299

In French, *Arègle*. Bishop of Chalon-sur-Saône and a contemporary of St Gregory of Tours, who knew him well. d. 580.

AGRICOLUS, ST, bp. September 2. SEPT., p. 23

He is said to have succeeded his father as bishop of Avignon and to have d. in 700. He has been venerated as patron saint of that city since 1647 only and information about him is very unreliable.

*AGRIPPINA, ST, virg. and mart. June 23. JUNE, p. 306

She is believed to have been a girl of good position who was executed for her faith in Rome in 262 (?). She is specially revered in Sicily, whither

her relics are supposed to have been translated (the Greeks say to Constantinople).

AIA, ST. April 18.   APR., p. 214

She was the wife of St Hydulphus of Hainault. d. *c.* 714.

*AICHARDUS, ST, ab. September 15.   SEPT., p. 181

He was for many years a monk at Ansion in Poitou and eventually became abbot of Jumiéges. St Aichardus was specially scrupulous in his observance of the Lord's Day. d. *c.* 687.

*AIDAN, ST, bp. August 31.   AUG., p. 394

St Aidan was sent from Iona to help the king St Oswald to spread the Faith among the people of Northumbria. He established his see at Lindisfarne (Holy Island), where he founded a monastery under the Celtic rule observed at Iona, and St Bede writes of the fruitfulness of his character and apostolate. St Aidan d. at Bamborough in 651, surviving St Oswald by only eleven days. His feast is kept in the dioceses of Argyll, Hexham, Lancaster, Liverpool, Middlesbrough, Northampton, and Portsmouth. *Edanus.*

AIDAN OF FERNS, ST, bp. January 31.   JAN., p. 398

Aidan (*Maedoc*) is venerated in Ireland as the first bishop at Ferns in county Wexford, where he had founded a monastery. When young he visited St David in Wales, and is alleged to have worked many strange miracles. d. 626.

*AIGULPHUS, ST, ab. and mart. September 3.   SEPT., p. 37

Aigulphus (in French, Ayou) was elected abbot of Lérins *c.* 670, and is said to have introduced the Benedictine rule there. There is considerable uncertainty about the circumstances of his death in 676. With four monks he is said to have been forcibly removed to an island near Corsica, where they were killed, perhaps by Moorish pirates.

AIGULPHUS, ST, bp. May 22.   MAY, p. 269

In French, *Aioul.* He was bishop of Bourges and d. in 836.

AILBE, ST, bp. September 12.   SEPT., p. 151

A commemoration of the feast of St Ailbe (*Albeus*) is made throughout Ireland but his recorded life is a confusion of valueless legends and contradictory traditions. He is venerated as the first bishop at Emly, in the early sixth century, and is the reputed author of a monastic rule.

AIMO TAPARELLI, BD. August 18.   AUG., p. 211

A confessor of the Order of Preachers, inquisitor general for Lombardy and Liguria, who d. at the age of one hundred in 1495. c.c. 1856.

AIRALDUS, BD, bp. January 2.   JAN., p. 41

Bishop of Saint-Jean de Maurienne in the twelfth century, but the details of his life have not been disentangled. c.c. 1863.

*ALBAN, ST, mart. June 22.   JUNE, p. 291

St Alban is venerated as the protomartyr of Britain and his feast is observed throughout England and Wales. He is said to have been a citizen of Verulamium (now Saint Albans) who was executed on Holmhurst Hill at that place in 304 for having sheltered a persecuted priest and declared his own Christianity. It has lately been suggested that Alban's death took place in South Wales, near Newport, and not at Verulamium. *Albanus.*

ALBERIC, ST, ab. January 26.   JAN., p. 321

One of the three founders of the Cistercians. Alberic was prior at

Molesmes when St Robert was abbot and St Stephen Harding a monk there. They found it impossible to restore discipline in this monastery, so in 1098 they took up their abode at Cîteaux, where Alberic soon became abbot, and no doubt had considerable influence on the development of Cistercian life, though he lived but a short time. The black and white Cistercian habit is said to have been revealed to Alberic in a vision by our Lady. d. 1109. *Albericus*.

ALBERT, ST, bp.   January 8.   JAN., p. 117

Patron saint of the archdiocese of Cashel, where he is said to have laboured when he came from England. Afterwards, it is related, he went with St Erhard to lead a wandering life on the continent and that Albert died at Ratisbon upon returning from Jerusalem. He probably lived and died in the seventh century but his true history is extremely obscure. *Albertus*.

ALBERT, ST, bp.   April 5.   APR., p. 63

He was bishop of Montecorvino. In old age, when he was blind, he was treated with the most amazing indignity and cruelty by his vicar-general or coadjutor and the man's friends. d. 1127.

†*ALBERT THE GREAT, ST, bp. and doct.   November 15.   NOV., p. 182

Albert was a Suabian by descent, joined the Dominicans, was a master of St Thomas Aquinas, and in 1245 was appointed regent of the house of studies in Cologne. He became provincial of his order in Germany, went to Rome to defend the mendicant friars against the attacks of the secular clergy, and in 1260 was made bishop of Regensburg (Ratisbon). He resigned two years later, and spent most of the rest of his life at the Cologne *studium*, though he played an active part in the Council of Lyons and went to Paris to defend some of the writings of St Thomas when they were attacked. Albert was called " the Great " and " the Universal Doctor " in his lifetime and his printed works fill thirty-eight quarto volumes, including treatises on logic, metaphysics, mathematics, ethics, and physical science, as well as biblical and theological works and sermons. But his principal fame is due to his application of Aristotelian methods and principles to the study of theology ; he was the chief pioneer and forerunner of the scholastic system that was brought to perfection by his pupil St Thomas. Albert d. at Cologne in 1280 and was bd. in 1622. He was equivalently canonized by being declared a doctor of the Church in 1931.

ALBERT OF BERGAMO, BD.   May 11.   MAY, p. 132

Albert was a peasant farmer who suffered much from a shrewish wife and jealous relatives. Late in life he lived at Cremona where he was credited with miracles. d. 1279. Bd Albert is venerated by the Dominicans as a tertiary of their order. c.c. 1748.

ALBERT OF JERUSALEM, ST, bp.   September 25.   SEPT., p. 318

Albert was an Italian canon regular who was called from the see of Vercelli to be Latin patriarch of Jerusalem in 1204. He was also papal legate and for nine years had to deal with a variety of matters which exercised his prudence and patience to the utmost, for the Latin kingdom in Palestine was already in dissolution. It was St Albert who gave their first written rule to the Frankish hermits on Mount Carmel, at the request of St Brocard. He was murdered at Acre in 1214 by a Hospitaller whom he had deposed from office.

*ALBERT OF LOUVAIN, ST, bp. and mart.   November 21. Nov., p. 264

He was b. *c.* 1166 at Mont César, Louvain, and in 1191 was elected bishop of Liége. The appointment was challenged on behalf of another

B   9

Albert and in the resulting politico-ecclesiastical dispute (Pope *versus* Emperor) St Albert was murdered at Rheims by three German knights in 1192.

*ALBERT OF TRAPANI, ST. August 7.   AUG., p. 86

This Albert was b. at Trapani in Sicily *c.* 1240. He became a Carmelite friar and was famous for his success with the Jews, for his missionary journeys, and for his miracles. d. 1306. c.c. 1453.

ALBINUS OF MAINZ, ST, mart. June 21.   JUNE, p. 279

According to tradition Albinus (or Albanus) was a Greek priest from Naxos who travelled across Europe and became a missionary among the Arian heretics around Mainz : here he was killed, either by heretics or barbarians, before 451. There is doubt if there be any historical foundation for this story.

ALCMUND, ST, mart. March 19.   MAR., p. 325

He was son or nephew of King Alchred of Northumbria, but it is not certain in what circumstances he was slain or why he was venerated as a martyr, first at Lilleshall and then at Derby. d. *c.* 800. *Alcmundus.*

ALCMUND, ST, bp. September 7.   SEPT., p. 77

He was the seventh bishop of Hexham and d. in 781. No details are known of his life.

ALDA, BD. April 26.   APR., p. 296

Or *Aldobrandesca.* Upon the death of her husband leaving her childless Bd Alda undertook a life of almsdeeds and mortification at Siena. d. 1309.

ALDEBRANDUS, ST, bp. May 1.   MAY, p. 17

A bishop of Fossombrone who died at the age of one hundred years early in the thirteenth century.

*ALDEGUND, ST, virg. January 30.   JAN., p. 385

An abbess of Maubeuge ; d. 684 from cancer of the breast. *Aldegundis.*

ALDEMAR, ST, ab. March 24.   MAR., p. 387

A monk of Monte Cassino who after a rather disturbed career founded a monastery at Bocchignano and other religious houses in the Abruzzi ; these he ruled with much success. d. *c.* 1080. *Aldemarus.*

*ALDHELM, ST, bp. May 25.   MAY, p. 303

B. in Wessex in 639 and educated at the monastery of Malmesbury and under St Adrian at Canterbury. He was given charge of the school and abbey at Malmesbury in middle life and was counsellor to King Ine. Aldhelm was the first English scholar of distinction, his vernacular hymns were treasured by King Alfred, and he did much for religion and education in Wessex, where he founded monasteries at Frome and Bradford-on-Avon. In 705 he became the first bishop of Sherborne. d. 709. A treatise on virginity and other works of St Aldhelm have come down to us. His feast is observed in the diocese of Clifton and he is commemorated in Southwark on May 28. *Aldelmus.*

ALDRIC, ST, bp. January 7.   JAN., p. 106

Chaplain to the Emperor Louis the Pious, and bishop of Le Mans in 832. He was noted alike for his public activities and private virtues. Some of his regulations for his cathedral and his three testaments are still extant. d. 856. *Aldericus.*

†*ALEXANDER and comps., SS, marts. May 3.   MAY, p. 40

Alexander, Eventius and Theodulus were three Roman martyrs (*c.* 113 ?) buried on the Via Nomentana ; nothing is known of them. The

Roman Martyrology erroneously identifies the Alexander with Pope St Alexander I.

*ALEXANDER, ST, bp. and mart. August 11. AUG., p. 132

Alexander, a charcoal-burner, was promoted from that trade to be bishop of Comana in Pontus ; he gave his life for Christ in 250.

*ALEXANDER and other bps., **SS.** August 28. AUG., p. 364

Alexander of Byzantium became patriarch of Constantinople in his seventy-fourth year, filled the office for twenty-three years, and d. in 340. He was a strong opponent of Arianism. In a common feast with him the Catholic Byzantines join two other patriarchs of Constantinople, John III (d. 577) and Paul IV (d. 784).

*ALEXANDER, ST, mart. December 12. DEC., p. 144

He suffered at Alexandria in 250 in company with St Epimachus (May 10) who is again mentioned in the Roman Martyrology on December 12 ; St Ammonaria and other virgin martyrs were put to death at the same time and place.

ALEXANDER AKIMETES, ST. January 15. JAN., p. 190

A somewhat turbulent archimandrite, best known for his institution of the " sleepless " monks (*akoimetoi*) who sang the Divine Office in relays without intermission day and night. d. 430.

ALEXANDER BRIANT, BD, mart. December 1. DEC., p. 23

He was a secular priest, arrested on the English mission and cruelly tortured to make him disclose the whereabouts of Father Persons, S.J. He was h.d.q. with Bd Ralph Sherwin and Bd Edmund Campion at Tyburn in 1581 and on the same charge. bd. 1886.

ALEXANDER RAWLINS, BD, mart. April 7. APR., p. 90

A secular priest, h.d.q. for his priesthood at York, 1595. bd. 1929.

*ALEXANDER SAULI, ST, bp. October 11. OCT., p. 159

B. at Milan in 1534. He joined the Barnabite clerks regular, was for many years the director of St Charles Borromeo, and was appointed bishop to reform the Corsican diocese of Aleria in 1569. He carried on this very difficult task for twenty years, and with such success that he was translated to Pavia, where he d. in the following year, 1593. cd. 1904.

ALEXANDER OF ALEXANDRIA, ST, bp. February 26. FEB., p. 355.

As archbishop of Alexandria he was a determined opponent of the heresy of Arius, against whom he wrote two encyclical letters. With his deacon St Athanasius he was the principal champion of orthodoxy at the first œcumenical council at Nicæa. d. 328.

*ALEXANDER OF JERUSALEM, ST, bp. and mart. March 18.

MAR., p. 309

He was bishop of his native city in Cappadocia and suffered imprisonment during the persecution of Severus. Some time after his release he was made coadjutor to the Bishop of Jerusalem—the first recorded example of an episcopal translation and coadjutorship. In the persecution under Decius he was again imprisoned and died in chains at Cæsarea in 251.

*ALEXANDRIA, MARTYRS OF, I. February 28. FEB., p. 380

In the year 261 Alexandria suffered from a terrible plague which had already devastated other parts of the empire. The Christians of the city visited and looked after the sick and comforted the dying regardless of their personal safety. Many of them, clergy and lay folk, themselves succumbed, and the Roman Church recognized their heroism by making a commemoration in her martyrology of those whom " the faith of religious persons acknowledges as martyrs."

*ALEXANDRIA, MARTYRS OF, II. March 17.   MAR., p. 298

The Roman Martyrology on March 17 mentions those Christians who were killed by the heathen mob at Alexandria when they refused to worship in the temple of Serapis, in 390.

†*ALEXIS, ST. July 17.   JULY, p. 224

St Alexis, " the Man of God," was one of the most popular of " popular saints," especially in the East, and his legends ramified all over Europe and hither Asia ; nevertheless the only things that are reasonably certain about his life are that he lived, died, and was buried at Edessa in Syria, probably early in the fifth century. Legend presents him as a sort of forerunner of St Benedict Joseph Labre. *Alexius.*

ALEXIS FALCONIERI, ST. *See* the Seven Holy Founders.

ALEYDIS, ST. *See* Adelaide (June 15).

ALFERICUS, ST, ab. April 12.   APR., p. 139

Alfericus or Alferius was founder of the great abbey of Cava, which within a few years of his death in 1050 had over thirty other establishments dependent on it in southern Italy and Sicily.

ALFWOLD, ST, bp. March 25.   MAR., p. 400

Last bishop of the see of Sherborne in Dorset ; he was noted for his simple life and his devotion to the memory of St Cuthbert. d. *c.* 1058. *Alfwoldus.*

*ALIPIUS, ST, bp. August 18.   AUG., p. 205

He was a close friend of St Augustine, under whom he studied in Africa, and after a severe struggle shared his master's conversion. He became bishop of Tagaste *c.* 393 and was Augustine's chief assistant in all his public work. d. *c.* 430.

ALLUCIO, ST. October 23.   OCT., p. 312

He began life as a herdsman in Tuscany and was appointed master of an almshouse at Val di Nievole, near Pescia, being in effect a second founder of the charity ; he was responsible for the undertaking of several other public works. d. 1134. c.c. by Pope Pius IX.

*ALMACHIUS, ST, mart. January 1.   JAN., p. 9

Otherwise *Telemachus.* Put to death by the people at Rome for protesting against gladiatorial sports, in consequence of which the Emperor Honorius is said to have abolished such spectacles, *c.* 400.

ALNOTH, ST. February 27.   FEB., p. 373

He was first a cowman on the land of St Werburg's monastery at Weedon and then a solitary in the woods of Stowe, near Bugbrooke in Northamptonshire. He was murdered by robbers *c.* 700 and for long was venerated in the neighbourhood, a feast being kept in his honour. His date is also given as November 25. *Alnothus.*

†*ALOYSIUS GONZAGA, ST. June 21.   JUNE, p. 269

Luigi Gonzaga was b. in 1568 in the castle of Castiglione in Lombardy. He is the classical example of a saint whose popular estimation has been seriously damaged by the inadequate presentation of biographers and the weak sloppiness of his pictorial representations : some recent writers have done their best to repair these mistakes. He was a lively boy of high birth, who refused to give in to the wickedness and mere worldliness of court life, and whom neither cajolery nor force could stop from serving God as a Jesuit. In 1585 he joined the Society at Rome ; within six years he sickened from nursing the plague-stricken, and d. 1591. cd. 1726. St Aloysius is the patron saint of youth.

ALOYSIUS TABATA, BD. May 11.   MAY, p. 134

A young Sicilian Carmelite of whom little is known. He d. in 1490 from the effects of a blow on the head from an assailant whom he refused to bring to justice. c.c. by Pope Gregory XVI.

ALPAIS, BD, virg. November 3.   NOV., p. 38

She was a bed-ridden peasant girl at Cudot in France whose patience and goodness made a very great impression on her contemporaries. d. 1211. c.c. 1874.

*ALPHÆUS and **ZACHÆUS, SS,** marts. November 17.   NOV., p. 217

Zachæus was deacon at Gadara beyond the Jordan and his cousin Alphæus was a reader and exorcist. They were beheaded at Cæsarea in 303.

*ALPHIUS, ST, mart. May 10.   MAY, p. 119

With his companions Philadelphus and Cyrinus, St Adelphus is venerated as a martyr in southern Italy and Sicily in 251, but the extant accounts of them are quite unreliable.

†*ALPHONSUS LIGUORI, ST, bp. and doct. August 2.   AUG., p. 11

B. of a distinguished family near Naples in 1696. He became a very successful advocate but gave up the law and received holy orders in 1726 : four years later he played a prominent part in the reorganization of the convent of Scala, near Amalfi, into the first house of Redemptoristine nuns. In 1732 St Alphonsus founded at Scala a new congregation of missioners to work among the peasants of the country districts, now known as the Redemptorists; this establishment was made in the face of huge difficulties, in the course of which Alphonsus was condemned, under a misapprehension, by Pope Pius VI and removed from its control ; the congregation was still riven by schism and opposition at the time of the founder's death. He had been appointed bishop of Sant' Agata de' Goti in 1762 and governed the small diocese with great wisdom and industry until 1775, when ill-health forced him to resign ; it was after this that the difficulties of the Redemptorists became even more distressing, but while dealing with them St Alphonsus found time to devote himself anew to ascetical and moral theology. His experience in a lay profession combined with natural common sense and sweetness of disposition helped much to make him the best known of all moral theologians. During the last eighteen months of his life he was tormented with the most fierce spiritual trials, but he died in peace in 1787, within two months of his ninety-first birthday. cd. 1839 and declared doctor of the Church in 1871.

ALPHONSUS NAVARETTE, BD, mart. June 1.   JUNE, p. 16

Bd Alphonsus was a Spanish Dominican who became a missionary in the Philippines and in 1611 was sent on to Japan. He was executed for his faith at Omura in 1617. One of the 205 martyrs of Japan bd. in 1867.

ALPHONSUS D'OROSCO, BD. September 19.   SEPT., p. 264

He was an Augustinian friar and was appointed preacher at the court of Philip II of Spain. Here he exercised a very beneficent influence for many years and wrote a number of mystical and other works. d. 1591. bd. 1882.

*ALPHONSUS RODRIGUEZ, ST. ˙ October 30.   OCT., p. 367

He was the son of a wealthy merchant of Segovia. After his business had failed and death had taken his wife and children Alphonsus, in 1571 at the age of forty-four, was accepted as a temporal coadjutor (lay-brother) of the Society of Jesus and sent to Majorca. For the rest of his life he was porter at the Montesion college there ; he was held in the deepest respect by the many and various people who got to know him at the door, one of the most famous who came to him for advice being St Peter Claver. St Alphonsus died after years of physical and spiritual suffering in 1617. cd. 1888. He must be distinguished from the other but uncanonized Jesuit Rodriguez (Alonso), and *see also* Paraguay, Martyrs of.

ALTMANN, BD, bp. August 8.   AUG., p. 97
He became bishop of Passau in 1065 and was one of the four south German bishops who opposed the emperor Henry IV on behalf of Pope St Gregory VII. He was driven from his see, but continued to exercise great influence from the borders of the diocese. d. 1091. c.c. by Pope Leo XIII.

ALTO, ST, ab. February 9.   SEPT., p. 63
Alto probably was an Irishman, who founded and governed a monastery at the place in Bavaria now known as Altomünster. d. *c.* 760.

ALVAREZ OF CORDOVA, BD. February 19.   FEB., p. 279
He entered the Dominican house at Cordova in 1368 and worked with great success in Andalusia and Italy. He became adviser to the Queen-mother of Spain, Catherine (daughter of John of Gaunt), and tutor to her son Juan II. He was a follower of Bd Raymund of Capua and founded a strictly observant Dominican priory near Cordova ; this was soon a centre of learning and religion, and of opposition to the Avignon pope Peter de Luna. Alvarez used himself to go questing for his house, and he set up stations of the cross that attracted many pilgrims. d. *c.* 1430. c.c. 1741.

AMADEUS, BD, bp. August 27.   AUG., p. 339
In 1139 St Bernard appointed this Amadeus to be abbot of the Cistercian house of Hautecombe in Savoy, and soon afterwards he was promoted to the see of Lausanne ; four years before his death he was made chancellor of the kingdom of Burgundy. d. 1159. c.c. 1910.

AMADEUS IX, BD. March 30.   MAR., p. 448
B. at Thonon in 1435 and succeeded to the dukedom of Savoy in 1455. Amadeus suffered from epilepsy, and eventually resigned his office in favour of his wife. In spite of his malady he led a very austere life and was revered as a saint after his death in 1472. c.c. 1666. Bd Amadeus is patron of the royal house of Savoy, of which he was an ancestor.

AMADEUS OF PORTUGAL, BD. August 10.   AUG., p. 126
He was the elder brother of Bd Beatrice da Silva. After ten years with the Hieronymites he joined the Friars Minor in Italy, where he initiated the reform known as " of Marignano " or " Amadeists." d. 1482. His popular cultus at Milan seems never to have been officially confirmed.

AMADOUR, ST. August 20.   AUG., p. 247
He is honoured in Quercy and the Limousin as the first hermit of Gaul and founder of the shrine of our Lady known as Rocamadour, but nothing whatsoever is known about him. *Amator.*

AMALBURGA, ST. July 10.   JULY, p. 131
Amalburga, or Amelia, was the wife of Count Witger and mother of St Gudule and others. When Witger became a monk she joined the convent of Maubeuge. d. 690.

AMALBURGA, ST, virg. July 10.   JULY, p. 132

Often confused with the above. She was a nun at Muensterbilsen in Flanders. d. c. 772.

*AMANDUS, ST, bp. February 6.   FEB., p. 91

A great missionary figure in the Merovingian epoch. After living as a solitary in Bourges for fifteen years he was consecrated bishop with no fixed see. He preached in Flanders and Carinthia, reproved King Dagobert for his crimes, and founded three monasteries in Flanders. d. 676.

*AMANDUS, ST, bp. June 18.   JUNE, p. 232

He was a bishop of Bordeaux whose wisdom and virtue is spoken of by St Paulinus of Nola, whom Amandus had prepared for baptism. d. c. 431.

*AMATOR OF AUXERRE, ST, bp. May 1.   MAY, p. 8

He was a bishop of Auxerre who during a long episcopate converted the remaining heathen in the diocese, built two churches, and performed many miracles. d. 418.

AMATUS, ST, ab. September 13.   SEPT., p. 162

While a monk of Luxeuil St Amatus (Amé) turned the heart of St Romaricus to God, and when this nobleman founded the monastery of Remiremont c. 620 Amatus was appointed the first abbot. d. c. 630.

*AMATUS, ST, bp. September 13.   SEPT., p. 163

It is not certain whether this Amatus was bishop of Sion in the Valais or of Sens, but he was driven from his see by the enmity of King Theodericus III and was confined in monasteries for the rest of his days. d. c. 690.

†*AMBROSE, ST, bp. and doct. December 7.   DEC., p. 93

He was b. c. 340 in Gaul, where his father was prætorian prefect, and became a barrister at Rome. Before he was thirty-five Ambrose was appointed governor of Liguria and Æmilia, with his headquarters at Milan, and he was called to be bishop by acclamation there in 374, although still only a catechumen. He proved to be one of the greatest and most beloved bishops of all time. He distributed his worldly wealth to the poor and set to work to administer his diocese, preaching and writing against the rampant Arianism with tremendous energy. He censured the Eastern emperor for his cruelty and defied the Western empress for her heresy ; he was at home to all comers ; and he wrote many homilies and treatises. So persuasive was Ambrose on the excellence of virginity that the civil authorities accused him of " anti-social " activities, to which he retorted that it is war, not maidenhood, that destroys peoples. St Ambrose was the first of the Fathers to use the Latin tongue with effect : as the Empire was declining in the West he inaugurated a new lease of life for its language, in the service of Christianity. One of his last treatises was " On the Goodness of Death," and soon after he died, on Good Friday, April 4, 397, being hardly fifty years of age : December 7 is the anniversary of his episcopal consecration. He is named in the canon of the Milanese Mass. *Ambrosius.*

AMBROSE AUTPERTUS, ST, ab. July 19.   JULY, p. 276

When he left the court of King Pepin the Short he became a monk at St Vincent's in the duchy of Benevento, where he spent the rest of his uneventful life. The writings of St Ambrose were very highly valued in the Middle Ages, and his learning was considerable. d. c. 778.

AMBROSE BARLOW, BD, mart. September 10.   SEPT., p. 136

He was professed a monk of St Gregory's at Douay in 1615 and worked on the English mission in his native Lancashire for twenty-four years.

After being in prison and released four times he was h.d.q. for his priest-hood at Lancaster in 1641. bd. 1929. Bd Ambrose was named titular cathedral-prior of Coventry a week before his execution.

AMBROSE SANSEDONI, BD. March 20. MAR., p. 342

He was a Dominican student with St Thomas under St Albert the Great and became a renowned preacher in Germany, France, and Italy. He fulfilled various missions for the Holy See and was Master of the Sacred Palace. His death in 1287 was hastened by the vehemence with which he preached against usury. c.c. 1622.

AMBROSE TRAVERSARI, BD, ab. November 20. NOV., p. 258

During thirty years as a Camaldolese monk at Florence he became a conspicuous religious and literary figure, a characteristic " all-round " man of the Renaissance : he wrote (especially in Greek), translated, and col-lected a good library. From 1431, when he was appointed abbot general of the Camaldolese, he was engaged in public affairs of church and state, in which he was as effective as he was as a scholar. d. 1439. Popular cultus.

AMICUS, ST. November 3. NOV., p. 31

He was a hermit and monk at Camerino, Torano dell' Aquila, and Avellano. d. c. 1045.

*AMMON, ST, mart. September 1. SEPT., p. 6

A deacon who suffered with several maidens at Heraclea c. 322.

*AMMON and his comps., **SS,** marts. December 20. DEC., p. 209

Ammon, Zeno, Ptolemy, and Ingenes, soldiers, with one Theophilus, were beheaded at Alexandria in 249 for encouraging a Christian confessor who showed signs of wavering at his trial.

AMMON THE GREAT, ST. October 4. OCT., p. 53

Ammon was one of the earliest and greatest of the hermit monks of the Nitrian desert, a life that he entered on after having lived for eighteen years with his wife as brother and sister. On the advice of St Antony he assembled the cells of his followers more or less together, under a general overseer. In his later years Ammon ate only once every three or four days. d. c. 350.

*AMPHILOCIUS, ST, bp. November 23. NOV., p. 276

Amphilocius, a close friend of St Basil the Great, was bishop of Iconium and showed great activity against the Macedonian heresy, in the course of which he wrote a work on the Holy Ghost which was approved by St Jerome. d. c. 400.

†*ANACLETUS, ST, pope and mart. *See* Cletus.

†*ANASTASIA, ST, mart. December 25. DEC., p. 244

Anastasia was martyred at Sirmium in Dalmatia, probably under Diocletian, but only worthless legends have survived concerning her. She was venerated in Rome in the fifth century and, under the influence of Byzantine officials there (Anastasia's relics had been translated to Con-stantinople), her memory became associated with the second Mass of Christmas ; she is still commemorated at that Mass in the Roman Missal, though the Byzantines keep her feast on December 22. She is named in the canon of the Mass.

*ANASTASIA and **CYRIL, SS,** marts. October 28. OCT., p. 348

The *passio* of this maiden and the boy who brought her water during her sufferings is a fictitious composition ; it is not certain that they ever existed.

ANASTASIA PATRICIA, ST, virg. March 10.   MAR., p. 169
    Hers is one of the several stories of women who lived disguised as monks
or hermits, in this case to escape marriage with the emperor Justinian.
The tale is in all probability nothing more than a pious romance.

ANASTASIUS. *See also* Astericus.

†***ANASTASIUS, ST,** mart. January 22.   JAN., p. 267
    A Persian convert at Jerusalem who became a monk in 621. He was
arrested and tortured at Cæsarea and then taken to the Persian king in
Assyria, by whose orders he was eventually slain in 628. A miraculous
picture of St Anastasius was put in as evidence at the seventh œcumenical
council at Nicæa in 787, which was held against Iconoclasm. This picture,
with the martyr's head, is said still to be at the monastery of SS Vincent
and Anastasius at Rome.

***ANASTASIUS I, ST,** pope. December 19.   DEC., p. 205
    Anastasius I, a Roman, is chiefly remembered for his condemnation of
the errors attributed to Origen. d. 401.

***ANASTASIUS I, ST,** bp. April 21.   APR., p. 251
    This Anastasius, patriarch of Antioch, was banished from his see for
many years by the Emperor Justin II for opposing the imperial politico-
theological opinions. He was a man of very great learning and piety.
d. 599.

***ANASTASIUS II, ST,** bp. and mart. December 21.   DEC., p. 218
    Sinaite monk who became patriarch of Antioch in 599. During the
rising of the Syrian Jews against the oppression of the emperor Phokas in
609 Anastasius was murdered by the mob and was looked on as a martyr.

***ANASTASIUS CORNICULARIUS, ST,** mart. August 21.   AUG., p. 258
    There has been a lot of confusion about this martyr. He seems to be a
duplication, with a different story, of St Anastasius the Fuller (September 7).

ANASTASIUS OF CLUNY, ST. October 16.   OCT., p. 229
    He was a monk first of Mont-Saint-Michel and then of Cluny, and d.
as a hermit near Toulouse in 1085.

***ANASTASIUS THE FULLER, ST,** mart. September 7.   SEPT., p. 74
    He plied his trade at Salona in Dalmatia, where in 304 he was put to
death by drowning for his confession of Christ. The proper date of his
feast is August 26.

***ANATOLIUS, ST,** bp. July 3.   JULY, p. 22
    He was a bishop of Laodicea, eminent as a philosopher and mathe-
matician, and at one time in charge of the Aristotelean school at Alexandria,
his native city. d. 283.

ANATOLIUS, ST, bp. July 3.   JULY, p. 25
    Nothing is known of the private life of this patriarch of Constantinople
and his public life is somewhat equivocal for one who is acclaimed as a
saint ; but the Bollandists have vindicated him and his feast is kept by
Byzantine Catholics in the East. He was appointed to the see of Constantinople in 449 and d. 458.

***ANDEOLUS, ST,** mart. May 1.   MAY, p. 7
    Nothing reliable is known of this martyr, who is said to have been put
to death near Viviers on the Rhône in 208.

ANDREW, ST. August 22.   AUG., p. 271
    He is said to have been an Irishman and archdeacon to St Donatus at
Fiesole at the end of the ninth century. His alleged relics are preserved

there, but the story is probably fictitious : it includes the miraculous transportation of Andrew's sister St Brigid to Fiesole. *Andreas.*

†*ANDREW, ST, ap. November 30.   Nov., p. 345

A confessor of the Order of Preachers, who was prior of the royal
Andrew, brother of St Peter, was the first of Christ's apostles in the order of time ; all that is certain about him is found in the gospels. He is said to have preached the gospel in Asia Minor and Greece and to have suffered martyrdom by crucifixion at Patras in Achaia. His alleged relics were stolen from Constantinople in 1210 and now rest in the cathedral of Amalfi in Italy. St Andrew is the patron saint of Scotland, Russia, and Greece ; his name occurs twice in the liturgy of the Roman Mass, in the canon and in the embolism of the Lord's Prayer.

ANDREW ABELLON, BD. May 17.   MAY, p. 223

A confessor of the Order of Preachers, who was prior of the royal friary of St Mary Magdalene at Saint-Maximin. d. 1450. c.c. 1902.

†*ANDREW AVELLINO, ST. November 10.   Nov., p. 111

B. near Naples in 1521. He was at first an ecclesiastical lawyer, and then, after being nearly killed by those who were interested in maintaining the disorder of a convent which he had been commissioned to reform, joined the Theatine clerks regular. He founded houses of this order in several parts of Italy, and his success as a preacher was confirmed by gifts of prophecy and miracle. St Andrew (christened Lancelot) was a personal friend and adviser of St Charles Borromeo. d. 1608. cd. 1712.

ANDREW BOBOLA, ST, mart. May 21.   MAY, p. 261

A Jesuit of Vilna who was especially successful in reconciling dissident Orthodox with the Holy See. His missionary labours naturally met with a great deal of opposition and in 1657 he was tortured and murdered by a gang of Cossacks at Janov, near Pinsk. cd. 1938.

ANDREW CACCIOLI, BD. June 3.   JUNE, p. 41

This Andrew was a well-to-do secular priest who gave all his riches to charity and became one of the first seventy-two followers of St Francis of Assisi. He was subjected to persecution and imprisonment for his active opposition to the innovations introduced among the Franciscans by Brother Elias. He founded a house of his order at Spello and was buried there after his death in 1254. c.c. by Pope Clement XII.

ANDREW CONTI, BD. February 15.   FEB., p. 234

He was a nephew of Pope Alexander IV but was himself a Franciscan lay-brother, held in great veneration both in life and after death. d. February 1, 1302. c.c. 1724.

†*ANDREW CORSINI, ST, bp. February 4.   FEB., p. 61

B. in Florence in 1302 of the great Corsini family. His early adolescence was dissipated and vicious, but the reproaches of his mother brought him round and he became a Carmelite friar. He studied in Paris and Avignon, was made prior at Florence, and then bishop of Fiesole. He was devoted to the causes of the poor and of peace in the quarrelsome Italian states, and was sent by Pope Urban V to pacify Bologna. St Andrew set the example of a prelate of a most noble house living according to the austerity of the religious rule he had professed. d. January 6, 1373. cd. 1629.

ANDREW DOTTI, BD. September 3.   SEPT., p. 40

A confessor of the Servite Order, wherein he was a disciple of St Philip Benizi and accompanied him on his preaching journeys. Bd Andrew was a figure of importance in the early days of the Servites, and ended his days as a solitary. d. 1315. c.c. 1806.

ANDREW FOURNET, ST. May 13.   MAY, p. 168

Andrew Hubert Fournet was b. in 1752 at Maillé, near Poitiers. After several false starts, he was ordained and made parish priest of his native town. After the revolution he worked untiringly as a missioner, preacher, and confessor, and with Elizabeth des Ages founded the congregation of Daughters of the Cross, in whose favour St Andrew's prayers several times miraculously increased food. d. 1834. cd. 1933.

ANDREW FRANCHI, BD, bp. May 30.   MAY, p. 365

He was a Dominican, who became bishop of Pistoia in 1378 and for twenty-three years was revered by his flock for his simplicity and justness. d. 1401. c.c. 1921.

ANDREW DE' GALLERANI, BD. March 19.   MAR., p. 326

A distinguished Sienese soldier who, having murdered a man, gave up the rest of his life to prayer and charity. d. 1251.

ANDREW HIBERNON, BD. April 18.   APR., p. 218

A Spanish Franciscan lay-brother who converted many Moors by his simplicity. d. 1602. c.c. 1791.

*ANDREW THE TRIBUNE, ST, mart. August 19.   AUG., p. 219

The authentic *acta* of this famous martyr have not survived, but he is said to have been an officer in the army of Maximian Galerius who became a Christian with a number of his comrades. They took refuge in the Taurus mountains but were tracked and put to death, *c.* 303.

ANDREW OF ANTIOCH, BD. November 30.   NOV., p. 349

This Andrew was b. at Antioch *c.* 1268 of Norman parents, a descendant of Robert Guiscard. He was a canon regular of St Augustine, and near the end of his life was sent into Europe to collect funds for the eastern houses of his order. He d. at Annecy in Savoy *c.* 1348, having earned a great reputation for holiness during the course of his travels.

ANDREW OF CRETE, ST, bp. July 4.   JULY, p. 36

Or " of Jerusalem." He was b. at Damascus, became a monk of Mar Saba and then at the Holy Sepulchre, and a deacon of the Great Church at Constantinople. From thence he was promoted to the archbishopric of Gortyna in Crete, where he distinguished himself as a preacher and a writer of hymns. He is said to have introduced the *kanon* into the Byzantine office. d. 740.

*ANDREW OF CRETE, ST, mart. October 20.   OCT., p. 277

Otherwise " the Calybite." He was a monk of Crete who went to Constantinople to take part in the Iconoclast controversy. He accused the emperor of heresy and was stabbed to death by a fanatical iconoclast while being led through the streets in derision, in 766.

ANDREW OF MONTEREALE, BD. April 12.   APR., p. 140

For fifty years Bd Andrew, an Augustinian friar, preached the gospel in Italy and France and was remarkable for his holiness and learning. d. 1480. c.c. 1764.

ANDREW OF PESCHIERA, BD. January 19.   JAN., p. 238

A Dominican friar who evangelized a part of southern Switzerland for forty-five years. d. 1485. c.c. 1820.

ANDREW OF RINN, BD, mart. July 12.   JULY, p. 162

A boy alleged to have been murdered by Jews out of hatred of the Faith at Rinn, near Innsbrück, in 1462. This is doubtful. Pope Benedict XIV allowed the continuation of the local *cultus* but refused a request for Andrew's canonization.

ANDREW OF STRUMI, ST, ab. March 10.   MAR., p. 173

Andrew, called " the Ligurian," was a chief supporter of the deacon Bd Arialdo and the church-reform party in the Milanese strife of the mid-eleventh century. After the murder of Arialdo, Andrew retired from the world to join the Vallombrosan monks. He became abbot of San Fedele at Strumi and divided his time between writing, governing his house, and public affairs ; he negotiated a peace between Florence and Arezzo, in consequence of which the prestige of his order was greatly increased. d. 1097.

*ANDRONICUS and ATHANASIA, SS. October 9.   OCT., p. 112

A man and wife of Antioch who, after the death of their two children, went their ways to lead a solitary life in the Egyptian deserts. Years later they met and occupied adjoining cells, Andronicus not recognizing his wife until after she was dead. Fifth century. These saints are particularly venerated in Egypt and Ethiopia.

ANGADRISMA, ST, virg. October 14.   OCT., p. 193

In French *Angadrème*. She was abbess of Oroër-des-Vierges, near Beauvais. d. *c.* 695.

†*ANGELA MERICI, ST, virg. May 31.   MAY, p. 370

She was b. near Brescia in 1470 or 1474, and for some years devoted herself to the education of young girls, the care of sick women, and similar work, in which she was joined by several companions. These she formed into a congregation under the patronage and title of St Ursula in 1535, the first specifically teaching order of women to be established in the Church ; it is now spread throughout the world. d. 1540. cd. 1807.

ANGELA OF FOLIGNO, BD. January 4.   JAN., p. 63

One of the great mystics and contemplatives of the middle ages. She was born of a good family at Foligno about the middle of the thirteenth century. She married and had several sons, but led a self-indulgent and perhaps sinful life until, as the result of a sudden conversion, she became a Franciscan tertiary. After the death of her husband and children she gradually stripped herself of all her possessions and became the leader of a large family of tertiaries, both men and women. At the request of her confessor, Friar Arnold, she dictated to him an account of her visions and ecstasies, from which we learn most that is known of her life. Her very remarkable visions are narrated in a restrained and convincing way, and she reveals clearly the spiritual heights and depths along which she was led. She died peacefully in 1309 and her *cultus* was confirmed in 1693.

ANGELINA OF MARSCIANO, BD. July 15.   JULY, p. 204

Her husband died when she was seventeen and she was inspired to establish a convent of regular tertiaries of St Francis at Foligno, the first of its kind, which was completed in 1397. Others soon followed, and at her death in 1435 there were 135 such houses ; they were formed into a congregation which still exists. c.c. 1825.

*ANGELO, ST, mart. May 5.   MAY, p. 75

This Angelo was an early member of the Carmelite Order who was killed at Leocata in Sicily in 1220 by a man whose wickedness he had denounced ; he is venerated as a martyr. *Angelus.*

ANGELO MAZZINGHI, BD. August 18. AUG., p. 209

Angelo Augustine Mazzinghi was b. in Florence in 1377 and was a model religious of the Carmelite Order. d. 1438. c.c. 1761.

ANGELO OF ACRI, BD. October 30. OCT., p. 371

After two unsuccessful efforts and then a stormy novitiate this Angelo was professed among the Capuchin friars. He began his public preaching in 1702, but it was not till 1711 at Naples that he was at all successful ; from then onwards he was famous all over southern Italy, and his preaching was supported by miracles. d. 1739. bd. 1825.

ANGELO DAL BORGO, BD. February 15. FEB., p. 235·

This Augustinian friar was a contemporary of St Nicholas of Tolentino and is said to have established houses of his order in England, but reliable particulars of his career are lacking. d. *c.* 1306. c.c. 1921.

ANGELO OF CHIVASSO, BD. April 12. APR., p. 140

Angelo was a senator of Piedmont who joined the Observantine friars minor at Genoa. His merits and abilities were recognized both by promotion to offices in the order and by his popularity among people of all ranks and kinds, and he was tireless in his efforts to save poor people from the clutches of usurious money-lenders. When over eighty Angelo preached among the Waldensians with considerable success. d. 1495.

ANGELO OF FOLIGNO, BD. August 27. AUG., p. 340

A confessor of the Augustinian friars, who founded three houses of his order in Umbria. d. 1312. c.c. 1891.

ANGELO OF FURCIO, BD. February 6. FEB., p. 95

A confessor of the order of Hermits of St Augustine who died in 1327, his cultus being approved by Pope Leo XIII.

ANGELO OF GUALDO, BD. February 14. FEB., p. 224

B. at Gualdo in Umbria *c.* 1265, and was distinguished all his life for his extreme simplicity, innocence, and gentleness. After making several pilgrimages he became a Camaldolese hermit. d. January 25, 1325. c.c. 1825.

ANGILBERT, ST, ab. February 18. FEB., p. 269

As a young man Angilbert was nicknamed " Homer " but his life at the court of Charlemagne was worthy neither of that name nor of his own subsequent career. He mended his ways and became abbot of Centula, near Amiens, where he is said to have introduced continual choir service in relays. He continued to take part in public affairs and was one of the witnesses of Charlemagne's will. d. 814. *Angilbertus.*

*ANIANUS, ST, bp. April 25. APR., p. 286

He is alleged to have been the helper and successor of St Mark as bishop of Alexandria and " a man well pleasing to God." First century.

*ANIANUS, ST, bp. November 17. NOV., p. 218

In French *Aignan.* He was a bishop of Orleans, and d. in 453.

†*ANICETUS, ST, pope and mart. April 17. APR., p. 195

St Anicetus was pope from about 152 till 160 ; he suffered under persecution but it is not certain that he actually gave his life for the Faith.

ANNAM, THE MARTYRS OF, I. July 11. JULY, p. 146

At the beginning of the nineteenth century Christianity made good progress in Indo-China, but this was followed from 1820 to 1841 by a period of violent persecution. Seventy-seven of the victims were beatified by Pope Leo XIII in 1900, including a number of Annamite lay people. *See also* BB Dominic Henarez, Ignatius Delgado, John Cornay, and Stephen Cuénot.

ANNAM, THE MARTYRS OF, II. November 6.   Nov., p. 79

A second group of martyrs in Annam, between 1745 and 1861, were beatified in 1906. Among them were Jerome Hermosilla, vicar apostolic of Eastern Tonkin, Valentine Berrio-Ochoa, vicar apostolic of Central Tonkin, and Peter Almato ; these three Spanish Dominicans were beheaded at Trong-thu in 1861. Vincent Liem, put to death in 1773, was the first Indo-Chinese Dominican to suffer martyrdom.

ANNE, ST, virg. July 23.   JULY, p. 334

She was a maiden of Constantinople (also called Susanna), who lived for over twenty years as a solitary on the Leucadian promontory in Epirus. d. *c.* 918. *Anna.*

†*ANNE, ST. July 26.   JULY, p. 366

Anne (Hannah =" grace ") is the name traditionally given to the mother of the Blessed Virgin Mary. Her *cultus* was known in the sixth century in the East and early in the eighth in the West, but it did not become widespread till the middle of the fourteenth.

ANNE MARY TAIGI, BD. June 9.   JUNE, p. 124

B. at Siena in 1769, daughter of a druggist whose business failed ; in 1790 she married Dominic Taigi, a servant at the Chigi palace in Rome. He was a good man but narrow, rather cantankerous and not spiritually intelligent, so that his tributes to his wife are the more valuable. Bd Anna Maria achieved holiness in the discharge of domestic duties and the bringing up of her children, but her light could not be hid and her counsel was sought by the great ones of Church and state. She read the minds of men and had the supernatural gift of foretelling the future. d. 1837. bd. 1920.

ANNE OF ST BARTHOLOMEW, BD, virg. June 7.   JUNE, p. 100

This Anne, ex-shepherdess, was a Carmelite lay-sister and the special companion of St Teresa of Avila, who died in her arms. She was sent to France with other reformed Carmelites in 1606, was promoted to the choir, and became prioress at Pontoise and Tours. In 1612 Bd Anne founded a Carmel at Antwerp that was primarily intended for refugees from England. d. 1626. bd. 1917. In making her foundations St Teresa declared that Sister Anne was more useful to her than anyone else.

ANNEMUNDUS, ST, bp. and mart. September 28.   SEPT., p. 347

Annemundus, Archbishop of Lyons, was friend and patron of the young St Wilfrid of York who was present when Annemundus was murdered at Chalon-sur-Saône in 657. St Bede and others call St Annemundus *Dalfinus* in error.

*ANNO, ST, bp. December 4.   DEC., p. 59

Anno was made archbishop elector of Cologne in 1056, but never succeeded in fully overcoming the prejudice against himself of his flock, which thought he was insufficiently well born to rule over them. Most of the events of his life belong to the troubled political history of the age, and they are not uniformly edifying ; Anno was canonized (in 1183) rather for the virtue of his private life and for his reforming energy in his diocese. d. 1075. *Annon.*

*ANSANUS, ST, mart. December 1.   DEC., p. 1

St Ansanus was martyred at Siena in 304 and is venerated as the apostle

of that city. He is said to have made so many converts that he was called
" the Baptizer."

*ANSBERT, ST, bp. February 9.   FEB., p. 144
   Abbot of St Wandrille and then archbishop of Rouen. He was banished
on a false accusation and d. in exile in Hainault *c.* 700. *Ansbertus.*

ANSEGISUS, ST, ab. July 20.   JULY, p. 295
   He was abbot of Saint-Germer, of Luxeuil, and finally of Fontenelle
and a characteristic example of the Benedictine working for Christianity
and civilization during the dark ages of Europe. Under his rule Fontenelle
became famous for its library and *scriptorium.* d. 833.

*ANSCHAR, ST, bp. February 3.   FEB., p. 54
   B. 801 near Amiens and was a monk first of Old and then of New
Corbie, whence he was taken by King Harold of Denmark to work among
the heathen Danes. He was appointed first archbishop of Hamburg and
legate of the Holy See, and for thirteen years preached and organized
missions in Scandinavia and northern Germany. In 845 the Northmen
destroyed Hamburg, and Sweden and Norway relapsed ; the see of
Bremen was united to that of Hamburg and St Anschar returned to
Denmark and set to work to restore his damaged missions. But Sweden
reverted completely to paganism after his death in 865. *Anscharius.*

ANSELM, ST, ab. March 3.   MAR., p. 41
   Anselm, Duke of Friuli, founded monasteries at Fanano and Nonantola,
the second of which he entered himself and governed as abbot until his
death in 803. To each of his monasteries he attached a hospital for the
sick. *Anselmus.*

†*ANSELM, ST, bp. and doct. April 21.   APR., p. 244
   B. at Aosta *c.* 1033, abbot of Bec in Normandy in 1078, and nominated
archbishop of Canterbury by King William Rufus in 1093. Almost at
once he angered William by opposing his spoliation of sees and abbeys
and his extortions from the clergy ; Anselm went to lay his case before the
Holy See in 1097 and had to remain abroad till William's death. He was at
the Council of Bari in 1098, where he resolved the theological doubts of the
Italo-Greek bishops. Difficulties arose with King Henry I because Anselm
refused to allow lay investiture of spiritual offices and he had to spend a
second period in exile. St Anselm was one of the first to oppose the selling of
men as chattels, and is regarded as the father of Scholasticism : his most
famous written work is on the Incarnation, *Cur Deus Homo ?* d. 1109.
Like St Albert the Great in our time he was declared a doctor of the Church
(in 1720) without having been formally canonized.

*ANSELM OF LUCCA, ST, bp. March 18.   MAR., p. 314
   After his nomination to the see of Lucca he for long refused to accept
investiture at lay hands—the emperor Henry IV—and he even withdrew
from his diocese for a time on this account. He naturally strongly supported
Pope Gregory VII in his campaign against lay investiture. Anselm was
a man of great learning, especially as a canonist and in scriptural matters.
He became papal legate in Lombardy, and worked hard to establish
stricter observance among monks and canons, though he had no success
with the canons of his own chapter. d. 1086.

ANSFRIDUS, ST, bp. May 11.   MAY, p. 130
   As a count of Brabant Ansfridus distinguished himself by the
suppression of brigands and pirates, but in 994 was made bishop of
Utrecht where he was greatly beloved by the citizens. d. *c.* 1009.

*ANSOVINUS, ST, bp. March 13.   MAR., p. 236

A hermit at Castel-Raymond, near Torcello, who was raised to the bishopric of Camerino ; he accepted the office only on condition that he should be exempt from the feudal duty of providing soldiers for the imperial army, which he considered unbecoming in a bishop. Many miracles are recorded of him. d. 840.

ANSTRUDIS, ST, virg. October 17.   OCT., p. 242

She was the daughter of St Salaberga and abbess of a convent at Laon, where she underwent some persecution from King Theodericus III. d. 688.

*ANTHELMUS, ST, bp. June 26.   JUNE, p. 354

B. in 1105, the son of a Savoyard nobleman, and became a secular priest. A chance visit to the charterhouse of Portes caused him to resign his offices and join the Carthusians, and in 1139 he was elected seventh prior of the Grande Chartreuse. He was responsible for the summoning of the first general Carthusian chapter at which the monks were organized into an order under a minister general, St Anthelmus being the first. He resigned in 1152 but seven years later emerged from his retirement to intervene on behalf of Alexander III against the antipope Victor ; much against his will he had to accept the bishopric of Belley in 1163. The diocese was in a disorderly state and after gentler methods had failed Anthelmus proceeded to deprivation and excommunication—including the Duke of Savoy, the sentence against whom he would not relax even at the bidding of the Holy See. He spent all his leisure at Carthusian monasteries and took a very active interest in certain women solitaries and in a leper hospital he had founded. On one occasion he was sent to England to try and bring about a reconciliation of King Henry II with St Thomas Becket. d. 1178.

*ANTHERUS, ST, pope and mart. January 3.   JAN., p. 50

Put to death after about six weeks' pontificate in 236, and buried in the cemetery of St Callistus.

*ANTHIMUS, ST, bp. April 27.   APR., p. 301

Bishop of Nicomedia, beheaded for confessing Christ in 303.

ANTONIA OF FLORENCE, BD. February 28.   FEB., p. 389

A young widow who was one of the first in Florence to become a regular tertiary of St Francis when Bd Angela of Foligno founded a convent there in 1429. Later she was made superioress at Aquila, and there with the help of St John Capistran she founded a community under the original rule of the Poor Clares. Her son and other relatives used to come and worry her with their disputes, for fifteen years she suffered from a painful disease, and she had numerous other difficulties all of which she overcame with quiet perseverance. d. 1472. c.c. 1847.

*ANTONINA, ST, mart. June 12.   JUNE, p. 152

Or *Antonia*. There is nothing but uncertainty about this martyr. She seems to be duplicated in the Roman Martyrology on March 1 and May 4 and is claimed by three different places called Cea ; actually she may have suffered at Nicomedia (in 304 ?).

†*ANTONINUS, ST, bp. May 10.   MAY, p. 116

Antoninus Pierozzi was b. in 1389 at Florence and was received into the Dominican Order by Bd John Dominic at Fiesole. While still young he was elected prior of the Minerva at Rome and in 1436 founded the friary of San Marco at Florence. In 1446 St Antoninus was made archbishop of

24

that city and, though delicate in health, he ruled with skill and vigour at a time of political crisis ; he was a people's prelate, too, loving and caring for the poor and oppressed and beloved in return. Antoninus was a moral theologian of some importance and a writer on local and international law. d. 1459. cd. 1523.

*ANTONINUS, ST, mart. September 2. SEPT., p. 22

The Antoninus, a martyr at Pamiers, mentioned by the Roman Martyrology on September 2, is probably a mistake for the Antoninus, a stonemason martyred at Apamæa in Syria, who is commemorated by the Byzantines on November 9.

*ANTONINUS OF SORRENTO, ST, ab. February 14. FEB., p. 221

With the bishop St Catellus he went to live on the mountain now called Monte Angelo, near Ancona, on account of the vision of St Michael that they had there. Later he became abbot of the monastery of St Agrippinus at Sorrento. d. 830. He is said to have been buried within the city wall and to have proved a powerful defence against attack.

†*ANTONY, ST, ab. January 17. JAN., p. 208

The patriarch of all monks, called "the Abbot." He was b. in Upper Egypt in 251 and when he was about twenty he gave away all his goods and lived in solitary places in the neighbourhood of his birthplace, Coma. When thirty-five he went into the desert and about 305 established a community of hermits in the Fayum and another soon after at Pispir. About 350 he was invited to Alexandria to preach against the Arians, and died in 356 in his hermitage on Mount Kolzim, near the Red Sea. He was 105 years old but in spite of the extraordinary austerity of his life all his faculties were unimpaired and he had suffered no sickness. St Athanasius wrote a biography of St Antony and gives many details of his life and miracles. He was famous throughout Egypt and beyond, and secular rulers and bishops as well as crowds of lesser folk sought him out to consult with him. Though St Antony was not by any means the first Christian recluse none before him had gathered them together into loose communities, and from the earliest times he was looked on as the father of Christian monasticism. *Antonius.*

ANTONY BALDINUCCI, BD. November 7. NOV., p. 90

He was b. at Florence, and joined the Society of Jesus in 1681. He worked for twenty years among the poor and distressed of Viterbo and Frascati, and his somewhat violent missionary methods bore good fruit. He rarely slept more than three hours and worked without ceasing for the rest of the twenty-four, so that he wore himself out when just over fifty. d. 1717. bd. 1893.

ANTONY BONFADINI, BD. December 1. DEC., p. 10

A confessor of the Friars Minor of the Observance who laboured in the Holy Land. d. 1482. c.c. 1901.

*ANTONY CAULEAS, ST, bp. February 12. FEB., p. 187

He was chosen patriarch of Constantinople in 888, and proved a vigorous prelate, forbidding the emperor Leo IV to contract a third marriage. d. *c.* 901.

ANTONY DELLA CHIESA, BD. July 28. JULY, p. 397

Bd Antony was b. in 1395, a collateral ancestor of Pope Benedict XV. He was a Dominican friar and a popular and effective preacher, especially against usury. He had the gift of discernment of spirits. d. 1459. c.c. 1819.

ANTONY CLARET, BD, bp. October 24.   OCT., p. 382

Antony Mary Claret was brought up to the trade of weaving in Spain, but became a secular priest in 1835. Fourteen years later he was mainly instrumental in founding the congregation of Missionary Sons of the Immaculate Heart of Mary (" Claretians "), which spread from Spain to America and elsewhere. Bd Antony was appointed archbishop of Santiago de Cuba, where several attempts were made on his life because of his drastic reforms ; in 1856 he was made confessor to Queen Isabella II and was exiled with her from Spain at the revolution of 1868. He had the gift of prophecy and of the healing of bodies. d. 1870. bd. 1934.

ANTONY GIANELLI, BD, bp. June 7.   JUNE, p. 102

B. 1789 at Cerreto, near Pavia. As a secular priest he organized a congregation of missioners and another of teaching sisters, and in 1838 was appointed bishop of Bobbio, in which office he gave an example of heroic virtue. d. 1846. bd. 1925.

ANTONY GRASSI, BD. December 13.   DEC., p. 159

He was a priest of the Oratory of Fermo in the Italian Marches, and its superior from 1635 until his death in 1671. An event that had a strong effect on his interior life was being struck by lightning in 1621, but in spite of this nerve-racking experience he was always noted for his unperturbable serenity. Bd Antony had the gift of reading consciences, and he had a way of dealing with people so gentle but effective that his influence extended far beyond his house and parish. Many miracles were attributed to his intercession and he was bd. in 1900.

ANTONY IXIDA, BD, mart. September 3.   SEPT., p. 41

A Japanese Jesuit who with five Franciscan and Austin friars was tortured for thirty-three days in a vain effort to make him apostatize. They were all burnt to death in 1632 and bd. with the other Japanese martyrs in 1867.

ANTONY MANZI, BD. February 1.   FEB., p. 19

Or *Manzoni*, called " the Pilgrim." A member of a good family of Padua who spent most of his life wandering over Europe as a simple pilgrim. On account of this vagabondish behaviour he was not well looked on by his relatives, especially by two sisters who were nuns. d. 1267.

ANTONY MIDDLETON, BD, mart. May 6.   MAY, p. 84

A secular priest, born at Middleton Tyas, h.d.q. at Clerkenwell, London, for his priesthood in 1590. bd. 1929.

ANTONY NEYROT, BD, mart. April 10.   APR., p. 116

This Antony, a Dominican friar, was carried off to Tunis by the Moors ; there he apostatized to Islam and took a wife. Within a few months he repented, resumed his preacher's habit, and witnessed to Christ before the Bey of Tunis. He was accordingly put to death, in 1460. c.c. by Pope Clement XIII.

ANTONY DE' PATRIZI, BD. April 27.   APR., p. 307

A confessor of the order of Hermit Friars of St Augustine. d. 1311.

ANTONY PAVONI, BD, mart. April 9.   APR., p. 109

A Dominican friar and inquisitor general for Liguria and Piedmont. After a vigorous sermon against heresy he was set upon and killed outside the church at Brichera, 1374.

ANTONY PRIMALDI, BD, mart. August 14.   AUG., p. 176

He was the leader of eight hundred citizens of Otranto, all men, who in a raid by the Turks in 1480 refused to apostatize to Islam in return for safety and were beheaded. Bd Antony was an aged artisan. c.c. 1771.

†*ANTONY ZACCARIA, ST. July 5. JULY, p. 51
Antony Mary Zaccaria was b. at Cremona in 1502 and became a secular priest, having originally intended to be a physician. In 1530 he founded a congregation of clerks regular, which in 1533 was approved by Pope Clement VII under the name of Clerks Regular of St. Paul, but from their headquarters at the church of St Barnabas at Milan they are commonly called Barnabites. St Antony died, worn out by his unceasing apostolic work, in 1539. cd. 1897.

ANTONY OF AMANDOLA, BD. January 28. JAN., p. 358
A friar of the Augustinian order, who d. 1350. His feast is kept by the order and at Ancona.

*ANTONY OF LERINS, ST. December 28. DEC., p. 268
Antony was born in Lower Pannonia and led an eremitical life in several places north of the Alps ; unable to find complete solitude he went into Gaul and became a monk of Lérins, where he d. c. 520.

†*ANTONY OF PADUA, ST. June 13. JUNE, p. 163
This great saint of Italy was by race a Portuguese, b. at Lisbon in 1195 ; in 1221 he left the Augustinian canons regular in order to become a Friar Minor. He is one of the most " popular " saints of the Church, with a great reputation for retrieving the lost belongings of careless people (cf., " . . . the Lord . . . shall place him over all his goods," in the communion verse of the saint's Mass), and he has always been famous as a wonder-worker. Whether he was the instrument of miracles during his lifetime has been much discussed ; to his contemporaries he was known, as well as for the holiness of his life, as a relentless and eloquent preacher against error and wickedness : he was indeed called the " hammer of heretics." A vision which, according to a late story, he received of the child Jesus is commemorated in all modern images of St Antony. He preached and taught in France as well as in Italy, and we are told that men closed their workshops and offices to go and hear him. d. 1231. cd. 1232.

ANTONY OF STRONCONE, BD. February 7. FEB., p. 110
Antony Vici became a Friar Minor of the Observance while very young and for more than ten years was engaged in combating the heretical Fraticelli. The rest of his life was spent in the solitude of the Carceri, near Assisi, where his reputation for virtue was very great. He d. at San Damiano in 1461. c.c. 1687.

*ANYSIA, ST, mart. December 30. DEC., p. 293
She is said to have been a young woman of Salonika who was in 304 killed by a soldier when she resisted his attempt to drag her to a pagan sacrifice.

*ANYSIUS, ST, bp. December 30. DEC., p. 294
He was an early bishop of Salonika, whose virtues were praised by Popes St Innocent I and St Leo the Great. d. c. 407.

*APHRAATES, ST. April 7. APR., p. 81
On April 7 the Roman Martyrology mentions a St Aphraates, a hermit in Syria, who opposed Arianism during the reign of the emperor Valens. Efforts have been made to identify him with the Aphraates of whom Theodoret writes. d. c. 345.

†*APOLLINARIS, ST, bp. and mart. July 23. JULY, p. 325

He was the first bishop of Ravenna and a famous early martyr, but it is not known in what persecution.

*APOLLINARIS, ST, bp. October 5. OCT., p. 59

He was the elder brother of St Avitus of Vienne and became bishop of Valence, of which diocese he is the principal patron under the popular form of his name, " Aiplonay." d. *c.* 520.

APOLLINARIS FRANCO, BD, mart. September 10. SEPT., p. 132

He was a Friar Minor and commissary general of his order's mission in Japan. With seventeen other Franciscan friars and twenty-two lay tertiaries he was cruelly tortured and put to death for refusing to apostatize (1617-1628). They were bd. with the other Japanese martyrs in 1867.

*APOLLINARIS SYNCLETICA, ST, virg. January 5. JAN., p. 78

The heroine of a religious romance who put on boy's clothes and lived undetected as the disciple of one of the saints Macarius in the Egyptian desert.

*APOLLINARIS THE APOLOGIST, ST, bp. January 8. JAN., p. 110

Claudius Apollinaris, Bishop of Hierapolis in Phrygia, was a teacher of the second century who was formerly greatly valued, but little is now known of his life and writings. He is called " the Apologist " from the *apologia* for the Christian faith which he addressed to Marcus Aurelius soon after the victory which the emperor had gained over the Quadi, at the intercession of the Christians as is alleged (" The Thundering Legion "). d. *c.* 175.

APOLLO, ST, ab. January 25. JAN., p. 305

After being a hermit in the Thebaid for many years became at a great age abbot over five hundred monks at Heliopolis ; many astonishing miracles are recorded of him. d. *c.* 395.

†*APOLLONIA, ST, virg. and mart. February 9. FEB., p. 138

This aged deaconess of Alexandria died by fire in the year 249. She is invoked against toothache, presumably because her teeth were knocked out by the heathen mob.

*APOLLONIUS THE APOLOGIST, ST, mart. April 18. APR., p. 209

Apollonius, a Roman senator, was denounced as a Christian by one of his own slaves ; an authentic account of his examination by the magistrate was discovered in an Armenian text in 1874 : it includes the *apologia* for Christianity from which the martyr gets his name. He was beheaded, *c.* 190.

*APPHIANUS, ST, mart. April 2. APR., p. 18

He was martyred at Cæsarea in 306 for trying to prevent the magistrate from offering public sacrifice to the heathen gods.

*AQUILA and PRISCA, SS, marts. July 8. JULY, p. 91

Aquila and his wife Prisca were disciples of St Paul who are mentioned in the *Acts of the Apostles* and elsewhere in the New Testament. There is a tradition that they were eventually martyred in Rome.

*AQUILINA, ST, mart. June 13. JUNE, p. 168

A young girl of Byblus in Syria who was martyred at the end of the third century ; she was formerly greatly venerated in the East but the account of her passion cannot be relied on.

*AQUILINUS, ST, bp. October 19. OCT., p. 264

After forty years in the service of Clovis II he retired with his wife to

Evreux and became bishop there ; it is said that he sought to live rather as a hermit than a bishop. d. *c.* 695.

*ARBOGAST, ST, bp. July 21.   JULY, p. 305

Great uncertainty surrounds the life of St Arbogast, who was a bishop of Strasburg in the sixth or seventh century. *Arbogastus.*

*ARCADIUS, ST, mart. January 12.   JAN., p. 147

A martyr in some city of Mauritania in Africa, perhaps under Diocletian. The extant account of his passion is not reliable.

*ARCADIUS, ST, mart. November 13.   NOV., p. 152

Arcadius and four other Spaniards (one of them a boy, Paulillus) were the protomartyrs of the Arian Vandal persecution, suffering death in North Africa in 437.

ARCHANGELA GIRLANI, BD, virg. February 13.   FEB., p. 210

B. at Trino in Italy in 1460 and became a Carmelite at Parma. She was a model of every religious virtue, and was sent at the wish of the Gonzagas to found a Carmel at Mantua, where she d. in 1494. c.c. by Pope Pius IX.

ARCHANGELO CANETULI, BD. April 16.   APR., p. 188

He was an Augustinian canon regular at Gubbio who was conspicuous for his holy life, prophetical gifts, and spirit of brotherly love. d. 1513.

ARCHANGELO OF CALAFATIMI, BD. July 30.   JULY, p. 418

He was a hermit in Sicily and afterwards a promoter of the Observant branch of the Franciscan Order in that island. d. 1460. c.c. 1836.

*ARCHELAUS, ST, bp. December 26.   DEC., p. 252

He was bishop of Kashkar in Mesopotamia and d. *c.* 278. The writings against Manichæism formerly attributed to him are the work of someone else.

*ARDALION, ST, mart. April 14.   APR., p. 159

One of several martyrs at different times who are said to have been converted while ridiculing Christianity on the stage ; *c.* 300.

ARDO, BD, ab. March 7.   MAR., p. 115

He followed St Benedict of Aniane in the abbacy of that monastery, and wrote a biography of his predecessor. He was venerated at Aniane and an office sung in his honour. d. 843.

ARETAS, ST. *See* Nagran, Martyrs of.

ARMEL, ST, ab. August 16.   AUG., p. 189

Armel (also *Ermel, Arthmael, Ermin,* etc.) was b. in South Wales, son of Hywel ap Emyr Llydaw and cousin of St Samson. He went over into Brittany and founded the monasteries of Saint-Armel-des-Boscheaux and Ploermel. d. *c.* 570.

*ARMOGASTES, etc., SS, marts. March 29.   MAR., p. 434

Armogastes was an official under the Vandal Genseric who, at the same time as SS Archinimus and Saturus, suffered greatly at the hands of the Arians. They all died soon after, *c.* 455, and are accounted martyrs.

ARNOLD, BD, ab. March 14.   MAR., p. 252

He was abbot of St Justina's at Padua and was persecuted by the tyrant Ezzelino de Romano, who kept him in prison eight years until his death in 1254 at the age of seventy. *Arnoldus.*

*ARNULFUS, ST, bp. July 18.   JULY, p. 254

In French *Arnoul.* He was a high official at the Austrasian court and his son married a daughter of Bd Pepin of Landen. About 610 Arnulphus became bishop of Metz and chief counsellor to Clothaire of Neustria. His last years were spent in a hermitage near the abbey of Remiremont. d. *c.* 640.

*ARNULFUS, ST, bp. August 15.   AUG., p. 184
He was abbot of Saint-Médard and then bishop of Soissons. He founded the abbey of Oudenbourg in Flanders, where he d. in 1087.

ARNULFUS OF VILLARS, BD. June 30.   JUNE, p. 398
A confessor of the Cistercian Order, who was a lay brother of very mortified and charitable life at Villars in Belgium. d. 1228.

*ARSACIUS, ST. August 16.   AUG., p. 188
He was a Persian soldier in the Roman army who was persecuted for the Faith and became a hermit at Nicomedia. He d. during the great earthquake in 358.

*ARSENIUS, ST. July 19.   JULY, p. 268
Called " the Great," " the Roman," or " the Deacon." As these names suggest he was a deacon of the city of Rome, and he was made tutor to Arcadius and Honorius, the sons of the Emperor Theodosius the Great. From Constantinople in 393 he retired to the desert of Skete, and spent the rest of his life as a solitary in various places in Egypt ; early writers about him all emphasize his gift of tears (" weeping over the feebleness of Arcadius and the foolishness of Honorius "). Arsenius d. at the Rock of Troë, near Memphis, *c.* 449.

ARTALDUS, BD, bp. October 7.   OCT., p. 88
He was a Carthusian monk, first at Portes and then at Valromey, in Savoy ; when over eighty he was called to be bishop of Belley. Here he was visited by St Hugh of Lincoln. d. 1206. c.c. 1834. In France he is called *Arthaud.*

ARTEMAS, ST, mart. January 25.   JAN., p. 303
This martyr is supposed to have suffered (*c.* 304 ?) at Pozzuoli, near Padua, where he was venerated in former times.

ARTHELAIS, ST, virg. March 3.   MAR., p. 39
She is alleged to have been a young girl who fled from Constantinople to Benevento to avoid the attentions of the emperor Justinian, but the extant record of her life is not trustworthy.

ARTHEMIUS, ST, bp. January 24.   JAN., p. 297
An early bishop of Clermont, venerated in that diocese. d. 396. *Artemius.*

*ARTHEMIUS, ST, mart. October 20.   OCT., p. 275
He seems to have been a veteran of the Roman army at Constantinople who was sent as prefect to Egypt ; here he took strong measures against the pagans and accordingly when Julian the Apostate came to the throne he was beheaded, in 363. Arthemius was an Arian and a persecutor of the orthodox, nor is there any record of his abjuring the heresy.

*ASAPH, ST, ab. May 11.   MAY, p. 14
Asaph, cousin of St Deiniol and St Tysilio, was founder of the monastery of Llanasa in north-east Flintshire and probably of Llanelwy, in the same county, where the cathedral city of Saint Asaph now stands. There is no trace of any bishop at Llanelwy before 1143. Sixth century. His feast is kept in the diocese of Menevia. *Asaphus.*

*ASCLAS, ST, mart. January 23.   JAN., p. 278
A martyr in Egypt, *c.* 287 (?).

ASICUS, ST, bp. April 27.   APR., p. 302

Asicus (Tassach), a copper-smith, was one of the earliest followers of St Patrick. d. *c.* 470. His feast is kept throughout Ireland as having been the first bishop of Elphin.

ASPASIUS, ST, bp. January 2.   JAN., p. 36

Bishop of Eauze (now Auch) ; d. *c.* 560.

ASTERICUS, ST, bp. November 12.   NOV., p. 148

He was first abbot of Martinsberg in Pannonia and a zealous evangelizer of the heathen Magyars. He worked hand in hand with the king St Stephen for the organization of the Hungarian church and became one of its first bishops ; he was afterwards advanced to the primatial see of Esztergom. d. *c.* 1040.

ASTERIUS, ST, bp. October 30.   OCT., p. 361

He was bishop of Amasea in Asia Minor and was a preacher of considerable power : twenty-one of his sermons are still in existence. d. *c.* 400.

*ATHANASIA, ST. August 14.   AUG., p. 174

She was widowed a few days after her marriage but married again. After a time her second husband wished to become a monk and Athanasia turned her own house into a convent and ruled it as abbess. The last seven years of her life were passed in a cell at Constantinople as adviser to the empress Theodora. d. 860.

†*ATHANASIUS, ST, bp. and doct. May 2.   MAY, p. 19

B. at Alexandria *c.* 297. The title St Athanasius earned for himself " Father of Orthodoxy," and the common saying " Athanasius against the world," indicate his life : he was the champion of Christian orthodoxy against Arianism from the day that, while still a deacon, he defended the deity of Jesus Christ at the Council of Nicæa. He was elected bishop of Alexandria in 328 and during an episcopate of over forty years he was five times driven into exile by heretics and politicians, spending a total of seventeen years away from his see, but never flagged in using all his powers —one of which was a humorous wit that was not always gentle—in support of the Catholic faith. d. 373. Athanasius is one of the four great Greek doctors of the Universal Church ; he is regarded as the father of scientific theology.

ATHANASIUS THE ATHONITE, ST, ab. July 5.   JULY, p. 53

Or " of Trebizond," from the place of his birth *c.* 920. He was a monk in Bithynia but migrated to Mount Athos and there in 961 founded the first monastery proper (" Laura ") in what has ever since been a wholly monastic republic. Athanasius was opposed by the solitaries already living there, but he had the support of the emperors Nicephoros Phocas and John Tzimisces, and at his death through an accident in 1003 was the superior-general of nearly sixty communities of hermits and monks on the Holy Mountain. Later they were involved in the schism of the Orthodox Church. St Athanasius is named in the preparatory part of the Byzantine eucharistic Liturgy.

*ATHANASIUS OF NAPLES, ST, bp. July 15.   JULY, p. 200

He was appointed to the see of Naples at the age of eighteen in 850 and after he had ruled it for twenty years he was driven into exile by his uncle Sergius, duke of Naples. During the troubles which followed Athanasius died at Veroli in 872.

*ATHENOGENES, ST, bp. and mart. July 16. JULY, p. 212

An Armenian bishop, of uncertain date, to whom St Basil attributes the authorship of the famous hymn *Phos hilaron* sung at Vespers in the Byzantine rite.

*ATTALAS, ST, ab. March 10. MAR., p. 171

A Burgundian monk who accompanied St Columbanus from Luxeuil to Bobbio. Attalas played a principal part in the founding of Bobbio and was its second abbot ; he had great trouble with the monks, many of whom found the rule too severe and left, spreading false stories about the abbot. d. 627.

ATTICUS, ST, bp. October 10. JAN., p. 114

He was intruded as bishop of Constantinople during the second banishment of St John Chrysostom, but repented of his opposition to that saint and lived a very holy life till his death on October 10, 425. He occurs in the *Acta Sanctorum* on January 8.

*ATTILANUS, ST, bp. October 5. OCT., p. 32

He was a disciple of St Froilan and became bishop of Zamora in Spain. d. 1009.

ATTRACTA, ST, virg. August 11. AUG., p. 134

Attracta (Athracht) was a solitary first at Killaraght, on Lough Gara, and then at Drum, near Boyle, during the fifth (?) century. Her feast is kept throughout Ireland.

*AUBIN, ST, bp. March 1. MAR., p. 4

Aubin (*Albinus*) was bishop of Angers in the first half of the sixth century. His very widespread cultus appears to be due to the unusually large number of miracles attributed to him. d. *c.* 554.

*AUDOENUS, ST, bp. August 24 AUG., p. 292

In French *Ouen.* While a layman and chancellor at the court of King Dagobert I he founded the abbey of Rebaix ; later he was ordained, and in 641 was made archbishop of Rouen. For forty-three years he played an active part in ecclesiastical and civil affairs, and was very zealous against simony and other abuses. d. 684.

AUDRY, ST. *See* Etheldreda.

†*AUGUSTINE, ST, bp. and doct. August 28. AUG., p. 346

B. at Tagaste in North Africa in 354. In spite of the influence of his mother St Monica he lived until the age of thirty-two a life defiled morally by licence and intellectually by Manichæism. After a great inward struggle he was converted at Milan, baptized by St Ambrose, and returned to Africa, where he established a sort of monastery. In 396 he became bishop of Hippo. Augustine was one of the greatest of the Latin doctors and his teaching on grace and the Church is profoundly influential still, even outside of Catholicism ; he refuted the heresy he had formerly held ; and by his establishment of communities of priests and of women he became the father of countless canons, friars, and other religious. He preached almost every day and his sermons are frequently read in the Divine Office. During his thirty-five years as bishop Augustine had always to be opposing one heresy or another : Manichæism, the Priscillianists, the Donatists, Pelagianism, the Arian Vandals ; he was one of the most outstanding intellects of history and one of the best regarded of men, for he is known by his own " Confessions." This and the *De Civitate Dei* are the most famous of his written works. d. 430. *Augustinus.*

AUGUSTUS CHAPDELAINE, BD, mart. February 27.   FEB., p. 375
B. in France in 1814, ninth child of a peasant. After being a country
curate he went as a missionary to China. After some years of devoted
work he was tortured and put to death most barbarously in 1856, the
required ransom of 300 taels not being forthcoming. bd. with other martyrs
in China in 1900.

AUGUSTINE GAZOTICH, BD, bp. August 3.   AUG., p. 36
He was a Dominican from Dalmatia who preached among the southern
Slavs and Magyars and in 1303 became bishop of Zagreb in Croatia.
Later he was translated to the see of Lucera (Nocera) in Italy. Bd
Augustine had the gift of healing in a marked degree. d. 1323. c.c. by
Pope Clement XI.

AUGUSTINE NOVELLO, BD. May 19.   MAY, p. 243
As Matthew of Taormina in Sicily he was chancellor to King Manfred
and was left for dead on the battlefield of Benevento. He recovered from
his wounds and became an Augustinian friar under the name of Augustine
Novello ; he helped to draft new constitutions for the order, became its
prior general, and was appointed papal penitentiary and legate. The last
nine years of his life he spent as a solitary. d. 1309. bd. 1759.

AUGUSTUS SCHÖFFLER, BD, mart. May 1.   MAY, p. 18
A priest of the Paris Society of Foreign Missions who was martyred
by beheading in Annam in 1851. bd. 1900.

AUGUSTINE OF BIELLA, BD. July 24.   JULY, p. 344
He was a confessor of the Dominican Order, who d. 1493. c.c. 1872.

†*AUGUSTINE OF CANTERBURY, ST, bp. May 26.   MAY, p. 330
With other monks of St Andrew's on the Coelian Hill Augustine was
sent by Pope St Gregory the Great to evangelize the English and strengthen
what remained of the British church. They landed at Ebbsfleet in 597, and
Augustine eventually established his episcopal see at Canterbury. He made
considerable progress in converting the English, but failed entirely with
the British Christians, whom he seems to have handled clumsily and
overbearingly. d. 605. As the apostle of the English his feast is kept in
England as a double of the second class on May 26 (in the general kalendar,
May 28) ; he was formerly generally called *Austin* in English.

AUNACHARIUS, ST, bp. September 25.   SEPT., p. 311
Also *Aunarius, Aunaire.* He became bishop of Auxerre *c.* 570 and
was one of the most influential and respected bishops of his time in France.
He enacted some very interesting disciplinary canons, throwing light on
current popular abuses. d. 605.

AUREA, ST, virg. March 11.   MAR., p. 197
A solitary at the convent of St Aemilian above the Upper Ebro in the
diocese of Calahorra, Spain. d. *c.* 1100.

AURELIUS, ST, bp. July 20.   JULY, p. 292
He became bishop of Carthage in 388 and had to oppose both the Donatist and Pelagian heresies, in which he was notably mild and conciliatory ;
but his adversaries were so violent that he had to ask the emperor Honorius
to put the civil law in force against them. d. 429.

***AURELIUS** and **NATALIA, SS,** marts. July 27.   JULY, p. 380
They were a Hispano-Moorish couple of good family at Toledo, who at
the time of Moorish persecution openly professed the Christian faith;
together with other martyrs they were beheaded *c.* 852.

AUSTIN. *See* Augustine.

*AUSTREBERTA, ST, virg. February 10. FEB., p. 150
Daughter of St Framechildis and the count palatine Badefrid. She became abbess of Port (Abbeville) and had then to undertake the reform of the abbey of Pavilly, in the course of which she offended its founder, one Amalbert, who threatened her life. But she continued her work unafraid and remained abbess of Pavilly until her death in 703.

*AUSTREGISILUS, ST, bp. May 20. MAY, p. 252
Abbot of Saint-Nizier at Lyons and then bishop of Bourges. d. 624. In France he is called *Outril.*

*AUSTREMONIUS, ST, bp. November 1. NOV., p. 10
Nothing certain is known of this saint except that he was a missionary in Auvergne (perhaps in the fourth century) where, as " St Stremoine," he is venerated as the first bishop of Clermont.

*AURELIAN, ST, bp. June 16. JUNE, p. 198
He became bishop of Arles in 546 and d. about three years later. *Aurelianus.*

*AUREUS and JUSTINA, SS, marts. June 16. JUNE, p. 196
Aureus, bishop of Mainz, with Justina his sister and others, was put to death during a barbarian invasion of the Rhineland, *c.* 460 (?). The accounts of these martyrs are conflicting.

AUTHBERTUS, ST, bp. September 10. SEPT., p. 131
He was the bishop of Avranches who founded the church of Mont-Saint-Michel early in the eighth century. In French, *Autbert.*

*AUTHBERTUS, ST, bp. December 13. DEC., p. 154
He was elected bishop of Cambrai in 633 and was notable for his encouragement of monasticism ; he was the first founder of the abbey of Saint Vedastus at Arras. d. 669.

*AUXENTIUS, ST. February 14. FEB., p. 219
A Persian soldier in the guards of the emperor Theodosius the Younger ; he became a hermit in Bithynia. Sozomen writes of his purity of life and steadfast faith. d. 473.

*AVENTINUS, ST, bp. February 4. FEB., p. 66
An early bishop of Chartres who succeeded his brother St Solennis. d. *c.* 520.

AVERTANUS, ST. February 25. FEB., p. 346
A Carmelite lay-brother of Limoges who died outside Lucca while on a pilgrimage to the Holy Land in 1380.

AVERTINUS, ST. May 5. MAY, p. 74
In the diocese of Tours Avertinus is venerated as a Gilbertine canon who was deacon to St Thomas Becket during his exile ; afterwards he was a solitary in Touraine. There is no reason to suppose that the hermit Avertinus had anything to do with the Gilbertine Order or with St Thomas. d. *c.* 1180 (?).

*AVITUS, ST, bp. February 5. FEB., p. 82
Avitus succeeded his father Isychius as bishop of Vienne in 490 and lived in the respect of both Christians and heathen. He left a number of written works, most of which are lost. His contemporaries refer to his learning and love of the poor. d. *c.* 519.

AVITUS, ST, ab. June 17. JUNE, p. 215
An abbot in the French province of Perche of whom no certain information is forthcoming. d. 530 (?).

AYBERT, ST. April 7. APRIL, p. 85
He was a monk and hermit in the diocese of Tournai, one of whose devotional practices is of significance in the controversy concerning the origins of the rosary. d. 1140.

BABYLAS, ST, bp and mart. January 24. JAN., p. 294

The most celebrated of the early bishops of Antioch after St Ignatius. St John Chrysostom praised him and St Aldehelm of Sherborne wrote an account of him in prose and verse. He was martyred c. 250.

BADEMUS, ST, ab. April 10. APR., p. 111

Bademus was founder and abbot of a monastery near Beth-Lapat in Persia ; during the persecution by Sapor II he was killed by an apostate at the order of the king, 376.

BAIN, ST, bp. June 20. JUNE, p. 253

A monk of Fontenelle who became bishop of Thérouanne, whence he evangelized the Pas de Calais. He is the patron of the town of Calais. d. c. 710. *Bagnus.*

*BALBINA, ST, virg. March 31. MAR., p. 452

A Roman maiden of the second century about whom nothing is known.

*BALDOMERUS, ST. February 27. FEB., p. 373

Otherwise *Galmier.* A locksmith who in the seventh century was famous at Lyons for his goodness, and was at length persuaded to enter a monastery. d. c. 660.

BALDWIN, ST, mart. October 16. JAN., p. 117

A seventh-century " martyr," archdeacon of Laon, honoured in the diocese of Soissons. *Bauduinus.*

BALREDUS, ST. March 6. MAR., p. 85

An anchorite who lived on the Bass Rock and elsewhere in ancient Northumbria. d. 756. He was venerated at Durham together with another anchorite, St Bilfrid. Some have identified Balredus with St Kentigern's successor Baldred.

BALTHASAR OF CHIAVARI, BD. October 17. OCT., p. 244

He was a Friar Minor and a fellow-preacher with Bd Bernardino of Feltre, venerated in the diocese of Pavia. d. 1492. c.c. 1930.

BAPTIST SPAGNUOLO, BD. March 20. MAR., p. 349

This Carmelite possessed the gift of counsel to such a degree that he was six successive times elected vicar general of the friars at Mantua. Eventually he was made prior general of the order, an office which he discharged with the same tact and success as the lesser one. Bd Baptist wrote over 50,000 lines of Latin verse, mostly with a specifically religious intention. d. 1516. bd. 1890. *Baptista.*

BAPTISTA VARANI, BD, virg. June 7. JUNE, p. 98

She was daughter of a prince of Camerino and, after leading the ordinary life of the world at her father's court, became a Poor Clare at Urbino in 1481. At once she had mystical revelations concerning the Passion which she embodied in a book called *I Dolori mentali di Gesù,* which contributed to the evolution of devotion to the Sacred Heart. After being transferred to a convent at Camerino she received other extraordinary graces, which

36

she wrote down in obedience to her confessor. Her " instructions " on the
spiritual life are marked by humour and common sense. d. 1527. c.c.
1843. *Battista*.

BARADATES, ST. February 22. FEB., p. 306

" The admirable Baradates," as Theodoret calls him in his *Philotheus*,
was a hermit in Syria in the fifth century. The Emperor Leo wrote to
consult him about the Council of Chalcedon.

†***BARBARA, ST,** virg. and mart. December 4. DEC., p. 53

St Barbara was one of the most popular saints of the Middle Ages, but
there is some doubt whether she ever existed and it is quite certain that her
extant legend is spurious. According to this she was shut up in a tower by
her father, who eventually killed her with his own hand for being a
Christian ; this is located at different places and various times—the Roman
Martyrology says at Nicomedia under Maximinus Thrax. St Barbara was
invoked against lightning and fire and by gunners, because it was said that
her father had been consumed by fire from heaven.

BARBASYMAS, ST, bp. and mart. January 14. JAN., p. 178

A metropolitan of Seleucia-Ctesiphon who in the persecution by the
Persians under Sapor II was imprisoned and tortured, and eventually
put to death with a number of companions in 346.

***BARBATUS, ST,** bp. February 19. FEB., p. 273

Bishop of Beneventum, which diocese was sunk in paganism and
indifference. He laboured in it for nineteen years to complete the work of
reclamation he had begun there as a priest. d. 682.

BARDO, ST, bp. June 15. JUNE, p. 188

Abbot of Kaiserwerth and of Horsfeld and then, in 1031, archbishop of
Mainz. At a time when great prelates were far too much concerned with
temporal affairs St Bardo's interests were always primarily spiritual, and
he was loved and trusted by his flock accordingly. His recreation was an
aviary of rare birds. d. 1053.

BARHADBESCIABAS, ST, mart. July 20. JULY, p. 291

He was deacon of the town of Arbela in Persia and was beheaded during
the persecution of Sapor II, in 355.

***BARLAAM, ST,** mart. November 19. Nov., p. 247

He was a martyr at Antioch, but when and in what circumstances is
not known ; his *acta* are spurious.

***BARLAAM** and **JOSAPHAT, SS.** November 27. Nov., p. 321

" SS Barlaam and Josaphat " (Joasaph) never existed. Their legend
is a Christianized version of that of Siddartha Buddha ; there has come
down to us, embedded in it, the text of the apology for Christianity of
Aristides the Athenian.

†***BARNABAS, ST,** ap. June 11. JUNE, p. 140

" He was a good man, full of the Holy Ghost and of faith " (Acts xi,
24) and, following the example of St Paul, the Church has always numbered
him among the Apostles because, although he was not one of the Twelve,
he was divinely set apart to accompany St Paul on his missionary journeys.
He is said to have been martyred in Cyprus *c.* 60, and is named in the
canon of the Roman Mass.

BARNARD, ST, bp. January 23. JAN., p. 288

B. 777 ; founded the abbeys of Ambronay and Romans ; archbishop
of Vienne in 810. Though somewhat imprudent in his political activities

he was one of the most influential as well as one of the most saintly prelates of his age. d. 841.

*BARONTIUS, ST. March 25.   MAR., p. 399

In middle age he retired with his son to the abbey of Lonrey and afterwards became a hermit near Pistoia. d. *c.* 725.

*BARSABAS, ST, mart. December 11.   DEC., p. 136

It is said that Barsabas was a martyr in Persia under Sapor II in 342, that he was an abbot and that his ten monks, and a layman who voluntarily joined them, suffered at the same time. But he is probably the same person as St Simeon Barsabæ (April 21).

*BARSANUPHIUS, ST. April 11.   APR., p. 124

He was an anchorite at Gaza, greatly revered in the East, but nothing more is known of him for certain. d. *c.* 540.

*BARSIMÆUS, ST, bp. and mart. January 30.   JAN., p. 384

Possibly a bishop of Edessa in the middle of the third century ; the story of his martyrdom under Trajan has been exploded.

BARTHOLOMEW, BD. June 24.   JUNE, p. 325

A native of Whitby who was ordained priest in Norway, became a monk of Durham, and spent forty-two years as a hermit on Farne island ; here he occupied St Cuthbert's old cell and his peaceful life was interrupted only by an unfortunate incident with a fellow-hermit who implied a doubt about the genuineness of Bartholomew's abstemiousness. d. 1193 (?). *Bartholomæus.*

†*BARTHOLOMEW, ST, ap. August 24.   AUG., p. 289

Beyond his existence as one of the Twelve, nothing is certainly known of this apostle : many scholars identify him with Nathanael. The stories of his missionary activity in India and martyrdom in Armenia are not reliable.

BARTHOLOMEW BREGANZA, BD, bp. October 23.   OCT., p. 314

He received the Preachers' habit from St Dominic and in 1233 founded at Bologna an association for the preservation of peace and public order (the "Fratres Gaudentes") which spread throughout Italy. He was made a bishop in Cyprus and in 1256 translated to Vicenza, where he was greatly venerated by the people. d. 1271. c.c. 1793.

BARTHOLOMEW FANTI, BD. December 5.   DEC., p. 81

He was a confessor of the Carmelite Order who lived and died at Mantua, where he was famed for miracles of healing. d. 1495. c.c. 1909.

BARTHOLOMEW PUCCI-FRANCESCHI, BD. May 23.   MAY, p. 28

After many years of married life he became a Franciscan friar at Montepulciano and a "fool for Christ's sake." d. 1330. c.c. 1880.

BARTHOLOMEW OF CERVERE, BD, mart. April 22.   APR., p. 263

He was killed by heretics at Cervere while performing the duties of inquisitor in Piedmont in 1466. c.c. by Pius IX.

*BARTHOLOMEW OF ROSSANO, ST, ab. November 11. NOV., p. 132

He was the fourth abbot of the Greek monastery of Grottaferrata, near Rome ; he was its lesser founder, carrying through the work begun by St Nilus. The disgraceful Pope Benedict IX ended his life in penitence under the influence of St Bartholomew. d. 1065.

BARTOLO BUONPEDONI, BD. December 14.   DEC., p. 168

After being a lay servant in a Benedictine monastery he became a secular priest and Franciscan tertiary ; he was appointed to the parish of

Peccioli, near Volterra, where he contracted leprosy or a similar disease in 1380. He thereupon went to a leper hospital, of which he was made master, and spent twenty years ministering to his fellow-sufferers with infinite patience. d. 1300. c.c. 1910.

BARTOLOMEA CAPITANIO, BD, virg. July 26. JULY, p. 370
Before her death at the age of twenty-six Bd Bartolomea had founded the congregation of Italian Sisters of Charity with the Venerable Vincenza Gerosa ; she also left a considerable body of spiritual writings. d. 1833. bd. 1926.

†*BASIL THE GREAT, ST, bp. and doct. June 14. JUNE, p. 172
B. at Cæsarea in Cappadocia in 329, son of saints and grandson of a martyr. Basil studied at Constantinople and Athens, visited the monasteries of the Near East, and established the first monastery in Asia Minor, on the river Iris in Pontus. In 370 he was appointed to the see of Cæsarea and proved to be one of the greatest of all bishops. He defended his huge province against the Arian heresy and defied the emperor in the process, wrote doctrinal works, numerous letters and homilies which are used in the Divine Office, founded the first recorded hospice for travellers, with a dispensary attached, and edited the eucharistic Liturgy which bears his name and is still used on certain days in the Byzantine rite. St Basil is regarded as the father of all Eastern monks, though his so-called rule is ascetical rather than legislative. He was one of the greatest of preachers and the Council of Chalcedon referred to him as " the minister of grace who has expounded truth to the whole earth " : in the East he is the first of the Three Holy Hierarchs, in the West one of the Four Greek Doctors. d. January 1, 379. *Basilius.*

*BASIL OF ANCYRA, ST, mart. March 22. MAR., p. 368
After an unwearying confession of the true faith against the Arians the priest Basil was put to death in 362 for opposing the emperor Julian the Apostate.

BASIL THE YOUNGER, ST. March 26. MAR., p. 412
A hermit near Constantinople, who was once tortured by the imperial officers on suspicion of being a spy. He was a hundred years old at his death in 952.

†*BASILIDES and Comps., **SS,** marts. June 12. JUNE, p. 151
Basilides seems to have been martyred at Rome, perhaps at the end of the third century ; his alleged companion St Quirinus is probably the Quirinus of June 4 ; SS Nabor and Nazarius may have belonged to Milan, but nothing is known of them. This group would appear to be the result of a confusion of names in the martyrologies.

BASILISSA. *See also* Basilla *and* Julian.

*BASILISSA and **ANASTASIA, SS,** marts. April 15. APR., p. 171
They are popularly supposed to be two Roman women who removed the bodies of SS Peter and Paul and had them buried, later suffering martyrdom themselves. But their existence is very doubtful.

*BASILLA, ST, virg. and mart. May 20. MAY, p. 251
A maiden who suffered martyrdom for Christ in Rome in 304. She is said to have broken off her engagement to the patrician Pompeius at her baptism.

BASINUS, ST, bp. March 4. MAR., p. 50
A bishop of Trier of whom very little is known. d. *c.* 705.

*BASOLUS, ST. November 26. Nov., p. 307

Basolus (Basle) was a monk and hermit at Vierzy in Champagne to whom many miracles were attributed. d. *c.* 600. His disciple St Sindulphus is also named in the Roman Martyrology.

*BATHILDIS, ST. January 30. JAN., p. 381

Bathildis was an English slave girl who became the wife of King Clovis II and mother of three kings, Clotaire III, Childeric II, and Thierry III. For eight years she was regent of France, taking St Eligius as her adviser, putting down slavery, and restoring monasteries. When Clotaire came of age she entered the convent of Chelles as a simple nun and d. there in 680. Her biography was written by a contemporary.

*BAUDELIUS, ST, mart. May 20. MAY, p. 252

Little is known of St Baudelius except that he suffered for Christ at Nîmes in the early centuries.

*BAVO, ST. October 1. OCT., p. 7

Bavo, or Allowin, patron of the dioceses of Ghent and of Haarlem, was a famous hermit in Brabant. He was a nobleman who, after having led a very irregular life, became a widower, was converted by St Amandus, and eventually led a solitary life in various places near Ghent and Liége. d. *c.* 653.

*BEAN, ST, bp. December 16.

The Roman Martyrology on December 16 makes mention of a St Bean, bishop in Ireland. The diocese of Aberdeen keeps the feast of St Bean, bishop of Mortlach at the beginning of the eleventh century, on October 26. *Beanus.*

BEATRICE D'ESTE, BD. January 18. DEC., p. 311

This Beatrice was a niece of the following. She was a Benedictine nun at Ferrara, probably after having been married and widowed. d. 1262. c.c. 1774. *Beatrix.*

BEATRICE D'ESTE, BD, virg. May 10. MAY, p. 123

She was left an orphan at the age of six and her relatives tried to use her for the aggrandizement of the family by arranging a marriage; Beatrice fled secretly and became a Benedictine nun, dying at the age of twenty in 1226. Her shrine is at Padua. c.c. 1763.

BEATRICE D'ORNACIEUX, BD, virg. February 13. FEB., p. 205

Bd Beatrice was a Carthusian nun of Parménie, of very austere life, who had numerous supernatural visions and also suffered from diabolical manifestations. She was one of the earliest to practise prayer before the Blessed Sacrament. Late in life she was sent with other nuns to make a new foundation at the house called d'Esmue and there she d. November 25, 1309. c.c. 1869.

BEATRICE DA SILVA, BD, virg. August 18. AUG., p. 210

Beatrice ("Brites") da Silva was b. in Portugal in 1424 and left the court of Isabel of Castile to found the Congregation of the Immaculate Conception ("Conceptionists") at Toledo; the institute was approved by the Holy See in 1489 and still exists in Spain, Italy, and elsewhere. d. 1490. c.c. 1926.

BEATUS, ST. February 19. FEB., p. 274

A priest of the Asturias who opposed the adoptionist errors of Helipandus of Toledo and was denounced as "a vagabond mountaineer who dared to set himself up against the archbishop of Toledo and the Church."

He wrote a book against Helipandus and represented the orthodox of Spain at the Council of Frankfort when Adoptionism was condemned. Beatus also wrote a commentary on the Apocalypse, which still exists. d. 789.

*BEATUS, ST. May 9. MAY, p. 110

A hermit, supposedly early but of uncertain date, at Beatenberg above the lake of Thun, who is venerated as the apostle of Switzerland. On May 9 another St Beatus is honoured at Vendôme.

†*BEDE THE VENERABLE, ST, doct. May 27. MAY, p. 322

The Venerable Bede, the only doctor of the Church of English birth, was b. at·Wearmouth in 673. From an early age he was brought up at, and all his life lived in, the monastery of that town and the adjoining abbey of Jarrow. St Bede was trained under St Benedict Biscop, ordained by St John of Beverley, and was always a simple and busy monk, a model of stability and detachment. He is best known as the author of the *Ecclesiastical History of the English People,* but the Bible was his principal study and he wrote on many and varied subjects; extracts from his homilies are read in the Divine Office of the Roman Church. d. 735. *Beda.*

BEE, ST. *See* Bega.

BEGA, ST, virg. September 6. OCT., p. 376

Bega is said to have been a seventh-century Irish maiden who established a nunnery on the promontory in Northumberland now called after her, St Bee's Head. She seems not to be the same as either the Bega or the Heiu mentioned by St Bede, but the whole matter is very confused and uncertain. The feast of St Bega is kept in the diocese of Lancaster.[1]

*BEGGA, ST. December 17. DEC., p. 195

She was sister of St Gertrude of Nivelles and spent most of her long life as a nobleman's wife " in the world." On becoming a widow in 692 she established and ruled over a convent at Andenne on the Meuse. d. 698.

†*BENEDICT, ST, ab. March 21. MAR., p. 352

B. at Norcia in Umbria *c.* 480. While a young man he fled from the licence of Rome and lived as a hermit at Subiaco; disciples gathered round, and about 525 he founded the monastery of Monte Cassino, for whose monks he wrote the rule which bears his name. That rule spread throughout Europe and became the norm for all Western monks; its followers taught the barbarians to work with hands and head, and to pray: but Benedict himself lived and legislated for those things immediately at hand —the formation of communities for the glory of God and the salvation of souls called to the cenobitical life. The little that is known about St Benedict personally mostly comes from the second book of St Gregory's *Dialogues,* where he appears as a man who was as lovable as he was great. As St Basil is Patriarch of the Monks of the East, so is St Benedict of those of the West—and the father of Western Europe as well. He was never a priest. d. *c.* 550. *Benedictus.*

*BENEDICT, ST. March 23. MAR., p. 381

A hermit in the Campagna who was marvellously preserved from a cruel death at the hands of the Goths. d. *c.* 550.

---

[1] In Butler's *Lives,* October volume, 1936 edition, the last large-type paragraph on p. 377 does not belong to St. Bega but to the end of the preceding account of St. Foillan p. 376.

*BENEDICT II, ST, pope. May 8.

This Benedict, a Roman, was elected to the apostolic throne in 684 but d. in the following year. During his pontificate of eleven months he upheld the cause of St Wilfrid of York.

*BENEDICT XI, BD, pope. July 7.

Benedict was the ninth master-general of the Dominicans, being then known as Nicholas Boccasini, and as cardinal bishop of Ostia and papal legate played a conspicuous part in the troubles between Pope Boniface VIII and King Philip IV of France. He was himself elected pope in 1303 but d. in the following year. In his private life he continued the penances and simplicity of a friar. bd. 1736.

*BENEDICT BISCOP, ST, ab. January 12.

Biscop Baducing, a Northumbrian by birth, after two journeys to Rome, received the monastic habit at Lérins. After another stay in Rome he returned to Northumbria and founded a monastery, St Peter's at Wearmouth, where St Bede was his pupil. He went again to Rome for books, relics, and other matters, and then founded a twin monastery, St Paul's at Jarrow. There was an abbot for each, but Benedict himself was in general control. Among his achievements was to bring from Rome the precentor of St Peter's to teach the English monks chant and cere-monial *more Romano ;* the constitutions of Wearmouth and Jarrow were drawn from those of seventeen monasteries that Benedict himself had visited. For the last three years of his life he was mostly confined to his bed, where he used to sing the Divine Office with monks who came to his cell for the purpose. St Benedict Biscop is one of the patrons of the English congregation of Benedictines. d. 690. His feast is kept in the dioceses of Southwark and Liverpool.

*BENEDICT JOSEPH LABRE, ST. April 16.

Labre is a representative example of those who, at all times in Christian history, have refused in the name of Christ to be " respectable." He was b. 1748, son of a prosperous French shopkeeper, and offered himself to several austere religious orders but proved unsuitable. He then began a series of pilgrimages on foot to the chief shrines of Western Europe, living almost literally on what he could pick up. From 1770 Labre lived in Rome, spending his days in the churches and his nights in the ruins of the Colosseum, and he was revered as a saint throughout the city. He was found dying on the steps of Santa Maria dei Monti, and was taken to the house of a friendly butcher where he d. 1783. His fame spread remarkably quickly, though the popular biographies of him (and not of him only) are apt to emphasize some of his less-important characteristics. cd. 1881.

BENEDICT RICASOLI, BD. January 20.

He left the Vallombrosan abbey of Coltiboni to live in a hermit's cell near by, from whence he would come at great feasts to exhort his brethren to perseverance. d. *c.* 1107. c.c. 1907.

*BENEDICT THE MOOR, ST. April 4.

Benedict the Moor, or " the Black," was in fact a Negro, whose parents were serfs near Messina in Sicily. He was invited to join with some hermits, and on the death of their superior was elected in his place. The com-munity was absorbed into the Friars Minor of the Observance and Benedict became a lay brother at Palermo, and in 1578, although he was illiterate and not a priest, was appointed guardian of the friary. He proved to be an ideal superior and showed many evidences of the direct supernatural help he received in the discharge of this and other offices. In his old age he returned to the kitchen, but was still sought there by his admirers. d. 1589. cd. 1809.

BENEDICT OF ANIANE, ST, ab. February 11.   FEB., p. 172
   The part played by Benedict of Aniane in the revival of monastic discipline in the eighth–ninth century has caused him to be called " the second father of Western monasticism." He was brought up at the court of Pepin and after taking part in several campaigns became a monk at Saint-Seine, near Dijon. Later he founded the monastery of St Saviour on the banks of the river Aniane in Languedoc, from whence he had the oversight of many monasteries in Provence, Languedoc, and Gascony. The emperor Louis the Débonnaire entrusted him with the reform of all the monastic houses of France and Germany and the bringing of monks and canons under uniform rules. The uniformity of discipline and central control was not carried to the length which St Benedict of Aniane seems to have desired, but the Synod of Aix-la-Chapelle over which he presided in 817 was a turning-point in the history of the Benedictines. d. 821.

*BENEDICT OF BENEVENTO, ST, mart. November 12.   NOV., p. 147
   This Benedict and his four companions were Benedictine monks, missionaries among the Slavs, who were massacred at their monastery near Gnesen in 1005.

*BENEDICT OF MILAN, ST, bp. March 11.   MAR., p. 194
   Benedict Crispus was archbishop of Milan for forty-five years in the seventh–eighth century. He wrote the epitaph for the tomb of the Anglo-Saxon prince Ceadwalla in St Peter's at Rome. d. 725.

BENEDICT OF URBINO, BD. April 30.   APR., p. 348
   A lawyer of Urbino who became a Capuchin at Fano in 1584. He was an effective preacher and accompanied St Laurence of Brindisi on his visitations in Austria and Bohemia. d. 1625. bd. 1867.

BÉNÉZET, ST. April 14.   APR., p. 162
   " Little Benedict the Bridge-builder " was a shepherd boy who was much concerned by the difficulties of people wanting to cross the Rhône. In consequence of a vision he went to the bishop of Avignon, who eventually agreed to help him build a bridge there. The work was done between 1177 and Bénézet's death in 1184, and is said to have been accompanied by many wonders. *Benedictus.*

*BENIGNUS, ST, mart. November 1.   NOV., p. 9
   Benignus is a third-century martyr venerated at Dijon from early times. The account of him that came into the hands of St Gregory of Tours, connecting the martyr with St Polycarp of Smyrna, is spurious : it is the first link in a chain of religious romances describing the alleged beginnings of the Church in parts of eastern France.

BENIGNUS, ST, bp. November 9.   NOV., p. 107
   St Benignus (Benen) was an early disciple of St Patrick and succeeded him as the chief bishop of the Irish church. He is said to have evangelized Clare and Kerry and to have had a monastery at Drumlease. There is no reason to suppose that Benen died near Glastonbury. d. *c.* 468.

BENINCASA, BD. May 11.   MAY, p. 134
   A Servite friar of Florence who lived as a solitary near Siena. d. 1426. c.c. 1829.

*BENJAMIN, ST, mart. March 31.   MAR., p. 451

A deacon martyred in Persia under Isdegerdes *c.* 421 for refusing to promise to keep silence about the Christian religion.

*BENNO, ST, bp. June 16.   JUNE, p. 200

He was made bishop of Meissen in 1066 and played a somewhat equivocal part in secular and ecclesiastical politics, being at one time imprisoned and at another deposed from his see. Later biographers speak very highly of him as a man and a bishop. d. 1106. His canonization in 1523 greatly annoyed Martin Luther.

BENNO, BD, bp. July 12.   JULY, p. 160

He was a monk and master builder to the emperor Henry III. In 1067 he was appointed bishop of Osnabrück and for a time was active in the struggle between Henry IV and Pope St Gregory VII. He founded the abbey of Iburg, and d. there in 1088.

BENNO, BD, bp. August 3.   AUG, p. 35

He was a hermit who in 927 was made bishop of Metz. After being attacked and blinded by his enemies he retired from the world, and formed a group of hermits from which eventually sprang the great Swiss abbey of Einsiedeln. d. 940.

BENTIVOGLIA DE BONIS, BD. January 2.   JAN., p. 42

A native of San Severino in the Marches of Italy and one of the early but more obscure Friars Minor. d. 1232. Cultus confirmed by Pope Pius IX. *Bentivolius.*

BENVENUTA BOJANI, BD, virg. October 30.   OCT., p. 364

She was a Dominican tertiary who lived in her own home at Cividale in northern Italy ; she is said to have been miraculously cured of a serious illness of five years' standing. d. 1292. c.c. 1763.

*BENVENUTUS, ST, bp. March 22.   MAR., p. 370

Benvenutus Scotivoli was a Friar Minor of Ancona who was bishop of Osimo from 1264 till his death in 1282. He is said to have been canonized less than four years after his death.

BENVENUTUS, BD. June 27.   JUNE, p. 363

He was a native of Gubbio and an unlettered soldier : he joined the Franciscans in 1222 and at his own request was set to care for lepers, whom he tended most lovingly. d. 1232. c.c. by Pope Gregory IX. ·

BENVENUTUS OF RECANATI, BD. May 21.   MAY, p. 261

A lay brother of the Conventual Friars Minor. d. 1289. c.c. by Pope Pius VII.

BEOCCA, etc., **SS,** marts. April 10.   APR., p. 112

During the ninth century the Danes raiding England showed special ferocity against representative Christians ; among their victims regarded as martyrs were the monks of Chertsey Beocca and Hethor, Abbot Hedda at Peterborough, Torthred and his companions at Thorney.

*BERARDUS, etc., **SS,** marts. January 16.   JAN., p. 205

Berardus with four other Friars Minor (Peter, Accursius, Adjutus, Otto) was sent by St Francis to preach to the Mohammedans of the west. They passed from Seville into Morocco, where they were put to death in 1220, the protomartyrs of the Franciscan Order. cd. 1481.

*BERCHARIUS, ST, ab. and mart. October 16.   OCT., p. 226

He was abbot of Hautvilliers and in 696 was stabbed by a monk whom he had reproved; Bercharius died from the wound and was mistakenly venerated as a martyr.

BERLINDA, ST, virg. February 3.   FEB., p. 53

Berlinda, daughter of Count Odelard, was disinherited by her father in a fit of rage, and she fled to the convent of Moorsel, near Alost in the Low Countries. On her father's death she became a solitary near his tomb at Meerbeke, giving her life to the poor and suffering. d. 702.

*BERNADETTE, ST, virg. April 16.   APR., p. 189

Bernadette Soubirous, daughter of a miller, was the child who, in 1858 at the age of fourteen, was chosen by God for the revelation to the world of the healing shrine of our Lady at Lourdes. For some years following she was the victim of much publicity, in which some Catholic ecclesiastics showed themselves extraordinarily lacking in sensibility at her expense. In 1866 Bernadette joined the Sisters of Notre Dame at Nevers, where she continued to do all she could to keep out of the public eye; she suffered much from ill health and d. at the age of thirty-five in 1879. cd. 1933. *Bernardetta, Bernarda.*

†*BERNARD, ST, ab. and doct. August 20.   AUG., p. 230

B. in 1090 near Dijon. When he was twenty-two Bernard joined the monastery and order of Cîteaux, in company with thirty other young noblemen, fifteen years after its foundation, and he formed and became abbot of the fourth house of the congregation, Clairvaux. His achievements were amazing: during his lifetime he established sixty-eight Cistercian monasteries, assisted at oecumenical and other councils, opposed and confuted Abelard, preached a crusade in France and Germany, wrote many treatises and sermons, particularly on the love of God and the *Song of Songs*, and engaged in complicated politics to preserve the peace of the Church—" he carried the twelfth century on his shoulders, and he did not carry it without suffering." Bernard defied princes and counselled popes, especially Bd Eugenius III, who had been one of his monks, and went on missions against the Albigensians in Cologne and Languedoc. d. 1153. cd. 1174. Declared a doctor of the Church (" The Honeysweet Doctor ") in 1830. *Bernardus.*

BERNARD SCAMMACCA, BD. February 16.   FEB., p. 247

He lived at Catania in Sicily and after an unruly youth became a Dominican friar. Details of his life are lacking, but marvels were reported of him both before and after his death. d. 1486. c.c. 1825.

*BERNARD TOLOMEO, BD, ab. August 21.   AUG., p. 266

B. in 1272 at Siena, where he was a man of public affairs till 1313 when, with other gentlemen, he retired to the desolate country near Mont' Amiata. They were given the Benedictine rule and white habit (instead of the usual black) by the Bishop of Arezzo, and thus began the now small monastic congregation called " of Monte Oliveto," of which several more houses were established almost immediately. In a great plague at Siena in 1348 the monks all nursed the sick, and their founder, Bd Bernard, was among those who were infected and died. c.c. 1644.

BERNARD THE PENITENT, BD. April 19.   APR., p. 230

Owing to his horrible crimes (unspecified) the Bishop of Miguelone in Provence in 1170 imposed severe penances on a young man called Bernard, who spent the rest of his life expiating his sins. He d. in a hermitage at Saint-Omer in 1182 and many wonderful cures were reported at his shrine.

BERNARD OF BADEN, BD. July 15. JULY, p. 206

In 1453 he handed over the rights of the margravate of Baden to his brother and went from court to court trying to organize a crusade against the Turks. He had no success, and d. in 1458. bd. 1481. Bd Bernard was patron of the former duchy of Baden.

*BERNARD OF CAPUA, ST, bp. March 12. MAR., p. 219

Bishop of Foro-Claudio, which see he transferred to Caleno (Carinola) hard by, where he is venerated as principal patron. d. 1109.

BERNARD OF CORLEONE, BD. January 19. JAN., p. 238

While in sanctuary after an assault on the police, Philip Latini underwent conversion and joined the Capuchins as a lay brother. His austerities were equalled only by his graces, and he had the unusual gift of healing animals by prayer. He d. at the friary of Palermo in 1667. bd. 1768.

*BERNARD OF MENTHON, ST. May 28. MAY, p. 337

He was for forty-two years vicar general to the bishop of Aosta, tirelessly visiting the most remote Alpine valleys of the diocese and being especially solicitous for the welfare of travellers. It was due to this that St Bernard established the two hospices on the great and little passes that bear his name, putting them in the charge of Augustinian canons regular. He d. probably in 1081, and in 1923 was named by Pope Pius XI patron saint of all mountaineers.

BERNARD OF OFFIDA, BD. September 1. SEPT., p. 12

He was a lay-brother of the Capuchins at Fermo, famous for his wisdom and miracles. d. 1694. bd. 1795.

*BERNARD OF PARMA, ST, bp. December 4. DEC., p. 63

While abbot-general of the Vallombrosan Benedictines this Bernard was created cardinal by Bd Urban II and entrusted with various legatine duties. He became bishop of Parma and was twice exiled for his opposition to usurped authority. He relinquished the temporal power which his predecessors in the see had obtained. d. 1133.

BERNARD OF THIRON, BD, ab. April 14. APR., p. 161

Also called " of Abbeville " ; he was founder of the abbey of Thiron, from which the reformed Benedictine Thironian congregation sprang. d. 1117. c.c. 1861.

BERNARDINO REALINI, BD. July 3. JULY, p. 32

B. in 1530 near Modena. He joined the Society of Jesus and after working for ten years among the poor of Naples he was made rector of the college at Lecce, where he remained for the rest of his life. d. 1616. Some curious phenomena are recorded concerning certain relics of his blood. Bd. by Pope Leo XIII. *Bernardinus.*

BERNARDINO OF FELTRE, BD. September 28. SEPT., p. 353

He was a Friar Minor of the Observance, clothed in 1456, and one of the outstanding Franciscans of his time in Italy. He preached almost extempore and with tremendous effect : " When he attacks wickedness he does not speak—he thunders and lightens " ; he had great influence with the civil authorities ; and he was the terror of evil-doers, who more than once tried to take his life. A famous activity of Bd Bernardino was the establishment of *montes pietatis,* charitable pawnshops that made loans on pledged objects at a very low interest to pay expenses : in this work he was an inveterate adversary of all usurers, whether Jewish or gentile. d. 1494. bd. 1728.

BERNARDINO OF FOSSA, BD. November 27.   Nov., p. 329
   He was a Friar Minor of the Observance, well known in Italy, Bosnia, and Dalmatia as a preacher and missioner. d. 1503. c.c. 1828.

†***BERNARDINO OF SIENA, ST.** May 20.   MAY, p. 246
   B. at Siena in 1380. Bernardino was a great preacher throughout Italy and a restorer of strict observance in the Franciscan order, especially in the matter of poverty. His vernacular sermons were written down and are as fresh and lively and applicable to-day as when they were first spoken ; his amusing pictures of such familiar things as a bachelor household, women's fashions, men's exactingness, " pious " superstitions, etc., have a bite in them—not for nothing is he called " the people's preacher." With St John of Capistrano he began the devotion to the Holy Name, displaying the monogram IHS for veneration and having it painted on houses. d. 1444. cd. 1450.

BERNO, BD, ab. January 13.   JAN., p. 164
   He was abbot of Gigny (which he probably founded), of Baume-les-Messieurs, and finally of Cluny, of which house he was the first ruler, from 910 to 917. Seeing the importance of the Cluniac Benedictine congregation strangely little is known of its first abbot general. d. 927.

*BERNWARD, ST, bp. November 20.   Nov., p. 257
   The name of Bernward is associated with the encouragement of ecclesiastical art in general and with metal-working in particular ; he was himself a good painter and metal-smith. He became bishop of Hildesheim in 993 ; his long episcopate was disturbed by a protracted dispute with St Willigis of Mainz, in which the conduct of Bernward was irreproachable. d. 1022. cd. 1193. *Bernwardus.*

BERTHA, ST. July 4.   'JULY, p. 36
   There are no very reliable particulars extant about this French widow and abbess. d. *c.* 725.

BERTHA DE ALBERTI, BD, virg. March 24.   MAR., p. 388
   Sometimes erroneously called " de Bardi." She was abbess of a Vallombrosan convent which she was sent to reform at Cavriglia. d. 1163.

BERTHALDUS, ST. June 16.   JUNE, p. 199
   In French *Berthaud*. He is said to have been a hermit in the Ardennes during the fifth–sixth century and to have been ordained priest, together with another hermit, St Amandus, by St Remigius.

BERTHOLD, ST. March 29.   MAR., p. 436
   Berthold is often called the founder of the Carmelite Order ; he seems to have been appointed the first general superior of the hermits on Mount Carmel by his brother Aymeric, Latin patriarch of Antioch, *c.* 1150. He rebuilt the monastery church and dedicated it in honour of Elias the Prophet. d. *c.* 1195. *Berthaldus.*

BERTHOLD OF GARSTEN, BD, ab. July 27.   JULY, p. 382
   He entered a monastery after the death of his wife and was commissioned to introduce the rule of St Benedict in the collegiate house of Steyer-Garsten. He enjoyed a great reputation as a confessor. d. 1142.

BERTILIA, ST, virg. January 3.   JAN., p. 56
   She led an uneventful life in the neighbourhood of Arras, and d. 705. She was married to a young nobleman (but in spite of this is venerated as a virgin), after whose death she became a solitary at Marœuil.

BERTILLA, ST, virg. November 5.   Nov., p. 62

When St Bathildis refounded the abbey of Chelles St Bertilla was made its abbess and her rule attracted subjects even from foreign lands ; her community eventually included two queens, St Hereswitha of the East Angles, and Bathildis herself. d. 692.

*BERTINUS, ST, ab. September 5.   Sept., p. 60

He was a monk of Luxeuil sent as a missionary to help St Omer among the Morini in Artois. With St Mommolinus he founded two monasteries, of one of which, Sithiu, he became abbot ; from thence he evangelized and civilized the heathen of the surrounding wet and marshy country. His community grew so large that he had to establish a daughter house, the church of which became the first cathedral of the diocese of Saint-Omer. St Bertinus, though probably not himself a Benedictine, was a characteristic example of the Benedictine missionary who civilized western Europe during the dark ages. d. *c.* 709.

BERTRAND, ST, bp. and mart. June 6.   June, p. 86

Or *Bertram.* After being for seventeen years auditor of the Rota in the papal court of Avignon, Bertrand was appointed patriarch of Aquileia ; in 1348 he transferred his residence to Udine, where he was a great benefactor of the town and patron of learning. He was set upon and murdered while on a journey in 1350, at the age of ninety, because he had resisted the simoniacal practices of the counts of Gorizia. c.c. by Pope Clement VIII. *Bertrandus, Bertichramnus.*

BERTRAND, ST, bp. June 30.   June, p. 396 ; July, p. 27

He was appointed bishop of Le Mans in 587 and had a troubled pontificate owing to political factions. He was a great benefactor of the poor, being specially interested in good agriculture and vine-growing, but his benefactions did not prevent him from having vast lands to dispose of in his will, which is extant. d. 623.

BERTRAND OF COMMINGES, ST, bp. October 16.   Oct., p. 229

St Bertrand was bishop of Comminges (now included in Toulouse) for fifty years, during which he showed himself a vigorous, enlightened, and fearless pastor and consequently encountered opposition, sometimes violent. Several miracles are related of him, one of which gave rise to the " great pardon " of Comminges. d. 1123. cd. 1167.

BERTRAND OF GARRIGA, BD. September 6.   Sept., p. 69

This Bertrand, a secular priest, was one of St Dominic's original group of preachers and helped in the first Dominican foundation at Paris. Later he rejoined his master and was the constant companion of his preaching, until Bertrand was made prior provincial of Provence where he spent the rest of his very active life. d. 1230. c.c. by Pope Leo XIII.

BERTULFUS, ST, ab. February 5.   Feb., p. 83

Otherwise *Bertoul, Berton.* He came from Pannonia into Flanders where he became a Christian and was for years steward to Count Wambert, whom he served with distinguished fidelity. After the count's death Bertulfus founded a small monastery at Renty and governed it till his death in 705.

BERTULFUS, ST, ab. August 19.   Aug., p. 223

He was abbot of Bobbio and obtained from Pope Honorius I the exemption of his monastery from episcopal control—the first recorded exemption of its kind. d. 640.

BETTELIN, ST. September 9.   SEPT., p. 102
Practically nothing is known about St Bettelin (Beccelin, Berthelm), except that he was a hermit at Croyland in the eighth century, succeeding St Guthlac there. This saint (or another of the same name) was patron of the town of Stafford. *Bertelmus.*

BEUNO, ST, ab. April 21.   APR., p. 251
St Beuno founded monasteries at Llanveynoe in Herefordshire, Llanymynech on the Severn and elsewhere, but his principal establishment was at Clynnog in Caernarvonshire where he is supposed to have been buried. In modern times he is best remembered for his alleged restoration to life of St Winefride and as the titular saint of the big Jesuit house in North Wales. d. *c.* 630. He is commemorated in the diocese of Menevia.

†*BIBIANA, ST, virg. and mart. December 2.   DEC., p. 25
Of the time at which this Roman martyr suffered and the circumstances of her passion nothing is certainly known. Her extant *acta* is a late, romantical and untrustworthy composition, which puts her death in the reign of Julian the Apostate.

*BIRINUS, ST, bp. December 5.   DEC., p. 78
Birinus was a missionary bishop from Rome who came to England and converted Cynegils, King of the West Saxons. He was given Dorchester in Oxfordshire for his see and from thence he converted many people and built churches for them, earning the title of Apostle of Wessex. d. *c.* 650. The feast of St Birinus is celebrated in the dioceses of Birmingham and Portsmouth.

BLAAN, ST, bp. August 11.   AUG., p. 136
Blaan (Blane) was a sixth-century Scottish bishop, trained by St Comgall and St Canice in Ireland ; he was buried at the place now called Dunblane. His feast is kept in the dioceses of Saint Andrews, Dunkeld, and Argyll. *Blaanus.*

BLÆSILLA, ST. January 22.   JAN., p. 267
Daughter of St Paula and a disciple of St Jerome. She d. at Rome at the age of twenty in 383.

†*BLAISE, ST, bp. and mart. February 3.   FEB., p. 48
It is supposed that St Blaise was bishop of Sebaste in Armenia and was martyred *c.* 316. There is no evidence for his cultus earlier than the eighth century, and credence cannot be given to his " acts." The Blessing of St Blaise against affections of the throat has reference to the statement that he saved the life of a boy who had got a fish-bone stuck in his throat. *Blasius.*

BOBO, ST. May 22.   MAY, p. 269
Bobo or Beuvon was a Provençal knight who fought against the marauding Saracens and later became a hermit. d. *c.* 985. His cultus in Lombardy is probably due to the miracles alleged at his tomb at Voghera.

BOËTHIUS. *See* Severinus Boëthius.

BOGUMILUS, ST, bp. June 10.   JUNE, p. 135
He was elected archbishop of Gnesen in 1167 but, refusing to countenance abuses that he found himself powerless to remedy, he resigned five later and became a Camaldolese hermit at Uniejow. d. 1182. c.c. 1925.

BOISIL, ST. *See* Boswell.

†*BONAVENTURE, ST, bp. and doct. July 14.   JULY, p. 177
B. near Viterbo in 1221. At thirty-six years of age Bonaventure

was elected minister general of the Franciscans, and he was nominated to, but refused, the archbishopric of York ; in 1273 he was created cardinal bishop of Albano. He was the greatest mystical theologian and among the greatest scholastics of the Middle Ages ; he wrote sermons and commentaries on the holy scriptures, and laboured for unity among the friars of his order, of whose founder he wrote a biography. Bonaventure was the outstanding figure at the second general council of Lyons in 1274 and played a big part in the reunion of the Orthodox Greeks thereat ; he was spared the sorrow of the speedy collapse of this work, for he died during the course of the council. cd. 1482. *Bonaventura.*

BONAVENTURE BADUARIO, BD. June 10.   JUNE, p. 137

A friar of St Augustine, the first member of that order to be made a cardinal. He was killed in Rome by an arrow in 1386, perhaps murdered because of his defence of the rights of the Church.

BONAVENTURE BUONACCORSI, BD. December 14.   DEC., p. 171

When nearing middle age he was converted by the preaching of St Philip Benizi and joined the Servite friars. He had been a violent partisan of the Ghibellines and now gave himself up to preaching brotherly love, civic unity, and peace. He made so great an impression that he was known as " il Beato " even during his lifetime. d. 1315. c.c. 1822.

BONAVENTURE TORNIELLI, BD. March 31.   MAR., p. 456

Bd Bonaventure became a Servite friar in 1448 and was specially commissioned by Sixtus IV to preach throughout the papal states and southern Italy ; this work he continued even after he had been elected vicar general of his order. d. 1491. c.c. 1911.

BONAVENTURE OF POTENZA, BD. October 26.   OCT., p. 341

He was a confessor of the Conventual Friars Minor in the kingdom of Naples. d. 1711. bd. 1775.

BONAVITA, BD. March 1.   MAR., p. 12

He was a blacksmith who lived and died in the little town of Lugo, near Ravenna, and was a devoted follower of St Francis of whose order he was a tertiary. d. 1375.

BONIFACE, ST, bp. March 14.   MAR., p. 251

All that can be safely affirmed of him is that he was a bishop who laboured in Scotland to introduce Roman, as opposed to Celtic, discipline and observances. Seventh century (?). *Bonifatius.*

†*BONIFACE, ST, bp. and mart. June 5.   JUNE, p. 58

The Apostle of Germany, who was b. probably at Crediton in Devonshire *c.* 680 and was christened Winfrid. He went to school at the monastery at Exeter and became a monk at Winchester. In 716 he left England to preach the gospel to the Germans and was a characteristic Benedictine missionary of the dark ages. He was consecrated bishop in Rome in 722 and laboured in Bavaria, Hesse, Thuringia, Westphalia, and elsewhere, establishing dioceses (he was made metropolitan in 731) and monasteries from whence the political, social and economic as well as the religious life of the people was formed and cared for. He placed these foundations in charge of other Englishmen and from 743 to 747 he could be spared to play a leading part in ecclesiastical reform in Gaul. His metropolitan see was fixed at Mainz and Pope St Zachary created him primate of Germany and apostolic delegate for Gaul as well. When over seventy St Boniface resigned his see and went to evangelize the Frieslanders ; he was murdered by the heathen in 754 while confirming some of his converts at Dokkum. With him perished clergy, monks, and others to the number of fifty-two.

*BONIFACE, ST, bp. and mart. June 19.　　　　　　JUNE, p. 242

He was b. at Querfurt, baptized Bruno, and became an ecclesiastic at the court of the emperor Otto III. In 996 he became a Camaldolese monk in Italy, changing his name to Boniface, and later went as a missionary to Prussia, being consecrated as a regionary bishop. He was slain by those whom he had gone to save in 1009.

*BONIFACE I, ST, pope. September 4.　　　　　　SEPT., p. 45

He became pope in difficult circumstances in 418, being opposed by one Eulalius. Boniface was a mild and peaceful man, but energetically upheld the rights of the Roman See against Constantinople and others. d. 422.

*BONIFACE IV, ST, pope. May 8.　　　　　　MAY, p. 99

Very little is known of this pope who ruled the Church from 609 till his death in 615. He consecrated the Pantheon in Rome as a Christian church in 609, and was the recipient of a famous letter from St Columbanus.

BONIFACE OF LAUSANNE, ST, bp. February 19.　　　FEB., p. 276

A native of Brussels who was made bishop of Lausanne c. 1230. His previous life as a university professor seems to have unfitted him for the episcopal office and he resigned in 1239. The last eighteen years of his life were spent as chaplain to the Cistercian nuns of Cambre, near Brussels, and in pastoral work around his native city. d. 1265.

BONIFACE OF SAVOY, BD, bp. March 13.　　　　MAR., p. 243

A member of the ducal house of Savoy and a Carthusian monk who became firstly bishop of Valence and then, in 1241, archbishop of Canterbury. He was a favourite with King Henry III (whose wife's uncle he was) but not with the bishops and abbots of England, with whom he entered on a dispute that was carried to Rome. He died in Savoy in 1270 and was buried at Haute Combe. Boniface was a man of great personal virtue and extraordinary generosity to the poor and needy, and after his death he was subject to a cultus in Savoy which was confirmed in 1830 ; but it never obtained in England.

†*BONIFACE OF TARSUS, ST, mart. May 14.　　MAY, p. 171

Boniface of Tarsus is said to have been martyred in that city in 306, but the extant story of his passion is fictitious.

BONITUS, ST, bp. January 15.　　　　　　JAN., p. 195

Bishop of Clermont, who resigned his see owing to a scruple of conscience. d. c. 710.

BONIZELLA, BD. May 6.　　　　　　　MAY, p. 83

On the death of her husband Bonizella Piccolomini left Siena and devoted herself and her wealth to the service of the poor in the district of Belsederio. d. 1300.

*BONOSUS and **MAXIMIAN, SS,** marts. August 21.　　AUG., p. 260

They were officers of the Herculean cohort at Antioch, who under Julian the Apostate refused to recognize the pagan military standard ; they were tortured and beheaded in 363.

BOSA, ST, bp. March 9.　　　　　　MAR., p. 154

When St Wilfrid of York was exiled and his diocese divided, Bosa, a monk of Whitby, was chosen bishop of the southern part, Deira, with the see at York. St Bede describes him as " beloved by God . . . a man of most unusual merit and holiness." d. 686.

BOSWELL, ST, ab. July 7. FEB., p. 319

Otherwise *Boisil.* An abbot of Melrose, who numbered St Cuthbert among his subjects. Cuthbert had a great admiration for him. St Boswell seems to have had the gift of knowledge of the future, and took a special delight in the gospel of St John. d. 664. Apparently his feast was kept in Durham on July 7 or 8.

BOTOLPH, ST, ab. June 17. JUNE, p. 220

St Botolph (Botulph, Botwulf), greatly venerated in pre-Norman England, was founder of a monastery at Ikanhoe, generally identified as Boston (Botolph's town) in Lincolnshire, in 654. He appears to have led a peaceful life and to have d. *c.* 680. His feast is still observed in the dioceses of Brentwood, Nottingham, and Northampton. *Botulphus.*

BOTWID, ST, mart. July 28. JULY, p. 397

Botwid was a Swede, converted to Christ in England, who preached in his own country ; he was basely murdered by a Finnish slave whom he had freed, in 1100.

*BOVA and **DODA, SS,** virgs. April 24. APR., p. 280

St Baldericus made his sister Bova abbess of a convent at Reims, and after her death in 673 she was succeeded by her niece Doda.

*BRAULIO, ST, bp. March 26. MAR., p. 410

He was bishop of Saragossa, a friend of St Isidore, a scholar, and a friend of the poor ; some of his letters and other writings have come down to us. d. 646. Patron saint of Aragon.

*BRENDAN, ST, ab. May 16. MAY, p. 206

Brendan the Voyager is one of the three most famous saints of Ireland. He was born probably near Tralee and for five years was in the charge of St Ita ; in 559 (?) he founded the monastery of Clonfert, and d. in 577 or 583 at Enach Duin. The voyages of St Brendan are now admitted to be fictitious, but he probably visited Scotland and perhaps Wales ; his journey to discover the isles of the blessed was known in most European languages in the Middle Ages. His feast is kept throughout Ireland. *Brendanus.*

*BRICE, ST, bp. November 13. NOV., p. 153

Although he was extravagant, contemptuous of his bishop St Martin, and even licentious, this cleric was raised to the see of Tours in succession to St Martin. He was an unsatisfactory bishop and after twenty years was driven from his diocese. He went to Rome, reformed his life completely, and after seventeen years of exile was restored to his bishopric. So strong was the impression made on his flock by his new manner of life that after his death in 444 Brice was revered as a saint ; his cultus spread all over northern Europe. *Britius.*

†*BRIDGET OF SWEDEN, ST. October 8. OCT., p. 90

She was b. in 1304 and before she was fifteen married Ulf Gudmarsson, Prince of Nierck, with whom she lived happily for twenty-eight years, having eight children, of whom one, Catherine, is also recognized as a saint. Bridget was a busy and accomplished housekeeper, giving much to the poor, and *c.* 1335 became chief lady-in-waiting to the queen of Magnus Eriksson, King of Sweden, whose court she unsuccessfully tried to induce him to purge. After her husband's death numerous and remarkable visions and revelations came to her, she became the adviser of popes and kings, and the devoted servant of the poor of Rome, whither she went to live. She d. there on July 23, 1373, and her body was taken home to the monastery of Wadstena of that order of nuns and canons (called after her "Bridgettines") which she had founded in 1344. The book of St Bridget's revelations has been translated into numerous languages. She was cd in 1391 and is the patron saint of Sweden. *Birgitta.*

BRIEUC, ST, ab. May 1.   MAY, p. 10

B. in Cardiganshire *c.* 420. He migrated to Brittany and founded two monasteries, one near Tréguier and the other where the town of Saint-Brieuc now stands. The saint is also known in Cornwall. d. *c.* 510. *Briocus.*

*BRIGID, ST, virg. February 1.   FEB., p. 10

Also *Bridget, Bride, Ffraid.* Brigid is among the greatest and most venerated of those many saints who gave glory to Ireland, but the numerous "lives" do not enable a connected account of her to be put together. She was born *c.* 450 at Faughart, near Dundalk, became a nun at an early age, and founded the monastery of Kildare, thereby becoming the spiritual mother of Irish nuns for many centuries. d. *c.* 525. Her memory in the hearts of the people was identified with a great spirit of charity, and the greater part of the numerous miracles attributed to her represent her responding to some appeal to her pity or her zeal for justice. " Everything that Brigid would ask of the Lord was granted at once," says the *Book of Lismore.* " For this was her desire : to satisfy the poor, to drive out every hardship, to spare every miserable man. . . . She is the Mary of the Gael." Her feast is kept throughout Ireland and Wales and in the dioceses of Birmingham and Portsmouth. *Brigida.*

BRIHTWALD, ST, bp. January 9.   JAN., p. 127

Otherwise *Brithwald.* He was abbot of Reculver and was made archbishop of Canterbury in 692. d. 731. He was a tactful and energetic prelate, but his claim to be counted a saint is somewhat questionable. *Britwaldus.*

BRIHTWOLD, ST, bp. January 22.   JAN., p. 272

A monk of Glastonbury and the last bishop of Ramsbury before that see was removed to Old Sarum. He was venerated by his contemporaries on account of his visions and prophecies. d. 1045.

BRITES, BD. *See* Beatrice da Silva.

BRITONIUS, ST, bp. May 5.   MAY, p. 70

Britonius, or Brito, while bishop of Trier, was a strong opponent of Priscillianism, but always refused to give up these heretics for punishment by the state. d. 386.

BROCARD, ST. September 2.   SEPT., p. 27

He was superior of the Frankish hermits on Mount Carmel and in 1210 gave them a rule drawn up by St Albert of Jerusalem. He guided the Carmelite Order during difficult times, and was greatly respected by the Mohammedans. d. 1231. *Brocardus.*

BRONISLAVA, BD, virg. August 30.   AUG., p. 388

She was a cousin of St Hyacinth and joined the Premonstratensian nuns in Poland ; later she became a solitary. d. 1259. c.c. 1839.

BRUDER KLAUS. *See* Nicholas von Flüe.

*BRUNO, ST., bp. May 27.   MAY, p. 222

This Bruno was bishop of Würzburg, and spent his private fortune on building the cathedral of St Kilian and other churches. He was killed by the collapse of a gallery while dining with the emperor Henry III at Bosenburg on the Danube in 1045.

†*BRUNO, ST. October 6. Oct., p. 68

He was b. in Cologne *c.* 1030, and from being chancellor of the diocese of Reims retired with six companions in 1084 to the solitude of La Grande Chartreuse in the mountains near Grenoble. Thus was founded the Carthusian Order, the most austere monastic organization in the Church, whose monks are semi-hermits. After only six years of this life Bruno was called to help the pope Bd Urban II in his reforms and his struggles with antipope and emperor, and, though he was allowed to live at last at a charterhouse which he founded at La Torre in Calabria, he was never fully released from this service : so did St Bruno display in himself the extremes of the contemplative and active ways of life. Moreover, his exile was the occasion of his original foundation spreading beyond France and becoming an order. d. 1101. St Bruno has never been formally canonized but his feast was extended to the whole Western church in 1623 ; in Calabria he enjoys all the veneration of a " popular " saint : the contrast of contemplative and active in his life is thus mirrored in the circumstances of his cultus.

BRUNO THE GREAT, ST, bp. October 11. Oct., p. 155

Though the epithet "the Great" would seem rather to belong to the founder of the Carthusians it was commonly given to his namesake and predecessor who became archbishop of Cologne in 953. This Bruno was brother of the emperor Otto I and actively co-operated with him in the religious and social building-up of Germany and the Empire. He was as capable a statesman as he was good a man, and was made co-regent of the Empire during Otto's absence in Italy in 961. Bruno was only forty when he d. in 965. c.c. 1870.

BRUNO OF QUERFURT, ST. *See* Boniface, St (June 19).

*BRUNO OF SEGNI, ST, bp. July 18. July, p. 255

He defended the doctrine of the Real Presence against Berengarius of Tours and was made bishop of Segni in 1080. Bruno was an extremely vigorous fighter against simony, and firmly rebuked Pope Paschal II for trying to enforce ecclesiastical privileges by force of arms. For a time he was abbot of Monte Cassino, but d. in his see in 1123. cd. 1183.

BUDOC, ST, bp. December 9. Dec., p. 116

St Budoc gives his name to several places in Devon and Cornwall, and according to a local story he was a hermit from Ireland. He may be the same as a Beuzec (or Budmael) venerated at Dol and elsewhere in Brittany. Seventh century (?).

*BURCHARD, ST, bp. October 14. Oct., p. 194

He went from Wessex to be a missionary in Germany and was appointed first bishop of Würzburg by St Boniface ; here he founded an abbey which afterwards bore his name. d. *c.* 754. *Burchardus.*

BURGUNDOFARA. *See* Fara.

CADFAN, ST, ab. November 1.   Nov., p. 13
    He founded the monastery of Towyn in Merionethshire, which persisted into the Middle Ages as a college of priests, and was the first abbot of Ynys Enlli (Bardsey). He died at the beginning of the sixth century.

CADOC, ST, ab. September 25.   JAN., p. 281
    St Cadoc was the founder of the great Welsh monastery of Llancarfan or Nantcarfan, not far from Cardiff. He is said to have founded other monasteries in Wales and Scotland. He died in the sixth century and, through reliance on a more than doubtful *passio*, is venerated as a bishop and martyr in the dioceses of Cardiff and Menevia. This martyrdom is alleged to have taken place on January 23. *Cadocus.*

CADROE, ST, ab. March 6.   MAR., p. 89
    Or *Cadroel.* He was the son of a Scottish chieftain, and educated at Armagh. He is alleged by his prayers to have saved London from destruction by fire. He journeyed from shrine to shrine in England and on the continent, and became abbot of Waulsort in the Ardennes. d. 976.

CÆSARIA, ST, virg. January 12.   JAN., p. 150
    Sister of St Cæsarius of Arles and abbess of the great monastery which her brother established in that city. Both Gregory of Tours and Venantius Fortunatus speak of her with admiration. d. *c.* 529.

*CÆSARIUS, ST. February 25.   FEB., p. 337
    Cæsarius, brother of St Gregory of Nazianzen, was a distinguished physician and public man, patronized by several of the Roman emperors. He elected to remain (so it seems) a catechumen nearly all his life, and was baptized only after a narrow escape in an earthquake, a few months before his death in 369. His name was inserted in the Roman Martyrology in virtue of his brother's panegyric.

*CÆSARIUS, ST, bp. August 27.   AUG., p. 333
    Cæsarius, a monk of Lérins, was made archbishop of Arles at the age of thirty in 500. He was the first " popular " preacher whose words have come down to us, in the form of short and homely homilies, and he took great pains for the fitting observance of corporate worship. He founded a famous monastery for women (which afterwards bore his name), putting it under the rule of his sister St Cæsaria. Side by side with his ecclesiastical labours as metropolitan of a large province, St Cæsarius had his share in the public upheavals of his time, and he sold the treasures of his churches to relieve the distress caused by the siege of Arles in 508. He is said to have been the first archbishop in western Europe to receive the *pallium* from the Holy See. d. 543.

*CÆSARIUS and **JULIAN, SS**, marts. November 1.   Nov., p. 8
    These martyrs at Terracina in Italy are mentioned in early martyrologies, but the particulars and date of their passion are not known. Their extant *acta* are not authentic.

†*CAIUS, ST, pope and mart. April 22.   APR., p. 255

Nothing is known of the life of this pope nor of his death in 296.

†*CAJETAN, ST. August 7.   AUG., p. 77

Cajetan (Gaetano) belonged to the nobility of Vicenza, where he was b. in 1480. He renounced his wealth and ecclesiastical dignities to devote himself to the poor and the suffering of his native town, and afterwards to the welfare of the pastoral office at large by founding in 1524 the first congregation of clerks regular : they were called " Theatines." St Cajetan was one of the most outstanding figures among the pre-Tridentine Catholic reformers, and his institution of pastoral clergy bound by vows and living in community was a very great force in the Counter-Reformation, most notably through the Jesuits. Cajetan was active with Bd John Marinoni in establishing those benevolent pawn-shops sanctioned some time before by the Fifth Lateran Council. d. 1547. cd. 1671. *Cajetanus.*

*CALEPODIUS, ST, mart. May 10.   MAY, p. 119

Calepodius, who gives his name to a Roman catacomb, is said to have been a priest who was martyred in 222.

†*CALLISTUS I, ST, pope and mart. October 14.   OCT., p. 188

Callistus (*Callixtus*) was a Christian slave who had an eventful youth in what may have been rather discreditable circumstances. Later he was made superintendent of the Christian cemetery on the Appian Way, which still is known by his name, San Callisto, and in 217 he was elected bishop of Rome. He condemned the errors of Sabellius, and by his gentleness towards sinners incurred the wrath of the rigorists. Callistus was probably martyred *c.* 222, but the extant account of his passion is worthless.

*CALOCERUS, ST, mart. April 18.   APR., p. 211

No reliable record of this martyr remains and nothing at all is known about him.

*CALOCERUS and PARTHENIUS, SS, marts. May 19.   MAY., p. 238

These brothers, martyred in 304, are alleged to have been eunuchs in the household of Tryphonia, wife of the emperor Decius.

CAMILLUS COSTANZO, BD, mart. September 25.   DEC. p. 321

An Italian Jesuit who was burnt to death at a slow fire in Japan in 1622. He had returned to the country after being banished thence as a Christian. bd. 1867.

†*CAMILLUS OF LELLIS, ST. July 18.   JULY, p. 242

Camillus was b. in the Abruzzi in 1550 and for years was a soldier and an inveterate gambler. After his reformation of life he tried to join the Capuchins, but was prevented by a disease of the feet which afflicted him for the rest of his life ; instead he became director of a hospital and established at many places in Italy houses of the Ministers of the Sick, a nursing congregation which he had founded and which still flourishes. His own grievous sufferings of body seemed only to encourage him to greater efforts for others. St Camillus was ordained by the last English bishop of the old hierarchy, Goldwell. d. 1614. cd. 1746. With St John-of-God he is the patron of the sick and of their nurses.

*CANICE, ST, ab. October 11.   OCT., p. 149

Canice (Cainneach, Kenny, Kenneth) was b. at Glengiven in Derry *c.* 515 ; he was a monk under St Cadoc in Wales and then at Clonard, whence he went to Glasnevin. He founded the monastery of Aghaboe and perhaps of Kilkenny, and was a zealous missionary in Scotland under St

Columba. d. 599. St Canice's feast is kept throughout Ireland and in the dioceses of St Andrews and Argyll. *Canicus.*

*CANTIUS and other marts., **SS.** May 31.   MAY, p. 374

Cantius and Cantianus with their sister Cantianella are said to have belonged to the Roman family of the Anicii ; they were put to death for not sacrificing to the gods in 304 (?).

*CANUTE, ST, mart. January 7.   JAN., p. 109

" Knud Lavard " was duke of Schleswig and spent a good deal of his life coping with Viking pirates. He was slain by a conspiracy of the Danes in 1130 and canonized in 1171 ; his feast was formerly a holy day of obligation in Denmark. *Canutus.*

†*CANUTE, ST, mart. January 19.   JAN., p. 233

Canute IV, King of Denmark, was a natural son of Sweyn III, whose uncle, Canute, had reigned in England. Having defended his country against aggressors he enacted severe laws to control his own jarls. In 1085 he was for the second time invited by the English to help them against the Norman conquerors, but whereas in 1069 he had been defeated, this time he was prevented from sailing by the treachery of his brother. St Canute was killed by rebels in 1086, and as this rebellion was concerned with the payment of tithes, which he had tried to enforce, he was accounted a martyr. Many miracles were recorded at his shrine.

*CAPRASIUS, ST. June 1.   JUNE, p. 4

A hermit on the island of Lérins who was the spiritual master and guide of St Honoratus who founded the great monastery there. d. 430.

*CAPRASIUS, ST, mart. October 20.   OCT., p. 274

According to a worthless legend he was the first bishop of Agen and, seeing the martyrdom of St Faith (October 6) from his hiding-place, he gave himself up and was executed.

CARADOC, ST. April 14.   APR., p. 162

He was a harper by profession, but became a hermit on Barry Island, at St Issels, and elsewhere in South Wales, where he suffered from the depredations both of sea-rovers and of the Normans. At his death in 1124 he was buried with great honour in the cathedral of St Davids. *Caractacus.*

CARANTOCK, ST, ab. May 16.   MAY, p. 203

This sixth-century Welsh abbot founded the church of Llangrannog and was associated with Crantock in Cornwall and Carhampton in Somerset. There is also a widespread cultus of him in Brittany. *Carantocus.*

CARILEFUS, ST, ab. July 1.   JULY, p. 6

In French, *Calais.* He founded and governed the abbey of Anisole in Maine. d. *c.* 536.

CARMES, MARTYRS DES. *See* September Martyrs.

*CARPUS and **PAPYLUS, SS,** marts. April 13.   APR., p. 146

A priest and deacon of Pergamos who were tortured and burnt alive either in the time of Marcus Aurelius or of Decius.

CARTHAGE, ST, bp. May 14.   MAY, p. 174

St Carthage (Carthach Mochuda) was a Kerry man and *c.* 590 founded a monastery at Rathin in Westmeath, for which he wrote a rule of life in verse ; he seems to have had episcopal charge of the neighbourhood. In 635 the community was expelled and Carthage led the monks to the banks of the Blackwater where they laid the foundation of the great

E

monastery and school of Lismore. d. 637. His feast is observed throughout Ireland. *Carthagus.*

CARTHUSIAN MARTYRS, THE. May 4. MAY, p. 58

The first monks of the Carthusian Order to suffer in England for refusal of King Henry VIII's Acts of Succession and Supremacy were John Houghton, prior of the London charterhouse, Robert Lawrence, prior of Beauvale, and Augustine Webster, prior of Axholme, who were h.d.q. at Tyburn on May 4, 1535. The following monks of the London charter-house suffered subsequently : Humphrey Middlemore, William Exmew, Sebastian Newdigate (Tyburn, June 19, 1535) ; John Rochester, James Walworth (York, May 11, 1537) ; John Davy, Thomas Green, William Greenwood, Robert Salt, Walter Pierson, Thomas Scryven, Thomas Reding (Newgate, June 6-16, 1537) ; Richard Bere, Thomas Johnson (Newgate, August-September, 1537) ; William Horne (Tyburn, August 11, 1540). bd. 1886-95. Bd John Houghton was the first of the English martyrs of the Reformation.

CASILDA, St, virg. April 9. APR., p. 106

She was a solitary, greatly revered at Burgos, Toledo, and elsewhere in Spain, but little is known of her true history. d. *c.* 1050.

†*CASIMIR, ST. March 4. MAR., p. 46

Casimir, patron saint of Poland and Lithuania, is often referred to as king of Poland and Hungary, though he never occupied the throne of either country. B. 1460, second son of Casimir IV of Poland. He was sent by his father to seize the crown of Hungary, but withdrew his troops without fighting, whereupon his father imprisoned him for three months. The remainder of Casimir's short life was spent in study and religious retirement. D. of consumption in 1483. cd. 1522. The Latin original of the hymn, " Daily, daily sing to Mary," often attributed to St Casimir, was written three centuries before his time. *Casimirus.*

CASPAR. *See also* Three Holy Kings.

CASPAR DE BONO, BD. July 14. JULY, p. 189

B. at Valencia in 1530. He was in the silk trade, a soldier, and finally a Minim friar, being twice corrector provincial of the Spanish province. d. 1604. bd. 1786. *Gasparus.*

CASPAR DEL BUFALO, BD. January 2. JAN., p. 45

B. in Rome in 1786, ordained 1808, and exiled with many other clergy by Napoleon. In 1814 he founded at Giano in the diocese of Spoleto the first house of the congregation of Missionaries of the Most Precious Blood for mission work at home. In spite of encouragement from the Holy See it met with endless difficulties at first, but before long the dramatic and tireless methods of the missioners had spread them all over Italy. Bd Caspar also founded works of charity in Rome to engage the activities of all sorts and conditions of people, and opened a chapel for night-long prayer and confession. His last mission was preached in Rome during the cholera outbreak of 1836, and he died in the following year at Albano. bd. 1904.

CASSIAN. *See also* John Cassian.

†*CASSIAN, ST, mart. August 13. AUG., p. 155

He was a schoolmaster at Imola. The Roman Martyrology states that, having refused to sacrifice to the gods, he was exposed naked among two hundred boys " by whom he had made himself disliked by teaching them," and these put him to death by stabbing him with their iron pens (in 304 ?). St Cassian is celebrated in a common feast with St Hippolytus, the priest, but they are unconnected. *Cassianus.*

*CASSIAN, ST, mart. December 3.   Dec., p. 47

When the centurion St Marcellus (October 30) was sentenced to death at Tangier in 298 the official shorthand-writer to the court, Cassian, threw down his pen and note-book in indignation at the injustice. He was at once arrested and a few weeks later executed. The short authentic *acta* of St Cassian are still in existence.

*CASSIUS, ST, bp. June 29.   June, p. 384

He was a bishop of Narni, of whose virtues St Gregory speaks in his *Dialogues.* d. 538.

CASTOR, ST, bp. September 2.   Sept., p. 23

He was a bishop of Apt and at his request St John Cassian wrote the *de Institutis Coenobiorum.* d. *c.* 425. *Castorius.*

CASTORA GABRIELLI, BD. June 14.   June, p. 180

She was wife and widow of a lawyer at Sant'Angelo in Vado in Umbria, where she was greatly revered for her goodness and charity. d. 1391.

*CASTULUS, ST, mart. March 26.   Mar., p. 409

A martyr in Rome under Diocletian in 286 ; a cemetery was named after his burial place on the Via Labicana.

*CASTUS and ÆMILIUS, SS, marts. May 22.   May, p. 267

Martyrs in Africa *c.* 250, who had given way for a brief period under torture.

*CATALDUS, ST, bp. May 10.   May, p. 122

St Cataldus presided over the monastic school of Lismore, but on his way back from a pilgrimage to Jerusalem was chosen bishop of Taranto, where he d. towards the end of the seventh century. Very little is known of the life of this saint, but his feast is kept throughout Ireland with that of St Conleth on May 10.

CATHERINE LABOURÉ, BD, virg. December 31.   Dec., p. 307

B. in the Côte d'Or in 1806, daughter of a yeoman farmer. She joined the Sisters of Charity of St Vincent de Paul in 1830 and there soon began the series of visions which has made her name famous : in consequence of them the first " miraculous medal " was struck, so called because of the circumstances in which its design became known. Little is recorded of Bd Catherine's personal life ; she was an unemotional and matter-of-fact religious. d. 1876 at the Enghien-Reuilly convent, where she was portress. bd. 1933.

*CATHERINE DEI RICCI, ST, virg. February 13.   Feb., p. 189

B. at Florence in 1522, and in 1535 became a regular tertiary of St Dominic. She filled the offices of novice-mistress and prioress, and her ecstasies and gift of miracles brought her to the notice of St Philip Neri. She had an extraordinary series of ecstasies in which she beheld and enacted the scenes of our Lord's passion, she is asserted to have had the *stigmata,* and on Easter day, 1542, we are told that she received the spiritual espousals. d. 1590. cd. 1746. *Catharina.*

CATHERINE TOMAS, ST, virg. April 1.   Apr., p. 11

Catherine was born in 1533 on the island of Majorca, where she spent her whole life. Remarkable tales are told of her precocious piety, and she eventually became a canoness of St Augustine at Palma. Here she was subject to a number of strange phenomena, both consoling and alarming, and during the later part of her life she was in ecstasy almost the greater part of her time. d. 1574. cd. 1930.

†*CATHERINE OF ALEXANDRIA, ST, virg. and mart. November 25.
Nov., p. 296

Though for long the object of a great and universal popular veneration St Catherine is now but little regarded ; her legend has been shown to be unreliable and not a single fact about her has been established. The traditional story is that she argued with fifty pagan philosophers and overcame them, that the wheel on which she was to be broken fell to pieces, and that she was then beheaded *c.* 310. A reputation for learning still clings to her and she is venerated as the patron saint of philosophers. Her alleged relics have been enshrined for nearly a thousand years at the Orthodox monastery of Mount Sinai.

*CATHERINE OF BOLOGNA, ST, virg. March 9.   MAR., p. 154

She was maid of honour to Margaret d'Este, and on Margaret's marriage joined a community of Augustinian nuns at Ferrara who later became Poor Clares. Catherine was baker, novice mistress, and then superioress of the daughter house at Bologna in 1457. From an early age she was subject to visions, both divine and diabolical, of which one of the child Jesus is particularly notable. Her religious life was one long intercession for the conversion of sinners, and she had unusual powers of healing the body as well. d. 1463. cd. 1712. St Catherine's body, shrunken and black with age, is preserved, sitting in a chair, in the chapel of the convent at Bologna.

*CATHERINE OF GENOA, ST. September 15.   SEPT., p. 183

Caterinetta Fieschi was b. in 1447 and at the age of sixteen was married to Julian Adorno, whose weak character was a cause of much unhappiness to her. In 1473 Catherine underwent a sudden conversion, gave herself to the care of the sick in a Genoese hospital, and recruited two friends and her husband to the same work. From this time on St Catherine led a most intense spiritual life, combined with unwearying and efficient activity in the hospital, and is a remarkable example of the Christian type of complete " other-worldliness " united with the most capable " practicality." She continued the same life after the death of her husband, and never became a religious or even a tertiary. St Catherine wrote a treatise on Purgatory and a Dialogue of the soul and the body, which the Holy Office declared were alone enough to prove her holiness : they are among the more important documents of mysticism. d. 1510. cd. 1737.

CATHERINE OF PALLANZA, BD, virg. April 6.   APR., p. 79

She was the first woman hermit in the mountain district above Varese, near Milan, where she lived a life of very great austerity and was soon joined by others. These she gathered into a community under the Augustinian rule. d. 1478.

CATHERINE OF PARC, BD, virg. May 4.   MAY, p. 56

She was the daughter of Jewish parents at Louvain and in the early thirteenth century ran away from home and became a Cistercian nun at Parc-aux Dames.

CATHERINE OF RACCONIGI, BD, virg. September 4.   SEPT., p. 52

She was a Dominican tertiary living in the world, who seems to have been favoured with remarkable mystical experiences from a very early age. She offered herself as a victim for the disorders of war, and many miracles are related of her. d. 1547. c.c. 1810.

†*CATHERINE OF SIENA, ST, virg. April 30.

APR., p. 337

Catherine, patroness of the City of Rome and one of the greatest women of Christendom, was b. at Siena in 1347 of middle-class parents. When sixteen she joined the third order of St Dominic, continuing to live at home, where her goodness attracted a circle of *Caterinati*, men and women, lay and clerical, who formed a sort of informal college and helped and hindered her in her work. From looking after the poor and sick she was drawn into politics, and as ambassadress of Florence persuaded Pope Gregory XI to abandon Avignon for Rome (she used to write to him as " my sweet babbo "). Then she was involved in the turmoil of the so-called great schism of the West, and in 1380 she died. Catherine left over 400 letters and a marvellous mystical work, her " Dialogue." cd. 1461.

*CATHERINE OF SWEDEN, ST. March 22.

MAR., p. 364

She was the fourth child of St Bridget of Sweden and married Eggard Lydersson, a very long-suffering man. He died while Catherine was in Italy with St Bridget, and henceforward for twenty-five years the lives of the two women were practically identified in charitable works, pilgrimages, and the welfare of the Bridgettine Order. After the death of her mother Catherine retired to the abbey of Wadstena, bringing with her a reputation for holiness and miracles. d. 1381. c.c. 1474.

CEADDA, ST. *See* Chad.

CEADWALLA, ST. April 20.

APR., p. 238

The king of the West Saxons who was converted by St Wilfrid and died while on a pilgrimage to Rome, where he was baptized by Pope St Sergius I, in 689 ; he is buried in the crypt of St Peter's. There is no evidence for any ancient cultus of Ceadwalla.

CECCO, BD. *See* Francis of Pesaro.

†*CECILIA, ST, virg. and mart. November 22.

Nov., p. 268

The maiden marriage of St Cecilia, the conversion of her husband St Valerian, his martyrdom with his brother St Tiburtius, and the attempted suffocation and beheading of Cecilia in her own house make up one of the best known stories of the early martyrs, but it has no historical value. Cecilia (who is named in the canon of the Mass) was certainly one of the most illustrious virgin martyrs of Rome, SS Valerian and Tiburtius certainly suffered about the same time, being buried in the cemetery of Præ-textatus and Cecilia in that of St Callistus, but in what circumstances and in what year of the second–third century is not known. The basilica of Santa Cecilia in Trastevere at Rome is built over the mansion of her family, and her relics with those of her companions rest beneath the high altar. Cecilia's being patron saint of musicians is unexplained except on the hypothesis of an inference unwarrantably drawn from a phrase occurring in her *acta* or in her office.

*CECILIUS, ST. June 3.

JUNE, p. 29

He was, in the words of the Roman Martyrology, " a priest of Carthage who brought St Cyprian to the faith of Christ." His name was probably really Cecilianus. d. *c.* 248 (?).

CEDD, ST, bp. October 26.

JAN., p. 102

A brother of St Chad of Lichfield. He was one of four monks sent from Lindisfarne to preach the gospel in the midlands of England, and afterwards was ordained bishop for the East Saxons among whom he founded two monasteries, of which one was at Tilbury. He also, in 658, established the monastery of Lastingham in Yorkshire. He was present at the Synod of Whitby, where he was among those who abandoned the Celtic usages for the Roman ones. He died at Lastingham on October 26, 664, but is named on January 7 in Wilson's English martyrology.

*CELESTINE I, ST, pope. July 27.   APR., p. 73
Celestine, born in Campania, became pope in 422. Of his private life nothing is known ; he encouraged the campaign of St Germanus of Auxerre against Pelagianism and commissioned Palladius to preach in Ireland a year or so before St Patrick began his work there. d. 432. *Cælestinus.*

†*CELESTINE V, ST, pope. May 19.   MAY, p. 234
Peter Morone was b. *c.* 1210 of peasant parents. After his ordination he received the Benedictine habit and lived as a hermit on Monte Morone, near Sulmona, where he formed the beginning of a small congregation of hermit-monks, later called "Celestines." In 1294, when he was over eighty years old, he was elected pope by acclamation ; he was utterly unequal to the task of ruling the Church and resigned the Holy See five months later. He returned to his hermitage, but was seized by his successor Boniface VIII (lest he should be used to create a schism) and d. after ten months' imprisonment in a castle near Anagni, in 1296. Dante in his *Inferno* condemns Peter Celestine as a coward ; the Church reveres him as a saint. cd. 1313.

*CELSUS, ST, bp. April 7.
Celsus (Cellach) was archbishop of Armagh and inaugurated the reform movement carried on there by St Malachy. d. 1129. Feast kept throughout Ireland.

CEOLFRID, ST, ab. September 25.   SEPT., p. 313
After being a monk at Gilling and Ripon he became abbot of Wearmouth and Jarrow, St Bede being among his monks. St Ceolfrid resigned his charge in 716 and set out on a pilgrimage to Rome, dying on the way at Langres in the same year ; he was carrying with him the manuscript of the Bible now famous as "Codex Amiatinus." The feast of this English abbot is still observed at Langres, under the name of "St Ceufroy." *Ceolfridus.*

CEOLWULF, ST. January 15.   JAN., p. 195
Ceolwulf was king of the Northumbrians, and ended his days as a monk at Lindisfarne. St Bede dedicated his *Ecclesiastical History* to him, and there was some cultus of him in the north after his death in 764.

CERATIUS, ST, bp. June 6.   JUNE, p. 80
In French *Cérase.* He was a bishop of Grenoble who d. *c.* 455.

*CERBONIUS, ST, bp. October 10.   OCT., p. 136
He is said to have become bishop of Piombino (Populonium) in Tuscany on being driven from his native Africa by the Vandals. He d. *c.* 575 in exile on Elba, whither he had been driven by the Goths.

CESLAUS, BD. July 17.   JULY, p. 240
He was admitted to the Order of Preachers by St Dominic at the same time as his brother St Hyacinth. He was a great preacher in Poland and neighbouring countries. d. 1242. c.c. 1713.

CETHEUS, ST. *See* Peregrinus (June 13).

*CHAD, ST, bp. March 2.   MAR., p. 16
Chad or Ceadda was brother of St Cedd, was trained with him at Lindisfarne under St Aidan, and became abbot of Cedd's monastery at

Lastingham. King Oswy appointed Chad to the see of York but he was removed by St Theodore in favour of St Wilfrid ; Chad took this so well that Theodore arranged for him to be bishop in Mercia. St Chad removed the episcopal seat from Repton to Lichfield but ruled there only a couple of years, dying in 672. Part of his relics are preserved in St Chad's cathedral, Birmingham, and his feast is observed in that diocese ; he is commemorated also in Hexham diocese. *Ceadda.*

*CHÆREMON, ST, bp. and mart. December 22.   DEC., p. 220

While bishop of Nilopolis this old man was driven by the persecution of Decius into the mountains of Arabia with one companion in 250 : they were never seen or heard of again.

CHAINOALDUS, ST, bp. September 6.   SEPT., p. 68

In French *Cagnoald* or *Cagnou.* When St Columbanus was exiled from Luxeuil St Chainoaldus accompanied him and helped in the foundation of Bobbio. He became bishop of Laon and d. in 633.

CHARLEMAGNE, BD. January 28.   JAN., p. 351

The life of Charlemagne (b. 742 ; king of the Franks, 768 ; first Holy Roman emperor, 800 ; d. 814) belongs to general history and his is a somewhat surprising name to find in a catalogue of saints. There does not seem to have been any noticeable popular cultus of him until 1166 when it developed under the unfortunate influence of Frederick Barbarossa and the antipope Paschal III. A feast in his honour was made obligatory on the whole of France in 1475. However, Pope Benedict XIV decided that the title " Blessed " might not improperly be accorded to so great a protector of the Church, and a feast of Charlemagne is observed to-day in Aachen and other German dioceses. *Carolus Magnus.*

†*CHARLES BORROMEO, ST, bp. November 4.   NOV., p. 42

Charles was b. in 1538, son of Count Gilbert Borromeo by a Medici mother. While still a child he received a rich abbey *in commendam*, he was a cardinal at twenty-two, and named archbishop of Milan soon after, although he was not ordained priest and bishop till 1563. Though the successful reassembling of the Council of Trent and a great deal of its work was due to him, his chief fame is as a bishop : his large and important diocese was in a scandalous state and his life's work was the re-ordering of it, which he began in 1566. Among his works was the establishment of the Confraternity of Christian Doctrine for instructing children, thus anticipating the Sunday schools of Robert Raikes by two hundred years, and he particularly provided for the proper carrying out of the sacred liturgy, to which he attached great importance. His reforms were not carried out without an attempt on his life, but his selflessness during the plague of 1576 put the seal on his great influence. St Charles was the first great prelate of the counter-reformation, incredibly hard-working, personally austere, devoted to anything that would forward the cause of true religion. d. 1584. cd. 1610. *Carolus.*

CHARLES SPINOLA, BD, mart. September 10.   SEPT., p. 134

Charles Spinola, S.J., with Sebastian Kimura the first Japanese Jesuit, and other Jesuits and lay people were martyred at Nagasaki in 1622 ; they were bd. with the other martyrs of Japan in 1867.

CHARLES OF BLOIS, BD. September 29.   SEPT., p. 372

He was b. *c.* 1316, nephew of Philip VI of France. On his marriage to Joan of Brittany in 1341 he claimed the dukedom of Brittany, and was at once involved in warfare with John de Montfort that lasted for the rest of his life, nine years of which Charles was a prisoner in the Tower of London. He was killed in battle in 1364 : many miracles were alleged at his tomb, and his ancient cultus among the Bretons was confirmed by the Holy See in 1904.

CHARLES THE GOOD, BD, mart. March 2. MAR., p. 19

He was the son of the martyred king of Denmark, St Canute, and was brought up by his relatives the Counts of Flanders. On returning from the Second Crusade he married Margaret, Countess of Amiens, and succeeded Robert II as count of Flanders, but had to fight against other claimants. Charles was so determined a defender of the poor that he was accused of an unfair prejudice against the rich, and during a famine in 1125 he was merciless to food-hoarders and " cornerers." This led directly to his death, for he was murdered by a conspiracy of clerical and secular profiteers in 1127. c.c. 1883.

CHARLES OF SEZZE, BD. January 6. JAN., p. 97

A lay-brother of the Observant branch of the Franciscans, who was well known in Rome in the seventeenth century. d. 1670. bd. 1882.

CHRISTIAN, BD, ab. March 18. MAR., p. 316

He was abbot of the first Cistercian monastery in Ireland, at Mellifont, to which he was sent from Clairvaux by St Bernard in 1142 at the request of St Malachy of Armagh. He is said also to have become papal legate and bishop of Lismore. d. 1186. *Christianus.*

CHRISTIANA. *See also* Nino.

*CHRISTINA, ST, virg. and mart. July 24. JULY, p. 337

The Christina mentioned in the Roman Martyrology on July 24 seems to have been a maiden martyred at Bolsena in Italy at an unknown date. But she has been confused with another virgin-martyr Christina, of Tyre, whose very existence is doubtful.

CHRISTINA CICCARELLI, BD. January 18. JAN., p. 227

An Augustinian nun at Aquila, remarkable for her humility and love of the poor. d. 1543. c.c. 1841.

CHRISTINA THE ASTONISHING, ST, virg. July 24. JULY, p. 339

This Christina was b. near Liége in 1150 and from the age of thirty-two was the subject of most extraordinary physical phenomena, which were written down by a contemporary Dominican. The evidence points to her having been a pathological case, and her local cultus seems never to have received official confirmation. d. 1224.

CHRISTINA OF SPOLETO, BD. February 13. FEB., p. 206

She was a daughter of a physician named Camozzi who lived near Lake Lugano, and after a very lively and rather disorderly youth she became a penitent about the age of twenty. After a few years of most undisciplined austerity she d. at Spoleto in 1458. c.c. 1834. The common story that this Christina was a Visconti who ran away from home and wandered about the shrines of Europe is discredited.

CHRISTINA OF STOMMELN, BD, virg. November 6. NOV., p. 75

Christina Bruso was b. in 1242 at Stommeln, near Cologne, where she lived for nearly the whole of her seventy years. Her life is one long record of astonishing phenomena : were it not for contemporary personal testimony she would have to be dismissed as a devout but mentally diseased sufferer from hallucinations, and even as it is it must be supposed that she was not morally responsible for some of her statements. d. 1312. Local veneration on account of Christina's personal virtues has been officially approved.

†*CHRISTOPHER, ST, mart. July 25.　　　　　　　　JULY, p. 358

St Christopher was a martyr, probably in the third century; otherwise nothing is known of him. The famous legend connected with his name grew up in the East during the sixth century and was unknown in the West before the ninth: even then it had not attained its final form. *Christophorus.*

CHRISTOPHER BALES, BD, mart. March 4.　　　　　　　MAR., p. 56

B. at Coniscliffe in co. Durham. Trained at the English College, Rome, ordained at Douai, and sent on the English mission in 1588. Condemned for his priesthood and h.d.q. in Fleet Street, 1590. bd. 1929.

CHRISTOPHER MACASSOLI, BD. March 11.　　　　　　MAR., p. 198

A priest of the order of Friars Minor, whose shrine is at Vigevano in the province of Milan. d. 1485. c.c. 1890.

CHRISTOPHER OF MILAN, BD. March 1.　　　　　　　MAR., p. 13

A Dominican preacher who exercised a very great influence in Liguria during the fifteenth century; at Taggia the people built a friary as a result of his preaching, and he was made the first prior. d. 1484. c.c. 1875.

CHRISTOPHER OF ROMANDIOLA, BD. October 31.　　OCT., p. 380

He was a parish priest in the diocese of Cesena who resigned his benefice and joined St Francis of Assisi; he established the Friars Minor in Gascony, at Cahors. d. 1272. c.c. 1905.

CHRODEGANG, ST, bp. March 6.　　　　　　　　　　MAR., p. 86

Chief minister to Charles Martel and then bishop of Metz. St Chrodegang is chiefly famous for his regulations for the life of secular clerics, whom he gathered together in chapters of canons with common life under a rule. He applied this first to his cathedral clergy and then to other churches, and this institution of secular canons spread all over Western Christendom. He also gave to his cathedral the pure Roman liturgy with the appropriate chant, Metz being probably the first church in the north to adopt them. The choir school that he established was for centuries the best known in Europe. d. 766.

CHROMATIUS, ST. August 11.　　　　　　　　　　　AUG., p. 128

He is said to have been prefect of Rome and father of the martyr Tiburtius (August 11), but there is no reliable evidence.

*CHROMATIUS, ST, bp. December 2.　　　　　　　　DEC., p. 27

He became bishop of Aquileia in 389 and was one of the most distinguished prelates of his time. He was a friend both of St Jerome and Rufinus, and a strong supporter of St John Chrysostom. Several of his scriptural treatises still exist. d. *c.* 407.

†*CHRYSANTHUS and DARIA, SS, marts. October 25.　OCT., p. 330

This husband and wife were early martyrs in Rome; they are said to have been stoned and buried in a sand-pit. The legend concerning them is fanciful, and nothing else is known of them.

†*CHRYSOGONUS, ST, mart. November 24.　　　　　　NOV., p. 292

This martyr is named in the canon of the Mass but nothing is known of him except that he probably suffered at Aquileia; he has been wrongly associated with St Anastasia (December 25).

CIARAN. *See* Kieran.

†*CLARE, ST, virg. August 12.　　　　　　　　　　AUG., p. 142

She was b. at Assisi *c.* 1193 and at the age of eighteen ran away from

65

home to join St Francis : her sister Agnes followed, and at San Damiano was established the first convent of Franciscan nuns, now called after her "Poor Clares"; she never left it again, except once to take dinner with St Francis and talk with him of God. From San Damiano St Clare wielded a great influence : bishops, cardinals, two popes came to consult her, the sick were brought to be tended by the nuns, and sometimes to be cured by her intercession. Similar convents were founded in other places and, Cardinal Ugolino having imposed a rule on them which forbade communal poverty, Clare had the bitterness for thirty-two years of struggling for the restoration of the true Franciscan rule for all. She was successful two days before her death in 1253. cd. 1255. *Clara*.

CLARE GAMBACORTA, BD. April 17. APR., p. 205
Clare was the daughter of Peter Gambacorta, who was at one time virtually the head of the state of Pisa. She was left a widow at fifteen and tried to join the Poor Clares, whereupon her father shut her up for five months. Then he relented and built a convent for Bd Clare and Bd Mary Mancini, who adopted the rule of the enclosed Dominicans. Clare had great financial difficulties to contend with in the conduct of the convent, and ill health that was brought on by seeing her brother cut down by a mob. d. 1419. c.c. 1830.

*CLARE OF MONTEFALCO, ST, virg. August 17. AUG., p. 197
She was abbess of a convent at Montefalco which during her lifetime exchanged the rule of the Franciscan tertiaries for that of the Augustinian nuns. She was noted for the faithfulness of her observance and the austerity of her penances, and for three physical phenomena of unusual interest : the incorruption of her body after death, the formation of a cross, etc., upon her heart, and the liquefaction of her blood. d. 1308. cd. 1881.

CLARE OF RIMINI, BD. February 10. FEB., p. 155
Clare Agolanti was twice married ; after her second widowhood she became a Franciscan tertiary and led a life of penance and alms-deeds. She founded a convent but never became a member of it herself. Some of her physical austerities were most extravagant and were so regarded even by her contemporaries of the fourteenth century. d. 1346. c.c. 1784.

CLARITUS, ST. May 25. MAY, p. 305
He is venerated by the Augustinian friars as the founder of a convent of nuns of their order wherein his own wife became a religious. d. 1348.

CLARUS, ST, ab. January 1. JAN., p. 19
Believed to have been abbot of the monastery of St Marcellus at Vienne in Dauphiny. d. *c.* 660.

*CLARUS, ST, mart. November 4. Nov., p. 56
He is said to have been a native of Rochester who became a hermit in France, and was murdered at the instigation of a woman whose advances he had refused. Early ninth century (?). He gave his name to Saint-Clair-sur-Epte.

*CLAUD, ST, bp. June 6. JUNE, p. 84
He was chosen bishop of Besançon in 685 after having been, as is said, abbot of Condat in the Jura mountains. He was already old, and resigned his see seven years later. d. *c.* 699. *Claudius*.

CLAUD DE LA COLOMBIÈRE, BD. February 15. FEB., p. 237
B. near Lyons in 1641 and entered the Society of Jesus at Avignon. He was tutor to the sons of the minister Colbert and then professor of

rhetoric at Avignon, where his preaching attracted much attention. At the age of thirty-three he was made superior of the college at Paray-le-Monial, where he met St Margaret Mary and was "her 'coadjutor' in propagating devotion to the Sacred Heart, and as one chosen by God to direct her in the time of her trouble and vexation of spirit." His next mission was as court preacher to Maria Beatrice d'Este, Duchess of York, and he made many converts in England. At the time of the Oates " plot " Bd Claud was condemned to death, but he was banished instead and returned to France. For the rest of his life he was an invalid, due largely to his imprisonment in England. d. 1682. bd. 1929.

CLAUDIA, ST. August 7.   Aug., p. 83
A woman mentioned by St Paul in his second letter to Timothy (iv, 21) ; that she was a Briton and the wife of Martial's Aulus Pudens has been asserted but is most improbable.

*CLAUDIUS and other marts., **SS.** August 23.   Aug., p. 283
Claudius, Asterius, and Neon were three brothers who were charged as Christians before the magistrate of Ægea in Cilicia by their mother-in-law, who hoped to inherit their estates ; two women, Domnina and Theonilla, were on trial as Christians at the same time. The men were crucified and the women scourged to death, in 303.

*CLAUDIUS and comps., **SS,** marts. December 3.   Dec., p. 46
Claudius, a Roman tribune, Hilaria his wife, their two sons and seventy soldiers are characters in the legend of SS Chrysanthus and Daria. Others are mentioned in the Roman Martyrology on December 1.

*CLAUDIUS and **MAXIMUS, SS,** marts. February 18.   Feb., p. 262
They were uncles of St Susanna (August 11), who were converted to Christianity by the example of their niece and put to death by an officer of Diocletian.

†*CLEMENT I, ST, pope and mart. November 23.   Nov., p. 273
Clement was the third successor of St Peter and the first after him about whom any information survives. A letter he wrote to the church at Corinth is extant and is one of the most important documents of sub-apostolic times. He is venerated as a martyr, c. 99, but the fact of his martyrdom is not certain. St Clement is named in the canon of the Mass. *Clemens*.

*CLEMENT MARY HOFBAUER, ST. March 15.   Mar., p. 254
He was the first to establish the Redemptorist congregation on this side of the Alps. He was a Slav, born in Moravia (real name, John Dvorak), the son of a grazier ; after being a baker and then a hermit he joined the Redemptorists at Rome in 1783 at the age of thirty-two. Four years later St Clement established a house of the congregation at Warsaw, primarily for the benefit of the Germans in that city. From 1787 till 1808 they preached five times a day, in Polish and German, and made numerous conversions of Protestants, Jews, and the lapsed. St Clement established an orphanage and schools and settled his congregation in several places, but much of his work was undone by Napoleon's suppression of the religious orders. He then retired to Vienna, where for twelve years he was the most respected and influential priest in the city ; he founded a college for boys and prepared the ground for the ultimate firm planting of the Redemptorists in the German lands. d. 1820. cd. 1909.

*CLEMENT OF ANCYRA, ST, bp. and mart. January 23. Jan., p. 279
We have no reliable knowledge of this saint or of his companion in martyrdom, St Agathangelus.

CLEMENT OF OKHRIDA, ST. *See* Seven Apostles of Bulgaria.

CLEMENT OF ST ELPIDIO, BD. April 8.   APR., p. 97

As prior general he drew up and revised the constitutions of the order of Hermit Friars of St Augustine in 1270 and 1284, and so is regarded as their second founder. d. 1291. c.c. 1572.

CLEOPATRA, ST. October 19.   OCT., p. 263

She is said to have been a widow who secured the body of St, Varus (October 19) and enshrined it at her home at Derâ'a in Syria. After the sudden death of her son, Varus appeared in a vision to comfort her.

†*CLETUS, ST, pope and mart. April 26.   APR., p. 289

Otherwise *Anacletus*. Nothing is known of him except that he died, probably by martyrdom, *c.* 91.

*CLODOALDUS, ST. September 7.   SEPT., p. 76

In French *Cloud*. He was a grandson of King Clovis. At the time of the murder of his two brothers he was taken to safety in Provence. Later he was ordained priest and founded a monastery at the place near Versailles now called Saint-Cloud. There he d. at the age of thirty-six, *c.* 560.

*CLODULFUS, ST, bp. June 8.   JUNE, p. 108

Clodulfus (Cloud, Ciou) was the son of St Arnulfus, bishop of Metz, and himself was appointed to that see, which he ruled for forty years. d. *c.* 692.

*CLOTILDE, ST. June 3.   JUNE, p. 32

Clotilde, b. at Lyons *c.* 474, was a daughter of Chilperic, ruler of that neighbourhood. She married Clovis, king of the Salian Franks, and helped to bring about her heathen husband's conversion. After his death in 511 her life was saddened by family feuds and the quarrels of her three sons and by the misfortunes of her unhappily married daughter. In old age St Clotilde went to live at Tours, where she spent the rest of her life in the service of God and the poor and suffering. d. 545. *Clotildis.*

*CODRATUS, ST, mart. March 10.   MAR., p. 166

Codratus, with four companions, was martyred at Corinth in 258 but the details of their passion are not reliable.

COEMGEN. *See* Kevin.

*COLETTE, ST, virg. March 6.   MAR., p. 95

Nicolette Boilet was b. 1381, the daughter of a carpenter at Corbie in Picardy. She was at first a Franciscan tertiary who lived as an ankress beside her parish church, but in 1406 she set out to walk to Nice to lay before Peter de Luna (who was acknowledged as pope in France) her scheme for the reform of the Poor Clares. He was so impressed that he made Colette superioress of the whole order with full powers to carry out the reform. This she proceeded to do by visiting all the convents in France, Savoy, Flanders, and Germany : some adopted her suggestions, others received her with contumely. In addition she founded seventeen new convents and some friaries. She also associated herself with St Vincent Ferrer in his efforts to heal the schism in the papacy. Colette exercised a notable influence by her simple goodness over people of high rank, like James of Bourbon and Philip the Good of Burgundy. She d. at Ghent in 1447. cd. 1807. *Coleta.*

COLMAN ELO, ST, ab. September 26.   SEPT., p. 324

This Colman was a nephew of St Columba, whom he visited on Iona. He founded monasteries at Lynally and at Muckamore, and the authorship of the *Alphabet of Devotion* is attributed to him. d. *c.* 610. The name of Colman was extraordinarily common in the early Irish church : there are ninety-six holy Colmans in the Martyrology of Donegal, 209 in the Book of Leinster, and many others. *Colmanus.*

COLMAN OF CLOYNE, ST, bp. November 24. NOV., p. 294
   He was a poet, royal bard at the court of Cashel, and was a heathen until middle age ; he is said to have been baptized by St Brendan. After he was ordained Colman preached in Limerick and the eastern parts of Cork, and founded the church of Cloyne, of which he is venerated as the first bishop. d. *c.* 600. His feast is observed throughout Ireland.

COLMAN OF DROMORE, ST, bp. June 7. JUNE, p. 91
   The founder of the monastery of Dromore in county Down during the sixth century and first bishop there. According to tradition he came to Ireland from Argyllshire. Feast kept throughout Ireland.

COLMAN OF KILMACDUAGH, ST, bp. October 29. OCT., p. 355
   He founded the monastery at Kilmacduagh and is venerated as the first bishop in those parts. He had previously been a hermit on Arranmore and at Burren in county Clare. d. 632. The feast of this Colman is observed throughout Ireland.

COLMAN OF LINDISFARNE, ST, bp. February 18. FEB., p. 268
   An Irish monk from Iona and the third bishop of Lindisfarne. During his short pontificate he took part in the Synod of Whitby in 664 and, rather than abandon Celtic in favour of Roman usages, he resigned his see and withdrew with his monks to Ireland. Here he established himself on Innisboffin, and later founded a separate monastery on the mainland for his English monks as they did not get on with their Irish brethren. d. 676.

*COLOMAN, ST, mart. October 13. OCT., p. 184
   Coloman, an Irish or Scottish pilgrim, was put to death in 1012 at Stockerau on the Danube on the unjust suspicion of being a spy. A popular cultus sprang up and his body was enshrined at the abbey of Melk. *Colomannus.*

*COLUMBA, ST, ab. June 9. JUNE, p. 114
   Colum, Colum-cille, the most famous of the saints of Scotland, b. at Garton in county Donegal *c.* 521. He studied at Moville and Clonard and left the monastery of Glasnevin to spend fifteen years preaching and founding churches and monasteries in various parts of Ireland. Then, in circumstances which are uncertain and have caused much discussion, he determined to leave his country. On Whitsun eve 563 he landed with twelve companions on the island of Iona (Hi) and there founded the monastery that was to be famous throughout western Christendom and from which he preached the gospel in Scotland, to the Picts in the north and to the Scots in the south : he is said to have penetrated even so far as Aberdeenshire. He revisited Ireland from time to time and folk of all kinds from all parts came to consult him at Iona ; his influence dominated the Church in Scotland, Ireland, and Northumbria, and his monastic rule influenced western Europe for long after his death, which took place in 597. " He had the face of an angel ; he was of an excellent nature, polished in speech holy in deed, great in counsel . . . loving unto all," is the verdict of his biographer Adamnan. St Columba's feast is kept throughout Scotland and Ireland.

*COLUMBA, ST, virg. and mart. September 17. SEPT., p. 228
   With other nuns of Tabanos she was driven from her convent by the

Moors. Having gone before the magistrate and denied Mohammed as a false prophet, she was beheaded at Cordova in 853.

COLUMBA OF RIETI, BD, virg. May 20.   MAY, p. 254
She was a Dominican religious of the third order at Perugia whose holiness and spiritual gifts caused her to be regarded in some sort as the city's patroness even in her lifetime. She was often consulted by the Perugian rulers, but is said to have been grievously persecuted by Lucrezia Borgia. d. 1501. c.c. 1627.

*COLUMBA OF SENS, ST, virg. and mart. December 31.   DEC., p. 300
She is said to have been a Spanish girl, put to death with other Christian Spaniards near Meaux c. 274. She is distinguished as " of Sens " because her shrine was there ; she had an extensive cultus in south-west Europe during the Middle Ages.

*COLUMBANUS, ST, ab. November 23.   NOV., p. 278
Columbanus was born in Leinster. He left Bangor c. 580 with a dozen monks and founded the great monastery of Luxeuil in the Vosges. When he was exiled for protesting against the disorders of the Austrasian court he went into Italy and there established the no less famous abbey of Bobbio. He was a somewhat intemperate upholder of Celtic customs, but the austere rule which he gave to his monks was exceedingly influential in western Europe during the sixth-seventh century, and his monasteries continued to exercise a great influence after they had become Benedictine. d. 615. The feast of St Columbanus is kept throughout Ireland ; the Roman Martyrology and the Benedictines commemorate him on November 21.

COMGALL, ST, ab. May 11.   MAY, p. 121
The feast of St Comgall is kept throughout Ireland as one of the four founders of monasticism in that country. He was b. in Ulster c. 516 and founded the great abbey of Benchor (Bangor), where he trained St Columbanus, giving to the monks a rule of his own composition. St Comgall seems to have made two missionary journeys into Scotland. d. c. 601. *Comgallus.*

COMGAN, ST, ab. October 13.   OCT., p. 182
An eighth-century Scottish abbot, brother to St Kentigern, whose feast is kept in the diocese of Aberdeen.

COMPIÈGNE, THE MARTYRS OF. July 24.   JULY, p. 350
Sixteen Carmelite nuns of Compiègne, together with a layman who befriended them, were guillotined in Paris in 1794 for being " enemies of the people " by reason of their religious belief and profession. They were bd. in 1906, the first victims of the French revolution to be so honoured.

CONAN, ST, bp. January 26.   JAN., p. 320
This Conan is believed to have been a bishop in the Isle of Man but nothing is known for certain about him. d. c. 648 (?).

*CONCORDIUS, ST, mart. January 1.   JAN., p. 9
A subdeacon martyred at Spoleto under Marcus Aurelius c. 178.

CONDEDUS, ST. October 21.   OCT., p. 291
Condedus, said to have been an Englishman, was a solitary in France and for a time a monk of Fontenelle ; he d. at a hermitage on an islet in the Seine at the end of the seventh century.

CONLETH, ST, bp. May 10.   MAY, p. 42
He was a priest and metal-worker at Old Connell on the Liffey and became a friend of St Brigid. He is venerated as the first bishop of Kildare

and his feast is kept throughout Ireland with that of St Cataldus on May 10. d. *c.* 519. *Conlethus.*

CONON, ST, ab. March 28. MAR., p. 429
Abbot of the Greek monastery of Nesi in Sicily, where he was revered for his holiness and miracles. d. 1236.

CONRAD, ST, mart. June 1. JUNE, p. 10
Or *Cuno.* He was appointed to the see of Trier by St Anno, arch-bishop of Cologne (his uncle), in defiance of the right of the Trier chapter to elect. The canons were supported by Count Theodoric, who seized Conrad and cast him from the battlements of the castle of Uerzig in 1066. *Conradus.*

***CONRAD, ST,** bp. November 26. Nov., p. 308
He became bishop of Constance in 934 and d. in 975. cd. 1123. Con-sidering the age in which he lived he seems to have kept remarkably aloof from secular politics.

CONRAD OF ASCOLI, BD. April 19. APR., p. 232
Conrad de' Milliani was a successful Franciscan missionary in Libya and later a counsellor of Cardinal Jerome Masci, whose election to the papacy Bd Conrad had foretold when a boy. d. 1289.

CONRAD OF BAVARIA, BD. February 14. FEB., p. 222
B. *c.* 1105, son of Henry the Black, Duke of Bavaria. He became a Cistercian monk at Clairvaux and died in Apulia on his way back from a pilgrimage to the Holy Land in 1154. c.c. 1832.

CONRAD OF OFFIDA, BD. December 14. DEC., p. 169
Bd Conrad was an early Friar Minor whose sympathies were with the " Spiritual " and eremitical movements in the order. He was accompanied in his preaching journeys by Bd Peter of Treja who shared his enthusiasm for evangelical poverty. Our Lady is said to have appeared to Bd Conrad one Candlemas day and to have laid the Holy Child in his arms. d. 1306· c.c. 1817.

***CONRAD OF PARZHAM, ST.** April 21. APR., p. 254
No life could be more simple and unsensational than that of St Conrad. He was b. at Parzham in Bavaria, became a Capuchin lay brother when he was thirty-one, and lived for forty years at the friary of Altötting. d. 1894. The fact that he was canonized only forty years after his death shows what an ineffaceable impression he made on his contemporaries.

CONRAD OF PIACENZA, ST. February 19. FEB., p. 277
He was a nobleman who was nearly ruined materially by restitution he made in consequence of an act of injustice. His wife became a Poor Clare and Conrad joined some hermits who lived under the rule of the third order of St Francis. To avoid publicity he removed to Sicily, where he lived for over thirty years and d. there in 1354. Many marvels are recounted of him. c.c. by Popes Leo X· and Paul III.

CONRAD OF SELDENBÜREN, BD. May 2. MAY, p. 31
He founded and endowed the abbey of Engelberg in 1082–1120, and became a lay-brother there. He was murdered at Zurich in 1126, having been sent there on business of the abbey.

CONRAN, ST, bp. February 14. FEB., p. 220
Nothing whatsoever is known about this alleged bishop in the Orkney Islands.

CONSTANTINE, ST, mart. March 11.   MAR., p. 189

There is very great uncertainty about this saint. He is said to have been a prince from Cornwall who was first a penitent in Wales and Ireland and then a missionary in Scotland, where he was murdered by pagan pirates in Kintyre, *c.* 598. Constantine used to be venerated as the first martyr in Scotland and his feast is still kept in the diocese of Argyll. *Constantinus.*

*CONSTANTINE, ST, bp. April 12.   APR., p. 135

He is the first bishop of Gap in France whose existence is certain, but nothing else is known of him. d. 529.

CONSTANTIUS OF FABRIANO, BD. February 25.   FEB., p. 348

Constantius Bernocchi was concerned in the reform of the Dominican friary of San Marco at Florence, and while a preacher in that city received the gift of prophecy. d. 1481. bd. 1811.

CONTARDO, ST. April 16.   APR., p. 186

St Contardo the Pilgrim belonged to the Este family of Ferrara and died while on a pilgrimage to Compostela in 1249 ; his tomb was honoured by miracles. *Contardus.*

CONVOYON, ST, ab. January 5.   JAN., p. 79

Founder of the monastery of Saint Saviour near Redon in Brittany in 831, a foundation which was carried out under great difficulties. d. 868. c.c. 1866.

CORBINIAN, ST, bp. September 8.   SEPT., p. 90

He was a Frankish hermit, and was sent by the Holy See to preach the gospel in Bavaria where he founded the see of Freising. The later years of his life were spent in semi-exile owing to the enmity of Duke Grimoald whose incestuous marriage he had opposed. d. 725. *Corbinianus.*

COREA, THE MARTYRS OF. September 21.   SEPT., p. 273

In 1925 there were beatified Laurence Imbert, titular bishop of Capsa and vicar apostolic of Corea, two other priests of the Paris Foreign Missions, and seventy-six Corean lay people, who gave their lives for Christ during the persecution of 1839. The three Europeans allowed themselves to be taken in order to avert a general massacre of Christians.

CORENTINUS, ST, bp. December 12.   DEC., p. 145

He is venerated as the first bishop of Cornouaille (Quimper) in Brittany, where he was a hermit at Plomodiern during the fifth century. Corentinus was known in the west and south of England, being called " St Cury " in Cornwall.

†*CORNELIUS, ST, pope and mart. September 16.   SEPT., p. 188

The pontificate of Cornelius is important in ecclesiastical history because of the appearance of the first antipope, Novatian, and the controversy about this man's rigorism in dealing with Christians who had weakened under persecution. The progress of the disputes showed clearly how all Christians recognized the necessity of being in communion with the true bishop of Rome. Pope St Cornelius was the first to suffer in the persecution of Gallus, in 253 : he probably d. of ill treatment in exile at Centumcellæ, though later accounts say that he was beheaded. This pope is named with his great supporter St Cyprian in the canon of the Mass.

†*COSMAS and **DAMIAN, SS,** marts. September 27.   SEPT., p. 331

They are the principal and best known of those saints venerated in the East as *anargyroi,* " moneyless ones," because they practised medicine without taking payment from their patients. They are said, with many legendary accretions, to have been twin Arab brothers, martyred in Cilicia under Diocletian, but their origin and true history are unknown.

COSMO DI CARBOGNANO, BD. *See* Gomidas.

CRESCENTIA HÖSS, BD, virg. April 5.　　　　　　　　　　APR., p. 67

This daughter of a weaver was admitted to a house of Franciscan regular tertiaries at Kaufbeuren at the request of the Protestant mayor, and was then neglected by the prioress and older nuns because she had not brought a dowry ! After a time they discovered that she had brought the dowry of holiness, and had the grace to make her first novice-mistress and then superioress. d. 1744. bd. 1900. Bd Crescentia's tomb is still a place of pilgrimage.

*CRESCENTIAN, ST, mart. June 1.　　　　　　　　　　JUNE, p. 3

He is said to have been a former soldier, beheaded for the faith at Saldo in Italy in 287, but his historical existence is doubtful. *Crescentianus.*

*CRESCENTIUS OF FLORENCE, ST. April 19.　　　　　　APR., p. 226

A young subdeacon of Florence, a disciple of the bishop St Zenobius and of St Ambrose. d. *c.* 396.

*CRETE, THE MARTYRS OF. December 23.　　　　　　DEC., p. 223

The group known as the Ten Martyrs of Crete (SS Theodulus and his companions) suffered death by beheading at Gortyna during the persecution under Decius in 250.

*CRISPIN and **CRISPINIAN, SS,** marts. October 25.　　OCT., p. 331

These famous martyrs, patron saints of shoemakers, were put to death at Soissons, probably *c.* 285, but the extant account of them cannot be relied on. They have a local traditional association with the town of Faversham in Kent. *Crispinus, Crispinianus.*

CRISPIN OF VITERBO, BD. May 21.　　　　　　　　　　MAY, p. 264

A Capuchin lay brother at various houses of his order in Italy, in al of which he was revered for his holy life and miracles. d. 1750. bd. 1806.

*CRISPINA, ST, mart. December 5.　　　　　　　　　　DEC., p. 74

St Augustine frequently mentions St Crispina, who was an African woman of rank, married and with several children. In 304 she was charged with ignoring the imperial commands to sacrifice to the gods, she was resolute in her disobedience, and was beheaded at Thebeste.

CRONAN OF ROSCREA, ST, ab. April 28.　　　　　　　APR., p. 319

There are no reliable accounts of the life of St Cronan, who founded several monasteries in Ireland. d. *c.* 626.

*CUCUFAS, ST, mart. July 25.

One of the most celebrated of the Spanish martyrs, b. of Punic descent in Africa ; he was tortured and beheaded at Barcelona in 304.

CUMIAN FADA, ST, ab. November 12.　　　　　　　　　NOV., p. 144

He had charge of the monastic school at Clonfert and founded a monastery at Kilcummin, where he was an active defender of the Roman computation of Easter against the Celtic usage. d. 662.

CUNCOLIM, THE MARTYRS OF. July 27.　　　　　　　JULY, p. 385

Rudolf Acquaviva and four other members of the Society of Jesus were slain at the Hindu village of Cuncolim in the district of Salsette, north of Bombay, in 1583 ; they had gone thither to choose a site for a church. They are usually called the Martyrs of Salsette. bd. 1893.

F　　　　　　　　　　　　　　73

*CUNEGUND, ST. March 3.   MAR., p. 33

Cunegund was the wife of the Holy Roman emperor St Henry II. A year after her husband's death she became a nun in the convent she had founded at Kaufungen, near Cassel. d. 1039. cd. 1200. St Cunegund had no children and she is commemorated liturgically as a virgin, but this seems to be an error. *Cunegundis.*

CUNEGUND, BD, virg. July 24.   JULY, p. 341

In Magyar *Kinga.* She was the daughter of Bela IV of Hungary and niece of St Elizabeth. She married Boleslaus II of Poland and together they took a vow of perpetual continency ; after his death she became a Poor Clare. d. 1292. c.c. 1690. She is a patron saint of Poland and Lithuania.

CUNGAR, ST, ab. November 27.   NOV., p. 326

Cungar (Cyngar) founded several churches in Wales and a monastery at Congresbury in Somerset, for which reason his feast is observed in the diocese of Clifton. He is the same as St Docco (Dochau). d. *c.* 520. *Cungarus.*

*CUNIBERT, ST, bp. November 12.   NOV., p. 142

He was bishop of Cologne and a chief minister during the minority of Sigebert of Austrasia ; but he did not live long to fulfil this office, dying with a great reputation of holiness *c.* 633. *Cunibertus.*

*CUTHBERT, ST, bp. March 20.   MAR., p. 327

While a monk at Melrose and Lindisfarne he made missionary journeys far and wide in Northumbria, and was then a solitary for ten years until 685, when he was consecrated bishop of Lindisfarne. He " continued to be the same man that he was before," but only ruled his see for two years, dying on Farne island in 687. St Cuthbert is one of the most famous of English saints (the claim that he was Irish is not established) : without intermission he preached, taught, distributed alms, and wrought so many miracles of healing that he was known during his lifetime as the " Wonder-worker of Britain." He travelled into the remoter parts of the north, visiting from cottage to cottage from Berwick to Solway Firth with the good news of Christ, and everywhere he was a welcome and honoured guest. His shrine at Durham was one of the most frequented in the Middle Ages ; his feast is kept to-day in the dioceses of Hexham, Lancaster, Birmingham, Liverpool, and Saint Andrews. *Cuthbertus.*

CUTHBERT MAYNE, BD, mart. November 29.   NOV., p. 341

Cuthbert Mayne, b. near Barnstaple in 1544, was the first seminary priest to suffer martyrdom. He was a convert minister, ordained at Douay, and in 1576 was sent on the mission in England. He was stationed at Mr Francis Tregian's mansion at Golden in Cornwall, where he was soon arrested. At Launceston assizes he was found guilty of various " offences " under 1 and 13 Elizabeth in such circumstances that a majority of the judges of the country thought the conviction could not stand. But the Privy Council directed that the sentence be carried out ; Bd Cuthbert was accordingly h.d.q. at Launceston in 1577. bd. 1886. His feast is kept in the dioceses of Westminster, Lancaster, Liverpool, Northampton, and Plymouth.

CUTHBURGA, ST. September 3.   AUG., p. 396

She was the wife of King Aldfrid of Northumbria, and she became a nun at Barking in Essex under St Hildelitha. Later she founded the abbey of Wimborne, with her sister St Quenburga, and ruled it as abbess till her death *c.* 725. SS Cuthburga and Hildelitha are celebrated in a common feast in the diocese of Brentwood.

CUTHMAN, ST. February 8. FEB., p. 123

He lived with his mother at Steyning in Sussex, where he appears to have built the first church. d. *c.* 900.

CYBI, ST, ab. November 8. NOV., p. 95

He is said to have been born in Cornwall, a nephew of St Cungar, and migrated to Wales where he was a missionary monk in Anglesey. His chief centre was at Holyhead, called in Welsh Caergybi, " Cybi's Stronghold." d. *c.* 555.

†*CYPRIAN, ST, bp. and mart. September 16. SEPT., p. 191

St Cyprian, bishop of Carthage, played an important part in the history of the Western church and the development of Christian thought in the third century, particularly in Africa. He was the first great Christian Latin writer, and his works include many letters and a famous treatise on the unity of the Church. Cæcilius Cyprianus was b. in proconsular Africa *c.* 210, became a lawyer, in due course was converted to Christianity and was consecrated bishop *c.* 249. He went into hiding during the persecution under Decius, supported Pope St Cornelius against the first antipope, Novatian, and was prominent in the controversy about the treatment of Christians who had lapsed or weakened under persecution. In the plague of 252–254 St Cyprian organized his flock in Carthage for the relief of the sufferers. He was arrested under the first edict of Valerian and beheaded in 258 : the early record of his trial and death is a document of very great interest. St Cyprian is named in the great intercession of the Roman Mass, which is the more notable because he had a serious disagreement with Pope St Stephen I concerning the validity of baptism given by heretics. *Cyprianus.*

†*CYPRIAN and JUSTINA, SS, marts. September 26. SEPT., p. 321

If there were ever a martyred Cyprian and Justina all trace of them has been lost, the story now connected with their names being an utterly fabulous moral tale. It concerns a magician of Antioch, Cyprian, who used his arts in vain to win a Christian maiden, Justina : himself being converted, they both died for Christ at Nicomedia by the command of the emperor.

†*CYRIACUS, LARGUS and other marts., SS. August 8. AUG., p. 94

St Cyriacus was a deacon, martyred at Rome in 304. With him suffered SS Largus, Smaragdus, and twenty others.

CYRICUS. *See* Quiricus.

CYRIL, ST. March 6. MAR., p. 92

He was prior general of the Carmelites in Palestine from *c.* 1232 to his death *c.* 1235. There has been some very peculiar confusion between him and two other SS Cyril, of Alexandria and of Jerusalem. This Cyril is sometimes called " of Constantinople." *Cyrillus.*

CYRIL, ST, mart. May 29. MAY, p. 348

A boy of Cæsarea in Cappadocia who became a Christian without his father's knowledge ; when he was turned out of his home he was arrested by the governor and killed (in 251 ?).

†*CYRIL and METHODIUS, SS. July 7. JULY, p. 67

These brothers are venerated with much enthusiasm as the apostles of the Slavs but there is much in their story as it has come down to us that is doubtful. Cyril (Constantine) was a secular priest and Methodius a monk in Greece, who in 863 were sent as missionaries into Moravia. Cyril died at Rome in 869, but his brother was consecrated bishop and sent back to Moravia and Pannonia with the permission of the Holy See to celebrate the liturgy in Slavonic. For this and other reasons Methodius incurred the opposition of the German bishops, who for a time put him in prison. He translated most of the Bible into Slavonic, as well as the *Nomokanon.* d. 885.

†*CYRIL OF ALEXANDRIA, ST, bp. and doct. February 9.

FEB., p. 134

B. at Alexandria *c.* 376 ; archbishop of that city 412. His name is bound up with the history of the early days of the Nestorian heresy, which he denounced to Pope St Celestine I. At the oecumenical council of Ephesus in 431, at which the heresy was solemnly condemned, St Cyril presided as representative of the Holy See, and the rest of his life was given over to the defence of the truth that in Jesus Christ there is but one divine person. He was a man of much vigour and determination, tending to the use of severe and hasty methods that were fruitful of trouble. Owing to the fact that the Monophysites (Copts, Syrians, and Ethiopians) base their heresy on a misinterpreted theological formula of St Cyril, he is venerated by them as their father and chief teacher. d. in June 444.

*CYRIL OF HELIOPOLIS, ST, mart. March 29.   MAR., p. 432

A deacon of Heliopolis in the Lebanon, martyred under Julian the Apostate, *c.* 362.

†*CYRIL OF JERUSALEM, ST, bp. and doct. March 18.   MAR., p. 305

He was b. about 315 and succeeded St Maximus as bishop of Jerusalem, but not a great deal is known of his life beyond that he had a stormy episcopate. The works for which he is famous are chiefly two series of instructions, one for catechumens in Lent before baptism and the other on the effects of baptism, confirmation, holy communion, and the offering for the living and the dead, with details of the customs of the Eastern Church. These writings are said to be " the earliest example extant of anything in the shape of a formal system of theology." St Cyril, a man of gentle and conciliatory disposition, d. in 387. Sixteen of his thirty-five years of episcopate had been spent in exile.

*CYRUS and JOHN, SS, marts. January 31.   JAN., p. 396

Physicians of Alexandria who went to Canopus to succour a woman and her three young daughters who were being persecuted for Christ's sake. They were all put to death, *c.* 303. SS Cyrus and John were greatly venerated in Egypt and the East generally.

DAGOBERT II, ST. December 23. DEC., p. 226

D Three French dioceses keep the feast of Dagobert II, King of Austrasia, son of St Sigebert III, but there seems no reason apart from popular tradition why he should be regarded as a saint. While in exile as a young man he became friendly with St Wilfrid of York, and he married an Englishwoman. His murder in 679 was popularly construed as martyrdom. *Dagobertus.*

DALMATIUS MONER, BD. September 26. SEPT., p. 329

The life of this Spanish confessor of the order of Friars Preachers was passed in the obscurity of his cell and the quiet discharge of his ordinary duties. d. 1341. c.c. 1721.

DAMASCUS, THE MARTYRS OF. July 10. JULY, p. 132

These were among the victims of the Druse rising against the Christians in the Lebanon in 1860. They were Emmanuel Ruiz, guardian of the Friars Minor at Damascus, and seven of his community with three Maronite laymen, all slain within the walls of the friary where they had been betrayed. They were offered the alternative of accepting Islam or death. bd. 1926.

†*DAMASUS I, ST, pope. December 11. DEC., p. 132

Damasus came to the papal chair in 366. He vigorously opposed Apollinarianism and other heresies and much increased the prestige of the Roman see ; he directed St Jerome to correct the Latin Bible ; and himself wrote inscriptions for buildings and for the tombs of the martyrs, many of which have survived. d. 384.

DAMIAN OF FINARIO, BD. October 26.

Damian dei Fulcheri was a Dominican friar known for his preaching throughout Italy. d. 1484. c.c. 1848. *Damianus.*

*DANIEL, ST, mart. October 10. OCT., p. 140

Seven Friars Minor, led by Brother Daniel, arrived in Morocco in 1227 to preach the gospel to the Moors. Within three weeks they were all beheaded at Ceuta for refusing to apostatize to Islam. cd. 1516.

*DANIEL STYLITES, ST. December 11. DEC., p. 138

He was the greatest and best-known of the pillar-saints after St Simeon the Elder, who was Daniel's inspiration. After being a hermit for some years near Constantinople he became a stylite, the emperor Leo I providing an arrangement of pillars which included a small shelter at the top. Here he was ordained priest by St Gennadius, and was as it were the oracle of Constantinople for many years ; on one occasion he came down to earth, *c.* 476, to rebuke the usurping emperor Basiliscus for supporting the monophysite heresy. d. 493.

*DASIUS, ST, mart. November 20. NOV., p. 252

He was a Roman soldier put to death at Durostorum (Silistria) in 303 for refusing to take part in heathen observances at the Saturnalia.

*DATIUS, ST, bp. January 14. JAN., p. 179

He became bishop of Milan about 530 and was much troubled by both

Goths and heretics. He was driven away to Constantinople, where he lived for the rest of his life and died in 552, after supporting Pope Vigilius against Justinian in the " Three Chapters " controversy.

DAVID, ST, bp. March 1.   MAR., p. 1

In Welsh, *Dewi Sant*. The patron saint of Wales lived in the fifth–sixth century. He founded a monastery at Mynyw (Menevia) in the far west of Pembrokeshire and is venerated as the first bishop in those parts, now called after him Saint Davids. The monks followed an extremely austere rule which included total abstinence from wine, whence they were called " the Watermen " ; this led to controversy between St David and St Gildas, who said that the Menevian monks were more ascetic than Christian. The story that David was acclaimed " primate of Wales " at the Synod of Brefi and that he was consecrated at Jerusalem is fictitious. His feast is kept in Wales and in the English dioceses of Westminster, Birmingham, and Portsmouth.

DAVID LEWIS, BD, mart. August 27.   AUG., p. 343

David Lewis (*alias* Charles Baker) was the last in order of time of the Welsh martyrs. He was b. in 1616 at Abergavenny, became a Jesuit, and was stationed at the Society's residence at the Cwm, near Monmouth. After the Titus Oates scare he was betrayed by an apostate and h.d.q. for his priesthood at Usk in 1679. bd. 1929.

DAVID OF SWEDEN, ST. July 15.   JULY, p. 204

According to legend this David was an English Benedictine who joined the mission of St Siegfried in Sweden and founded a monastery at Monken-torp. He is said to have been the first bishop of Västeräss. d. *c.* 1080.

*DAVINUS, ST. June 3.   JUNE, p. 39

A wealthy young Armenian pilgrim who, having visited the Holy Land and Rome, set out for Compostella ; he d. on the way at Lucca in 1051, and was revered there as a saint.

DECLAN, ST, bp. July 24.   JULY, p. 338

A fifth-century missionary in Ireland who was bishop in the district of Ardmore. His feast is kept throughout Ireland. *Declanus*.

DEICOLUS, ST, ab. January 18.   JAN., p. 227

He left Ireland with St Columbanus, but when his master left France he stayed behind and founded the abbey of Lutra, or Lure. d. *c.* 625.

DEINIOL, ST, bp. September 11.   SEPT., p. 144

Deiniol the Elder was a son of St Dunawd and father of St Deiniol the Younger (Deiniolen). He afterwards became a monk and founded the monastery of Bangor Fawr on the Menai Straits, where eventually was the mediæval see of Bangor. He was probably the founder of Bangor Iscoed on the Dee also. d. *c.* 584. Deiniol's feast is kept in the diocese of Menevia.

DELPHINA, BD. December 9.   SEPT., p. 334

Delphina of Glandèves, lady of Puy-Michel, was the wife of St Elzear and is said to have been a member of the third order of St Francis. She survived her husband for some thirty-five years, first in attendance on Queen Sanchia of Naples and then in retirement in her native Provence. d. *c.* 1358. c.c. by Pope Urban VIII.

*DELPHINUS, ST, bp. December 24.   DEC., p. 233

Delphinus, bishop of Bordeaux, is now chiefly remembered as a correspondent of St Ambrose and a strong influence in the conversion of St Paulinus of Nola. d. 404.

DEMETRIAN, ST, bp. November 6. Nov., p. 73

He was abbot of the monastery of St Antony in Cyprus and then bishop of Khytri for many years. He is one of the most venerated of Cypriote saints. d. *c.* 912. *Demetrianus.*

*DEMETRIUS, ST, mart. October 8. Oct., p. 101

He was probably a deacon martyred during the persecution of Diocletian at Sirmium in Dalmatia, but the centre of his cultus was at Salonika. Later fictitious legends made Demetrius a proconsul and a great warrior-saint, in which capacity he received the most solemn cultus all over the East: he is even named in the preparation of the Byzantine Liturgy.

DEMETRIUS, ST, bp. October 9. Oct., p. 109

He is reputed the twelfth bishop of Alexandria and was a close friend of Origen, whom later he had to banish for being irregularly ordained. Demetrius had the gift of reading men's secret sins and thoughts. d. 231.

DENIS. *See* Dionysius.

DEOCHAR, ST, ab. June 7. June, p. 93

Or *Gottlieb.* Abbot of a monastery founded by Charlemagne at Herrie-den in Franconia. d. *c.* 832.

DEODATUS, ST, ab. April 24. Apr., p. 279

In French *Dié.* He is said to have been the first hermit in the neighbourhood of Blois, and founded the monastery round which the town of Saint-Dié grew up. d. *c.* 525.

DEODATUS, ST, bp. June 19. June, p. 240

In French *Dié, Didier.* He became bishop of Nevers in 655 but after some years retired to the Vosges mountains as a solitary. Later he was abbot of a community at Ebersheim, near Strasbourg, and then returned to the Vosges, where Saint-Dié is now on the site of his cell. He is said to have helped in the founding of the neighbouring abbey of Jointures, but this is doubtful. d. 679.

*DEOGRATIAS, ST, bp. March 22. Mar., p. 369

While bishop of Carthage he ransomed numerous captives who had been brought from Italy by Genseric and given to the Vandals and Moors as slaves. d. 457.

DESIDERATUS, ST, bp. May 8. May, p. 98

A bishop of Bourges during the sixth century. His brothers Desiderius and Deodatus are also venerated locally as saints.

DESIDERIUS, BD, bp. January 20. Jan., p. 248

Or *Didier.* A bishop of Thérouanne who founded the Cistercian abbey of Blandecques, " Blandyke," a word having significance for the *alumni* of Jesuit schools. d. 1194.

*DESIDERIUS, ST, bp. and mart. May 23. May, p. 281

In French *Didier.* He was bishop of Vienne and his zeal for clerical discipline and against simony and profligacy at the court brought down on him the anger of Queen Brunhildis. In 608 he was murdered for rebuking the wickedness of King Theodoric, at the place now called Saint-Didier-sur-Chalaronne.

DESIDERIUS OF CAHORS, ST, bp. November 15. Nov., p. 188

Desiderius followed his brother St Rusticus as bishop of Cahors in 630, and worked most zealously for the spiritual and temporal betterment of his diocese. d. 655.

DEUSDEDIT, ST, bp. July 14. JULY, p. 185

The sixth archbishop of Canterbury and the first Englishman to occupy the see. Nothing is known of his episcopate. d. 664.

*DEUSDEDIT, ST, pope. November 8.

Deusdedit, also called Adeodatus I, was pope from 615 till his death in 618. He worked nobly for the stricken during a plague, but otherwise little is known of him.

DIANA, CECILIA and **AMATA, BB,** virgs. June 9. JUNE, p. 121

Three original members of the first house of Dominican nuns at Bologna in 1222. Diana was a Bolognese whose family violently tried to prevent her becoming a religious : she d. 1236. The other two were Romans from the San Sisto convent, of which Cecilia was in a sense the foundress ; d. 1282. Of Amata practically nothing is known. bd. 1891.

DIDACUS, BD. March 24. MAR., p. 390

A Capuchin of Cadiz, famous for his sermons about the Most Holy Trinity, who ministered throughout Spain, but especially in Andalusia. d. 1801. bd. 1894.

†*DIDACUS, ST. November 13. NOV., p. 151

This Didacus (Diego) was born of lowly parents in Spain c. 1400, and became a Friar Minor of the Observance at Arizafa. He was simply a lay brother, but his ability and goodness were so remarkable that he was appointed guardian of the chief friary in the Canary Islands, at Fortaventura, in 1445. Later he was recalled to Spain, where he d. at Alcalá in 1463. cd. 1588.

DIDACUS CARVALHO, BD, mart. February 25. FEB., p. 351

B. at Coimbra in 1578. He was a Jesuit missionary in the Far East, chiefly in Japan, for fifteen years and the first priest to celebrate Mass in Hokkaido, the northern island. When a crisis of persecution came in 1623 Father Carvalho and a number of his flock were arrested and taken in the most barbarous manner to Sendai. Three attempts were made to make him and nine Japanese laymen apostatize by leaving them standing naked in freezing water, and they all died from the effects of this exposure, the Jesuit last of all. d. 1624. bd. 1867.

DIDIER. *See* Desiderius, Desideratus.

*DIDYMUS and **THEODORA, SS,** marts. April 28. APR., p. 317

The story of Theodora and her rescue from a brothel by Didymus, for which they were both executed at Alexandria, is probably a purely fictitious narrative.

DIEMUT, BD, virg. March 29. MAR., p. 436

Diemut or Diemoda was a solitary at Wessobrunn in Bavaria. She employed her time in copying manuscripts, some of which still exist. d. c. 1130.

*DIONYSIA and other marts., **SS.** December 6. DEC., p. 89

On December 6 and 7 are commemorated certain martyrs in Africa at the hands of the Arian king Hunneric in 484. Principal among them are St Dionysia, her young son Majoricus, and her sister Dativa.

†*DIONYSIUS, ST, bp. and mart. October 9. OCT., pp. 107, 110

This saint figures in the Roman liturgy as a composite of Dionysius the Areopagite, a disciple of St Paul (Acts xvii, 34), Dionysius, bishop of Paris (" St Denis of France "), who with Rusticus and Eleutherius is said to have been martyred at Paris c. 275, and pseudo-Dionysius, the fifth-century mystical writer. It was a project of Pope Benedict XIV to suppress this anomalous feast.

*DIONYSIUS, ST, pope.   December 26.   DEC., p. 251

He was a Roman priest who came to the chair of Peter in 259 and restored the Roman church after Gallienus stopped the persecution. St Dionysius was not the first pope to die in peace, but he is the earliest to whom the title " martyr " is not accorded liturgically. d. 269.

DIONYSIUS and **REDEMPTUS, BB,** marts. November 29. Nov., p. 343

Bd. Dionysius (Peter Berthelot) was a French ship-master and trader, who became a Carmelite at Goa in 1635. When an embassy was sent thence to Sumatra in 1638 Dionysius went with it in the combined capacities of pilot and chaplain. The embassy was not welcome and among those put to death by the Sumatrans were the chaplain and his *socius*, Brother Redemptus. bd. 1900.

*DIONYSIUS THE GREAT, ST, bp. November 17.   Nov., p. 213

This Dionysius became bishop of Alexandria in 247, after being head of the catechetical school there, and governed his diocese from Libya during the persecution of Decius ; he was again exiled for a time under Valerian. He was very active in the controversies that troubled the Church at that time (Novatianism, Chiliasm, etc.), and was called by St Athanasius " the teacher of the whole Church." d. 265.

*DIONYSIUS OF CORINTH, ST, bp. April 8.   APR., p. 93

A great leader of the Church in the second century, who from his see at Corinth wrote letters to other churches, some of which have come down to us. In the East he is venerated as a martyr because he suffered much for the Faith. d. *c.* 180.

*DIONYSIUS OF MILAN, ST, bp. May 25.   MAY, p. 301

He was made bishop of Milan in 351 and four years later was banished for upholding the cause of St Athanasius against the Arian emperor Constantius. d. *c.* 359.

DISIBOD, ST, bp. September 8.   SEPT., p. 87

He is said to have been a bishop of Dublin who was forced by persecution to flee to Germany, where he founded the monastery of Disibodenberg, near Bingen. d. *c.* 700.

DISMAS, ST. *See* the Good Thief.

DOCCO, ST. *See* Cungar.

DODO, BD. March 30.   MAR., p. 447

He was a hermit at various places in Friesland and was reputed to have received the stigmata—possibly a case of older date than that of St Francis. d. 1231.

DOGMAEL, ST. June 14.   JUNE, p. 177

A Welsh monk, of the house of Cunedda, who founded churches in Pembrokeshire, Brittany, and elsewhere. 5th–6th century.

*DOMETIUS THE ILLUSTRIOUS, ST, mart. August 7. AUG., p. 83

A Persian monk who was stoned to death for the Faith at Nisibis, *c.* 362.

†*DOMINIC, ST. August 4.   AUG., p. 43

He was born at Calaruega in Spain in 1170 and became an Augustinian canon regular at Osma. At that time the Albigensian heresy was going from strength to strength in the face of slack Catholicism in south-western Europe and in 1206 Dominic founded a convent at Prouille whose first nuns were converts from this heresy ; this was the germ of the Dominican

A DICTIONARY OF SAINTS

Order. After a further ten years' preaching he established the Friars Preachers, first to combat Albigensianism and then to preach and teach throughout Europe, to hand on to others the fruits of contemplation. This new order was as successful as that of the contemporary Franciscans, and together they left an ineffaceable mark on the later Middle Ages. The Order of Preachers was confirmed by the Holy See in 1216 and within a few years it had spread all over Europe : it is still world-wide. Both during his life and since his death few saints have excited such personal affection as St Dominic—and few been so reviled by the ignorant : " Nothing disturbed the even temper of his soul," said one who knew him, " except his quick sympathy with every sort of suffering "—the beauty of holiness is remarkably apparent in him. d. 1221 (in another friar's bed and another's habit—because he had none of his own). cd. 1234. *Dominicus.*

DOMINIC and **GREGORY, BB.** April 26.   APR., p. 295
Two Spanish Dominicans who preached in the villages of the Pyrenees ; they were killed by a fall of rock near Besiano in 1300, and have been venerated there ever since. c.c. by Pius IX.

DOMINIC HENAREZ, BD, bp. and mart. July 11.   JULY, p. 146
He was a Spanish Dominican, auxiliary bishop to Bd Ignatius Delgado in Eastern Tonkin, who was beheaded with his catechist Bd Francis Chien in 1838 during the Annamite persecution. bd. 1900.

*DOMINIC LORICATUS, ST. October 14.   OCT., p. 195
When Dominic discovered that his ordination had been obtained by a simoniacal gift by his father he refused to exercise his priesthood and became a hermit monk under St Peter Damian at Fonte Avellano. His physical mortifications were altogether extraordinary, and he was called *Loricatus,* " the Mailed," because he wore a rough iron coat of mail next his skin. d. 1060.

DOMINIC SPADAFORA, BD. October 3.   OCT., p. 37
A confessor of the Order of Preachers in Sicily and Italy. d. 1521. bd. 1921.

DOMINIC VERNAGALLI, BD. April 20.   APR., p. 241
A Camaldolese monk, founder of a hospital in Pisa. d. 1218. c.c. 1854.

*DOMINIC DE LA CALZADA, ST. May 12.   MAY, p. 148
St Dominic of the Causeway is so called from the road which he made for pilgrims on their way to Compostella. He was a hermit in the wooded wilderness of Bureba in north-eastern Spain, and it was there that he made his road. d. *c.* 1109.

*DOMINIC OF SILOS, ST, ab. December 20.   DEC., p. 211
He was a monastic reformer in Navarre until the enmity of King Garcia III forced him to migrate to Castile, where he restored and became abbot of Silos. d. 1073. It was after Dominic of Silos that the founder of the Order of Preachers was named in consequence of Bd Joan of Aza's vision at the saint's shrine.

*DOMINIC OF SORA, ST, ab. January 22.   JAN., p. 271
The founder of several Benedictine monasteries in Italy. d. 1031.

*DOMINICA, ST, virg. and mart. July 6.   JULY, p. 60
This saint, the best known of several of the name, is said on very little little authority to have been martyred in Campania under Diocletian. She may be the same as St Cyriaca (=Dominica), venerated in the East on the same date as a martyr at Nicomedia.

82

DOMITIAN, ST, bp. May 7. MAY, p. 87
He was bishop of Maestricht and evangelized the Meuse valley, where his relics are still venerated at Huy. d. *c.* 560. *Domitianus.*

*DOMITILLA, ST, mart. May 12. MAY, p. 139
Her name is associated in the Roman liturgy with SS Nereus and Achilleus, who were buried in the cemetery of Domitilla on the Via Ardeatina. There seem to have been two patrician ladies named Flavia Domitilla who suffered for the Faith, a niece of the emperor Domitian and her own niece by marriage.

*DOMNOLUS, ST, bp. May 16. MAY, p. 208
He was bishop of Le Mans ; d. in 581.

DONALD, ST. July 15. JULY, p. 197
He lived at Ogilvy in Forfarshire during the eighth century, and after the death of his wife led a sort of community life with his nine daughters (the " Nine Maidens "). *Donaldus.*

DONAN, ST, mart. April 17. APR., p. 197
Donan was a monk of Iona under St Columba. He established a monastery on the island of Eigg in the Inner Hebrides, and with his monks was massacred by Danish raiders *c.* 616. Their feast is kept in the diocese of Argyll. *Donnanus.*

*DONATIAN and **ROGATIAN, SS,** marts. May 24. MAY, p. 290
Gallo-Roman brothers who refused to sacrifice to the gods and so were beheaded at Nantes, probably in 289 or 304.

*DONATUS, ST, bp. October 22. OCT., p. 302
According to the tradition of Fiesole Donatus was an Irish pilgrim who was miraculously indicated as their bishop and was accordingly elected. He wrote a preface to Coelan's *Life of St Brigid.* d. 876. The feast of St Donatus is observed throughout Ireland.

†*DONATUS OF AREZZO, ST, bp. and mart. August 7.
Donatus is said to have been b. at Nicomedia and to have come to Arezzo during the persecution of Diocletian, where he was made bishop and martyred under Julian in 362, with the monk St Hilarinus.

DORCHESTER MARTYRS, THE. July 4. JULY, p. 47
On July 4, 1594, there suffered at Dorchester in Dorset, John Cornelius (*alias* Mohun), condemned for his priesthood ; Thomas Bosgrave, gentleman, for aiding and abetting Cornelius ; and John Carey and Patrick Salmon, servants, for the same. All these martyrs, except Mr. Bosgrave, were of Irish parentage. Another martyr who died at Dorchester was Hugh Green, a secular priest, on August 19, 1642. All were bd. in 1929.

†*DOROTHEA, ST, virg. and mart. February 6. FEB., p. 88
A martyr at Cæsarea in Cappadocia *c.* 303, whose story as it has come down to us is mainly apocryphal.

DOROTHEA OF MONTAU, ST. October 30. OCT., p. 365
She was a peasant girl of Montau in Prussia, and married a swordsmith named Albert : by her sweetness of character she modified his surly disposition and, when eight of their nine children had died, they used to go on pilgrimages together to various shrines. After the death of Albert, Dorothy became a recluse at Marienwerder and during the few months of life left to her acquired a great reputation for holiness and supernatural enlightenment. d. 1394. This mystic still has a cultus in central Europe, but her canonization, though begun, was never carried through.

*DOROTHEUS, ST, mart. June 5. JUNE, p. 65

He was a priest of Tyre, driven into exile under Diocletian. He attended the Council of Nicæa, but under Julian the Apostate was arrested at Varna on the Black Sea and beaten to death, *c.* 362. That is the story, but this martyr has not been certainly identified.

DOROTHEUS, ST, ab. June 5. JUNE, p. 67

Called " the Archimandrite." He was first a monk near Gaza, but of what monastery he became archimandrite is not known. His spiritual writings were much valued by Abbot de Rancé who had them translated into French. d. during first half of seventh century. There is no evidence of cultus.

DOROTHEUS THE THEBAN, ST. June 5. JUNE, p. 66

He was an anchorite some way out of Alexandria and the first master of Palladius when he went among the Egyptian monks, but it does not appear that he ever had any cultus as a saint, though he was, Palladius tells us, a very holy man.

DOROTHEUS THE YOUNGER, ST, ab. January 5. JUNE, p. 67

B. at Trebizond and became first a monk at Samsun on the Black Sea and then founder of a monastery at Khiliokomos near by. He had the gifts of prophecy and miracles. 11th century.

DOROTHY. *See* Dorothea.

DOSITHEUS, ST. February 23. FEB., p. 318

A rich young man who was converted to Christianity at Jerusalem and became a monk at Gaza, where he lost his health and scandalized his fellows by being unable to fast and work miracles. But, as his abbot pointed out, he had completely surrendered his own will. d. *c.* 530.

DOUAY, THE MARTYRS OF. October 29. OCT., p. 357

More than 160 " seminary priests " from the English College at Douay were put to death in England and Wales during the century following its foundation in 1568. Over eighty of them (many of whom are referred to in this volume under their proper names) have been beatified as martyrs, and a collective feast is kept in their honour in the dioceses of Westminster and Hexham.

DRAUSIUS, ST, bp. March 7. MAR., p. 113

Bishop of Soissons in the seventh century. After his death *c.* 674 he was specially invoked against the machinations of enemies, and St Thomas Becket is said to have visited his shrine before returning to martyrdom in England.

DRITHELM, ST. September 1. SEPT., p. 9

He was a Northumbrian who, in consequence of a vision (narrated by St Bede), divided his goods between his wife, his children, and the poor, and was admitted a monk of Melrose. Here he lived a life of great austerity in a special cell near the monastery. d. *c.* 700.

*DROCTOVÆUS, ST, ab. March 10. MAR., p. 170

In French *Drotté*. He was abbot of the monastery of St Vincent and the Holy Cross at Paris, and d. *c.* 580.

*DROGO, ST. April 16. APR., p. 184

Drogo, a Fleming, left his home and inheritance to be a shepherd in France, an occupation which he varied by pilgrimages to Rome until they were ended by a bodily affliction that made him a most unpleasant sight ; he then shut himself up in a cell adjoining the church at Sebourg. d. 1186.

St Drogo is a patron of shepherds and is invoked against hernia and gravel.

DROSTAN, ST, ab.   July 11.

JULY, p. 137

An abbot of Deer whose feast is kept in the dioceses of Aberdeen and Argyll. d. *c.* 610. *Drostanus.*

DUBRICIUS, ST, bp.   November 14.

NOV., p. 174

In Welsh *Dyfrig.* His principal monasteries were at Henllan and Moccas from whence he made many religious settlements in what are now the borders of Herefordshire and Monmouthshire. He had some jurisdiction over the monks of Caldey and made St Samson abbot there, later consecrating him bishop. In mediæval legend St Dubricius was " archbishop of Caerleon " and crowned King Arthur at Colchester. d. on Bardsey *c.* 545. His feast is observed on Caldey Island and in the archdiocese of Cardiff.

*DUNSTAN, ST, bp.   May 19.

MAY, p. 239

Dunstan, the most famous of the Anglo-Saxon saints, was b. near Glastonbury and was appointed abbot of that monastery in 943. He gradually superseded its secular occupants by Benedictine monks and made it a centre of learning and religious observance. Dunstan was chief adviser to King Edred and initiated a vigorous policy of national unification and moral reform. For a time he was banished by King Edwy, but returned under Edgar and was made successively bishop of Worcester and London and primate at Canterbury. He was appointed papal legate in 961 and, with St Ethelwold of Winchester and St Oswald of York, carried on his far-reaching reforms with increased zeal. On the death of Edgar in 979 St Dunstan retired and spent the remainder of his life in pastoral work, recreating himself with smithing, painting and music, in all of which he was skilled. d. 988. His feast is kept by the English Benedictines and in the dioceses of Westminster, Birmingham, Brentwood, Clifton, and Southwark. *Dunstanus.*

DURHAM MARTYRS, THE.   July 24.

JULY, p. 346

Four martyrs were put to death in the county palatine of Durham during the year 1594. On February 4 at Durham, John Speed, a layman, was hanged for helping priests ; on July 24 at Durham, a secular priest, John Boste, was h.d.q. for his priesthood ; on July 26 at Gateshead another secular priest, John Ingram, was likewise executed ; and on the same day at Darlington a layman, George Swallowell, was h.d.q. for being reconciled to the Church. All were bd. in 1929.

DUTHAC, ST, bp.   March 8.

MAR., p. 136

An Irish priest who became bishop of Ross in Scotland, where his memory is preserved in several place-names, *e.g.* Kilduthie. d. *c.* 1065. His feast is kept in the diocese of Aberdeen. *Duthacus.*

*DYMPNA, ST, virg.   May 15.

MAY, p. 191

The relics of St Dympna and of St Gerebernus were discovered at Gheel, near Antwerp, in the thirteenth century and so many miracles of curing insanity, epilepsy, etc., were reported at their new tomb that St Dympna has ever since been venerated as a patroness of lunatics ; there is a large and well-equipped asylum at Gheel to-day which had its origin soon after the finding of the relics. The feast of St Dympna is kept throughout Ireland because of the popular story that she was an Irish princess and Gerebernus her chaplain, but the true story of these saints is not known.

EADBERT, ST, bp. May 6. MAY, p. 81
Eadbert succeeded St Cuthbert in the see of Lindisfarne ; he was remarkable for his knowledge of Holy Scripture and for his generosity to the poor. d. 698. Though there seems to have been no cultus of him in the past, St Eadbert is now commemorated in the diocese of Hexham. *Eadbertus.*

EANSWIDA, ST, virg. September 12. SEPT., p. 153
She was the granddaughter of St Ethelbert, King of Kent, and founded a convent near Folkestone of which she was the first abbess. d. *c.* 640.

EATA, ST, bp. October 26. OCT., p. 340
He was an English disciple of St Aidan and became abbot of Melrose ; in 678 he was made bishop of part of St Wilfrid's diocese of York, and later exchanged with his pupil St Cuthbert for the see of Hexham. St Bede calls him " a most venerable man, meek and simple." d. 685. St Eata's feast is kept in the diocese of Lancaster.

EBBA THE ELDER, ST, virg. August 25. AUG., p. 308
She was a sister of St Oswald of Northumbria and founded the monastery of Coldingham (*cf.* St Abb's Head), over which she ruled as abbess ; but she seems to have been a not very successful superioress. d. 683.

EBERHARD, ST. June 22. JUNE, p. 295
B. at Nuremberg *c.* 1087. He gave up a canonry at Bamberg to take the Benedictine habit, was made abbot of Biburg, and in 1146 archbishop of Salzburg. He was a successful reformer of both clergy and laity in his diocese and was one of the few German bishops who refused to support the antipope Victor at the word of the emperor Frederick Barbarossa. d. 1164.

EBERHARD, BD, ab. August 14. AUG., p. 175
He joined his friend Bd Benno in his hermitage at Einsiedeln in 934 and built at his own expense a monastery and church there ; he is venerated as the first abbot of Einsiedeln. d. 958.

EBERHARD OF MARCHTAL, BD, ab. April 17. APR., p. 204
He was appointed abbot of the monastery of Marchtal in Suabia when it was handed over to the Premonstratensians in 1166. d. 1178.

*EBRULFUS, ST, ab. December 29. DEC., p. 285
In French *Evroult.* From being in the service of King Clotaire I he became a hermit in the forest of Ouche in Normandy where a community grew up of which he was elected abbot. d. 596.

EBSDORF, THE MARTYRS OF. February 2. FEB., p. 41
The army of King Louis III under Duke St Bruno was caught in ice and snow in the winter of 880 by the Northmen and overwhelmed. Bruno, with two bishops, eleven noblemen, and others were among the slain and were venerated as martyrs. This took place on the marshy heath of Lüneburg at Ebsdorf in Saxony.

EDBURGA, ST, virg. December 12. DEC., p. 148

This Edburga probably succeeded St Mildred as abbess of Minster-in-Thanet ; she is chiefly known as a friend and correspondent of St Boniface. d. 751.

EDBURGA OF WINCHESTER, ST, virg. June 15. JUNE, p. 187

This Edburga, granddaughter of Alfred the Great, daughter of Edward the Elder, and abbess at Winchester, was venerated principally at Pershore in Worcestershire, where her relics were enshrined ; the miracles alleged here were chiefly responsible for her fame. d. 960.

EDGAR, ST. July 8. JULY, p. 97

The reign of King Edgar was certainly a peaceful and prosperous one for England but, though he was venerated in the past at Glastonbury abbey, he was a popular hero rather than the sort of person who would to-day be considered a likely candidate for canonization. The religious revival during his reign was principally due to St Dunstan, whom Edgar recalled from exile and promoted to the episcopate. d. 975. *Edgarus.*

EDITH OF POLESWORTH, ST. July 15. JULY, p. 197

She may have been the widow of Sithric the Dane, king of Northumbria, whose name was Edith and who was buried at Tamworth, near Polesworth, probably before 950. *Editha.*

*EDITH OF WILTON, ST, virg. September 16. SEPT., p. 210

She was the daughter of King Edgar and St Wilfrida, and while still a baby was taken to the convent of Wilton, which she never left. She chose to be professed at the age of fifteen, and refused the government of three abbeys, remaining a simple nun at Wilton. She d. at the age of twenty-two in 984. St Edith's feast is celebrated in the diocese of Clifton.

EDMUND, ST, mart. November 20. NOV., p. 254

When the Danes invaded East Anglia in 870 they slew St Edmund, who had become king of the East Angles when a youth in 855. According to tradition he was shot to death with arrows at Hoxne in Norfolk, having refused proposals from the Danes that were inconsistent with religion and justice. His shrine gave its name to the town and abbey of Bury St Edmund's. His feast is kept in the dioceses of Westminster, Birmingham, and Northampton, and by the English Benedictine congregation. *Edmundus.*

EDMUND ARROWSMITH, BD, mart. August 28. AUG., p. 371

He came of a recusant yeoman family in Lancashire, was ordained in 1612 and worked on the English mission for fifteen years, during which he was received into the Society of Jesus. He was indicted in 1628 for being a priest and for reconciling converts, and was h.d.q. at Lancaster. bd. 1929. Cures of ill-health are attributed to Bd Edmund's hand, preserved in the church of St Oswald at Ashton-in-Makerfield.

EDMUND CAMPION, BD, mart. December 1. DEC., p. 17

Bd Edmund, b. in London *c.* 1540, was a " Bluecoat boy " ; he had a brilliant career at Oxford, was reconciled to the Catholic Church, and joined the Society of Jesus at Rome. After working in Bohemia he was sent on the English mission in 1580. After labouring most successfully for over a year, Campion was betrayed in Norfolk and taken to the Tower of London ; he was accused of complicity in a bogus plot, racked in the hope of making him betray his associates, and h.d.q. at Tyburn in 1581. The feast of Bd Edmund is observed by the Society of Jesus and in the dioceses of Northampton, Portsmouth, Prague, and Brünn.

EDMUND CATHERICK, BD, mart. April 13. APR., p. 153

B. in Yorkshire *c.* 1605. He was a secular priest on the English mission for seven years and was h.d.q. for his priesthood at York in 1642. bd. 1929.

*EDMUND RICH, ST, bp. November 16. Nov., p. 198

B. at Abingdon in 1180. He taught theology at Oxford, was a canon of Salisbury and apostolic delegate to preach the crusade in England, and was elected archbishop of Canterbury in 1233. Edmund's zeal for good discipline and monastic observance and his resistance against the encroachment of royal powers involved him in trouble with his chapter, with the monasteries, and with King Henry III, and his difficulties were much increased by the opposition he encountered from the papal legate in England. In 1240 he retired to the Cistercian abbey of Pontigny in France, and died in the same year. cd. 1246. St Edmund's feast is kept throughout England and by the Cistercians.

†*EDWARD THE CONFESSOR, ST. October 13. Oct., p. 177

He was b. at Islip, near Oxford, in 1004, son of King Ethelred the Redeless, and succeeded Hardicanute on the throne of England in 1042. Edward was gentle, generous, without ambition, given to much prayer and to hunting, and his kingdom had peace and good government under his rule. He was the first king to touch for the " king's evil," and his ring (subject of a well-known legend) wedded every sovereign of England to his people from Richard I to James II. In commutation of a vow to go on pilgrimage to Rome, he refounded the abbey of Westminster, and was buried in its church in 1066 ; his body still rests in its shrine beyond the sanctuary of the choir. Edward's sanctity was widely recognized during his lifetime and he was cd. in 1161 ; his feast is observed throughout the Western church on October 13, the anniversary of the translation of his relics in 1163 (the day of his death was January 5). *Edwardus.*

*EDWARD THE MARTYR, ST. March 18. MAR., p. 312

There was formerly considerable cultus of this English king, though there is little reason to regard him as a martyr. At the age of sixteen he was murdered at the instigation of his stepmother Elfrida to open the way to the throne for her son Ethelred. This was in 979. Part of Edward's relics were buried at Wareham and part at Shaftesbury. Elfrida repented and founded the convents of Amesbury and Wherwell in reparation. St Edward's feast is kept in the diocese of Plymouth.

EDWARD COLEMAN, BD, mart. December 3. DEC., p. 49

The first victim of the Titus Oates " plot " was a gentleman of Suffolk, Mr. Edward Coleman. He was h.d.q. at Tyburn in 1678 on a false charge of conspiring with a foreign power to restore the Catholic Church in England. bd. 1929.

EDWARD JONES, BD, mart. May 6. MAY, p. 84

A Welsh secular priest, h.d.q. in Fleet Street, London, for his priesthood in 1590. bd. 1929.

EDWARD OLDCORNE, BD, mart. April 7. APR., p. 91

B. at York, ordained in Rome, and admitted to the Society of Jesus. He worked as a priest in the English midlands for seventeen years and was h.d.q. at Worcester in 1606 for alleged complicity in the Gunpowder Plot. bd. 1929.

EDWARD POWELL, BD, mart. July 30. JULY, p. 423

A Welshman, fellow of Oriel, canon of Salisbury, and one of Catherine's counsel in Henry VIII's nullity suit. He was in prison for six years, condemned by attainder for denying the king's spiritual supremacy, and h.d.q. at Smithfield, London, in 1540. His feast is kept in Wales with Bd Richard Featherstone. bd. 1886.

EDWIN, ST, mart. October 12.

Oct., p. 164

Edwin became effective king of Northumbria in 616, married as his second wife Ethelburga of Kent, and was himself baptized by her chaplain St Paulinus at York in 627. St Bede records that there was perfect peace wherever the rule of King Edwin extended. The Mercians and Welsh marched against him in 633 and he was slain in the ensuing battle. Edwin was venerated as a martyr in England, but he seems to have had no liturgical cultus. *Edwinus.*

*EGBERT, ST, April 24.

Apr., p. 281

Egbert was an English monk of Lindisfarne who, after studying in Ireland, went to Iona with the object of inducing the monks there to celebrate Easter according to the Roman reckoning. He was successful only on the day of his death in 729. St Egbert's feast is observed in the dioceses of Hexham and Argyll. *Egbertus.*

EGWIN, ST, bp. January 11.

Jan., p. 146

Egwin became bishop of Worcester in 692 and by his severity against vice incurred the enmity of some of his flock. He made two pilgrimages to Rome, and after the first one founded, with King Kenred of Mercia, the famous abbey of Evesham. He d. December 30, 717; January 11 is probably the date of the translation of his relics to a better shrine at Evesham in 1183. *Egwinus.*

*ELESBAAN, ST, October 27.

Oct., p. 322

Elesbaan was the Aksumite Ethiopian king who recovered power in Himyar after the massacre of the Martyrs of Nagran (October 24). He seems to have made amends for his cruel and revengeful spirit by later becoming an exemplary monk at Jerusalem, but he is for several reasons an equivocal figure to find in the Roman Martyrology.

*ELEUTHERIUS, ST, bp. and mart. February 20.

Feb., p. 284

He is venerated as the first bishop of Tournai, who died from wounds inflicted by certain heretics in the year 532. The available information about him is not reliable.

*ELEUTHERIUS, ST, mart. April 18.

Apr., p. 212

The story of the martyrdom of Eleutherius, his mother Anthia, and eleven others in Illyria during the second century, has been shown to be a pious romance of Greek origin.

†*ELEUTHERIUS, ST, pope and mart. May 26.

May, p. 316

He occupied the chair of St Peter from 175 to 189, but there is little reliable information about him. He is venerated as a martyr.

*ELEUTHERIUS, ST, ab. September 6.

Sept., p. 67

An abbot near Spoleto at the end of the sixth century, of whose virtues and miracles St Gregory the Great writes in his *Dialogues.*

*ELEUTHERIUS, ST, mart. October 2.

Oct., p. 16

He was martyred at Nicomedia, *c.* 303; he had nothing to do with the burning of Diocletian's palace there.

ELFLEDA, ST, virg. February 8.

Feb., p. 120

Or *Ethelfleda.* She was the daughter of King Oswy of Northumbria and St Eanfleda. She became a nun at Hartlepool and succeeded St Hilda as abbess of Whitby. She took a prominent part in the affairs of

G

the time and appeared at synods on behalf of St Wilfrid of York. St Bede gives an account of a meeting between St Elfleda and her friend St Cuthbert that took place at Coquet island. d. 714.

*ELIAS, etc., SS, marts. February 16. FEB., p. 243

Five Egyptians, viz., Elias, Jeremias, Isaias, Samuel, and Daniel, on their return from visiting the Christian confessors in the mines of Cilicia, were arrested at Cæsarea in Palestine and brought before the governor with St Pamphilus and others. After torture they were all beheaded in 309. One Porphyrius, who said that the bodies ought to be buried, was burned alive for so doing. There is an account of these martyrs by Eusebius who was living in Cæsarea at the time.

*ELIAS, ST. July 20. JULY, p. 284

The Holy Machabees are the only "Old Testament saints" commemorated liturgically throughout the Western church, but the feast of St Elias the Thesbite is kept by the Latins of Jerusalem, in Bosnia, and by the Carmelite Order. Elias, otherwise Elijah, was one of the greatest of the Hebrew prophets, and is specially associated with Mount Carmel (III and IV Kings). He d. *c.* 880 B.C.

ELIAS OF BOURDEILLES, BD, bp. July 5. JULY, p. 56

He was count of Bordeilles in Périgord and joined the Friars Minor. King Louis XI made him the royal confessor and archbishop of Tours, and in 1483 he was created cardinal. Among the works of Elias was a written defence of St Joan of Arc. He d. 1484. His title to be regarded as a saint is somewhat equivocal, and the process of his beatification has not been proceeded with.

*ELIGIUS, ST, bp. December 1. DEC., p. 3

Eligius, called in French *Eloi*, is the patron saint of metal-workers. He was himself a metal-smith of very great skill, and was made master of the mint at Paris by King Clotaire II. He became a person of importance at the court, where he consorted with Audoenus, Desiderius of Cahors, and others who were afterwards venerated as saints. In 641 Clovis II appointed Eligius to the see of Noyon and Tournai, where he was as good a bishop as he had been a layman. He evangelized a considerable part of Flanders, founded a house of nuns under St Godeberta, and was the valued counsellor of the queen-regent St Bathildis, whose solicitude for slaves he shared. d. 660.

*ELIZABETH, ST. November 5.

Nothing is known about the mother of St John the Baptist except what can be gleaned from the Gospel of St Luke. Her feast is kept by the Maronites and Copts and by the Latins of Palestine.

ELIZABETH THE GOOD, BD, virg. November 25. Nov., p. 301

She was b. in 1386 at Waldsee in Würtemberg and passed her life in a small community of Franciscan tertiaries near by. She was one of the last of the mediæval women mystics connected with the mendicant orders who were remarkable for their physical austerities, visions, and other abnormal phenomena. Bd Elizabeth received the *stigmata* and is reputed to have gone very long periods without any natural food. d. 1420. c.c. 1766. *Elisabeth.*

ELIZABETH PICENARDI, BD, virg. February 20. FEB., p. 290

She was a Servite tertiary at Mantua, and several young girls banded themselves together to live in community under her direction. d. 1468. bd. 1804.

†*ELIZABETH OF HUNGARY, ST. November 19.   NOV., p. 241

B. at Presburg in 1207, daughter of King Andreas II of Hungary and niece of St Hedwig. At the age of fourteen Elizabeth married Louis IV, landgrave of Thuringenland, and bore him three children, living happily until in 1227 he went crusading and died at Otranto : " The world," cried Elizabeth, " is dead to me, and all that was joyous in the world." Her subsequent life was full of suffering, a great deal of which was caused by the rigour and roughness of the director, Conrad of Marburg, to whom she had submitted herself ; she abandoned all state, put on the dress of the Franciscan third order, and devoted herself to the poor, the sick, and the aged, continuing the work she had already begun with the encouragement of Louis. St Elizabeth died when still only twenty-four, in 1231. cd. 1235.

†*ELIZABETH OF PORTUGAL, ST. July 8.   JULY, p. 87

B. 1271, daughter of King Pedro III of Aragon, and was married to King Denis of Portugal, who was the source of considerable unhappiness to his wife, for he was selfish and dissolute. Elizabeth was particularly noted as a peacemaker—between her son Alphonso and his father, between Ferdinand IV of Castile and his cousin, and between Ferdinand and James II of Aragon. After the death of Denis she retired to a Poor Clare convent as a tertiary. In 1336 she set out to restrain her son, who was threatening war against his son-in-law the King of Castile ; she was very ill at the time, but succeeded in reconciling them before death overtook her. cd. 1625. In her own country St Elizabeth is known by the Spanish form of her name, *Isabella*.

*ELIZABETH OF SCHÖNAU, ST, virg. June 18.   JUNE, p. 233

Elizabeth was professed a nun at the Benedictine monastery of Schönau in 1147. From the age of twenty-three she was subject to extraordinary supernatural manifestations, accounts of which she wrote down ; she was the inculpable means of a further fictitious elaboration of the legend of St Ursula. For the last seven years of her life she was abbess of the nuns at Schönau, her brother Egbert, who wrote a memoir of her, governing the monks. d. 1164.

ELMO, ST. *See* Erasmus (June 2), Peter Gonzalez.

*ELPHEGE, ST, bp. and mart. April 19.   APR., p. 228

A monk of Deerhurst, raised to the bishopric of Winchester in 984 and translated to Canterbury in 1006. He was deeply beloved, and when the Danes raided Kent in 1011 he was urged to take refuge. Elphege refused and appealed to the invaders to moderate their savagery ; they replied by imprisoning him and demanding a huge ransom. Elphege retorted that the country was too poor to pay such a sum and the Danes accordingly killed him, at Greenwich in 1012. In St Anselm's opinion St Elphege was a martyr in that he died rather than connive at injustice, and he has always been venerated as such. His feast is kept in the dioceses of Westminster, Birmingham, Clifton, Portsmouth, and Southwark. *Elphegus*.

ELPHEGE OF WINCHESTER, ST, bp. March 12.   MAR., p. 218

Also called " the Elder " or " the Bald," to distinguish him from St Elphege the martyr. He became bishop of Winchester in 935 and helped on the religious vocation of his young kinsman St Dunstan, whom he ordained and whose future greatness he prophesied. d. 951.

ELSTAN, ST, bp. April 6.   APR., p. 77

Elstan, or Elfstan, succeeded St Ethelwold both as abbot of Abingdon and bishop of Winchester. d. 981.

*ELZEAR, ST. September 27.   SEPT., p. 334

He was b. in Provence in 1285 and inherited the barony of Ansouis and the county of Ariano ; he married Bd Delphina of Glandèves. In the management of his territories in France and Italy and the conduct of his household Elzear was a most excellent example of the Christian nobleman, and he was chosen to be tutor to Prince Charles of Naples as well as for certain diplomatic missions. An old tradition says that St Elzear was a Franciscan tertiary and that for the last eight years of his life he lived in a brotherly relation with his wife. d. 1323. cd. 1369. *Elzearius.*

EMEBERT, ST, bp. January 15.   JAN., p . 195.

A seventh-century bishop of Cambrai, honoured in some Belgian dioceses.

†*EMERENTIANA, ST, virg. and mart. January 23.   JAN., p. 279

A Roman martyr of unknown date ; she has come to be regarded as the foster-sister of St Agnes.

*EMERICUS, BD. November 4.   NOV., p. 58

B. in 1007, the only son of St Stephen of Hungary ; he predeceased his father in 1031. Though much venerated by the Magyars little is known about Emericus.

EMETERIUS and **CHELIDONIUS, SS,** marts. March 3.   MAR., p. 36

Martyrs at Santander in Spain in 304.

*EMILIAN CUCULLATUS, ST. November 12.   NOV., p. 141

St Emilian-of-the-Cloak, San Millan de la Cogolla, was a famous early saint of Spain, where he was a hermit and a monk in the mountains near Burgos and elsewhere. d. *c.* 572.

EMILY BICCHIERI, BD, virg. August 19.   AUG., p. 228

She was b. at Vercelli in 1238 and, wishing to be a nun, her father built a convent for her and some companions, which was put under the direction of the Friars Preachers ; according to some, this was the first house of Dominican regular tertiaries. Bd Emily was a tactful and enlightened prioress, and is said to have had the gift of miracles. d. 1314. c.c. 1769. *Aemilia.*

EMMA, ST. *See* Hemma.

*EMMERAMUS, ST, bp. and mart. September 22.   SEPT., p. 290

He was a native of Poitiers who went to preach the gospel in Bavaria. He died towards the end of the seventh century, from injuries received when attacked while on the way to Rome, and was venerated as a martyr ; but the motive and circumstances of his murder are a mystery.

*EMYGDIUS, ST, bp. and mart. June 25.   JUNE, p. 332

The legend of St Emygdius states that he was a German Christian who came to Rome and was sent as missionary bishop to evangelize the people of the Ancona Marches ; there he was beheaded with three companions in 304. This saint is invoked in Italy against earthquakes, and his cultus in this form has spread to San Francisco and Los Angeles in U.S.A.

*ENCRATIA, ST, virg. and mart. April 16.   APR., p. 179

Otherwise *Enchratis, Engrazia.* In some way unknown this Spanish girl bore such energetic witness to her faith that she was known as the " vehement maiden." She was mutilated by pagans at Saragossa, but seems to have survived the terrible torture. Date uncertain (304 ?).

A DICTIONARY OF SAINTS

ENDA, ST, ab. March 21.
MAR., p. 361

Enda, or *Endeus*, is said to have been persuaded to become a monk by his sister St Fanchea. He established himself with his disciples on Arranmore, where they led a very penitential life. d. *c.* 590.

*ENECO, ST, ab. June 1.   JUNE, p. 9

Or *Iñigo*. An Aragonese hermit who was appointed abbot of Oña and filled the office with great distinction, his influence extending over the whole countryside. d. 1057. cd. *c.* 1259.

*ENGELBERT, ST, bp. and mart. November 7.   Nov., p. 88

After being the rather unworthy holder of four valuable benefices he incurred excommunication, and when this was lifted he was made archbishop of Cologne at the age of thirty in 1216. From then on Engelbert's personal life appears to have been blameless, but it is doubtful if his cultus would either have arisen or been officially recognized had he not come to a violent end in 1225 on account of his defence of the rights of a nunnery. *Engelbertus.*

ENGELMUND, ST. June 21.   JUNE, p. 281

An English Benedictine and the most successful of St Willibrord's missionaries in the Netherlands, where his centre was at Velsen, near Haarlem. d. c. 720. *Engelmundus.*

ENGLISH MARTYRS OF 1588. October 1.   OCT., p. 11

In the renewal of persecution that followed the defeat of the Armada, a number of people were put to death in addition to those who suffered in London (*q.v.*). The following were bd, in 1929 : Robert Wilcox, Edward Campion (*vere* Edwards), and Christopher Buxton, secular priests, h.d.q. for their priesthood at Canterbury, October 1, 1588 ; Robert Widmerpool, gentleman, hanged at Canterbury at the same time for sheltering a priest ; Ralph Crockett, Edward James (Chichester, Oct. 1), John Robinson (Ipswich, Oct 1), and William Way (Kingston-on-Thames, Sept. 23), all secular priests, h.d.q. for their priesthood.

*ENNODIUS, ST, bp. July 17.   JULY, p. 231

Magnus Felix Ennodius, of a Gallo-Roman family, is chiefly remembered for his writings, hymns, letters, and an account of his own life and conversion ; he was one of the last representatives of the ancient school of rhetoric. He was made bishop of Pavia *c.* 514, and was entrusted with two missions to the East by the Holy See. d. 521.

*EPARCHIUS, ST, ab. July 1.   JULY, p. 8

In French *Cybard*. He renounced his right to the duchy of Périgord and became a monk at Sessac. d. 581.

†*EPHRAEM, ST, doct. June 18.   JUNE, p. 226

Called " the Syrian," " the Deacon," and " the Harp of the Holy Ghost." B. at Nisibis in Mesopotamia *c.* 300 and became the greatest theologian, preacher, and poet of the Syrian church. He was probably head of the famous episcopal school at Nisibis, but after that city was captured by the Persians he became a hermit or monk near Edessa. Ephraem was the first Christian writer of hymns, which he undertook in the first place in opposition to local heretics who were spreading their doctrines by means of sung verses. He also wrote commentaries on the Scriptures and homilies, some of these also in metre, and his writings are extensively used in the various Syriac liturgies. Shortly before his death there was a terrible famine in Mesopotamia in which Ephraem was the leader in organizing relief and help for the sick, which included the provision of 300 ambulances, *i.e.* litters. He seems to have d. in his hermit's cave a very short time afterwards, in 373, though some writers claim that he lived on till 378 or 379. His body is said to rest in the church of the dissident Armenians at Urfa (Edessa). St Ephraem was proclaimed a doctor of the Church by Pope Benedict XV in 1920.

*EPHYSIUS, ST, mart. January 15.   JAN., p. 186
A martyr venerated in Sardinia of whom nothing certain is known.

*EPIPHANIUS, ST, bp. January 21.   JAN., p. 259
A bishop of Pavia who rebuilt the city after it had been destroyed by Odoacer. The fever from which he died was brought on by a journey into Burgundy to ransom some prisoners in 496.

*EPIPHANIUS, ST, bp. May 12.   MAY, p. 141
B. in Palestine *c.* 310. As abbot of a monastery at Eleutheropolis he stood up to imperial persecution and wrote and preached against the errors of his age till he came to be regarded as the '' oracle of Palestine.'' In 367 he became bishop of Salamis in Cyprus, but the later years of his life were clouded by the results of several headstrong actions on his part. The fame of St Epiphanius rests chiefly on his writings, which make him one of the fathers of the Church. d. 403.

*EPIPODIUS and **ALEXANDER, SS,** marts. April 22.   APR., p. 256
Two young friends who were martyred at Lyons in 178.

*EQUITIUS, ST, ab. August 11.   AUG., p. 135
He founded a number of religious houses in Italy during the lifetime of St Benedict. d. March 7, *c.* 540.

†*ERASMUS, ST, bp. and mart. June 2.   JUNE, p. 25
Erasmus or Elmo was formerly widely venerated as the patron of sailors (*cf.* '' St Elmo's Fire ''). Nothing is actually known of his history but he is said to have been bishop at Formiæ in the Campagna (where his relics were until 842), martyred in 303.

ERCONGOTA, ST, virg. July 7.   JULY, p. 75
She was the daughter of St Sexburga and went over to France to be a nun at Faremoutier. d. *c.* 660.

*ERCONWALD, ST, bp. May 13.   APR., p. 345
He founded the monastery of Chertsey and that of Barking, over which he put his sister, St Ethelburga, as abbess ; in 675 he was appointed bishop of London. d. *c.* 686. His feast is kept in the dioceses of Westminster and Brentwood. *Erconvaldus.*

EREMBERT, ST, bp. May 14.   MAY, p. 175
A monk of Fontenelle who became bishop of Toulouse and d. *c.* 672.

ERHARD, ST, bp. January 8.   JAN., p. 118
This saint had a very strong *cultus* around Ratisbon, where what purport to be his crozier and part of his skull are still preserved. He is stated to have baptized St Odilia, and is sometimes described as an Irishman. He seems to have lived in the seventh century. *Erhardus.*

*ERIC, ST, mart. May 18.   MAY, p. 228
Eric IX was elected king of Sweden in 1150 ; he was known as '' the Lawgiver '' from his codification of the laws and customs of his kingdom. He was a man of much personal goodness, who spread the Faith in Sweden and beat off the attacks of the heathen Finns. He was murdered by invading Danes, assisted by rebels against his just rule, in 1160. c.c. in thirteenth century. St Eric is the principal patron of Sweden. *Ericus.*

ERKEMBODEN, ST, bp. April 12. APR., p. 138

Abbot of Sithiu at Saint-Omer and bishop of Thérouanne. d. 714.

ERMENGILDE, ST. February 13. FEB., p. 202

Or *Ermenilda*. Daughter of King Ercombert of Kent and St Sexburg, and wife of King Wulfhere of Mercia by whom she was the mother of St Werburg. On the death of her husband in 675 she became a nun and was abbess of Milton and Ely. d. 703. *Hermengildis*.

ERMENTRUDE, ST, virg. June 30. JUNE, p. 397

She was a relative of St Rupert who helped in his missionary work in Bavaria by conducting a religious house for women at Salzburg. d. *c.* 718. Also called *Ehrentraud, Erentrudis*.

ERMINOLD, ST, mart. January 6. JAN., p. 92

He is venerated as a martyr but his death in 1121 resulted from the conspiracy of a criminal faction of the monks of Prüfening who resented his strict rule as abbot of that monastery.

*ERMINUS, ST, ab. April 25. APR., p. 287

Abbot of Lobbes in Hainault. d. 737.

ESKILL, ST, bp. and mart. June 12. JUNE, p. 161

Eskill was an Englishman and a missionary bishop in Sweden with St Siegfrid. He was stoned to death for protesting against a heathen festival at Strengnäs *c.* 1080. Eskilstuna is the place where his body was enshrined.

ESTERWINE, ST, ab. March 7. MAR., p. 114

He was appointed by his kinsman, St Benedict Biscop, to be abbot of Wearmouth, which he governed for four years. d. 686. *Esterwinus*.

*ETHBIN, ST. October 19. OCT., p. 264

He was a monk at Taurac in Brittany ; on being driven out by the Franks he took refuge in Ireland and d. there *c.* 580. *Ethbinus*.

ETHELBERT, ST, mart. May 20. MAY, p. 253

He succeeded his father Ethelred as king of the East Angles and was treacherously murdered at the instigation of the wife of Offa of Mercia in 793. Ethelbert was buried at Hereford and he had considerable *cultus* as a martyr. His feast is still kept in the dioceses of Cardiff and Northampton. *Edilbertus*.

*ETHELBERT OF KENT, ST. February 25. FEB., p. 334

Ethelbert, whose wife Bertha was a Christian, was ruling in Kent and far beyond when Pope St Gregory sent St Augustine to evangelize the English. Ethelbert received the missionaries well and was himself baptized on Whit-Sunday in 597 ; unlike many other monarchs he did not try to impose the new religion on his subjects by force. He founded Christ Church cathedral and the abbey of SS Peter and Paul at Canterbury, the see of Rochester and St Andrew's cathedral, and endowed these and other churches. He was a declarer of law, and his " Dooms " are the first known written laws given in England. d. 616. St Ethelbert is commemorated liturgically in the dioceses of Westminster, Southwark, Nottingham, and Northampton.

ETHELBURGA, ST. April 5. APR., p. 61

St Ethelburga was the daughter of King Ethelbert of Kent and Queen Bertha and was married to the pagan King Edwin of Northumbria. She was accompanied to his court by St Paulinus as chaplain, and Edwin was in due course baptized, with many of his people. After his death Ethelburga became abbess of Lyminge in Kent. d. *c.* 647. *Edilburga*.

*ETHELBURGA, ST, virg. July 7. JULY, p. 75

She was a daughter of King Anna of the East Angles and became a nun at Faremoutier in France, succeeding her half-sister, St Sethrida, as abbess. d. *c.* 664.

ETHELBURGA, ST, virg. October 11. OCT., p. 151

When St Erconwald founded the double monastery of Barking in Essex he set his sister Ethelburga over it as abbess : she, in the words of St Bede, " behaved in all respects as became the sister of such a brother " and several marvels are recorded of her life and death. d. *c.* 678. St Ethelburga's feast is kept in the diocese of Brentwood.

*ETHELDREDA, ST. June 23. JUNE, p. 305

Etheldreda (Audry) was daughter of King Anna of the East Angles and married Prince Tonbert, who died three years later ; she then retired to the isle of Ely and after five years married again, young Prince Egfrid of Northumbria : however, she refused to consummate the marriage and, with the support of St Wilfrid, received the veil of a nun. About 672 she founded a double monastery at Ely (from which arose Ely cathedral) and governed it till her death in 679, setting a high example of asceticism and prayerfulness. A very large number of churches were dedicated in honour of this princess, whose feast is still observed in the dioceses of Westminster, Birmingham, Liverpool, Hexham, and Northampton. *Ediltrudis.*

ETHELNOTH, ST, bp. October 29. OCT., p. 356

Ethelnoth the Good was archbishop of Canterbury in the days when the Danish Canute governed England ; he translated the relics of his martyred predecessor, St Elphege, from London to Canterbury. d. 1038. There is no evidence of *cultus*. *Ædelnodus.*

ETHELWALD, ST. March 23. MAR., p. 381

He followed St Cuthbert in the occupation of the hermitage on Farne island where Cuthbert died, and St Bede relates a miracle he performed on a storm of wind. d. 699. *Ethelwaldus.*

ETHELWOLD, ST, bp. February 12. FEB., p. 186

Ethelwold was a disciple of St Cuthbert and from being abbot of Old Melrose was promoted to the bishopric of Lindisfarne in 721. He was living in the time of St Bede, who speaks of his worthiness. d. *c.* 740.

*ETHELWOLD, ST, bp. August 1. AUG., p. 8

A monk of Glastonbury, who became abbot of Abingdon in 955 and bishop of Winchester in 963. With St Dunstan and St Oswald of York he was one of the leaders of the religious revival in England at this period, and restored a number of monastic houses, often replacing secular canons by Benedictine monks : among them were Newminster, Chertsey, Milton Abbas, and Peterborough. He is said to have translated the Rule of St Benedict into English, and was fittingly called " the father of monks." d. 984.

*EUCHERIUS, ST, bp. February 20. FEB., p. 287

A monk of Jumièges who was appointed bishop of Orleans in 721. Having opposed the confiscation of church revenues by Charles Martel, he was exiled in 737 first to Cologne and then to Liége. St Eucherius was so well loved in the places of his banishment that he was allowed by those responsible for him to retire to a monastery, where he died in 743.

*EUCHERIUS, ST, bp. November 16. NOV., p. 195

By his wife Galla he had two sons, Salonius and Veranus, both bishops and both venerated as saints. Later in life Eucherius became a solitary and, c. 434, bishop of Lyons, of which see he was the best-known pastor after St Irenæus. His writings include a book in praise of the solitary life. d. c. 449.

*EUGENDUS, ST, ab.   January 1.   JAN., p. 10
Otherwise *Oyend*. Abbot of Condate, near Geneva, later called after him Saint-Oyend, and then Saint-Claude. d. c. 510.

EUGENE, ST, bp.   August 23.   AUG., p. 286
Eugene (Eoghan, Owen) is venerated as the first bishop at Ardstraw in Tyrone, predecessor of the see of Derry. He lived during the sixth century, and his feast is kept throughout Ireland. *Eugenius.*

*EUGENIA, ST, virg. and mart.   December 25.   DEC., p. 242
The legend of Eugenia is like that of St Marina and others, the tale of a woman disguised as a monk and accused of a crime she could not commit. It has been arbitrarily attached to the name of St Eugenia who was a third-century (?) martyr in Rome, buried in the cemetery of Apronian on the Via Latina.

*EUGENIUS, ST, bp.   July 13.   JULY, p. 167
Eugenius was elected bishop of Carthage in 481 and the whole of his episcopate was one long struggle with the oppressions of the Arian Vandal kings. He was exiled for several years in the desert of Tripoli where he shared the great hardships of his flock. He was recalled by Gontamund in 488 and allowed to reopen the Catholic churches, but was banished again eight years later. St Eugenius d. at Albi in 505.

*EUGENIUS I, pope.   June 2.
Eugenius was pope from 654 till his death in 657. He was generous and gentle, but firmly opposed the Monothelism of the Byzantine emperor, who threatened to roast the pope alive. It was probably this pope who received St Wilfrid on his first visit to Rome.

*EUGENIUS III, BD, pope.   July 8.   JULY, p. 103
St Antoninus called him " one of the greatest and one of the most afflicted of the popes." He was abbot of the Cistercian monastery of St Anastasius (Tre Fontane) at Rome and was elected to the Holy See in 1145. His election was at once challenged by the political Romans and he was in exile from the city, with a short break, for seven years. Some of the minor troubles of his pontificate were concerned with England, e.g. the affair of St William of York. Eugenius at all times had the support and help of his master St Bernard, and it was said of him that he had " no arrogance, no domineering, no regality : justice, humility, and reason claimed the whole man." d. 1153. c.c. 1872.

*EUGENIUS OF TOLEDO, ST, bp.   November 13.   NOV., p. 155
He was a musician, poet, and archbishop of Toledo ; d. 657. Another Eugenius, martyr, is miscalled " of Toledo " in the Roman Martyrology on November 15.

*EULALIA, ST, virg. and mart.   December 10.   DEC., p. 120
Eulalia was the most celebrated virgin martyr of Spain. She suffered at Merida in 304, and Prudentius wrote a hymn in her honour.

*EULALIA OF BARCELONA, ST, virg. and mart.   February 12.
                                                                       FEB., p. 180
She was the same as St Eulalia of Merida, who was martyred in 304, but she is venerated as a local saint and patroness at Barcelona.

*EULAMPIUS and **EULAMPIA, SS,** marts. October 10.   OCT., p. 135
This brother and sister probably suffered martyrdom by the sword at Nicomedia under Gallienus, *c.* 310.

*EULOGIUS, ST, mart. March 11.   MAR., p. 185
He was a prominent and distinguished priest of Cordova at the time of the Moorish persecution in the middle of the ninth century. He wrote *The Memorial of the Saints*, a record of the sufferings of Christians at that time, and was foremost in encouraging them to constancy. At length he was arrested for protecting a convert from Islam, a girl called Leocritia who was herself martyred, and was beheaded in 859. A short biography of St Eulogius was written by his friend Paul Alvarez.

*EULOGIUS, ST, bp. September 13.   SEPT., p. 160
He was patriarch of Alexandria and a personal friend of St Gregory the Great, who wrote and told him about the beginnings of the conversion of the English. d. 607.

EUNAN, ST. *See* Adamnan.

†*EUPHEMIA, ST, virg. and mart. September 16.   SEPT., p. 205
Beyond the fact of her martyrdom nothing whatever is known of St Euphemia except that her cultus was widespread at an early date. Legends cluster round her name and she was greatly venerated in the East, especially at Chalcedon. She is still named in the canon of the Ambrosian Mass.

*EUPHRASIA, ST, virg. March 13.   MAR., p. 231
Euphrasia or Eupraxia refused to leave the convent in Egypt where she had been brought up to marry the senator to whom she had been betrothed and spent the rest of her life there in great austerity and humility. There is a more or less contemporary Greek record of her. d. *c.* 420.

EUPHROSYNE, ST, virg. February 11.   FEB., p. 168
There are no authentic accounts of the life of St Euphrosyne, who in the East is called " Our Mother," and there is reason to doubt whether she ever existed. The " history " of her which we have is only a replica of the legend of St Pelagia (October 8).

*EUPLIUS, ST, mart. August 12.   AUG., p. 149
He was a deacon at Catania in Sicily who was seized with a copy of the gospels on him ; he refused under torture to sacrifice to the gods and was beheaded, in 304.

EUROSIA, ST, virg. June 25.   JUNE, p. 337
She is venerated in Spain as a victim of the Moors in the eighth century and her *cultus* was introduced by Spanish soldiers into northern Italy. There is no mention of her before the fifteenth century and it is likely that she is a fictitious character.

EUSEBIA, ST, virg. March 16.   MAR., p. 280
Eldest daughter of St Adalbald and St Rictrude, and succeeded her grandmother St Gertrude as abbess of Hamage at a very early age. d. *c.* 680.

EUSEBIUS, ST, ab. January 23.   JAN., p. 280
A fourth-century monk who lived on Mount Coryphe, near Antioch.

EUSEBIUS, ST, mart. January 31.   JAN., p. 401
An Irish monk at St Gall in Switzerland, who became a hermit in the Vorarlberg. He was murdered by a peasant whose wicked life he had rebuked, in 884.

*EUSEBIUS, ST, mart. August 14.   AUG., p. 170
He was a priest put to death early in the persecution of Diocletian, but

he is surrounded with obscurity and there seems to be no evidence of *cultus*.

†*EUSEBIUS, ST. August 14.   Aug., p. 169

A priest of a patrician family in Rome who about the middle of the fourth century founded the " parish church " called after him *titulus Eusebii*.

*EUSEBIUS, ST, pope. August 17.   Sept., p. 323

Eusebius, a Greek, was pope for a few months only, dying in exile in Sicily in 310.

*EUSEBIUS and other marts., SS. September 8.   Sept., p. 86

Eusebius, Nestabus, Zeno, and Nestor were slain by a mob at Gaza in 362, they having been concerned in the destruction of a pagan temple there.

*EUSEBIUS OF CREMONA, ST, ab. March 5.   Mar., p. 58

He went with St Jerome to Palestine and was sent by him to Europe to collect funds for the hostel for pilgrims. Eusebius was involved in a dispute about the teaching of Origen, which was carried on with considerable bitterness. He died, probably in Italy, *c.* 423. The tradition that he founded the monastery of Guadalupe in Spain is unreliable.

*EUSEBIUS OF SAMOSATA, ST, bp. and mart. June 21.   June, p. 277

This Eusebius, bishop of Samosata, was a friend of St Basil and a vigorous opponent of the Arian heresy, on account of which he was exiled by the emperor Valens. He was killed by an Arian woman who threw a tile at his head, *c.* 379.

†*EUSEBIUS OF VERCELLI, ST, bp. and mart. December 16.

Dec., p. 178

He was b. in Sardinia *c.* 283 and became the first known bishop of Vercelli. His life was chiefly spent in struggling with Arianism ; for defying the emperor Constantius on this account he was banished with St Dionysius of Milan and Lucifer of Cagliari. He was taken to Palestine and other places in the East, where his sufferings were such that he is venerated as a martyr. He was eventually allowed to return to his see and d. there on August 1, *c.* 370. Eusebius was the first bishop who lived with his clergy under a rule and he is therefore honoured by canons regular as their co-founder with St Augustine.

EUSEUS, ST. February 15.   Feb., p. 236

A hermit who lived near Serravalle in Piedmont during the fourteenth century. Nothing certain is known of him.

†*EUSTACE, ST, mart. September 20.   Sept., p. 266

Eustace is among the most famous martyrs of the Church, but there is nothing that can be said of him with any sort of certainty and even his existence has been called in doubt. His vision of a stag with a crucifix between its antlers is a seventh-century legend, afterwards borrowed and incorporated into that of St Hubert. *Eustachius*.

EUSTATHIUS, ST, bp. July 16.   July, p. 213

He was translated to the see of Antioch in 323, and proved to be one of the doughtiest opponents of Arianism. In 331 he was deposed by an heretical synod and banished. He d., still in exile, *c.* 335.

*EUSTOCHIUM, ST, virg. September 28.   Sept., p. 343

Eustochium Julia was the daughter of St Paula and she accompanied her mother to Palestine, where she collated manuscripts for St Jerome's translation of the Bible. On Paula's death Eustochium succeeded to the direction of the community of women at Bethlehem, where she d. in 420.

EUSTOCHIUM CALAFATO, BD, virg. February 1.   FEB., p. 20

Daughter of the Countess Matilda of Calafato. She became a Poor Clare of the Conventual observance near Messina in 1446, and desiring a more austere life she founded some years later an Observant convent at a place called the Maidens' Hill. Of this she became abbess and attracted numerous subjects by her virtues. d. 1468. c.c. 1782.

EUSTOCHIUM OF PADUA, BD, virg. February 13.   FEB., p. 207

Eustochium was the daughter of an erring nun at Padua in the fifteenth century. Her own life was normal until she herself became a nun, when she became subject to the most violent attacks, during the course of which she displayed remarkable phenomena which are witnessed to by contemporary evidence. This lasted four years but she was eventually admitted to vows, when she seems to have recovered and to have earned the veneration of her fellow nuns. Her last years were bedridden and she died at the age of twenty-six in 1469. The *cultus* of this Eustochium at Padua has never received the formal approval of the Church.

*EUSTOCHIUS, ST, bp. September 19.   SEPT., p. 256

He succeeded St Brice in the see of Tours in 444, and d. in 461.

*EUSTORGIUS II, ST, bp. June 6.   JUNE, p. 81

He became bishop of Milan in 512. He was described as a man of great virtue, an excellent shepherd of his people, and his life and episcopate were uneventful. d. 518.

*EUSTRATIUS, ST, mart. December 13.   DEC., p. 151

This martyr, with St Orestes, a soldier, and others, suffered at Sebaste, in Armenia in 303.

EUTHYMIUS, ST, ab. October 15.   OCT., p. 215

Called "the Thessalonian" or "the New." While still under twenty he left his wife and child and became a monk at Mount Olympus in Bithynia. Later he went to Mount Athos to learn the eremitical life and after being a solitary in several places revived the monastery of St Andrew, near Salonika. He also started a convent near by and, when these were both established, went to end his days on Athos. d. 886.

*EUTHYMIUS THE GREAT, ST, ab. January 20.   JAN., p. 244

B. at Melitene in Armenia in 378. He was ordained at home and went to be a monk near Jerusalem, ever withdrawing further into the wilderness towards Jericho. He was a stout opponent of the Nestorian and monophysite heresies, and induced the Empress Eudoxia to give up the latter. At different times he founded two monasteries and a *laura* of hermitages. He foretold the day of his death, which happened in 473, and he was honoured as a saint immediately after.

EUTROPIUS. *See also* Tigrius.

*EUTROPIUS, ST, bp. and mart. April 30.   APR., p. 344

He is honoured as the first bishop of Saintes, where he is supposed to have been martyred in the third century.

*EUTROPIUS, ST, bp. May 27.   MAY, p. 327

He was bishop of Orange at a time when the diocese had been laid waste by the Visigoths. d. *c.* 476.

*EUTYCHIAN, ST, pope and mart. December 7.

Eutychian became pope *c.* 275 and d. *c.* 283. Nothing is known of his life. He is called a martyr in the Roman Martyrology, but this is almost certainly an error. *Eutychianus.*

*EUTYCHIUS, ST, mart. March 14.   MAR., p. 251

This Eutychius (or Eustathius) was, with several companions, put to death by the Mohammedans in Mesopotamia for refusing to abjure Christ, in 741.

EUTYCHIUS, ST, bp. April 6.   APR., p. 74

Eutychius, patriarch of Constantinople from 552, is honoured in the East for his resistance to the emperor Justinian's interference in theological controversies. He was consequently banished from his see for twelve years. d. 582.

EVA OF LIÉGE, BD, virg. May 26.   MAY, p. 318

A recluse of Liége who on the death of Bd Juliana of Cornillon successfully took up her work in favour of a liturgical feast of the Blessed Sacrament. d. c. 1266. c.c. 1902.

*EVAGRIUS, ST, bp. March 6.   MAR., p. 80

A bishop of Constantinople, exiled by the Arians. d. c. 380.

EVANGELIST and **PEREGRINUS, BB.** March 20.   MAR., p. 341

Schoolboy friends who together became Austin friars ; they were both endowed with the same miraculous gifts and virtues, and died within a few hours of one another, c. 1250. c.c. by Pope Pius VI. *Evangelista.*

†*EVARISTUS, ST, pope and mart. October 26.   OCT., p. 338

He was the fourth successor of St Peter and is said to have been an Hellenic Jew ; he d. c. 107 ; his martyrdom is not certain.

EVERARD HANSE, BD, mart. July 30.   JULY, p. 426

A Northamptonshire man, a convert and a secular priest, who at his examination in London as a suspected person was tricked into denying the royal supremacy in religion. He was accordingly h.d.q. at Tyburn in 1581. bd. 1886. His feast is kept in the diocese of Northampton. *Everardus.*

*EVERGISLUS, ST, bp. and mart. October 24.   OCT., p. 321

He is venerated as bishop of Cologne and a martyr at the hands of heathen robbers during the fifth century, but it is likely that he lived a hundred or more years later and died in his bed. He has been confused, too, with a St Ebregisilus of Maestricht.

EVERILDIS, ST, virg. July 9.   JULY, p. 108

She was the seventh-century foundress of a convent at Everingham (Everildsham), near York.

EVERMARUS, ST, mart. May 1.   MAY, p. 15

The villagers of Rousson, near Tongres, hold a procession on May 1 every year in honour of St Evermarus, who is said to have been a pilgrim killed by robbers in the neighbourhood c. 700.

EVERMOD, ST, bp. February 17.   DEC., p. 312

A Premonstratensian canon, a personal disciple of St Norbert, who became abbot of Gottesgnaden, of Magdeburg, and bishop of Ratzeburg. He was an apostle of the Wends. d. 1178. *Evermodus.*

*EVODIUS, ST, bp. May 6.   MAY, p. 80

Evodius preceded St Ignatius in the see of Antioch, being ordained perhaps by St Peter himself ; he is said to have been one of the seventy disciples appointed by our Lord. d. c. 64 (?).

*EWALDS, THE TWO, marts. October 3. Oct., p. 29

Ewald the Fair and Ewald the Dark were brothers from Northumbria, missionaries in Westphalia. They were martyred, traditionally at Aplerbeke, near Dortmund, *c.* 695.

*EXPEDITUS, ST. April 19. Apr., p. 225

There is good reason to doubt whether a martyr of this name ever existed ; but the story which traces devotion to him to the receiving by a Paris convent of a package of relics marked *spedito* has been completely disproved.

*EXUPERANTIUS, ST, bp. May 30. May, p. 361

He had a peaceful and uneventful episcopate as bishop of Ravenna and d. in 418.

*EXUPERIUS, ST, bp. September 28. Sept., p. 342

In French *Spire*. He became bishop of Toulouse *c.* 405 and was noted for his great generosity in alms-giving, sending gifts as far as Egypt and Palestine. d. *c.* 415.

FABIAN, ST, pope and mart. January 20. JAN., p. 241

He was martyred under Decius in 250 after being pope for fourteen years; St Cyprian wrote that the glory of his death corresponded with the purity and goodness of his life. *Fabianus.*

FABIOLA, ST. December 27. DEC., p. 259

She was a Roman patrician who divorced her dissolute husband and united herself with another man; after his death she did public penance for this and devoted her time and wealth to works of charity, establishing the first-known Christian public hospital in the West. She was associated in her good works with St Pammachius. In 395 she visited her friend St Jerome at Bethlehem, but he dissuaded her from trying to settle down there—she was too lively. St Fabiola d. *c.* 400 and all Rome attended her funeral.

FACHANAN, ST, bp. August 14. AUG., p. 173

He was probably the first bishop in the district of Ross. He was the founder of the great monastic school at what is now Rosscarbery in county Cork, where he made St Brendan one of the teachers. St Fachanan d. near the end of the sixth century, and his feast is kept throughout Ireland.

*FAITH, ST, virg. and mart. October 6. OCT., p. 75

The legend of St Faith and of the miracles at her shrine was unusually popular in the Middle Ages. She may have been martyred at Agen but the date is problematical. *Fides.*

*FAITH, HOPE, and **CHARITY, SS,** marts. August 1. AUG., p. 8

The maidens Faith, Hope, and Charity, with their mother Wisdom are said to have been martyred at Rome under Hadrian. They, or a similar group, are venerated in both West and East (Pistis, Elpis, Agape, Sophia), but the story is probably a myth.

FANCHEA, ST, virg. January 1. JAN., p. 18

Otherwise *Faenche, Fainche,* etc. Sister of St Enda. She is said to have founded a convent at Rossory in Fermanagh and to have been buried at Killane. d. *c.* 585 (?).

*FANTINUS, ST. August 30. AUG., p. 388

He was abbot of the Greek monastery of St Mercury in Calabria, which was destroyed by the Saracens *c.* 980. Fantinus d. soon after.

*FARA, ST, virg. April 3. APR., p. 36

Fara was the sister of St Cagnoaldus and St Faro and in face of bitter opposition she became a nun; the monastery which she ruled for thirty-seven years afterwards became famousu nder the name of Faremoutier. d. 657.

*FARO, ST, bp. October 28. OCT., p. 350

From being chancellor at the court of King Dagobert I he became a priest of the diocese of Meaux and *c.* 626 was made bishop of that see. He befriended St Fiacre when he arrived from Ireland, and founded a monastery for monks from Luxeuil. d. *c.* 675.

FASTRED, BD, ab. April 21. APR., p. 253

He was a disciple of St Bernard who made him first abbot of Cambron ; afterwards he ruled Clairvaux and then Citeaux itself. d. 1163.

†*FAUSTINUS and **JOVITA, SS,** marts. February 15. FEB., p. 227

Brothers who were martyred at Brescia (*c.* 121 ?). They are chief patrons of that city.

FAUSTUS, ST, bp. September 28. SEPT., p. 345

From being abbot of Lérins he was promoted to the see of Riez, where he was as good a bishop as he had been an abbot. He was a strong opponent of Arianism and Pelagianism, but in certain of his writings himself propounded semipelagian error : for some years he was exiled from his see by the Arian king Euric. d. *c.* 493.

*FAUSTUS and his comps., **SS,** marts. October 13. OCT., p. 181

SS Faustus, Januarius, and Martial gave their lives for Christ in 304 ; Prudentius calls them the Three Crowns of Cordova, where they suffered.

FEARGAL, ST. *See* Virgilius (of Salzburg).

*FEBRONIA, ST, virg. and mart. June 25. JUNE, p. 330

Legend states that St Febronia was a nun at Nisibis in Mesopotamia, learned in the Scriptures and beautiful of body, who was lopped limb by limb for refusing to renounce Christ and marry the nephew of the Roman magistrate. This story was widely diffused, especially in the East, but there is good reason to doubt whether Febronia ever existed.

FECHIN, ST, ab. January 20. JAN., p. 247

Said to have been a Connacht man. He founded a community of monks in Westmeath, probably at Fobhar (Fore), and d. during the great plague of 665. The name " Ecclefechan " testifies to his cultus in Scotland.

FELAN, ST, ab. January 9. JAN., p. 126

Otherwise *Fillan, Foilan.* Son of St Kentigerna. He was abbot of a monastery near Saint Andrews and afterwards went to live near a church he founded in Fifeshire ; d. *c.* 710 and was buried in Strathfillan. The *Aberdeen Breviary* relates some extravagant miracles of him. At the battle of Bannockburn Robert Bruce had with him a relic of St Felan, to whose intercession he attributed the victory. The diocese of Dunkeld keeps his feast on January 19. *Foelanus.*

FELICIA MEDA, BD, virg. October 5. OCT., p. 65

B. at Milan in 1378. After governing the Poor Clare convent of St Ursula for fourteen years she was sent to found a new house at Pesaro, where she was as successful and reverenced as she had been at Milan. d. 1444. c.c. 1812.

†*FELICISSIMUS and **AGAPITUS, SS,** marts. August 6. AUG., p. 72

They were deacons of Pope St Sixtus II and were martyred in 258 on the same day as that pope and four other Roman deacons.

FELICIAN, ST, bp. and mart. January 24. JAN., p. 296

An early bishop of Foligno and the traditional apostle of Umbria. After being bishop for more than fifty years he died from ill treatment while being taken to Rome for martyrdom, *c.* 254. *Felicianus.*

FELICITAS. *See also under* Perpetua.

†*FELICITAS, ST, mart. November 23. JULY, p. 127

She was martyred in Rome with her sons during the second century, but it is unlikely that these sons are identical with the so-called Seven Brothers.

*FELICULA, ST, mart. June 13. JUNE, p. 167
She is thought to have been the foster-sister of St Petronilla (May 31) and to have suffered death for Christ a few days after her.

*FELIX, ST, bp. March 8. MAR., p. 131
Felix converted the East Anglian prince Sigebert who was in exile in Burgundy, and afterwards accompanied him to England and preached the gospel with great success in Suffolk, Norfolk, and Cambridgeshire, establishing schools on the French model. Felix (whose name is found in Felixstowe) settled his episcopal see at Dunwich, a place now washed away by the sea. d. 648. His feast is kept in the diocese of Northampton.

*FELIX, etc., SS, marts. April 23. APR., p. 266
The priest Felix with his deacons Fortunatus and Achilleus were martyred at Valence c. 212.

*FELIX, ST, bp. and mart. October 24. OCT., p. 317
Felix, bishop of Thibiuca in Africa, was beheaded in 303, one of the first of Diocletian's victims, for refusing to deliver up the sacred books. He probably suffered at Carthage ; certainly not in Italy, as a later version of his *passio* has it.

†*FELIX I, ST, pope and mart. May 30. MAY, p. 360
Felix I was pope from 269 to 274. His veneration as a martyr is almost certainly a mistake due to confusion with another Felix.

†*FELIX II, ST, pope and mart. July 29. JULY, p. 404
This Felix was not a martyr nor was he a pope, though he was wrongly intruded into the see of Rome in the year 355. How his name got into the Roman Martyrology has been the subject of a great deal of discussion. d. 365.

*FELIX III, ST, pope. March 1.
This Felix was pope from 483 till his death in 492. His pontificate was mostly taken up with disturbances concerning the monophysite heresy, and little is known about the man himself.

*FELIX IV, ST, pope. September 22. SEPT., p. 288
Properly Felix III. During his pontificate of four years he was revered as a man of great simplicity, humility, and kindness to the poor ; he built the basilica of SS Cosmas and Damian. d. 530.

†*FELIX and **ADAUCTUS, SS,** marts. August 30. AUG., p. 383
Felix was a Roman priest who was beheaded for his faith in 304. A man who suffered with him is said to have been called Adauctus (*i.e.* the one added) because his name was not known.

*FELIX and **CYPRIAN, SS,** bps. and marts. October 12. OCT., p. 162
These two bishops and hundreds of other clergy and lay people of Africa were driven into the desert and there left to perish by the Vandals under the Arian king Hunneric, c. 484.

*FELIX and **FORTUNATUS, SS,** marts. June 11. JUNE, p. 143
Brothers from Vicenza who suffered martyrdom at Aquileia in 296 (the date is uncertain).

FELIX OF BOURGES, ST, bp. January 1. JAN., p. 18
Bishop of Bourges, where he d. c. 580.

*FELIX OF CANTALICE, ST. May 18. MAY, p. 230
B. in 1513 at Cantalice in Apulia, the child of peasant farmers. After a narrow escape from death, from bolting bullocks when he was ploughing, Felix became a Capuchin lay brother. He lived for forty years in Rome,

begging for his friary from door to door, and was held in great regard by St Philip Neri and the people of the City. d. 1587. There is record of a large number of miracles at his shrine. cd. 1724.

FELIX OF NANTES, ST, bp. July 7. JULY, p. 74
Felix was a man of learning and one of the most eminent of the bishops of Nantes, but little is now known of his life. d. January 8, 584.

FELIX OF NICOSIA, BD. June 1. JUNE, p. 17
Felix was b. at Nicosia in Sicily and was apprenticed to a shoemaker. After several fruitless attempts he was admitted as a Capuchin lay brother : he reclaimed numerous sinners and was a devoted friend of the poor and sick, and had the gift of healing both bodies and souls. d. 1787. bd. 1888.

*FELIX OF NOLA, ST. January 14. JAN., p. 173
Priest at Nola, near Naples, where his father, a Romano-Syrian soldier, was a landowner. Felix suffered persecution under Decius, but himself escaped from prison and rescued his bishop in miraculous circumstances. He was known far and wide for his generosity to the poor, and refused to go to law to recover his impounded estate. d. c. 260. Over a century later St Paulinus of Nola wrote of the crowds that came from all over Italy to the shrine of St Felix, of the miracles that took place there, and of the assistance he had himself received from Felix's intercession.

*FELIX OF TRIER, ST, bp. March 26. MAR., p. 409
A most holy man and extremely generous to the poor ; he resigned his see of Trier because the circumstances of his election were looked on with suspicion by the Holy See and St Ambrose. Sulpicius Severus speaks of him with much respect. d. c. 400.

†*FELIX OF VALOIS, ST. November 20. NOV., p. 251
Felix of Valois is venerated as co-founder of the Trinitarians with St John of Matha, but his career is as uncertain as are the beginnings of that order. He is said to have organized the Trinitarians in France, beginning the work when he was already seventy years old. d. 1212. c.c. 1666.

*FERDINAND III, ST. May 30. MAY, p. 362
Ferdinand became king of Castile in 1217, when he was eighteen, and of Leon in 1230. For twenty-seven years he was engaged in almost uninterrupted warfare against the Mohammedans in Spain, campaigns which culminated in the capture of Seville in 1249. This successful crusading was the basis of the veneration of St Ferdinand in Spain, but he was as well an admirable ruler and virtuous man. By his second wife, Jane of Ponthieu, he was the father of Eleanor, wife of Edward I of England. d. 1252. cd. 1671. *Ferdinandus.*

FERDINAND OF ARAGON, ST. June 27. JUNE, p. 363
His relics are preserved at Cornello in Italy ; local tradition says he was bishop of Cajazzo during the thirteenth century.

FERDINAND OF PORTUGAL, BD. June 5. JUNE, p. 70
Prince Ferdinand the Constant was b. at Santarem in 1402, son of King John I of Portugal and Philippa, daughter of John of Gaunt. With his brother Henry the Navigator he led an expedition against the Moors in Africa ; they were defeated at Tangier and Ferdinand and others were given up as hostages. At Arzilla he was imprisoned with a great deal of cruelty, but all his concern was for his companions and he was never heard to speak a hard word against his captors. He was allowed to die of neglected dysentery in 1443 after over five years of confinement. c.c. 1470.

FERGUS, ST, bp. November 27.   Nov., p. 327
The feast of this eighth-century bishop is kept by the diocese of Aberdeen ; he was an Irish missionary in Perthshire, Caithness, Buchan, and Forfarshire. *Fergustus.*

FERREOLUS, ST, bp. January 4.   JAN., p. 61
Became bishop of Uzès in 553 and is said to have got into trouble for trying to convert the local Jews. He founded a monastery and wrote a rule for it. d. 581.

FERREOLUS, BD, bp. and mart. January 16.   JAN., p. 204
A seventh-century bishop, supposedly of Grenoble, whose ancient cultus was confirmed in 1907.

*FERREOLUS, ST, mart. September 18.   SEPT., p. 246
The cultus of this martyr is ancient, but little is known of him except that he was put to death near Vienne on the Rhône (in 304 ?).

*FERREOLUS and **FERRUTIO, SS,** marts. June 16.   JUNE, p. 196
A priest and deacon who laboured as missionaries around Besançon for thirty years and then were martyred, *c.* 212.

*FIACRE, ST. August 30.   AUG., p. 386
He was a hermit at Kilfiachra in Ireland who went over to France where he was given land for a hermitage by St Faro of Meaux ; here he lived, greatly revered by the people, for the rest of his life and d. *c.* 670. St Fiacre's shrine, at the place in Seine-et-Marne that bears his own name, is still resorted to and he is invoked against all sorts of physical ills. His feast is kept throughout Ireland on September 1. *Fiacrius.*

*FIDELIS, ST, mart. October 28.   OCT., p. 349
Fidelis was a martyr at Como (in 303 ?), where his tomb was venerated in the sixty century.

†*FIDELIS OF SIGMARINGEN, ST, mart. April 24.   APR., p. 276
Mark Rey was born of a middle-class family at Sigmaringen in south Germany in 1577 and for some time practised as an advocate, especially on behalf of poor people. Then he joined the Capuchins, receiving the name of Fidelis, and for ten years wrote and preached against Calvinism, notably among the Swiss of the Grison Alps. His opponents raised the peasants against him by putting about the story that he was a political agent of the Austrian emperor, and he was set upon and killed between Seewis and Grüsch in 1622. cd. 1745.

*FIDOLUS, ST, ab. May 16.   MAY, p. 204
Fidolus (in French *Phal*) was ransomed from captivity by Aventinus, abbot of Aumont, and himself rose to rule that abbey, which was afterwards known as Saint-Phal. d. *c.* 540.

FINA, SANTA. *See* Seraphina.

FINAN, ST, bp. February 17.   FEB., p. 253
Finan, an Irish monk from Iona, succeeded St Aidan as bishop at Lindisfarne and for ten years efficiently and peacefully governed his huge diocese. He baptized Peada, King of the Middle English, and Sigbert, King of the East Angles, and sent missionaries into their territories. d. 661. His feast is kept in the diocese of Lancaster. *Fionanus.*

FINBAR, ST, bp. September 25.   SEPT., p. 312
Fionnbharr (=White Head) is venerated as the founder of the city and see of Cork, he having established a monastery at the mouth of the river Lee which exerted a strong influence all over the south of Ireland ; he

founded a dozen other churches as well, and seems also to have preached in Scotland. Accounts of St Finbar are full of conflicting statements and decorated with surprising wonders. He is said to have d. at Cloyne, *c.* 623. His feast is kept throughout Ireland. *Finnbarrus.*

FINIAN LOBHAR, ST, ab. March 16. MAR., p. 279

The records of this saint are conflicting and untrustworthy : even the century of his birth is uncertain. His name is associated with the monastery of Clonmore and he is said to have been made abbot of Swords by St Columba. d. *c.* 560 (?). *Finianus.*

FINIAN OF CLONARD, ST, bp. December 12. DEC., p. 146

This Finian (Findan) was the outstanding figure among the holy men of Ireland in the period following the death of St Patrick. He was b. at Myshall in county Carlow and became a monk ; after a long sojourn in Wales he returned to Ireland and founded a number of churches, monasteries, and schools, the greatest of which was Clonard. Here the so-called Twelve Apostles of Ireland studied under Finian, and be became known as the " Teacher of the Saints of Ireland " ; Clonard was famous for its biblical studies for several centuries. At the same time Finian continued his missionary work, and made a foundation at Achonry in Connacht. d. *c.* 552. The feast of St Finian of Clonard is kept throughout Ireland.

FINIAN OF MOVILLE, ST, bp. September 10. SEPT., p. 127

He was b. near Strangford Lough, was a monk in Scotland, and ordained in Rome. When he returned to Ireland he brought with him biblical manuscripts that led to the famous incident of the psalter of St Columba, who was a disciple of Finian. He established the monastery of Moville in county Down, which was one of the great schools of Ireland for several centuries. d. *c.* 575. In Ireland and elsewhere St Finian is wrongly identified with St Frigidian of Lucca.

*FINTAN, ST, ab. February 16. FEB., p. 251

He was trained by St Columba of Tir da Glas and settled at Clonenagh in Leix as an anchorite. But he soon had many disciples, with whom he lived a life of very great rigour, so that the monks of neighbouring monasteries protested. Clonenagh was held in high repute and its monks are referred to in an early litany. The memory of Fintan is preserved in several stories of his austerity and marvels. d. 603. St Fintan's feast is kept throughout Ireland and in the diocese of Argyll. *Fintanus.*

FINTAN, ST. November 15. NOV., p. 189

He is said to have been carried off from Leinster by Norse raiders. He escaped and became a monk, first at Farfa and then at Rheinau in the Black Forest. d. 879.

FINTAN MUNNU, ST, ab. October 21. OCT., p. 290

This Fintan was one of the most austere of the early Irish monks. He founded the monastery of Taghmon in county Wexford about the beginning of the seventh century. According to Scottish tradition (in which he is called St Mundus) he lived in Iona and elsewhere in Scotland for a time. d. *c.* 635.

*FIRMINUS I, ST, bp. and mart. September 25. SEPT., p. 310

He was probably simply a missionary bishop in Gaul, martyred during the third century, but he is venerated as the first bishop of Amiens.

FIRMINUS II, ST, bp. September 1. SEPT., p. 5

He is honoured as third bishop of Amiens, but he may be the same person as the preceding.

FLANNAN, ST, bp. December 18. DEC., p. 200

Flannan is venerated as the first bishop of Killaloe, during the seventh century, and his feast is kept throughout Ireland. *Flannanus.*

*FLAVIAN, ST, bp. and mart. February 18. FEB., p. 264

Flavian began his career as patriarch of Constantinople by refusing to acknowledge his promotion in 447 by making a present to the Emperor. He condemned the monophysite teachings of Eutyches and received from Pope St Leo the famous " Dogmatic Letter " confirming the condemnation. At the " Robber Synod " of Ephesus in 449 St Flavian appealed from it to the Holy See, whereupon the monophysite Dioscoros and his followers beat him and drove him into exile ; he died of his injuries three days later. There is, however, some conflict of evidence as to the occasion and manner of his death. Flavian was proclaimed a saint and a martyr at the Council of Chalcedon in 451. *Flavianus.*

*FLAVIAN and **ELIAS, SS,** bps. July 20. JULY, p. 294

Flavian, patriarch of Antioch, and Elias, patriarch of Jerusalem, are named together in the Roman Martyrology, they having been driven into exile by the emperor Anastasius for upholding the Council of Chalcedon. They d. in 512 and 518 respectively.

*FLORA and **MARY, SS,** virgs. and marts. November 24. Nov., p. 295

Flora and Mary were Christian maidens of Cordova who gave themselves up to the Moors during the persecution under Abderrahman II ; they were beheaded in 851.

FLORA OF BEAULIEU, BD, virg. June 11. JUNE, p. 146

A hospitaller nun of the order of St John of Jerusalem at the convent of Beaulieu near Rocamadour. A number of spiritual trials and surprising physical phenomena are narrated of her by a biography whose value is uncertain. d. 1347.

*FLORENTIUS, ST, bp. and mart. January 3. JAN., p. 50

A bishop of Vienne, said to have been martyred *c.* 275.

*FLORENTIUS, ST, bp. November 7. Nov., p. 83

He was made bishop of Strasburg *c.* 678, after being a missionary in Alsace. He is said to have been an Irishman. d. *c.* 693.

*FLORIAN, ST, mart. May 4. MAY, p. 53

He was a Roman military officer and official who suffered death for Christ in 304 at Lorch in Austria. He is a patron of Poland and Upper Austria. *Florianus.*

FLORIBERTUS, ST, bp. April 27. APR., p. 303

A bishop of Liége who was, among more amiable characteristics, " vehement in correcting." d. 746.

*FLORUS and **LORUS, ST,** marts. August 18. AUG., p. 199

According to a rather unreliable Greek tradition these martyrs were brothers and both stone-masons : they handed over a temple on which they had been working to Christian worship and were accordingly put to death by the heathen, in Illyria during the second century. Their veneration was nothing to do with the worship of Castor and Pollux.

*FLOSCULUS, ST, bp. February 2. FEB., p. 50

Or *Flou.* A fifth-century bishop of Orleans of whom nothing is known.

FOILLAN, ST, bp. and mart. October 31. OCT., p. 375

He was a brother of St Fursey and when Burghcastle was destroyed by the Mercians he crossed over to France with his other brother, St Ultan, and founded the abbey of Fosses. Foillan exercised considerable influence at the convent of Nivelles, and going from thence to Fosses one night *c.* 655 he and his companions were murdered by robbers. St Foillan is venerated as "bishop and martyr" but nothing is known of his alleged episcopate and the circumstances of his death hardly constitute martyrdom.[1] *Foelanus.*

FORANNAN, ST, ab. April 30.   APR., p. 346
He was one of the several Irish abbots of Waulsort in Belgium, where he introduced the rule of St Benedict. d. 982.

†*FORTY MARTYRS, THE. March 10.   MAR., p. 161
These were among the most greatly venerated bodies of martyrs in early times and in the East to-day. They were soldiers at Sebaste (Sivas) in Lesser Armeria who were left naked on the ice of a frozen pond, baths of hot water beii.g put on the banks as a temptation to apostatize. One failed to support the ordeal, but his place was taken by one of the guards who was converted by the heroism of the rest. This was during the persecution by Licinius in 320. The Forty Martyrs are spoken of by St Basil, St Gregory of Nyssa, St Gaudentius of Brescia, the historian Sozomen, and others.

†*FOUR HOLY CROWNED MARTYRS, THE. November 8. Nov., p. 93
There is confusion and uncertainty about the martyrs called the Four Holy Crowned Ones. They may have been four who suffered at Albano *c.* 305 (SS Severus and companions) or others in Pannonia about the same time (SS Claudius and companions) : or they may have been neither. A basilica was dedicated in their honour in Rome in the fifth century.

FOURTEEN HOLY HELPERS, THE. August 8.   AUG., p. 96
A feast in honour of this group of saints is celebrated in various parts of Germany on August 8 and other dates. The usual fourteen names are Achatius, Barbara, Blaise, Catherine, Christopher, Cyriacus, Denis, Erasmus, Eustace, George, Margaret, Pantaleon, Vitus (all martyrs), and Giles. In France the Holy Helpers are fifteen, the extra one being our Lady

FRANCA VISALTA, ST, virg. April 26.   APR., p. 294
As abbess of St Syrus at Piacenza St Franca was persecuted on account of her strict discipline, and eventually was transferred to take charge of a new Cistercian community at Pittoli. d. 1218. c.c. by Pope Gregory X.

FRANCES D'AMBOISE, BD. November 4.   NOV., p. 59
Frances was the wife of Duke Peter of Brittany, after whose death in 1457 she increased the charitable works for which she was already known. She helped Bd John Soreth to introduce the Carmelite nuns into France, and herself joined the order at Vannes ín 1468. d. 1485. bd. 1863. *Francisca.*

†*FRANCES THE ROMAN, ST. March 9.   MAR., p. 141
She was b. in Rome in 1384 and married at an early age to Lorenzo de Ponziani. She led a life of great devotion and penance, but without singularity or excess ; she patiently bore terrible distresses in the death of her children, Lorenzo's banishment, and the confiscation of their estates : and contrived in forty years never to annoy her husband. On his death Frances joined the community of Benedictine oblates of the Tor de' Specchi which she had founded in 1433 for retirement and charitable works

---

[1] In Butler's *Lives*, October volume, 1936 edition, the last large-type paragraph on p. 377 belongs to the end of the account of St. Foillan on p. 376.

(this community still exists). d. 1440. cd. 1608. A biography of St Frances, with many particulars of visions and miracles, was written by John Matteotti who was her confessor for the last ten years of her life.

†*FRANCIS BORGIA, ST. October 10.   OCT., p. 124

B. at Gandia in Aragon into the noble family of de Borja in 1510. For nearly twenty years Francis led the life appropriate to a great nobleman, holding office at the court of the emperor and administering his Spanish estates. On the death of his wife in 1546 he relinquished these estates (he was then duke of Gandia) and joined the Society of Jesus. First as a preacher and then as provost general of his order he became one of the chief instruments of the counter-Reformation, a worthy lieutenant of Pope St Pius V ; he established the Jesuits throughout western Europe, sent missionaries to the Americans, and more than counterbalanced the evil justly associated with the name of Borgia. St Francis was the typical patrician saint, humble, determined, mortified, attracting all ranks by his kindness and courtesy. d. 1572. cd. 1670. *Franciscus.*

†*FRANCIS CARACCIOLO, ST. June 4.   JUNE, p. 46

B. in the Abruzzi in 1563 of the noble Neapolitan family of the Caraccioli. He became a priest in gratitude for being cured of a disease akin to leprosy and in 1588 founded with John Augustine Adorno the order of Minor Clerks Regular. The life of St Francis was one of prayer and penance combined with the establishment of the new congregation in Italy and Spain, where its members worked as missioners and in prisons and hospitals. They met with a good deal of opposition, and overwork led Francis to resign the government of the society. He refused several bishoprics and passed his last years in preaching and contemplation. d. 1608. cd. 1807.

FRANCIS DICKENSON, BD, mart. April 30.   APR., p. 348

He was a secular priest, born in Yorkshire, who was h.d.q. for his priesthood at Rochester in 1590. bd. 1929.

FRANCIS GALVEZ, BD, mart. December 4.   DEC., p. 64

A Castilian Friar Minor of the Observance who was martyred by burning at Tokio in 1623. bd. 1867

*FRANCIS JEROME, ST. May 11.   MAY, p. 136

B. in 1642 near Taranto, ordained priest in 1666, and became a Jesuit in 1670. St Francis Jerome spent his life as a missioner in the kingdom of Naples, where from the outset his preaching attracted huge congregations and produced remarkable conversions : he once brought twenty Turkish prisoners to the Faith. Many miracles were attributed to him. d. 1716. cd. 1839.

FRANCIS PACHECO, BD, mart. June 20.   JUNE, p. 264

This Portuguese Jesuit was martyred at Nagasaki in Japan in 1626 together with two other Jesuits from Europe, a Japanese Jesuit, four Japanese laymen and a Korean. They were all burned alive. bd. 1867.

FRANCIS PAGE, BD, mart. April 20.   APR., p. 243

He belonged to a Protestant family at Harrow-on-the-Hill, was reconciled to the Church, and ordained at Douai ; h.d.q. for his priesthood at Tyburn in 1602. bd. 1929.

FRANCIS PATRIZZI, BD. May 12.   MAY, p. 149

He was received into the Servite Order by St Philip Benizi and soon became famous as a missioner and preacher. d. 1328. c.c. 1743.

FRANCIS POSSADAS, BD. September 20.   SEPT., p. 269

A confessor of the Order of Preachers who was well known all over the south-west of Spain during the second half of the seventeenth century. d. 1713. bd. 1818.

FRANCIS REGIS CLET, BD, mart. February 17.   FEB., p. 256

B. at Grenoble in 1748. He joined the Lazarists and went as a missionary to China in 1791. Sporadic persecution was going on, and for three years he worked under the greatest difficulties and entirely alone. Persecution intensified in 1818 and Bd Francis was betrayed to the mandarin. In spite of his age, seventy-two, he was tortured and then strangled, near Hankow, 1820. bd. with seventy-six other martyrs in China, 1900.

*FRANCIS SOLANO, ST. July 24.   JULY, p. 347

He was b. in 1549, joined the Observant Franciscans, and for years exercised his ministry in southern Spain. In 1589 he was sent as a missionary to South America and for twenty years he was a power among the Indians and the Spanish colonists : his denunciations of the corruptions of Lima brought panic to the citizens. St Francis had the gift of tongues, and many other miracles were related of him. d. 1610. cd. 1726. The Franciscans keep his feast on July 13.

†*FRANCIS XAVIER, ST. December 3.   DEC., p. 34

Francis Xavier was b. in Navarre in 1506 of noble parents and was by nature aristocratic, refined, and ambitious. In 1534 he became the second of St Ignatius Loyola's original seven followers and proved to be perhaps the greatest individual missionary to the heathen since St Paul. He set out on his first journey, to the East Indies, in 1540, and within ten years he had made most successful visits to India, Ceylon, and other East Indian islands, Malaya, and Japan ; like many missionaries before and since he found that the greatest difficulty in the way of his apostolate was presented by the trading and political Europeans, but he received great supernatural assistance. Francis Xavier d. on the island of Sancian in 1552, when about to enter China. He was cd. in 1662 and Pope Pius X named him patron of foreign missions and of all works for the spreading of Christianity. The body of St Francis was brought to Goa, where it still lies in the church of the Child Jesus.

FRANCIS-XAVIER BIANCHI, BD. January 31.   JAN., p. 404

B. in 1743 at Arpino and became a Barnabite clerk regular, in spite of great opposition from his family. He overworked himself in his ministry, added severe austerities to already bad health, and at last lost the use of his legs. He inspired boundless veneration in Naples and miracles were attributed to him. d. 1815. bd. 1893.

†*FRANCIS OF ASSISI, ST. October 4.   OCT., p. 38

It has been said of St Francis that he entered into glory in his lifetime, and that he is the one saint whom all succeeding generations have agreed in canonizing : but often this is rather on account of the listening birds, the hunted leveret, the falcon, and the nightingale in the ilex-grove (nothing extraordinary in his day, when Nature was still natural) than for those qualities which earned him canonization. He was b. at Assisi in 1181, the son of a merchant. After a pleasure-seeking youth he left his home, and in 1209 founded the order of Friars Minor, capturing the imagination of his time by presenting poverty, chastity, and obedience in terms of the troubadours and courts of love : numerous followers were soon forthcoming. In 1219 he went to the East to try to evangelize the

Mohammedans, but without success, either among the crusaders or their infidel opponents. There were considerable internal difficulties in the new order, but in 1224 Francis's labours were supernaturally recognized by the imprinting of the *stigmata* of the Passion on his body—the first recorded and most famous example of this phenomenon. The Franciscan nuns were established in concert with St Clare in 1212. St Francis d., still in deacon's orders, in 1226. cd. 1228.

FRANCIS OF CALDEROLA, BD. September 13.   DEC., p. 320
A confessor of the Franciscan order who had a special gift for reconciling enemies; d. 1507. c.c. by Pope Gregory XVI.

FRANCIS DE CAPILLAS, BD, mart. January 15.   JAN., p. 196
A Spanish Dominican from the Philippines who went as a missionary to the Chinese province of Fo-Kien and was there martyred in 1648, the protomartyr of China in these later times. bd. 1909.

FRANCIS OF CAMPOROSSO, BD. September 16.   SEPT., p. 218
He was a Capuchin lay brother, who for many years begged alms for his brethren in the city of Genoa where he was greatly loved and respected by the people. He d. while nursing cholera victims in 1866. bd. 1929.

FRANCIS OF FABRIANO, BD. April 22.   APR., p. 262
B. 1251 and became a Friar Minor; he wrote a treatise in defence of the Portiuncula indulgence and is said to have been the first Franciscan to form a library. d. *c.* 1322.

†*FRANCIS OF PAOLA, ST. April 2.   APR., p. 13
B. at Paola in Calabria in 1416. He was founder of the order of Minim friars, so called because they wished to be the least of all friars, which took its rise with the hermits that Francis attracted to his solitude in 1436. The order spread quickly with the fame of its founder, who was gifted with powers of miracle and prophecy, but it did not lack set-backs, St Francis being at one time threatened with imprisonment by the King of Naples. He was specially sent for by the dying Louis XI of France and was honoured by his two successors, who would not let him return to Italy. d. at Plessis 1507. cd. 1519. The Minim friars still exist.

FRANCIS OF PESARO, BD. August 13.   AUG., p. 166
This Francis ("Bd Cecco") was an early Franciscan tertiary who lived with others in community. A number of very remarkable occurrences are associated with his name. d. 1350. c.c. by Pope Pius IX.

†*FRANCIS OF SALES, ST, bp. and doct. January 29.   JAN., p. 362
B. in Savoy in 1567, eldest son of the Seigneur de Nouvelles. He was a student of law at Paris and Padua, but decided to become a priest and was ordained in 1593. He was sent as a missionary to the Protestants of the Chablais where, after a poor start, he was notably successful. In 1599 he was nominated coadjutor of the bishop of Geneva, and in 1602 succeeded to the see. St Francis established a seminary at Annecy, organized conferences and synods of his clergy, and insisted on simple preaching and religious instruction. He met St Jane Frances de Chantal in 1604 and with her founded the order of Visitation nuns. He was one of the finest bishops and most attractive men that Christianity has ever produced and his effect on the indifferent and on Protestants was most marked: "The man who preaches with love," he said, "preaches adequately against the heretics, even though he never utters a controversial word"; Cardinal du Perron said that he (the Cardinal) could confute

Protestants, but Mgr de Sales could convert them. Of St Francis's written works the most famous are his treatise on the love of God and the *Introduction to the Devout Life*—a book which were it rewritten and published to-day with a new title would creature a furore. St Francis was only fifty-six when he died in 1622. cd. 1665 ; declared doctor of the Church in 1877, and patron saint of journalists and other writers in 1923.

FRANCO LIPPI, BD. December 11. DEC., p. 140
While a fugitive from justice he joined a band of *condottieri* and until middle-age led a most evil life. He was brought to penitence by a temporary blindness and when he was over sixty-five was admitted to the Carmelite Order as a lay-brother, in which capacity he edified Siena as much as he had formerly scandalized it. d. 1291. c.c. 1670. *Francus.*

FREDERICK, BD, bp. May 27. MAY, p. 328
He was appointed bishop of Liége in 1119 in place of the simoniacal Alexander, but d. in 1121, it is said poisoned by Alexander's supporter the Count of Louvain. *Fridericus.*

*FREDERICK, ST, bp. and mart. July 18. JULY, p. 256
He became bishop of Utrecht in 820 and was murdered in church at Maastricht in 838, it is said by men from Walcheren where Frederick had worked hard to extirpate the custom of incestuous marriages.

FREDERICK OF RATISBON, BD. November 29. NOV., p. 340
He is a confessor of the Augustinian friars, a lay brother of their order at Ratisbon (Regensburg). d. 1329. c.c. 1909.

*FREDIANO, ST, bp. March 18. MAR., p. 310
Frediano (*Frigdianus*), an Irishman, went on pilgrimage to Italy and became a hermit there on Monte Pisano. He was elected bishop of Lucca, where he rebuilt his cathedral after it had been burned by the Lombards and converted many of the invaders. He formed the clergy of the city into a community of canons regular, which enjoyed a great reputation, and centuries later became part of the Canons Regular of the Lateran. St Gregory in his *Dialogues* narrates the miracle of St Frediano diverting the course of the river Serchio which threatened Lucca. d. 588.

*FRIDESWIDE, ST, virg. October 19. OCT., p. 265
The legend of St Frideswide is late and untrustworthy, but she undoubtedly founded a nunnery at Oxford and d. there *c.* 735. Early in the twelfth century the monastery was refounded for Austin canons, and their theological school was probably the germ of the university. St Frideswide's feast is observed in the archdiocese of Birmingham and also at Borny in Artois, under the corrupt name *Frévise. Fredeswinda.*

FRIDOLIN, ST. March 6. MAR., p. 80
Fridolin was a wandering Irish priest who founded the abbey of Seckingen on the Rhine at an unknown date during the Merovingian period. Other particulars of his life are considered unreliable. He may have d. *c.* 538. *Fridolinus.*

FRODOBERTUS, ST, ab. January 8. JAN., p. 117
Abbot of the monastery of Moutier-la-Celle, near Troyes, of which he was the founder. d. *c.* 673.

*FROILAN, ST, bp. October 3. OCT., p. 32
He was bishop of Laon and one of the principal restorers of monasticism in Spain. d. 1006. *Froilanus.*

*FRONTO AND GEORGE, SS, bps.   October 25.   Oct., p. 333
These saints were early apostles of Périgueux, but their story has been completely overlaid with worthless legend.

*FRUCTUOSUS, ST, bp. and mart.   January 21.   Jan., p. 256
Fructuosus, Bishop of Tarragona in Spain, with his deacons Augurius and Eulogius, was arrested in 259 during the persecution of Valerian, and all three were burnt alive.   There is an authentic account extant of the bishop's examination by the Roman governor and of the subsequent martyrdom.

*FRUCTUOSUS, ST, bp.   April 16.   Apr., p. 181
Fructuosus was a Visigoth of high rank.   He devoted his estates to the poor, to freed slaves, and to endowing religious houses, some of which sheltered whole families.   He himself was abbot of Complutum and in 656 was made archbishop of Braga, in the direction of which diocese he met with opposition that amounted to persecution.   d. 665.

*FRUMENTIUS, ST, bp.   October 27.   Oct., p. 343
A youth from Tyre who was wrecked on the Ethiopian coast and, with another young man, St Aedesius, was taken to the royal court at Aksum, where both in time became officials.   Frumentius was, c. 340, consecrated bishop at Alexandria by St Athanasius, and sent back to preach the gospel with Aedesius in Ethiopia.   The missionaries had considerable success, converting two kings and many of the people, and Frumentius is venerated as the apostle of that country.   d. c. 380.

FULBERT, ST, bp.   April 10.   Apr., p. 114
Fulbert was a pupil of Gerbert at Rheims and a very distinguished scholar ; under his care the cathedral school at Chartres became the chief one in France, and in due course he was promoted to the bishopric of that city.   He was author of the hymn, " Chorus novæ Hierusalem."   d. 1029

FULGO OF NEUILLY, BD.   March 2.   Mar., p. 22
He was parish priest at Neuilly-sur-Marne and a famous preacher throughout north-western France.   He was regarded with suspicion by some because he lived in a quite ordinary way, with no unusual ascetic practices.   He was ordered by Pope Innocent III to preach the Fourth Crusade, but was saved by death from participating in that disastrous expedition.   d. 1201.

*FULGENTIUS, ST, bp.   January 1.   Jan., p. 11
B. in Africa in 468 of a senatorial family.   Became a monk and abbot, and suffered under Arian persecution.   Bishop of Ruspe in 508, but was banished by the Arians with other bishops to Sardinia, where Fulgentius wrote a number of treatises, especially against Arianism.   He finally returned to his diocese on the death of King Thrasimund in 523, and retired to a remote monastery a year before his death in 533.   The theological and controversial writings of St Fulgentius are of considerable importance.

FULRAD, ST, ab.   July 16.   July, p. 217
He was abbot of Saint-Denis, near Paris, and held several responsible offices under the Frankish kings.   Fulrad was the delegate of King Pepin for the handing over to the Holy See of the exarchate of Ravenna and the duchy of the Pentapolis in 756.   d. 784.

*FURSEY, ST, ab.   January 16.   Jan., p. 203
B. near Lough Corrib (on Inisquin ?) and established a monastery at

Rathmat (Killursa ?) which soon became popular. Then he returned home and began to experience the remarkable ecstasies of which St Bede and others write. St Fursey came to England, where land was given him for a monastery at Burgh Castle, near Yarmouth, and then went on to Gaul where he founded another monastery, at Lagny. He died *c.* 648, and was buried at Péronne. His feast is observed in the diocese of Northampton and throughout Ireland. *Furseus.*

FUSCIAN and his comps., **SS,** marts. December 11. Dec., p. 135

Fuscian and Victorius are said to have been early missionaries in Gaul who were martyred near Amiens *c.* 287. Gentian, an old man, was killed while defending them from arrest. *Fuscianus.*

GABRIEL THE ARCHANGEL, ST. March 24.   MAR., p. 384

†*   The angel of the Annunciation (Luke i, 26 ; *see also* Daniel ix, 21 and Luke i, 10, 19). His feast was added to the general calendar of the Western church in 1921.

GABRIEL FERRETTI, BD. November 12.   NOV., p. 150

A confessor of the Franciscan Order at Ancona ; d. 1456. c.c. by Pope Benedict XIV.

GABRIEL MARY, BD. August 27.   AUG., p. 341

Gilbert Nicolas was b. near Clermont in 1463, joined the Friars Minor, and became the confessor and helper of Bd Joan of Valois. The nickname of " Gabriel ab Ave Maria " was given to him by Pope Alexander VI. d. 1532.

*†GABRIEL OF THE SORROWS, ST. February 27.   FEB., p. 377

Francis Possente was born of a middle-class family at Spoleto in 1838 ; his childhood was entirely normal and he went to the Jesuit school in that town. There were apparently no clear indications of religious vocation in his youth, but after two serious illnesses and the death of his sister he entered the novitiate of the Passionists, taking the name of Gabriel-of-our-Lady-of-Sorrows. He was then eighteen and the remaining six years of his life is simply a record of an extraordinary effort to attain perfection in and by small things. The parallel between this saint and St Teresa of Lisieux is obvious. An outstanding characteristic was his continual cheerfulness. In 1860 St Gabriel developed consumption, and he died two years later at Isola di Gran Sasso in the Abruzzi. He had not been ordained to the priesthood. cd. 1920.

*GALATION and **EPISTEME, SS,** marts. November 5.   NOV., p. 61

They are the hero and heroine of what is nothing more than a Christian continuation of the romance of Clitophon and Leucippe. Misled, possibly, by the example of some Eastern menologies, Cardinal Baronius unfortunately inserted their names in the Roman Martyrology.

*GALDINUS, ST, bp. April 18.   APR., p. 215

He was archdeacon of Milan, was created cardinal in 1165, and archbishop in the following year. The career of Galdinus was cast in extremely disturbed days and their hardships damaged his health, but such was his determination in discharging his office that he is reckoned the third of the great Milanese archbishops, after St Ambrose and St Charles Borromeo. d. 1176.

*GALL, ST, bp. July 1.   JULY, p. 7

He was bishop of Clermont, but very little is known of his life. d. *c.* 552. *Gallus.*

*GALL, ST. October 16.   OCT., p. 223

Gall is the best known of the twelve monks who left Ireland with St Columbanus ; he shared his master's exile from Luxeuil, but stayed on in Switzerland when Columbanus went into Italy. Gall was a missionary hermit in several places, particularly at a place on the Steinach where the great abbey and town of Saint-Gall subsequently sprang up. d. *c.* 640. The feast of St Gall is kept throughout both Switzerland and Ireland.

*GALLA, ST.   October 5. Oct., p. 60

She was the widow of a citizen of Rome (and sister-in-law of Boethius), whose life and death is briefly referred to by St Gregory in his *Dialogues*. d. *c.* 550.

*GALLICANUS, ST, mart.   June 25. June, p. 333

It is not certain who this Gallicanus was, of whom it is said that he was a man of consular rank and of large charities, but probably he was the Roman consul with Symmachus in 330. He was not a martyr.

GANDULPHUS OF BINASCO, BD.   April 3. Apr., p. 42

He became a Friar Minor during the lifetime of St Francis and went to preach and pray in the island of Sicily, where he is greatly venerated. d. 1260.

GARIBALDUS, ST, bp.   January 8. Jan., p. 120

One of the three bishops whom St Boniface consecrated in Bavaria *c.* 740. Nothing more is known of him.

*GATIAN, ST, bp.   December 18. Dec., p. 200

He is venerated as founder and first bishop of the see of Tours, who d. probably *c.* 337. *Gatianus.*

GAUCHERIUS, ST, ab.   April 9. Apr., p. 106

He founded the abbey of St John at Aureil for canons regular of St Augustine, and was the benefactor of St Stephen of Grammont at Muret. d. 1140.

*GAUDENTIUS, ST, bp.   October 25. Oct., p. 334

He was consecrated bishop of Brescia by St Ambrose *c.* 387, and was called by Rufinus " the glory of the teachers of the age wherein he lived." He was one of the bishops sent to the East by Pope St Innocent I to defend the cause of St John Chrysostom. d. *c.* 410. The Canons Regular of the Lateran keep the feast of another Gaudentius, bishop of Rimini, on October 14.

*GAUGERICUS, ST, bp.   August 11. Aug., p. 137

Gaugericus (Géry) was for thirty-nine years bishop of the united sees of Cambrai and Arras ; the beginning of the city of Brussels is attributed to him. d. *c.* 625.

*GELASIUS I, ST, pope.   November 21. Nov., p. 262

During his pontificate of less than five years Gelasius, of African descent, showed himself one of the most capable and vigorous popes of the fifth century. The so-called Gelasian Sacramentary is of later date than him. d. 496.

*GEMINIAN, ST, bp.   January 31. Jan., p. 397

A fourth-century bishop of Modena who opposed the heresy of Jovinian. d. *c.* 348.

GEMMA, BD, virg.   May 12. May, p. 150

A recluse who lived and died at Salmona in the Abruzzi, where her relics are still venerated. d. 1429. c.c. 1890.

GEMMA GALGANI, BD, virg.   April 11. Dec., p. 314

This young girl was b. at Camigliano in Tuscany in 1878 and d. at Lucca in 1903. Her short life was a story of earnest religion and continuous suffering, both physical and spiritual, but spiritually her normal state was one of peace, during which she used to experience many ecstasies. She had periodically recurring stigmata between 1899 and 1901. bd. 1933.

GENESIUS, ST, bp.   June 3.   JUNE, p. 37
Bishop of Clermont in Auvergne. He was learned, benevolent, and surpassingly good, beloved by old and young, rich and poor. d. 662.

*GENESIUS OF ARLES, ST, mart. August 25.   AUG., p. 305
This Genesius (Gènes) is patron saint of Arles, near which city he gave his life for Christ c. 303. He was an official shorthand-writer, who protested against taking down a decree against Christians.

*GENESIUS THE COMEDIAN, ST, mart. August 25.   AUG., p. 303
He is said to have been converted, and subsequently martyred, while taking part in a burlesque of Christian rites in Rome in the days of Diocletian. Substantially the same story is told of three other names and it is very uncertain how much truth there is in it.

*GENEVIÈVE, ST, virg. January 3.   JAN., p. 52
Principal patroness of Paris. She was born c. 422 at the village of Nanterre near Paris, and at an early age attracted the notice of St Germanus of Auxerre when he preached there. When she was fifteen she was consecrated a virgin by the bishop of Paris, after which she led a very austere life and undertook long journeys for charitable objects. She was persecuted for a time, but vindicated by St Germanus. When Paris was captured by the Franks and threatened by the Huns, Geneviève stirred up the inhabitants to defence both by word and example, and Clovis himself is said to have consulted her. St Geneviève died c. 500, her body was solemnly enshrined, and in later centuries many miracles in favour of the city of Paris were attributed to her intercession. Recent attacks on the authenticity of the records of St Geneviève have not received the support of most competent critics. *Genovefa.*

GENGULPHUS, ST. May 11.   MAY, p. 128
In French *Gengoul.* He was a Burgundian nobleman who is said to have been murdered by his wife's paramour in 760 ; the wonders credited to his relics led to a considerable cultus and Hroswitha of Gandersheim wrote a verse account of his " martyrdom."

GENNADIUS, ST, bp. May 25.   MAY, p. 304
He was abbot of San Pedro de Montes and bishop of Astorga in Spain. d. 936.

GENTILIS, BD, mart. September 5.   SEPT., p. 64
He was an Italian Friar Minor who went as a missionary among the Mohammedans and was eventually martyred in Persia in 1340. c.c. by Pope St Pius V.

GENULFUS, ST, bp. January 17.   JAN., p. 218
Genulfus is honoured in Cahors as its first bishop, in the third century, but there is no evidence for this attribution.

†*GEORGE, ST, mart. April 23.   APR., p. 264
There is every reason to believe that St George was a martyr who suffered at Diospolis (Lydda, Ludd) in Palestine, probably before the time of Constantine ; beyond this there seems nothing that can be affirmed with confidence. He is the subject of numerous legends, of which the dragon story is comparatively a late one. The East revered him in early times as a patron of soldiers and he was known in England long before he

was adopted as her patron in the late Middle Ages ; he was declared to be Protector of the Kingdom of England by Pope Benedict XIV. *Georgius.*

GEORGE NAPPER, BD, mart. November 9.   Nov., p. 109

George Napper (Napier) was a secular priest, b. at Holywell manor, Oxford, in 1550, h.d.q. for his priesthood at Oxford in 1610. bd. 1929.

GEORGE OF AMASTRIS, ST, bp. February 21.   FEB., p. 295

He was first a hermit on Mount Sirik, then a monk of Bonyssa, and finally bishop of Amastris on the Black Sea. He was a true father of his people, and on one occasion the successful defence of the city against the Saracens was due to his influence over the inhabitants. d. *c.* 825.

GEORGE THE YOUNGER, ST, bp. April 7.   APR., p. 84

Three eighth–ninth century bishops of Mitylene, the capital of Lesbos, were named George and were venerated as saints. The best known of them, " the Younger," was exiled for opposing Iconoclasm, his tomb becoming illustrious for miracles. d. *c.* 816.

GERALD, ST, ab. March 13.   MAR., p. 235

One of the Lindisfarne monks who accompanied St Colman to Ireland after the Synod of Whitby. He became abbot of the house for English monks that Colman founded, " Mayo of the Saxons." d. 732. *Gerardus.*

GERALD, ST, ab. April 5.   APR., p. 62

He was appointed abbot of Saint Vincent's at Lâon, but as the monks were unwilling to submit to proper discipline he resigned. With three companions he founded the abbey of Sauve Majeure, near Bordeaux, and governed it till his death in 1095. He instituted the practice of celebrating Mass and Office for the deceased for thirty days after the death of a member of the community.

GERALD OF AURILLAC, ST. October 13.   OCT., p. 182

Gerald, Count of Aurillac, b. in 855, lived a holy life " in the world " at a time of considerable degeneracy and disorder. He was very generous to the poor, lived according to a daily rule, and founded a monastery for Benedictines on his estate. For the last seven years of his life he was blind. d. 909. St Gerald is the patron saint of Upper Auvergne.

GERARD, BD. June 13.   JUNE, p. 171

This Gerard was the second brother of St Bernard, whom he joined at Clairvaux, and became his right-hand man. d. 1138. One of St Bernard's sermons is in praise of his dead brother. *Gerardus.*

GERARD, ARDWYNE, and comps., **SS.** August 11.   DEC., p. 317

Gerard, Ardwyne, Bernard, and Hugh are venerated in certain places in Italy as English pilgrims to the shrine of St Michael at Monte Gragano who were famed for their goodness. Nothing is known about them and their very existence is doubtful.

GERARD CAGNOLI, BD. January 2.   JAN., p. 43

A lay-brother of the Order of Friars Minor, to whose intercession numerous miracles were attributed ; until he was forty he led a wandering life in Sicily. d. 1345. c.c. 1908.

*GERARD MAJELLA, ST. October 16.   OCT., p. 231

He was apprenticed to a tailor, entered the service of a bishop, followed his trade for some years and then, at the age of twenty-three, was received by the Redemptorists as a lay-brother, " a perfect model for those in that office," said Pope Pius IX. He soon attracted the notice of St Alphonsus Liguori, who deliberately shortened his novitiate. Brother

Gerard was attached to various houses of his congregation in the neighbourhood of Naples, and his simple but sufficient goodness was recognized even to the extent of allowing him to be in effect spiritual director of several convents of nuns. There are over twenty examples of his having brought secret sinners to repentance by reading their consciences, and numerous supernatural physical phenomena are related of him, especially " bilocation." He was also the agent of several miracles of healing, multiplying of food, etc., but, like other saints, the biggest miracle of all was his own character. d. 1755. cd. 1904.

*GERARD SAGREDO, ST, bp. and mart. September 24.   SEPT., p. 303
He was abbot of San Giorgio Maggiore at Venice and later became apostle of a large part of Hungary, where he was made first bishop of Csanad by the prince St Stephen. During a resurgence of paganism St Gerard was killed by rebel soldiers and his body thrown into the Danube at Buda in 1046. He was declared a martyr by Pope St Gregory VII.

*GERARD OF BROGNE, ST, ab.   October 3.   OCT., p. 30
He founded a monastery on his estate at Brogne in Flanders and became its abbot. He was so successful as a superior that he was called upon to reform the life and rule of a score of monasteries, and he introduced the Rule of St Benedict into several houses of regular canons. d. 959.

GERARD OF MONZA, BD.   June 6.   JUNE, p. 84
Gerard Tintorio was a young bourgeois of Monza in Lombardy who expended his fortune on building a hospital, to the service of which he devoted his whole life. d. 1207. c.c. 1582.

*GERARD OF TOUL, ST, bp.   April 23.   APR., p. 268
As bishop of Toul he was famed for the charity shown during the famine of 982 and for his establishments of Greek and Irish monks who did much for religion and learning in the diocese. d. 994.

GERARD OF VILLAMAGNA, BD.   May 23.   MAY, p. 286
A Tuscan solitary, who is venerated as a tertiary of the Order of St Francis. d. 1245. c.c. 1833.

*GERASIMUS, ST, ab.   March 5.   MAR., p. 60
He was a disciple of some of the great fifth-century monks in Egypt and Palestine, and himself established a large settlement of hermits near Jericho. As a monastic leader in Palestine he was second only to St Sabas. d. *c.* 475.

*GEREMARUS, ST, ab.   September 24.   SEPT., p. 302
In French *Germer*. He was the husband of the lady Domana, also venerated as a saint, and after the death of their two children they both went " into religion." Geremarus became abbot of Pentale on the Seine. d. *c.* 658.

*GEREON, ST, mart.   October 10.   OCT., p. 134
Gereon and his companions probably represent a band of martyrs of unknown date venerated at Cologne, where their tomb was known in the fifth century ; but their association with the Theban Legion is fictitious.

GERIUS, BD.   May 24.   MAY, p. 291
Nothing can be asserted positively about Bd Gerius except that he is the age-long patron of Monte Santo, near Loreto. He is said to have been a hermit from France. d. 1298 (?). c.c. 1742.

GERLAC, ST. January 5. JAN., p. 79

A Dutch soldier of disorderly life who was recalled to decent behaviour by the sudden death of his wife. He did seven years' penance in Rome and then returned to his native place, Valkenberg, where he lived for seven more years in a hollow tree adjoining St Gerlac's well. Neighbouring monks were so scandalized by this way of life that they are said to have refused him the sacraments when he was dying *c.* 1170, so, says tradition, God supplied them miraculously. *Gerlacus.*

GERLANDUS, ST, bp. February 25. FEB., p. 343

Nothing definite can be stated about this saint except that he was a Norman who became bishop of Girgenti in Sicily at the end of the eleventh century. d. 1104.

GERLANDUS, ST. June 18. JUNE, p. 236

A member during the thirteenth century of one of the military orders, probably the Templars ; he is venerated at Caltagirone in Sicily.

GERMAIN. *See* Germanus.

*GERMAINE COUSIN, ST, virg. June 15. JUNE, p. 191

Germaine was b. *c.* 1579 at Pibrac, near Toulouse, daughter of a farm-labourer. She had ill-health and a paralysed hand, she was ignored by her father and badly treated by her stepmother. As soon as she was old enough she was set to mind sheep and was thus employed for the rest of her short life. She was well known throughout the neighbourhood for her efficiency in her work, her religious devotion, her patience under unkindness, her care for young children and for those even poorer than herself, and several miraculous happenings were associated with her name. Germaine was found dead on her pallet beneath the stairs on June 15, 1601. Forty-three years later her body was accidentally exhumed and found to be incorrupt. cd. 1867. *Germana.*

*GERMANICUS, ST, mart. January 19. JAN., p. 230

A young martyr at Smyrna who when thrown to the beasts encouraged them to attack him in the year 156. The letter in which this is narrated is one of the most authentic extant memorials of early Church history.

GERMANUS, ST, mart. February 21. FEB., p. 294

With his young brother Numerian he entered the abbey of Romberg (later Remiremont) in the Vosges, and later went on to Luxeuil, whence he was made abbot of the new foundation at Granfel in the Val Moutier. Among his works here was to remake the road through the valley. He, with his prior St Randoald, was murdered by the followers of a local magnate whose oppression of the people St Germanus had rebuked, *c.* 677.

*GERMANUS, ST, bp. May 12. MAY, p. 146

He became patriarch of Constantinople in 715 and as an energetic defender of the veneration of images came into collision with the emperor Leo III the Isaurian ; he was compelled to resign in 730, and d. in 732. A few of St Germanus's writings are still extant.

GERMANUS, ST, bp. July 3. JULY, p. 26

He is said to have been a nephew of St Patrick and a missionary monk in Ireland, Wales, and Brittany. Then he became bishop in the Isle of Man, where his memory is still preserved, under the forms " Germain " and " Jarman," in several place names. d. *c.* 474.

*GERMANUS, ST, bp. October 30. OCT., p. 363

This Germanus was bishop of Capua and a friend of St Benedict. He was probably the legate sent by Pope St Hormisdas to heal the Acacian Schism at Constantinople, where he experienced ill-treatment from the heretics. d. *c.* 540.

*GERMANUS OF AUXERRE, ST, bp. July 31. JULY, p. 442.

By his mission against the Pelagian heresy St Germanus strengthened and consolidated the Church in Britain after the withdrawal of the Romans. He became bishop of Auxerre after a secular career in Gaul, and was sent into Britain in 429 and again in 447 ; thereafter the Church in these islands remained practically free from heresy for a space of eleven hundred years. It is recorded that by a ruse of St Germanus the Britons gained a great victory over marauding Picts and Saxons—the " Alleluia Victory." d. 448. His feast is kept on various dates in the dioceses of Plymouth, Portsmouth, Birmingham, Westminster, and in Wales.

*GERMANUS OF PARIS, ST, bp. May 28. MAY, p. 334

B. 496 near Autun. As bishop of Paris he was one of the most venerated churchmen of his age and he converted the last heathen in several parts of France ; he worked hard to check the licentiousness of the nobles and is said miraculously to have healed King Childebert I. d. 576.

GERMERIUS, ST, bp. May 16. MAY, p. 205

Germerius was bishop of Toulouse for fifty years during the sixth century ; his cultus goes back to very early times. d. 560 (?).

GEROLDUS, ST. April 19. APR., p. 227

The tomb of St Geroldus and his two sons is still a place of pilgrimage near Mitternach. In middle age he became a hermit there and after his death in 978 his hermitage was occupied by his two sons Cuno and Ulric, monks from Einsiedeln.

*GERONTIUS, ST, bp. and mart. May 9. MAY, p. 114

A bishop of Cervia in the province of Ravenna, murdered on the highway by " ungodly men " in 501.

†*GERTRUDE THE GREAT, ST, virg. November 16. Nov., p. 192

From her childhood Gertrude lived at the nunnery of Helfta in Saxony, and her life was without exterior incident except for the supernatural revelations that made her name famous ; these began at the age of twenty-six. Gertrude was of considerable intellectual ability, as her writings show, but only the second book of the work commonly called the *Revelations of St Gertrude* is hers. She was the pupil of St Mechtilde, and with both the love of the Sacred Heart of Jesus was a frequently recurring theme. For the last ten years of her life Gertrude suffered greatly from physical ill-health. d. October 17, 1302. Her feast was given to the whole Western church in 1677. The monastery of Helfta has been claimed both for the Benedictines and the Cistercians. *Gertrudis.*

GERTUDE OF ALTENBERG, BD, virg. August 13. AUG., p. 165

She was the third daughter of St Elizabeth of Hungary and became abbess of Altenberg, where she was one of the first in Germany to get permission for the feast of Corpus Christi. d. 1297. c.c. by Pope Clement VI.

*GERTRUDE OF NIVELLES, ST, virg. March 17. MAR., p. 299

Younger daughter of Pepin of Landen and Bd Ida, b. at Landen in 626. She was made abbess of her mother's foundation at Nivelles, and both abbey and abbess became very famous ; the Irish saints Foillan and Ultan settled near by on land given by St Gertrude. d. 659. A good deal of folk-lore grew up around this Gertrude, who is honoured as a patroness of travellers and gardeners and invoked against the ravages of rats and mice ; fine weather on her feast is regarded as a good omen.

GERTRUDE VAN OOSTEN, BD, virg.   January 6.   JAN., p. 93
   A *béguine* at Delft in Holland who, in 1340, received the stigmata of our Lord's passion, which at first used to bleed seven times a day. She led a life of suffering for eighteen years, was much sought after, and had a strange knowledge of people's thoughts and distant events. Her name, " van Oosten," is said to be a nickname from her frequent repetition of the hymn, " Het daghet in den Oosten," " The day breaks in the East." d. 1358.

†*GERVASE and PROTASE, SS, marts.   June 19.   JUNE, p. 239
   The alleged relics of these martyrs were discovered by St Ambrose at Milan in 386, but even then nothing was remembered of them except their names and a vague tradition of their martyrdom. Their *acta* are fictitious, but it is believed that they were genuine martyrs who suffered during the second century. *Gervasius, Protasius.*

GERVINUS, ST, ab.   March 3.   MAR., p. 41
   Canon of Reims, monk of St Vannes at Verdun, and abbot of Saint-Riquier ; he visted England several times, where he enjoyed the confidence of St Edward the Confessor. d. 1075.

*GETULIUS, ST, mart.   June 10.   JUNE, p. 132
   Getulius is said to have been the husband of St Symphorosa and to have been martyred at Tivoli with his brother and an official whom he had converted *c.* 120.

GIBRIAN, ST.   May 8.   MAY, p. 98
   He was the eldest of an Irish family alleged to have migrated from Ireland to Brittany and then to have settled as solitaries in the forest around the Marne. d. *c.* 515 (?). *Gibrianus.*

GILBERT, ST, bp.   April 1.   APR., p. 9
   He was formerly honoured in Scotland as a zealous upholder of Scottish ecclesiastical independence of the archbishop of York. He was bishop of Caithness and d. 1245. *Gilbertus.*

*GILBERT OF SEMPRINGHAM, ST, ab.   February 16.   FEB., p. 73
   Founder of the only religious order of English origin. He was born at Sempringham in Lincolnshire, where he became parson in 1123. He drew up a rule for seven women who wanted to live in community, and this developed into the Gilbertine Order of both canons and nuns. It was very successful at first, but at the dissolution had only four greater houses and twenty-one lesser ones. Most of the monasteries were double, the canons following the rule of St Augustine, with additions, and the nuns a form of the Cistercian recension of that of St Benedict. The order was governed by a supreme master or prior general, an office which St Gilbert himself held till he lost his sight. He died in 1189, at the age of 106. Ireland was the only country outside England where the Gilbertines had any foundations (two), and no attempt has ever been made to re-establish the order since its dissolution. St Gilbert's feast is observed in the dioceses of Birmingham (Feb. 4), Nottingham, and Northampton.

*GILDARD, ST, bp.   June 8.   JUNE, p. 108
   Or *Godard.* He is said to have been bishop of Rouen and to have d. *c.* 514. That he was the twin brother of St Médard is a fable. *Gildardus.*

GILDAS, ST. January 29. JAN., p. 378

Called " the Wise." This sixth-century saint is chiefly known as the author of an " Epistle " in which he violently attacks his contemporaries, clerical and lay ; his authorship of a part of it, however, has been questioned. He was a pupil of St Illtyd, and he may have written his epistle while living solitary on the island of Flatholm in the Bristol Channel. The last years of his life were spent at the monastery of Ruys in Brittany, where he died honoured in Wales, Ireland, Scotland, and Brittany.

†*GILES, ST, ab. September 1. SEPT., p. 1

The legend of St Giles (*Ægidius*), with the incident of the wounded hind, was one of the most popular of the Middle Ages, but it derives chiefly from a tenth-century biography that is utterly untrustworthy. Giles was probably a Provençal and abbot of a monastery on the Rhône, who d. *c.* 712. Over 160 churches were dedicated in his honour in England alone before the Reformation, and he was invoked as the patron of cripples, beggars, and blacksmiths.

GILES MARY, BD. February 7. FEB., p. 114

Giles Mary of St Joseph was a rope-maker who joined the Alcantarine Friars Minor at Naples when he was twenty-five, and spent the rest of his life as porter of the friary. d. 1812. bd. 1888.

GILES OF ASSISI, BD. April 23. APR., p. 272

One of the two most famous of the early followers of St Francis of Assisi. At first he accompanied Francis on his preaching journeys, but afterwards made several long pilgrimages and went to preach (unsuccessfully) to the Mohammedans in Tunis ; the latter part of his life was spent in Italy again. Giles was exceedingly simple and single-minded, but endowed with a supernatural wisdom that caused him to be consulted by people of all kinds. d. at Perugia in 1262. c.c. by Pope Pius VI.

GILES OF LORENZANA, BD. January 28. JAN., p. 360

B. *c.* 1443 in the kingdom of Naples, where he was a farm-hand. He became a Franciscan lay-brother, and d. 1518. c.c. 1880.

GILES OF PORTUGAL, BD. May 14. MAY, p. 178

According to tradition this Giles was a medical student who became enmeshed in the practice of black magic. In consequence of a dream he gave this up and became an exemplary Dominican friar at Valencia. d. 1265.

*GISLENUS, ST, ab. October 9. OCT., p. 114

In French *Ghislain*. He was abbot of a monastery at Saint-Ghislain, near Mons, but there is no satisfactory account of his life. He is said to have had great influence on the family of St Vincent Madelgarus. d. *c.* 680.

*GLYCERIA, ST, virg. and mart. May 13. MAY, p. 158

A Christian maiden who suffered martyrdom at Heraclea in the Propontis *c.* 177.

*GOAR, ST. July 6. JULY, p. 62

He was a secular priest of Aquitaine who took to the solitary life near Oberwesel on the Rhine, but the extant particulars of his life are unhistorical. d. *c.* 575.

GOBAN, ST, mart. June 20. JUNE, p. 253

He was an Irish disciple of St Fursey in East Anglia and followed him to France ; he was murdered by barbarians at the place now called Saint-Gobain *c.* 670.

GODEBERTA, ST, virg. April 11. APR., p. 126

She was abbess of a convent at Noyon which was endowed by King Clovis II, and directed by St Eligius. d. *c.* 700.

GODELEVA, ST, mart. July 6. JULY, p. 65

Godeleva was married at the age of eighteen to Bertulf of Ghistelles, and throughout the two years of her wedded life was treated by her husband with great neglect and cruelty, of which the reasons are unexplained. In 1070 he had her strangled and drowned ; fourteen years later the bishop of Tournai enshrined Godeleva's body in the church of Ghistelles, and she has been venerated as a martyr in the neighbourhood ever since,

*GODFREY, ST, bp. November 8. Nov., p. 100

From the abbacy of Nogent he was raised to the see of Amiens in 1104. He was noted for the severity of his discipline, which indeed seems to have been excessive, and it was said that there was not a parish in his diocese in which his life was safe. But he was as inflexible with himself as he was with others. d. 1115. *Godefridus.*

GODFREY OF CAPPENBERG, BD. January 13. JAN., p. 165

He was count of Cappenberg and a big landowner in Westphalia. Coming under the influence of St Norbert he, in the face of violent opposition from his relatives, turned his castle of Cappenberg into a Premonstratensian monastery, built a convent for his wife and his two sisters, and himself became a Premonstratensian canon. He d. 1127, at the age of thirty and while still in minor orders.

GODRIC, ST. May 21. MAY, p. 258

He was first a sailor on the northern seas and then house-steward to a landowner in his native Norfolk. After several pilgrimages he became a hermit at Finchale in co. Durham where he lived for sixty years and d. in 1170. St Godric was endowed with extraordinary powers, especially of prevision. *Godericus.*

GOERICUS, ST, bp. September 19. SEPT., p. 257

Also called *Abbo.* In thanksgiving for the restoration of his sight he became a priest, and succeeded St Arnulphus as bishop of Metz. d. 647.

GOHARDUS, ST, bp. and mart. June 25. JUNE, p. 338

Guichard, Gundard. A bishop of Nantes who, in 843 was slain by raiding Normans while celebrating Mass ; many monks and priests were killed with him.

GOMIDAS, BD, mart. November 5. Nov., p. 64

Gomidas Keumurjian was b. in Constantinople *c.* 1656, married at the age of twenty, and was ordained priest in the dissident Armenian church. With his family he came into Catholic communion *c.* 1696, at a time when the number of Armenian reconciliations was causing alarm among the dissidents. In 1707 Gomidas was denounced to the Turkish authorities as a European agent who was subverting the allegiance of the people, and the vizir, somewhat unwillingly, condemned him to death ; he was beheaded at Parmak-Kapu on the outskirts of Constantinople. bd. 1929, A son of Bd Gomidas took the surname of " Carbognano ", by which his father is sometimes called. *Cosmas.*

GONSALVO OF AMARANTHA, BD. January 16. JAN., p. 206

A Portugese priest who became a Dominican, but was allowed to live as a hermit. d. 1259 (?). c.c 1560.

*GOOD THIEF, THE. March 25. MAR., p. 396
A number of legends have grown up around the repentent thief who died beside our Lord on the cross, and to whom the name of Dismas has been given. Nothing is known about him.

*GORCUM, THE MARTYRS OF. July 9. JULY, p. 121
Nineteen priests and religious who were taken by the Calvinists in Gorcum, near Dordrecht, and hanged on account of their religion in 1572. The leader of the martyrs was Nicholas Pieck, guardian of the Observant Franciscan friary at Gorcum, and ten others belonged to his community. cd. 1867.

†*GORDIAN and **EPIMACHUS, SS,** marts. May 10. MAY, p. 120
Epimachus is said to have been martyred at Alexandria in 250 and his body taken to Rome, while Gordian was later beheaded at Rome and buried in the same tomb as Epimachus. These martyrs certainly existed, but their extant *acta* are spurious. *Gordianus.*

*GORDIUS, ST, mart. January 3. JAN., p. 51
An ex-soldier of Cæsarea in Cappadocia who became a hermit. Under the persecution of Diocletian he gave himself up and was beheaded, *c.* 304.

*GORGONIA, ST. December 9. DEC., p. 115
She was the eldest child of St Gregory Nazianzen senior and St Nonna and was married to one Vitalian, by whom she had three children. She was noted for her love for the Church's public worship and for her generosity to the needy. d. *c.* 374.

†*GORGONIUS and other marts., **SS.** September 9. SEPT. p., 93
Dorotheus and Gorgonius were freedmen in the imperial palace at Nicomedia. When they saw a fellow-servant, Peter, tortured for his Faith they protested to the emperor, and were themselves put to death in 304.

GOTHARD, ST, bp. May 4. MAY, p. 55
Gothard (Godehard) while abbot of Nieder-Altaich in Bavaria was commissioned by the emperor St Henry to reform the Benedictine monasteries in several German dioceses. He became bishop of Hildesheim in 1022 and was one of the outstanding prelates of that see. d. 1038. cd. 1131. The Pass of St Gothard takes its name from a chapel built thereon and dedicated in honour of this saint.

GOTTESCHALC, ST, mart. June 7. JUNE, p. 94
He was a Wendish prince who repudiated Christianity because his father was murdered by Christian Saxons. He married Canute's grandniece, spent some time in England where he returned to Christianity, and later recovered his own territories, encouraging missionaries and establishing monasteres in them. He was slain at Lenzen in 1066 during a rising fomented by his brother-in-law. There seems to be no solid reason for regarding Gotteschalc as either a saint or a martyr.

*GRATA OF BERGAMO, ST. May 1. MAY, p. 8
From the conflicting accounts of this holy woman it is not even possible to determine whether she lived in Bergamo in the fourth century or in the eighth.

GRATIA OF CATTARO, BD. November 16. NOV., p. 205
For thirty years he was a fisherman in the Adriatic and then joined the Augustinian friars as a lay-brother, in which capacity miracles were recorded of him. d. 1509. c.c. 1889.

†*GREGORY THE GREAT, ST, pope and doct. March 12. MAR., p. 202

Gregory, the first monk to become pope, was b. in Rome in the middle of the sixth century, son of a patrician and of a saint, Sylvia. After being papal legate at Constantinople he was elected to the supreme pontificate in 590 and proved to be the outstanding pope of the first thousand years of Christianity : some of his activities have their effect in the Church and the world to-day. Gregory sent St Augustine with other Benedictines to convert the English, he encouraged monasticism, maintained the primacy of the Roman see in East and West, enforced the discipline of the clergy, reformed and cared for the Roman liturgy and chant, defended central Italy against the Lombards, was a fine administrator—and with it all was a great mystic. Six of his written works, including the famous *Dialogues* and a book of homilies on the gospels much used in the Divine Office, have come down to us ; he was the fourth of the doctors of the Western church. " It is impossible to conceive what would have been the confusion, the lawlessness, the chaotic state of the Middle Ages without the mediæval papacy : and of the mediæval papacy the real father is Gregory the Great " (Milman). St Gregory d. in 604 and his body rests in St Peter's at Rome. *Gregorius.*

*GREGORY II, ST, pope. February 13. FEB., p. 202

He became pope in 715 and was specially solicitous about the affairs of the Eastern church. He encouraged the monks of St Benedict and re-established their abbey of Monte Cassino, and consecrated St Corbinian and St Boniface for Germany. Gregory had dealings with England over the Easter dispute, firmly opposed the Iconoclasm of the emperor Leo, and checked the Lombard advance in Italy. d. February 10, 731.

*GREGORY III, ST, pope. December 10. DEC., p. 122

The pontificate of Gregory III, a Syrian, was troubled at the beginning by the iconoclasm of the emperor Leo the Isaurian and at its end by incursions of the Lombards. He sent St Willibald to help St Boniface in Germany. d. 741.

†*GREGORY VII, ST, pope. May 25. MAY, p. 295

He was b. in Tuscany *c.* 1020 of poor parents and was baptized Hildebrand. His story belongs to the general history of the Church. After discharging various responsible offices at Rome he was elected pope by acclamation in 1073. Few men have been so admired by his friends and so bitterly attacked by his foes, both during life and after death. But his was an ungrateful and huge task, to reform the Church, enforce celibacy among the Latin clergy, resist the encroachments of the temporal power, and consolidate that of the Church, eliminate simony and abolish lay investiture. All admit that Gregory proved himself a stern Christian and a very great man. He d. in exile at Salerno in 1085. cd. 1728.

*GREGORY X, BD, pope. January 10. JAN., p. 135

While archdeacon of Liége Theobald Visconti preached the crusade and himself visited the Holy Land, where he was when elected pope in 1271 (he was not even a priest at the time). He at once summoned the fourteenth oecumenical council, which met at Lyons in 1274, and a temporary reunion of the Eastern Orthodox with the Catholic Church took place thereat. He also put an end to the interregnum in the Empire by approving the election of Rudolf of Habsburg as emperor. d. 1276. Miraculous cures were attributed to Gregory in his lifetime, and his name was added to the Roman Martyrology by Pope Benedict XIV.

GREGORY BARBARIGO, BD, bp. June 18.   JUNE, p. 237

B. at Venice in 1625. He was bishop first of Bergamo and then of Padua and was created cardinal in 1660, being looked on as another St Charles Borromeo. His charities were enormous, he founded a college and a seminary, which he equipped with a printing-press and a fine library, and was an earnest worker for the reconciliation of the dissident Byzantines. d. 1697. bd. 1761.

GREGORY LOPEZ, BD. July 20.   JULY, p. 297

He left his native Spain *c.* 1563 and became a hermit among the Indians of Mexico, where the Spanish colonists were very censorious of his way of life. He was vindicated by the Archbishop of Mexico City, and at his death in 1596 he was widely respected and loved. Miracles were reported at his tomb and his cultus spread all over Mexico, but it has never been officially confirmed.

GREGORY MAKAR, ST, bp. March 16.   MAR., p. 281

He is said to have been an Armenian monk and bishop of Nicopolis, who fled from his see and wandered across Europe into France. At Pithiviers in the diocese of Orleans he settled down as a hermit and received great respect for his austerities and miracles. d. *c.* 1010.

†*GREGORY NAZIANZEN, ST, bp. and doct. May 9.   MAY, p. 105

He was b. at Arianzus in Cappadocia *c.* 329, son of St Gregory the Elder and St Nonna, and read law for ten years at Athens. Instead of taking up his profession he joined St Basil in his retreat in Pontus and later was ordained by his father, who was bishop of Nazianzus. He was consecrated bishop but refused a diocese until in 380 he reluctantly accepted the see of Constantinople, which was then greatly troubled by the Arian heresy. A month later St Gregory resigned and retired to Nazianzus. He d. at his birthplace in 390. Gregory was gentle, retiring, and peace-loving and was most effective when writing. His works were particularly directed against Arianism, especially his five *Theological Discourses* ; he also wrote homilies, poems, and letters in large numbers. He was one of the greatest of theologians, called, in fact, " the Divine " (*Theologos*), one of the four great Greek doctors of the Universal Church, and the third of the Three Holy Hierarchs of the Byzantines.

†*GREGORY THAUMATURGUS, ST, bp. November 17.   Nov., p. 209

He was b. in Pontus *c.* 213 and studied under Origen. At the age of forty he became bishop of his native Neocæsarea ; it is said that when elected his diocese contained seventeen Christians, and when he died there were seventeen pagans : his missionary methods included the association of games and merry-making with great feast days—a proceeding not so common then as later. Gregory's name, " the Wonder-worker," explains itself, though but few reliable particulars of his miracles have survived. d. *c.* 270.

*GREGORY THE ILLUMINATOR, ST, bp. September 30. SEPT. p. 385

He is venerated as the apostle of the Armenians, but the particulars of his life are somewhat uncertain. He seems to have converted King Tiridates, to have been consecrated bishop by the archbishop of Cæsarea, and to have set up his see at Ashtishat where, with the aid of Greek and Syrian missionaries, he set himself to organize his church, strengthen the converts, and win over waverers. He consecrated his son Aristakes to succeed him, retired to a hermitage, and d. there *c.* 330. Armenian legends about St Gregory are full of very astonishing incidents, patently fictitious.

*GREGORY OF GIRGENTI, ST, bp. November 23.   Nov., p. 283

He was Byzantine bishop of Girgenti in Sicily, now best remembered for his commentary on the book of *Ecclesiastes*. d. *c.* 638.

GREGORY OF LANGRES, ST, bp. January 4.   Jan., p. 60

Great-grandfather of St Gregory of Tours. He was *comes* of the district round Autun, and after the death of his wife was, late in life, made bishop of Langres. As a civil governor he was known for his severity, as a bishop for his mildness and charity. d. 539.

*GREGORY OF NYSSA, ST, bp. March 9.   Mar., p. 150

One of that great Christian family at Cæsarea in Cappadocia of which his brother St Basil the Great is the most famous. St Gregory was at first a professor of rhetoric and married a lady named Theosebia ; then he was ordained priest, and in 372 was appointed bishop of Nyssa on the edge of Lower Armenia. The diocese was a hotbed of Arianism, but Gregory was wanting in tact and inexperienced in handling affairs, and for some time was (unjustly) excluded from his see. After Basil's death he came to the fore as a mainstay of orthodoxy and exerted great influence at the second oecumenical council (Constantinople II). Of Gregory's voluminous writings the chief is an instruction on the Christian faith called his Catechetical Discourse ; a number of his sermons and letters also are extant. d. *c.* 395.

*GREGORY OF SPOLETO, ST, mart. December 24.   Dec., p. 232

A priest at Spoleto said to have been beheaded in 304 for refusing to sacrifice to Jove, Minerva, and Æsculapius. A fanciful passage in his *acta* states that he was saved from being roasted alive by an earthquake that destroyed a quarter of the town. His existence is doubtful.

*GREGORY OF TOURS, ST, bp. November 17.   Nov., p. 219

Georgius Florentius took the name of Gregory when he became bishop of Tours in 573. He was one of the most effective bishops of his day, but he is now best remembered as an historian and hagiographer. Both St Gregory the Great and St Odo of Cluny spoke highly of his personal virtues. d. 594.

*GREGORY OF UTRECHT, ST, ab. August 25.   Aug. p. 309

He was a monk under St Boniface, who made him abbot of St Martin's at Utrecht. After the death of Boniface in 754 Gregory administered the diocese as well for twenty-two years, but was apparently never consecrated bishop. Under his rule St Martin's abbey became a great missionary centre and a nursery of saints. d. *c.* 776.

GREGORY OF VERUCCHIO, BD. May 4.   May, p. 57

He was dismissed for some improper reason from the Augustinian friary which his mother had founded at Verucchio and was given shelter by the Franciscans at Monte Carnerio, near Reati. Here he became a hermit and d. at a great age in 1343. c.c. 1769.

GRIMBALD, ST, ab. July 8.   July, p. 97

Grimbald was a monk of Saint-Bertin whence he was invited to England by Alfred the Great. He was made abbot of the secular canons at Newminster in Winchester, and d. 903.

GRIMONIA, ST, virg. and mart. September 7.   Sept., p. 73

She is venerated in Picardy, but the facts about her are hard to come by : she may have been a solitary from Ireland who at some unknown date lost her life in defending her chastity.

GUALA ROMANONI, BD, bp. September 3. SEPT., p. 39

He was an early disciple of St Dominic in Italy and first prior of the Preaching Friars at Brescia. He was appointed papal legate to Savoy and then bishop of Brescia, a charge he afterwards resigned on account of civil strife. d. 1244. c.c. 1868.

GUALFARDUS, ST. April 30. APR., p. 347

He was a saddler from Augsburg who plied his trade in Verona, till his discovery that he was looked on as a saint made him hide away as a hermit in a remote place. d. 1127. He is the patron of saddlers.

GUALTERIUS. *See* Walter.

GUARINUS, ST, bp. January 6. JAN., p. 92

Abbot of Aulps, near Geneva, who affiliated his monastery to Clairvaux but was taken away from it to be bishop of Sion in the Valais. St Bernard had a great esteem for St Guarinus. d. 1150.

*GUARINUS, ST, bp. February 6. FEB., p. 93

An Augustinian canon of Bologna who for his ability and virtue was appointed cardinal bishop of Palestrina by Pope Lucius II. d. 1159.

GUDULE, ST, virg. January 8. JAN., p. 119

Daughter of St Amalberga and brought up at Nivelles under the care of her cousin St Gertrude. She led an austere life of prayer and good works in the house of her father, Count Witger, and died about the year 712. The relics of St Gudule were eventually translated in 1047 to the collegiate church in Brussels which now bears her name. She is the patroness of the city. *Gudula.*

GUIBERT, ST, ab. May 23. MAY, p. 282

Guibert gave his estates to found a monastery at what is now Gembloux, himself becoming a monk at Gorze. He had to defend his establishment against his brother-in-law and also against the emperor Otto I, and was a missionary among the pagan refugees in Brabant. d. 962. *Guibertus.*

GUIDO. *See* Guy.

*GUMMARUS, ST. October 11. OCT., p. 154

Gummarus (Gomer) served in the court of Pepin, where he married the lady Gwinmaria. She was of an extravagant and perverse disposition and Gummarus was an example of heroic virtue particularly in respect of his troublesome wife ; but at length she became too much for him, a separation was arranged, and he d. as a solitary *c.* 774.

GUNDEBERT, ST, mart. April 29. APR., p. 328

Little is known of this seventh-century saint. According to one account he went as a monk from France to Ireland and was there killed by heathen raiders.

GUNDLEUS, ST. March 29. MAR., p. 435

Gwynllyw, anglicized as Woollos and latinized as Gundleus, is said to have been the husband of St Gladys and father of St Cadoc, and to have ended his life as a hermit in south-west Wales. Sixth century. There is an old church dedicated in his honour at Newport.

GUNTHER, BD. October 9. OCT., p. 117

Until he was fifty this Gunther, who was a cousin of St Stephen of Hungary, led the life of a worldly and ambitious nobleman. He then became a monk at Niederaltaich, but his conversion was incomplete and he continued to give free play to his ambitions. In 1008 he entered on an eremitical life, and from thenceforward made ample amends for his former excesses. d. 1045.

*GUNTRAMNUS, ST. March 28. Mar., p. 426

Guntramnus, or Gontran, king of Burgundy, was honoured as a saint by his subjects after his death and his name has found its way into the Roman Martyrology ; but it is more than doubtful if his claims to holiness would obtain formal canonization for him to-day. d. 592.

*GURIAS and **SAMONAS, SS,** marts. November 15. Nov., p. 186

Gurias and Samonas were tortured and beheaded for the Faith at Edessa in 306.

GURVAL, ST. June 6. June, p. 82

Or *Gudwall*. He founded the monastery of Plécit at Locoal Meudon and several other churches in Brittany but there is no trustworthy account of his life. Sixth century (?).

GUTHLAC, ST. April 12. Apr., p. 136

Guthlac left the abbey of Repton to become a hermit in the middle of the Lincolnshire fens ; he lived thus for over fifteen years, following so far as possible the examples of the fathers of the eastern deserts. He had remarkable influence over wild nature. Guthlac was honoured in his life and still more after his death in 714 ; a monastery grew up around his tomb and dwelling-place which became the great abbey of Croyland. *Guthlacus*.

GUY, ST, ab. March 31. Mar., p. 453

Guy was abbot first of St Severus at Ravenna and then of Pomposa, near Ferrara. For some reason he was persecuted by Archbishop Heribert of Ravenna, but both St Peter Damian and the emperor Henry III had a more just opinion of St Guy, to whom many miracles were attributed. d. 1046. *Guido*.

*GUY, ST. September 12. Sept., p. 154

Guy (Wye), commonly called the Poor Man of Anderlecht, was lay sacristan of a church at Laeken, in Belgium, lost all his money in an investment, became a pilgrim, and ended his days *c.* 1012 in the public hospital at Anderlecht, near Brussels. He led a hidden life of much simplicity and mortification, and was credited with many miracles.

GUY MARAMALDI, BD. June 25. June, p. 344

A confessor of the Order of Preachers well known as a theologian and preacher around Naples and Ragusa. d. 1391. c.c. 1612.

GUY OF CORTONA, BD. June 16. June, p. 202

Guido Vignotelli sold all that he had and gave the proceeds in alms at the word of St Francis of Assisi ; he became a hermit near his native town. d. *c.* 1245.

GWEN, ST, mart. October 18. Oct., p. 254

She was reputed to be a daughter of Brychan Brycheiniog and mother of Caradog Fraichfrâs, and to have been murdered by the heathen Saxons at Talgarth *c.* 492. Also called *Gwenllian*. Another St Gwen (Wenn), mother of St Cybi, was commemorated on October 18 in Cornwall. *Candida*.

H

ADRIAN. *See* Adrian.

HALWARD, ST, mart. May 14. ~~~~~~~~~~~~~ MAY, p. 177

The true history of St Halward (Hallvard), patron of Oslo in Norway, is obscure. According to tradition he was murdered early in the eleventh century for refusing to give up to her pursuers a woman who asked his protection.

HARTMANN, BD, bp. December 23. ~~~~~~~~~~~~~~ DEC., p. 227

While a canon of Salzburg cathedral he introduced life under a rule among the chapter and later was called to be provost of the canons regular at Klosterneuburg : in 1140 he was elected bishop of Brixen and continued to do much for the canonical life in Germany. d. 1164. c.c. 1784. *Hartmannus.*

HARVEY, ST. *See* Hervæus.

HATTO, BD. July 4. ~~~~~~~~~~~~~~~~~~~~~~~~~~~~ JULY, p. 40

Hatto endowed the Benedictine monastery of Ottobeuren in Suabia and became a monk therein. d. 985. His title to be included in a list of saints is somewhat dubious.

*HEDDA, ST, bp. July 7. ~~~~~~~~~~~~~~~~~~~~~~~~~ JULY, p. 75

He was a monk who was made bishop of the divided diocese of Wessex in 676 and removed its see from Dorchester to Winchester. He was one of the first benefactors of the abbey of Malmesbury and assisted King Ine in the drawing-up of his laws. d. 705. The feast of St Hedda is kept by the archdiocese of Birmingham.

HEDWIG, BD. February 28. ~~~~~~~~~~~~~~~~~~~~~~~ FEB., p. 387

B. in 1371, and was accepted as queen of Poland, in succession to her father Louis, at the age of thirteen. For political reasons she married Jagiello, Duke of Lithuania (instead of the William of Austria whom she preferred), and thus hastened the conversion of the heathen Lithuanians. She seems to have been a very saintly woman and a most capable sovereign, but the cause of her beatification, though introduced, has never been completed ; nevertheless she is commonly called " Blessed " in Poland. d. 1399. *Hedwigis.*

†*HEDWIG, ST. October 16. ~~~~~~~~~~~~~~~~~~~~~~~ OCT., p. 218

Hedwig (Jadwiga), of Moravian descent and aunt of St Elizabeth of Hungary, was b. in Bavaria *c.* 1174. She married Henry the Hairy, Duke of Poland, by whom she had seven children, who were from time to time the occasions of a good deal of trouble for their parents. Hedwig was the devoted assistant of her husband in the governing of his realm and together they founded several religious houses. After Henry's death in 1238 she passed most of her time with the Cistercian nuns at Trebnits, near Breslau, following their exercises and caring for the sick and needy. d. 1243. cd. 1267. St Hedwig is the patron saint of Silesia.

*HEGESIPPUS, ST. April 7. ~~~~~~~~~~~~~~~~~~~~~~~~ APR., p. 83

He is chiefly remembered as the father of ecclesiastical history, on the strength of a work of which only a few chapters survive. St Jerome testifies to his humble and apostolic spirit, " which he expressed by the simplicity of his writing." Hegesippus was a Jew of Jerusalem, but spent twenty years of his life in Rome. d. *c.* 180.

HEIMRAD, ST. June 28. JUNE, p. 371

Heimrad was a Suabian priest who wandered about Europe, mostly in Germany ; his strange behaviour caused him to be regarded by some as a saint and by others as a lunatic. d. 1019. Many miracles were reported at his tomb at Wolfhagen in Hesse-Nassau, but his cultus is a purely popular one.

HELDRAD, ST, ab. March 13. MAR., p. 237

A Provençal nobleman who provided a church, hospice and small-holdings for the people of Lambesc, near Aix. He afterwards was a monk and then abbot of Novalese at the foot of the Alps, where he seems to have anticipated on the Mount Cenis pass the work of the canons of the Great St Bernard. d. *c.* 842.

***HELEN, ST.** August 18. AUG., p. 201

She was b. *c.* 250, probably in Bithynia (certainly not in Britain). She married Constantius Chlorus, by whom she was the mother of the emperor Constantine the Great, and became a Christian at the Edict of Milan in 313. St Helen was most liberal in alms and was responsible for the building of many churches, especially in Palestine, and her name is traditionally associated with the finding of the True Cross in a rock-cistern near Mount Calvary. d. *c.* 330. St Helen's feast is kept in the dioceses of Brentwood, Liverpool, and Salford. *Helena.*

HELEN DUGLIOLI, BD. September 23. SEPT., p. 300

The devotion to this Helen at Bologna is a typical example of spontaneous popular cultus. She lived an uneventful life, married happily for thirty years to a citizen of that place, and d. in 1520. c.c. 1828.

HELEN ENSELMINI, BD, virg. November 6. NOV., p. 74

She received the Poor Clare habit from St Francis himself at Arcella, near Padua ; she was bed-ridden, blind, and dumb before her death at the age of thirty-four in 1242. c.c. 1695.

HELEN OF SKÖFDE, ST, mart. July 31. JULY, p. 447

She was the widow of a Swedish nobleman, who put her time and property at the service of the poor and of religion. She was unjustly put to death in a family feud *c.* 1160. Her cultus was approved in 1164 on the strength of the miracles alleged at her tomb.

HELEN OF UDINE, BD. April 23. APR., p. 274

After leading a very happy married life for twenty-five years Helen Valentini's husband died, and she decided to withdraw from the world ; she became a tertiary of the Augustinian friars and was noted for her benefactions to the needy and suffering and for the austerities which she inflicted on herself. d. 1458. c.c. 1848.

HELIER, ST, mart. July 16. JULY, p. 216

A sixth-century hermit on the island of Jersey, said to have been murdered by heathen whom he tried to convert. He is commemorated in the diocese of Portsmouth. *Helerius.*

***HELIODORUS, ST,** bp. July 3. JULY, p. 24

He was a friend of St Jerome and accompanied him to the East. Later he returned to his home at Aquileia and was appointed bishop of Altino, where he proved to be one of the finest prelates of his time, co-operating with St Ambrose in combating Arianism.   d. *c.* 390.

*HELLADIUS, ST, bp.   February 18.   FEB., p. 267
    While minister of public affairs at the court of the Visigothic kings Helladius would slip away to the monastery of Agallia, and eventually he became a monk and then abbot there.   In 615 he was recalled to public life in the capacity of archbishop of Toledo.   d. 633.

HEMMA, ST.   June 29.   JUNE, p. 386
    Hemma was the wife of William, landgrave of Friesach, with whom she lived in great content.   But her two sons were murdered and her husband died on a journey and for twenty-two years she lived a disconsolate widow.   She founded a great double monastery at Gurk, in Carinthia. d. 1045.

HENRY ST.   January 16.   JAN., p. 205
    A Dane who became a hermit on Cocket island off the coast of Northumberland.   He d. in 1127 and was buried in the abbey church of Tynemouth. *Henricus.*

HENRY, ST, bp. and mart.   January 19.   DEC., p. 311
    An Englishman who became bishop of Upsala in 1152.   He accompanied St Eric of Sweden in an expedition against the Finns and remained in their country to organize the Church there.   He was murdered in 1156 (?) by a Finn whom he had penanced for murder, and was venerated as a martyr and patron saint of Finland.

†*HENRY II, ST.   July 15.   JULY, p. 190
    Henry the Good, b. in Germany in 972, became Holy Roman Emperor in 1002 and his career belongs to the general history of Europe.   Common accounts of his ascetic practices do not entirely accord with what is certainly known of his character and life : he was a temporal sovereign and a layman and his ways were not those of the cloister, and he was far from being an upholder of ecclesiastical aggrandizement in temporal affairs.   He identified himself with those ideas of ecclesiastical reform which radiated from the abbey of Cluny.   d. 1024.   cd. 1146.   Henry's wife Cunegund is also numbered among the saints.

HENRY SUSO, BD.   March 2.   MAR., p. 27
    The most famous pupil of Meister Eckhart, b. at Bihlmeyer, near Constance.   He became a Dominican at an early age and was one of the greatest mystics of that order.   He was a preacher for thirty-six years, underwent many grievous trials and received great consolations : but how far his alleged autobiography is authentic is a subject of dispute.   *The Book of the Eternal Wisdom* is the best known of his writings.   d. 1365. c.c. 1831.

HENRY WALPOLE, BD, mart.   April 7.   APR., p. 90
    B. in Norfolk and educated at Cambridge and Gray's Inn ; he was reconciled to the Church and became a Jesuit in 1584.   H.d.q. for his priesthood at York, 1595.   bd. 1929.

HENRY ZDIK, BD.   bd. June 25.   JUNE, p. 342
    He was appointed bishop of Olmütz in 1126 and received the Premonstratensian habit in Jerusalem ; on his return he founded the abbey of Strahov (which still exists) for canons of his order as an example for the relaxed clergy of his diocese.   He is venerated in Czechoslovakia.   d. 1150.

HENRY THE SHOEMAKER, BD. June 9.   JUNE, p. 123

Henry Michael Buche was a shoemaker at Arlen in Luxemburg. In 1645 he migrated to Paris where, with the help of Baron de Renti, he formed an association among his fellow-tradesmen whose members undertook a strict way of life and much charitable work. d. 1666. There is apparently no evidence of cultus.

HENRY OF TREVISO, BD. June 10.   JUNE, p. 130

Henry of Treviso (or " of Bolzano " ; often called " San Rigo ") was a labourer in that town and when he could no longer work subsisted on alms. His death in 1315 was the sign for an enthusiastic popular cultus and 276 miracles are said to have been wrought through his relics. c.c. by Pope Benedict XIV.

HERBERT, ST. March 20.   MAR., p. 337

He was a priest, a friend of St Cuthbert, who lived as a solitary on St Herbert's Island in Derwentwater. He died on the same day as his friend in 687. The present Catholic church at Windermere is dedicated in honour of St Herbert. *Herbertus.*

HERCULANUS, BD. June 1.   JUNE, p. 13

Also called *Peigaro.* One of the foremost preachers of the Franciscan Order in Italy during the fifteenth century. d. 1451. bd. 1860.

*HERCULANUS, ST, bp. and mart. November 7.   Nov., p. 82

He was a bishop of Perugia who was killed by the invading Goths in 549. Another St Herculanus of Perugia, alleged martyr under Domitian, is probably a duplication of this one.

HERIBALDUS, ST, bp. April 25.   APR., p. 287

Abbot of St Germanus at Auxerre and then bishop of the same city. d. *c.* 857.

*HERIBERT, ST, bp. March 16.   MAR., p. 282

Heribert was elected archbishop of Cologne in 998 and was one of the most distinguished of the prelates of that city. He was imperial chancellor and therefore closely connected with the politics of his day, but this did not in any degree make him neglectful of his diocese. The cultus of St Heribert was greatly encouraged by the monks of Deutz, a monastery that he founded in collaboration with Otto III and where he was buried. d. 1021. *Heribertus.*

HERLUIN, BD, ab. August 26.   AUG., p. 319

He was founder and first abbot of Bec, which became one of the most influential monasteries of the Middle Ages and gave Lanfranc and St Anselm to England. But there has been no proper cultus of Herluin. d. 1078.

*HERMAGORAS, ST, bp. and mart. July 12.   JULY, p. 156

He is venerated as the first bishop of Aquileia, with his deacon and fellow-martyr Fortunatus, but nothing is known about them.

HERMANN JOSEPH, BD. April 7.   APR., p. 86

B. at Cologne *c.* 1150. From about his seventh year until his death at a great age Bd Hermann was the recipient of numerous visions which made him famous beyond the borders of Germany. He became a Premonstratensian canon regular at Steinfeld and was a model religious—and a clever mechanic. Certain writings are attributed to him, but the " revelations " about St Ursula are probably not his. d. 1241. *Hermanus.*

†*HERMENGILD, ST, mart. April 13.   APR., p. 143

Hermengild was son of the Visigothic king of Spain Leovogild, by his
first wife, and was brought up an Arian but became a Catholic on his
marriage to the daughter of Sigebert of Austrasia. When Leovogild called
on his son to give up his dignities in consequence of his conversion Hermengild refused ; moreover, he took up arms and marched against his father
and stepmother and the Arian forces. He was captured and, upon refusing
to revert to Arianism, was put to death by his father, at the instigation of
the stepmother, in 585. The question of whether Hermengild was entitled
to be honoured as a martyr has been much discussed ; but it seems certain
that when the general calendar is revised this will be one of the first feasts
to be suppressed. *Hermenegildus.*

*HERMENLAND, ST, ab. March 25.   MAR., p. 397

First abbot of Aindre when it was founded by St Pascharius ; he had
the gift of prophecy and could read men's minds. d. *c. 720. Hermene-
landus.*

*HERMES, ST, mart. August 28.   AUG., p. 363

He was a martyr in Rome who was venerated there and elsewhere
in very early times ; other martyrs of the same name, commemorated on
August 24 and 25, are probably duplicates of this one.

HERVÆUS, ST, ab. June 17.   JUNE, p. 217

Hervé is the most popular saint of Brittany after St Yves. According
to mediæval tradition he was born blind but became abbot of Plouvien ;
he transferred his community (or part of it) to Lanhouarneau where he
passed the rest of his life and was famous for miracles. Sixth century.

*HESYCHIUS, ST, mart. June 15.   JUNE, p. 183

A companion of St Julius (May 27), martyred shortly after him at
Durostorum.

*HESYCHIUS, ST. October 3.   OCT., p. 28

He was a disciple of St Hilarion, whom he accompanied from Palestine
into Egypt. When Hilarion fled to Sicily, Hesychius spent three years
searching for him and after his master's death conveyed his body back to
Majuma, near Gaza, where he himself d. at the end of the fourth century.

HIDULFUS, ST, bp. July 11.   JULY, p. 139

He was a bishop (of what diocese is not known—perhaps an auxiliary)
who retired to the Vosges mountains and there founded the abbey of Moyenmoutier *c. 676.* At his death *c. 707* he was abbot both of Moyenmoutier
and of Galilée (now Saint-Dié).

†*HILARION, ST, ab. October 21.   OCT., p. 279

Hilarion the Abbot was the first hermit of Palestine, where he was b.
near Gaza *c. 291.* He became a Christian at Alexandria and went to live
in the desert of Sinai. His holiness attracted followers and his miracles
trippers, who were such a nuisance that he had to travel about to avoid
them in his old age. When his monastery at Gaza was destroyed under
Julian the Apostate Hilarion proceeded to Egypt, Sicily, Dalmatia, and
Cyprus, where he d. *c. 371.* A good deal is learned of this saint from
St Jerome, who had his information from St Epiphanius who knew Hilarion
personally.

*HILARUS, ST, pope. February 28.   SEPT., p. 126

Hilarus was a Sardinian and was papal legate at the " Robber Synod
of Ephesus," from which he escaped with difficulty. He was elected pope

in 461 and his chief work was to strengthen ecclesiastical discipline in Gaul and Spain. d. 468.

HILARUS, ST, ab. May 15. MAY, p. 191

Disciples gathered round his hermitage on the river Ronco in Italy and he formed them into a community, naming the monastery Galeata ; it was afterwards known as Sant' Ilaro and passed into the hands of the Camaldolese monks. d. 558.

HILARY. *See also* Hilarus.

*HILARY OF ARLES, ST, bp. May 5. MAY, p. 70

This Hilary became a monk of Lérins under his relative St Honoratus whom he accompanied to Arles when Honoratus became bishop there. He succeeded to that see, which he administered with a zeal not always tempered with discretion and was twice reproved by the Holy See for his hasty conduct ; nevertheless he was always regarded in his diocese after his death in 449 as " Hilary of sacred memory," and in these words Pope St Leo I referred to him. *Hilarius.*

†*HILARY OF POITIERS, ST, bp. and doct. January 14. JAN., p. 167

He was born of pagan and noble parents and was married some years before he became a Christian. In 353 he was chosen bishop of his native Poitiers and he threw himself whole-heartedly into the campaign against Arianism, in consequence of which he was exiled to Phrygia by the Emperor Constantius in 356. He continued the controversy in the East, till at last in 360 he was allowed to return to Poitiers, the Arians hoping he would be less troublesome there. Most of St Hilary's writings are concerned more or less directly with the Arian controversy ; he introduced Greek Trinitarian speculation into the West. d. *c.* 368. Declared a doctor of the Church in 1851.

HILDA, ST, virg. November 17. NOV., p. 221

Hilda, kinswoman of St Edwin of Northumbria, lived " in the world " till she was thirty-three and then became abbess, first at Hartlepool and afterwards of the double monastery of Whitby (Streaneshalch). The success of her rule and the love which she inspired in her subjects may be clearly seen in the pages of St Bede's *Ecclesiastical History* : among her monks were St Wilfrid of York, St John of Beverley, and the poet Cædmon. At the great synod at Whitby in 664 St Hilda and her community supported the Celtic customs in dispute. d. 680. Her feast is observed in the diocese of Middlesbrough.

HILDEGARD, BD. April 30. APR., p. 345

Hildegard was one of the several successive queens of Charlemagne, by whom she had eight children, but not much is known of her personal life. She was a close friend of St Lioba and was honoured as the second founder of the abbey of Kempten, where her tomb was a place of pilgrimage. d. 783. *Hildegardis.*

*HILDEGARD, ST, virg. September 17. SEPT., p. 229

She was b. in 1098, became a nun at an early age, and was made abbess of Bd Jutta's community at Diessenberg. She moved her nuns to a desolate place on the Rupertsberg, near Bingen, in circumstances of great difficulty, and from there founded a daughter house and made numerous journeys among the ecclesiastical centres of the Rhineland. Hildegard was the first of the great German mystics, a poetess and a prophetess, a physician and a political moralist, who rebuked popes and princes, bishops and lay-folk, with complete fearlessness and unerring justice. In 1147 the pope, Bd

Eugenius III, authorized the prudent publication of her visions and revelations, in which a renewed interest has been taken in recent years ; among her other written works are books on medicine and natural history. Hildegard's mystical writings have provoked comparison both with Dante and William Blake, and in her own day she was called the " Sibyl of the Rhine " : she was alike one of the greatest figures of the twelfth century, of the followers of St Benedict, and of the women of all time. d. 1179.

HILDEGUND, ST. February 6. FEB., p. 94

Upon the death of her husband Count Lothair she, not without family difficulties, turned her castle of Meer, near Cologne, into a convent of Premonstratensian nuns, of which she became prioress. d. 1183. *Hildegundis.*

HILDEGUND, ST, virg. April 20. APR., p. 240

Of the several women of whom it is related that they lived disguised in a monastery of men, Hildegund is almost the only one in whose story there seems to be a measure of truth. After extraordinary adventures she is said to have died a novice in the Cistercian abbey of Schönau in 1188. Her cultus has never been formally approved.

HILDELITHA, ST, virg. March 24. MAR., p. 386

She was an English nun at Chelles or Farmoutiers who came to England to train St Ethelburga as abbess at Barking ; she succeeded her pupil in that office and d. *c.* 717. Her feast is kept in the diocese of Brentwood with St Cuthburga on September 3.

HIMELIN, ST. March 10. MAR., p. 172

A Scots or Irish priest who, returning from a pilgrimage to Rome, is said to have performed a miracle of turning water into wine just before death overtook him at Vissenaeken, near Tirlemont in Belgium, where he is still venerated ; *c.* 750.

†*HIPPOLYTUS, ST, mart. August 13. AUG., p. 152

The Hippolytus celebrated by the Western church on August 13 is a Roman priest who lived during the early part of the third century, a man of great learning and the most important theological writer in the early days of the Roman church. For a time he allowed himself to be put forward as an antipope, but he was reconciled with the Church, was exiled to Sardinia for the Faith, and d. of ill treatment there *c.* 235. He has been confused liturgically with the Hippolytus mentioned in the unreliable *acta* of St Laurence.

†*HIPPOLYTUS, ST, bp. and mart. August 22. AUG., p. 268

There is great uncertainty about this martyred bishop of Porto : he may be identical with the Hippolytus of August 13. But he is commemorated together with St Timothy and St Symphorian on the 22nd.

HIPPOLYTUS GALANTINI, BD. March 20. MAR., p. 351

A silk-weaver at Florence who founded an institute to teach the Christian religion to children and ignorant adults : it was imitated all over Italy. d. 1619.

*HOMOBONUS, ST. November 13. NOV., p. 163

Homobonus was a merchant of Cremona, married, and successful in his commerce. His charity and justice in spiritual and temporal matters so impressed his fellow-citizens that, two years after his death in 1197, they petitioned the Holy See for his canonization which duly took place in 1199.

*HONORATUS, ST, bp. January 16.   JAN., p. 200

A Gallo-Roman of consular family who c. 400 founded the great abbey of Lérins after having studied monasticism in Greece. St Hilary of Arles gives an attractive account of the monks and their abbot. Honoratus very unwillingly accepted the bishopric of Arles three years before his death in 429.

*HONORATUS, ST, bp. May 16.   MAY, p. 208

He gives their names to the Faubourg and Rue St Honoré in Paris, but little is known of him except that he was bishop of Amiens and d. c. 600. St Honoratus is regarded in France as patron of bakers and all trades that deal in flour.

HONORIUS, BD, mart. January 9.   JAN., p. 128

A merchant who was murdered in 1250 (?) ; the miracles reported at his tomb caused him to be honoured as a saint in the diocese of Poitiers. Pope Eugenius IV is said to have approved the cultus in 1444.

*HONORIUS, ST, bp. September 30.   SEPT., p. 388

He was the fifth archbishop of Canterbury, one of St Augustine's Roman monks, who succeeded St Justus c. 627. One of his most important known acts was the consecration of St Felix as bishop of the East Angles ; he also consecrated the first English bishop, St Ithamar of Rochester. d. 653. St Honorius is commemorated in the dioceses of Southwark and Nottingham.

*HORMISDAS, ST, pope. August 6.   AUG., p. 74

He became pope in 514 and is famous in ecclesiastical history as the author of the confession of faith called the Formula of Hormisdas, whose acceptance in 519 at Constantinople ended the monophysite Acacian schism. d. 523.

*HORMISDAS, ST, mart. August 8.   AUG., p. 95

He was a noble Persian youth who, because he was a Christian, was sentenced to be an army camel-driver, c. 420. It is not known when or how he suffered death.

HOSANNA OF CATTARO, BD, virg. April 27.   APR., p. 308

Catherine Cosie was the daughter of dissident Orthodox parents in Montenegro. She was reconciled with the Catholic Church at Cattaro, and became a Dominican tertiary living in seclusion : it was then that she took the name of Hosanna. d. 1565. c.c. 1928.

*HOSPITIUS, ST. May 21.   MAY, p. 260

A hermit at Cap-Saint-Hospice between Villefranche and Beaulieu. d. 581.

HROZNATA, BD, mart. July 19.   JULY, p. 278

After the sudden death of his wife and child he founded the abbey of Tepl in Bavaria for Premonstratensians and himself joined the community. His death in 1217 is attributed to the malice of private enemies. c.c. 1897.

*HUBERT, ST, bp. November 3.   NOV., p. 28

He was in the service of Pepin of Heristal and after the death of his wife received holy orders. (A conversion in similar circumstances to that of St Eustace was afterwards attributed to him.) He followed St Lambert as bishop of Maestricht c. 708 and transferred the see to Liége, of which city he is honoured as the founder. Hubert was a zealous missionary in the Ardennes and is the patron saint of those who hunt in that forest. d. 727. *Hubertus.*

HUGH, BD, ab. April 1.   APR., p. 8

He was a relative of St Hugh of Grenoble and abbot of the Cistercian house of Bonnevaux ; he is said to have introduced devotion to the Crown of Thorns in France. d. 1194. *Hugo.*

HUGH FARINGDON, BD, ab. and mart. November 15.   DEC., p. 13

Hugh Faringdon (*vere* Cook) was elected abbot of Reading in 1520. For some time he was on terms of excessive friendship with King Henry VIII, but at the dissolution he refused to surrender his monastery. He was condemned to death, probably for denying the royal supremacy, and was h.d.q. at Reading on November 15, 1539. With him suffered two other priests, who may have been monks of his abbey, BB John Eynon and John Rugg. bd. 1895. The feast of these martyrs is kept by the diocese of Portsmouth on November 14 and by Westminster and the English Benedictines on December 1.

HUGH OF ANZY, BD. April 20.   APR., p. 239

He had a great reputation for wisdom and miracles and was in much request to assist in the reorganization and reform of monastic houses. He d. prior of Anzy-le-Duc *c.* 930.

*HUGH OF CLUNY, ST, ab. April 29.   APR., p. 329

During the sixty years that he was abbot of Cluny he raised its prestige to extraordinary heights : he was an adviser of nine popes, consulted and respected by all the sovereigns of western Europe, and had the ultimate control over two hundred monasteries ; in 1068 he fixed the usages for the whole Cluniac congregation and during his rule its first English house was founded, at Lewes. One of his monks said of him, " It is hard to say which was the greater, his prudence or his simplicity. . . . He was never angry, except against sin." He introduced the singing of *Veni Creator* during Terce at Whitsuntide. d. 1109. cd. 1120.

HUGH OF FOSSE, BD, ab. February 10.   FEB., p. 153

This Hugh was the principal assistant of St Norbert in the establishment of the Canons Regular of Prémontré. He joined Norbert in 1119 and went preaching with him in Hainault and Brabant, and after the founding of Prémontré had much of the responsibility of conducting that house. When St Norbert was appointed archbishop of Magdeburg Bd Hugh became abbot general of the Premonstratensians and over one hundred houses of the order were begun during his thirty-five years of administration. A letter from St Bernard to Bd Hugh suggests that he was a man of somewhat impetuous disposition. d. 1164. c.c. 1927.

*HUGH OF GRENOBLE, ST, bp. April 1.   APR., p. 1

B. 1052. While canon of the chapter of Valence he earned so great a reputation that in 1080 he was appointed bishop of Grenoble in view of the disorders that required remedying in that diocese. He was very successful in the task and pope after pope refused his application to be allowed to resign. It was this St Hugh who welcomed St Bruno and his monks and gave them the land of La Grande Chartreuse. d. 1132. The holiness of his life was so patent that he was canonized by Pope Innocent II only two years after his death.

*HUGH OF LINCOLN, ST, bp. November 17.   Nov., p. 222

Hugh was b. in Burgundy in 1140 and was professed as a canon regular, but afterwards joined the Carthusians at the Grande Chartreuse. In 1175 he was sent to England to found the first charterhouse there, at Witham in Somerset, which he did under great difficulties. He was elected bishop of Lincoln in 1181, and was at the same time a vigorous defender of the rights of the people and a valued adviser of King Henry II ; he gained the respect also of Richard I by withstanding unjust exactions. Much of the present cathedral of Lincoln is due to St Hugh, who found the church almost in ruins. He was a notable defender of the Jews against official oppression and popular spite. d. 1200. cd. 1220. Hugh's feast is observed in the dioceses of Westminster, Birmingham, Clifton, Northampton, and Nottingham, and by the Carthusians.

HUGH OF LINCOLN, ST, mart. August 18. AUG., p. 208
" Little St Hugh " was a nine-year-old boy at Lincoln who in 1255 was killed by Koppin (or Jopin) and other Jews, eighteen of whom were hanged for their crime. It is impossible to tell now whether they were really guilty, but the universal mediæval conviction that Hugh was murdered out of hatred of the Faith is recognized in the diocese of Nottingham, where his feast is still observed on August 18.

*HUGH OF ROUEN, ST, bp. April 9. APR., p. 105
He lived in days when pluralism was common and was at the same time archbishop of Rouen, bishop of Paris and Bayeux, and abbot of Fontenelle and Jumièges : but in his hands neither power nor wealth were abused and he was venerated as a saint accordingly. d. 730

HUGOLINO MAGALOTTI, BD. December 11. DEC., p. 141
A secular tertiary of the Friars Minor who led a life of prayer and manual work in Italy. d. 1373. c.c. 1856. *Hugolinus.*

HUGOLINO ZEFFERINI, BD. March 22. MAR., p. 371
There is very little information to be had about this Augustinian friar : it is not clear whether he belonged to Cortona or to Mantua or even whether he lived in the fourteenth or fifteenth century. c.c. 1804.

HUGOLINO OF GUALDO, BD. January 1. JAN., p. 24
An Augustinian friar at Gualdo in Umbria of whom little is known. d. 1260. c.c. 1919.

HUMBERLINE, BD. August 21. AUG., p. 265
She was the only sister of St Bernard, and when her father and five brothers went to Cîteaux in 1113 she inherited their lands and married a nobleman. St Bernard dissuaded her from a very worldly life and after some years she became a nun ; she died (in 1135 or 1141) abbess of Jully, a Benedictine convent from whence the first house of Cistercian nuns was established, at Tart near Langres. c.c. 1703. The Cistercians keep her feast on February 12. *Humbelina.*

HUMBERT OF ROMANS, BD. July 14. JULY, p. 187
Fifth master general of the Dominicans. In this office he devoted himself to the encouragement of studies, to the final revision of his order's liturgy, and to the development of missions in the East. He resigned from the generalate at a general chapter in London in 1263, and d. at Valence in 1277. Though commonly called " Blessed," his cultus has never been confirmed. *Humbertus.*

HUMBERT OF SAVOY, BD. March 4. MAR., p. 54
Humbert III, Count of Savoy, was an ancestor of the present Italian royal house. He was b. 1136, and was a capable and just ruler. He was married three, or even four times, and in his old age retired to the abbey of Haute Combe. It was probably here that he died, in 1188. c.c. 1838.

HUMILIS, BD. November 27. Nov., p. 331

Humilis of Bisignano was an Observant Franciscan lay-brother, very celebrated for miracles. He was consulted by Popes Gregory XV and Urban VIII. d. 1637. bd. 1882.

HUMILITAS, ST. May 22. MAY, p. 271

B. at Faenza in 1226. Both she and her husband became religious. Humilitas living for twelve years as a recluse; she then left her cell to direct the first house of Vallombrosan nuns at Malta, near Faenza, founding a second, at Florence, before her death in 1310.

HUMPHREY. *See also* Onuphrius.

HUMPHREY, ST, bp. March 8. MAR., p. 134

A monk of Prüm, who became bishop of Thérouanne in 856. His diocese was overrun by the Normans and Humphrey wanted to resign, but he persevered and lived to restore the diocese. In his later years he was as well abbot of St Bertin's at Saint-Omer. Also called *Hunfrid*. d. 871. *Onuphrius.*

HUNNA, ST. April 15. APR., p. 174

She was the wife of an Alsatian nobleman and was known to her neighbours as " the Holy Washerwoman " because of her willingness to lend a hand with any job. d. 679. cd. 1520.

†*HYACINTH, ST. August 17. AUG., p. 192

He was a Polish Dominican who is venerated as the Apostle of the North. He received the habit from St Dominic himself and preached with very great success in many countries of northern and central Europe, being credited with numerous miracles. But the details of his history are confused and uncertain. d. 1257. cd. 1594. *Hyacinthus.*

*HYACINTHA MARISCOTTI, ST. virg. January 30. JAN., p. 386

St Hyacintha presents the unusual case of a religious who began by being scandalously unfaithful to rule, was converted to better ways, relapsed, and so far recovered as to attain to heroic virtue. She belonged to a noble family at Vignarello, and when her younger sister was married was so annoyed and troublesome that her family insisted on her becoming a nun in a convent of Franciscan regular tertiaries at Viterbo. d. 1640. cd. 1807.

†*HYGINUS, ST, pope. January 11. JAN., p. 144

He was pope probably from 138 to 142 and is sometimes described as a martyr, but there is no early evidence for this.

*HYPATIUS, ST, ab. June 17. JUNE, p. 213

He was abbot of a monastery at Chalcedon and an early opponent of the Nestorian heresy. d. 446 (?).

I**A, ST,** virg. February 1. FEB., p. 15

This Irish maiden gave her name to St Ives in Cornwall (but not to the St Ives in Huntingdonshire), whither she came in the sixth century with SS Fingar, Piala, and other missionaries, and landed at the mouth of the Hayle river.

*IA, ST, virg. and mart. August 4. AUG., p. 55

She was a Greek slave, put to death with many other Christians in Persia during the persecution by King Sapor II, in 360.

IDA OF BOULOGNE, BD. April 13. APR., p. 148

Ida was descended from Charlemagne and married Eustace II, Count of Boulogne ; by him she was the mother of Godfrey and Baldwin de Bouillon. After the death of her husband she utilized much of her great property in helping the poor and founding monasteries. d. 1113.

IDA OF HERZFELD, ST. September 4. SEPT., p. 48

Ida was of royal birth and brought up at the court of Charlemagne ; on the death of her husband Egbert she retired from the court, passing the rest of her days in good works. Her biography consists mostly of improbable miracles. d. c. 813.

IDA OF LOUVAIN, BD, virg. April 13. APR., p. 150

The extant biography of this Ida, who entered a Cistercian convent at Roosendael, is full of surprising marvels, but is not a document that can be regarded with much confidence. Her cultus has survived to this day in Louvain. d. c. 1300 (?)

IDA OF TOGGENBURG, BD. November 3. NOV., p. 39

Ida is said to have been the childless wife of a Count Henry of Toggen-burg, from whom she suffered most malignant persecution. She ran away from home in fear of her life and eventually her husband agreed to her retiring to a nunnery at Fischingen. d. 1226. c.c. 1724.

IBAR, ST, bp. April 23. APR., p. 267

He was a missionary in Ireland before St Patrick, by whom he was probably consecrated bishop. Ibar established a monastery on Beg-Eire (Beggary). d. c. 499.

IDESBALD, ST, ab. April 18. APR., p. 214

Abbot of the Cistercian monastery of our Lady of the Dunes between Dunkirk and Nieuport. d. 1167.

†*IGNATIUS, ST, bp. and mart. February 1. FEB., p. 1

Ignatius, bishop of Antioch, surnamed "the God-bearer," was sent to Rome c. 107 to be executed as a Christian. On the way he wrote four letters from Smyrna to various churches and at Troas three more. These letters are still in existence and in them can be recognized the whole system of Christian doctrine as we know it to-day. Little is known of Ignatius himself except from these letters ; his journey to Rome was a sort of triumphal progress : he was killed by wild beasts in the arena. St Ignatius is named in the canon of the Mass.

*IGNATIUS, ST, bp. October 23. OCT., p. 308

This Ignatius was one of the best bishops who ever ruled the see of Constantinople and his story is part of general Church history. His refusal of holy communion to Bardas Cæsar, on account of open incest, led to his expulsion from the patriarchal throne and the intrusion of Photius. Ignatius was restored in 867, after receiving very harsh usage, and he spent the remaining years of his life in discharging his office with vigilance and energy, though not without a dispute with Pope John VIII. d. 877.

IGNATIUS AZEVEDO, BD, mart. July 15. JULY, p. 207

He joined the Society of Jesus at Coïmbra in 1548, attained office therein, and was greatly reverenced. In 1570 he was sent to Brazil in charge of a band of missionaries ; on the way their ship was stopped by a French privateer, whose Huguenot skipper had all the forty Jesuits, save one, put to death out of hatred of their faith. c.c. 1854.

IGNATIUS DELGADO, BD, bp. and mart. July 11. JULY, p. 146

Ignatius Delgado y Cebrian was a Spanish Dominican, vicar apostolic of Eastern Tonkin, who died in prison from exposure and ill-treatment in Annam in 1838, after having worked in that country for nearly fifty years. bd. 1900.

†*IGNATIUS OF LOYOLA, ST. July 31. JULY, p. 429

Ignatius was born at the castle of Loyola in 1491, a nobleman of Spain, and was bred to arms. After being wounded in battle against the French he heard the call of God and, after a pilgrimage to the Holy Land, studied for holy orders. The lessons Ignatius had learned as a soldier he employed in the service of the Church, and in 1534 he began the foundation of the company of spiritual soldiers whose characteristic virtue was to be obedience : they were to be ready to go wherever the good of the Church required (originally they had intended to be missionaries in Palestine), and for four hundred years its members have distinguished themselves in all fields, but especially in the education of boys and in foreign missions. The character of Ignatius was strong and determined, a prominent note being the simplicity of his aim—the greater glory of God. He and the Society of Jesus played a very conspicuous part in the counter-reformation, and his *Spiritual Exercises* continues to be a religious work of vast influence. From 1541 St Ignatius directed his society from Rome, and before his death his missionaries were found in the East Indies, Ethiopia, the Congo, South America, and elsewhere. d. 1556. cd. 1622.

*ILDEPHONSUS, ST, bp. January 23. JAN., p. 286

Nephew of St Eugenius of Toledo whom he succeeded in that see about 657. The writings of St Ildephonsus are notable for the fervour of their language concerning our Lady, and they had a marked effect on Spanish piety. Our Lady is said to have appeared to him in vision and to have given him a chasuble. d. 667.

ILLTYD, ST, ab. November 6. NOV., p. 70

St Illtyd (Iltyd, Illtud) was one of the greatest of the Welsh saints, but the details of his life are uncertain. He is said to have been cousin to King Arthur, to have married one Trynihid, and to have been captain of the guard to Paul of Penychen. But " the desert " called both him and his wife, and Illtyd founded the great monastery of Llanilltyd Fawr (Llantwit Major), which became a nursery of saints. According to some the original foundation was on Caldey Island. The Life of St Samon

calls Illtyd " of all the Britons the most learned in the Scriptures." d. *c.*
505. St Illtyd is said to be the original of the Sir Galahad of the Arthurian
romances. His feast is kept in the archdiocese of Cardiff and on Caldey.
Iltutus.

IMELDA, BD, virg. May 13.   MAY, p. 164
 She was the daughter of Count Egano Lambertini, of Bologna, who is
stated to have received her first holy communion miraculously at the age
of eleven and to have died immediately after, in 1333. c.c. 1826.

INDRACTUS, etc., **SS,** marts. February 5.   FEB., p. 84
 According to the legend Indractus was an Irishman treacherously
killed in England by heathen Saxons, together with his sister Dominica
and others *c.* 710. Their bodies were said to be buried at Glastonbury.

INES DE BENIGANIM, BD, virg. January 21.   JAN., p. 262
 B. near Valencia in 1625 and became an Augustinian hermitess at
Beniganim. Her name in religion was Josepha Maria, but in Spain she is
called as above. d. 1696. bd. 1888.

*INGENUINUS, ST, bp. February 5.   FEB., p. 83
 Bishop of Seben in the Tirol, who transferred the see to Brixen. He
appears to have died in exile, *c.* 605.

*INNOCENT, ST, bp. April 17.   APR., p. 197
 He was bishop of Tortona in Italy in the time of Constantine the
Great. d. *c.* 350. *Innocentius.*

†*INNOCENT I, ST, pope. July 28.   JULY, p. 392
 He was pope for sixteen years, during which time Alaric the Goth
sacked Rome. Innocent was a powerful upholder of the prerogatives of
the Roman see and a protector of St John Chrysostom. d. 417.

*INNOCENT V, BD, pope. June 22.   JUNE, p. 297
 In the age of St Thomas and St Albert the Great friar Peter of Tarentaise
was an eminent theologian. After holding office in his order he was made
archbishop of Lyons in 1272 and took a leading part at the oecumenical
council in that city on behalf of the reunion of the dissidents of the East.
In 1276 he was elected pope as Innocent V, the first Dominican to occupy
the pontifical throne, and his short rule was chiefly marked by his efforts
on behalf of peace, especially among the Italian states. d. 1277. c.c. 1898.

†*INNOCENTS, THE HOLY, marts. December 28.   DEC., p. 263
 The children murdered by order of King Herod as recorded in St
Matthew's Gospel, ii, 16–18. Their number is not known, but it cannot
have been large, legends to the contrary notwithstanding. They are
venerated as martyrs, *flores martyrum,* who died not only for Christ, but
instead of him ; their feast in the Latin rite presents some interesting
ritual peculiarities.

*IRENÆUS, ST, bp. and mart. March 24.   MAR., p. 384
 He was bishop of Sirmium, the capital of Pannonia, and was arrested
during the persecution of Diocletian : his mother, his wife, his children,
and his friends begged him to sacrifice to the gods, but he remained firm
and was beheaded in 304.

†*IRENÆUS, ST, bp. and mart. June 28.   JUNE, p. 365
 He was b. in Asia Minor *c.* 125, being a pupil of St Polycarp, who was
a disciple of St John the Divine. From his writings he is accounted a
father of the Church, for he laid the foundations of Christian theology :
he already speaks of the primacy of the Roman see and the duty of unity

therewith, and was a principal opponent of Gnosticism. He came as a missionary to Gaul and was made bishop of Lyons. d. *c.* 202. A late tradition says that he was martyred, but this is highly improbable. The feast of St Irenæus was extended to the whole Western church only in 1922, whereas it had been celebrated in the Eastern churches from early times.

*IRENÆUS and **MUSTIOLA, SS,** marts. July 3. JULY, p. 21
Irenæus was a deacon martyred during the third century at Chiusi; the matron Mustiola is said to have ministered to him and others in prison.

IRMENGARD, BD, virg. July 16. JULY, p. 218
Great-granddaughter of Charlemagne and abbess of Chiemsee; d. 866. c.c. 1928. *Hermenegardis.*

*IRMINA, ST, virg. December 24. DEC., p. 234
She was the eldest daughter of St Dagobert II. According to tradition she became a nun after undergoing a tragic love-affair; she was a zealous supporter of the missionary St Willibrord. d. *c.* 708.

ISAAC, ST, ab. May 30. MAY, p. 360
He warned the Arian emperor Valens to his face for the oppression of Catholics, and narrowly escaped death; later he became abbot of a large community of monks which he founded at Constantinople. d. *c.* 410.

*ISAAC, ST, mart. June 3. JUNE, p. 38
He was a Christian notary under the Moorish government in Spain, but gave up his post to be a monk. Having denounced Mohammed during a debate with the chief magistrate of Cordoba he was tortured and put to death in 851.

*ISAAC JOGUES, ST, mart. March 16. MAR., p. 269
One of the principal of the Martyrs of North America (q.v.). With other Jesuits he arrived in Canada in 1636 and was seized by the Mohawks while on his way to relieve distress in the Huron country. He was tortured but escaped, and later returned to work among the Indians. He was tomahawked in an Iroquois village on October 18, 1646. cd. 1930.

ISAAC THE GREAT, ST, bp. September 9. SEPT., p. 94
This Isaac (Sahak, Sahag) was called to rule the Armenian church *c.* 390, he being son of the katholikos St Nerses the Great. During his rule he did away with the custom of married bishops, confirmed the autonomy of his church, founded many monasteries, and with St Mesrop laid the foundations of Armenian vernacular literature: he translated a large part of the Bible himself. For some years Isaac was practically also civil ruler of his people. d. *c.* 440, aged over one hundred years.

*ISAAC OF SPOLETO, ST. April 11. APR., p. 125
Isaac was a Syrian who fled from monophysite persecution and took up his abode in a cave on Monte Luco at Spoleto; he was regarded as the unofficial superior of the other hermits there. d. *c.* 550.

ISABELLA. *See also* Elizabeth of Portugal.

ISABELLA OF FRANCE, BD, virg. February 26. FEB., p. 366
She was sister to St Louis of France. She refused several marriages, gave away much in alms, financed knights to go on the crusades, and after the death of her mother, Blanche of Castile, founded the Poor Clare monastery of Longchamps where she lived in retirement as a secular. d. 1270. bd. 1520.

ISAIAH BONER, BD. February 8. FEB., p. 128

An Augustinian friar and doctor of divinity of the University of Cracow. He was famous for his enthusiasm in expounding the Bible and the devotion that he kindled in his hearers. d. 1471.

*ISCHYRION, ST, mart. December 22. DEC., p. 220

An Egyptian official who was impaled for his faith in Christ in 250.

†*ISIDORE, ST, bp. and doct. April 4. APR., p. 45

St Isidore presided over the see of Seville in the sixth–seventh century, but no satisfactory early account of his life exists. It is known that he was a very learned man, an ardent educationist, and an encourager of monasticism ; he has sometimes been called the " schoolmaster of the Middle Ages." Among his writings are a sort of general encyclopædia and works of history, geography, astronomy, biography, and theology. At the Council of Toledo in 633 St Isidore was responsible for the decree that there should be a cathedral school in every diocese, where the liberal arts, Hebrew, and Greek should be taught. The completion of the Mozarabic liturgical rite is also attributed to him, and he finally converted the Visigoths from the Arian heresy. d. 636. c.c. 1598. Declared a doctor of the church by Pope Benedict XIV. *Isidorus.*

*ISIDORE OF ALEXANDRIA, ST. January 15. JAN., p. 189

He passed most of his life as governor of the hospital at Alexandria, but having incurred the anger of St Jerome (who suspected him of Origenism) he went away to Constantinople, where he d. 404.

*ISIDORE OF CHIOS, ST. mart. May 15. MAY, p. 189

Isidore was a martyr on Chios (in 251 ?), but the details of his passion appear to be fictitious.

*ISIDORE THE LABOURER, ST. May 15. MAY, p. 194

The patron of Madrid spent his life as a labourer on an estate just outside the city and exemplified Christian perfection in this simple calling. His wife is also popularly venerated, as Santa Maria de la Cabeza. d. 1130. The miracles attributed to St Isidore's intercession gave an impetus to his cultus, and he was cd. in 1622.

*ISIDORE OF PELUSIUM, ST, ab. February 4. FEB., p. 65

An abbot in Egypt, much admired by St Cyril of Alexandria ; a number of his letters are still preserved. d. *c.* 450.

ISNARDO, BD. March 22. MAR., p. 370

Isnardo of Chiampo received the religious habit from St Dominic himself and founded the first house of the Friars Preachers in Pavia. In spite of his austere life he was excessively fat and people used to ridicule him about it when he was preaching. d. 1244. c.c. 1919. *Isnardus.*

ISRAEL, BD. December 31. DEC., p. 306

A canon regular, provost of the house of Dorat in the Limousin, who d. in 1014. Little is recorded of his life.

ITA, ST, virg. January 15. JAN., p. 191

Otherwise *Ida, Mida,* etc. The most popular Irish woman saint after St Brigid. B. near Drum, co. Waterford. Wishing to dedicate herself to God she migrated to Hy Conaill, south-west of Limerick, where she gathered round her a large community of maidens. d. *c.* 570. Many anecdotes and miracles are related of St Ita, some of them edifying, some preposterous. Her feast is observed throughout Ireland.

ITHAMAR, ST, bp. June 10. JUNE, p. 133

He was the third bishop of Rochester and the first Englishman to occupy an English see, but nothing much more is known about him. d. *c.* 656.

IVES, ST, bp. April 24. APR., p. 280

The town of St Ives in Huntingdonshire takes its name from a local hermit who, according to the mediæval legend, was a Persian bishop who had fled from his own country during the seventh century. What element of truth there is in this story is not known. He had nothing to do with St Ives in Cornwall (*see* Ia).

*IVO HÉLORY, ST. May 19. MAY, p. 242

He was b. near Tréguier in Brittany and became an ecclesiastical and civil lawyer. As diocesan " official," first of Rennes and then of Tréguier, he protected orphans, defended the poor, and administered justice with an impartiality and kindliness that made him greatly respected and loved. The last fifteen years of his life were spent in parish work in Brittany, and he built a hospital out of his legal fees. d. 1303. cd. 1347. St Ivo is the patron saint of lawyers.

IVO OF CHARTRES, ST, bp. May 23. MAY, p. 284

Ivo was promoted from being provost of the Augustinian canons regular of Saint-Quentin to be bishop of Chartres in 1091, where he was one of the most venerated prelates of his age. He was involved in difficulties with his sovereign, King Philip, who wanted to contract an adulterous union, and strongly opposed the rapacity and simony of certain legates and other papal ecclesiastics. St Ivo was a voluminous writer, and some of his works have survived. d. 1115.

JACOBINUS DE CANEPACI, BD. March 3.   Mar., p. 45
A Carmelite lay-brother who died at Vercelli in 1508. c.c. 1845.
JACOPONE DA TODI, BD. December 25.   Dec., p. 246
Jacopone is famous as the putative author of the hymn " Stabat Mater dolorosa," and he certainly wrote many religious *laude* in Italian. In his own day he was well known, first as a " fool for Christ's sake," half-crazed by the tragic death of his young wife, and then as an irrepressible Franciscan Spiritual who made a written attack on Pope Boniface VIII, for which he was imprisoned. d. 1306. His cultus at Todi has not been confirmed.

JAMES. *See also* Didacus.

JAMES, ST, bp. January 16.   Jan., p. 202
Traditionally regarded as the first bishop of Tarentaise and a disciple of St Honoratus at Lérins. d. 429 (?). *Jacobus.*

JAMES BELL, BD, mart. April 20.   Apr., p. 242
A secular priest under Queen Mary who conformed to the state church under Elizabeth. He repented of so doing and on that account was h.d.q. at Lancaster in 1584. bd. 1929.

JAMES BENEFATTI, BD, bp. November 26.   Nov., p. 311
Bd James, a Dominican, was made bishop of his native Mantua in 1303. Immediately after his death in 1338 he was venerated as a saint, though from time to time his memory was almost forgotten. c.c. 1859.

JAMES BERTONI, BD. May 30.   May, p. 366
James Philip Bertoni was a confessor of the Order of Servants of Mary at Faenza. d. 1483. c.c. 1766.

JAMES BIRD, BD, mart. March 25.   Mar., p. 402
A young layman, nineteen years old, h.d.q. at Winchester in 1593 for being reconciled to the Catholic Church. bd. 1929.

JAMES CAPOCCI, BD, bp. March 14.   Mar., p. 253
A learned Augustinian friar who was promoted to be archbishop of Naples. d. 1308. c.c. 1911.

JAMES DUCKETT, BD, mart. April 19.   Apr., p. 233
Duckett, a London bookseller, born near Kendal, was hanged at Tyburn in 1602 for dealing in books with which " he furnished Catholics as well for their own comfort and instruction as for the assistance of their neighbours' souls." He had previously served a total of nine years' imprisonment on similar charges. bd. 1929.

*JAMES INTERCISUS, ST, mart. November 27.   Nov., p. 322
This James was martyred in Persia in 421. He is called *Intercisus,* " the Cut-to-Pieces," because he was put to death by his body being dismembered into twenty-eight parts.

JAMES SALÈS, BD, mart. February 7.   Feb., p. 112
B. in Auvergne in 1556, the son of a manservant, and became a Jesuit. In 1592, in company with William Saultemouche, a temporal coadjutor

of the Society, he went to conduct missions and preach at Aubenas, a town of the Cévennes, where the Calvinists were very active. One night a gang of Huguenots came to plunder the church ; the two Jesuits were seized and brought before an assembly of ministers who disputed with Father Salès about the Holy Eucharist. He was set upon and killed by the Huguenot soldiers, and Saultemouche was stabbed to death in trying to defend him ; 1593. Both were bd. 1926.

JAMES SALOMONIUS, BD. May 31.   MAY, p. 376

A confessor of the Order of Preachers ; he was prior of several houses in Italy and ended his life in semi-solitude at Forli. d. 1314. c.c. 1526.

JAMES STREPAR, BD, bp. October 21.   OCT., p. 292

He was a Polish Franciscan, a successful missionary among the schismatics and pagans of western Russia, and in 1392 was appointed archbishop of Halitch. d. c. 1410. c.c. 1791.

JAMES THOMPSON, BD, mart. November 28.   NOV., p. 337

He was a secular priest (alias Hudson), hanged for his priesthood at York in 1582. bd. 1895.

*JAMES THE ALMSGIVER, BD. January 28.   JAN., p. 355

James was a young Lombard lawyer and priest who bought a decayed hospital and restored it for the use of the poor. Discovering that in the past its revenues had been improperly appropriated by the bishops of Chiusi he applied to the then bishop for restitution. It was refused, and Bd James obtained judgements against the see in both ecclesiastical and civil courts. Thereupon the bishop had him waylaid and murdered in 1304. James has been claimed as a tertiary of their order both by the Servites and Franciscans.

†*JAMES THE GREATER, ST, ap. July 25.   JULY, p. 354

All that is known about St James, brother of St. John the Apostle, is to be found in the gospels. He was a fisherman from Bethsaida. Outside of Spain almost all scholars of consideration and critical students of history agree that this apostle never preached the gospel in Spain ; and there is a like agreement that his relics were not conveyed thither after his death and enshrined at Santiago de Compostela.

†*JAMES THE LESS, ST, ap. May 1.   MAY, p. 3

James the Less, i.e. the younger, was the apostle who became first bishop of Jerusalem. He was martyred c. 62 by the Jews, being stoned to death or, as some say, thrown from a pinnacle of the temple. St James was the writer of the epistle in the Bible that bears his name.

JAMES OF BITETTO, BD. April 27.   APR., p. 307

Or " of Illyricum " (Dalmatia), his native country. A lay-brother of the Observant Franciscans, who spent most of his life at the friary of Bitetto, near Bari. d. c. 1485. bd by Pope Innocent XII.

JAMES OF CERQUETO, BD. April 17.   APR., p. 205

A hermit friar of St Augustine who d. in 1367, and whose tomb was honoured with miracles. c.c. 1895.

JAMES OF CERTALDO, BD. April 13.   APR., p. 150

He was a monk in the Camaldolese monastery at Volterra, where he acted as parish priest. d. 1292.

*JAMES DELLA MARCA, ST. November 28.   NOV., p. 335

James Gangala was b. in the March of Ancona in 1391. He abandoned the law to become a Franciscan, and he was a fellow-worker of St. John of Capistrano in spreading the Observant reform and in apostolic work in central and northern Europe : his preaching brought both Bd Bernardino of Fossa and Bd Bernardino of Feltre into the Franciscan order, and it is said that not a day passed in forty years without his preaching the word of God. He was a strong supporter of the establishment of charitable pawn-shops (*montes pietatis*). d. 1476. cd. 1726.

JAMES OF MEVANIA, BD. August 23. AUG., p. 287

He was prior of the first Dominican friary in his native town of Mevania (Bevagna) in Umbria, where he was very active in combating a local antinomian sect. d. 1301. c.c. 1400.

*JAMES OF NISIBIS, ST, bp. July 15. JULY, p. 193

James was a Syrian monk who became bishop of Nisibis in Mesopotamia, but much of the traditional story of his life has been shown to be untrue. His learning and writings rank him after St Ephraem among the doctors of the Syrian church, and he is greatly venerated by the Armenians, for whom he wrote treatises of instruction. He d. probably *c*. 338.

JAMES OF OLDO, BD. April 19. APR., p. 217

Or "of Lauda." He was a wayward and pleasure-loving young man of Lodi whose life was changed in rather striking circumstances. His wife and he then became Franciscan tertiaries and James was eventually ordained priest. d. 1404.

JAMES OF ULM, BD. October 11. OCT., p. 158

James Griesinger left the army of Naples and became a Dominican lay-brother at Bologna ; he was a master in the art of painting on glass, and during his fifty years of religious life that was his principal employ-ment. d. 1491. bd. 1825.

JAMES OF VORAGINE, BD, bp. July 13. JULY, p. 172

Bd James was a Dominican friar and in 1292 he was appointed arch-bishop of Genoa, but his claim to fame is the authorship of the *Legenda Sanctorum*, now known everywhere as "The Golden Legend." Of this extraordinarily popular book Caxton issued the first printed English edition at Westminster in 1483, when it had already been translated into five vernacular languages. Bd James d. *c*. 1298. c.c. 1816.

JANE. *See also* Joan, Jeanne.

†*JANE FRANCES DE CHANTAL, ST. August 21. AUG., p. 251

Jane Frances Frémyot was b. at Dijon in 1572 and in 1592 married the Baron de Chantal, with whom she lived happily for eight years, having four children. After her husband's death St Jane Frances, under the direction of St Francis de Sales, founded and presided over the Visitation nuns, of whom 66 convents were established during her lifetime : it was a congregation on entirely new lines, and met with much opposition, for it welcomed especially widows and those whose poor health prevented them from entering the other religious orders. St Jane Frances was an uncompromising, sensitive, rather intense person, who suffered a great deal in body and mind during her last years ; St Francis, who loved her dearly, said she was "the perfect woman, whom Solomon hardly found in Jerusalem." d. December 13, 1641. cd. 1767. *Joanna*.

JANE SCOPELLI, BD, virg. July 9. JULY, p. 108

She founded a Carmelite convent at Reggio, insisting that it should be endowed with freely given alms and not with the property she had inherited : it took forty years to establish. d. 1491. c.c. 1771.

JANE OF PORTUGAL, BD, virg. May 12.   MAY, p. 150

B. 1452, daughter of Alphonso V of Portugal. It was her wish to be a nun, and at the age of nineteen she entered the Dominican convent at Aveiro, but her father would not let her be professed and she was continually subject to annoyance from her relations who wanted her to make a political marriage. d. 1490. c.c. 1693.

JANE OF TOULOUSE, BD, virg. March 31.   MAR., p. 455

She was affiliated to the Carmelites by St Simon Stock at Toulouse and was the first tertiary of that order ; she is reckoned the foundress of the Carmelite third order accordingly. She used to train young boys with a view to their becoming friars, and her shrine at Toulouse was thronged with pilgrims. d. 1286. c.c. 1895.

†*JANUARIUS, ST, bp. and mart. September 19.   SEPT., p. 251

Januarius (Gennaro) was bishop of Benevento, put to death for Christ at Pozzuoli during the persecution of Diocletian, but otherwise nothing is known of him or of those who suffered with him. All the fame of Januarius rests on the phenomenon called the liquefaction of the alleged relic of his blood which is preserved in the cathedral of Naples, a happening of which there are records for the past four hundred years.

*JAPAN, THE MARTYRS OF. February 5.   FEB., p. 86

Six Franciscans, three Jesuits and nineteen lay people, put to death out of hatred of the faith (by a kind of crucifixion) at Nagasaki in 1597. All were Japanese except some of the friars ; three of them were boys between twelve and fifteen. cd. 1862.

JARLATH, ST, bp. June 6.   JUNE, p. 81

St Jarlath is venerated as founder of the see of Tuam, where he probably ruled a community of monks as their abbot-bishop. Little is known of him, but his monastic school was far-famed, among his pupils being St Brendan of Clonfert. d. *c.* 550. St Jarlath's feast is kept throughout Ireland. *Jarlathus.*

*JASON, ST, bp. July 12.   JULY, p. 155

St Paul's host at Salonika (Acts xvii, 5–9). He is said to have become bishop of Tarsus and to have died on the island of Corfu.

JEANNE. *See also,* Joan, Jane.

JEANNE DE LESTONNAC, BD. February 2.   FEB., p. 42

She was a niece of Montaigne and wife of Gaston de Montferrant, by whom she had four children. At the age of forty-seven, when her husband was dead and her children provided for, Mme de Lestonnac became a Cistercian nun. The life was too much for her health and she left, but in 1606 she founded an institute of Religious of Notre Dame whose object was the education of girls of all social classes especially in view of the Calvinism rampant in Bordeaux at that time. The institute prospered, but Bd Jeanne was removed from its control by the wicked intrigues of one of the sisters ; this womane ventually repented, but only a few years before the death of Bd Jeanne in 1640. bd. 1891. *Joanna.*

JEANNE DE MAILLÉ, BD, virg. March 29.   MAR., p. 438

Jeanne Marie was the daughter of the Baron of Maillé ; she is said to have lived in virginity with her husband until his death in 1362. She then became a Franciscan tertiary and lived a very mortified and charitable life, suffering much from ill health. The closing years of her life she passed as a solitary at Tours. Some people regarded Bd Jeanne Marie as mad,

and she received much unkindness from her relatives. d. 1414. c.c.
1871.

JERMYN GARDINER, BD, mart. March 7. Mar., p. 199

A layman, secretary to Stephen Gardiner, Bishop of Winchester, h.d.q.
with Bd John Larke in 1544. bd. 1886. *Germanus.*

†*JEROME, ST, doct. September 30. Sept., p. 374

Eusebius *Hieronymus* Sophronius, the father of the Church most
learned in the Bible, was b. *c.* 342 at Stridonium in Dalmatia. After a
varied life of study, solitude, activity, and travel he retired to Bethlehem
in 385, where he carried on his great work of revising and re-translating
the Latin Bible. He was helped in this by some of the famous circle of
women whom he had directed at Rome, notably St Paula. From history
and his extant letters St Jerome is seen to have been an outspoken man
who made enemies as well as great friends (he referred to St Augustine as
a "little Numidian ant," and to emenders of biblical texts as "presumptuous
blockheads ") : he was no admirer of moderation, whether in virtue or
against evil ; and his breach with his old friend Rufinus over the errors
of Origen is an unhappy story. But if he was swift to anger he was also
swift to remorse, even more severe on his own shortcomings than on those
of others. d. 420. St Jerome is often represented in pictures as a cardinal,
because of services he discharged for Pope St Damasus. *Hieronymus.*

JEROME and **VALENTINE, BB.** *See* Annam, Martyrs of, II.

JEROME DE ANGELIS, BD, mart. December 4. Dec., p. 64

A Sicilian Jesuit who was martyred by burning at Tokio in 1623.
bd. 1867.

†*JEROME EMILIANI, ST. July 20. July, p. 282

B. at Venice in 1481, and became a soldier of the Republic and a
loose liver. He was brought to reason by a miraculous deliverance from
captivity, received holy orders, and gave himself to all kinds of charitable
works throughout the Venetian territory ; at Bergamo he started one
of the first institutions to shelter penitent prostitutes. In 1532 St Jerome
founded a congregation of Clerks Regular, primarily to care of orphans,
the Somaschi, so called from the place of their first establishment, Somascha
in Lombardy. d. 1537. cd. 1767. St Jerome was named the patron saint
of orphans and abandoned children in 1928.

JEROME RANUZZI, BD. December 11. Dec., p. 142

A confessor of the Servites, who was for a time personal adviser to
Count Frederick of Montefeltro. d. 1455. c.c. 1775.

†*JOACHIM, ST. August 16. Aug., p. 186

Joachim is the name traditionally given to the father of our Lady.
According to the apocryphal Gospel of James he was a man of great wealth
whose long childlessness was broken by the birth of Mary to him and St
Anne, his wife.

JOACHIM PICCOLOMINI, BD. April 16. Apr., p. 186

He belonged to the great Piccolomini family of Siena and joined the
Servite Order, being distinguished therein for his devotion and goodness.
d. 1305. bd. by Pope Paul V.

JOAN. *See also* Jane, Jeanne.

JOAN SODERINI, BD, virg. September 1. Sept., p. 11

B. at Florence in 1301. She joined the Servite regular tertiaries and was the constant personal attendant of St Juliana Falconieri during her last illness. d. 1367. c.c. 1827. *Joanna.*

JOAN THOURET, BD, virg.   August 25.   AUG., p. 312

Jeanne Antide Thouret was b. near Besançon in 1765, daughter of a tanner. In 1787 she became a Sister of Charity of St Vincent de Paul ; these were dispersed at the revolution and Bd Joan, who had not made her profession, eventually started a school and other good works at Besançon at the request of the vicar general. By 1807 her helpers numbered a hundred and formed the new institute of Daughters of Charity, which three years later Bd Joan established at Naples as well. For some time, owing to the action of the Archbishop of Besançon, there was schism among the nuns, but Bd Joan was faithful to the directions of the Holy See and her foundation grew and prospered. d. 1826. bd. 1926.

*JOAN OF ARC, ST, virg.   May 30.   MAY, p. 355

B. at Domrémy in 1412, daughter of a peasant farmer. When she was seventeen, as a result of supernatural " voices," she induced Charles VII of France to entrust her with the leadership of an army against the English invaders. Her military successes enabled Charles to be crowned at Rheims within a few months. In 1430 Joan was captured by the Burgundians and sold to the English, who conspired with the unscrupulous bishop of Beauvais, Cauchon, to bring her before an ecclesiastical court which had been carefully " packed." This court decided that her " voices " were diabolical and that Joan was a heretic ; she was then handed over to the secular arm and was burnt alive at Rouen, May 31, 1431. A revision of her " trial " declared her innocent in 1456, and she was cd. in 1920. It must be noted that Joan was canonized as a holy maiden, and not as a martyr (which she was not) as is often supposed.

JOAN OF AZA, BD.   August 8.   AUG., p. 99

She was a noble Spanish lady, wife of Felix de Guzman, who became the mother of two sons and a daughter and finally (by promise) of that St Dominic who founded the Order of Preachers. She d. towards the end of the twelfth century. c.c. 1828.

JOAN OF ORVIETO, BD, virg.   July 23.   JULY, p. 335

Bd Joan, usually called " Vanna," was a Dominican tertiary who led a life of devotion to God and care of the poor at Orvieto. d. 1306. c.c. 1754.

JOAN OF SEGNA, BD, virg.   November 17.   Nov., p. 229

A number of miracles are related of this Franciscan tertiary, but very little is known of her life. She was a peasant girl at Segna, near Florence. d. 1307. c.c. 1798.

JOAN OF VALOIS, BD.   February 4.   FEB., p. 74

She was the daughter of King Louis XI and was misshapen in body. Her father married her to Louis of Orleans, who afterwards obtained a declaration of the nullity of the union. Bd Joan thereupon went to live in retirement at Bourges, where, with the help of the Franciscan Gabriel Mary, she founded the order of nuns of the Annunciation of our Lady (Annonciades) in 1500. d. 1504.

*JOANNICIUS, ST.   November 4.   Nov., p. 57

After being a soldier in the imperial army, Joannicius, at the age of forty, received the monastic habit ; he was a notable opponent of Iconoclasm, and one of the leading monks of his age, living in various monasteries in Bithynia. Among his disciples was St Euthymius the Thessalonian. d. 846.

JOAVAN, ST, bp. March 2. MAR., p. 15

An Irishman who was a disciple of his uncle St Paul of Leon in Britain and Brittany; he was consecrated bishop for Leon, but d. soon after, *c.* 576.

†*JOHN, ST, ap. and evang. December 27. DEC., p. 254

St John, " the disciple whom Jesus loved," is often distinguished in English as " the Divine," *scl.,* " the Theologian." He was a Galilean fisherman and younger brother of St James the Greater; to him was committed the care of His blessed Mother by our Lord on the cross. St John was the author of the gospel which bears his name, of three canonical epistles, and of the Apocalypse. He is the only one of the Twelve Apostles who is certainly known not to have been a martyr, dying at Ephesus *c.* 100, at a great age. The feast called of " St John before the Latin Gate," kept in the Western church on May 6, probably commemorates the dedication of a church at the place by the Porta Latina at Rome where, according to an old but unreliable tradition, the apostle was thrown into a vat of boiling oil by order of the emperor Domitian and was delivered unharmed. *Joannes.*

†*JOHN I, ST, pope and mart. May 27. MAY, p. 327

He became pope in 523 and three years later went as head of an embassy to the emperor Justin .I at Constantinople from Theodoric the Goth. On his return to Ravenna the pope was thrown into prison by Theodoric on suspicion of having conspired with Justin. John d. a few days later as a result of this treatment, but his claim to be venerated as a martyr has been contested.

JOHN and **PETER, BB,** marts. September 3. SEPT., p. 38

St Francis of Assisi sent John of Perugia and Peter of Sassoferrato into Spain to preach the gospel to the Moors. They were seized in a mosque at Valencia and, upon refusing to accept Islam, were beheaded, in 1231. bd. 1783.

JOHN and **PETER, BB,** marts. May 22. MAY, p. 272

John de Cetina and Peter de Duenas were Franciscan friars martyred by Mohammedans at Granada in 1397.

†*JOHN and **PAUL, SS,** marts. June 26. JUNE, p. 346

These martyrs, named in the canon of the Mass, suffered in Rome, perhaps under Julian the Apostate in 362. Their so-called " acts " are a pious fiction.

JOHN, SERGIUS, etc., **SS,** marts. March 20. MAR., p. 340

Twenty monks of the monastery of St Sabas in the Jordan valley were killed and many more wounded out of hatred of the Faith when the Arabs raided their house in 796. The story is told in detail by one of the monks who escaped, Stephen the Poet.

JOHN ALMOND, BD, mart. December 5. DEC., p. 82

He was b. at Allerton, near Liverpool, and worked on the English mission as a secular priest for ten years. He was h.d.q. for his priesthood at Tyburn in 1612. bd. 1929.

JOHN AMIAS, BD, mart. March 16. MAR., p. 288

Amias or Anne was a clothmonger at Wakefield who on the death of his wife went to the college at Rheims and was ordained. He was h.d.q. for his priesthood with Bd Robert Dalby at York in 1589. bd. 1929.

JOHN BECHE, BD, ab. and mart. December 1. DEC., p. 14

John Beche (or Thomas Marshall) was translated in 1533 from the abbacy of St Werburgh's, Chester, to St John's, Colchester. He was a friend of More and Fisher, and refused to deliver up his monastery at the dissolution. He was condemned in the same way and for the same reason as BB Richard Whiting and Hugh Faringdon, and was h.d.q. at Colchester a fortnight after them in 1539. bd. 1895. His feast is observed in the dioceses of Westminster and Brentwood and by the English Benedictines.

*JOHN BERCHMANS, ST. November 26. Nov., p. 312

He was b. in 1599, son of a master-shoemaker at Diest in Flanders. He joined the Society of Jesus at the age of seventeen and was sent to Rome for his novitiate ; many testimonies to the perfection of his life still exist, and from them it appears that he closely anticipated " the little way " of St Teresa of Lisieux. Assiduous study during the heat of a Roman summer undermined his health and he died at the age of twenty-two in 1621. Numerous miracles were attributed to his intercession and his cultus quickly spread to his native Flanders. cd. 1888.

JOHN BODEY, BD, mart. November 2. Nov., p. 23

He was a layman, a fellow of New College, Oxford, who was h.d.q. at Andover in 1583 for denying the royal supremacy in spiritual matters. bd. 1929.

JOHN BONNARD, BD, mart. May 1. MAY, p. 18

John Louis Bonnard was a priest of the Paris Society of Foreign Missions who was martyred by beheading in Annam in 1852. bd. 1900.

*JOHN BONUS, BD. October 23. OCT., p. 312

He, until he was about forty years old, lived a depraved life, making his living as an entertainer in the houses of the Italian nobles. A dangerous illness changed his heart and he became a hermit near Cesena, where a number of other penitents joined him ; these Bd John formed into a congregation (the " Boniti ") which later formed one of the constituent elements of the Augustinian hermit friars. Their founder led a most austere life and received many supernatural enlightenments. d. 1249. c.c. 1483.

*JOHN CAMILLUS BONUS, ST, bp. January 10. JAN., p. 133

A bishop of Milan who was a strenuous defender of orthodoxy against the monothelite heresy. St Charles Borromeo translated his relics to a more worthy shrine. d. c. 660.

†*JOHN BOSCO, ST. January 31. FEB., p. 21

B. in 1815, son of a Piedmontese peasant. After difficulties he became a priest and started boys' club and school work in Turin which was soon in a very flourishing state. Don Bosco as well made his name as a preacher, showed himself a born leader of boys, and before long miracles of healing were reported of him. He built a church in honour of St Francis of Sales, and here in 1854 he laid the foundations of the Salesian Congregation. In 1858 it received its preliminary approbation from the Holy See and permission to ordain its members in view of a college for late vocations that Don Bosco had established. The society grew apace, and it sent missionaries to Patagonia. Don Bosco also founded the Daughters of St Mary Auxiliatrix to do for girls what the Salesians were doing for boys, and an association of lay people to help in these educational works. He also undertook the building of new churches, and when he went abroad to collect for these he was everywhere acclaimed as a saint and a wonderworker and money poured in. But Don Bosco was wearing himself out with work, his strength gave way altogether, and he died in 1888 : the whole of Turin was present at his funeral. cd. 1934. The Salesians have now over 10,000 religious in all parts of the world.

JOHN BOSTE, BD, and others. *See* Durham Martyrs.

*JOHN BRÉBEUF, ST, mart. March 16.   MAR., p. 267

One of the principal of the Martyrs of North America (q.v.). He landed at Quebec with two other Jesuits in 1615 and laboured among the Hurons and other Indians for thirty-four years. In 1649 he was put to death with the most atrocious tortures by the Iroquois, together with St Gabriel Lalemant.

JOHN DE BRITTO, BD, mart. February 4.   FEB., p. 77

B. in Portugal in 1647 and went to India as a Jesuit missionary. He became superior of the Madura mission and followed the example of Father de Nobili, living the life of an Indian in all things lawful. In 1686 he was tortured in the Maravar country for preaching against Siva, and his recovery thereafter was deemed miraculous. He refused to return to Europe and in 1693 was put to death because he had opposed the worship of the gods of the country. bd. 1853.

*JOHN CALYBITES, ST. January 15.   JAN., p. 191

After being a monk at Gomon on the Bosphorus he returned home and lived disguised as a beggar outside his parents' house in a little hut, whence his name (*kalybe*). The same idea of disguise occurs in other legends, *e.g.* of St Alexis. d. *c.* 450.

†*JOHN CANTIUS, ST. October 20.   OCT., p. 272

He was born at Kenty in Silesia *c.* 1395 and for practically his whole life occupied the chair of Sacred Scripture in the University of Cracow. He imposed on himself penitential conditions of life and his goods were always at the disposition of the poor, who were continually clearing him right out. d. December 24, 1473. cd. 1767. St John Cantius is the only confessor-not-a-bishop who has different hymns for Matins, Lauds, and Vespers in the Roman Breviary.

JOHN CASSIAN, ST, ab. July 23.   JULY, p. 330

B. in the East *c.* 360. He was a monk in Egypt and elsewhere but eventually arrived at Marseilles where he founded a house of monks and another of nuns, which he directed from the abbey of Lérins. For the guidance of his communities Cassian wrote two books, his *Institutes* and his *Conferences*, which were influential far beyond anything within the intention of the author, and through St Benedict John Cassian left his mark on all Christendom. d. *c.* 433.

†*JOHN CHRYSOSTOM, ST, bp. and doct. January 27.   JAN., p. 327

B. at Antioch *c.* 344. After his ordination in 386 he soon developed that great gift of eloquence which obtained for him the name of Chrysostom, "Golden Mouth." He was called to be archbishop of Constantinople in 398. He undertook the reform of the great diocese, founded hospitals and homes for the sick and needy, adjusted the troubles of the church of Ephesus, and sent missionaries to the Goths. The principal Byzantine Liturgy bears his name, as having been revised by him. In 403 at the Synod of the Oak a gathering of St John's enemies got him banished from his see. He was soon recalled, but, having had occasion to rebuke the empress, he was exiled again, being sent into the depths of Armenia. From thence it was ordered that he should be removed to Pytius in Colchis, but at his age he succumbed to the weather of winter during the journey and

d. at Comana in Pontus on September 14, 407. January 27, his feast day in the West, is the anniversary of the translation of his relics to the church of the Apostles at Constantinople in 438. St John Chrysostom was the most prolific preacher of the four great Greek doctors of the Church and the first of the three outstanding hierarchs of the Eastern church. During his later years he seems to have been sometimes rather unnecessarily violent and provocative in his language ; but the story of his banishment is one of the most flagrant injustice, which the Roman see tried in vain to remedy.

*JOHN CLIMACUS, ST, ab. March 30. MAR., p. 442

He is sometimes called John the Scholastic but the more usual name comes from his book the *Climax of Perfection* or *Ladder of Paradise*, a mystical work intensely popular in both East and West in the Middle Ages. He was a monk of the monastery of Mount Sinai and afterwards a solitary in the same neighbourhood. Some years before his death he was made abbot at Sinai, and his fame as a holy man spread throughout Palestine and Arabia. d. *c.* 605 or *c.* 675.

*JOHN COLOMBINI, BD. July 31. JULY, p. 447

He was a merchant of Siena who for two-thirds of his life was an eminent citizen of that town, and avaricious, ambitious and bad-tempered. About 1344 he underwent a sudden conversion ; after some years he arranged to separate from his wife, and formed a small society of men who preached penance and specialized in composing business and other private disputes. They were nicknamed the " Gesuati " and in 1367 were approved by Pope Urban V as an institute of lay-brothers, though formally called Apostolic Clerks of St Jerome ; in 1668 they were dissolved. Bd. John d. in 1367 and was bd. by Pope Gregory XIII.

JOHN CORNAY, BD, mart. February 8. FEB., p. 131

A French missionary in Annam, b. at Loudun in 1809. When a brigand chief denounced the Christians of Ban-no the Abbé Cornay was betrayed by the chief's wife ; he was kept in a cage, often in irons and cruelly beaten, for three months—and when he was examined by the mandarins he was expected to sing to them as the beauty of his voice was well known. He was beheaded on September 20, 1837. bd. 1900 with a number of fellow-martyrs.

JOHN CORNELIUS, BD, and others. *See* Dorchester Martyrs.

†*JOHN DAMASCENE, ST, doct. March 27. MAR., p. 413

He was born in Damascus about 676, son of a Christian official at the court of the khalifa, and after a good education succeeded to his father's post. John filled this for three years and then became a monk in the monastery of St Sabas near Jerusalem. He boldly defended the veneration of images against the emperor, Leo the Isaurian, wrote numerous works summing up and expanding the theology of the first Christian centuries, and was the greatest hymn-writer of the Eastern church (with the possible exception of St Romanus). St John Damascene was the last of the Greek fathers and the first of the Christian Aristotelians. He died at Mar Saba *c.* 749 and his relics were eventually translated to Moscow. He was proclaimed a doctor of the Church in 1890.

JOHN DOMINICI, BD, bp. June 10. JUNE, p. 138

B. at Florence in 1376 and became one of the most distinguished Dominicans of his era. He was the leader in the restoration of discipline to his order in Italy and was keenly interested in the education of the young. He was appointed archbishop of Ragusa and cardinal in 1408 and was instrumental in ending the Great Schism of the West ; as papal legate in Bohemia he preached against the Hussites. Bd. John wrote two educational treatises of importance. d. 1419. c.c. 1832.

JOHN DUCKETT, BD, mart. September 7. SEPT., p 78

He was a kinsman of Bd James Duckett and became a secular priest in 1639. While ministering in county Durham he was arrested for his priesthood and h.d.q. at Tyburn in 1644. bd. 1929.

†*JOHN EUDES, ST. August 19. AUG., p. 213

He was the son of a yeoman farmer, and was b. at Ri in France in 1601. He was ordained priest in 1625 and for twenty years was a member of the French Oratory, engaged on mission work and study, and he twice distinguished himself by his fearlessness in attending victims of the plague. St John Eudes was the greatest " home missioner " of the seventeenth century, and an apostle of devotion to the Sacred Heart. But the work of his life was the foundation of the Sisters of our Lady of Charity of the Refuge, from whom sprang the Good Shepherd nuns, and of a congregation for the sanctification of the clergy and aspirants to the priesthood (Congregation of Jesus and Mary, " Eudists "), in connexion with which he established six seminaries. d. 1680. cd. 1925.

JOHN FELTON, BD, mart. August 8. AUG., p. 100

Felton was a layman, living in Southwark, who was h.d.q. in St Paul's churchyard in 1570 for affixing to the door of the Bishop of London's house a copy of the bull of Pope St Pius V whereby Queen Elizabeth was excommunicated.

JOHN FINCH, BD, mart. April 20. APR., p. 242

A yeoman farmer of Eccleston in Lancashire who was h.d.q. at Lancaster in 1584 for being reconciled to the Church and for sheltering priests.

*JOHN FISHER, ST, bp. and mart. June 22. JUNE, p. 300

B. in 1469, son of a draper at Beverley in Yorkshire. He was educated at Cambridge and in later life became chancellor of that university, which owes much to him. In 1502 he was appointed chaplain to the king's mother, Lady Margaret Beaufort, and in 1504 bishop of Rochester. He was a most devoted bishop at a time when bishops often were not, and so keen a scholar that he began to learn Greek when he was forty-eight and collected one of the finest libraries in Europe. Fisher was a reformer but he preferred prayer before controversy and martyrdom before violence. He opposed Henry VIII's nullity suit and ecclesiastical supremacy and was in consequence attainted of misprision of treason ; he was committed to the Tower and in 1535 beheaded on Tower Hill : though only sixty-six years old he was almost too weak to walk. cd. 1935. The feast of St John of Rochester is kept on various dates throughout England.

JOHN FOREST, BD, mart. May 22. MAY, p. 276

John Forrest was a Franciscan friar of the Observance at Greenwich and confessor to Catherine of Aragon. In common with his fellow-Observants he strongly opposed the queen's " divorce " and was consequently kept in a state of semi-captivity. In 1538 he was tried for denouncing the king's supremacy over the Church and was burnt at Smithfield. His feast is observed by the Friars Minor.

JOHN GRANDE, BD. June 3. JUNE, p. 42

He gave up the linen trade in Seville, changed his surname to Pecador,

" the Sinner," and occupied a hermitage near Marcena. Then it was revealed to him that he was called to serve God in other ways and he went to Xeres and devoted himself to the care of the sick, suffering and afflicted in the prison. His services in the public hospital caused him to be put in charge of a new one that was founded, and he joined the Hospitallers of St John of God and gathered a band of young helpers round him. Bd John never lost his interest in prisoners, when the English stormed Cadiz he looked after three hundred fugitive Spanish soldiers, and he is said to have foretold the destruction of the Armada. d. 1600. bd. 1853.

†*JOHN GUALBERT, ST, ab. July 12.   JULY, p. 150
He was born of noble parents at Florence towards the end of the tenth century and was bred to arms. Having for love of virtue relinquished his obligation in a blood-feud, his action was miraculously recognized by Almighty God, and he shortly after became a Benedictine. Dissatisfied with the observance of his monastery, he started a house of stricter life at Vallis Umbrosa, near Fiesole, from which developed the Vallombrosan congregation of monks, which he directed until his death in 1073. cd. 1193.

JOHN HAILE, BD, mart. May 4.   MAY, p. 58
He was a secular priest, vicar of Isleworth, Middlesex, who was h.d.q. at Tyburn in 1535, one of the first group of English martyrs of the Reformation.

JOHN HOUGHTON, BD. For this and other English Carthusian martyrs *see* Carthusian Martyrs.

JOHN IRELAND, BD, mart. March 7.   MAR., p. 199
A secular priest, chaplain to St Thomas More, who was h.d.q., with Bd John Larke in 1544. bd. 1929.

JOHN JONES, BD, mart. July 12.   JULY, p. 162
John Jones (*alias* Buckley) was b. at Clynnog Fawr and became a Franciscan. In 1592 he was sent from Rome on the English mission and was arrested and tortured in 1596. H.d.q., for his priesthood at St Thomas Waterings in the Old Kent Road, London, in 1598. bd. 1929.

JOHN KEMBLE, BD, mart. August 22.   AUG., p. 275
For fifty-three years he worked as a secular priest in Monmouthshire and Herefordshire, from his headquarters at Pembridge Castle. In his eighty-first year he was convicted for his priesthood and h.d.q. at Hereford in 1679. bd. 1929.

JOHN LARKE, BD, mart. March 11.   MAR., p. 199
Rector of St Ethelburga's, Bishopsgate, then of Woodford, Essex, and then of Chelsea, to which he was nominated by St Thomas More. He was h.d.q. at Tyburn in 1544 for denying the royal supremacy. His feast is observed in the diocese of Brentwood.

JOHN DU LAU, BD. *See* September Martyrs.

*JOHN LEONARDI, ST. October 9.   OCT., p 122
He was apprenticed to a druggist at Lucca *c.* 1550, but became a secular priest and founded the small congregation of Clerks Regular of the Mother of God. For some reason this undertaking was unpopular in Lucca, and Bd John had to carry on his work, with the encouragement of the Holy See, elsewhere. He was helped by St Philip Neri, St Joseph Calasanctius, and Cardinal Baronius, and Pope Clement VIII commissioned him to superintend the reform of the monks of Vallombrosa and Monte Vergine. d. 1609. cd. 1938.

JOHN LICCIO, BD. November 14.   Nov., p. 181
    A confessor of the Order of Preachers in Sicily ; d. 1511. c.c. 1753.

JOHN LLOYD, BD, mart. July 22.   JULY, p. 323
    A Breconshire man and a secular priest in South Wales. He was h.d.q. for his priesthood after the Oates " plot " at Cardiff in 1679. bd. 1929.

JOHN LOCKWOOD, BD, mart. April 13.   APR., p. 153
    B. 1561 in Yorkshire. He was a secular priest on the English mission for forty-four years and was h.d.q. for his priesthood at York in 1642. He was eighty-one years old. bd. 1929.

JOHN MARINONI, BD. December 13.   DEC., p. 158
    He was chaplain to a hospital at Venice, then a canon of St Mark's cathedral, and finally, in 1530, a Theatine Clerk Regular. Bd John was an associate of St Cajetan, with whom he went to Naples and helped in the establishment of *montes pietatis*. d. 1562. c.c. 1762.

*JOHN MARK, ST, bp. September 27.   SEPT., p. 333
    The " John, surnamed Mark " referred to in Acts xii has been conjecturally identified by many writers with St Mark the evangelist ; but liturgical tradition in both East and West regards him as a separate person, who became bishop at Byblos in Phoenicia.

JOHN MASSIAS, BD. September 18.   SEPT., p. 249
    He was b. in Spain in 1585 and emigrated to Peru where, after working on a cattle ranch, he became a Dominican lay-brother at Lima. His physical austerities had to be restrained by his superior and miracles were attributed to him by the poor of the city. d. 1645. bd. 1837.

JOHN NELSON, BD, mart. February 3.   FEB., p. 59
    A Nelson of Skelton, Yorkshire. Went to Douay at the age of forty and was ordained in 1576. In the same year he was arrested in London and sentenced for refusing the oath of supremacy. H.d.q. at Tyburn 1578. Bd John was received into the Society of Jesus shortly before his death. bd. 1886.

*JOHN NEPOMUCEN, ST, mart. May 16.   MAY, p. 199
    He was b. in Bohemia *c.* 1345 and his appellation is derived from the name of his native town, Nepomuk. He had a distinguished ecclesiastical career and eventually became chaplain to Queen Sophia, second wife of Wenceslaus IV of Bohemia ; according to strong local tradition Wenceslaus, who unjustly suspected his wife of infidelity, had St John drowned in the Moldau for refusing to disclose Sophia's confessions, in 1393. But no mention of this is made in contemporary documents, and other incidents occurred which could easily account for the undoubted murder of St John by the king. There has been acrimonious controversy on the subject. John Nepomucen was cd. in 1729.

JOHN OGILVIE, BD, mart. March 10.   MAR., p. 178
    He was son of the head of the younger branch of the Ogilvies and of a daughter of Lady Douglas of Lochleven ; he was brought up a Calvinist and sent abroad to be educated ; received into the Church at the Scots College, Louvain, at the age of seventeen in 1596. Ogilvie joined the Society of Jesus and, after a dozen years in Austria and France, was allowed to return to Scotland in 1613. He worked zealously among the Catholics for some time and made a few converts, but was betrayed in Glasgow and arrested. In a vain attempt to make him betray his co-religionists he was

forcibly kept from sleep for eight days and nights on end. He was eventually hung at Glasgow for denial of the royal supremacy in religion, 1615. bd. 1929.

JOHN PAYNE, BD, mart. April 2.   APR., p. 24
 B. at Peterborough. He was a priest from Douai who had his head-quarters with the Petres at Ingatestone in Essex. After imprisonment and torture he was condemned at Chelmsford on a trumped up charge of conspiracy and h.d.q. in that town in 1582. He is commemorated liturgically in the dioceses of Northampton and Brentwood.

JOHN PELINGOTTO, BD. June 1.   JUNE, p. 12
 He was the son of a merchant of Urbino, who became a Franciscan tertiary and gave up all his life to prayer and almsdeeds. d. 1304. c.c. 1918.

JOHN PERBOYRE, BD, mart. September 11.   SEPT., p. 147
 John Gabriel Perboyre held responsible posts in the Lazarist congregation for ten years before he was sent as a missionary to China in 1835. Persecution was renewed four years later, and Bd John was strangled in 1840, after undergoing incredible tortures. He was the first missionary in China to be beatified, in 1889.

JOHN PLESINGTON, BD, mart. July 19.   JULY, p. 279
 B. near Garstang and worked on the mission in North Wales and Cheshire. H.d.q., for his priesthood at Chester after the Oates " plot " in 1679. bd. 1929.

JOHN ANGELO PORRO, BD. October 24.   OCT., p. 328
 A confessor of the Servite Order who d. at Milan in 1506. c.c. 1737.

JOHN RAINUZZI, BD. JUNE 8.   JUNE, p. 112
 He is called " the Almsgiver " and is supposed to have d. at Todi in 1330 but the evidence concerning him is scanty and unsatisfactory.

*JOHN FRANCIS REGIS, ST. June 16.   JUNE, p. 205
 B. in 1597 and when eighteen joined the Society of Jesus at Béziers. He early showed his influence for good over people, especially children, and after his ordination in 1631 he was sent out to give missions. He worked unwearyingly, mainly among the poorer folk of Languedoc and Auvergne ; no hardships, from weather, travelling or any cause, could deter him, and he changed the lives of many and brought many Huguenots back to the Church. At Le Puy he established a refuge for penitent women, which was the occasion of his being slandered and of other difficulties being put in his way ; he also set up a granary for the poor, and miraculously increased its contents. d. 1640. cd. 1737.

JOHN DE RIBERA, BD, bp. January 6.   JAN., p. 96
 Son of a grandee of Spain and promoted to the archbishopric of Valencia in 1568, an office of very great difficulty and responsibility which he filled for forty-two years. His diocese was full of Moriscos and Jews whose activities caused him great alarm and he was one of those responsible for the deportation of Moriscos from Valencia in 1609. Bd John's public acts and political views were not all on the same level of enlightenment with the personal virtues which caused his beatification in 1796. d. 1611.

JOHN RIGBY, BD, mart. June 21.   JUNE, p. 284
 A layman, b. at Harrock Hall, Wigan, who was h.d.q. at Southwark in 1600 for being reconciled to the Holy See. bd. 1929.

JOHN ROBERTS, BD, mart. December 10.   DEC., p. 127
 B. at Trawsfynydd in Merioneth in 1577. He was received into the

Church abroad and professed a Benedictine at Compostella in 1600. Bd John was the chief assistant of Dom Augustine Bradshaw in the founding of the monastery of St Gregory at Douai, now Downside Abbey ; at the same time he was engaged on the mission in England and several times imprisoned and released ; his efforts for the sick during the plague of 1603 made his name known throughout the land. He was h.d.q. for his priesthood at Tyburn in 1610. bd. 1929. Bd John Roberts is an outstanding figure among the numerous Welsh martyrs.

JOHN RUYSBROECK, BD. December 2. DEC., p. 30

John Ruysbroeck, b. near Brussels in 1293, is one of the most famous of mystical writers. After his ordination he lived with his uncle, a secular canon, and then with others they withdrew to Groenendael in the forest of Soignies and formed a community of contemplative Augustinian canons regular. Bd John was an exemplary religious and he exercised a great influence on his contemporaries : among his writings are the *Adornment of the Spiritual Marriage* and the *Book of the Spiritual Tabernacle*. d. 1381. c.c. 1908. *Rusbrochius.*

JOHN SARKANDER, BD, mart. March 17. MAR., p. 302

Parish priest at Holleschau in Moravia. During the Thirty Years' War he was accused by the Hussites of conspiring to bring Polish troops into the country and ordered to disclose the confessions of his penitent Baron von Lobkovitz, governor of Moravia. On his refusal he was thrice racked and otherwise tortured, and died as the result, after a month's lingering in agony. d. 1620. bd. 1859.

JOHN SLADE, BD, mart. October 30. OCT., p. 366

A schoolmaster who was h.d.q. at Winchester in 1583 for having denied the royal supremacy in spiritual matters. bd. 1929.

JOHN SORDI, BD, bp. and mart. March 16. MAR., p. 285

Also known as John Cacciafronte, after his stepfather. He was Benedictine abbot of St Lawrence's at Cremona and bishop of Mantua, but resigned the see to his predecessor, who had for a time followed the antipope Victor. John was then made bishop of Vicenza, and was murdered in 1183 by a man whom he had rebuked for embezzling episcopal revenue. He was at once acclaimed a martyr by the people of his diocese.

JOHN SORETH, BD. July 30. JULY, p. 419

John Soreth was prior general of the Carmelites from 1451 to 1471, and was a forerunner of St Teresa in his efforts for the reform of that order, establishing houses of strict observance in every province. He inaugurated the first convents of Carmelite nuns, in the Netherlands *c.* 1452, a movement which quickly spread to other countries. d. 1471. c.c. 1865.

JOHN SOUTHWORTH, BD, mart. June 28. JUNE, p. 373

This John was b. in Lancashire, ordained at Douai, and in 1619 sent on the English mission. He worked in London and Lancashire and in 1627 was sentenced to death but reprieved ; he was in prison again in 1632 and four years later was most active on behalf of the victims of an outbreak of plague. In 1654 he was h.d.q. at Tyburn for his priesthood. bd. 1929. Bd John's relics were found at Douai in 1927 and in 1930 were solemnly enshrined in Westminster cathedral.

JOHN STONE, BD, mart. May 12. MAY, p. 152

An Austin friar h.d.q. at Canterbury, probably in 1539, for denying the royal supremacy.

JOHN STOREY, BD. June 1.   JUNE, p. 14

B. *c.* 1504. As " the most noted civilian and canonist of his time " Storey was appointed the first regius professor of civil law at Oxford. After 1537 he married, practised as a barrister, and entered parliament. Under Edward VI he opposed the Act of Uniformity and under Elizabeth the Supremacy bill and was imprisoned. He escaped abroad but was kidnapped, brought back, and condemned on a false charge of treason. h.d.q. at Tyburn, 1571.

JOHN WALL, BD, mart. August 22.   AUG., p. 274

A Lancashire man (*alias* Johnson, Webb, Dormer) who became a secular priest and then a Franciscan, with the name of Father Joachim-of-St-Anne. After working in Worcestershire for over twenty years he was h.d.q. for his priesthood at Worcester in 1679. bd. 1929.

JOHN ZEDAZNELI, ST. November 4.   Nov., p. 55

He was the leader of that band of Syrian monks, evangelists in Georgia (Iberia), that included St Khio Mghvimeli, St David Garedjeli, and St Antony of Martkofi. They were the fathers of a very flourishing monasticism in Georgia. Sixth century.

*JOHN THE ALMONER, ST, bp. January 23.   JAN., p. 282

Made patriarch of Alexandria *c.* 608. when one of his first deeds was to distribute 80,000 pieces of gold to hospitals and monasteries ; charity on this scale was continued throughout his pontificate. The whole of St John's life was to match . He d. in 616 (?) at Cyprus while on the way to visit the emperor at Constantinople.

†*JOHN THE BAPTIST, ST. June 24.   JUNE, p. 319

The forerunner of the Messias, Christ himself saying of him that, " Among those that are born of women there is not a greater prophet " (Luke vii, 28). St Augustine and other doctors are of the opinion that John was sanctified from original sin in his mother's womb, and the Church, contrary to her usual custom, celebrates with a feast his birthday in the flesh on June 24—one of the earliest and greatest of Christian festivals. The Baptist's (*i.e.*, Baptizer) life is narrated in the gospels, especially by St Luke, his death on account of his protest against the wickedness of Herod constituting him a martyr : his beheading is commemorated on August 29. St John is the first in the second series of saints named in the canon of the Mass ; before the Reformation over 500 English churches were dedicated in his honour.

JOHN BAPTIST. *See* at the end of the Johns.

†*JOHN OF THE CROSS, ST, doct. November 24.   Nov., p. 287

John de Yepes was b. in the province of Old Castile in 1542, the son of a weaver of good family. He became a Carmelite friar in 1563 and was selected by St Teresa to be the first member of the first friary of the reformed observance, at Duruelo. The more public side of his life was in establishing this reform among the men Carmelites, and he underwent much persecution, including imprisonment at Toledo. It is as a supreme mystic that the Church calls St John a " doctor," his teaching being contained in half a dozen treatises, some poems, and a few letters (*The Ascent of Mount Carmel, The Dark Night of the Soul, The Spiritual Canticle,* etc.). He was a faithful follower of ancient tradition, but he writes of God from experience and with hardly any reference to the mystical writings of his predecessors. St John was treated with great inhumanity by his superiors during the last months of his life, and died at

Ubeda on December 14, 1591. cd. 1726. Declared doctor of the Church in 1926.

*JOHN JOSEPH OF THE CROSS, ST. March 5.   MAR., p. 66

Charles Gaetano was b. in the island of Ischia in 1654. He became a Franciscan of the Alcantarine reform, was master of novices at Naples, guardian at Piedimonte de Alife, and held other offices. When the Spanish friars in Italy separated from the Italians, St John Joseph was mainly instrumental in forming the Italian Alcantarine province and successfully conducted it through its difficult beginnings. He had the gift of miracles and other supernatural endowments. d. 1734. cd. 1839.

JOHN THE DWARF, ST. September 15.   SEPT., p. 178

John Kolobos, " the Dwarf," was a disciple of St Poemen in the desert of Skete. He was famous among the Egyptian monks of the fifth century, and amusing stories are told of his absentmindedness. He was by nature quick-tempered and conceited, yet was known among his fellows for his equability and humility.

†*JOHN OF GOD, ST. March 8.   MAR., p. 119

B. in Portugal in 1495 and for forty years led an adventurous and varied life as shepherd, soldier, peddler, and looking after Christian slaves among the Moors. He then settled down in Granada to tend the sick and dying, and laid the foundations of the order of Hospitallers of St John-of-God. This was in 1540 ; St John d. in 1550, and the order, which still flourishes, was not properly organized till twenty years later. He was cd. in 1690 and later named (with St Camillus of Lellis) patron of hospitals, nurses, and the sick.

JOHN OF THE GRATING, ST, bp. February 1.   FEB., p. 17

He received this name, *de Craticula*, from the metal railings that surrounded his tomb. He was a Breton and a disciple of St Bernard at Clairvaux. He founded Cistercian houses at Bégard and Buzay in Brittany and became bishop of Aleth, which see he removed to Saint-Malo. d. 1170.

JOHN THE IBERIAN, ST, ab. July 12.   JULY, p. 158

John the Iberian (Georgian), also called " the Hagiorite," parted from his wife and family and became a monk in Bithynia, with his son St Euthymius. Thence they went to the monastery of St Athanasius on Mount Athos and there, c. 998, founded the still-existing monastery of Iviron for men of the Iberian nation. d. c. 1002.

JOHN DELLA PACE, BD. November 12.   NOV., p. 149

John Cini was a soldier, living at Pisa. In 1296 he became a Franciscan tertiary and established several religious and charitable organizations, including a confraternity of flagellants. d. 1332. c.c. 1856.

*JOHN THE SILENT, ST, bp. May 13.   MAY, p. 161

B. in 454 at Nicopolis in Armenia, where he established a monastery which he directed till he was made bishop of Colonia. After nine years he resigned and became a monk under St Sabas near Jerusalem ; here he passed the rest of his life, living for long periods as a solitary in the desert. d. 558.

JOHN THE SPANIARD, BD. June 25.   JUNE, p. 343

A confessor of the Carthusian Order. He was first a monk at Montrieu in France, then of the Grande Chartreuse under St Anthelmus, and was the first prior of the charterhouse of Reposoir, near the lake of Geneva. Bd John drew up constitutions for the Carthusian nuns. d. 1160. c.c. 1864.

JOHN OF ALVERNIA, BD. August 9.   AUG., p. 120

B. at Fermo in 1259, became a Friar Minor in 1272, and was sent to La Verna, where he lived a semi-eremitical existence, preaching throughout the neighbouring country and northern Italy. He had the gift of infused knowledge of things and of souls. d. 1322. c.c. 1880.

JOHN OF AVILA, BD. May 10.   MAY, p. 124

This John, a secular priest of the diocese of Seville, was one of the most powerful religious influences in sixteenth-century Spain as a preacher, writer, and adviser of saints and sinners. His unfulfilled ambition was to be a missionary in Mexico : instead he was appointed missioner in Andalusia, where his fiery zeal made him enemies among the rich, who at one time delated him to the Inquisition—he was acquitted. Bd. John's letters are among the classics of Spanish literature. d. 1569. bd. 1894.

*JOHN OF BERGAMO, ST, bp. and mart. July 11.   JULY, p. 138

He was elected bishop of Bergamo c. 656, and was a man of great holiness and learning. He is erroneously venerated as a martyr at the hands of the Arians : he d. in peace c. 690.

*JOHN OF BEVERLEY, ST, bp. May 7.   MAY, p. 89

B. at Harpham and educated at Canterbury under SS Theodore and Adrian. He became a monk of Whitby, was made bishop of Hexham and subsequently of York. St Bede, who was ordained by St John, testifies to his holiness, as does Bd Alcuin. In 717 John retired to the monastery he had founded at Beverley and d. there in 721. His shrine was a favourite pilgrimage place before the Reformation, and his feast is now kept by the dioceses of Hexham (May 7), Liverpool, Leeds, Middlesbrough, and Lancaster (October 25).

JOHN OF BRIDLINGTON, ST. October 11.   OCT., p. 157

Little is known of the life of John Thwing, who studied at Oxford University and joined the Augustinian canons at Bridlington. In due course he became prior and ruled the house for seventeen years, dying in 1379. Many miracles were recorded at his tomb and he seems to have been canonized by a bull of Pope Boniface IX in 1403. St John's feast is celebrated by the Canons Regular of the Lateran and in the diocese of Middlesbrough.

†*JOHN OF CAPISTRANO, ST. March 28.   MAR., p. 421

B. at Capistrano in the Abruzzi in 1386. John was a lawyer and became governor of Perugia, but at the death of his wife when he was thirty he joined the Franciscans. He was a disciple and companion of St Bernardine of Siena in his preaching and in the establishment of the Observant reform. In 1451 he was sent by Pope Nicholas V into Bohemia to reconcile the Hussites; his methods of fulfilling that mission have been severely criticized. John was an active leader of the Hungarian resistance under Hunyady Janos against the Turks who were threatening their country, and was in Belgrade during the siege. d. October 23, 1456. cd. 1724.

*JOHN OF CHINON, ST. June 27.   JUNE, p. 362

He was a hermit at Chinon during the sixth century and had a wide reputation as healer and seer.

JOHN OF DUKLA, BD. October 1.   OCT., p. 11

He was a Polish confessor of the Observant branch of the Friars Minor, and a successful missioner in Galicia. d. 1484. c.c. 1739.

*JOHN OF EGYPT, ST. March 27.   MAR., p. 416

This John was the most famous of the desert hermits after St Antony : he was consulted by emperors and his praises were sung by St Jerome, Palladius, St John Cassian, St Augustine, and many others. He was a carpenter, born near Assyut, and went into the desert when he was twenty-five. He was noted for miracles of healing and for remarkable prophecies. Palladius gives an account of a visit that he paid to St John. d. 394.

JOHN OF FABRIANO, BD. March 11.   MAR., p. 198

John Baptist Righi was a Friar Minor of great natural ability who from humility refused to acquire more learning than was needful for ordination ; he led a life of great physical rigour. d. at Massaccio in 1539. c.c. 1903.

†*JOHN OF ST FACUNDO, ST. June 12.   JUNE, p. 149

This John was b. at Sahagun in Spain in 1419 and educated at the Benedictine abbey of San Fagondez. He was ordained priest and received several benefices, but he gave them up (his conscience being touched in the matter of pluralism), and in 1463 became an Augustinian friar. He was a very effective preacher in the city of Salamanca, which at that time was peculiarly in need of an apostle. d. 1479. cd. 1690.

JOHN OF THE GOTHS, ST, bp. June 26.   JUNE, p. 351

This John, bishop of the Goths on the north of the Black Sea, is honoured in the East because of his defence of the veneration of holy images against the iconoclasts. He was eventually driven from his diocese by the invading Khazars. d. at Amasia in Asia Minor *c.* 800.

JOHN OF GORZA, ST, ab. February 27.   FEB., p. 374

A large owner of land near Metz, who in 933 revived the almost extinct abbey of Gorza. After being elected abbot in 960 he introduced reforms which spread to many other Benedictine houses. On one occasion he was sent on an imperial mission to the court of the khalif Abd-ar-Rahman at Cordova. d. 974.

†*JOHN OF MATHA, ST. February 8.   FEB., p. 115

John of Matha came from Provence and was an exceptionally holy and zealous man. He founded the Trinitarian Order for the redemption of captives, which was approved by Pope Innocent III, and he died at Rome on December 17, 1213. This is practically all that is known for certain of St John of Matha, as it seems that his more extended biographies are based on spurious records. The Trinitarians still exist as a small order of mendicant friars engaged in teaching, nursing, and other work.

JOHN OF MEDA, ST. September 26.   SEPT., p. 328

This John is associated with the early days of the religious movement known as that of the *Humiliati*, but little is known of him. d. 1159 (?).

*JOHN OF NICOMEDIA, ST, mart. September 7.   SEPT., p. 73

" A man of secular dignity " who, when the edict of Diocletian against the Christians was published in Nicomedia, tore it down and was punished with death, in 303.

JOHN OF PARMA, BD. March 20.   MAR., p. 344

B. 1209 and became seventh minister general of the Friars Minor, in which capacity he made a visitation in England. He governed his order with great firmness in very troubled times for ten years, and was sent as papal legate to the Emperor and patriarch of Constantinople. For the last thirty years of his life he lived in retirement at the hermitage of Greccio. d. 1289. c.c. 1777.

JOHN OF PRADO, BD, mart. May 24. MAY, p. 293

B. 1584 and joined the barefooted Franciscans of the strict observance. He was sent as a missionary with special powers to the Mohammedans of the Barbary coast, where he was martyred with two other friars in 1631. bd. 1728.

*JOHN PENARIENSIS, ST. March 19. MAR., p. 323

He is said to have been a Syrian refugee from monophysite persecution who founded religious houses at Spoleto and Pesaro during the sixth century.

JOHN OF PENNA, BD. April 3. APR., p. 43

The story of Bd John of Penna (or Pinna), who spent his life in France and Italy, fills chapter 45 of the *Little Flowers of St Francis*. d. 1271. c.c. by Pope Pius VII.

JOHN OF PULSANO, ST, ab. June 20. JUNE, p. 256

He was b. at Matera in the kingdom of Naples and became a monk at a monastery where his austerity made him unpopular. After wandering about and suffering a good deal of persecution he settled at Pulsano, near Monte Gargano, where he founded a monastery which prospered and was at one time the mother-house of a small Benedictine congregation. d. 1139.

*JOHN OF REOMAY, ST, ab. January 28. JAN., p. 348

This John was one of the pioneers of monasticism in France ; he founded the monastery of Reomay under the inspiration of the Egyptian St Macarius, which afterwards became the Benedictine Moutier-Saint-Jean. d. *c.* 544.

JOHN OF RIETI, BD. August 9. AUG., p. 121

A confessor of the order of Hermit Friars of St Augustine. d. *c.* 1350. c.c. 1832.

JOHN OF SAHAGUN, ST. *See* John of St. Facundo.

JOHN OF SALERNO, BD. August 9. AUG., p. 118

John Guarna was prior of the first Dominicans in Etruria and founded the famous friary of Santa Maria Novella at Florence in 1221. d. 1242. c.c. 1783.

JOHN OF TOSSIGNANO, BD, bp. July 24. JULY, p. 343

John Tavelli, a member of the now extinct order of the Gesuati, was chosen bishop of Ferrara in 1431. He is chiefly remembered for his translations of books of the Bible, etc., into Italian. d. 1446. c.c. Pope Benedict XIV.

JOHN OF TRIORA, BD, mart. February 13. FEB., p. 212

John Lantrua was b. in Liguria in 1760, became a Friar Minor in 1777 and a missionary in China in 1799. It was a time of almost unremitting persecution in that country, but he worked there under the greatest difficulties for fifteen years before he was arrested. He was strangled at Ch'angsha Fu on February 7, 1816. bd. 1900.

JOHN OF VALENCE, BD, bp. March 21. MAR., p. 362

A Cistercian monk, abbot of Bonneval, who was elected to the see of Valence in 1141. d. 1146. c.c. 1901. *See also* April volume, p. 294.

JOHN OF VALLOMBROSA, BD. March 10. MAR., p. 175

This John was a Vallombrosan monk who became a secret necromancer ; on being discovered he was imprisoned for a time and on his release was a changed man. He was given permission to live as a solitary, and he turned his considerable intellectual abilities to better use. He enjoyed the friendship of St Catherine of Siena. d. *c.* 1380.

JOHN OF VERCELLI, BD. December 1.   DEC., p. 8

He became the sixth master general of the Order of Preachers in 1264 and discharged his office with much energy and enlightenment. He fulfilled various missions for the Holy See, including drawing up the *schema* for the second oecumenical council of Lyons, and was one of the early propagators of devotion to the holy name of Jesus. d. 1283. c.c. 1903.

JOHN OF VILNA, etc., **SS,** marts. April 14.   APR., p. 165

John, Antony, and Eustace, Lithuanians of high rank, were cruelly put to death out of hatred of the faith by pagans at Vilna in 1342.

JOHN OF WARNETON, BD, bp. January 27.   JAN., p. 347

He was a pupil of St Ivo of Chartres, a monk of Mont-Saint-Eloi, archdeacon of Arras, and finally bishop of Thérouanne ; it required a papal order to make him accept this last dignity. He was a firm, but gentle prelate and refused to take any action against some people who tried to murder him. d. 1130.

JOHN BAPTIST OF THE CONCEPTION, BD. February 14. FEB., p. 225

Reformer of the Trinitarian Order, b. in Spain in 1561. In 1597 he formed a community of reformed Trinitarians at Valdepeñas, which was approved at Rome. This caused a rift within the order and Bd John Baptist was subjected even to personal violence by followers of the old ways. But thirty-four Trinitarian houses accepted the reform, and were made into a separate province, before his death at Cordova in 1613. bd. 1819. *Joannes Baptista.*

JOHN BAPTIST MACHADO, BD, mart. May 22.   MAY, p. 277

He was a Portuguese Jesuit and a missionary in Japan and was martyred near Nagasaki in 1617, together with the Franciscan Bd Peter and a Japanese youth, Bd Leo. bd. 1867.

*JOHN BAPTIST ROSSI, ST. May 23.   MAY, p. 279

This secular priest was b. in the diocese of Genoa in 1698 and spent all his life in Rome where he was first curate and then a canon at the collegiate church of Sta Maria in Cosmedin. St John was specially noted for his work among the sick in hospitals, among the labourers in the City, and among homeless women, for whom he established a hospice. So sought after was he as a confessor that he was dispensed from his obligation of choir office. d. 1764. cd. 1881.

†*JOHN BAPTIST DE LA SALLE, ST. May 15.   MAY, p. 183

B. at Rheims in 1654 and ordained at the age of twenty-six when he was already a canon of the cathedral chapter. The whole of his life was devoted to education, especially of the poor, and the establishment of the congregation of the Brothers of the Christian Schools : but he was not simply an administrator and organizer, he was a thinker and initiator of the first importance in the history of the education of the young. He set out his revolutionary system in the *Manual for Christian Schools*, among whose innovations was class instead of individual teaching and the learning of reading first in the vernacular instead of in Latin. Of course he experienced bitter opposition from schoolmasters, and at one moment the very existence of his congregation was in danger. d. 1719. cd. 1900.

†*JOHN BAPTIST VIANNEY, ST. August 9.   AUG., p. 103

John Mary Baptist Vianney was b. at Dardilly in 1786. While an ecclesiastical student he was conscripted for the army and for over a year was, more or less accidentally, a deserter in hiding. His studies were so unsatisfactory that there was considerable difficulty about his ordination, which eventually took place in 1815. Three years later M. Vianney was appointed *curé* of Ars, an obscure village near Lyons : here the rest of his life was spent and from thence his name sounded throughout the world. He was absorbed in his parish, but people came from all parts of Europe to his confessional ; he had gifts of healing and hidden knowledge, and was tormented by evil spirits ; to any but spiritual means to spiritual ends he was indifferent ; his clothes were ragged, his food poor, sleep insufficient, he had no learning—and the Church has exalted him with Pope Gregory VII and Philip Neri. In the twelve months before his death in 1859 over a thousand pilgrims came to Ars. cd. 1925. Named principal patron saint of parochial clergy in 1929.

JOLENTA OF HUNGARY, BD. June 15.   JUNE, p. 190
    Niece of St Elizabeth of Hungary and sister of Bd Cunegund. She was happily married to Duke Boleslas the Good of Halicz and in widowhood became a Poor Clare at Gnesen. The Poles call her Bd Helena. d. 1299.

*JONAS AND BARACHISIUS, SS, marts. March 29.   MAR., p. 430
    During the persecution of king Sapor these two Persian monks were tortured in divers ways and put to most cruel deaths, in 327. There is an extant account of their passion which seems to have been written by an eye-witness.

JORDAN OF PISA, BD. March 6.   MAR., p. 93
    Jordan of Pisa was one of the makers of the modern Italian language, being the first to use the Tuscan dialect instead of Latin in his sermons. He received the Dominican habit at Pisa in 1280, and when he was lector there Santa Maria Novella at Florence attained the greatest celebrity as a place of studies. Jordan was a great upholder of the value of preaching, and was a fine preacher himself—sometimes for two hours on end. The Confraternity of the Holy Redeemer that he founded at Pisa still exists there with its original constitutions. d. 1311. c.c. 1833. *Jordanus.*

JORDAN OF SAXONY, BD. February 15.   FEB., p. 232
    He joined St Dominic in 1220 and while yet a novice was summoned to the first general chapter of his order at Bologna. At the third chapter he was elected second master general, and his time of office saw a great extension of the order. Among the priories founded were those of Ratisbon, Constance, Bâle, Freiburg, and Strasbourg, and the friars reached Denmark. Bd Jordan was an eloquent preacher (a sermon of his attracted Albert the Great to the Dominicans) and his words were such that their effect did not wear off : he was much esteemed by Pope Gregory IX. Bd Jordan was drowned while on the way to Palestine in 1237. c.c. 1828.

†*JOSAPHAT, ST, bp. and mart. November 14.   Nov., p. 169
    Josaphat Kuntsevich was b. of Catholic parents at Vladimir, c. 1582. He became a monk of the Byzantine rite and abbot of Vilna at the time when the Orthodox dioceses of the province of Kiev were newly reunited with the Holy See. Josaphat's life was devoted to maintaining and spreading this union in the face of acute difficulties from Catholics as well as schismatics. In 1617 he was appointed archbishop of Polotsk, and he added very necessary diocesan reform to his work of unity. He consistently refused to be dragged into politics and other civil activities, and his combination of gentleness and firmness, knowledge and goodness gained

him many followers. But secular interests were against him, a schismatic reaction set in, and in 1623 he was murdered by a mob at Vitebsk in Russia. St Josaphat was canonized in 1867, and his feast extended to the whole Western church in 1882.

†*JOSEPH, ST. March 19.   MAR., p. 318

Husband and guardian of the Blessed Virgin Mary, and foster-father of our Lord Jesus Christ. All that is known of this " just man " is contained in chapters i and ii of the gospels of St Matthew and St Luke ; other early works contain particulars that are not reliable. Devotion to St Joseph is relatively recent, but the unerring instinct for holiness of the Christian folk at large has in the past 400 years raised him to the highest rank of the Church's saints. He has two feasts, on March 19 and, a solemnity as patron of the Universal Church, ten days after Low Sunday. *Josephus.*

*JOSEPH BARSABAS, ST. July 20.   JULY, p. 290

The disciple of our Lord who was put in competition with St Matthias to succeed Judas Iscariot in the apostleship. His feast is kept by the Latins of Jerusalem.

†*JOSEPH CALASANCTIUS, ST. August 27.   AUG., p. 324

Joseph Calasanza, one of the foremost figures in the educational activities of the Counter-reformation, was the son of an Aragonese nobleman, b. in 1556. The first years of his priestly life were spent in pastoral and administrative work in his own country, but in 1592 he went to Rome and remained there, working for the free schooling of poor and neglected children. In face of great difficulties he established a congregation for the purpose, the Clerks Regular of the Religious Schools, or " Piarists." On one occasion one of his subordinates caused St Joseph to be brought before the Holy Office and afterwards to be removed from control of the congregation, until he was restored by a special commission. Joseph's patience under these trials caused Pope Benedict XIV to refer to him as " a second Job." d. 1648. cd. 1767.

JOSEPH COTTOLENGO, BD. April 29.   APR., p. 334

In 1827 Canon Joseph Benedict Cottolengo founded at Turin, without a penny of capital, a small hospital for the poor. It grew, and during the cholera epidemic in 1831 was transferred to the suburb of Valdocco and called the Little House of Divine Providence. It then grew even more quickly and branched into schools, almshouses, refuges, orphanages, asylums, workshops, conducted by several religious institutes which Bd Joseph inaugurated. It is significant that for this vast and complex organization he kept no books or accounts and invested no money—he spent it as it came in. To-day the Cottolengo Charitable Institute, which seeks out the most abandoned and miserable, has branches in British East Africa, Palestine, Switzerland, and Aust⁻⁾ᵃ. Bd Joseph d. in 1842 and was bd. in 1917.

*JOSEPH ORIOL, ST. March 23.   MAR., p. 378

This Joseph was the son of humble parents at Barcelona, and was enabled by his parish priest to be ordained. He lived throughout his adult life on bread and water and engaged in the cure of souls : he was especially successful with soldiers and children. At one time he was strongly moved to go on the foreign missions, but while on his way to Rome he fell ill and had a vision in consequence of which he returned to his home. St Joseph had the gifts of miracle and prophecy in an eminent degree. d. 1702. cd. 1909.

JOSEPH PIGNATELLI, BD. November 11. Nov., p. 133

In the twenty years that followed the suppression of the Society of Jesus by Pope Clement XIV in 1773, Father Joseph Pignatelli lived at Bologna and devoted himself to studying the history of the order and spiritually and materially aiding its former members. In 1799 he was allowed to organize a quasi-novitiate and continued to work unceasingly for the restoration of the Society; so far as the kingdom of Naples was concerned this took place in 1804, and Father Joseph was named provincial, first of Naples and then of Italy. This priest of "manly and vigorous holiness" d. 1811. bd. 1933.

JOSEPH TOMMASI, BD. January 1. Jan., p. 24

B. 1649, son of the Duke of Palermo, and became a Theatine clerk regular. In 1673 he was definitely established at Rome, where he soon won the reputation of a saint and also of a very fine scholar. His liturgical writings show him to have been a man of profound learning, critical spirit, and independence of judgement. He was the confessor of Cardinal Albani and required his penitent to accept the papacy under pain of mortal sin, and Clement XI, in his turn, imposed the cardinalate on Joseph Tommasi (properly *Tomasi*). In his titular church of San Martino ai Monti he would allow no music but plain chant, and would himself conduct the catechism classes there. Miracles are said to have taken place even before his death in 1713. bd. 1803.

*JOSEPH OF ARIMATHÆA, ST. March 17. Mar., p. 296

All that is known about Joseph of Arimathæa is to be found in the gospels in connection with our Lord's passion and burial. But he has been the subject of numerous legends: that which makes him the founder of the monastery of Glastonbury is of special interest in Great Britain, but there is not a shred of truth in the story.

†*JOSEPH OF CUPERTINO, ST. September 18. Sept., p. 239

Joseph Desa was b. in 1603, and after some difficulty (as a youth he was not "bright") was received by the Conventual Franciscans as a lay tertiary servant; in 1625 he was admitted to the novitiate, and in due course professed and ordained. From this time onward St Joseph's life was one long succession of ecstasies, miracles of healing, and supernatural happenings on a scale not paralleled in the reasonably authenticated biography of any other saint. For example, during the seventeen years he was at the friary of Grotella, in southern Italy, over seventy occasions of levitation are recorded, and he is the classical example of this class of phenomenon. These manifestations were troublesome to some members of his order and during the later years of his life St Joseph was subjected to very severe treatment. He bore it with patience, increased his remarkable physical mortifications, and died peacefully in 1663. cd. 1767.

*JOSEPH OF LEONESSA, ST. February 4. Feb., p. 76

B. in 1556 and professed as a Capuchin at Leonessa in Italy in 1574. He was sent on the mission in Turkey where he ministered to the galley slaves, reconciled apostates to Islam, and was imprisoned and tortured. He d. after an operation for cancer, 1612. cd. 1745.

*JOSEPH OF PALESTINE, ST. July 22. July, p. 316

He was a well-known Jew of the Biblical school at Tiberias who became a Christian. The emperor Constantine gave him the rank and title of *comes*, "count," with authority to build churches in Galilee. This Joseph did in face of much opposition from the Jews. Under the Arian emperor

Constantius he retired to Scythopolis, where he sheltered St Eusebius of Vercelli, St Epiphanius, and other orthodox refugees. d. *c.* 356.

JUDAS QUIRIACUS, ST, bp. and mart. May 4.   MAY, p. 51

This saint, the patron of Ancona, may have been an early bishop who met his death while on pilgrimage to Jerusalem, but the local legend makes him a bishop of Jerusalem martyred under Julian the Apostate.

JUDE, ST. *See* Simon and Jude.

JUDICAËL, ST. December 16.   DEC., p. 152

Judicaël, ruler of Brittany, was venerated in that country both as a national hero and as an unusually holy man. He harried the Franks, until St Eligius brought about a treaty with him, and resigned the throne in his old age, retiring to the monastery of Gaël, near Vannes. d. *c.* 650.

*JUDOC, ST. December 13.   DEC., p. 152

Judoc, or Josse, was the younger brother of St Judicaël. In his later years he became chaplain to Count Haymo of Ponthieu and was then a hermit at Villiers-Saint-Josse and near Saint-Josse-sur-Mer. d. *c.* 669. St Judoc is named in several English mediæval kalendars and his relics are said to have been translated to Hyde Abbey at Winchester. *Judocus.*

*JULIA, ST, virg. and mart. May 22.   MAY, p. 266

She was put to death in Corsica, probably by Saracen marauders in the sixth or seventh century.

JULIA OF CERTALDO, BD, virg. February 15.   FEB., p. 237

Julia was a domestic servant who, at the age of eighteen in 1337, joined the Augustinian third order at Florence. Then she returned to her home at Certaldo and lived as an ankress in a cell adjoining a church. d. 1367, c.c. 1819.

*JULIAN, ST, mart. January 9.   JAN., p. 124

With his wife Basilissa he converted his house into a hospital (so that he has been confused with Julian the Hospitaller) and was eventually a martyr with others (304 ?). Basilissa died in peace. The historical existence of this couple is doubtful. *Julianus.*

*JULIAN, ST, bp. January 27.   JAN., p. 345

Venerated as the first bishop of Le Mans (third century ?), but nothing is known of him. His feast was kept throughout the south of England in the Middle Ages.

*JULIAN, CRONION and **BESAS, SS,** marts. February 27.   FEB., p. 371

Three martyrs at Alexandria in 250 ; Julian was so gouty that he could not walk and Cronion was one of his bearers ; Besas, a sympathetic soldier, was killed by the mob.

*JULIAN SABAS, ST. January 17.   JAN., p. 218

A Mesopotamian solitary who went to Antioch to refute a false charge of Arianism and preached with great effect in that city. d. 377.

JULIAN OF ST AUGUSTINE, BD. April 8.   APR., p. 98

A tailor's apprentice at Medina Cœli in Castile who became a Franciscan lay-brother. His extraordinary devotions and weird austerities at first gave the impression that he was mad and he was twice turned away from the order. Eventually he became an eloquent and well-known preacher. d. 1606. bd. 1825.

JULIAN THE HOSPITALLER, ST. February 12.   FEB., p. 184

According to an old but probably fictitious legend, St Julian in error slew his own parents and as a penance built a hospice by the side of a river where he tended the poor and rowed travellers across. In consequence many hospitals were dedicated in his honour, and he was looked on as a patron of innkeepers, travellers, and boatmen. There has been a good deal of confusion between this Julian and other saints of the same name.

*JULIAN OF ANTIOCH, ST, mart. March 16.　　　MAR., p. 275

The panegyric preached on him by St John Chrysostom suggests that this martyr was the most important of the many named Julian. He suffered at Anazarbus in Cilicia in 250 (?), and his body was afterwards enshrined in a basilica at Antioch.

*JULIAN OF BRIOUDE, ST, mart. August 28.　　　AUG., p. 363

Or " of Auvergne." Julian was one of the most famous martyrs of Gaul ; he was a soldier, put to death near Brioude in 304.

JULIAN OF NORWICH, BD, virg. May 13.　　　MAY., p. 165

The title " Blessed " is often given to Dame Julian, who was a recluse at Norwich and died with a great reputation for holiness c. 1423. The book in which she narrates her visions, *Revelations of Divine Love*, is the tenderest and most beautiful exposition in the English language of God's loving dealings with man.

*JULIAN OF TOLEDO, ST, bp. March 8.　　　MAR., p. 132

Julian, Archbishop of Toledo, was a person of very great civil and ecclesiastical power in the Spain of his day, and was the first bishop to exercise a primacy over the whole country. He called several important synods and was a voluminous writer, and he revised the Mozarabic liturgy. It is said that Julian was a Jew by race, and he encouraged the sovereigns to revive the laws against the Jews. d. 690.

JULIAN OF VALLE, BD. May 11.　　　MAY, p. 133

Three feasts are held annually at Valle in Istria in honour of this Franciscan, but beyond the fact that he was a local man and must have died early in the fourteenth century nothing is known about him. c.c. 1910.

*JULIANA, ST, virg. and mart. February 16.　　　FEB., p. 245

Apparently she was martyred in the neighbourhood of Naples, perhaps at Cumae in 305, but nothing certain is known.

†*JULIANA FALCONIERI, ST, virg. June 19.　　　JUNE, p. 245

Juliana was b. in 1270 at Florence and followed her uncle St Alexis Falconieri into the Order of Servites, becoming a tertiary and still living at home. In 1304 she established a community, the sisters working in a hospital, and St Juliana is honoured as the foundress of all women religious of the Servite Order, of whom the tertiaries are known as " Mantellate." The collect of her feast refers to the miraculous holy communion said to have been granted to her on her death-bed. St Juliana's mortifications seriously impaired her health, and she d. 1341. cd. 1737.

JULIANA OF CORNILLON, BD, virg. April 5.　　　APR., p. 65

Juliana was a nun of Cornillon, near Liége, and to her more than anybody else the institution of the feast of Corpus Christi is due. Her suggestion met with a certain amount of opposition, but the feast was formally adopted in the diocese of Liége in 1246. But Juliana was driven from her convent on a false charge and had to take refuge in a monastery near Namur, and then as a recluse at Fosses. d. 1258. c.c. 1869. Juliana's mission, which she claimed had been revealed to her by our Lord, was carried on by her friend the recluse Eva, at whose request Pope Urban IV sanctioned the feast ; in 1312 it was obligatory throughout the Western church.

JULIE BILLIART, BD, virg. April 8. APR., p. 99

Marie Rose Julie Billiart was the daughter of a peasant farmer at Cuvilly in Picardy. She showed signs of unusual goodness at an early age, particularly by the patience with which she bore a nervous malady brought on by an attempt on her father's life. After the French Revolution she went to Amiens, where she laid the foundations of the Institute of Notre Dame for the education of girls and the training of religious teachers. In 1804 Bd Julie was miraculously cured of her illness and the establishment of her congregation went on apace, spreading to Ghent, Namur, and Tournai ; for a time it was set back by the bad behaviour of a young priest, confessor to the sisters at Amiens, but Mother Julie was fully vindicated, and she spent the last seven years of her life in still further extending her foundations. d. 1816. bd. 1906. " Mother Julie," said the Bishop of Namur, " is one of those people who can do more for the Church of God in a few years than others can do in a century."

*JULITTA, ST, mart. July 30. JULY, p. 416.

She was a wealthy woman of Cæsarea in Cappadocia, who was denounced as a Christian by a man who coveted her property. She was sentenced to be burnt, walked into the flames, and was choked by the smoke, c. 303.

*JULIUS I, ST, pope. April 12. APR., p. 130

Julius I, a Roman, became pope in 337. Three years later he held a synod against the Arians, his subsequent letter to the opponents of St Athanasius being, in the words of Mgr Batiffol, " a model of gravity, wisdom, and charity." St Julius built several churches in Rome. d. 352.

*JULIUS and AARON, SS, marts. July 3. JULY, p. 23

According to tradition they were martyrs for Christ at Caerleon-upon-Usk c. 305. Their feast is observed in the diocese of Cardiff.

*JULIUS OF DUROSTORUM, ST, mart. May 27. MAY, p. 326

He was a veteran soldier of the Roman army who was put to death for professing Christianity at Durostorum (now Silistra, in Rumania) c. 302. Other members of his legion suffered about the same time.

*JUSTA and RUFINA, SS, virgs. and marts. July 19. JULY, p. 266

Martyrs in 287 at Seville in Spain, where they are greatly venerated. In the course of ages one of them seems to have undergone a change of sex, for Justa was originally called Justus.

†*JUSTIN, ST, mart. April 14. APR., p. 155

St Justin, called " the Philosopher," was b. at Nablus in Palestine c. 100, of pagan parents. He became a Christian when about thirty years old as a result of reading the Scriptures and observing the fortitude of the martyrs. He had deeply studied the philosophies of Greece and became the first great Christian apologist, both against the Jews and the heathen ; certain of his writings are extant. He was martyred in Rome, by beheading, c. 165. *Justinus.*

*JUSTINA, ST, virg. and mart. October 7. OCT., p. 85

She was martyred at Padua, probably during the persecution of Diocletian ; a mediæval forgery associates her with St Prosdocimus, " a disciple of the blessed Peter."

JUSTINA OF AREZZO, BD, virg. March 12. MAR., p. 221

A Benedictine nun of Arezzo who became a recluse at Civitella. Miracles of healing were attributed to her. d. 1319. c.c. by Pope Leo XIII.

A DICTIONARY OF SAINTS

*JUSTUS, ST, mart. October 18.   Oct., p. 253

Justus is said to have been put to death for Christ at Beauvais in 287 at the age of nine. This young martyr was formerly famous all over north-western Europe, but the extension of his cultus was in some measure due to confusion with other saints of the same name. His legend as it has come down to us is fabulous.

*JUSTUS, ST, bp. November 10.   Nov., p. 116

Justus was appointed by St Augustine to be the first bishop of Rochester, and in 624 he became archbishop of Canterbury. Pope Boniface V, in sending Justus the *pallium*, wrote commending his work. d. *c.* 627. His feast is observed in the diocese of Southwark.

*JUSTUS and PASTOR, SS, marts. August 6.   Aug., p. 73

Prudentius numbers these two among the most glorious martyrs of Spain : they suffered at Alcalá in 304.

JUSTUS OF LYONS, ST, bp. October 14.   Oct., p. 191

As bishop of Lyons he assisted at the Synod of Aquileia against the Arians, where he gained the respect of St Ambrose. He did not return to his see, but retired to Egypt, where he d. *c.* 390.

*JUSTUS OF URGEL, ST, bp. May 28.   May, p. 333

The first recorded bishop of Urgel in Spain ; he wrote a treatise on the *Song of Songs.* d. *c.* 550.

JUTTA, BD. January 13.   Jan., p. 166

Otherwise *Ivetta.* Jutta was left a widow when she was eighteen. For ten years she nursed the sick in the lazar-house of her native Huy, near Leyden, and then became an ankress in a cell close by. Here she lived forty years till her death in 1228. She had the power of reading thoughts, and by her prayers converted her father and son to better living.

JUTTA, ST. May 5.   May, p. 76

The life of St Jutta (Judith) bears a resemblance to that of St Eliza-beth of Hungary. Jutta was a Thuringian of noble family whose husband died while on a pilgrimage to the Holy Land ; after all her children had been provided for she became a poor pilgrim and wandered into Prussia, where she settled as a solitary near Kulmsee. She lived here four years till her death in 1260 ; many miracles were recorded at her grave, and she is venerated as patroness of Prussia.

JUTTA, BD, virg. December 22.   Dec., p. 221

Jutta was the recluse who brought up St Hildegard, who said of her that she " overflowed with the grace of God like a river fed by many streams." She formed her followers into a community under the Rule of St Benedict. d. 1136.

JUVENAL ANCINA, BD, bp. August 31.   Aug., p. 397

B. at Fossano in 1545. He was professor of medicine at the University of Turin and went to Rome as the private physician of the Savoyard ambassador in 1575. Three years later he joined the congregation of the Oratory, was ordained, and sent to Naples, where he was soon respected and loved by the whole city. Bd Juvenal was torn between desire for the contemplative life and for active work among the poor ; he disappeared for five months for fear he would be made a bishop, and eventually, in 1602, he was, of Saluzzo in Piedmont. On returning from his first episcopal visitation, which was marked by miracles, Bd Juvenal was poisoned by a friar whose evil life the bishop had rebuked, in 1604. bd. 1869. *Juvenalis.*

*JUVENAL OF NARNI, ST, bp.   May 3.   MAY, p. 41

He is venerated as the first bishop of Narni but he has been confused with other bishops of the same name and little reliable information is available about him. d. *c.* 376.

*JUVENTINUS, ST, mart.   January 25.   JAN., p. 303

With St Maximinus was an officer in the army of Julian the Apostate. For criticizing the laws against Christians and refusing to sacrifice to idols they were beheaded at Antioch in 363.

KENAN, ST, bp. November 24. NOV., p. 293

This Kenan was a disciple of St Patrick, who established him as the first bishop at Duleek in Meath. d. *c.* 500.

KENELM, ST, mart. July 17. JULY, p. 234

There is no early historical evidence for the story of Kenelm, who is said to have succeeded to the crown of Mercia at the age of seven and to have been killed in the forest of Clent by order of his ambitious sister, *c.* 820. There was considerable cultus of St Kenelm in the past (his shrine was at Winchcombe) and he is still commemorated in the dioceses of Birmingham and Clifton. *Kenelmus.*

KENNETH, ST. *See* Canice.

KENNOCH, ST, virg. March 13 MAR., p. 240

The life of this Scottish maiden is wrapped in very great obscurity and there is some doubt if she ever existed. According to the Aberdeen Breviary she was a solitary in Fifeshire and died at an advanced age in 1007.

KENTIGERN, ST, bp. January 13. JAN., p. 162

Otherwise *Mungo*="darling." According to Scottish tradition he was brought up by St Serf, near whose monastery his mother was cast up by the sea. Kentigern became the leader of a small religious community at Glasgow and was consecrated bishop there, the first. What with a flock that was part pagan and part Pelagian and the political upheavals of Strathclyde, St Kentigern led a very disturbed life, and on one occasion had to flee into Wales. Many exaggerated miracles are related of Kentigern, one of which is perpetuated in the ring and fish on the arms of the city of Glasgow. He died while taking a bath, 603. His feast is kept throughout Scotland on January 14, and in the dioceses of Liverpool, Lancaster, Salford, and Menevia. *Kentigernus.*

KENTIGERNA, ST. January 7. JAN., p. 105

Mother of St Felan. When her husband died she went from Ireland to Scotland and lived as a hermitess on an island in Loch Lomond, where a church bears her name. d. 734.

KESSOG, ST, bp. March 10. MAR., p. 168

Kessog, or Mackessog, was an Irish missionary bishop in Scotland. There is great uncertainty about his life and death (according to one account he was martyred at Bandry), but he certainly was very greatly venerated in Scotland in earlier ages. d. *c.* 560.

KEVIN, ST, ab. June 3. JUNE, p. 35

Kevin (Caoimhghin) was one of the great sixth-century saints of Ireland and founder of the famous monastery of Glendalough. How much fact underlies the legends that compose his extant biographies is uncertain. He is said to have been a Leinster man and his name means "well-begotten"; remarkable miracles are recorded of him, and his great soul-friend was St Kieran of Clonmacnois. St Kevin's feast is observed throughout Ireland. *Coemgenus.*

KEYNE, ST, virg. October 8. OCT., p. 104

St Keyne's cultus was well known in parts of South Wales and the west of England (her holy well is near Liskeard in Cornwall), but it is difficult to find out anything authentic about her. She is said to have been a daughter of Brychan of Brecknock and to have occupied a hermitage at Keynsham in Somerset during the fifth century. She is commemorated in the diocese of Clifton. *Keyna.*

*KIERAN, ST, ab. September 9. SEPT., p. 96

This Kieran (*Queranus*), sometimes called " the Younger," was b. in Connacht. He went to the monastic school at Clonard, where he was one of the " Twelve Apostles of Ireland," and then lived for some time with St Enda on Inishmore. In consequence of a vision Kieran left the Arans, wandered across Ireland, and eventually founded the great monastery of Clonmacnois. The biographies of St Kieran speak much of his virtues and the miracles to which they gave rise. He apparently ruled Clonmacnois for only a short time, and d. *c.* 556 (?). His feast is kept throughout Ireland.

KIERAN OF OSSORY, ST, bp. March 5. MAR., p. 62

Very conflicting accounts of this Kieran appear in the various " lives." He was probably one of the twelve whom St Patrick consecrated to the episcopate and he is venerated as the first bishop in Ossory and founder of the monastery of Saighir. He has wrongly been identified with the Cornish St Piran. d. *c.* 530. His feast is kept throughout Ireland. *Kiranus.*

*KILIAN, ST, bp. and mart. July 8. JULY, p. 94

Kilian, with Coloman, Totnan, and others, were Irish missionaries sent from Rome to preach the gospel in Franconia and East Thuringia, where they were martyred *c.* 689. St Kilian is venerated as the apostle of Thuringia, and his feast is kept throughout Ireland. *Chilianus.*

KILIAN, ST. November 13. NOV., p. 154

This Kilian was a relative of St Fiacre and was a missionary in Artois during the seventh century.

KYNEBURGA, ST. March 6. MAR., p. 83

She was a daughter of the pagan Penda of Mercia, and was married to Alcfrid, King of Bernicia. In later life she founded and governed the abbey of Castor in Northamptonshire. Here she was joined by her sister Kyneswide and her kinswoman Tibba. Kyneburga d. *c.* 680. These three holy women were all buried in Peterborough minster, which the two princesses had helped to endow ; their relics were twice removed during the Danish invasions, but brought back under King Henry I, when a feast of their translation was instituted.

KYNESWIDE, ST. *See* Kyneburga.

LADISLAUS, ST. June 27. JUNE, p. 358

Ladislaus I, King of Hungary, extended the borders of his state, kept its enemies at bay, made of it a politically great nation, ushered in an era of peace, and fostered Christianity in every part of his dominions—in fact, was the complete national hero. He belonged to the house of Arpad and became king in 1077; he allied himself by marriage with Rupert of Suabia against the emperor Henry IV. He established the bishoprics of Zagreb and Nagy Varad, gave full liberty to Jews and Mohammedans, refused to recognize political suzerainty in the Holy See, and was chosen commander-in-chief of the first Crusade. But he d. before it set out, on July 30, 1095. cd. 1192. In Magyar he is called *Laszlo*.

LADISLAUS OF GIELNIOW, BD. May 11. MAY., p. 135

B. in 1440, became an Observant Franciscan at Warsaw, and as minister provincial sent a picked body of friars to evangelize Lithuania. He himself preached with much effect in every part of Poland. The flooding of the Pruth and Dneister and the consequent overthrow of the Tartars and Turks in 1498 were attributed by the Poles to the prayers of Bd Ladislaus. d. 1505. bd. 1586.

*****LÆTUS, ST,** and comps., bps. and marts. September 6. SEPT., p. 66

Lætus, bishop of Leptis Minor, was burned alive *c.* 484, one of the first victims of the Vandal Huneric. There are commemorated with him St Donatian and other African bishops, who were driven into the desert by Huneric and left there to die.

*****LAMBERT, ST,** bp. April 14. APR., p. 160

Abbot of Fontenelle and then bishop of Lyons; d. 688. *Lambertus*.

LAMBERT, ST, bp. May 26. MAY, p. 317

A monk of Lérins who became bishop of Vence in 1114. d. 1154.

*****LAMBERT, ST,** bp. and mart. September 17. SEPT., p. 224

Lambert (*Landebertus*) became bishop of Maestricht *c.* 668, but in 674 was exiled from his see for seven years by the tyrannical Ebroin. On his return he was active in evangelizing the heathen of the Low Countries. Lambert was murdered *c.* 700. There is some uncertainty about the circumstances leading to his death, but he has been ever since venerated as a martyr.

LAMLISS, ST. *See* Laserian.

*****LANDELINUS, ST,** ab. June 15. JUNE, p. 186

B. *c.* 625 near Bapaume. As founder of the great abbeys of Lobbes and Saint-Crespin and of two lesser houses, St Landelinus was held in much honour, but very little is known of his life. d. *c.* 686.

LANDERICUS, ST, bp. April 17. APR., p. 198

He was the eldest son of St Vincent Madelgarus and became bishop of Metz; when Vincent died he resigned his see and took over his father's abbey at Soignies. d. *c.* 700.

LANDERICUS, ST, bp. June 10. JUNE, p. 134

In French *Landry*. He became bishop of Paris in 650 and is said to have established the first real hospital in that city. d. *c.* 661.

*LANDOALD, ST. March 19. MAR., p. 324

A Roman priest, missionary in the country of Maestricht, who founded the church at Wintershoven. His servant Adrian, who was murdered by robbers while carrying alms to his master, was venerated as a martyr. d. *c.* 668. *Landoaldus*.

LANFRANCUS, BD, bp. June 23. JUNE, p. 310

His fifteen years of episcopate at Pavia were troubled by heretics and by the attempts of the civil authorities to lay hands on ecclesiastical property. At length he decided to resign and join the Vallombrosan monks, but he d. first, in 1194.

LANUINUS, BD. April 14. APR., p. 160

A Carthusian monk who accompanied St Bruno to Calabria and succeeded him in the rule of the two Italian charterhouses ; he was appointed visitor apostolic of all monastic houses in Calabria. d. 1120. c.c. 1893.

LASERIAN, ST, bp. April 18. MAR., p. 39 ; APR., p. 213

Otherwise *Lasairian, Molaisse*, and (probably) *Lamliss*. He is said to have twice visited Rome and on the second occasion was appointed legate to Ireland by Pope Honorius I ; in this capacity he practically settled the dispute about the date of Easter in the south of Ireland, where he always upheld the Roman observance. d. 639. His feast is kept throughout Ireland as bishop at Leighlin. *Laserianus*.

†*LAURENCE, ST, mart. August 10. AUG., p. 123

There are few Christian martyrs whose names are so famous as that of St Laurence, who was one of the seven deacons of Rome under Pope St Sixtus II. He was put to death, according to tradition, by being roasted on a grid-iron, three days after that pope in 258. His death, says Prudentius, was the death of idolatry in Rome, which from that time began to decline. He was buried on the Via Tiburtina, where is now the fifth patriarchal basilica, of St Laurence-outside-the-walls, and is named in the canon of the Mass. *Laurentius*.

LAURENCE IMBERT, BD. *See* Corea, Martyrs of.

†*LAURENCE JUSTINIAN, ST, bp. September 5. SEPT., p. 54

He was one of the Giustiniani of Venice, b. there in 1381. He became a canon at a local collegiate church, was advanced to the provostship, and turned the chapter into a community of canons regular. In 1433 he was appointed bishop of Castello, and he founded fifteen religious houses in that diocese. In 1451 he was translated to the see of Grado, whose archbishop had the title of patriarch, and its residence was at the same time transferred to Venice, whence St Laurence is sometimes reckoned the first patriarch of Venice. In public life he was a zealous and generous prelate, in private a mortified and humble priest, who wrote several books on mystical contemplation. d. 1455. cd. 1690.

LAURENCE LORICATUS, BD. August 16. AUG., p. 189

A hermit near Subiaco ; he was called Loricatus, " the cuirassier," because of the coat of mail studded with spikes which he wore next his skin. d. 1243. c.c. 1778.

*LAURENCE O'TOOLE, ST, bp. November 14. Nov., p. 175

Lorcan o Tuathail was b. in 1128, probably near Castledermot. He became abbot of Glendalough at the age of twenty-five and archbishop of Dublin eight years later. St Laurence did much to spread the canonical life among his clergy, but his reforms were handicapped by the upheavals of the times ; he had to negotiate with " Strongbow," rallied the Irish chieftains against him, and in 1171 submitted to King Henry II of England. In 1179 he went to Rome for the Lateran Council and was appointed papal legate in Ireland. Laurence was much employed as go-between by Henry and the Irish chiefs, and in 1180 he d. in Normandy while on his way to see the king on behalf of Ruaidri O'Conor. cd. 1226. St Laurence's feast is kept throughout Ireland and by the Canons Regular of the Lateran.

*LAURENCE OF BRINDISI, ST. July 22.   JULY, p. 321
He was b. in 1559, became a Capuchin Franciscan, and in his studies showed a marvellous aptitude for languages. With Bd Benedict of Urbino he established the Capuchins in Germany, he preached in several countries of central Europe, and was for a term minister general of his order. St Laurence was chaplain general to the forces of the Archduke Matthias against the Turks and the victory of Stuhlweissenburg was attributed to his prayers, example, and tactical advice. During the later years of his life he was much in demand among secular princes as a diplomat and peace-maker. d. 1619. cd. 1881.

*LAURENCE OF CANTERBURY, ST, bp. February 2.   FEB., p. 39
One of the monks who accompanied St Augustine to England. After being sent back to Rome to get further instructions from Pope St Gregory he succeeded Augustine as second archbishop of Canterbury. Owing to the obstinacy of King Eadbald in upholding paganism Laurence was tempted to retire to France, but he was rebuked by St Peter in a dream and was successful in winning over Eadbald. d. 619. Feast kept in the dioceses of Westminster and Southwark.

LAURENCE THE ILLUMINATOR, ST, bp. February 3.   FEB., p. 50
One of a band who fled from Syria in 514 to escape the persecution of the monophysite Severus of Antioch. They came to Rome where Laurence was ordained and sent to preach in Umbria. He was bishop of Spoleto for twenty years, when he founded the abbey of Farfa and retired thereto. He is called " the Illuminator " because of his gift for healing blindness, both physical and spiritual. d. 576.

LAURENCE OF RIPPAFRATTA, BD. September 28.   SEPT., p. 352
Bd Laurence was an able lieutenant of Bd John Dominic in his reforming activities among the Dominicans : he was novice-master at Cortona, where he trained St Antoninus, Fra Angelico, and Benedict of Mugello, and later vicar general of the reformed friaries. d. 1457. c.c. 1851.

LAURENCE OF VILLAMAGNA, BD. June 6.   JUNE, p. 86
He belonged to the family of Mascoli and was one of the best known Franciscan preachers of his time. d. 1535. c.c. 1923.

*LAZARUS, ST, bp. February 11.   FEB., p. 170
Bishop of Milan while the Goths were ravaging Italy ; he had much to suffer at their hands, but he ruled his flock prudently and faithfully. d. March 14, c. 450.

*LAZARUS, ST, bp. and mart. December 17.   DEC., p. 190
Nothing at all is known of the life of Lazarus subsequent to his being raised from the dead as narrated in the Gospel of St John, cap. xi. The

tradition of the East is that he died bishop at Kition in Cyprus. His presence and martyrdom at Marseilles is first heard of in the eleventh century ; this baseless story seems to have arisen from the existence of a fifth-century bishop of Aix called Lazarus.

*LEANDER, ST, bp. February 27.   FEB., p. 369

He was brother to St Isidore and St Fulgentius and preceded the first of these in the see of Seville. Leander was banished after the martyrdom of St Hermengild by his Arian father, King Leovigild ; on his return he was instrumental in retrieving the Visigoths from Arianism, and was responsible for two great synods at Toledo in 589 and the following year. He was a close friend of St Gregory the Great, whom he persuaded to write his *Moralia,* but very little of St Leander's own writing has come down to us. d. 596.

LEBUINUS, ST. November 12.   NOV., p. 145

Lebuinus (Lebwin, Liafwin) was a monk of Ripon who went as a missionary to the borders of Westphalia. He founded the church at Deventer, from whence he preached the gospel among the Saxons as well as the Frisians. d. *c.* 773.

*LEGER, ST, bp. and mart. October 2.   OCT., p. 17

He was called from his monastery in Poitou in 663 to be bishop of Autun and a counsellor of St Bathildis, regent for King Clotaire III. In the upheavals that followed the death of Clotaire, Leger incurred the enmity first of Childeric II and then of Ebroin ; he gave himself up to the troops of the latter rather than bring disaster on his flock, his eyes were put out, and he was interned at Fécamp. In 679 a court of bishops, creatures of Ebroin, pronounced St Leger to be deposed and he was executed secretly. The struggle between St Leger and Ebroin is a famous incident of Merovingian history, but it is not obvious why the bishop should be venerated as a martyr : his spreading of the Rule of St Benedict among the monasteries of his diocese was probably more useful than the political activities that led to his death. *Leodegarius.*

LEO, BD, ab. February 26.   FEB., p. 364

Monk of Anchin, abbot of Lobbes, and finally abbot of the great monastery of Saint-Bertin ; among St Bernard's letters are two addressed to him. It was he who, on behalf of Count Thierry, brought back from Jerusalem the alleged relic of our Lord's blood which ever since has been kept in the chapel of St Blaise at Bruges. d. 1163.

*LEO, ST, ab. May 25.   MAY, p. 302

This Leo (in French *Lyé*) was abbot of Mantenay in the diocese of Troyes. d. *c.* 550.

†*LEO THE GREAT, ST, pope and doct. April 11.   APR., p. 119

The wisdom of Pope Leo I, his successful defence of the Catholic faith against heresy, and his intervention with Attila the Hun and Genseric the Vandal raised the prestige of the Holy See to great heights and earned him the title of " the Great," which is shared by only two other popes, Gregory I and Nicholas I. He was elected to the supreme pontificate in 440. Theologically his greatest achievement was in respect of Monophysism : in a letter to St Flavian, Patriarch of Constantinople, he clearly defined the true faith concerning the natures of our Lord, condemning Nestorianism on the one hand and Monophysism on the other : this, the " Dogmatic Letter " or " Tomos " of St Leo was acclaimed as the teaching of the Church at the oecumenical council of Chalcedon in 451. The gospel for the proper Mass of St Leo is, significantly enough, from Matt. xvi, recording our Lord's promises to St Peter; Leo's numerous sermons are utilized for lessons in the Divine Office. d. 461. He was declared a doctor of the Church in 1754.

†*LEO II, ST, pope. July 3. JULY, p. 19

He was a Sicilian and succeeded to the papal throne in 681. During his short pontificate he confirmed the condemnation, by the third general council of Constantinople, of his predecessor Pope Honorius I for "hedging" when he ought to have denounced outright the monothelite heresy. d. 683.

*LEO III, ST, pope. June 12. JUNE, p. 157

He was a Roman, elected to the Holy See in 795, and the story of his pontificate belongs to general ecclesiastical history. He was the object of a vicious attack by relatives of his predecessor. Among the acts of Leo III was the coronation of Charlemagne as Holy Roman Emperor and a refusal to allow the liturgical innovation of the addition of the word "Filioque" to the Nicene Creed. d. 816.

*LEO IV, ST, pope. July 17. JULY, p. 235

Leo IV became pope in 847 and his relatively short pontificate was a full one. His benefactions to churches take up 28 pages in the *Liber Pontificalis*, he brought the relics of many saints into the City, and stood godfather at the confirmation of young Alfred of England when he came to Rome. From this pope the Leonine City—the part of Rome including St Peter's and the Vatican—gets its name, he having surrounded it with a wall. d. 855.

*LEO IX, ST, pope. April 19. APR., p. 221

On the death of Damasus II in 1047 the Alsatian bishop of Toul, Bruno, was elected in his place and took the name of Leo IX. He was greatly concerned for the reformation of morals, especially by the suppression of simony, and twice condemned the heresy of Berengarius about the Holy Eucharist. Leo was a man of much energy and several times crossed the Alps on ecclesiastical and political missions, but in 1053 he was taken prisoner by the Normans for resisting their ravages in southern Italy. Leo was released on account of his shattered health, and he d. 1054. He it was who first proposed that the election to the papacy should be entirely in the hands of the Roman cardinals.

LEO and PAREGORIUS, SS, marts. February 18. FEB., p. 260

After Paregorius had suffered martyrdom at Patara in Lycia his friend Leo was emboldened publicly to destroy some of the illuminations in the Temple of Fortune. Whereupon he was brought before the governor, sentenced, and executed. It is likely that this story is a pious romance.

*LEO OF SENS, ST, bp. April 22. APR., p. 258

He was bishop of Sens; d. 541.

LEOBINUS ST, bp. March 14. MAR., p. 249

Otherwise *Lubin*. He was a peasant lad of Poitiers who became a hermit, priest, abbot of Brou, and finally bishop of Chartres. d. c. 556.

*LEOCADIA, ST, virg. and mart. December 9. DEC., p. 111

The cultus of St Leocadia at Toledo has a respectable antiquity, but there is little certain known about her. She is said to have died in prison for the Faith in that city in the persecution of Diocletian.

PONTIUS, BD, ab. November 26. Nov., p. 310

The memory of Pontius of Faucigny, abbot of the canons regular at Abondance in the Chablais, was greatly revered by St Francis de Sales. Pontius was also for a time abbot of the monastery of St Sixtus, which he founded. d. 1178. c.c. 1896.

*POPPO, ST, ab. January 25. Jan., p. 307

He was first a soldier and pilgrim and then a monk under Abbot Richard of Saint-Vannes, for whom he reformed several monasteries, including that of Saint-Vaast at Arras. Poppo himself became abbot of Stavelot and was a sort of general superior of a group of monasteries in Lotharingia, as well as an adviser to the Emperor St Henry II. d. 1048.

*PORCARIUS, ST, mart. August 12. Aug., p. 151

Second abbot of Lérins who, with nearly all his monks, was massacred by Moors c. 732.

*PORPHYRIUS, ST, bp. February 26. Feb., p. 359

After years as a hermit in the desert of Skete and the Jordan valley he was consecrated bishop of Gaza in 395. These were the days of the last efforts of paganism in the East and Porphyrius concentrated all his efforts on uprooting it, getting permission from the empress Eudoxia to destroy the temples in Gaza. It is not surprising to learn that the worshippers lost no opportunity of harassing the bishop and his flock. On the site of the temple of Marnas a great church was built which Porphyrius consecrated in 408. He d. in 420 and his biography, written by his deacon Mark, is a very valuable historical document.

*POSSIDIUS, ST, bp. May 16. May, p. 203

Possidius, bishop of Calama in Numidia, was closely associated with St Augustine in his struggles against heresy and suffered personal violence. He was driven from his see by the Arian Genseric and d. in exile c. 440.

*POTAMIANA, ST, virg. and mart. June 28. June, p. 369

She would not purchase her freedom at the price of her chastity and was lowered slowly into a cauldron of boiling pitch at Alexandria in 202. Her mother, St Marcella, was martyred at the same time.

*POTAMION, ST, bp. and mart. May 18. May, p. 227

He was bishop of Heraclea in Egypt and was savagely tortured during the persecution of Maximinus Daia in 310 ; he met his death at the hands of the Arians c. 340.

*POTHINUS, ST, bp. and mart. June 2. June, p. 20

St Pothinus was the first bishop of Lyons and the leader of those martyrs under the bitter persecution of Marcus Aurelius in 177 whose sufferings are recorded in a contemporary letter which has been called "the jewel of the Christian literature of the second century." Pothinus had probably "listened to those who had seen the Apostles" ; in his ninetieth year he was mishandled by a mob and died in prison from his injuries. Among the other martyrs of Lyons and Vienne were SS Vettius, Sanctus, a deacon, Maturus, a neophyte, Attalus, and Blandina, a slave girl.

*POTITUS, ST, mart. January 13. Jan., p. 161

A martyr of unknown history who is honoured in the diocese of Naples ; he is said to have been a young boy.

*PRÆJECTUS, ST, bp. and mart. January 25. Jan., p. 306

Otherwise *Priest, Prest, Preils, Prix.* Bishop of Clermont c. 666.

He was slain by one Agritius, who had an imaginary grievance against him, in 676. There is a contemporary account of his life and achievements.

*PRÆTEXTATUS, ST, bp. and mart. February 24.   Feb., p. 331

Prætextatus, called *Prix* in France, was chosen bishop of Rouen in 549. Chilperic, king at Soissons, charged him with acts calculated to encourage rebellion and he was banished. After Chilperic's death he returned to his see, but was pursued by the enmity of his widow, the wicked queen Fredegonda, with whom the bishop had often to remonstrate. She eventually caused him to be murdered in 586. St Gregory of Tours witnesses to the falseness of the calumnies made against St Prix by his enemies.

†*PRAXEDES, ST, virg. July 21.   July, p. 301

Legend has it that Praxedes was the sister of St Pudentiana, and that she helped and sheltered Christians during the persecution under Marcus Antoninus ; but her extant *acta* have been officially declared to be spurious.

†*PRIMUS and FELICIAN, SS, marts. June 9.   June, p. 118

Brothers who were martyred and buried at Nomentum, near Rome, *c.* 297. The legendary details of their passion are unreliable.

†*PRISCA, ST, virg. and mart. January 18.   Jan., p. 225

The St Prisca, virgin and martyr, mentioned in the Roman Martyrology on January 18 has not been satisfactorily identified.

PRISCILLA. *See also* Aquila and Prisca.

*PRISCILLA, ST. January 16.   Jan., p. 200

It is likely that St Priscilla was the wife of Manius Acilius Glabrio and mother of the senator Pudens ; she gives her name to the most ancient of the Roman catacombs, above which was her villa in which it is believed that St. Peter made his headquarters.

*PRISCUS, ST, mart. May 26.   May, p. 317

Priscus and other citizens of Besançon were martyred at Auxerre *c.* 272.

†*PROCESSUS and MARTINIAN, SS, marts. July 2.   July, p. 15

Roman martyrs of uncertain date. The story that they were the gaolers of St Peter and St Paul in the Mamertine prison is a baseless legend.

*PROCLUS, ST, bp. October 24.   Oct., p. 318

He became patriarch of Constantinople in 434 and was distinguished for the gentle way in which he dealt with Nestorians and other heretics, saving the Armenian church from the errors of its East Syrian and Persian neighbours. According to tradition he added the singing of the Trisagion to the Liturgy in miraculous circumstances. St Cyril of Alexandria and others speak highly of the goodness of Proclus. d. July 24, 447.

*PROCOPIUS, ST, mart. July 8.   July, p. 92

There is extant a contemporary account, written by Eusebius, bishop of Cæsarea, of the passion of St Procopius, who was the first victim of the Diocletian persecution in Palestine. He was in reader's orders at Scythopolis and was beheaded in 303 at Cæsarea Maritima for refusing to sacrifice to the emperors. The simple narrative of Eusebius was the seed of nonsensical later legends, in the course of whose evolution St Procopius was split up into three different people, none of whom remotely resembled him.

*LIVINUS, ST, bp. and mart. November 12.   Nov., p. 143

He is said to have been a missionary bishop from Dublin, martyred near Alost in Brabant in 657, but he may be the same as St Lebuinus. His feast is kept throughout Ireland.

LODOVICA ALBERTONI, BD. January 31.   Jan., p. 403

B. in Rome in 1473 ; she was happily married and had three daughters ; when her husband died in 1506 she became a Franciscan tertiary and spent all her money on the poor, so that at the last she had herself to be supported by her family. d. 1523. c.c. 1671.

LOMAN, ST, bp. February 17.   Feb., p. 250

According to legend Loman was a nephew of St Patrick and went with him to Ireland. When the convert Feidlimid gave Patrick land for a church at Trim, Loman was made bishop there. d. *c.* 450.

*LOMBARDS, MARTYRS UNDER THE. March 2.   Mar., p. 14

St Gregory in his *Dialogues* speaks of a number of Christians in Campania who were slain by the Lombards *c.* 579 for refusing idolatrous worship. They are mentioned in the Roman Martyrology on March 2.

LOMER, ST, ab. January 19.   Jan., p. 231

A priest of Chartres who became a monk and founded the abbey of Corbion ; d. *c.* 590.

LONDON MARTYRS OF 1582, THE. May 28, 30.   May, pp. 341, 367

On May 28, 1582, three secular priests were h.d.q. at Tyburn for exercising their priesthood, viz., Thomas Ford, John Shert (both Oxford men), and Robert Johnson (formerly a manservant). Two days later there were four more victims : William Filby, Luke Kirby, and Laurence Richardson (*alias* Johnson), who were secular priests, and Thomas Cottam, Jesuit. All these martyrs were ostensibly executed for being concerned in a bogus plot called the conspiracy of Rheims and Rome.

LONDON MARTYRS OF 1588, THE. August 28, etc.   Aug., p. 368
                                                     Oct., p. 66

The defeat of the Armada in July 1588 was followed by a severe persecution of Catholics in London, where three groups of martyrs suffered. On August 28, BB William Dean, William Gunter, Robert Morton, Thomas Holford, James Claxton (secular priests), Thomas Felton (a Minim friar), and Hugh More, a layman ; on August 30, Richard Leigh (secular priest), Edward Shelley, Richard Martin, John Roche, and Margaret Ward (lay people) ; on October 5, William Hartley, John Hewett (secular priests), and the layman Robert Sutton. All these were bd. in 1929.

LONDON MARTYRS OF 1591, THE. December 10.   Dec., p. 124

A stricter enforcement of the laws against Catholics in 1591 led to seven martyrdoms in London on December 10. At Gray's Inn Fields, Edmund Genings, a secular priest, was h.d.q. for his priesthood and a layman, Swithin Wells, was hanged for harbouring him. At Tyburn, Eustace White and Polydore Plasden, secular priests, were h.d.q. for their priesthood and three more layman, Brian Lacey, John Mason, and Sidney Hodgson, were hanged for helping priests. bd. 1929.

*LONGINUS, ST, mart. March 15.   Mar., p. 259

This is the name given to the soldier who pierced the side of our Lord on the cross. There are several legends about him and his alleged subsequent martyrdom, but the truth about his life is not known.

LOUIS IV, BD. September 11.　　　　　　　　　SEPT., p. 145

Louis (Ludwig), Landgrave of Thuringia, was the beloved husband of St Elizabeth of Hungary. He d. at Otranto while going on the crusade in 1227. His popular cultus in Germany has never been officially confirmed, but seems to be eminently well deserved. *Ludovicus.*

†*LOUIS IX, ST. August 25.　　　　　　　　　AUG., p. 294

He was b. at Poissy in 1215 and succeeded to the throne of France when he was eleven. King Louis IX was a characteristic example of the good and great mediæval layman : indifferent to comfort, humbly devoted to the poor and to religious, the father of eleven children, and a fighting man who admirably governed and consolidated his own kingdom. He defeated King Henry III of England at Taillebourg in 1242 and concluded an honourable treaty with him sixteen years later. Twice St Louis went crusading to the East, intent only on the Holy Places, ignoring political combinations, and achieving nothing : during the first venture he was captured by the Saracens in Egypt, and at the second he met his death, at Tunis, from the plague, in 1270. cd. 1297.

LOUIS ALLEMAND, BD, bp. September 16.　　　　SEPT., p. 215

This Louis was made archbishop of Arles in 1423 and cardinal soon after, and played a prominent part in the troubled ecclesiastical affairs of his day. He was a leader of the " conciliarists," took part in the setting up of the antipope Felix " V " by the Council of Ferrara, and was excommunicated and deprived of the cardinalate by Eugenius IV ; he was restored by Nicholas V and, deeply repenting of his schismatic activities, retired to Arles where he administered his diocese with the virtue that had always characterized his private life. d. 1450. c.c. 1527. Bd Louis Allemand is an outstanding example of how the Church in practice and not simply in theory looks so far as possible at the hearts rather than the exterior actions of men.

*LOUIS BERTRAND, ST. October 9.　　　　　　OCT., p. 118

He was b. at Valencia in 1526, joined the Dominicans, and was sent to preach the gospel in South America in 1562. He worked in what is now Colombia for seven years, making numerous converts among the Indians both there and in some of the West Indian islands. On his return to Spain St Louis achieved fame as a preacher and was active in keeping up the primitive spirit of his order. d. 1581. cd. 1671.

LOUIS DUFRESSE, BD, bp. and mart. September 14.　SEPT., p. 172

Louis Gabriel Taurin Dufresse, titular bishop of Tabraca, was a most effective missionary in China for nearly forty years, being appointed vicar apostolic in 1801. He was beheaded for being a " foreign preacher " at Ch'in-Tu in 1815. bd. 1900.

LOUIS GRIGNION DE MONTFORT, BD. April 28.　APR., p. 322

He was b. in 1673 and, after undergoing great hardships, became a secular priest. While chaplain to a hospital at Nantes he laid the foundations of the congregation of Sisters of the Divine Wisdom, but was forced to resign his post. He then became a missionary preacher and again met with much opposition, but he received the approval of the Holy See and carried on with his forceful methods of combating sin. Shortly before his death Bd Louis founded the first establishment of the Missionary Priests of Mary. He was a great admirer of the Order of Preachers, of which he was a tertiary, and very zealous in encouraging the use of the rosary. d. 1716. bd. 1888.

Q

QUADRATUS, ST, bp. May 26. MAY., p. 315

Bishop of Athens and the first of the great line of Christian apologists, with a treatise written for the emperor Hadrian. d. *c.* 129.

*QUENTIN, ST, mart. October 31. OCT., p. 374

The story of the passion of St Quentin has come down to us in a variety of embellished forms, but he seems certainly to have been an authentic martyr at the town on the Somme which is now called by his name. He is said to have been a missionary from Rome, who suffered in 287. *Quinctinus.*

*QUIRICUS and **JULITTA, SS,** marts. June 16. JUNE, p. 194

According to their fictitious legend Julitta was a widow of noble birth from Iconium who fled from persecution but was martyred at Tarsus. Her three-year old son Quiricus had previously had his brains dashed out by an infuriated magistrate whose face he had scratched. Nothing is known about them really : it is likely that Quiricus was a real martyr around whom the legend subsequently grew up.

*QUIRINUS, ST, bp. and mart. June 4. JUNE, p. 50

Quirinus was bishop of Siscia (Sisak in Croatia) and during the persecution under Diocletian fled from the city. He was captured and brought back, but in spite of cruel beating refused to sacrifice to the gods. He was sent to the governor of Pannonia Prima at Sabaria (Szombathely in Hungary) and there, since he still refused to sacrifice, he was drowned in the river Raab in 308.

*QUITERIA, ST, virg. and mart. May 22. MAY, p. 267

This saint is much venerated on the borders of France and Spain, but nothing more is certain about her.

RABANUS MAURUS, BD, bp. February 4. FEB., p. 69

This prolific writer was one of the most learned men of his age. He was b. *c.* 784 probably at Mainz and was educated at Fulda and Tours where he became deeply attached to Alcuin. He learned Greek, Hebrew, and Syriac and was made master of the monastery school at Fulda (being for a time called off to help in the building of a new abbey). Rabanus became abbot of Fulda in 822, and it was probably then that he wrote his homilies and drew up his martyrology. After a fruitful rule he gave up the office, only to be made archbishop of Mainz when he was seventy-one. He was as energetic as he was learned, assisting at numerous synods and having 300 poor fed at his house every day. d. 856.

RADBOD, ST, bp. November 29. NOV., p. 340

He was the great-grandson of the last pagan king of the Frisians (also called Radbod) and he became bishop of Utrecht in 900. Some hymns and other poems that he wrote are still in existence. d. 918.

*RADEGUNDE, ST. August 13. AUG., p. 157

St Radegunde is one of the best-known figures of the sixth century in France. She had the misfortune to be one of the numerous wives of King Clothaire I, and when he murdered her brother she separated herself from him and was consecrated a deaconess by St Médard. She played a considerable part in religious and secular affairs, especially on behalf of peace, and was the foundress of the great monastery of the Holy Cross at Poitiers. d. 587. There are several churches dedicated in this saint's honour in England, and she is one of the titulars of Jesus College, Cambridge. *Radegundis.*

RALPH, ST, bp. June 21. JUNE, p. 283

Though probably not a monk he received several abbacies and in 840 was made bishop of Bourges ; he was active in public affairs, a man of learning, and founder of several religious houses. He compiled a book of pastoral instructions for the use of his clergy, which was rediscovered early in the seventeenth century. d. 866. *Radulphus.*

RALPH ASHLEY, BD, mart. April 7. APR., p. 92

A Jesuit lay-brother h.d.q. at Worcester in 1606 for being found in attendance on Bd Edward Oldcorne. bd. 1929.

RALPH CORBY, BD, mart. September 7. SEPT., p. 79

Vere Corbington. He was a Jesuit who ministered in the county of Durham. After some years he was condemned for his priesthood and h.d.q. at Tyburn in 1644. bd. 1929.

RALPH SHERWIN, BD, mart. December 1. DEC., p. 16

After being ordained at Douay and studying at the English College in Rome, Bd Ralph came on the English mission in 1580. Within a few months he was arrested and tortured, and in 1581 was h.d.q. at Tyburn for " complicity " in a fictitious plot. bd. 1886. Bd Ralph was the proto-

and for thirty-nine years she suffered without a word of complaint. The people of Ferrara did not even realize that she was still alive, and the announcement of her death in 1544 caused an outburst of popular veneration. This cultus continued, and was officially confirmed in 1710.

LUDAN, ST. February 12. FEB., p. 188

According to tradition he was an Irish or Scots pilgrim who died by the wayside in Alsace on his way back from Jerusalem, and was buried at Scherkirchen. d. 1202.

*LUDGER, ST, bp. March 26. MAR., p. 404

Ludger, the apostle of Saxony, was trained in the abbey school of Utrecht and for three and a half years studied under Alcuin in England. He was a missionary in Friesland until Saxon raids drove him out. He returned in 787 and worked first in north-east Friesland (including Heligoland) and then in north-west Saxony or Westphalia. He founded a monastery of canons regular at Münster, and when he was consecrated bishop in 804 he settled his see there. Ludger's gentleness, persuasiveness, and personal attraction were strikingly successful in reconciling the Saxons, especially when contrasted with the results of Charlemagne's repressive measures. d. 809. *Ludgerus.*

LUDMILA, ST, mart. September 16. SEPT., p. 209

She was the widow of Borivoj, Duke of Bohemia, and was entrusted with the upbringing of the young prince Wenceslaus. It was feared that under her influence he would seize the government of Bohemia during his minority and finally establish Christianity there ; Ludmila was accordingly strangled by two of the heathen party at Tetin in 921.

LUDOLPHUS, ST, bp. March 29. MAR., p. 438

A Premonstratensian canon and bishop of Ratzeburg, who suffered persecution from Duke Albert of Sachsen-Lauenberg. d. 1250.

LUFTHILD, ST, virg. January 23. JAN., p. 288

She inspired considerable local devotion around Cologne, but nothing certain is known of her life. d. 850 (?)

†*LUKE, ST, evang. October 18. OCT., p. 249

He was a Greek of Antioch, a physician by profession, and the companion of St Paul during part of his missions and his captivity at Rome. He wrote the Acts of the Apostles and the gospel which bears his name. It does not seem that he was a martyr or a painter of pictures. It is not known where or when he died. *Lucas.*

LUKE BELLUDI, BD. February 17. FEB., p. 256

B. in 1200 and received the habit of the Friars Minor from St Francis himself at Padua. He was a close friend of St Antony, after whose death Bd Luke was instrumental in building the great basilica at Padua in his honour. d. 1285. c.c. 1927.

LUKE THE YOUNGER, ST. February 7. FEB., p. 107

Also called Thaumaturgus, "the Wonderworker." He was a Greek, brought up in Thessaly, who after many difficulties succeeded in being a hermit near Corinth, where he was famed for his austerity and miracles. After his death *c.* 946 his cell on Mount Joannitza was called Soterion, the Place of Healing.

*LULLUS, ST, bp. October 16. OCT., p. 227

Lullus was a monk of Malmesbury, who joined St Boniface in Germany and became his archdeacon and right-hand man. After a visit to Rome he was consecrated bishop as coadjutor, and succeeded Boniface in the see of Mainz, where he was a most energetic pastor for thirty years. St Lullus had in his day a great reputation for learning. d. 786.

*LUPICINUS, ST, ab. March 21. FEB., p. 382

Brother of St Romanus (February 28) and co-founder of monasteries with him. He was excessively austere and saw to it that all the monks tried to emulate him. d. *c.* 480.

*LUPUS, ST, bp. July 29. JULY, p. 405

In French *Leu, Loup.* He married a sister of St Hilary of Arles, but after a time they parted by mutual consent and Lupus became a monk at Lérins. He was chosen bishop of Troyes in 426, and may have accompanied St Germanus of Auxerre to Britain to combat the Pelagian heresy. d. 478.

*LUPUS OF SENS, ST, bp. September 1. SEPT., p. 7

He was a monk of Lérins and became archbishop of Sens in 609. In consequence of slander Lupus was banished from his see by King Clotaire, but was recalled at the request of St Winebald and the people. d. 623.

*LUTGARDIS, ST, virg. June 16. JUNE, p. 203

Lutgardis was a Benedictine nun at Tongres who afterwards undertook the even more austere life of the Cistercians. An account of her inner life and mystical experiences was written by the contemporary Thomas of Chantimpré. She was blind for eleven years before her death in 1246. Lutgardis is one of the most sympathetic figures among the mediæval women mystics.

*LUXORIUS and other marts, **SS.** August 21. AUG., p. 259

Luxorius was a converted soldier who was put to death in 303 at Forum Trajanum in Sardinia. The youths Cisellus and Camerinus are said to have suffered with him.

LYDWINA OF SCHIEDAM, BD, virg. April 14. APR., p. 166

Bd Lydwina is described in her proper office as " a prodigy of human suffering and of heroic patience." B. 1380, the daughter of a labourer. An accident while skating in 1396 brought on disease and illness of the most agonizing kind, and she became completely bed-ridden ; when she was nineteen the symptoms became more revolting and more painful. Lydwina bore it all with extraordinary patience, and about 1407 she began to receive visions, but then incurred the suspicion of her parish priest : one trial was spared her—she was never neglected or misunderstood by her family. After hardly sleeping for seven years Bd Lydwina d. 1433. c.c. 1890.

LYONS AND VIENNE, THE MARTYRS OF. *See* Pothinus, bp. and mart.

his body into the Rhine—but this seems insufficient reason for venerating him as a martyr.

REMACLUS, ST, bp. September 3.   SEPT., p. 35

He was abbot of several monasteries in Austrasia before he became bishop of Maestricht in 652. After ten years he resigned and retired to the abbey of Stavelot, where his reputation drew many recruits to the community. d. *c.* 668.

*REMBERT, ST, bp. February 4.   FEB., p. 72

A disciple of St Anschar and his successor as archbishop of Hamburg and Bremen. He preached among the Slavs and Vandals, sold sacred vessels to ransom prisoners among the Northmen, and wrote a biography of St Anschar. d. June 11, 888. *Rembertus.*

REMIGIUS, ST, bp. January 19.   JAN., p. 233

A son of Charles Martel, made archbishop of Rouen in 755. d. *c.* 772.

†*REMIGIUS, ST, bp. October 1.   OCT., p. 1

Remigius (Remi), a great apostle of the French, was illustrious for his learning, eloquence, and miracles during an episcopate of seventy years in the see of Rheims, but his biographical sources are rather unsatisfactory. The great event of his life was the baptism at Rheims of the Frankish king Clovis in 496. d. January 13, *c.* 533.

*RENÉ GOUPIL, ST, mart. March 16.   MAR., p. 271

One of the most remarkable among the Martyrs of North America (q.v.). His health had caused him to fail in his efforts to be a Jesuit, so he became a surgeon and went to America as a lay assistant to the missionaries. He was assistant to St Isaac Jogues and was the first of the group of martyrs to suffer, being tomahawked on September 29, 1642, for having traced the sign of the cross on the brow of some children. *Renatus.*

*REPARATA, ST, virg. and mart. October 8.   OCT., p. 98

She was put to death at Cæsarea in Palestine *c.* 250, but the extant account of her passion is spurious.

*RESTITUTA, ST, virg. and mart. May 17.   MAY, p. 219

An African girl who died for Christ during the persecution of Valerian or Diocletian, at Carthage or elsewhere.

*RESTITUTA OF SORA, ST, virg. and mart. May 27.   MAY, p. 325

Nothing is known of the passion of this Roman patrician at Sora in 271 (?).

*RHIPSIME, ST, virg. and mart. September 29.   SEPT., p. 365

SS Rhipsime, Gaiana, and their maiden companions have been from early times venerated as the protomartyrs of the Armenian church, *c.* 290, but nothing at all is now known of their history or the circumstances of their passion. They are referred to in the legend of St Gregory the Illuminator. *Ripsimis.*

*RICHARD, ST. February 7.   FEB., p. 106

A saint whose feast is kept at Lucca in Italy, where it is said that he was an English prince, and father of SS Willibald, Winebald, and Walburga, who d. at Lucca while on a pilgrimage to Rome in 722. But this story has been shown to be not worthy of credence. *Richardus ; Reccaredus.*

*RICHARD, ST, bp. June 9.   JUNE, p. 120

It seems to be agreed that this St Richard was an Englishman and bishop of Andria in Italy, but his reputed *acta* are spurious. These state that he flourished in the middle of the fifth century, but the twelfth is more likely.

RICHARD FEATHERSTONE, BD, mart. July 30.   JULY, p. 424

He was archdeacon of Brecon and tutor to the Princess Mary. After speaking in convocation in favour of the validity of Queen Catherine's marriage he was attainted for high treason and h.d.q. at Smithfield, London, in 1540. bd. 1886. His feast is kept in Wales with Bd Edward Powell.

RICHARD GWYN, BD, mart. October 17.   OCT., p. 245

Alias White. He was b. at Llanidloes in 1537, went to St John's College, Cambridge, repudiated Protestantism, married, and became a schoolmaster. He was imprisoned as a recusant and during four years in jail wrote many religious poems in Welsh that are still extant. Bd Richard was h.d.q. at Wrexham in 1584, the protomartyr of Wales. bd. 1929.

RICHARD HERST, BD, mart. August 29.   AUG., p. 379

Richard Herst (Hurst, Hayhurst) was a farmer near Preston who was hanged at Lancaster in 1628, ostensibly for murder (it was not even manslaughter) ; his real offence was being a Catholic recusant. bd. 1929.

RICHARD KIRKMAN, BD, mart. August 22.   AUG., p. 273

A secular priest, tutor in the household of Dymoke of Scrivelsby, who was h.d.q. at York in 1582 for denying the Queen's supremacy in spiritual matters.

RICHARD LANGLEY, BD, mart. December 1.   DEC., p. 24

A Yorkshire gentleman who was hanged at York in 1586 for sheltering priests in his house. bd. 1929.

RICHARD NEWPORT, BD, mart. May 30.   MAY, p. 369

Alias Smith. A secular priest from Northamptonshire, h.d.q. for his priesthood at Tyburn in 1612.

RICHARD REYNOLDS, BD, mart. May 4.   MAY, p. 58

Bridgettine monk of Syon Abbey, Middlesex, who was h.d.q. at Tyburn for denying the royal supremacy, one of the first group of English martyrs, 1535.

RICHARD ROLLE, BD. September 29.   SEPT., p. 367

Richard Rolle had a very considerable popular cultus in the past, but it has not yet been confirmed by ecclesiastical authority, though preparations for his canonization were begun soon after his death. He was b. at Thornton in Yorkshire *c.* 1300 and spent most of his life as a hermit, at Hampole and elsewhere in that county. More interest has been taken in recent years in Rolle than in any other English uncanonized saint, on account of the unique position which he holds among English mystical writers. His best known work is the *Fire of Love,* and he seems as a man to have been as personally attractive as his writings. d. 1349.

RICHARD THIRKILD, BD, mart. May 29.   MAY, p. 353

B. in co. Durham and ordained abroad in 1579 when he was already an old man. H.d.q. for his priesthood at York in 1583.

RICHARD WHITING, BD, ab. and mart. November 15.   DEC., p. 10

The last abbot of Glastonbury came to that office in 1525. At the dissolution he refused to surrender his monastery to the Crown and he was sentenced to death for high treason, his offence apparently being that he recanted the oath recognizing the King's supremacy in spiritual matters.

MAGDALEN PANATTIERI, BD, virg. October 13.   OCT., p. 185
She was a Dominican tertiary who lived a life of usefulness and charity
in her own home at Trino-Vercellese in north-western Italy. Her life was
notably lacking in external eventfulness. d. 1503. c.c. by Pope Leo XII.

MAGENULPHUS, ST. October 5.   OCT., p. 61
Magenulphus (Meinulf, Méen) was brought up at the court of Charlemagne, was ordained, and founded a monastery for women on his estate at
Bödeken, Westphalia, of which province he is accounted one of the apostles.
d. *c.* 857.

*MAGLORIUS, ST, bp. October 24.   OCT., p. 325
Maglorius (Mælor) was a son of St Umbrafel, uncle of St Samson, and
is said to have succeeded his cousin as abbot and bishop at Dol. Afterwards he retired to the Channel Islands, where he built a monastery on
Sark. d. *c.* 586. St Maglorius is commemorated in the diocese of Portsmouth.

*MAGNERICUS, ST, bp. July 25.   JULY, p. 365
He was the first Frank to be made bishop of Trier, and was a man of
" shining piety and sound learning." d. 596.

MAGNUS, ST, mart. April 16.   APR., p. 183
Magnus, son of Erlin, co-earl of the Orkneys, was plotted against and
captured by the king of Norway, Magnus Barefoot. He escaped to the
protection of King Malcolm III of Scotland, at whose court he repented
of his youthful excesses and began a life of prayer and penance. In 1116
St Magnus was killed by his cousin Hakon for political ends, but was
nevertheless venerated as a martyr. The cathedral of Kirkwall, where he
was buried, was dedicated in his honour, and his feast is still observed in
the diocese of Aberdeen.

MAHARSAPOR, ST, mart. October 10.   OCT., p. 136
After three years of cruel imprisonment he was put to death for
confessing Christ in Persia in 421.

MAIMBOD, ST, mart. January 23.   JAN., p. 289
A wandering Irish missionary in the diocese of Besançon, killed by
pagans while preaching near Kaltenbrunn in Alsace, *c.* 880.

*MAJOLUS, ST, ab. May 11.   MAY, p. 129
In French *Maieul*. He became head of the congregation of Cluny in
965 and was a worthy peer of the great early Cluniac abbots. He had the
confidence of the emperors and the empress St Adelaide was anxious that
he should be chosen pope, but by preference Majolus was a scholar and an
administrator. d. 994.

*MALACHY, ST, bp. November 3.   NOV., p. 32
Malachy o'More (Maolmhaodhog ua Morgair) was b. at Armagh in
1094 and became vicar general to the archbishop St Celsus. He distinguished himself by his zeal and vigour and became in turn abbot of Bangor,
bishop of Connor, and primate at Armagh, where he continued the much-
needed restoration of discipline and superseded the Celtic liturgy by the
Roman. In 1138 he resigned and made a pilgrimage to Rome in the course
of which he visited Clairvaux ; here he became very friendly with St
Bernard and arranged for the first Cistercian foundation in Ireland,
Mellifont. On a second journey to Rome he died in St Bernard's arms at
Clairvaux in 1148. cd. 1190, the first Irishman to be formally canonized.
The " prophecies " found in Rome in 1590 and attributed to St Malachy

were not written by him. His feast is observed by the Cistercians and the Canons Regular of the Lateran, as well as throughout Ireland. *Malachias*.

MALARD, ST, bp. January 15. JAN., p. 194
Bishop of Chartres in the seventh century.

*MALCHUS, ST. October 21. OCT., p. 288
Malchus, a monk in the desert of Chalcis, was kidnapped by Bedouin and made to wander with them over their grounds beyond the Euphrates. He was given a woman to wife, but she was already married and they lived as brother and sister, and eventually escaped together. Malchus returned to his monastery and died there towards the end of the fourth century. St Jerome had this story from the lips of St Malchus himself.

*MALO, ST, bp. November 15. NOV., p. 187
He was a monk of Llancarfan who went to Brittany and was a missionary bishop, first where the town of Saint-Malo now stands and then near Saintes. d. 621. *Maclovius, Machutus*.

MALRUBIUS, ST, ab. April 21. APR., p. 253
An Irish monk of Bangor who went as a missionary among the Picts, establishing a monastery at Applecross ; there are several places named after him in the neighbourhood. d. 722. His feast is kept in the diocese of Aberdeen.

*MAMAS, ST, mart. August 17. AUG., p. 195
He was a shepherd at Cæsarea in Cappadocia and was martyred there c. 275. His feast is widely observed in the East.

*MAMERTUS, ST, bp. May 11. MAY, p. 126
St Mamertus, archbishop of Vienne, is chiefly remembered as the originator of the days of penance and supplication called rogation days which are still observed before the feast of the Ascension. d. c. 475.

MANECHILDIS, ST, virg. October 14. OCT., p. 192
She was one of six sisters, all of whom are venerated as saints in different parts of Champagne. She is said to have become a solitary, and is called in France *Ménéhould*. d. c. 490.

MANNES, BD. July 30. JULY, p. 417
He was an elder brother of St Dominic and one of the sixteen original members of the Order of Preachers. d. c. 1230. c.c. 1834.

*MAPPALICUS, ST, mart. April 17. APR., p. 196
Mappalicus and others were martyred at Carthage for refusing to sacrifice to the gods during the persecution under Decius, c. 250.

*MARCELLA, ST. January 31. JAN., p. 398
Called by St Jerome the " glory of the ladies of Rome." After the early death of her husband she lived a retired life of prayer and alms-deeds. When the Goths plundered Rome in 410 they beat St Marcella to make her disclose the whereabouts of her supposed wealth, but she induced them to spare her ward St Principia from outrage. Marcella died soon after in the same year.

*MARCELLINA, ST, virg. July 17. JULY, p. 229
She was the elder sister of St Ambrose and received the veil of a consecrated virgin c. 353. d. c. 398.

*MARCELLINUS, ST, mart. April 6. APR., p. 72
Marcellinus, with his brother the judge Apringius, attempted to enforce the decisions of a conference at Carthage against the Donatists with a

*ROBERT OF CHAISE DIEU, ST, ab. April 17. APR., p. 199
Robert de Turlande was founder and first abbot of Chaise Dieu in the Auvergne, which at his death in 1067 had over 300 monks.

ROBERT OF KNARESBOROUGH, BD. September 24. SEPT., p. 305
Robert Flower was b. at York *c.* 1160. After being a postulant at Newminster he became a hermit, eventually making his home in a cave by the river Nidd, near Knaresborough ; here he earned a great reputation for holiness, and after his death in 1218 (or 1235 ?) was the object of a considerable cultus, which was never officially confirmed. This Robert has been sometimes confused with St Robert, Abbot of Newminster, who d. many years before him.

*ROBERT OF MOLESMES, ST, ab. April 29. APR., p. 332
While abbot of Molesmes he received permission, with two of his monks, St Stephen Harding and Bd Alberic, to leave the monastery and retire to the forest of Citeaux ; here in 1098 the foundations of the Cistercian congregation were laid. Only a year later St Robert had, under obedience, to return to Molesmes, and he ruled that abbey successfully till his death in 1110. But he never ceased to long for Citeaux.

*ROBERT OF NEWMINSTER, ST, ab. June 7. JUNE, p. 96
B. at Gargrave in Yorkshire, where he was rector before joining the Benedictines at Whitby. He took part in the founding of Fountains abbey, which became Cistercian, and from thence was appointed first abbot of Newminster in Northumberland. It was said of St Robert that he was "modest in his bearing, gentle in companionship, merciful in judgement," and he ruled his abbey successfully for many years, founding a daughter house at Pipewell in Northamptonshire. d. 1159. His feast is observed by the Cistercians.

*ROCH, ST. August 16. AUG., p. 190
Pronounced "Rock." All that is known with certainty of the life of this much venerated saint is that he was b. at Montpellier and nursed the sick during a plague in Italy in the fourteenth century. He is invoked against pestilence and skin diseases. *Rochus.*

ROCH GONZALEZ, BD. *See* Paraguay, Martyrs of.

RODERICUS and **SOLOMON, SS,** marts. March 13. MAR., p. 239
A priest of Cabra who was betrayed by his Mohammedan brother and put to death for the Faith, together with one Solomon, at Cordova in 857.

ROGER OF ELLANT, BD. January 4. JAN., p. 63
An Englishman who became a Cistercian monk at Lorroy in France and from thence founded the new monastery of Ellant in the diocese of Rheims. d. 1160. *Rogerus.*

ROGER LE FORT, BD, bp. March 1. MAR., p. 10
Roger was son of the Lord of Ternes in the Limousin and attained in his youth both to scholastic and ecclesiastical distinction. His election to the see of Orleans is said to have been made in error, but he was an excellent bishop and was translated first to Limoges and then to the metropolitan see of Bourges. He established the feast of our Lady's conception in his dioceses and by will left all his property for the education of poor boys. d. 1367.

ROGER OF TODI, BD. January 28. JAN., p. 354
A personal follower of St Francis of Assisi, who appointed him spiritual

director of the Poor Clare convent at Rieti. d. 1237. Cultus confirmed by Pope Benedict XIV.

ROMÆUS, ST. March 4.　　　　　　　　　　　　MAR., p. 55

He was a Carmelite lay brother and the companion of St Avertanus (February 25) ; he caught the plague while nursing him, and d. a week later, 1380.

*ROMANUS, ST, ab. February 28.　　　　　　　　FEB., p. 382

Romanus retired from his monastery to a solitude in the Jura mountains where he was joined by his brother Lupicinus. Together they founded the monasteries of Condate and Leuconne for men and La Beaume (St Romain-de-la-Roche) for women, and each governed one monastery directly with joint authority over the whole congregation. These religious strove in all things to imitate the monks of the Eastern deserts, but the climate obliged them somewhat to mitigate their austerities. St Romanus d. c. 460, and was buried at La Beaume, where his sister was abbess.

*ROMANUS, ST. May 22.　　　　　　　　　　　　MAY, p. 268

A monk who encouraged and helped St Benedict when he first fled from Rome to Subiaco. d. c. 550

†*ROMANUS, ST, mart. August 9.　　　　　　　　AUG., p. 113

He was a doorkeeper of the Roman church who, together with the priest Severus and the clerics Claudius and Crescentius, was martyred at the same time as St Laurence in 258.

*ROMANUS, ST, bp. October 23.　　　　　　　　OCT., p. 306

He was bishop of Rouen for ten years and d. in 639. The chapter of Rouen formerly had the privilege of releasing a prisoner condemned to death every year on the feast of the Ascension in honour of this saint.

*ROMANUS and **BARULA, SS,** marts. November 18.　NOV., p. 234

St Romanus was a Palestinian deacon martyred at Antioch in 304. Nothing certain is known of his companion Barula.

ROMANUS THE MELODIST, ST. October 1.　　　　OCT., p. 6

Romanus, a Syrian Jew, was one of the clergy of the church of Constantinople, probably during the sixth century, and the greatest of the Greek hymn writers : about a thousand hymns are attributed to him.

*ROMARICUS, ST, ab. December 8.　　　　　　　DEC., p. 109

He was a monk of Luxeuil, formerly a Merovingian nobleman, who with St Amatus (September 13) founded the abbey of Remiremont (*Romarici mons*) in the Vosges. Romaricus succeeded Amatus as its abbot. d. 653.

†*ROMUALD, ST, ab. February 7.　　　　　　　　FEB., p. 97

B. c. 951 of the Onesti, dukes of Ravenna. To expiate his part in a duel in which his father had killed his opponent he became a monk and then a hermit. For thirty years he wandered about reforming monasteries and establishing hermitages in northern Italy and southern France, the best known and most lasting of his foundations being that of the Camaldolese hermit monks, which began a revival in the eremitical life of the West. This took place at Camaldoli, near Arezzo, in 1009, and the order still exists as an independent branch of the Benedictines. There seems to have been a tendency both to restlessness and harshness in Romuald's character, but he attracted many during his life. d. June 19, 1027, his feast on February 7 being the anniversary of the translation of his relics. *Romualdus*.

†*MARGARET MARY, ST, virg. October 17.   OCT., p. 236

Margaret Mary Alacoque was b. in Burgundy in 1647 and joined the Visitation Order at the age of twenty-four. She was an exemplary religious and was chosen by God to be the recipient of a number of revelations and visions : these had reference particularly to the love of the Heart of Jesus for man, and in 1675 it was made known to her that it was the divine will that a liturgical feast should be kept in honour of the Sacred Heart and in reparation for man's ingratitude. From these visions, and the consequent activity of Bl Claude de la Colombière and others, devotion to the Sacred Heart became public and, in time, universal. St Margaret Mary also underwent considerable trials : she was tempted to despair, vainglory, and self-indulgence, and suffered from bodily sickness and misunderstanding by her fellows. She d. at the convent of Paray-le-Monial in 1690. cd. 1920.

MARGARET POLE, BD, mart. May 28.   MAY, p. 339

Margaret Plantagenet, niece of Edward IV and Richard III, married Sir Reginald Pole ; when she was left a widow with five children Henry VIII created her countess of Salisbury in her own right, and she was governess to Princess Mary. She retired from court when the king married Anne Boleyn, and the opposition of her fourth son (afterwards Cardinal Pole) to the royal supremacy further angered Henry against her. Bd Margaret was lodged in the Tower of London but never brought to trial ; an act of attainder was passed against her and she was beheaded on Tower Green in 1541 at the age of seventy. Bd Margaret's feast is kept in the dioceses of Westminster, Birmingham, Brentwood, Clifton, and Portsmouth.

*MARGARET THE BAREFOOTED, ST. August 27.   AUG., p. 341

A woman of Sanseverino who suffered for years from the ill-treatment of her husband. d. 1395.

MARGARET OF CITTÀ-DI-CASTELLO, BD, virg. April 13.
                                                          APR., p. 152

She was a foundling, brought up by various families in Città-di-Castello, who spent her life looking after children for their mothers. She d. at the age of thirty-three in 1320. c.c. 1609.

*MARGARET OF CORTONA, ST. February 22.   FEB., p. 307

"The Magdalen of the Seraphic Order" was a farmer's daughter from Laviano in Tuscany. For nine years she was the mistress of a young nobleman, and in his sudden and violent death Margaret saw the judgement of God. She went with her young son to Cortona and lived for three years under the care of two ladies there ; then she became a tertiary of St Francis, devoted herself to the care of the sick, and started a hospital staffed by a community of tertiaries that she founded for the purpose. Her life was now as austere as it had formerly been easy, and her confessor narrates some remarkable visions and supernatural communications. Slanderous tongues and other trials induced her to live a more retired life, but later she renewed her activities and made many conversions of hardened sinners ; penitents came to her even from France and Spain. The people hailed her as a saint on the day of her death in 1297, but she was not formally canonized until 1728.

MARGARET OF ENGLAND, ST, virg. February 3.   FEB., p. 55

A Cistercian nun of Seauve Benite who was greatly venerated in the diocese of Puy-en-Velay in the Middle Ages under the above title. There is reason to think that she was actually of Hungarian birth, though her mother, with whom she went on pilgrimage to the Holy Land, was probably of English extraction. d. 1192.

MARGARET OF HUNGARY, BD, virg. January 26.   JAN., p. 323

Daughter of Bela IV, King of Hungary. She made her profession as a Dominican nun into the hands of Bd Humbert of Romans. The details of her extraordinary life of self-crucifixion are set out in the depositions of the witnesses for her beatification, seven years after her death, which are still in existence. Some of them have been described as " horrifying " and verging on fanaticism, and there was apparently a certain element of wilfulness in her self-immolation. There can be little doubt that Margaret shortened her life by her austerities. She d. 1270. The process of beatification referred to above was never finished, but her cultus was confirmed in 1789.

MARGARET OF LORRAINE, BD. November 6.   Nov., p. 78

She was left a widow with three small children at the death of René of Alençon and devoted herself solely to their upbringing, to the care of their estates, and to relief of the needy. She retired to a Poor Clare convent at Argentan in 1519 and d. in 1521. c.c. 1921.

MARGARET OF LOUVAIN, BD, virg. and mart. September 2.

            SEPT., p. 26

She was a maidservant at an inn at Louvain who was murdered by robbers whom she had seen kill and rob her employers. Marvels are said to have accompanied the finding of her body. d. 1225. c.c. 1905.

MARGARET OF RAVENNA, BD, virg. January 23.   JAN., p. 289

A young woman of Russi, near Ravenna, almost or quite blind, who suffered much injustice at the hands of her neighbours, though later many of them gathered round her to form a religious confraternity. d. 1505. Her biography is given in the Bollandist *Acta Sanctorum* but her cultus seems never to have been formally confirmed.

MARGARET OF SAVOY, BD. November 23.   Nov., p. 285

Bd Margaret was related to the principal royal houses of Europe and married Theodore Paleologus, Marquis of Montferrat, in 1403. She was noted for her wide charity to the common people, and after her husband's death in 1418 she took the habit of the Dominican third order and established a house of tertiary sisters at Alba in Liguria. After twenty-five years of good works the community was transformed into one of contemplative Preacheresses, and Bd Margaret directed it for another sixteen years. Many ecstasies and miracles were reported of her and she suffered a good deal of persecution, especially from Philip Visconti, whom she had refused to marry in 1418. d. 1464. c.c. 1669.

†*MARGARET OF SCOTLAND, ST. June 10.   JUNE, p. 128

B. in exile *c.* 1050, granddaughter of King Edmund Ironside of England, and in 1070 married King Malcolm III Canmore of Scotland. Both in her private life and public activity she worked unostentatiously and without singularity for the advancement of religion by the spiritual and temporal care of her people. She had six sons and two daughters, one of whom was " Good Queen Maud," wife of Henry I. Margaret d. November 16, 1093, and was buried at the abbey of Dunfermline which she had founded; while on her death-bed she heard of the treacherous murder of her husband by the English at Alnwick. A priest who knew her well wrote that, " So pleasant was she even in her severity that all around her loved her, men as well as women, loved her while they feared her and in fearing loved her."

SABAS, ST, bp. January 14. JAN., p. 181

In Slavonic *Sava*. B. 1174, youngest son of the first Serbian sovereign, Stephen I Nemanya. At the age of seventeen he became a monk at Mount Athos and founded the monastery of Khilandari, which still exists. In 1207 he returned to Serbia to help his brother Stephen II. He organized the first Serbian hierarchy of bishops, being himself appointed its metropolitan by the patriarch of Constantinople, and gave new life to religion in his country by establishing small houses of missionary monks. From Pope Honorius III Sava obtained the recognition of Stephen II as king and a crown for his coronation at Zitcha. d. 1237 in Bulgaria and was eventually buried at the Serbian monastery of Milochevo, but his relics were destroyed in 1594 by the Turks. St Sava is one of the principal patrons of Yugoslavia.

*SABAS, ST, mart. April 12. APR., p. 129

Sabas was a Christian Goth in what is now Rumania and belonged to the order of readers. In 372 he was seized by heathen Gothic soldiers and, upon his refusing to eat food that had been sacrificed to idols, was tortured and then drowned in the river Mussovo, near Tirgovist.

†*SABAS, ST, ab. December 5. DEC., p. 66

St Sabas, one of the greatest of the early monks, was b. in Cappadocia in 439. After being a monk and solitary in various places for years he founded a large *laura* or semi-eremitical monastery in a most wild gorge between Jerusalem and the Dead Sea ; in 493 he was appointed superior general over all the monks of Palestine ; and he played an active part in the public ecclesiastical history of his time in the Near East. d. 532. The monastery he founded still exists, called after him Mar Saba, and is one of the two oldest occupied monasteries in the world , its monks belong to the dissident Eastern Orthodox Church.

†*SABINA, ST, mart. August 29. AUG., p. 377

She is the titular saint of the ancient church of St Sabina on the Aventine at Rome, but nothing is certainly known about her. Sabina is named in the canon of the Ambrosian Mass..

*SABINIAN, ST, mart. January 29. JAN., p. 374

He is believed to have been a martyr at Troyes in the early centuries. *Sabinianus*.

SABINUS, ST, bp. January 17. JAN., p. 219

Bishop of Piacenza and a close friend of St Ambrose. When deacon he was sent on a mission to Antioch by Pope St Damasus. d. 420.

*SABINUS, ST, bp. February 9. FEB., p. 143

Bishop of Canosa in Apulia and a friend of St Benedict. He was sent by the Holy See on a mission to Constantinople, and while at Myra in Lycia had a vision of St Nicholas. d. *c.* 566. The body of St Sabinus was eventually translated to Bari, where his relics were lost for a time and found in 1901.

*SABINUS, ST, bp. and mart. December 30. DEC., p. 292
Sabinus, alleged bishop of Assisi, was put to death for Christ with several converts in 303.

*SACERDOS, ST, bp. May 5. MAY, p. 73
Sacerdos (also Serdon, Sardot, Sadroc) was bishop of Limoges during the early sixth century.

SADOC, BD, mart. June 2. JUNE, p. 27
Sadoc was one of the first Dominicans in Hungary, where he preached and then founded a house of his order at Sandomir in Poland. In 1260 the town was ravaged by the Tartars and Sadoc and all his friars were slain while singing *Salve Regina*. c.c. by Pope Pius VII.

*SADOTH, ST, bp. and mart. February 20. FEB., p. 283
He became bishop of Seleucia-Ctesiphon, the primatial see of Persia, during the persecution of Sapor II. He cared for his flock from a place of hiding, and then was arrested with 128 others. All were put to death, St Sadoth and eight others after five months' imprisonment at Beit-Lapat, 345.

SAHAK. *See* Isaac.

*SALABERGA, ST. September 22. SEPT., p. 289
She was the mother of St Beauduin and St Anstrudis ; after her second widowhood she became abbess of the monastery of St John which she had founded at Laon. d. *c.* 665.

SALOME, BD. November 17. NOV., p. 228
After the death of her husband, Coloman of Hungary, she joined the Poor Clares and died abbess of Zavichost in Poland in 1268. c.c. by Pope Clement X.

SALOME and JUDITH, SS. June 29. JUNE, p. 384
These two women are said to have been English recluses of royal blood at the monastery of Ober Altaich in Bavaria during the ninth century. The tradition is a late one, but it has been suggested that one of them may have been Eadburga, the rather shocking daughter of Offa of Mercia, who was driven out of England and may have repented in this fashion.

SALVATOR OF ORTA, BD. March 18. MAR., p. 317
A Spanish Franciscan lay brother of the Observance, who lived at Orta, Barcelona, Cagliari, and other friaries in the sixteenth century. d. 1567. c.c. by Pope Clement XI.

*SALVIUS, ST, bp. January 11. JAN., p. 146
Otherwise *Sauve*. Bishop of Amiens in the seventh century, famous for miracles. d. *c.* 625. A relic of this saint was formerly treasured at Canterbury cathedral.

*SALVIUS, ST, bp. September 10. SEPT., p. 129
Salvius became bishop of Albi in 574 ; he showed special devotedness to his flock during an epidemic in the year of his death, 584.

SALVIUS, ST. October 28. OCT., p. 349
This Salvius (in French *Saire*) seems to have been a sixth-century hermit at Saint-Saire in Normandy.

*SALVIUS and SUPERIUS, SS, marts. June 26. JUNE, p. 350
Their legend states that they were a bishop and his disciple who were murdered by an official's son near Valenciennes *c.* 768 for the sake of the bishop's gorgeous and valuable girdle. The story is not well attested—but there is a lesson in it.

John Maro, reputed patriarch of Antioch in the seventh century, probably never existed.

*MAROLUS, ST, bp. April 23.　　　　　　　　　　　Apr., p. 267

A Syrian priest who became archbishop of Milan ; Ennodius praises him in a poem. d. 423.

†*MARTHA, ST, virg. July 29.　　　　　　　　　　　July, p. 399

Martha was the sister of Mary (identified in the West with the Magdalen) and of Lazarus, " careful and troubled about many things." The story that she died in the south of France deserves no credence.

*MARTIAL OF LIMOGES, ST, bp. June 30.　　　　　　June, p. 393

Though well known as the reputed apostle of the Limousin and first bishop of Limoges there are no reliable particulars of the life of St Martial, his legend being an extravagant forgery. He probably d. c. 250. *Martialis*.

†*MARTIN I, ST, pope and mart. November 12.　　　　Nov., p. 136

He was a Tuscan and became pope in 649. Immediately after his election he condemned the Monothelite heresy in the teeth of the emperor, Constans II. Martin was therefore seized by the imperial exarch, taken to Constantinople, most cruelly treated and banished to the Chersonese, where he died of ill-treatment and starvation in 655. He was the last pope to date to die for the Church. *Martinus*.

MARTIN PORRES, BD. November 5.　　　　　　　　　Nov., p. 63

He was b. in Lima in 1569, son of a Spanish knight and a Panama Indian, and is the first " half-caste " whose heroic virtue has been officially recognized by the Church. Martin was a tertiary and infirmarian in the Dominican friary of the Rosary at Lima and was a friend to all the poor in the city, especially the African slaves and including the stray cats and dogs. d. 1639. bd. 1837.

MARTIN OF BRAGA, ST, bp. March 20.　　　　　　　Mar., p. 336

He was a zealous missionary in Spain and bishop first of Mondonedo and then of Braga. Martin was a man of great learning and was compared by Fortunatus with his namesake of Tours ; some of his works, including a description of peasant customs and superstitions, are extant. d. 580.

*MARTIN OF TONGRES, ST, bp. June 21.　　　　　　June, p. 276

He is venerated as the apostle of the Hesbaye district of Brabant, where he preached the gospel probably during the first half of the fourth century.

†*MARTIN OF TOURS, ST, bp. November 11.　　　　　Nov., p. 120

He was b. in Upper Pannonia c. 316, son of a Roman officer. Martin was sent into the army, but refused to fight against German invaders on the ground that a Christian should not engage in war. He became a disciple of St Hilary of Poitiers and for ten years lived as a recluse, founding a community of hermit-monks which later became the Benedictine abbey of Ligugé. He became bishop of Tours much against his will c. 371 and continued his monastic life as much as possible, establishing the monastery of Marmoutier near his episcopal city. He strongly opposed Ithacius of Ossanova for invoking the civil power and the death penalty against heretics, and protected the Priscillianists against persecution. St Martin was the pioneer of monasticism in Gaul and as such had considerable influence on the Celtic churches. He was, very properly, one of the most venerated of saints in Europe during the Middle Ages. d. 397.

*MARTIN OF VERTOU, ST, ab. October 24. OCT., p. 327
This rather nebulous saint was a hermit and missionary in Poitou in the sixth century and is said to have founded several monastic communities.

†*MARTINA, ST, virg. and mart. January 30. JAN., p. 383
There is some doubt whether this martyr ever existed for, though her alleged relics were found in 1634, there is no trace of any early devotion to her in Rome, where she is supposed to have suffered.

MARTINIAN, ST. February 13. FEB., p. 197
He is alleged to have been a hermit at the " Place of the Ark," near Cæsarea in Palestine, and to have been fruitlessly tempted by a woman called Zoe to give up that life and come to live with her. Instead he converted her and sent her to St Paula's convent at Bethlehem. But there is reason to doubt whether Martinian ever existed.

*MARTINIAN and others, **SS,** marts. October 16. OCT., p. 222
Martinian, his fellow-servant the maiden Maxima, and others were beaten and otherwise ill-treated for their loyalty to Christ by the Vandals in Africa. They were cruelly put to death in 458, except Maxima, who died in peace.

MARTIUS, ST, ab. April 13. APR., p. 148
St Martius, or Mars, was abbot of Clermont and is spoken of by St Gregory of Tours in his *Vitæ Patrum.* d. 530.

*MARUTHAS, ST, bp. December 4. DEC., p. 57
Maruthas, a doctor of the Syrian church, was bishop of Maiferkat in Mesopotamia. He compiled the *passiones* of the martyrs under Sapor and wrote liturgical hymns in their honour, as well as other works. He worked very hard for the organization of the Church in Persia and eastern Syria, visiting Constantinople twice (where he was much valued by St John Chrysostom) and convening the synod of Seleucia in 410 whose work lasted until the Mohammedan invasion. d. *c.* 415.

†*MARY, THE BLESSED VIRGIN. August 15. AUG., p. 177
Mary was a Jewish maiden of the house of David, whose parents are commonly referred to as St Joachim and St Anne ; at her conception she was preserved by God from all stain of original sin (the Immaculate Conception). Mary was betrothed to a carpenter, St Joseph ; at the annunciation the Second Person of the Blessed Trinity took flesh in her womb by the power of the Holy Ghost, but her marriage to Joseph took place ; in due course she gave birth at Bethlehem to Jesus, the God-Man, and so is properly called the Mother of God. Both before and after her miraculous childbearing she was a virgin and so remained all her days, and she was for her whole life absolutely sinless. For the thirty years before the public ministry of Jesus began Mary lived the outward life of any other Jewish woman of the common people ; she was present at His crucifixion, when He confided her to the care of the apostle St John ; on the day of Pentecost the Holy Ghost descended on her with the apostles and other disciples in the upper room at Jerusalem, and that is the last reference to her in the Bible. The rest of Mary's earthly life was probably passed mainly at Jerusalem. There, it is believed, she died, and it is a traditional belief of the Church that her body was preserved from corruption and soon after taken into Heaven and reunited to her soul by an unique anticipation of the general resurrection : the celebration of this event, commonly called in the West our Lady's Assumption, is her principal feast throughout the

years. He d. in London, clothed in the monastic habit, in 694 and was buried in St Paul's. There seems to have been no cultus of St Sebbe in the past, but his feast is now kept in the diocese of Brentwood on September 1. *Sebbus.*

SECHNALL, ST, bp. November 27.   Nov., p. 324

He was a disciple of St Patrick and was made bishop at Dunshaughlin in Meath. He wrote the earliest known Latin hymn written in Ireland, *Audite, omnes amantes Deum.* d. *c.* 450. *Secundinus.*

*SECUNDUS, ST, mart. June 1.   June, p. 3

An alleged martyr at Amelia in 304 who is the patron of several places in central Italy : but his historical existence is doubtful.

*SECUNDUS and **ALEXANDER, SS,** marts. August 26.   Aug., p. 317

They are said to have been soldiers in the Theban Legion (September 22) put to death at Ventimiglia and near Bergamo respectively. Their extant story is worthless.

SENAN, ST, bp. March 8.   Mar., p. 127

Senan, the most famous of the Irish saints of that name, was trained as a monk at Kilmanagh in Ossory. He is said then to have visited Rome and on his way back to have stayed with St David in Wales (there are also traces of him in Cornwall). He made several religious foundations and finally established a monastery on Inis Cathaig, now called Scattery Island, in the Shannon estuary. Here St Senan d. *c.* 560. He is commemorated to-day throughout Ireland. *Senanus.*

*SENATOR, ST, bp. May 28.   May, p. 333

A legate of Pope St Leo I to Constantinople, afterwards bishop of Milan. d. 475.

SENOCH, ST, ab. October 24.   Oct., p. 324

He was a hermit at what is now Saint-Senou in Touraine and d. in 579. His biography was written by St Gregory of Tours, who knew him personally.

SENORINA, ST, virg. April 22.   Apr., p. 260

Abbess first at Venaria and then at Basto in Portugal. d. 982.

SEPTEMBER, THE MARTYRS OF. September 2.   Sept., p. 28

These are 191 of the many people put to death in France on September 2–3, 1792, by the mob, with the approval of the Legislative Assembly, for refusing the oath and constitution of the clergy which had been condemned by the Holy See. Among them were John du Lau, Archbishop of Arles, Francis de la Rochefoucauld, Bishop of Beauvais, and his brother Louis, Bishop of Saintes, Charles de la Calmette, Count of Valfons, and other prelates, priests, and religious. 120 of them perished at the Carmelite Church in the rue des Rennes at Paris. bd. 1926.

*SEQUANUS, ST, ab. September 19.   Sept., p. 256

Also *Seine, Sigon.* He was a monk of Réomé who founded a monastery at the place now called Saint-Seine near the source of the river of that name. d. *c.* 580.

SERAPHINA, ST, virg. March 12.   Mar., p. 220

St Seraphina is specially venerated, as " Santa Fina," at San Geminiano in Tuscany. She was a young girl who suffered from a complication of painful and repulsive diseases, which she bore with wonderful cheerfulness in God's name. After the death of her parents she had only one friend to look after her properly, and she died in her youth in 1253.

SERAPHINA SFORZA, BD. September 9.   SEPT. p. 104

She received considerable persecution from her husband Alexander Sforza, Lord of Pesaro, and eventually left him and became a Poor Clare. Her prayers brought her husband to repentance before his death. d. 1478. c.c. 1754.

*SERAPHINO, ST. October 12.   OCT., p. 176

His life was of that uneventfulness which one associates with the vocation of a lay brother (in this case of the Capuchins), though he reached spiritual heights and many miracles are recorded of him. He d. at Ascoli-Piceno in Italy in 1604. cd. 1767.

*SERAPION, ST, bp. March 21.   MAR., p. 360

Serapion was bishop of Thmuis in Lower Egypt and played a considerable part in the ecclesiastical affairs of his day. His writings are lost but the *Euchologium* which he edited was discovered and published in the nineteenth century. d. *c.* 370.

*SERAPION, ST, bp. October 30.   OCT., p. 358

This bishop of Antioch d. *c.* 212. He is chiefly remembered for his theological writings.

*SERAPION, BD, mart. November 14.   NOV., p. 180

He is said to have been b. in England, to have joined the Mercedarians in Spain, and to have been crucified by the Moors for preaching the gospel while a hostage among them in 1240. c.c. 1728. Another Serapion, martyr at Alexandria *c.* 250, is mentioned in the Roman Martyrology on November 14.

SERENICUS, ST, ab. May 7.   MAY, p. 88

After being a hermit with his brother St Serenus he was made abbot by a community near Hyesmes on the Sarthe. d. *c.* 669.

SERENUS, ST, mart. February 23.   FEB., p. 316

Called " the Gardener " because he lived as an anchorite in a garden which he tended at Mitrovicza (Sirmium) in Yugoslavia. Having drawn attention by an alleged insult to the wife of a Roman officer he was arrested and found to be a Christian, and having refused to sacrifice to the gods he was beheaded in 302. But it is not certain to what extent this story is genuine.

SERENUS, ST. May 7.   MAY, p. 88

He was brother to St Serenicus and spent his life as a hermit in various parts of France. d. *c.* 669

SERF, ST, bp. July 1.   JULY, p. 10

There are several legends about St Serf, connecting him with Scotland and the Orkneys, but they are extravagant and even the century of his life is uncertain. He d. and was buried at Culross. *Servanus.*

*SERGIUS I, ST, pope. September 8.   SEPT., p. 88

Sergius I was pope from 687 till his death in 701 and his life is a part of general ecclesiastical history. His cultus began immediately after his death. He had a number of interesting contacts with England.

†*SERGIUS and BACCHUS, ST, marts. October 7.   OCT., p. 84

They were officers of the Roman army in Syria. On refusing to sacrifice to the gods in 303 St Bacchus was beaten to death and St Sergius was beheaded a week later, at Resapha in Mesopotamia.

SERLO, BD ab. March 3.   MAR., p. 43

A monk of Mont-Saint-Michel in Normandy to whom William the Conqueror confided the abbey of Gloucester : he received the abbatial

✱MARY OF CERVELLIONE, BD, virg. September 19. SEPT., p. 263
Also called *Maria de Socos*, " of Help." She is venerated as the first nun of the order of our Lady of Ransom (Mercedarians). Very little is known about her. d. 1290. c.c. 1690.

✱MARY OF EGYPT, ST. April 2. APR., p. 19
According to the earliest reference Mary of Egypt was an actress and courtesan who fled into the desert beyond Jordan to expiate her sins ; she was found dead by two disciples of St Cyriacus, *c.* 500. Round this narrative there grew up an elaborate legend which attained enormous popularity in the Middle Ages.

MARY OF OIGNIES, BD. June 23. JUNE, p. 311
She was b. at Nivelles in Belgium and displayed precocious piety as a child. Having been persuaded against her inclination to marry, it is said she induced her husband not to consummate the marriage, and they turned their house into a leper hospital. This they looked after themselves and Mary practised great austerities and was often visited by visions and ecstasies. Later her husband let her go to live in a cell adjoining a church at Oignies. This Mary and other Netherland mystics are important in the history of the evolution of Catholic devotion during the Middle Ages, and she is one of the first of whom details of certain strange phenomena (*e.g.* knowledge of what was happening at a distance) are forthcoming. An account of her life was written by Cardinal James de Vitry, who knew her intimately. d. 1213.

✱MATERNUS, ST, bp. September 14. SEPT., p. 169
He was the first bishop of Cologne of whom there is any certain knowledge, and is heard of in connection with the Donatist controversy. d. *c.* 325. St Maternus was given mythical associations with St Peter in a ninth-century biography.

✱MATILDA, ST. March 14. MAR., p. 246
She was the wife of King Henry the Fowler, and mother of, among others, the Emperor Otto I, St Bruno, Archbishop of Cologne, and Hedwige, who became mother of Hugh Capet. Matilda suffered much from the behaviour of her sons Otto and Henry (" the Quarrelsome "), who resented the amount of money she spent on religious and charitable works. Her widowhood lasted for thirty-two years, of which the latter part was spent in retirement at one or other of the convents she had established. d. at Quedlinburg 968. *Mathildis.*

✱MATRONA, ST, virg. and mart. March 15. MAR., p. 260
Said to have been the serving-maid of a Jewess who caused her to be martyred for her Christianity at Salonika in 350 (?). Two other Matronas are mentioned in the *Acta Sanctorum* on March 15, one a girl of Barcelona who was martyred at Rome and the other a maiden of Capua who was invoked locally against dysentery.

†✱MATTHEW, ST, ap. and evang. September 21. SEPT., p. 270
Beyond what is told in the Bible (*e.g.* that he was a tax-collector by profession) no more is known of St Matthew except that he wrote the gospel that bears his name. The scene of his preaching is not known, nor is it certain that he died a martyr. *Matthæus.*

MATTHEW CARRERI, BD. October 7. OCT., p. 89
A confessor of the Friars Preachers. Once, while on a voyage from Genoa to Pisa, he offered himself to some pirates in exchange for a captured woman and her daughter. d. 1470. c.c. 1482.

MATTHEW OF GIRGENTI, BD, bp.   February 3.   FEB., p. 58
 He left the Conventual Franciscans to join the Observants and became
a close friend of St Bernardino of Siena whom he accompanied on his
preaching journeys in Italy. He became a noted preacher himself, and
when he returned to his native Sicily he was appointed bishop of Girgenti.
He set about reforming his diocese and so made enemies whose slander
made it necessary for him to go to Rome to clear himself ; but his reforms
stirred up so much strife that he offered the resignation of his see, which
was accepted. Bd Matthew was then refused admittance to the friary
he had himself founded because they feared he was too much of a firebrand.
d. 1450. c.c. 1767.

MATTHIA NAZZAREI, BD, virg.   December 30.   DEC., p. 296
 She was an early nun and abbess of the famous Poor Clare Convent at
Matelica in the March of Ancona. d. 1300. In consequence of the marvels
that took place at her tomb when it was opened in 1756 the Holy See
confirmed her ancient cultus in 1765.

†***MATTHIAS, ST,** ap.   February 24.   FEB., p. 325
 The apostle of Christ who took the place of Judas Iscariot. Apart
from the reference in the *Acts of the Apostles* there is no reliable source
of information concerning him. He is said to have been martyred in
Colchis, *c.* 50.

***MATURINUS, ST.**   November 1.   NOV., p. 12
 Nothing is known of the true life of St Maturinus (Mathurin), whose
cultus still exists in the dioceses of Sens and Meaux.

MAUGHOLD, ST, bp.   April 25.   APR., p. 286
 Maughold is said to have been a brigand, converted by St Patrick,
who was sent to the Isle of Man as a missionary and became bishop there.
d. *c.* 498. He is commemorated in the diocese of Liverpool on April 27.
Maccaldus.

MAURA, ST, virg.   September 21.   SEPT., p. 272
 She passed her life in prayer and good works, living in her own home
at Troyes, where she d. while still young in 850.

MAURA AND BRIGID, SS, virg. and marts. July 13.   JULY, p. 166
 There is an old cultus of these maidens in Picardy, who according to
legend were British princesses murdered on their way home from a pilgrimage to Rome during the fifth century. Scholars have found it
impossible to give a satisfactory account of them from the sources
available.

MAURICE. *See also* Theban Legion.

MAURICE, ST, ab.   October 13.   OCT., p. 184
 A confessor of the Cistercian Order, monk of Langonet in Brittany
and then abbot of Carnoët. d. 1191. He may be the " St Mawes " of
Cornwall. c.c. by Pope Clement XI. *Mauritius.*

MAURICE OF HUNGARY, BD.   March 20.   MAR., p. 347
 Maurice Csaky, of the royal house of Hungary, became a Dominican
at the same time as his wife also entered religion ; his reputation was such
that he is still venerated by the Magyars. d. 1336.

***MAURILIUS, ST,** bp.   September 13.   SEPT., p. 159
 He was a disciple of St Martin of Tours and a zealous missionary,
who occupied the see of Angers for thirty years. d. *c.* 430.

verse ; as a bishop he was noted for the simplicity and sincerity of his daily life. d. *c.* 488.

SIGEBERT III, ST. February 1. FEB., p. 16

After the death of his father, Dagobert I, Sigebert governed Austrasia, his brother Clovis ruling in the rest of France. The reign of Sigebert was notably peaceful, and the young man gave himself up to good government and charitable works. Among his monastic foundations were Stavelot and Malmédy. d. 656. *Sigisbertus.*

SIGFRID, ST, bp. February 15. FEB., p. 230

Sigfrid, or Siegfried, is venerated as the apostle of Sweden, but his history is obscure. He seems to have been a priest of York or Glastonbury who went as missionary bishop to Scandinavia. Sigfrid converted King Olav of Sweden and established bishops in East and West Gothland. His own centre was at Wexiow, and when it was plundered and his three nephews murdered by the heathen, he refused to let the culprits be punished or to accept compensation from Olav. d. 1045. Sigfrid is said to have been canonized by the English pope Adrian IV in 1158. *Sigfridus.*

SIGFRID, ST, ab. August 22. AUG., p. 270

He was appointed abbot of Wearmouth, as coadjutor to St Benedict Biscop, in 686, and d. in 689. There is no trace of any liturgical cultus of St Sigfrid.

SIGIRANUS, ST, ab. December 5. DEC., p. 79

Sigiranus (Cyran) was archdeacon of Tours, of which see his father was bishop, but his desire was for the contemplative life. He accordingly founded and directed the abbeys of Meobecq and Lonrey. d. *c.* 655.

SIGISBERT, BD. July 11. JULY, p. 138

A disciple of St Columbanus who was a missionary in Switzerland and founded the monastery of Dissentis. d. *c.* 636. c.c. 1905. *Sigisbertus.*

*SIGISMUND, ST, mart. May 1. MAY, p. 12

Sigismund was a king of Burgundy, of Vandal extraction, and corresponding instincts : he had one of his sons strangled for rebuking his stepmother. At the same time Sigismund was a benefactor of the Church and founded the great monastery of St Maurice at Agaunum in Valais. After he had been defeated in battle by the sons of Clovis, he lived in hiding in a monk's habit near Agaunum, but was found and put to death by King Clodomir in 523. Thereafter he was revered as a martyr. *Sigismundus.*

*SILAS, ST. July 13. JULY, p. 164

Silas (Sylvanus) was a principal companion of St Paul of whom mention is made in the New Testament.

†*SILVERIUS, ST, pope and mart. June 20. JUNE, p. 250

Silverius was the son of Pope St Hormisdas and was chosen pope in 536 while still a subdeacon. He refused to restore the heretical bishop Anthimos to Constantinople at the request of the monophysite empress Theodora ; accordingly a charge of treason was trumped up against him and he was carried away prisoner. He d. of ill-treatment, or was murdered, on an island off Naples *c.* 537.

SILVESTER, BD. June 9. JUNE, p. 122

A wool-carder who in middle age became a Camaldolese lay brother at Florence. He was quite illiterate but so endowed with infused wisdom that he was often consulted by learned men. d. 1348.

†*SILVESTER I, ST, pope. December 31. Dec., p. 298

Silvester, a Roman, became pope in 314, less than a year after the emperor Constantine had granted toleration to Christianity. He is remembered rather on account of the events which followed this, including the Council of Nicæa, than of his personal life and achievements, of which little is known ; but doubtful and spurious legends are not lacking. It is not true, for example, that Constantine granted numerous rights to Silvester and his successors and endowed the Church with the lands of Italy, or that Silvester baptized the emperor. d. 335.

†*SILVESTER GOZZOLINI, ST, ab. November 26. Nov., p. 303

He was b. at Osimo in 1177 and deserted first the law and then a secular canonry to become a hermit. In 1231 he organized his followers into a congregation under the Rule of St Benedict at Monte Fano, near Fabriano, which soon had ten houses—the first of the Italian Benedictine reforms. St Silvester governed his monks with great wisdom and holiness for thirty-six years, and d. 1267. Equivalently cd. 1598. A few small monasteries of Sylvestrines (" Blue Benedictines ") still exist.

*SILVIN, ST, bp. February 17. Feb., p. 253

A regionary bishop who preached the gospel to the heathen in the region of Thérouanne. He is said to have lived for forty years on fruit and vegetables and to have owned nothing except his clothes and a horse. d. *c.* 720. *Silvinus.*

†*SIMEON, ST, bp. and mart. February 18. Feb., p. 259

Said to have been a relative of our Lord (Matt. xiii, 55). He succeeded St James as bishop at Jerusalem and was crucified at a great age, *c.* 107.

*SIMEON, ST. June 1. June, p. 7

He was b. at Syracuse in Sicily and became a monk and hermit in Palestine. He was sent on a mission by the abbot of Sinai to Duke Richard II in Normandy. After many adventures he reached Rouen and eventually settled down as a recluse at Trier, where he was venerated by all as a saint and a wonder-worker. d. 1035. cd. 1042.

*SIMEON, ST. July 26. July, p. 368

He was an Armenian who was a pilgrim in Europe, where he earned a reputation for miracles and for heroic charity. d. 1016.

*SIMEON, HOLY. October 8. Oct., p. 97

Holy Simeon, the just and devout man who awaited the consolation of Israel (Luke ii, 25), is named in the Roman Martyrology and his feast is observed in certain places.

SIMEON and other abbots, **BB.** November 16. Nov., p. 1??

During the twelfth-thirteenth century the abbey and congregation of Cava in Italy was governed by a remarkable series of abbots of much holiness and wisdom. There are particularly venerated the fifth to the eleventh abbots, Simeon, Falco, Marinus, Benincasa, Peter II, Balsamus, and Leonard, and the fifteenth, Leo II. This ancient cultus was confirmed in 1928.

*SIMEON BARSABÆ, ST, bp. and mart. April 21. Apr., p. 249

One of the longest individual entries in the Roman Martyrology is devoted to St Simeon Barsabæ, bishop of Seleucia-Ctesiphon, and his companions, martyrs in Persia in 341 during the persecution of King Sapor II.

nuisance to his richer friends. For all that he was one of the most distinguished and worthy churchmen of his time. d. 1036.

MEL and his comps., **SS**, bps.   February 6.   FEB., p. 89
SS Mel, Melchus, Munis, and Rioch are said to have been the sons of Conis and Darerca, sister of St Patrick, whom they accompanied to Ireland as missionaries. Mel is venerated as the first bishop at Ardagh, but the records of these saints are conflicting and largely legendary. Fifth century. *Melchus.*

*MELANIA THE YOUNGER, ST. December 31.   DEC., p. 301
She belonged to the Roman patrician family of the Valerii and was a granddaughter of St Melania the elder. She married her cousin Pinian *c.* 406, and after the death of their two children and the Visigothic invasion they lived abroad : eventually St Pinian became a monk at Jerusalem and Melania joined a community of women near by. They especially occupied themselves with the care of the poor and the copying of books. d. 439. The memory of this St Melania was revived in modern times by Cardinal Rampolla.

*MELANIUS ST, bp.   January 6.   JAN., p. 90
A bishop of Rennes, for whom King Clovis, after his conversion, had great respect. d. *c.* 530.

†*MELCHIADES, ST, pope and mart.   December 10.   DEC., p. 118
Melchiades (more properly Militiades) is chiefly remembered because it was during his short pontificate that the emperor Constantine granted toleration to the Church. He was an African, and is venerated as a martyr because he had suffered many things during the persecution of Maximian. d. 314.

*MELETIUS, ST, bp.   February 12.   FEB., p. 180
When he became archbishop of Antioch in 360 his diocese was divided by the Arian heresy and the whole of his pontificate of twenty years was troubled by this and other difficulties. Meletius was several times banished by the imperial power, and at one time there were three Catholic bishops disputing the see of Antioch ; Meletius slowly gained the bulk of Eastern support and he presided at the second oecumenical council, held at Constantinople in 381. He died while the council was still sitting.

MELITO, ST, bp.   April 1.   APR., p. 5
A bishop of Sardis in Lydia whose writings were praised by Eusebius and others. d. *c.* 180.

*MELLITUS, ST, bp.   April 24.   APR., p. 279
Mellitus followed St Augustine to England in 601 and was made the first bishop of London. He was banished for refusing holy communion to the apostate sons of King Sigebert of the East Saxons, but was recalled to be archbishop of Canterbury in 619. d. 624. His feast is kept in the dioceses of Westminster, Brentwood, and Southwark.

*MELLONUS, ST, bp.   October 22.   OCT., p. 301
Or *Melanius.* He is venerated as the first bishop of Rouen, at the beginning of the fourth century. He is said to have been a Briton, born near Cardiff, where there is a district called St Mellon's.

*MENAS, ST, bp.   August 25.   AUG., p. 306
He became patriarch of Constantinople in 536, and at the instance of the emperor Justinian condemned in synod a number of propositions of Origen. Menas was also concerned in the affair of the Three Chapters in the monophysite controversy. d. 552. *Mennas.*

†***MENAS, ST**, mart. November 11. Nov., p. 125
All that is probably certain about St Menas is that he was an Egyptian, martyred and buried at Karm aba-Mina, near Alexandria, perhaps *c.* 295. He was afterwards made into a " warrior saint," put to death in Phrygia and buried in Egypt, and his cultus was widespread in the East.

*****MENAS** and his comps., **SS**, mart. December 10. Dec., p. 121
Menas, Hermogenes, and Eugraphus were put to death by beheading at Alexandria *c.* 310. No reliance can be put on their *passio*, which was falsely ascribed to St Athanasius.

*****MENODORA**, etc., **SS**, marts. September 10. Sept., p. 121
The sisters Menodora, Metrodora, and Nymphodora are the subjects of a Greek legend which makes them martyrs in Bithynia under Diocletian.

*****MERCURIUS, ST**, mart. November 25. Nov., p. 298
He is said to have been a Scythian officer in the Roman army, beheaded for the Faith at Cæsarea in Cappadocia *c.* 250. He was afterwards revered in the East as a " warrior-saint."

MERIADEC, ST. June 7. June, p. 90
Meriadocus, Meriasek. This saint, probably a Welshman, is greatly venerated in Brittany, but his history is only conjectural : it is not even certain in which century he lived (5th or 6th ?). The parish church of Camborne in Cornwall is dedicated in his honour and he is the subject of the Cornish miracle-play, *Beunans Meriasek.*

MESROB, ST. November 25. Nov., p. 300
He was a monk and missionary in Armenia under St Isaac the Great ; to him is attributed the invention of the Armenian alphabet, the translation of the New Testament into that language, and the organization of studies and schools throughout the country, so that he is called in the Armenian liturgy, " Mesrob the Teacher." d. 441.

*****METHODIUS, ST**, bp. June 14. June, p. 178
Called " the Confessor." He was a strong opponent of the iconoclast heresy and was sent to Rome to report on the persecution to the Holy See. On his return to Constantinople in 821, he was thrown into prison, and remained there for seven years. In 842 he was made patriarch, and among his acts was to institute the Feast of Orthodoxy, still observed by the Byzantines, to commemorate the vindication of the true doctrine concerning holy images by the second Council of Nicæa. d. 847.

*****METHODIUS, ST**, bp. and mart. September 18. Sept., p. 247
He was bishop of Olympus in Lycia. Particulars are wanting of his life and martyrdom (*c.* 311), and his fame rests on his writings, especially his treatise on the Resurrection and the *Banquet of the Ten Virgins.*

*****METROPHANES, ST**, bp. June 4. June, p. 52
He was bishop of Byzantium (Constantinople) in the days of Constantine and probably the first bishop of that see. He had a great reputation for holiness throughout the Christian East, but little is known about him. d. 325.

†***MICHAEL THE ARCHANGEL, ST.** September 29. Sept., p. 361
St Michael is regarded traditionally as the chief of the archangels, the protector of the Church and her members against the attacks of Satan, the conductor of the souls of the dead, and, in the East, the patron of the sick. The occurrence of his name in the blessing of incense at Mass is a

A DICTIONARY OF SAINTS

death of St Antony. " His zeal against vice was without bitterness."
d. *c.* 429.

*SIXTUS I, ST, pope and mart. April 6.   Apr., p. 70

Sixtus I was pope from 117 to 127 ; he was a Roman by birth, but we have no particulars of his life or alleged martyrdom. The Sixtus named in the canon of the Mass is probably not this one, but Sixtus II. *Xystus.*

†*SIXTUS II, ST, pope and mart. August 6.   Aug., p. 71

He succeeded Pope St Stephen I in 257 and in the following year was seized and beheaded while preaching to the Christian assembly. Sixtus II was the most highly venerated among the popes martyred after St Peter, and he is named in the canon of the Mass.

*SIXTUS III, ST, pope. August 19.   Aug., p. 221

Sixtus III was pope from 432 till his death in 440. He banished the heretic Nestorius, built or restored several basilicas, and dedicated a number of churches, but of his personal life nothing is now known.

*SOCRATES AND STEPHEN, SS, mart. September 17.   Sept., p. 223

The Roman Martyrology commits itself to the statement that these martyrs suffered in Britain. Nothing is known of them, but Bithynia would seem to be the more likely scene of their passion.

SOLA, ST. December 3.   Dec., p. 48

Sola (or Solus) was an English disciple of St Boniface in Germany. He was a hermit, and on the piece of land given to him by Charlemagne grew up the abbey of Solnhofen, a dependency of Fulda. d. 794.

SOLANGIA, ST, virg. and mart. May 10.   May, p. 122

She is venerated in the French province of Berry as a shepherdess who was killed by a young nobleman when she resisted his attempts on her chastity, *c.* 880.

SOLOMON, ST, mart. June 25.   June, p. 339

This Solomon was the ruler of Brittany who successfully defended his country against both Franks and Northmen ; he did penance for the crimes of his earlier years and after his assassination in 874 was venerated as a martyr. There are many Breton legends about this national hero, who is called Selyf in their speech. *Salomon.*

*SOPHRONIUS, ST, bp. March 11.   Mar., p. 190

He was the patriarch of Jerusalem who convened a synod to condemn Monothelism, and sent a legate to urge the Holy See to do the same, which happened at a synod at the Lateran in 649. But before that Sophronius had been driven from his see when the Saracens took Jerusalem in 638, and he is thought to have died of grief very soon after. This saint is generally identified with Sophronius the Sophist, who was fellow-hermit and pilgrim with John Moschus, author of the *Spiritual Meadow.*

†*SOTER, ST, pope and mart. April 22.   Apr., p. 255

Very little is known about this pope and there are no particulars of his martyrdom ; d. 174.

*SOTERIS, ST, virg. and mart. February 10.   Feb., p. 148

A martyr at Rome, under Diocletian in 304, of whom St Ambrose speaks.

*SOZON, ST, mart. September 7.   Sept., p. 75

According to a Greek legend Sozon was a young Cilician shepherd who smashed an idol with his crook and was accordingly burned, at Pompeiopolis in 304.

*SPECIOSUS, ST. March 15.   MAR., p. 261
A monk who received the habit from St Benedict himself and died in the monastery at Capua *c.* 545.

*SPERATUS, ST, mart. July 17.   JULY, p. 226
Speratus and six other men and five women are known as the Scillitan Martyrs from the place of their passion, Scillium in Africa, in 180. Their *acta* are unusually free from later editorial "improvement."

*SPES, ST, ab. March 28.   MAR., p. 426
An abbot of Campi in central Italy who for many years of his life was deprived of sight. d. *c.* 513.

*SPEUSIPPUS, etc., SS, marts. January 17.   JAN., p. 217
According to a probably fictitious legend Speusippus, Eleusippus, and Meleusippus were three twin brothers who, with their grandmother Leonilla, suffered martyrdom at Langres under Marcus Aurelius.

*SPIRIDION, ST, bp. December 14.   DEC., p. 163
Spiridion, shepherd of sheep and pastor of souls, figures in numerous stories of marvels. He became bishop of Tremithus in Cyprus and was mutilated during the persecution of Galerius; he was present at the Council of Nicæa and is said there to have converted a heathen philosopher. d. *c.* 348.

†*STANISLAUS, ST, bp. and mart. May 7.   MAY, p. 85
Stanislaus Szczepanovsky was b. in 1030 and appointed bishop of Cracow in 1072. He proved to be an exemplary bishop, to the extent of excommunicating his prince, Boleslaus II the Cruel, for his oppressive rule and evil life. In revenge Boleslaus with his own hand murdered the bishop while he was celebrating Mass on May 8, 1079. Pope Gregory VII laid Poland under an interdict for this crime, and Innocent IV cd. Stanislaus in 1253; but some Polish historians allege that the bishop had plotted to dethrone his sovereign.

*STANISLAUS KOSTKA, ST. November 13.   NOV., p. 165
B. in 1550, son of a Polish senator. He made up his mind to be a Jesuit, and was received into the Society at the age of seventeen in the face of angry opposition from his family. Stanislaus was more than a model novice, but before the year was out he had died, on August 15, 1568. He was indeed " made perfect in a short while and fulfilled many times by the angelic innocence of his life." cd. 1726.

STEPHANA QUINZANI, BD, virg. January 2.   JAN., p. 44
B. in 1457 near Brescia, and was a secular Dominican tertiary until she was enabled to found a convent of that order. A contemporary account (1497) is extant, signed by twenty-one witnesses, describing in detail one of the ecstasies in which Bd Stephana represented in her own person the different stages of the passion of Christ. d. 1530. Cultus confirmed by Pope Benedict XIV.

STEPHEN, ST, bp. and mart. June 2.   JUNE, p. 26
Very little is known of this St Stephen, who is venerated as first bishop of Helsingborg in Sweden. He is said to have been a monk of New Corbie in Saxony and eventually slain by the heathen in 1075 (?) at Upsala or Nora. *Stephanus.*

†*STEPHEN, ST, mart. December 26.   DEC., p. 249
The martyrdom of Stephen, the first deacon and the Church's first martyr for Christ, whom St Luke calls " a man full of faith and of the

Ireland, who evangelized various parts of his native land. d. at Rossmarkie
c. 572 ; his shrine was at Mortlach, *i.e.* Murlach. *Moluanus.*

MOLUA, ST, ab.   August 4.   AUG., p. 56
This Molua (Lugaidh Maccan) founded many monasteries in Ireland,
the chief of which was at Kyle in the Slieveblooms. His identity with the
Scottish St Moloc has not been established. d. 605.

MOMMOLINUS, ST, bp.   October 16.   OCT., p. 225
A monk of Luxeuil who became bishop of Noyon and Tournai c. 659.
d. c. 686.

*MONEGUNDIS, ST.   July 2.   JULY, p. 16
A woman of Chartres who, after the death of her two daughters, shut
herself up in a cell ; later she migrated to Tours and followed the same
way of life : her cell there became the nunnery and collegiate church of
St. Pierre-le-Puellier. d. 570.

†*MONICA, ST.   May 4.   MAY, p. 46
St Monica was born of Christian parents at Tagaste in north Africa
in 332, and married a pagan husband who hampered her in the Christian
upbringing of their three children. He was converted by her gentleness
and prayers just before his death, and thenceforward her life was the story
of the conversion of her elder son, Augustine, afterwards the holy bishop
of Hippo and doctor of the Church. She followed him to Rome and to
Milan (where St Ambrose was her friend and helper), and there her prayers
and sufferings were rewarded ; it was not possible " that the son of such
tears should perish." St Monica d. at Ostia Tiberina on the way back to
Africa with St Augustine in 387 ; the translation of her relics from Ostia
to Rome in 1430 seems to have been the occasion of the beginning of her
cultus.

*MONTANUS, ST, and other marts.   February 24.   FEB., p. 326
In 259 there was an insurrection at Carthage, which the procurator
Solon unjustly blamed upon the Christians. Montanus, Lucius, and six
others, all disciples of St Cyprian, were arrested, and we have a reliable
contemporary account of their sufferings and death, written in part by
one of the martyrs. After being kept in prison with hardly any food or
drink for several months they were beheaded. One of them, Julian, was
reprieved because of his popularity with the people, but he insisted that the
plea made for him, that he was not a deacon and therefore not liable to
the death penalty, was false ; and accordingly three days later he, too, was
beheaded.

MORANDUS, ST.   June 3.   JUNE, p. 39
He was b. near Worms and after his ordination became a Cluniac
monk. While serving the church of Altkirch in Alsace he distinguished
himself as a missioner all over the neighbouring countryside. d. c. 1115.

MORICUS, BD.   March 30.   MAR., p. 447
He is said to have been the fifth recruit to join the Friars Minor, and
is honoured among the Franciscans. d. 1236.

*MOSES, ST, bp.   February 7.   FEB., p. 105
An Arabian missionary bishop among the nomadic tribes of the Syro-
Arabian desert. d. c. 372. *Moyses.*

*MOSES, ST, mart.   November 25.   NOV., p. 299
He was a priest at Rome and one of the first to be arrested in the
Decian persecution ; he died after a year's imprisonment c. January 1, 251.

A DICTIONARY OF SAINTS

*MOSES THE BLACK, ST, mart. August 28. AUG., p. 366
Moses was an Ethiopian, first a slave and then a brigand in Egypt ; he was converted, became a monk and priest in the desert of Skete, and in old age was murdered by robbers against whom he refused to defend himself. He was one of the most remarkable figures among the Desert Fathers during the fourth century.

*MOUNT SINAI, THE MARTYRS OF. January 14. JAN., p. 176
During the fourth century several groups of solitaries on Mount Sinai and in the near-by desert of Raithu were put to death by Bedu Arabs. They are mentioned in the Roman Martyrology and commemorated in the Byzantine rite.

*MUCIUS, ST, mart. May 13. MAY, p. 159
A priest who was put to death for the Faith at Constantinople in 304.

MUNCHIN, ST, bp. January 2. JAN., p. 36
The traditional patron of the diocese of Limerick, of whom practically nothing is known. He is said to have lived in the sixth–seventh century, but it is doubtful if he ever was a bishop.

MUNDUS, ST, ab. April 15. APR., p. 174
There is difficulty in identifying this tenth-century abbot, once venerated as the patron of Argyllshire ; some have thought him the same as St Fintan Munnu.

MUNGO, ST. *See* Kentigern.

MURTAGH, ST, bp. August 12. AUG., p. 150
Murtagh (Muredach) is venerated liturgically throughout Ireland as the first bishop in Killala, probably in the sixth century. *Muredachus.*

MYLOR, ST, martyr. October 1. OCT., p. 9
The story of the martyred prince Melorus (Mélar in Brittany, Mylor in Cornwall) is a mediæval fable worked up out of several Celtic elements ; whether it has any foundation in fact is not known. Its events were localized both in Brittany and Cornwall, and he was one of the titulars of the abbey of Amesbury, which claimed his relics.

NABOR and FELIX, SS, marts. July 12. JULY, p. 157
Martyrs under Diocletian at Milan, where they have an ancient cultus and are named in the canon of the Ambrosian Mass.

*NAGRAN, THE MARTYRS OF. October 24. OCT., p. 322
Nagran (Nedjran), in south-western Arabia, was the scene in 523 of a massacre of Ethiopian and other Christians by Jews and heathen Arabs, a leader among the victims being the chief of the Beni Harith, Abdullah ibn Kaab (called in the Roman Martyrology St " Aretas "). This massacre made a deep and awful impression which lasted for many generations in the East : Mohammed mentions it in the Koran.

*NARCISSUS, ST, bp. October 29. OCT., p. 353
When he was already very old Narcissus was made bishop of Jerusalem at the end of the second century. He retired from his see for a time in consequence of a false accusation made against him. He was greatly venerated by his people, who narrated several miracles of him. d. c. 220.

*NARCISSUS and FELIX, SS, marts. March 18. MAR., p. 310
Nothing certainly true is known about these martyrs, who are mixed up with the fictitious part of the legend of St Afra.

NATALIS PINOT, BD, mart. February 21. FEB., p. 297
Natalis (Noel) Pinot, b. at Angers in 1747, was parish priest of Louroux-Béconnais. At the time of the French Revolution he was one of those who refused to take the illegal oath. The court forbade him to minister in his parish for two years, but he continued to do so secretly and afterwards openly. He was eventually arrested when vested for Mass and, after again refusing the oath, was guillotined, still in his vestments, twelve days later, 1794. bd. 1926.

NATHALAN, ST, bp. January 19. JAN., p. 231
According to the ancient Aberdeen Breviary Nathalan, believing that " amongst the works of man's hands the cultivation of the earth approaches nearest to divine contemplation," gave himself up to that occupation in which he earned a great reputation for holiness and miracles. While on a pilgrimage to Rome he was made bishop, and on his return founded churches in Scotland. d. 678. His cultus was confirmed for the diocese of Aberdeen in 1898. *Nathalanus.*

NATHY and PHELIM, SS. August 9. AUG., p. 114
St Nathy was a monk and priest at Achonry and St Phelim was probably a regionary bishop in the Breffney country. Though not associated with one another, so far as is known, these two sixth-century saints are celebrated throughout Ireland by a common feast. *Natheus.*

†*NAZARIUS and CELSUS, SS, marts. July 28. JULY, p. 388
The only certain thing about these martyrs is that St Ambrose searched for and found their reputed relics at Milan, where they are supposed to have suffered.

NECTAN, ST. June 17. JUNE, p. 216

Nectan was venerated as a martyr at his shrine at Hartland in Devon and elsewhere in the west of England during the Middle Ages, but nothing at all is known about him. He may have been a missionary from Ireland in the sixth century as his name appears in the Martyrologies of Donegal and Tallaght.

NECTARIUS, ST, bp. October 11. OCT., p. 148

He succeeded St Gregory Nazianzen as archbishop of Constantinople and ruled for sixteen years. d. 397.

*NEMESIAN, ST, mart. September 10. SEPT., p. 120

The Roman Martyrology on September 10 names Nemesian, Bishop of Tubunæ, and eight other African bishops who with numerous lower clergy and lay people suffered under the persecution of Valerian in 257. *Nemesianus.*

*NEMESIUS, ST, mart. December 19. DEC., p. 204

He was an Alexandrian who in 250, upon being acquitted on a charge of theft, was condemned as a Christian and executed with a number of criminals.

NEOT, ST. July 31. JULY, p. 446

Nothing is certainly known of St Neot : according to mediæval legends he was a monk of Glastonbury in the ninth century who became a hermit at the place now called Saint Neot in Cornwall.

NEPOTIAN, ST. May 4. MAY, p. 54

There does not appear to have been any cultus of this young man, who was first an officer in the imperial bodyguard and was then ordained priest by his uncle St Heliodorus of Altino. d. 395. *Nepotianus.*

*NERONIAN MARTYRS, THE. June 24. JUNE, p. 322

On June 24 the Roman Martyrology mentions " the first fruits with which Rome, so fruitful in that seed, peopled Heaven," namely, those Christians who in the year 64 were put to death with refinements of cruelty by order of Nero on a false charge of having set fire to the city. That Nero himself had fired it is by no means certain.

NERSES, ST, bp. and mart. November 20. NOV., p. 253

He was bishop of Sahgerd in Persia and, with his disciple St Joseph, was beheaded under Sapor II in 343 for refusing false worship. A number of other martyrs are referred to in the *passio* of St Nerses.

NERSES THE GREAT, ST, bp. and mart. November 19. NOV., p. 250

This Nerses married a princess of the Mamikonian family, by whom he was the father of St Isaac the Great. After the death of his wife he became, *c.* 363, katholikos, or chief bishop of the Armenian church and laboured to spread Christianity among the common people, but some of his reforms displeased King Arshak, who banished him. The succeeding monarch, Pap, was atrociously wicked and would neither behave himself nor submit to the religious discipline that Nerses imposed on him ; in the end, Pap poisoned the bishop in 373.

NERSES GLAIÉTSI, ST, bp. August 13. AUG., p. 164

Nerses Glaiëtsi (" the Gracious ") was the most famous writer of the twelfth-century Armenian renaissance and a fervent upholder of the unity of the Church. He became chief bishop of his people, as Nerses IV, in 1166, maintained the communion of his see with the Roman church, and worked for the reconciliation of the Orthodox Greeks. d. 1173.

NERSES LAMBRONAZI, ST, bp.   July 17.   JULY, p. 239
He was Armenian archbishop of Tarsus and played a chief part in
the events which led up to the reunion of Little Armenia with the Holy
See in 1198. St Nerses d. in the same year. Among other literary works he
translated the Rule of St Benedict into Armenian.

†*NEREUS and **ACHILLEUS, SS,** marts. May 12.   MAY, p. 139
Two Roman soldiers who on becoming Christians left the army and
were martyred. First century (?). Their extant *acta* are legendary.

***NESTOR, ST,** bp. and mart. February 26.   FEB., p. 357
Bishop of Magido in Pamphylia, put to death for the Faith by crucifixion in 251.

***NICANDER** and **MARCIAN, SS,** marts. June 17.   JUNE, p. 211
These martyrs, formerly soldiers in the Roman army, were put to death
by beheading, probably somewhere in what is now Rumania or Bulgaria,
but at an uncertain date (303 ?).

***NICARETE, ST,** virg. December 27.   DEC., p. 260
She came from Nicomedia and was a supporter of St John Chrysostom
at Constantinople ; like St Olympias she suffered persecution and exile
in consequence. She died early in the fifth century.

***NICASIUS, ST,** bp. and mart. December 14.   DEC., p. 165
He was a bishop of Rheims who, with his sister St Eutropia and several
members of his clergy, was killed by invading barbarians while defending
his flock, in 407 or 451.

***NICEPHORUS, ST,** mart. February 9.   FEB., p. 139
It appears that Nicephorus, who was said to be a martyr at Antioch
c. 260, was the hero of a pious romance whose object was to teach the
lesson of forgiveness of injuries.

***NICEPHORUS, ST,** bp. March 13.   MAR., p. 227
B. 758. He was an official at the imperial court at Constantinople
and distinguished himself as an opponent of Iconoclasm ; while still a
layman he was elected patriarch of Constantinople in 806, and incurred
the strong disapproval of St Theodore and his Studite monks. At the
second outbreak of Iconoclasm, under the emperor Leo the Armenian,
Nicephorus was exiled and spent the last fifteen years of his life in a monastery he had founded on the Bosphorus. d. June 2, 828. March 13 is the
anniversary of the translation of his relics to the church of the Apostles
at Constantinople in 846.

***NICETAS, ST,** ab. April 3.   APR., p. 37
He was abbot of Medikion on Mount Olympus in Bithynia, who with
his monks was much persecuted for his opposition to the iconoclastic
emperor Leo and his intruded patriarch of Constantinople. He spent many
years in prison. d. 824.

NICETAS, ST. October 6.   OCT., p. 76
He was a young patrician of Constantinople who became a monk
there and distinguished himself by his opposition to the Iconoclasts He
d. in exile in Paphlagonia c. 838.

***NICETAS THE GOTH, ST,** mart. September 15.   SEPT., p. 177
He was one of the Eastern Goths put to death c. 378 by King Athanaric
who wished to exterminate Christians from his dominions. Nicetas was a

priest and may have been (in ignorance and good faith) an Arian. In the East he is called " the Great."

*NICETAS OF REMESIANA, ST, bp.   June 22.   JUNE, p. 293
This Nicetas was an exceedingly successful missionary in the country now called Rumania and Yugoslavia. It is strongly held by some scholars that he was the author of the thanksgiving hymn, " Te Deum." d. c. 414.

NICETIUS, ST, bp.   February 8.   FEB., p. 119
A holy bishop of Besancon, a friend of St Gregory the Great and of St Columbanus. d. c. 611.

*NICETIUS, ST, bp.   April 2.   APR., p. 23
This Nicetius, or Nizier, was bishop of Lyons for twenty years and d. in 573.

*NICETIUS, ST, bp.   December 5.   DEC., p. 76
Nicetius was the last Gallo-Roman bishop of Trier, being named to that see c. 532. He fearlessly opposed the cruelty of the Frankish nobles and even excommunicated Clotaire I for his crimes, so that for a time the bishop was banished. Nicetius was tireless in restoring to discipline a diocese that had suffered much from civil disorder, and he founded a school for young clerics. d. c. 566.

†*NICHOLAS, ST, bp.   December 6.   DEC., p. 84
Although St Nicholas was, and still is, one of the most popular of saints both in the East and the West no more is certainly known of him than that he was bishop of Myra in Lycia in the fourth century and that his alleged relics, stolen by Italian merchants in 1087, now rest at Bari, whence in the West he is often called " of Bari." The varied and in parts fantastic legends of St Nicholas are first heard of some five hundred years after his death ; his patronage of children seems to have arisen from his restoring to life three murdered boys who had been pickled in a brine-tub ! (St Nicholas=Sint Klaes=Santa Klaus.) He is also a patron of sailors, of captives, of several countries and provinces (including Russia), of many cities and dioceses (including Galway), and of churches innumerable. *Nicolaus.*

*NICHOLAS I, ST, pope.   November 13.   NOV., p. 157
Nicholas the Great came to the papal chair in 858 and ruled for nine years. The chief event of his pontificate was the dispute with Photius at Constantinople. In other struggles this pope stood up to the great ones of the earth in defence of the integrity of Christian marriage, the protection of the weak, and the equality of all before the divine law: he rebuked emperors and kings and archbishops impartially. Nicholas was " patient and temperate, humble and chaste, beautiful in face and graceful in body . . . the champion of the people." d. 867.

*NICHOLAS ALBERGATI, BD, bp.   May 9.   MAY, p. 114
Bd. Nicholas was a Carthusian monk. In 1417 he was appointed bishop of Bologna and in 1426 a cardinal, and had so great a reputation as a mediator that he was called " the angel of peace." He played a prominent part in the Council of Florence, dying at Siena in 1443. c.c. 1744.

NICHOLAS FACTOR, BD.   December 23.   DEC., p. 230
A confessor of the Friars Minor of the Observance in Spain, with whose name many marvels are associated. d. 1583. St Paschal Baylon and St Louis Bertrand gave evidence for his beatification in 1786.

NICHOLAS VON FLUE, BD. March 22. MAR., p. 372

He was the son of a farmer, b. in Unterwalden in 1417, and twice fought in the military forces of his canton, where he was appointed magistrate and deputy for Obwalden in public affairs. He married when a young man and had ten children, several of whom distinguished themselves. When he was fifty Nicholas heard a call from God, left his family with their consent, and spent nineteen years as a hermit at Ranft. When the Swiss Confederation was convulsed with dissensions in 1481 it consulted Bd Nicholas, and it is possible that he helped to draw up the Edict of Stans. d. 1487. As " Bruder Klaus " Bd Nicholas was and is honoured throughout Switzerland as a patriot and a saint : ecclesiastics, politicians, historians, and poets of all beliefs have sung his praises. c.c. 1669.

NICHOLAS HERMANSSÖN, BD, bp. July 24. JULY, p. 342

He was bishop of Linköping in Sweden and a counsellor of St Bridget, a poet and liturgist, an upholder of clerical celibacy, and a father to the poor and oppressed. d. 1391. His formal canonization by Pope John XXIII has not been established.

NICHOLAS MYSTICUS, ST, bp. May 15. MAY, p. 194

He was banished from the patriarchal see of Constantinople by the emperor Leo the Wise for refusing to recognize his fourth marriage (fourth marriages were forbidden in the Eastern church). d. 925.

NICHOLAS OWEN, BD, mart. March 12. MAR., p. 222

It has been said that probably no single person did more for the preservation of the Catholic religion in England during the penal times than this workman, who in the reign of James I saved the lives of uncounted priests by his great skill in devising hiding-places for them. After he had worked in this way for years he was admitted to the Society of Jesus as a temporal coadjutor, and was the companion of Fr Henry Garnett. Owen was twice imprisoned and tortured ; after his third arrest the torments inflicted in a vain attempt to make him betray his fellows and admit complicity in the Gunpowder Plot were so barbarous that he died under them—literally torn in pieces. This was in the Tower of London in 1606. bd. 1929.

NICHOLAS PALEA, BD. February 14. FEB., p. 224

Having heard St Dominic preach at Bologna he joined the Friars Preachers and founded priories at Perugia in 1233 and Trani in 1254. He became prior provincial of the Roman province and was " a holy and prudent man, well versed in sacred lore." d. 1255. c.c. 1828.

***NICHOLAS PEREGRINUS, ST.** June 2. JUNE, p. 27

Nicholas the Pilgrim was a young Greek who wandered about southern Italy carrying a cross and crying out " Kyrie eleison." He was generally treated as a tramp or a lunatic, but after his death at Trani in 1094 miracles were alleged at his tomb and he was cd. in 1098.

NICHOLAS STUDITES, ST, ab. February 4. FEB., p. 71

A native of Crete who became abbot of the Studion at Constantinople during the iconoclast persecution ; together with the patriarch Nicephorus and others he was banished for opposing Iconoclasm, first under the emperor Leo and then under Michael the Stammerer. He continued to be a leader of orthodoxy, until he was again exiled for supporting the patriarch St Ignatius against Photius. He was at last restored to freedom and died among his monks in 863.

NICHOLAS TAVIGLI, BD, mart. December 5. DEC., p. 81

For twenty years he was a Franciscan missionary among the Paterine heretics of Bosnia ; he then went to Palestine, where he was martyred for preaching to the Mohammedans in 1391. c.c. by Pope Leo XIII.

NICHOLAS OF FORCA-PALENA, BD. October 1. OCT., p. 10

He founded a society of hermits under the patronage of St Jerome in Naples, Florence, and Rome, which was later amalgamated with the Hieronymites. d. 1449. c.c. 1774.

†*NICHOLAS OF TOLENTINO, ST. September 10. SEPT., p. 115

He was b. near Fermo in Italy in 1245 and became a friar of the Augustinian Order. He led an uneventful life, distinguished for his patience and humility and unwearying assiduity in preaching; he was stationed at Tolentino for thirty years, where he was known as much for his selfless work in the slums as for his many miracles. d. 1305. cd. 1446.

†*NICOMEDES, ST, mart. September 15. SEPT., p. 176

Nicomedes was venerated as a martyr at Rome at an early date, but nothing is known of his passion.

*NICOMEDIA, THE MARTYRS OF. December 25. DEC., p. 243

According to a Greek tradition, accepted by the Roman Martyrology, many thousands of Christians were burned alive in their church at Nicomedia while celebrating the feast of Christmas in 303, by order of Diocletian. But there are difficulties in the way of accepting the story in the form in which it has been preserved.

*NICON METANOITE, ST. November 26. NOV., p. 309

He was first a monk at Khrysopetro and then a missionary, in Armenia, for twenty years in Crete, and in Greece. He received the name "Meta-noite " from his frequent calls to penance. d. 998.

*NILUS THE ELDER, ST, ab. November 12. NOV., p. 139

He was an imperial official at Constantinople, who in middle life retired with one of his sons to the monastery at Mount Sinai, where he achieved a reputation as a theological, biblical, and ascetical writer. d. c. 430.

*NILUS THE YOUNGER, ST, ab. September 26. SEPT., p. 325

After a careless youth he became a monk and then abbot of the Byzantine monastery of St Adrian, near San Demetrio Corone in Calabria. The community was driven out by the Saracens c. 981, and for fifteen years lived at Vellelucio on lands given by the abbey of Monte Cassino. In 1004 St Nilus was taken ill in the Alban hills and had a vision that here was the final abiding-place of his monks ; he died very soon after, but the migration was carried out, and thus was established the still flourishing Greek monastery of Grottaferrata, near Rome : St Nilus is accounted its first abbot.

*NINIAN, ST, bp. September 16. SEPT., p. 207

The "first authentic personage that meets us in the succession of Scottish missionaries." He was a bishop from Britain who established his see at Whithern (*Candida Casa*, the White House) in Wigtownshire. A monastery was attached, and Ninian and his monks preached the gospel among the northern Britons and the Picts, for whom he had to consecrate several bishops (Ninian himself is said to have been consecrated in Rome). d. 432 (?). The feast of St Ninian (Ninnidh) is kept throughout Scotland and in the dioceses of Lancaster and Hexham. *Ninianus.*

NINNOC, ST. June 4. JUNE, p. 54

He was probably the missionary who evangelized the district of Lan-

Ninnoc in Brittany during the fifth century but nothing is known about him. The Bretons venerate him as an abbess but it is unlikely that Ninnoc was a woman.

*NINO, ST, virg. December 15.   DEC., p. 173

Nino is said to have been a slave girl, brought as a captive into Georgia (Iberia), who by her goodness, teaching, and miracles brought about the conversion of many people, and eventually of the king and queen, in the earlier part of the fourth century. She is venerated as the Apostle of Georgia and it is possible that the story had some basis in fact, but it has become overlaid by many and contradictory legends. The Roman Martyrology, not knowing the maiden's local name, calls her " St Christiana." The Armenians associate her with the legend of their SS Rhipsime and Gaiana.

NOEL. *See* Natalis.

NONIUS, BD. November 6.   NOV., p. 78

Nuñez Alvarez de Pereira is a national hero of Portugal, having with King John I overcome the armies of Castile and established a Portuguese sovereign state. After the death of his wife in 1422 Nonius entered the Carmelite Order as a lay-brother at Lisbon. d. 1431. c.c. 1918.

*NONNA, ST. August 5.   AUG., p. 67

She converted her pagan husband, who is now known as St Gregory Nazianzen the Elder, and they were the parents of the younger saint of that name, of St Gorgonia, and of St Cæsarius, the last two of whom predeceased her. d. 374.

NONNUS, ST, ab. June 14.   JUNE, p. 177

Also *Nennus, Nem, Nehemias.* One of the abbots who ruled in Aran after the death of St Enda. d. 654 (?).

†*NORBERT, ST, bp. June 6.   JUNE, p. 74

Norbert was b. of a princely family at Xanten in 1080 and received holy orders as a means to worldly advancement. In 1115 he was converted by a narrow escape from death : he left the court of the emperor, was ordained priest and, after vainly trying to reform the chapter of canons at Xanten of which he was a member, became a wandering preacher. At Prémontré in Lâon he founded in 1120 a community of canons regular of strict observance which, under the name of Premonstratensians or Norbertines, spread with great rapidity ; Norbert himself, however, was obliged to accept the bishopric of Magdeburg, where he was a vigorous reformer and more than once was the object of physical violence. He took an important part in the politics of the time and persuaded the emperor Lothair II to lead an army into Italy to reinstate the exiled Pope Innocent II. By his preaching against certain heresies St Norbert did much to forward the external cultus of the Blessed Sacrament. d. 1134. cd. 1582. *Norbertus.*

*NORTH AMERICA, MARTYRS OF. March 16.   MAR., p. 266

A group of Jesuits with two laymen who were martyred by the Indians at various dates between 1642 and 1649. They were SS John Brébeuf, Isaac Jogues, René Goupil (qq.v.), John Lalande, Antony Daniel, Gabriel Lalemant, Charles Garnier and Noel Chabanel. Their ceaseless labours in an unknown land, the shocking tortures some of them suffered, and their noble deaths excited the admiration of the historian Francis Parkman, who devoted a volume to the Jesuits in North America. These martyrs were canonized in 1930. Their feast is kept on March 16 by the Society of Jesus and on September 26 by the Church in North America.

NOTBURGA, ST, virg. September 14.   SEPT., p. 170

Notburga was a younger contemporary of St Zita, and led a similar life in Bavaria, where she was a servant first in a noble family and then to a farmer. In later life she returned to the service of Count Henry, by whose wife she had been dismissed for giving away food to the poor. d. 1313. c.c. 1862.

NOTHELM, ST, bp. October 17.   OCT., p. 243

He was elected archbishop of Canterbury in 734 and was St Bede's source for the records and traditions of that church when he was writing his *Ecclesiastical History.* d. *c.* 740.

NOTKER BALBULUS, BD. April 6.   APR., p. 76

This monk of Saint Gall, famous in the history of liturgical hymnody, is still honoured as a saint in Switzerland, one who was, in the words of a contemporary, " weakly in body but not in mind, stammering of tongue but not of intellect, pressing forward boldly in things divine—a vessel filled with the Holy Ghost without equal in his time." d. 912. c.c. 1512.

NOVELLONE, BD. July 27.   JULY, p. 383

A shoemaker of Faenza, and a Franciscan tertiary, who made numerous pilgrimages and was greatly revered locally. After his wife's death he became a hermit. d. 1280. c.c. 1817.

*NUNILO and **ALODIA, SS,** virgs. and marts. October 22. OCT., p. 301

They were the daughters of a Christian mother at Huesca in Spain and suffered from the brutality of a Mohammedan stepfather. They were beheaded for their faith during the persecution of Abderrahman in 851.

†*NYMPHA, ST, virg. November 10.   NOV., p. 114

She seems to have been a native of Palermo and may have been martyred there *c.* 313. St Nympha is commemorated with SS Tryphon and Respicius because the reputed relics of all three were enshrined at the hospital of Santo Spirito in Sassia at Rome.

OBICIUS, ST. February 4.   FEB., p. 74

A knight of Brescia who was nearly drowned in battle and had a vision of Hell which changed his life. He d. c. 1200 and miracles were reported at his tomb.

ODA, BD, virg. April 20.   APR., p. 239

Oda publicly refused the husband offered to her and entered a convent of Premonstratensian canonesses. d. 1158.

ODDINO BARROTTI, BD. July 21.   JULY, p. 305

He was a parish priest and gild chaplain at Fossano in Piedmont, whose devoted life and activities have never been forgotten in that town. d. 1400. c.c. 1808.

*ODILIA, ST, virg. December 13.   DEC., p. 155

According to tradition Odilia was the daughter of a Frankish lord who insisted that she be brought up away from her family because she was blind from birth. She recovered her sight miraculously, was reconciled with her father, and founded a nunnery at his castle of Hohenburg (Odilienberg) which she ruled till the end of her days. d. *c.* 720. St Odilia, who is the subject of several legends, is the patron saint of Alsace, and the Odilienberg has again become a popular place of pilgrimage in modern times ; the water of her well is used for unhealthy eyes. *Othilia.*

*ODILO, ST, ab. January 1.   JAN., p. 21

Succeeded St Majolus as abbot of Cluny in 994, and was one of its great early abbots ; under his rule the number of Cluniac houses rose from 37 to 65. He was active in promoting the " peace of God " and instituted the annual commemoration of all the faithful departed. d. 1049.

ODO, BD, bp. June 19.   JUNE, p. 243

This Odo was a distinguished scholar, director of the cathedral school at Tournai, where he attracted students from foreign lands. Becoming dissatisfied with this life he founded a community of Benedictines, from which he was removed after thirteen years to be bishop of Cambrai. But he refused to receive secular investiture from the emperor and was exiled. d. 1113.

ODO OF NOVARIA, BD. January 14.   JAN., p. 179

A Carthusian and prior of Geyrach in Slavonia, whence he was driven by the persecution of the local bishop. Odo became chaplain to a convent at Tagliacozzo in Italy, where he lived to be nearly a hundred and d. in 1200. There is an official account by his contemporaries of his manner of life and the miracles attributed to him.

ODO THE GOOD, ST, bp. July 4.   JULY, p. 41

B. in East Anglia, probably of Danish parents. While bishop of an unidentified see in Wessex he was present at the battle of Brunanburh, and in 942 was made archbishop of Canterbury, in which capacity he took a leading part in the legislation of Kings Edmund and Edgar. St Odo is said to have been the agent of a miracle in vindication of the Real Presence. d. 959.

*ODO OF CLUNY, ST, ab. November 18.   Nov., p. 236

Odo was the second and one of the greatest abbots of Cluny. He succeeded St Berno in 927 and dedicated his life to the reform of the monasteries of France ; his union of some of these houses under his own control was the beginning of the Cluniac congregation. By his regulation of the life of St Paul's-outside-the-Walls of Rome he carried the spirit of Cluny beyond the borders of France, and his influence was felt elsewhere in Italy. d. 942.

ODORIC OF PORDENONE, BD. January 28.   Jan., p. 356

This Franciscan friar made one of the most remarkable journeys of the Middle Ages. He left his friary at Udine about 1317 and went to northern China via Armenia, Baghdad, Malabar, Ceylon, Sumatra, and Java. He was in Peking for three years and came home via Lhasa. Odoric dictated an account of his adventures to one of his brethren but does not say much about his missionary activities while on his travels ; later accounts state that they were considerable. d. 1331. c.c. 1755. *Odericus*.

ODULPHUS, ST. June 12.   June, p. 159

He was the foremost helper of St Frederick in the completion of the evangelization of the Frisians. He was a native of Brabant and d. at Utrecht *c.* 855. The relics of St Odulphus are said to have been taken to Evesham abbey in 1034.

OENGUS, ST. *See* Aengus.

*OLAV, ST, mart. July 29.   July, p. 408

In 1013 he helped Ethelred of England against the Danes and two years later succeeded to the crown of Norway, of which country he is venerated as the apostle. He fetched over a number of priests and monks from England but his zeal for Christianity was misliked by many and he was driven from his kingdom. In an attempt to recover it he was killed at the battle of Stiklestad in 1030. St Olav had formerly a considerable cultus in England. *Olavus*.

OLGA, ST. July 11.   July, p. 140

She was a Scandinavian who married Igor, Grand Duke of Kiev ; after his assassination she became a Christian, and her grandson St Vladimir began the conversion of the Russian people. d. 969.

OLIVE, ST, virg. and mart. June 10.   June, p. 135

Olive of Palermo is an imaginary person, heroine of a romance of martyrdom among the Mohammedans, by whom, curiously enough, her name is held in veneration at Tunis. *Olivia*.

OLIVER PLUNKET, BD, bp. and mart. July 11.   July, p. 141

B. in 1629 at Loughcrew in Meath. After his ordination at Rome in 1654 he was appointed a professor in the College *de Propaganda Fide* and in 1669 was named archbishop of Armagh. Disorder, enforced neglect and clerical timidity characterized the Church in Ireland at this time, and Plunket set himself to remedy them with great zeal, though his efforts were weakened by a dispute with Peter Talbot, Archbishop of Dublin, which was carried on with notable charity on both sides. Bd Oliver was on excellent terms with the Protestant bishops and others, but in 1673 renewed persecution drove him into hiding. After Oates's " plot " he was betrayed by apostates and shut up in Dublin Castle. His first trial for " conspiring against the State " collapsed for lack of evidence, so he was sent to London, where the grand jury returned " no true bill " ; he was not released, and by a flagrantly unjust court was found guilty. He was h.d.q. in London in 1681, the last Catholic to die for his Faith at Tyburn. Bd Oliver was the first of the Irish martyrs to be beatified, in 1920. His feast is kept throughout Ireland and also in the diocese of Clifton, his relics being enshrined at Downside abbey. *Oliverius.*

*OLLEGARIUS, ST, bp. March 6.   MAR., p. 90

Or *Oldegar.* He was a canon regular and governed two monasteries in France before he was appointed bishop of Barcelona in his native land. Thence he was promoted to the archiepiscopal see of Tarragona, and was very active against the Moors who had devastated the diocese. d. 1137.

*OLYMPIAS, ST. December 17.   DEC., p. 191

She married Nebridius, prefect of Constantinople, but he died very soon after and his widow consecrated herself and her fortune to the service of religion. Olympias was a close personal friend of St John Chrysostom and when he was exiled she suffered cruel persecution for her loyalty to him : her household was sold up and the community of women that she directed was dispersed. She withdrew to Nicomedia and there d. July 25, 408, being not much more than forty years old.

*OLYMPIAS and **MAXIMUS, SS,** marts. April 15.   APR., p. 171

These are martyrs said to have been put to death in Persia, *c.* 251. Their existence is very doubtful.

*OMER, ST, bp. September 9.   SEPT., p. 99

In Latin *Audomarus.* After being twenty years a monk of Luxeuil he was appointed to the missionary bishopric of Thérouanne in Belgic Gaul. The diocese was full of vice and error and Omer gathered round him a notable band of holy monks to deal with the situation. He helped in the establishment of the abbey of Sithiu, round which grew up the town now called Saint-Omer. d. *c.* 670.

*ONESIMUS, ST, mart. February 16.   FEB., p. 242

The runaway slave who is the subject of St Paul's epistle to Philemon, said to have been martyred *c.* 90. The Roman Martyrology confuses him with another Onesimus, who was bishop at Ephesus after St Timothy.

*ONUPHRIUS, ST. June 12.   JUNE, p. 153

According to a certain abbot who met him St Onuphrius was a solitary in the Egyptian desert for seventy years : he dressed only in his own abundant hair and a loin-cloth of leaves. d. *c.* 400 (?). This saint was a popular character in the West during the Middle Ages.

OPPORTUNA, ST, virg. April 22.   APR., p. 260

She was a sister of St Chrodegang of Séez and was abbess of the Benedictine convent at Montreuil. d. *c.* 770.

*OPTATUS, ST, mart. April 16.   APR., p. 178

St Optatus with seventeen others was put to death for the Faith at Saragossa in 304.

*OPTATUS, ST, bp. June 4.   JUNE, p. 52

Optatus, bishop of Mileve in North Africa, was illustrious for his refutation of the errors of the Donatist schismatics ; he wrote six treatises against them, in vigorous and spirited but conciliatory terms. St Augustine couples him with St Hilary and St Cyprian (like them he was a convert from paganism) and St Fulgentius puts him in the same rank as St Ambrose and St Augustine. d. *c.* 387.

ORINGA A CRUCE, BD, virg. January 4.   JAN., p. 69

Otherwise *Christiana*. The leader of a band of devout women who lived under the Rule of St Augustine at Castello di Santa Croce in the valley of the Arno in the thirteenth century. d. 1310.

ORSISIUS, ST, ab. June 15.   JUNE p. 185

Orsiesius, Horsi-isi. A close disciple of St Pachomius, whom he followed as abbot of Tabenna. He wrote an ascetic treatise which St Jerome translated into Latin. d. *c.* 380.

OSANNA ANDREASI, BD, virg. June 20.   JUNE, p. 258

B. at Mantua in 1449 and related to the ducal family there. In consequence of a vision while a child she became a Dominican tertiary, very active in the corporal works of mercy and strongly imbued with the spirit of Savonarola. She was allowed many remarkable mystical experiences, for which there is contemporary evidence, and her " spiritual conversations " were written down by her close friend Dom Girolamo ; these still exist. Osanna was a force in Mantuan society, and when Duke Frederick went to the wars in 1478 he put her in charge of his family and practically of his office. d. 1505. c.c. by Pope Leo X.

OSBURGA, ST, virg. March 28.   MAR., p. 428

Osburga was a famous abbess at Coventry but no details of her life are known ; she d. *c.* 1016, or perhaps much earlier. Her feast is still kept in the diocese of Birmingham.

*OSMUND, ST, bp. December 4.   DEC., p. 61

This Osmund came to England with the Normans and was nominated bishop of Salisbury (Old Sarum) in 1077. He finished its cathedral and instituted a chapter of secular canons, but his great achievement was the drawing up of the ordinal of services for his diocese which was the basis of that " Sarum use " which spread throughout England and beyond and was normal in Great Britain until after the reign of Queen Mary. St Osmund was of a quiet and conciliatory disposition, and liked to spend his leisure copying and binding books. d. 1099. cd. 1457. His feast is kept in the dioceses of Westminster, Clifton, and Plymouth. *Osmundus*.

*OSWALD, ST, mart. August 9.   AUG., p. 115

Oswald was formerly venerated as one of the great national heroes of England, and his cultus extended so far as Switzerland. He defeated and slew in battle the Welsh king Cadwalla near Hexham in 635 and rightfully ascended the throne of Northumbria. Oswald had been baptized at Iona and received from there the bishop St Aidan to evangelize his kingdom, giving him the island of Lindisfarne for his headquarters. So great was the power and influence of St Oswald that he had some sort of nominal overlordship of the other English kings. He was killed in 642 fighting at Maserfield against the pagan Penda of Mercia and his Welsh Christian allies. He at once received cultus as a martyr, and his feast is still kept in the dioceses of Argyll, Westminster, Hexham, Lancaster, Liverpool, Middlesbrough, and Shrewsbury, and commemorated in Nottingham on August 5. *Oswaldus*.

OSWALD OF WORCESTER, ST, bp. February 28.   FEB., p. 384

He was nephew of St Odo of Canterbury, became dean of Winchester, and then a monk at Fleury. Under St Dunstan he was appointed to the see of Worcester and continued to administer it after he was promoted in 972 to the archbishopric of York. He was a strong supporter of Dunstan's reforms, helped to found the abbey of Ramsey, and founded the monastery at Worcester that afterwards became the cathedral priory. d. 992.

OSWIN, ST, mart. August 20. AUG., p. 248

He became king of Deira in 642 and was murdered at Gilling in Yorkshire by order of his cousin Oswy in 651. A monastery was built at Gilling, where St Oswin's tomb was illustrious for miracles until the incursions of the Danes caused the relics to be translated to Tynemouth. *Oswinus.*

OSYTH, ST, virg. and mart. October 7. OCT., p. 87

According to her legend St Osyth was a nun, at the place now called Saint Osyth at the mouth of the Colne in Essex, who was murdered by Danish marauders *c.* 675.

OTTERAN, ST, ab. October 27. OCT., p. 345

Otteran (Odhran) was an abbot from Meath who went to Iona with St Columba and was the first to die there, in 563. Although this is practically all that is known of the saint his feast is observed throughout Ireland. *Otteranus.*

*OTTO, ST, bp. July 2. JULY, p. 17

Otto was bishop of Bamberg under the emperor Henry IV and laboured to reconcile that sovereign and his successor with the Holy See. He is said to have conducted a very successful mission among the Pomeranians, and is venerated as their apostle. d. 1139. cd. 1189. *Otho.*

OUDOCEUS, ST, bp. July 2. JULY, p. 17

In Welsh *Euddogwy.* A disciple and nephew of St Teilo and perhaps his successor as abbot of Llandeilo Fawr. He is one of the four name saints of Llandaff cathedral but was never " bishop of Llandaff." Sixth century.

OUEN, ST. *See* Audoenus.

OWEN, ST. March 3. MAR., p. 40

Owen, or Ouini, was steward of the household of St Etheldreda and afterwards became a monk at Lastingham. He was a friend of St Chad, who on becoming bishop in Mercia established him with other monks in a house near Lichfield. d. 680. *Audoenus.*

OXFORD UNIVERSITY, THE MARTYRS OF. December 1. DEC., p. 24

Over forty members of the University of Oxford have been beatified as martyrs during the English persecution. A feast in their honour is kept in the diocese of Birmingham.

PACHOMIUS, ST, ab. May 9. MAY, p. 111

The founder of Christian communal (as opposed to eremitical) monasticism. He was b. in the Upper Thebaid *c.* 292 and after being discharged from the army became a Christian and a hermit in the desert. In 318 he began his first monastery at Tabenna, near the Nile, and subsequently established six others, organizing them on a communal basis and providing a written rule to be observed by all. This was the first example of a number of religious houses grouped together with a common rule and a general superior. Pachomius was never a priest and would not present his monks for ordination, though he welcomed priests to join them. Before his death at Pabau in 346 he had seven thousand monks in his communities. Pachomius is one of the four outstanding figures in the early history of Christian monasticism, and St Benedict made considerable use of the Egyptian rule when drawing up his own.

*PACIAN, ST, bp. March 9. MAR., p. 149

He was bishop of Barcelona in the fourth century and a voluminous writer, but few of his works have come down to us. He was the author of the famous declaration, " My name is Christian, my surname Catholic. . . ." d. *c.* 390. *Pacianus.*

*PACIFICUS, ST. September 24. SEPT., p. 308

This Pacificus, called " of San Severino " after his birthplace, was a Friar Minor of the Observance. In 1688, at the age of thirty-five, he became deaf and blind and almost a cripple : he had perforce to give up his successful active work, and passed the rest of his days in prayer, penance, and alms-deeds. On several occasions he displayed the gift of prophecy. d. 1721. cd. 1839.

PACIFICUS OF CERANO, BD. June 8. JUNE, p. 112

Pacificus Ramota was b. in Novara in 1424 and become a Franciscan friar. He laboured in Italy and Sardinia and wrote a treatise on moral theology highly thought of by his contemporaries. d. 1482. c.c. 1745.

PADARN, ST, ab. April 15. APR., p. 172

Padarn, with other monks from Brittany, including SS Cadfan, Tydecho, and Cynllo, landed near Aberystwyth and there founded Llanbadarn Fawr, *i.e.* the Great Monastery of Padarn, whence he evangelized the country round about. Fifth century. *Paternus.*

*PALÆMON, ST. January 11. JAN., p. 145

The companion of St Pachomius in the desert ; when Pachomius went away to make his great foundation at Tabennisi Palæmon accompanied him, and d. soon after, *c.* 330.

PALLADIUS, ST, bp. July 7. JULY, p. 72

Palladius was a deacon in Rome who was consecrated and sent as the first bishop to the Irish *c.* 430. He landed near Wicklow and founded three churches, but his mission was a failure and he soon crossed over into

Scotland, where he d. at Fordun, near Aberdeen, in 432. His feast is observed in the diocese of Aberdeen.

PAMBO, ST. July 18.   JULY, p. 252

Pambo was b. *c.* 315 and was one of the founders of the Nitrian group of monasteries in Egypt. He followed the usual austere life of the desert fathers, but had a less narrow outlook than many early monks on other ways of life : " Seek never to offend your neighbour " was his first theme. Among those who visited his cell were Rufinus and St Melania the Elder. d. *c.* 390.

*PAMMACHIUS, ST. August 30.   AUG., p. 384

He was a learned and charitable Roman layman, a close friend of St Jerome, who married the second daughter of Jerome's other great friend, St Paula. When he was a widower he joined with St Fabiola in founding the first pilgrim's hostel in the West, at Porto. d. 410.

*PAMPHILUS, ST, bp. April 28.   APR., p. 319

This bishop of Sulmona and Corfinium in the Abruzzi was denounced by his flock as an Arian—apparently because he sang Mass before daybreak on Sundays. d. *c.* 700.

*PAMPHILUS, ST, mart. June 1.   JUNE, p. 1

He is described by Eusebius as " the most illustrious martyr of his day for philosophical learning and for every virtue." He was b. at Beirut, studied at Alexandria, and ordained at Cæsarea in Palestine, where he lived. He was reputed the greatest biblical scholar of his age and was well known for his munificence and because he treated slaves and dependents as his brothers. He was tortured for refusing to sacrifice to the gods of Rome and after two years of imprisonment was beheaded at Cæsarea in 309.

*PANCRAS, ST, bp. and mart. April 3.   APR., p. 36

According to the Sicilian legend he was a disciple of St Peter and became first bishop of Taormina, being at the last stoned to death by brigands. *Pancratius.*

*PANCRAS, ST, mart. May 12.   MAY, p. 140

There is no reliable information about this St Pancras, who gave his name to a church and so to a borough and railway station in London. The well-known story of the boy martyr is a fabrication, but a martyr called Pancras was certainly buried in the cemetery of Calepodius in Rome.

PANCRATIUS. *See* Pancras.

*PANTÆNUS, ST. July 7.   JULY, p. 71

Pantænus was a converted Stoic philosopher who was made head of the famous catechetical school at Alexandria *c.* 175, where he was the first to use Greek philosophy in the study of theology. Little is known of his life, though he is said to have been at one time a missionary, probably in the Yemen and Ethiopia. d. *c.* 200.

†*PANTALEON, ST, mart. July 27.   JULY, p. 373

There is known to have been a martyr of this name *c.* 305, but the legends which have survived about him are late and valueless. He is a patron saint of physicians, as it is said he practised their art without taking payment. His early cultus is connected with Nicomedia in Bithynia.

PAOLA GAMBARA-COSTA, BD. January 31.   JAN., p. 401

B. near Brescia in 1473. She was a Franciscan tertiary and there is extant the rule of life drawn up for her by Bd Angelo of Chiavasso at her marriage. Her husband was annoyed by what he regarded as excessive charities dispensed by Bd Paola, and even put another woman in charge of his household, but in time Paola regained his affection. d. 1515. c.c. 1845.

*PAPHNUTIUS, ST, bp. September 11.　　　　　　SEPT., p. 140

Sometimes distinguished as " Paphnutius the Great." He was an Egyptian bishop in the Upper Thebaid, and was deprived of an eye and was lamed in the persecution under Maximinus. He was a notable opponent of Arianism, and is said to have defended the marriage of clergy at the Council of Nicæa (he was himself a monk). d. c. 356.

PARAGUAY, THE MARTYRS OF. November 17.　　　Nov., p. 230

Roch Gonzalez, Alphonsus Rodriguez, and John de Castillo, Jesuits, founded the " reduction " of the Assumption on the Ijuhi river in Paraguay in 1628. From thence the All-Saints' mission was established, and the local chief murdered all three fathers in the same year. bd. 1934.

*PARISIUS, ST. June 11.　　　　　　　　　　JUNE, p. 145

A Camaldolese monk near Treviso, venerated in that order ; little information about him has survived. d. 1267.

*PASCHAL I, ST, pope. February 11.　　　　　　MAY, p. 176

Paschal I occupied the papal chair from 817 till his death in 824 and is specially remembered for having removed from the catacombs to various Roman churches the relics of St Cecilia and of many other martyrs ; but the grounds on which his name is included in the Roman Martyrology are obscure. *Paschalis.*

†*PASCHAL BAYLON, ST. May 17.　　　　　　MAY, p. 214

He was b. in Aragon in 1540, the child of peasants, and was a shepherd until he became a lay brother of the Alcantarine reform of the Friars Minor. He led an uneventful life of prayer and work. On account of his devotion to the Blessed Sacrament and his defence of true eucharistic doctrine before a Calvinist mob he has been declared by the Holy See to be the patron of eucharistic congresses and confraternities. d. May 15, 1592. cd. 1690.

PASCHASIA, ST, virg. and mart. January 9.　　　JAN., p. 123

A virgin martyr honoured in Dijon in very early times ; later said to be a convert of St Benignus. d. 178 (?).

PASCHASIUS RADBERTUS, ST, ab. April 26.　　　APR., p. 293

St Paschasius is best known as a prolific writer, especially of biblical commentaries. He was novice-master at New Corbie and, though not a priest, abbot of Old Corbie, an office which he found uncongenial. d. c. 851.

PATERNUS, ST. April 10.　　　　　　　　　APR., p. 115

Little is known of this Paternus except that he was an Irish anchorite at Paderborn who lost his life when the town was burnt down in 1058. He was greatly revered by St Peter Damian and Bd Marianus Scotus.

*PATERNUS, ST, bp. April 16.　　　　　　　　APR., p. 180

In French *Pair.* After many years as a monk and hermit he was made bishop of Avranches at the age of seventy. d. c. 574. *See also* Padarn.

*PATIENS, ST, bp. January 8.　　　　　　　　JAN., p. 113

Said to have been the fourth bishop of Metz and to have occupied that see for fourteen years in the second century.

*PATIENS, ST, bp. September 11.　　　　　　SEPT., p. 143

An archbishop of Lyons, whom St Sidonius Apollinaris calls a " holy, active, ascetic, and merciful man," famed for his generosity to the poor. d. c. 491.

PATRICIA, ST, virg. August 25. DEC., p. 317

A maiden venerated as one of the patrons of Naples whither, according to her legend, she had fled from Constantinople in order to become a nun. d. *c.* 665.

†*PATRICK, ST, bp. March 17. MAR., p. 289

The patron saint and apostle of Ireland was a Romano-Briton, but the place of his birth *c.* 389 is unknown. In 405 he was carried off as a slave to Ireland but escaped after six years. About 432, having been consecrated bishop by St Germanus at Auxerre, he returned to Ireland to take up the work of the missionary Palladius who had been sent by Pope St Celestine I but had soon died. The data of Patrick's labours supplied by his biographers are confused, sometimes contradictory, and often legendary. He travelled to every part of the land, converting chiefs and people by his example and teaching : to impress the heathen Irish it was needful that the word should be confirmed by the signs which followed, and everywhere miracles supported his preaching. In some accounts of his life the space allotted to these is somewhat excessive : only by reference to his own writings can the deep and lasting impression that he made be understood. Patrick established the primatial see of Ireland at Armagh about the year 444, probably after a visit to Pope St Leo I. d. *c.* 461 at Saul on Strangford Lough. His body was translated to the cathedral of Down in 1186. *Patricius.*

*PATROCLUS, ST, mart. January 21. JAN., p. 258

He was a Christian of Troyes of exceptional charity and goodness, who was martyred either in 259 or 275 by beheading.

*PAUL, ST, bp. February 8. FEB., p. 119

A bishop of Verdun whose name is preserved at the hill called Paulberg, near Trier, where he was at one time a hermit. d. *c.* 649. *Paulus.*

*PAUL, ST, bp. June 7. JUNE, p. 88

This Paul was bishop of Constantinople from *c.* 336. He is a figure in church history but is otherwise little known. About the year 350 he was deported from his see by the Arians and is said to have been strangled at Kukusus in Armenia.

†*PAUL, ST, ap. June 29. JUNE, p. 388

The Apostle of the Gentiles, a tent-maker by trade from Tarsus in Cilicia, whose life is related in the Acts of the Apostles and his doctrine set forth in his Epistles. He was well educated and as Saul the Pharisee bitterly persecuted the Christian Jews, only to be touched by the hand of the Lord and converted on the road to Damascus. His mission to the Gentiles was accomplished in three famous journeys over western Asia Minor and Greece, " in perils of robbers, from my own nation, from the Gentiles, in the city, in the wilderness, in the sea, from false brethren ; in labour and painfulness," beaten, stoned, shipwrecked, imprisoned. Having been imprisoned at Cæsarea in consequence of a tumult raised by the Jews at Jerusalem, Paul, as a Roman citizen, appealed from the procurator Festus to the emperor ; accordingly he was taken to Rome, where " he remained two whole years in his own hired lodging, and he received all that came in to him." He was probably acquitted, made a fourth missionary journey, to Macedonia, and then returned to Rome, where he was martyred about the same time as St Peter. There is a reliable tradition that he was beheaded on the Ostian Way, where the basilica and abbey of St Paul-outside-the-Walls now stand. Apart from his personal missionary work St Paul has had through his letters an influence on Christianity and Christians that only increases as the years and centuries go by. In every liturgical office of St Peter in the Roman rite a commemoration is made of St Paul, and *vice versa*, and the whole office of June 30 is devoted to his honour.

*PAUL I, ST, pope. June 28. JUNE, p. 370

He succeeded his brother Stephen III as pope in 757 and reigned for ten years. He rebuilt the church of San Silvestro in Capite (the English church in Rome) and gave it to monks of the Greek rite. A contemporary speaks of his kindness and wide-spiritedness. d. 767.

PAUL NAVARRO, BD, mart. November 16. NOV., p. 208

An Italian Jesuit martyr who was put to death by burning at Ximabara in Japan in 1622. bd. 1867.

*PAUL OF CRETE, ST, mart. March 17. MAR., p. 302

He was martyred in the island of Cyprus during the iconoclast persecution for refusing to trample on a crucifix, *c.* 760.

†*PAUL OF THE CROSS, ST. April 28. APR., p. 313

Paul was b. at Ovada in Piedmont in 1694 and after an exemplary youth set to work, in consequence of a series of visions, to establish the congregation of clerks regular whose rule he had framed before he himself was ordained. By 1737 the first house (" retreat ") of the Barefooted Clerks of the Cross and Passion (Passionists) was in being and, with some setbacks, the congregation made steady progress. St Paul himself preached throughout the Papal States and Tuscany, and among his practices was to pray daily for the reconciliation of the English. He was endowed with gifts of prophecy and healing, and crowds flocked to his sermons and confessional. St Paul d. on October 18, 1775. cd. 1867.

†*PAUL THE HERMIT, ST. January 15. JAN., p. 182

This Paul is venerated as the first hermit. B. *c.* 230, he went into the Theban desert at the age of twenty-two and lived alone in a cave for ninety years. Here he was found by St Antony, who on a second visit found Paul dead, *c.* 342. The account of his life edited by St Jerome is a classic of desert-father literature ; numerous stories of varying value are told of St Paul.

PAUL OF LATROS, ST. December 15. DEC., p. 175

He was for many years a hermit in a cave on Mount Latros in Bithynia, where he attracted a number of followers. For a time he was a monk of Karia and worked in the kitchen, where the sight of the fire reminded him so forcibly of Hell that he burst into tears every time he looked at it. d. 956.

PAUL OF LEON, ST, bp. March 12. MAR., p. 213

Paul Aurelian was a Romano-Briton and a fellow of SS David, Samson, and Gildas under Illtyd at Llantwit Major. When sixteen he retired to Caldey Island, whence he went as a missionary, eventually to Brittany. With his companions he founded a monastery at Porz-Pol on the isle of Ouessant, and later settled at Ocismor (now called Saint-Pol-de-Léon), where he was consecrated bishop by order of King Childebert. d. *c.* 573.

*PAUL OF NARBONNE, ST. March 22. MAR., p. 367

A Roman missionary in Gaul, who died at Narbonne where he had worked, *c.* 290.

*PAUL THE SIMPLE, ST. March 7. MAR., p. 110

Leaving his wife on account of her unfaithfulness he became, although already an old man, a disciple of St Antony in the Egyptian Thebaid. He is mentioned in the *Lausiac History* of Palladius. d. *c.* 339.

*PAULA, ST. January 26.   JAN., p. 316

We learn about St Paula from the letters of St Jerome, whose disciple she was. She was of a noble Roman family, born in 347, and married Toxotius, by whom she had five children, among them St Blæsilla and St Eustochium. After the death of her husband when she was thirty-two Paula lived for a time in retirement and then went to Palestine. She settled near St Jerome at Bethlehem, forming a community of religious women, building a monastery for men, and establishing a hospital. St Paula lived this life of good work and devotion for some twenty years and d. in 404, being buried in the basilica of the Nativity near to the birthplace of Christ, where her empty tomb is still to be seen.

PAULA FRASSINETTI, BD, virg. June 11.   JUNE, p. 147

B. at Genoa in 1809. While living with her brother who was parish priest at Quinto she found her vocation in the schooling of poor children ; she founded a society for the work, which developed into the congregation of Sisters of St Dorothy, which has spread beyond Italy. d. 1882. bd. 1930.

*PAULINUS, ST, bp. October 10.   OCT., p. 137

He was one of the monks of St Andrew's on the Cœlian sent from Rome in 601 to join St Augustine in England. After twenty-four years of missionary work in Kent he evangelized the southern parts of Northumbria, and baptized King Edwin at York on Easter day, 627. Paulinus was archbishop of that city but he was driven out by the Mercians, who killed St Edwin, and for the last ten years of his life he administered the see of Rochester. d. 644. His cultus was formerly very widespread ; his feast is now observed in the dioceses of Hexham, Lancaster, Leeds, Liverpool, Middlesbrough, Nottingham, and Southwark.

PAULINUS OF AQUILEIA, ST, bp. January 28.   JAN., p. 349

B. *c.* 726 near Friuli, and as he grew up acquired a great reputation for learning. He was greatly respected by Charlemagne and about 776 was promoted to the important see of Aquileia. Paulinus was joined with Alcuin in the business of confuting the adoptionist heresy then being preached in Spain, and preached the gospel to the Avars and other heathens. He also wrote a work of religious direction for the use of Duke Henry of Friuli. d. 804.

†*PAULINUS OF NOLA, ST, bp. June 22.   JUNE, p. 287

He was b. into a patrician family at Bordeaux *c.* 354, was educated by Ausonius, and inherited great wealth. After his retirement from state service he was converted to Christianity by his Spanish wife and St Delphinus of Bordeaux, and the couple gave away much of their wealth in charity. At the age of forty Paulinus was ordained priest and retired to Nola in Italy where he built churches, an aqueduct, and other public works and *c.* 409 was made bishop. A number of letters and poems written by him are preserved and they amply explain the affection and veneration that Paulinus enjoyed even during his lifetime. d. 431.

*PAULINUS OF TRIER, ST, bp. August 31.   AUG., p. 393

While bishop of Trier he was expelled from his see with other bishops for supporting St Athanasius against the Arianizing emperor Constantius in 355. He was banished to Phrygia, where he d. in 358 ; his relics were brought back to Trier in 396 and there they remain.

PEGA, ST, virg. January 8. JAN., p. 120

She was the sister of St Guthlac and lived as a hermitess in North-amptonshire. She is said to have d. in Rome *c.* 719.

*PELAGIA, ST, virg. and mart. June 9. JUNE, p. 119

This is the historical Pelagia from whose simple story a whole cycle of extravagant fables has been evolved. She was a young Christian girl of Antioch who, when soldiers were sent to arrest her, jumped from the top of the house to avoid dishonour and was killed, *c.* 311. St John Chrysostom states that she acted under divine inspiration, and she is named in the canon of the Milanese Mass.

*PELAGIA THE PENITENT, ST. October 8. OCT., p. 102

In origin this Pelagia (or Margaret) is probably the same as the virgin martyr Pelagia mentioned in the Roman Martyrology on June 9; the fiction that she was a repentant courtesan of Antioch who lived disguised as a male solitary at Jerusalem seems to have been the starting-point of the similar romances that are associated with the names of Marina, Euphrosyne, Theodora, etc.

*PELAGIA OF TARSUS, ST, virg. and mart. May 4. MAY, p. 52

Pelagia was probably no more than the heroine of a pious romance according to which she was roasted to death for refusing to marry the emperor Diocletian.

*PELAGIUS, ST, mart. June 26. JUNE, p. 352

Pelagius was a young boy left as a hostage among the Moors at Cordoba. He was offered liberty and other inducements if he would accept Islam and commit other shameful sins; on his stubborn and repeated refusals he was put to death in 925.

*PELEUS, ST, mart. September 19. SEPT., p. 255

The Egyptians Peleus, Nilus, and Elias, priests, and a layman had been sentenced to hard labour in the quarries and were burned *c.* 310, probably at Phunon, near Petra, for conducting divine worship in the place of their detention.

PEPIN OF LANDEN, BD. February 21. FEB., p. 293

The life of Pepin of Landen, mayor of the palace to Clotaire II, Dago-bert and St Sigebert and practically ruler of their dominions, belongs to general history. He was married to Bd Itta, was father of St Gertrude of Nivelles and St Begga, and was " a lover of peace, the constant defender of truth and justice." d. 646. His feast used to be kept at Nivelles.

*PEREGRINUS, ST, bp. and mart. May 16. MAY, p. 202

He was the first bishop of Auxerre, who converted most of the city's inhabitants and was beheaded for the Faith *c.* 261 by the Roman governor .

*PEREGRINUS, ST, bp. and mart. June 13. JUNE, p. 170

Peregrinus (properly Cetheus) was bishop of Amiternum (Aquila); he was put to death by the Lombards *c.* 600 for asking for mercy for a con - demned captive.

*PEREGRINUS LAZIOSI, ST. May 1. MAY, p. 33

B. at Forli in 1260. During a popular rising he struck St Philip Benizi across the face and, Philip turning his other cheek, was seized with remorse. Peregrinus joined the Servites, and at the height of his success as a friar was stricken with cancer of the foot; but on the night before it was to be amputated he was completely cured in his sleep. d. 1345. cd. 1726. St Peregrinus is invoked against cancer.

PEREGRINUS DE FALERONE, BD. September 6. DEC., p. 318

A personal disciple of St Francis of Assisi and a confessor of the Friars Minor. d. 1240.

*PERGENTINUS and **LAURENTINUS, SS,** marts. June 3. JUNE, p. 30

Said to have been brothers at Arezzo who were martyred there in 251. Their real existence is quite uncertain.

†*PERPETUA, SS, and other marts. March 6. MAR., p. 72

Vivia Perpetua was a young married woman of good family and Felicitas, also married, was a slave girl who with other catechumens were imprisoned at Carthage in 203. Eventually they were thrown to the beasts and those not thus killed were slain by the sword. The "acts" of these martyrs are one of the greatest and most moving hagiological treasures that have come down to us ; in the fourth century they were read publicly in the churches of Africa. They were written by Saturus, one of the martyrs, and completed by an eye-witness. SS Perpetua and Felicitas are named in the canon of the Roman Mass ; their companions were SS. Saturus, Saturninus, Revocatus, and Secundulus (the last named died in prison)

*PERPETUUS, ST, bp. April 8. APR., p. 94

He ruled the diocese of Tours successfully for thirty years during the fifth century. The document purporting to be his will is now known to be a forgery of the seventeenth century. d. c. 494.

*PERSIAN MARTYRS, THE 120. April 6. APR., p. 71

The 120 martyrs in Persia mentioned in the Roman Martyrology on April 6 are believed to have suffered at Seleucia under King Sapor in 345.

†*PETER, ST, ap. June 29. JUNE, p. 376

Simon Peter, leader or " prince " of the Apostles, was a fisherman on the Sea of Galilee, where he lived with his wife at Bethsaida. The most important and striking of the events of his life in Palestine as narrated in the gospels is his confession of faith in our Lord and Christ's subsequent charge to him, " Thou art Peter and upon this Rock I will build my Church . . ." (Matt. xvi, 15–19) ; in striking contrast is his thrice-repeated denial of his Master at the house of Caiphas. Peter's pre-eminent position among his fellows is clear both before and after our Lord's ascension. He may have been for a time bishop at Antioch but it was at Rome that he established his permanent see, a fact that is no longer seriously questioned by anyone. He was martyred c. 67, being crucified head downwards in the Circus of Nero on the Vatican hill, where his body now rests beneath the basilica that bears his name ; from that day to this there has been an unbroken succession of supreme pontiffs of the Universal Church, bishops of Rome and inheritors of the unique responsibility and powers confided by Jesus Christ to St Peter. The joint feast of St Peter and St Paul has been kept at Rome on June 29 probably at least since the beginning of the fourth century. *Petrus.*

*PETER, ST, mart. March 12. MAR., p. 212

A chamberlain in the household of Diocletian, martyred at Nicomedia with Migdonius and others in 303.

PETER, BD. March 23. MAR., p. 382

This Hermit of St Augustine seems to have been venerated chiefly on account of the wonders reported at his tomb at Gubbio. d. c. 1250 (?). c.c. by Pope Pius IX.

*PETER and other marts., **SS.** June 7.   JUNE, p. 94
Other martyrs amongst the Moors of Spain in 851, following on the execution of SS. Isaac (June 3) and Sancho (June 5). Peter was a priest of Ecija.

*PETER ARBUEZ, ST, mart. September 17.   SEPT., p. 236
Peter Arbuez, a canon regular, was provincial inquisitor for the kingdom of Aragon, around whom an undeserved legend of cruelty has grown up. He discharged the office for only a few months, preaching against bogus Christians and apostates among the Moors and the Jews, and against their characteristic vices : he was responsible for no sentence of death and only two arrests were made at his instance. But his influence was feared by the crypto-Jews and they contrived his murder in 1485. cd. 1867.

*PETER ARMENGOL, BD. April 27.   APR., p. 306
In the form that it has come down to us the story of Bd Peter, a Mercedarian who worked among the Moors, is of very doubtful authenticity. d. 1304. c.c. 1688.

*PETER BALSAM, ST, mart. January 3.   JAN., p. 48
Probably identical with the Peter Abselamus whom Eusebius describes as having been burnt to death for the faith at Cæsarea, in the year 311. Another account says that he was crucified.

†*PETER CANISIUS, ST, doct. April 27.   APR., p. 297
Canisius was born at Nijmwegen, then in Germany, in 1521, and after a lively youth joined the Society of Jesus. His energies were devoted to rebuilding the Church in the Empire after the onslaughts of the " reformers." He went to and fro in Germany, Austria, Switzeriand, and the Tyrol, Poland and Bohemia, preaching, instructing, arbitrating, above all writing a great catechism and other works and reforming and establishing universities and schools. In an age of violence he stands out as a man of moderation, who consequently did more to restore the Faith and purify lives in south and west Germany than any other. He was one of the originators of the "Catholic press," and was the first literary Jesuit. d. 1597. He was the first saint to be declared a doctor of the Church at his canonization (in 1925).

PETER CHANEL, BD, mart. April 28.   APR., p. 324
Peter Louis Marie Chanel was b. in France in 1803, the son of a peasant. After some years of pastoral and professorial work he went at the head of a band of Marist missionaries to the Pacific in 1836. He was put to death by a savage chief out of hatred of the Faith on Fortuna island in 1841, the first martyr of Oceania. Within five months the whole island was Christian. bd. 1889.

†*PETER CHRYSOLOGUS, ST, bp. and doct. December 4.   DEC., p. 51
He was b. at Imola in 406 and became deacon to the bishop of that town. St Peter was made archbishop of Ravenna c. 433, but little is known of his life beyond his assiduity in expounding the Christian religion by writing and preaching. His gifts as an orator earned him his name, Golden Speech ; a large number of his sermons are still in existence. d. c. 450. St Peter was declared a doctor of the Church in 1729.

*PETER CLAVER, ST. September 9.   SEPT., p. 106
Peter Claver, the Apostle of the Negroes, was a young Jesuit at Palma and was fired by St Alphonsus Rodriguez with the desire to work for souls in the New World. He went to Colombia in South America in 1610 and

soon saw that the people who most needed his ministrations were the Negro slaves, who were shipped from West Africa in great numbers and under the most ghastly conditions, both spiritual and physical. Claver declared himself to be " the slave of the Negroes for ever," and this is just what he was. He cared both for souls and bodies, brought numerous Negroes to a knowledge of Christianity and love of Christ by his careful instruction, and followed them up after they had been dispersed from the port to the mines and plantations. He nursed the sick and diseased whom others could hardly bear even to look at, but for the last four years of his life was himself a sick man and was often left in his cell alone, neglected by his brethren, in the most amazing fashion : since his death in 1654 he has never been forgotten, and never will be. bd. 1888. St Peter Claver was declared patron of all enterprises in favour of the Negroes in 1896.

†*PETER DAMIAN, ST, bp. and doct. February 23.   FEB., p. 312

He was born at Ravenna in 1007, an unwanted child, ill-treated, set to herd pigs and similar jobs, until he was put to school by a brother. He joined the hermit monks of Fonte Avellino, was soon famous for his learning, and became abbot. Among his disciples were St Ralph of Gubbio, St Dominic Loricatus, and St John of Lodi. In 1057 he was made cardinal bishop of Ostia. Whether as hermit or cardinal his time was devoted to writing, preaching and otherwise actively working against the clerical abuses of his time, simony, incontinence, luxury, slackness, and against the schisms of antipopes. d. 1072. Declared doctor of the Church in 1828. Invoked against headaches.

PETER JULIAN EYMARD, BD. August 3.   AUG., p. 38

B. in France in 1811 and ordained in 1834, being a member of the Society of Mary. After over twenty years of apostolic work he was dispensed from his vows and in 1857 founded the congregation of Priests of the Blessed Sacrament, whose ordinary sacerdotal work is subordinated to their chief object of maintaining " perpetual adoration." The new foundation was beset with many difficulties, in coping with which Father Eymard was encouraged by St John Vianney ; it received the approval of the Holy See during his lifetime. d. 1868. bd. 1925.

PETER FABER, BD. August 11.   AUG., p. 138

Peter le Fèvre, the senior of the first companions of St Ignatius Loyola, was the first among the Jesuits to come to grips with the Protestant Reformation. He was sent by the Holy See to the Diet of Worms in 1540, and worked with tremendous energy, ability, and no little success to purify and strengthen the Catholics of the Rhineland, Spain, and Portugal. He d. in 1546 while on his way to the Council of Trent. c.c. 1872.

*PETER FOURIER, ST. July 7.   JULY, p. 83

B. in Lorraine in 1565. He became an Augustinian canon regular and was given cure of souls at Mattaincourt in the Vosges, where he did marvellous work in a very troublesome parish. Here he founded the Canonesses Regular of St Augustine of the Congregation of Notre Dame for the education of girls, and himself instructed the early aspirants in pedagogical method, in which he was a pioneer ; he was also very urgent for free schooling for the poor. In 1622 the Holy See appointed Fourier visitor apostolic of his order and he organized the Lorraine houses into a reformed congregation, of which he was made superior general. The great disappointment of his life was that his efforts to do something for the education of boys were not successful. d. 1640. cd. 1897.

PETER GAMBACORTA, BD. June 17.   JUNE, p. 224

B. at Pisa in 1355, son of the ruler of the republic. In 1380 he founded a small community of hermit-monks, called Poor Brothers of St Jerome, and not even the assassination of his father and two brothers could draw him from his retreat : like his sister Bd Clare Gambacorta he freely forgave the murderers. d. 1435.

PETER GONZALEZ, BD. April 14.   APR., p. 163

Bd Peter was Dominican chaplain at the court of Ferdinand III of Leon and Castile, where he was a zealous reformer, and afterwards a preacher among the Moors of Cordova and the peasants of Galicia. d. 1246. c.c. 1741. Portuguese sailors invoke him as " St Elmo," by confusion with St Erasmus (June 2).

*PETER IGNEUS, BD, bp. February 8.   FEB., p. 124

To demonstrate that Peter of Pavia had become bishop of Florence by simony, this Peter, a monk of Vallombrosa, passed through fire unharmed, whence his second name. There is a remarkable contemporary account of this. Peter was later appointed cardinal bishop of Albano, and sent on missions to foreign states by the Holy See. d. c. 1089.

†*PETER MARTYR, ST. April 29.   APR., p. 326

Peter of Verona was b. in that town in 1206 ; he joined the Friars Preachers and was appointed inquisitor of Lombardy. He preached far and wide in mid and northern Italy against evil-living Catholics and the heresies of Catharism (which his parents had professed). By Catharists he was murdered while travelling from Como to Milan on April 6, 1252, and was cd. as a martyr in the following year. This St Peter must not be confused with Peter Martyr Vermigli, who was a Protestant leader in the sixteenth century.

†*PETER NOLASCO, ST. January 28.   JAN., p. 391

B. in Languedoc c. 1189. The spectacle of the sufferings of Christian slaves among the Moors in Spain fired him with the resolve to work for the redemption of such captives and he was associated with the beginnings of the Mercedarian Order which existed for that purpose. By the Mercedarians he is regarded as their principal founder. The details of his life, however, are obscure. d. December 25, 1258. cd. 1628.

PETER PAPPACARBONE, ST. ab. March 4.   MAR., p. 52

He left the abbey of Cava, which his uncle St Alferius had founded, to be a monk at Cluny. He was recalled to be made bishop of Policastro, but resigned, and was appointed third abbot of Cava. He had great difficulty in imposing the severe observance of Cluny, but was successful and his monastery became very famous. d. 1123.

PETER PARENZI, ST, mart. May 22.   MAY, p. 270

He was governor of Orvieto and was killed by Catharist heretics in 1199 because of the severity with which he had proceeded against them.

*PETER PASCHASIUS, BD, bp. and mart. December 6. DEC., p. 91

Peter Pasqualez was b. at Valencia and became a priest c. 1250. After filling a number of responsible offices he was appointed to the see of Jaen, which at that time was still under Moorish domination. His activity in ransoming captives and preaching to the infidels caused him to be imprisoned ; here he wrote a treatise against Islam, in consequence of which he was imprisoned and died, or was killed, in jail in 1300, at the age of seventy-three. c.c. 1673.

PETER PETRONI, BD. May 29.   MAY, p. 352

Bd Peter joined the Carthusians at Maggiano, near Siena, when he was seventeen. He brought about the conversion of Boccaccio. d. 1361.

PETER REGALATUS, ST. May 13.   MAY, p. 167

A Franciscan friar of Valladolid who became superior of some friaries noted for the austerity of their regime ; hence his name, " rule-enforcer." d. 1456. cd. 1746.

PETER RODRIGUEZ, BD, mart. June 11.   JUNE, p. 144

The leader of a band of Portuguese officers who were murdered during an armistice by Moors at Tavira in 1242. There seems no justification for their veneration as martyrs and their cultus has not been confirmed by authority.

PETER ROQUE, BD, mart. March 1.   DEC., p. 313

B. at Vannes in 1758, where he was ordained, and afterwards joined the Lazarists at Paris. He refused to take the " constitutional " oath and was martyred by the guillotine in 1796. bd. 1934.

PETER SANZ, BD, bp. and mart. May 26.   MAY, p. 320

A Spanish Dominican, vicar apostolic of Fu-kien, who was martyred at Foochow in China in 1747 ; his four fellow-Dominican missionaries were put to death in the following year. They were all beatified in 1893.

PETER TECELANO, BD. December 10.   DEC., p. 123

He was a comb-maker of Siena. After the death of his wife he became a Franciscan tertiary, went to live near the friary, and there carried on his trade till the end of his long life. His days were simple and uneventful, but he attained a high degree of contemplative prayer. d. 1287. c.c. 1802.

PETER THOMAS, ST, bp. January 28.   JAN., p. 94

B. in France in 1305, became a Carmelite, and eventually was sent as procurator of that order to the papal court at Avignon. Here he attracted notice and from that time forward most of his life was spent in missions and negotiations for the Holy See. In the discharge of these duties he was notable for the simplicity of his manner of living and the confidence which his goodness inspired in others. He had to visit Italy, Serbia, Hungary, Constantinople, Palestine, and Cyprus and, surprisingly enough, was virtually in charge of the military expedition against Alexandria in 1365. Here he was wounded and died three months later at Cyprus, January 6, 1366. St Peter Thomas was consecrated bishop of Patti in 1354, and was promoted to the archbishopric of Candia and to be titular Latin patriarch of Constantinople. His feast was approved for the Carmelites in 1608.

*PETER URSEOLUS, ST. January 10.   JAN., p. 134

B. 928 in Venice, and at the age of twenty was admiral of the Venetian fleet. After the murder of the doge Peter Candiani IV in 976, Urseolus was appointed to the office, and safely guided Venice through a great political crisis. Then, when he had been doge for only two years, he suddenly disappeared, not even his wife and son knowing where he had gone. He was eventually found at the abbey of Cuxa, on the border of France and Spain. He continued to live here for a time in austere retirement ; then he became a complete solitary and so died, in 987. There is evidence that his sudden fleeing from the world was not so unpremeditated as it seemed. His son in his turn became one of the greatest of the doges of Venice.

PETER WRIGHT, BD, mart. May 19.   MAY, p. 244

He was a Northamptonshire Jesuit who was a chaplain in the royalist army during the Civil War ; he was h.d.q. for his priesthood at Tyburn in 1651.

PETER THE HERMIT, BD. July 8.   JULY, p. 100

Peter the Hermit, an ex-soldier, is known for his fiery and successful preaching of the Crusade in Europe ; he returned to the profession of arms and accompanied the first expedition to the East, where he took part in the siege of Antioch and the capture of Jerusalem in 1099. During the subsequent ecclesiastical squabbles he came back to Flanders and founded a monastery of canons regular at Huy. d. 1115. Peter's name is found in some old Flemish calendars.

PETER OF JEREMIAS, BD. March 10.   MAR., p. 176

He was a law-student at Bologna who in consequence of a vision gave up that profession and joined the Friars Preachers. He soon had a considerable reputation as a preacher and theologian, and was summoned by the Holy See to the Council of Florence. Though always engaged in active duties he was by nature a contemplative and ascetic. d. 1452 at Palermo, where he was prior. c.c. 1784.

PETER THE VENERABLE, BD, ab. December 29.   DEC., p. 287

At the age of thirty in 1122 Bd Peter was called to the abbacy of Cluny, and during his rule the great Cluniac congregation reached a point of influence and prosperity that it never again touched. Peter was a generous friend of Abelard, and himself was involved in a controversy with St Bernard about monastic observance. d. 1156.

†*PETER OF ALCANTARA, ST. October 19.   OCT., p. 255

He was b. at Alcantara in Spain in 1499. He became a Franciscan of a reformed branch of the order and in 1554 began a yet more severe reform, whose members were referred to as Alcantarines and existed until the union of the Observants in 1897. St Peter was one of the great Spanish mystics of that time ; St Teresa, whom he encouraged and defended in her reform of the Carmelites, said of him that his austerities and penances were " incomprehensible to the human mind," and his treatise on prayer was very greatly valued. d. 1562. cd. 1669.

†*PETER OF ALEXANDRIA, ST, bp. and mart. November 26. Nov., p. 304

The twelve years of this Peter's episcopate were darkened by continual struggles with schism, heresy, and persecution, crowned by his own death for Christ in 311. By the Copts he is called the " Seal and Complement of the Persecution," because he was the last martyr put to death by public authority at Alexandria.

PETER OF ATHOS, ST. June 12.   JUNE, p. 155

He is reputed to have been the first Christian solitary on Mount Athos, and to have d. there c. 743. His story in the Greek *Menæa* is fictitious.

*PETER OF BRAGA, ST, bp. April 26.   APR., p. 291

Principal patron of Braga and bishop there, probably in the fourth century. Nothing is known of his life.

PETER OF CASTELNAU, BD. January 15.   JAN., p. 196

A Cistercian monk who was appointed by Innocent III apostolic delegate and inquisitor for the Albigensians. He was slain by these heretics in 1208. His feast is kept by the Cistercians and some French dioceses.

PETER OF CHAVANON, ST. September 11.   SEP., p. 145

He was a secular priest who founded a monastery of Augustinian canons regular at Pébrac in Auvergne ; he ruled it with such success that he was entrusted with the reform of several collegiate chapters. d. 1080.

PETER OF JUILLY, BD. June 23.   JUNE, p. 309
He was an Englishman and a friend of St Stephen Harding, whom he afterwards joined at the abbey of Molesme. At their own request he was made chaplain to the nuns at Juilly, and there he d. in 1136.

*PETER OF LAMPSACUS, ST, mart. May 15.   MAY, p. 190
This Peter was martyred at Lampsacus in 251 and is commemorated with other martyrs, who suffered at Troas. But the details of their story are not trustworthy.

PETER OF LUXEMBURG, BD, bp. July 4.   JULY, p. 44
He was a son of Count Guy of Luxemburg and before he was eighteen years old had been made canon of Notre Dame de Paris and other cathedrals, archdeacon of Dreux, bishop of Metz, and cardinal of the Roman Church ; as he was not yet a priest he had to have an auxiliary bishop to perform most of his duties. In spite of such glaring pluralism (common in his day) he was a young man of great holiness of character, but was cut off in his youth in 1387. cd. 1527.

PETER OF MOGLIANO, BD. July 30.   JULY, p. 422
He was an Observant Franciscan and a preaching companion of St James della Marca ; it was said of him that he would die laughing. d. 1490. c.c. 1760.

PETER OF POITIERS, ST, bp. April 4.   APR., p. 51
He was bishop of Poitiers and is venerated in that diocese, particularly for his merciless denouncement of wickedness in high places. d. 1115.

PETER OF RUFFIA, BD, mart. November 7.   NOV., p. 90
He was a Dominican, murdered by some sectaries in 1365, while discharging the office of inquisitor general in Piedmont and Lombardy. c.c. 1856.

*PETER OF SEBASTE, ST, bp. January 9.   JAN., p. 121
Brother of St Basil the Great and St Gregory of Nyssa. He succeeded Basil as abbot of the monastery which their mother had founded and was made bishop of Sebaste in 380, when he had to combat the Arian heresy. Gregory of Nyssa testifies to his brother's great holiness. d. c. 391.

PETER OF TARENTAISE, BD. *See* Innocent V, Bd.

*PETER OF TARENTAISE, ST, bp. May 8.   MAY., p. 102
Peter, a Cistercian monk, was appointed archbishop of Tarentaise in 1142 and found his diocese in a deplorable state. After thirteen years of reorganization he disappeared, but was found living as a lay brother in a Swiss monastery, whereupon he had to return to his see. He zealously opposed the antipope Victor, and was commissioned to try to bring about a reconciliation between King Louis VII of France and Henry II of England ; he was unsuccessful in his efforts and d. in 1175 while on his way back to Tarentaise. St Peter's custom of distributing free bread and soup during the weeks preceding the harvest was carried on until the French Revolution. He was one of the great figures of the Cistercian Order. cd. 1191.

PETER OF TIFERNO, BD. October 21.   OCT., p. 294
A confessor of the Dominican Order at Cortona. d. 1445. c.c. by Pope Pius VII.

PETER OF TREJA, BD. February 20. FEB., p. 289

He was an early Franciscan, who after a long life of labour, adorned by miracles and the gift of prophecy, d. in 1304. c.c. 1793.

PETROC, ST. June 4. JUNE, p. 55

Petroc (Pedrog) was one of the most active missionary saints in Cornwall during the sixth century, but nothing much is known about him : he probably came to Cornwall from Wales. At least twenty-seven churches in that county and Devon were dedicated in his honour and he gave his name to Padstow (Petrocstow) : the modern Catholic church there is " St Petroc's." *Petrocus.*

PETRONAX, ST, ab. May 6. MAY, p. 82

He re-established the abbey of Monte Cassino in 717 and ruled it till his death thirty years later.

†*PETRONILLA, ST, virg. and mart. May 31. MAY, p. 373

The date and history of her passion are unknown, but she was certainly not St Peter's daughter, as she is called in the Roman Martyrology.

PETRONILLA OF TROYES, BD, virg. May 14. MAY, p. 179

She was the first abbess of the convent of Poor Clares at Moncel in Burgundy founded by King Philip le Bel. d. 1355.

*PETRONIUS, ST, bp. October 4. OCT., p. 55

He is said to have become bishop of Bologna c. 430, and to have founded the monastery of St Stephen there, whose buildings reproduced the general lines of the Holy Places at Jerusalem, a monument which still exists in a modified form. d. c. 445 (?).

PHARAILDIS, ST, virg. January 4. JAN., p. 61

Otherwise *Varelde, Verylde, Veerle.* The accounts of this popular Belgian saint are confusing and improbable. The main tradition is that she was married against her will and, having dedicated her maidenhood to God, refused to live with her husband, who treated her with great cruelty. A number of miracles are recorded of St Pharaildis, who d. c. 740.

*PHILASTRIUS, ST, bp. July 18. JULY, p. 250

He was a bishop of Brescia whom St Gaudentius praises in a panegyric for his " modesty, quietness, and sweetness towards all men." He wrote a book against Arianism and other heresies, and was notably generous not only to the poor, but to tradesmen and others who lacked capital. d. c. 387.

*PHILEAS, ST, bp. and mart. February 4. FEB., p. 63

Phileas was arrested soon after being made bishop at Thmuis in Egypt. From his prison at Alexandria he wrote a letter to his flock describing the sufferings of the Christian prisoners. He was beheaded together with a Roman official named Philomorus in 304.

*PHILEMON and APOLLONIUS, SS, marts. March 8. MAR., p. 125

Philemon was an Egyptian musician and entertainer who was converted to Christianity by Apollonius, a deacon from Antinoe. They were both seized under Diocletian and drowned at Alexandria, c. 305.

*PHILEMON and APPIA, SS, marts. November 22. Nov., p. 271

Appia is supposed to have been the wife of that Philemon to whom St Paul addressed a letter about a runaway slave. They are said to have been martyred at their home at Colossæ in Phrygia.

*PHILIBERT, ST, ab. August 20. AUG., p. 249

He founded the abbey of Jumièges and other religious houses, and was one of the ecclesiastics who stood up to the notorious Ebroin, mayor of the palace to Thierry III, for which he was imprisoned and banished for some years. d. 684. *Philibertus*.

†*PHILIP, ST, ap. May 1.   MAY, p. 1
The apostle Philip is mentioned several times in the gospel of St John. According to an old tradition he preached the gospel in Phrygia after Pentecost, and d. at Hierapolis. It is not known for certain whether he was martyred. *Philippus*.

†*PHILIP BENIZI, ST. August 23.   AUG., p. 278
B. at Florence in 1233, and gave up the medical profession to become a lay brother of the Servants of Mary. He was taken away from his gardening to receive holy orders, and was in due course promoted to the generalate of the order, to his great discomfort. Philip's reputation for holiness spread, and in 1268 the cardinals were for making him pope ; he fled by night and hid in a cave till the suggestion was withdrawn. From year to year he travelled Europe visiting the houses of his order and working for peace between Guelfs and Ghibellines, and he assisted at the second general Council of Lyons, where he is said to have shown the gift of tongues. St Philip was the chief propagator and the best-known saint of the Servite Order. d. 1285. c.c. 1671.

PHILIP EVANS, BD, mart. July 22.   JULY, p. 323
B. at Monmouth in 1645, became a Jesuit, and worked on the mission in South Wales. He was h.d.q. for his priesthood after the Oates " plot " at Cardiff in 1679. bd. 1929.

PHILIP HOWARD, BD, mart. October 19.   OCT., p. 269
Philip Howard, Earl of Arundel and Surrey, for some years was neglectful of his estates, his wife, and his religion, but he mended his ways in 1581 and was reconciled to the Church with his wife, Anne Dacre. In 1585 he was committed to the Tower of London, and in 1589 sentenced to death ; the sentence was not carried out and he died in the Tower at the age of thirty-eight, after ten years' imprisonment, in 1595. bd. 1929.

†*PHILIP NERI, ST. May 26.   MAY, p. 310
B. at Florence in 1515. For eighteen years he was a layman in Rome, beginning that work for souls which was to earn him the title of apostle of the City. After ordination he gathered some companions around him who formed the nucleus of the Congregation of the Oratory, and continued to live very simply, at the service of all, from the pope to a pot-boy. To Archbishop Ullathorne he was the " most extraordinary being of whom we have an account " : he was an unusually fine, almost fastidious, man, and converted renaissance Rome by influencing individuals rather than by exterior legislation or public exhortation ; religious controversy he avoided. d. 1595. cd. 1622.

PHILIP POWEL, BD, mart. June 30.   JUNE, p. 400
B. at Trallwng in Breconshire, educated at Abergavenny grammar school, and became a Benedictine at St Gregory's, Douay, in 1619. He was a priest for twenty years in Devonshire, and was then arrested on shipboard while on his way to Wales. h.d.q. for his priesthood at Tyburn in 1646. bd. 1929.

*PHILIP THE DEACON, ST. June 6.   JUNE, p. 79
He was one of the seven deacons chosen by the Apostles and baptized the eunuch of Queen Candace of Ethiopia (Acts vi, viii). First century.

*PHILIP OF GORTYNA, ST, bp.   April 11.   APR., p. 124
Bishop in Crete during the second century; by his training of his flock he exercised great influence in the eastern Mediterranean. d. *c.* 180.

*PHILIP OF HERACLEA, ST, bp. and mart.   October 22.   OCT., p. 295
The martyrdom in 304 of Philip, bishop of Heraclea, with whom suffered the priest Severus and the cleric Hermes, who had been a magistrate, is one of the best attested episodes of the Diocletian persecution. Philip, an aged man, refused to give up the sacred books or to sacrifice to the gods, and Hermes followed his example; after persuasion and torture had failed they were burned to death. Severus, who had been in hiding and gave himself up, suffered on the following day.

PHILIP OF PIACENZA, BD.   May 24.   MAY, p. 292
A confessor of the Hermit Friars of St Augustine. d. 1306.

PHILIP OF ZELL, ST.   May 3.   MAY, p. 43
This Philip was an Englishman who lived as a hermit near Worms and is said to have had great influence over King Pepin. After his death a monastery was built on the site of his cell and the town of Zell grew up around it. Eighth century.

PHILIPPA MARERI, BD, virg.   February 16.   FEB., p. 245
Fired by meeting St Francis of Assisi in her parents' home she became a solitary on Mount Marerio in the diocese of Rieti. Her brother Thomas, who had previously opposed her vocation, then gave her a site for a convent, where Bd Philippa formed a community of Franciscan nuns under the direction of Bd Roger of Todi. d. 1236.

*PHILOGONIUS, ST, bp.   December 20.   DEC., p. 209
Philogonius, a barrister, was elected bishop of Antioch in 318, and was imprisoned for the Faith; he was highly spoken of by St John Chrysostom. d. 324.

PHILOMENA, ST, virg. and mart.   August 11.   AUG., p. 129
Philomena (Philumena) is the name given to a saint of unknown date and history, venerated as a virgin martyr; whose cultus is due to the discovery of the relics of a young woman in the catacomb of St Priscilla at Rome in 1802. They were translated to Mugnano in the diocese of Nola in 1805, and from that day on miracles and many graces, spiritual and temporal, were attributed to the invocation of Philomena, the name which appeared on the *loculus* wherein the relics were found. Her cultus was greatly advanced by (among others) St John Vianney, and her feast was authorized in 1837 by Pope Gregory XVI.

PHOCAS, ST, mart.   March 5.   MAR., p. 58
Said to have been martyred at Antioch *c.* 320, and formerly invoked against snake-bite.

PHOCAS THE GARDENER, ST, mart.   July 23.   JULY, p. 327
All that is certainly known of this Phocas is that he lived, was martyred, and is greatly venerated in the East. According to legend he was a market-gardener at Sinope in Pontus. There is confusion between him and St Phocas, bishop of Sinope and martyr, whom the Roman Martyrology names on July 14.

PHŒBADIUS, ST, bp.   April 26.   APR., p. 290
Or *Fiari*. Bishop of Agen and a formidable opponent of Arianism. d. *c.* 395.

*PHŒBE, ST. September 3.   SEPT., p. 32

She is mentioned by St Paul in the last chapter of his epistle to the Christians at Rome. There is no reason to suppose that she was ever his wife.

*PHOTINA, ST, mart. March 20.   MAR., p. 335

According to a fable popular in the East she was the Samaritan woman with whom our Lord talked at the well, being afterwards martyred with others at Rome. Cardinal Baronius would seem to have entered her name in the Roman Martyrology by an oversight.

*PIERIUS, ST. November 4.   NOV., p. 54

A priest of Alexandria, famed for his learning and goodness. d. *c.* 310.

*PIONIUS, ST, mart. February 1.   FEB., p. 8

Pionius, a priest of Smyrna, was arrested while observing with friends the anniversary of the martyrdom of St Polycarp. After a long cross-examination they refused with violence to sacrifice in the pagan temple and were condemned to die. St Pionius was burnt alive and we have an eye-witness's account of his death. d. 251.

*PIRMINUS, ST, ab. November 3.   NOV., p. 31

First abbot of Reichenau, and a missionary in Baden. Being driven out by the civil power, he founded other monasteries elsewhere, and d. in 753. He wrote a popular work of religious instruction.

†*PIUS I, ST, pope and mart. July 11.   JULY, p. 136

The conflicts which he sustained obtained him the title of martyr liturgically, and some authorities maintain that he actually died by the sword, *c.* 154.

†*PIUS V, ST, pope. May 5.   MAY, p. 64

Michael Ghislieri was b. in Piedmont in 1504 ; he joined the Dominicans, was made a bishop in 1556 and a cardinal in the following year, and in 1565 was elected to the Holy See as Pius V. He was an austere and severe man raised up by God when austerity and severity were particularly needed. He enforced the reforms of the Council of Trent, combated Protestantism in the Empire and France, organized resistance against the threatening Turks (battle of Lepanto), excommunicated Queen Elizabeth of England, reformed the public worship of the Roman rite, and reproved by example prelatical luxury, insisting strongly that bishops and other beneficed clergy must reside in their cures. d. May 1, 1572. cd. 1712. St Pius V was one of the great figures of the Counter-reformation.

PLACIDUS, BD, mart. July 11.   JULY, p. 138

A disciple of Bd Sigisbert, martyred in Switzerland *c.* 625. c.c. 1905.

†*PLACIDUS, ST, mart. October 5.   OCT., p. 57

He was the young disciple of St Benedict who was miraculously saved from drowning by St Maurus. In the twelfth century he became identified with another Placidus, who with his companions was martyred probably over two hundred years before the Benedictine Placidus was born. This error has been perpetuated in the Roman office of his feast, but the Benedictines suppressed his proper office in 1915 ; it is likely that the feast will be eventually given up altogether.

*PLATO, ST, ab. April 4.   APR., p. 49

Abbot of Symboleon on Mount Olympus in Bithynia and then of Sakkudion, near Constantinople. He suffered persecution and imprisonment for opposing the divorce and subsequent attempted marriage of the

emperor Constantine Porphyrogenitus. d. 813. St Plato's funeral panegyric, preached by St Theodore Studites, is the main source of knowledge
of him.

PLECHELM, ST, bp. July 15.   JULY, p. 198
    He was a Northumbrian who went into the Low Countries with St
Wiro and became the apostle of Guelderland. d. *c.* 730.

*PLUTARCH, ST, mart. June 28.   JUNE, p. 368
    A pupil of Origen who was martyred with other students from the
catechetical school at Alexandria in 202. *Plutarchus.*

*POEMEN, ST, ab. August 27.   AUG., p. 331
    Poemen was one of the most celebrated of the Fathers of the Desert.
He retired to Skete during the second half of the fourth century and
became abbot of a group of hermits who lived in the ruins of a heathen
temple at Terenuth. He was present at the death of St Arsenius, and
himself d. *c.* 450.

*POLLIO, ST, mart. April 28.   APR., p. 317
    He was a lector of the church of Cybalæ in Pannonia, martyred in
304.

†*POLYCARP, ST, bp. and mart. January 26.   JAN., p. 309
    One of the most famous of the Apostolic Fathers and a disciple of St
John the Evangelist, who appointed him bishop of Smyrna *c.* 96. St
Ignatius on the way to martyrdom recommended him to his own church
of Antioch, and soon after Polycarp at his request wrote a letter on
Ignatius's behalf to the Philippians : in St Jerome's time this letter was
still publicly read in the churches of Asia. Another extant letter, written
in the name of the church of Smyrna, describes Polycarp's martyrdom.
After St Germanicus had been put to death he was seized by the crowd
and brought before the proconsul, where he confessed himself a Christian
and refused to give divine honours to the emperor. The games being over,
the people clamoured for him to be burned alive, and this was done, the
old man meeting his death with calmness and fortitude, in 156 (or 166).
Polycarpus.

*POLYEUCTUS, ST, mart. February 13.   FEB., p. 196
    Polyeuctus was martyred at Melitene in Armenia *c.* 259 and a church
was dedicated in his honour there before 377. Corneille in his tragedy,
Polyeucte, makes use of elements that are found in the martyr's *acta,* but
are fictitious.

POMPILIO PIROTTI, BD. July 15.   JULY, p. 210
    Pompilio Maria Pirotti was a confessor of the Piarist congregation,
who taught school and preached missions in the kingdom of Naples. d.
1756. bd. 1890.

†*PONTIAN, ST, pope and mart. November 19.   NOV., p. 248
    He was pope from *c.* 230 to *c.* 236. He was exiled to Sardinia by the
emperor Maximinus, and is said to have died there from ill-treatment.
Pontianus.

*PONTIUS, ST. March 8.   MAR., p. 124
    He was the deacon of St Cyprian of Carthage and went with him into
exile at Curubis. Pontius was the author of the *Life and Passion of
Cyprian,* which is still extant. d. *c.* 260.

*PONTIUS, ST, mart. May 14.   MAY, p. 173
    A martyr of the third (?) century at Cimella (Cimiez, near Nice).

PONTIUS, BD, ab. November 26. Nov., p. 310

The memory of Pontius of Faucigny, abbot of the canons regular at Abondance in the Chablais, was greatly revered by St Francis de Sales. Pontius was also for a time abbot of the monastery of St Sixtus, which he founded. d. 1178. c.c. 1896.

*POPPO, ST, ab. January 25. Jan., p. 307

He was first a soldier and pilgrim and then a monk under Abbot Richard of Saint-Vannes, for whom he reformed several monasteries, including that of Saint-Vaast at Arras. Poppo himself became abbot of Stavelot and was a sort of general superior of a group of monasteries in Lotharingia, as well as an adviser to the Emperor St Henry II. d. 1048.

*PORCARIUS, ST, mart. August 12. Aug., p. 151

Second abbot of Lérins who, with nearly all his monks, was massacred by Moors c. 732.

*PORPHYRIUS, ST, bp. February 26. Feb., p. 359

After years as a hermit in the desert of Skete and the Jordan valley he was consecrated bishop of Gaza in 395. These were the days of the last efforts of paganism in the East and Porphyrius concentrated all his efforts on uprooting it, getting permission from the empress Eudoxia to destroy the temples in Gaza. It is not surprising to learn that the worshippers lost no opportunity of harassing the bishop and his flock. On the site of the temple of Marnas a great church was built which Porphyrius consecrated in 408. He d. in 420 and his biography, written by his deacon Mark, is a very valuable historical document.

*POSSIDIUS, ST, bp. May 16. May, p. 203

Possidius, bishop of Calama in Numidia, was closely associated with St Augustine in his struggles against heresy and suffered personal violence. He was driven from his see by the Arian Genseric and d. in exile c. 440.

*POTAMIANA, ST, virg. and mart. June 28. June, p. 369

She would not purchase her freedom at the price of her chastity and was lowered slowly into a cauldron of boiling pitch at Alexandria in 202. Her mother, St Marcella, was martyred at the same time.

*POTAMION, ST, bp. and mart. May 18. May, p. 227

He was bishop of Heraclea in Egypt and was savagely tortured during the persecution of Maximinus Daia in 310 ; he met his death at the hands of the Arians c. 340.

*POTHINUS, ST, bp. and mart. June 2. June, p. 20

St Pothinus was the first bishop of Lyons and the leader of those martyrs under the bitter persecution of Marcus Aurelius in 177 whose sufferings are recorded in a contemporary letter which has been called " the jewel of the Christian literature of the second century." Pothinus had probably " listened to those who had seen the Apostles " ; in his ninetieth year he was mishandled by a mob and died in prison from his injuries. Among the other martyrs of Lyons and Vienne were SS Vettius, Sanctus, a deacon, Maturus, a neophyte, Attalus, and Blandina, a slave girl.

*POTITUS, ST, mart. January 13. Jan., p. 161

A martyr of unknown history who is honoured in the diocese of Naples ; he is said to have been a young boy.

*PRÆJECTUS, ST, bp. and mart. January 25. Jan., p. 306

Otherwise *Priest, Prest, Preils, Prix.* Bishop of Clermont c. 666.

He was slain by one Agritius, who had an imaginary grievance against him, in 676. There is a contemporary account of his life and achievements.

*PRÆTEXTATUS, ST, bp. and mart. February 24.　　FEB., p. 331

Prætextatus, called *Prix* in France, was chosen bishop of Rouen in 549. Chilperic, king at Soissons, charged him with acts calculated to encourage rebellion and he was banished. After Chilperic's death he returned to his see, but was pursued by the enmity of his widow, the wicked queen Fredegonda, with whom the bishop had often to remonstrate. She eventually caused him to be murdered in 586. St Gregory of Tours witnesses to the falseness of the calumnies made against St Prix by his enemies.

†*PRAXEDES, ST, virg. July 21.　　JULY, p. 301

Legend has it that Praxedes was the sister of St Pudentiana, and that she helped and sheltered Christians during the persecution under Marcus Antoninus ; but her extant *acta* have been officially declared to be spurious.

†*PRIMUS and **FELICIAN, SS,** marts. June 9.　　JUNE, p. 118

Brothers who were martyred and buried at Nomentum, near Rome, *c.* 297. The legendary details of their passion are unreliable.

†*PRISCA, ST, virg. and mart. January 18.　　JAN., p. 225

The St Prisca, virgin and martyr, mentioned in the Roman Martyrology on January 18 has not been satisfactorily identified.

PRISCILLA. *See also* Aquila and Prisca.

*PRISCILLA, ST. January 16.　　JAN., p. 200

It is likely that St Priscilla was the wife of Manius Acilius Glabrio and mother of the senator Pudens ; she gives her name to the most ancient of the Roman catacombs, above which was her villa in which it is believed that St. Peter made his headquarters.

*PRISCUS, ST, mart. May 26.　　MAY, p. 317

Priscus and other citizens of Besançon were martyred at Auxerre *c.* 272.

†*PROCESSUS and **MARTINIAN, SS,** marts. July 2.　　JULY, p. 15

Roman martyrs of uncertain date. The story that they were the gaolers of St Peter and St Paul in the Mamertine prison is a baseless legend.

*PROCLUS, ST, bp. October 24.　　OCT., p. 318

He became patriarch of Constantinople in 434 and was distinguished for the gentle way in which he dealt with Nestorians and other heretics, saving the Armenian church from the errors of its East Syrian and Persian neighbours. According to tradition he added the singing of the Trisagion to the Liturgy in miraculous circumstances. St Cyril of Alexandria and others speak highly of the goodness of Proclus. d. July 24, 447.

*PROCOPIUS, ST, mart. July 8.　　JULY, p. 92

There is extant a contemporary account, written by Eusebius, bishop of Cæsarea, of the passion of St Procopius, who was the first victim of the Diocletian persecution in Palestine. He was in reader's orders at Scythopolis and was beheaded in 303 at Cæsarea Maritima for refusing to sacrifice to the emperors. The simple narrative of Eusebius was the seed of nonsensical later legends, in the course of whose evolution St Procopius was split up into three different people, none of whom remotely resembled him.

*PROCULUS, ST, mart.   June 1.   JUNE, p. 5
   He is said to have been an officer in the Roman army, martyred at
Bologna in 304 (?).

PROCULUS, ST, bp. and mart.   June 1.   JUNE, p. 5
   A bishop of Bologna who was martyred by the Goths in 542.

*PROSDOCIMUS, ST, bp.   November 7.   Nov., p. 82
   He is venerated as the first bishop of Padua, but is wrongly supposed
to have been a disciple of St Peter from Antioch.

*PROSPER OF REGGIO, ST, bp.   June 25.   JUNE, p. 334
   He was a bishop of Reggio in Emilia during the fifth century. The
Roman Martyrology mistakenly identifies him with Prosper of Aquitaine.

PROTERIUS, ST, bp. and mart.   February 28.   FEB., p. 381
   Proterius was elected patriarch of Alexandria when Dioscoros, the
Eutychian heretic, was deposed by the Council of Chalcedon. The schis-
matic party was so violent that Proterius was in danger throughout his
pontificate, and eventually he was killed by the mob in a church on
Good Friday in 458. He was recognized as a martyr first by the bishops of
Thrace.

PROTHADIUS, ST, bp.   February 10.   FEB., p. 149
   A bishop of Besançon who d. 624 ; practically nothing is known of
him.

†*PROTUS AND HYACINTH, SS, marts.   September 11.   SEPT., p. 139
   By tradition they were brothers and servants in the house of St Basilla,
martyred *c.* 257. Their *acta* are fictitious, but the indubitable relics of St
Hyacinth were discovered in the cemetery of St Basilla at Rome in 1845.

PRUDENTIA, BD, virg.   May 6.   MAY, p. 83
   Bd Prudentia Castori was a hermitess of St Augustine at Milan and
Como, chiefly known for the miracles recorded at her tomb. d. 1492.

PRUDENTIUS, ST, bp.   April 6.   APR., p. 74
   Prudentius, bishop of Troyes, was one of the most learned prelates
of the Gallican church in the ninth century ; he played a notable part in
the controversies about predestination. d. 861.

*PRUDENTIUS, ST, bp.   April 28.   APR., p. 320
   Bishop of Tarazona in Spain during the eighth century. His so-called
" acts " are spurious.

*PTOLOMÆUS, ST, mart.   October 19.   OCT., p. 262
   He was put to death *c.* 165 for being a Christian and instructing a
woman in the faith. One Lucius and an unnamed man, both of whom
protested at the injustice of the sentence, were executed at the same time.

*PUBLIA, ST.   October 9.   OCT., p. 112
   She was a widow, the leader of a community of women at Antioch,
who was put to death by Julian the Apostate *c.* 370 ; he overheard them
singing psalm 115 (113) and interpreted certain passages therein as an
insult to himself.

PUBLIUS, ST, ab.   January 25.   JAN., p. 304
   He founded monasteries for Greeks and Syrians in Syria, and d. *c.* 380.

†*PUDENTIANA and **PUDENS, SS,** marts.   May 19.   MAY, p. 237
   The Roman Martyrology names as martyrs in Rome the maiden
Pudentiana (Potentiana) and her father Pudens, a senator. Opinions are
divided as to whether this is the Pudens mentioned in 2 Timothy iv, 21.

*PULCHERIA, ST, virg. September 10.   SEPT., p. 121
    The story of St Pulcheria, Eastern empress with her brother Theodosius II and then with Marcian, belongs to general secular and ecclesiastical history. She was a firm opponent of Monophysism, and she and Theodosius were the first rulers of Constantinople who were Greek rather than Latin. d. 453. Her feast is observed in many places in the East.

QUADRATUS, ST, bp.   May 26.   MAY., p. 315
Bishop of Athens and the first of the great line of Christian apologists, with a treatise written for the emperor Hadrian. d. c. 129.

*QUENTIN, ST, mart.   October 31.   OCT., p. 374
The story of the passion of St Quentin has come down to us in a variety of embellished forms, but he seems certainly to have been an authentic martyr at the town on the Somme which is now called by his name. He is said to have been a missionary from Rome, who suffered in 287. *Quinctinus.*

*QUIRICUS and **JULITTA, SS,** marts.   June 16.   JUNE, p. 194
According to their fictitious legend Julitta was a widow of noble birth from Iconium who fled from persecution but was martyred at Tarsus. Her three-year old son Quiricus had previously had his brains dashed out by an infuriated magistrate whose face he had scratched. Nothing is known about them really : it is likely that Quiricus was a real martyr around whom the legend subsequently grew up.

*QUIRINUS, ST, bp. and mart.   June 4.   JUNE, p. 50
Quirinus was bishop of Siscia (Sisak in Croatia) and during the persecution under Diocletian fled from the city. He was captured and brought back, but in spite of cruel beating refused to sacrifice to the gods. He was sent to the governor of Pannonia Prima at Sabaria (Szombathely in Hungary) and there, since he still refused to sacrifice, he was drowned in the river Raab in 308.

*QUITERIA, ST, virg. and mart.   May 22.   MAY, p. 267
This saint is much venerated on the borders of France and Spain, but nothing more is certain about her.

RABANUS MAURUS, BD, bp. February 4. FEB., p. 69

This prolific writer was one of the most learned men of his age. He was b. *c.* 784 probably at Mainz and was educated at Fulda and Tours where he became deeply attached to Alcuin. He learned Greek, Hebrew, and Syriac and was made master of the monastery school at Fulda (being for a time called off to help in the building of a new abbey). Rabanus became abbot of Fulda in 822, and it was probably then that he wrote his homilies and drew up his martyrology. After a fruitful rule he gave up the office, only to be made archbishop of Mainz when he was seventy-one. He was as energetic as he was learned, assisting at numerous synods and having 300 poor fed at his house every day. d. 856.

RADBOD, ST, bp. November 29. NOV., p. 340

He was the great-grandson of the last pagan king of the Frisians (also called Radbod) and he became bishop of Utrecht in 900. Some hymns and other poems that he wrote are still in existence. d. 918.

*RADEGUNDE, ST. August 13. AUG., p. 157

St Radegunde is one of the best-known figures of the sixth century in France. She had the misfortune to be one of the numerous wives of King Clothaire I, and when he murdered her brother she separated herself from him and was consecrated a deaconess by St Médard. She played a considerable part in religious and secular affairs, especially on behalf of peace, and was the foundress of the great monastery of the Holy Cross at Poitiers. d. 587. There are several churches dedicated in this saint's honour in England, and she is one of the titulars of Jesus College, Cambridge. *Radegundis.*

RALPH, ST, bp. June 21. JUNE, p. 283

Though probably not a monk he received several abbacies and in 840 was made bishop of Bourges ; he was active in public affairs, a man of learning, and founder of several religious houses. He compiled a book of pastoral instructions for the use of his clergy, which was rediscovered early in the seventeenth century. d. 866. *Radulphus.*

RALPH ASHLEY, BD, mart. April 7. APR., p. 92

A Jesuit lay-brother h.d.q. at Worcester in 1606 for being found in attendance on Bd Edward Oldcorne. bd. 1929.

RALPH CORBY, BD, mart. September 7. SEPT., p. 79

Vere Corbington. He was a Jesuit who ministered in the county of Durham. After some years he was condemned for his priesthood and h.d.q. at Tyburn in 1644. bd. 1929.

RALPH SHERWIN, BD, mart. December 1. DEC., p. 16

After being ordained at Douay and studying at the English College in Rome, Bd Ralph came on the English mission in 1580. Within a few months he was arrested and tortured, and in 1581 was h.d.q. at Tyburn for " complicity " in a fictitious plot. bd. 1886. Bd Ralph was the protomartyr of the " Venerabile " and his feast is kept in the diocese of Nottingham, within whose borders he was born.

RAMBERT, ST, mart. June 13. JUNE, p. 170

He was one of the many victims of Ebroin, mayor of the palace to Thierry III of Austrasia ; Ebroin feared that Rambert's virtues and abilities would make him a serious rival and had him ambushed and killed in the Jura mountains *c.* 680. But this appears insufficient reason for venerating him as a martyr. *Ragnebertus.*

†*RAPHAEL THE ARCHANGEL, ST. October 24. OCT., p. 316

He is called the " Healer of God " (see the book of *Tobias*) and is identified with the angel of the healing sheep-pool (John v, 1–4). His feast was extended to the whole Western church in 1922. *Raphaël.*

RATHO, BD. May 17. MAY, p. 221

Ratho (also *Rasso*, etc.) gives his name to the healing shrine of Grafrath in Bavaria. He was count of Andechs and, after fighting in several campaigns, founded a Benedictine abbey at Wörth where he himself became a monk. d. 953.

RAYMUND LULL, BD, mart. July 3. JULY, p. 29

B. *c.* 1233 on Majorca. When he was about thirty he was converted by a series of visions from his irregular life and determined to devote himself to the conversion of the Moors. He provided for his family, and after years of preliminary study crossed to Africa, where he was ill-treated, imprisoned, and deported ; this happened again some years later. In spite of receiving no encouragement from the Holy See or anywhere else he made a third attempt, and was stoned to death at Tunis in 1315. Bd Raymund realized that it was hopeless to try to convert the Mohammedans, knowing nothing of their religion and culture, and he spent many years travelling to the chief European centres of learning to encourage such studies and in a huge literary activity in Latin, Catalan and Arabic. His feast is kept by the Friars Minor, of which order he was a tertiary. *Raymundus.*

†*RAYMUND NONNATUS, ST. August 31. AUG., p. 390

He succeeded St Peter Nolasco as ransomer and master general of the Mercedarians, and his career shares the obscurity of the early days of that order. He is said at one time to have been a voluntary prisoner among the Moors to ransom other captives, and to have been made a cardinal just before his death in 1240. c.c. 1657.

RAYMUND OF CAPUA, BD. October 5. OCT., p. 63

Bd Raymund is famous as the spiritual guide and right-hand man of St Catherine of Siena, seconding her efforts which led to the return of Pope Gregory XI to Rome in 1377. After her death he was elected master general of the Dominicans and his reforms within the order earned him the title of its second founder. He wrote biographies of St Catherine and of St Agnes of Montepulciano. d. 1399. bd. 1899.

RAYMUND OF FITERO, BD, ab. February 6. FEB., p. 94

When in 1157 the Moors threatened an attack on Calatrava Abbot Raymund got permission from King Sancho of Castile to add Calatrava to the possessions of the abbey of Fitero if he could hold it against the Mohammedans. Raymund manned the city with a large army and the Moors did not attack, but from among his recruits Raymund formed a military order for its defence, known as the Military Order of the Knights of Calatrava. d. 1163. c.c. 1719.

†*RAYMUND OF PEÑAFORT, ST. January 23.   Jan., p. 273

From being a dignitary of the church of Barcelona he became a Dominican in 1222 and preached among the Jews and Moors. He was summoned to Rome by Pope Gregory IX, where he gave himself to the study of canon law : his five books of decretals were the best arranged part of the canon law until its codification in our own day. In 1238 he was elected master general of his order, and encouraged St Thomas Aquinas to write the *Contra Gentiles*. He was taken by King James to the island of Majorca where he undertook the reformation both of the king and of the islanders. St Raymund's part in the foundation of the Mercedarian Order is a matter of dispute. He died at the age of a hundred in 1275 and was followed to his grave by two kings and their families. cd. 1601.

RAYMUND OF TOULOUSE, ST. July 8.   July, p. 101

He was a singer in the church of St Sernin at Toulouse, noted for his benefactions, especially towards the Jews. After the death of his wife he received a canonry at St Sernin and restored the common life to the chapter. d. 1118.

*RAYNERIUS, ST. June 17.   June, p. 221

In Italian *Raniero*. After a dissipated youth at Pisa he was converted and a trading journey into Palestine confirmed him in his new and austere way of life. On his return he lived a retired existence, first in one monastery and then in another. Both before and after his death St Raynerius had a great reputation for miracles, healing the sick through the instrumentality of blessed water, whence he was called " de Aqua." d. 1160. cd. by Pope Alexander III. *Rainerius*.

RAYNERIUS INCLUSUS, BD. April 11.   Apr., p. 128

Raynerius *Inclusus* is so called because he spent twenty-two years shut up in a cell adjoining the cathedral of Osnabrück; to this self-imposed imprisonment he added other austerities. d. 1237.

RAYNERIUS OF AREZZO, BD. November 3.   Nov., p. 41

A confessor of the Friars Minor of whom little is known. d. 1304. c.c. 1802. There was also a Bd Raynerius among the Capuchins, who d. in 1586.

*REGINA, ST, virg. and mart. September 7.   Sept., p. 72

Regina (Reine) was venerated as a maiden martyr in France at an early date, but nothing is known of her history.

REGINALD OF ORLEANS, BD. February 17.   Feb., p. 255

B. in 1183 in Languedoc. He taught canon law at Paris for five years and met St Dominic at Rome in 1218, when he immediately joined his new order of friars. Bd Reginald organized the priory in connection with the University of Bologna, but his career was early cut short as he d. in 1220. c.c. 1875. *Reginaldus*.

*REINELDIS, ST, virg. and mart. July 16.   July, p. 216

A daughter of St Amalburga, said to have been murdered by the Huns at Saintes, near Hal, *c.* 710.

REINOLD, ST, mart. January 7.   Jan., p. 107

According to tradition he belonged to the family of Charlemagne and was a monk of St Pantaleon's at Cologne. Being in charge of some building operations there he incurred the hostility of the masons by trying to make them work harder ; so they killed him with their hammers and flung his body into the Rhine—but this seems insufficient reason for venerating him as a martyr.

REMACLUS, ST, bp. September 3. SEPT., p. 35

He was abbot of several monasteries in Austrasia before he became bishop of Maestricht in 652. After ten years he resigned and retired to the abbey of Stavelot, where his reputation drew many recruits to the community. d. *c.* 668.

*REMBERT, ST, bp. February 4. FEB., p. 72

A disciple of St Anschar and his successor as archbishop of Hamburg and Bremen. He preached among the Slavs and Vandals, sold sacred vessels to ransom prisoners among the Northmen, and wrote a biography of St Anschar. d. June 11, 888. *Rembertus.*

REMIGIUS, ST, bp. January 19. JAN., p. 233

A son of Charles Martel, made archbishop of Rouen in 755. d. *c.* 772.

†*REMIGIUS, ST, bp. October 1. OCT., p. 1

Remigius (Remi), a great apostle of the French, was illustrious for his learning, eloquence, and miracles during an episcopate of seventy years in the see of Rheims, but his biographical sources are rather unsatisfactory. The great event of his life was the baptism at Rheims of the Frankish king Clovis in 496. d. January 13, *c.* 533.

*RENÉ GOUPIL, ST, mart. March 16. MAR., p. 271

One of the most remarkable among the Martyrs of North America (q.v.). His health had caused him to fail in his efforts to be a Jesuit, so he became a surgeon and went to America as a lay assistant to the missionaries. He was assistant to St Isaac Jogues and was the first of the group of martyrs to suffer, being tomahawked on September 29, 1642, for having traced the sign of the cross on the brow of some children. *Renatus.*

*REPARATA, ST, virg. and mart. October 8. OCT., p. 98

She was put to death at Cæsarea in Palestine *c.* 250, but the extant account of her passion is spurious.

*RESTITUTA, ST, virg. and mart. May 17. MAY, p. 219

An African girl who died for Christ during the persecution of Valerian or Diocletian, at Carthage or elsewhere.

*RESTITUTA OF SORA, ST, virg. and mart. May 27. MAY, p. 325

Nothing is known of the passion of this Roman patrician at Sora in 271 (?).

*RHIPSIME, ST, virg. and mart. September 29. SEPT., p. 365

SS Rhipsime, Gaiana, and their maiden companions have been from early times venerated as the protomartyrs of the Armenian church, *c.* 290, but nothing at all is now known of their history or the circumstances of their passion. They are referred to in the legend of St Gregory the Illuminator. *Ripsimis.*

*RICHARD, ST. February 7. FEB., p. 106

A saint whose feast is kept at Lucca in Italy, where it is said that he was an English prince, and father of SS Willibald, Winebald, and Walburga, who d. at Lucca while on a pilgrimage to Rome in 722. But this story has been shown to be not worthy of credence. *Richardus; Reccaredus.*

*RICHARD, ST, bp. June 9. JUNE, p. 120

It seems to be agreed that this St Richard was an Englishman and bishop of Andria in Italy, but his reputed *acta* are spurious. These state that he flourished in the middle of the fifth century, but the twelfth is more likely.

RICHARD FEATHERSTONE, BD, mart. July 30.   JULY, p. 424

He was archdeacon of Brecon and tutor to the Princess Mary. After speaking in convocation in favour of the validity of Queen Catherine's marriage he was attainted for high treason and h.d.q. at Smithfield, London, in 1540. bd. 1886. His feast is kept in Wales with Bd Edward Powell.

RICHARD GWYN, BD, mart. October 17.   OCT., p. 245

Alias White. He was b. at Llanidloes in 1537, went to St John's College, Cambridge, repudiated Protestantism, married, and became a schoolmaster. He was imprisoned as a recusant and during four years in jail wrote many religious poems in Welsh that are still extant. Bd Richard was h.d.q. at Wrexham in 1584, the protomartyr of Wales. bd. 1929.

RICHARD HERST, BD, mart. August 29.   AUG., p. 379

Richard Herst (Hurst, Hayhurst) was a farmer near Preston who was hanged at Lancaster in 1628, ostensibly for murder (it was not even manslaughter) ; his real offence was being a Catholic recusant. bd. 1929.

RICHARD KIRKMAN, BD, mart. August 22.   AUG., p. 273

A secular priest, tutor in the household of Dymoke of Scrivelsby, who was h.d.q. at York in 1582 for denying the Queen's supremacy in spiritual matters.

RICHARD LANGLEY, BD, mart. December 1.   DEC., p. 24

A Yorkshire gentleman who was hanged at York in 1586 for sheltering priests in his house. bd. 1929.

RICHARD NEWPORT, BD, mart. May 30.   MAY, p. 369

Alias Smith. A secular priest from Northamptonshire, h.d.q. for his priesthood at Tyburn in 1612.

RICHARD REYNOLDS, BD, mart. May 4.   MAY, p. 58

Bridgettine monk of Syon Abbey, Middlesex, who was h.d.q. at Tyburn for denying the royal supremacy, one of the first group of English martyrs, 1535.

RICHARD ROLLE, BD. September 29.   SEPT., p. 367

Richard Rolle had a very considerable popular cultus in the past, but it has not yet been confirmed by ecclesiastical authority, though preparations for his canonization were begun soon after his death. He was b. at Thornton in Yorkshire *c.* 1300 and spent most of his life as a hermit, at Hampole and elsewhere in that county. More interest has been taken in recent years in Rolle than in any other English uncanonized saint, on account of the unique position which he holds among English mystical writers. His best known work is the *Fire of Love,* and he seems as a man to have been as personally attractive as his writings. d. 1349.

RICHARD THIRKILD, BD, mart. May 29.   MAY, p. 353

B. in co. Durham and ordained abroad in 1579 when he was already an old man. H.d.q. for his priesthood at York in 1583.

RICHARD WHITING, BD, ab. and mart. November 15.   DEC., p. 10

The last abbot of Glastonbury came to that office in 1525. At the dissolution he refused to surrender his monastery to the Crown and he was sentenced to death for high treason, his offence apparently being that he recanted the oath recognizing the King's supremacy in spiritual matters.

Bd Richard was h.d.q. at Glastonbury in 1539. With him suffered BB John Thorne and Roger James, monks of the same abbey. bd. 1895. The feast of these martyrs is kept in the dioceses of Westminster (December 1) and Clifton (November 15), and by the English Benedictines on the first date.

*RICHARD OF CHICHESTER, ST, bp.   April 3.   APR., p. 38

Richard de Wyche (*i.e.* Droitwich), after coping with a decayed family estate, went to Oxford, Paris, and Bologna to study. He became chancellor of Oxford University and diocesan chancellor to St Edmund of Canterbury, after whose exile Richard was ordained and became parish priest of Deal. In 1244 he was appointed bishop of Chichester by Bd Boniface of Canterbury (" of Savoy ") in opposition to King Henry III's unworthy candidate. He was prevented by force from taking possession of his see and had to administer it from a country rectory for two years. St Richard was a stern reformer of his clergy, a great almsgiver and simple in his own habits. d. 1253. cd. 1262. St Richard is commemorated in the dioceses of Southwark, Westminster, and Birmingham.

RICHARDIS, ST.   September 18.   SEPT., p. 248

Richardis was the wife of the emperor Charles the Fat. She was falsely accused of unfaithfulness to her husband and is said to have cleared herself by ordeal by fire. But the two separated and Richardis retired to a convent, where she d. *c.* 895. Her cultus was approved by Pope St Leo IX in 1049 and her feast is still observed in two French dioceses.

*RICHARIUS, ST, ab.   April 26.   APR., p. 292

In French *Riquier*. He was converted by two Irish priests and himself studied in England. Richarius was a very successful preacher and induced King Dagobert to found a monastery for him at Celles. He ended his life as a hermit, *c.* 645.

RICHIMIRUS, ST, ab.   January 17.   JAN., p. 221

He founded a monastery at an unidentified place on the river Loire and was its abbot until his death in 715. His memory has practically died out.

RICTRUDIS, ST.   May 12.   MAY, p. 145

Rictrudis was the wife of the Frankish St Adalbald to whom she bore four children, all of them venerated as saints. After the murder of her husband, King Clovis II tried to force her to marry again, but with the assistance of St Amand she was enabled to become a nun and d. abbess of Marchiennes in 688.

RIEUL, ST, bp.   March 30.   MAR., p. 445

He is venerated as the first bishop of Senlis, in the third century. *Regulus.*

*RIGOBERT, ST, bp.   January 4.   JAN., p. 62

Little is known of this archbishop of Rheims except that he was banished from his see for a time by Charles Martel. d. *c.* 745. *Rigobertus.*

*RITA OF CASCIA, ST.   May 22.   MAY, p. 273

The current account of St Rita is based on a biography written nearly 150 years after her death. She was b. into a peasant home in 1381 and married a brutal and dissolute husband ; after his violent death she, with great difficulty, was admitted to the convent of the Augustinian nuns at Cascia. She was a most mortified religious, with a special devotion to the passion of our Lord, the contemplation of which often sent her into ecstasy. d. 1457. cd. 1900.

RIZZERIO, BD. February 7. FEB., p. 108

Rizzerio or Richarius was one of the two young men who offered themselves to St Francis of Assisi after his famous sermon at Bologna (he is referred to in the *Fioretti* as " Rinieri "). He was one of the most loved followers of Francis and became minister provincial of the friars in the Marches. d. 1236. c.c. 1836.

ROBERT ANDERTON, BD, mart. April 25. APR., p. 288

A secular priest, born at Chorley, who was h.d.q. for his priesthood in the Isle of Wight in 1586. bd. 1929. *Robertus.*

†*ROBERT BELLARMINE, ST, bp. and doct. May 13. MAY, p. 153

B. in 1542 at Montepulciano and entered the Society of Jesus in 1560. He had a career of the greatest distinction, teaching theology at Louvain, teaching and preaching in Rome, working on the Vulgate Bible, rector of the Roman College : in 1598 he was made a cardinal, " as he had no equal for learning." For three years he occupied the archbishopric of Capua and gave up all other activities to look after his flock ; he then became head of the Vatican Library and took a prominent part in all the affairs of the Holy See. Among other controversies he answered King James I of England and the Scottish jurist Barclay. St Robert was one of the greatest polemical theologians the Church has ever produced and her foremost teacher against the doctrines of the Protestant reformers ; his best-known writings are the four volumes of *Disputations*, his catechism of Christian doctrine, and the devotional works of his later years. d. September 17, 1621. cd. 1930. Declared doctor of the Church 1931.

ROBERT DALBY, BD, mart. March 16. MAR., p. 288

Dalby (or Drury) was a convert minister who went to the Rheims college and was ordained priest. He was h.d.q. for his priesthood with Bd John Amias at York in 1589. bd. 1929.

ROBERT SOUTHWELL, BD, mart. February 21.

He was b. at Horsham St Faith's in Norfolk in 1561 and became a Jesuit at Rome at the age of seventeen ; he came on the English mission in 1586. Southwell was a poet and prose-writer (best known for " The Burning Babe " and *Triumphs Over Death* respectively), who in all probability had an effect on the work of Shakespeare himself. He was betrayed to the state in 1592 and imprisoned for three years before he was brought to trial, being tortured thirteen times. h.d.q. for his priesthood at Tyburn 1595. bd. 1929.

ROBERT WATKINSON, BD, mart. April 20. APR., p. 243

A secular priest of Hemingworth in Yorkshire, h.d.q. for his priesthood at Tyburn in 1602. bd. 1929.

ROBERT OF ARBRISSEL, " BD," ab. February 25. FEB., p. 344

Founder of the monastic congregation of Fontevrault. As chancellor and vicar general at Rennes he was so vigorous in putting down abuses that he was forced to leave Brittany. In 1099 he established adjoining communities of men and women in the valley of Fontevrault under the Rule of St Benedict ; their life was extremely austere, and the abbess was the supreme superior. He made other foundations, and after a stormy and difficult career retired to Fontevrault where he lived as a simple monk until his death in 1116. Robert is usually called " Blessed," but attempts in the seventeenth and nineteenth centuries to get his cultus confirmed were not successful.

*ROBERT OF CHAISE DIEU, ST, ab. April 17.   APR., p. 199
Robert de Turlande was founder and first abbot of Chaise Dieu in the Auvergne, which at his death in 1067 had over 300 monks.

ROBERT OF KNARESBOROUGH, BD. September 24.   SEPT., p. 305
Robert Flower was b. at York *c.* 1160. After being a postulant at Newminster he became a hermit, eventually making his home in a cave by the river Nidd, near Knaresborough ; here he earned a great reputation for holiness, and after his death in 1218 (or 1235 ?) was the object of a considerable cultus, which was never officially confirmed. This Robert has been sometimes confused with St Robert, Abbot of Newminster, who d. many years before him.

*ROBERT OF MOLESMES, ST, ab. April 29.   APR., p. 332
While abbot of Molesmes he received permission, with two of his monks, St Stephen Harding and Bd Alberic, to leave the monastery and retire to the forest of Citeaux ; here in 1098 the foundations of the Cistercian congregation were laid. Only a year later St Robert had, under obedience, to return to Molesmes, and he ruled that abbey successfully till his death in 1110. But he never ceased to long for Citeaux.

*ROBERT OF NEWMINSTER, ST, ab. June 7.   JUNE, p. 96
B. at Gargrave in Yorkshire, where he was rector before joining the Benedictines at Whitby. He took part in the founding of Fountains abbey, which became Cistercian, and from thence was appointed first abbot of Newminster in Northumberland. It was said of St Robert that he was " modest in his bearing, gentle in companionship, merciful in judgement," and he ruled his abbey successfully for many years, founding a daughter house at Pipewell in Northamptonshire. d. 1159. His feast is observed by the Cistercians.

*ROCH, ST. August 16.   AUG., p. 190
Pronounced " Rock." All that is known with certainty of the life of this much venerated saint is that he was b. at Montpellier and nursed the sick during a plague in Italy in the fourteenth century. He is invoked against pestilence and skin diseases. *Rochus.*

ROCH GONZALEZ, BD. *See* Paraguay, Martyrs of.

RODERICUS and SOLOMON, SS, marts. March 13.   MAR., p. 239
A priest of Cabra who was betrayed by his Mohammedan brother and put to death for the Faith, together with one Solomon, at Cordova in 857.

ROGER OF ELLANT, BD. January 4.   JAN., p. 63
An Englishman who became a Cistercian monk at Lorroy in France and from thence founded the new monastery of Ellant in the diocese of Rheims. d. 1160. *Rogerus.*

ROGER LE FORT, BD, bp. March 1.   MAR., p. 10
Roger was son of the Lord of Ternes in the Limousin and attained in his youth both to scholastic and ecclesiastical distinction. His election to the see of Orleans is said to have been made in error, but he was an excellent bishop and was translated first to Limoges and then to the metropolitan see of Bourges. He established the feast of our Lady's conception in his dioceses and by will left all his property for the education of poor boys. d. 1367.

ROGER OF TODI, BD. January 28.   JAN., p. 354
A personal follower of St Francis of Assisi, who appointed him spiritual

director of the Poor Clare convent at Rieti. d. 1237. Cultus confirmed by Pope Benedict XIV.

ROMÆUS, ST. March 4. MAR., p. 55

He was a Carmelite lay brother and the companion of St Avertanus (February 25) ; he caught the plague while nursing him, and d. a week later, 1380.

*ROMANUS, ST, ab. February 28. FEB., p. 382

Romanus retired from his monastery to a solitude in the Jura mountains where he was joined by his brother Lupicinus. Together they founded the monasteries of Condate and Leuconne for men and La Beaume (St Romain-de-la-Roche) for women, and each governed one monastery directly with joint authority over the whole congregation. These religious strove in all things to imitate the monks of the Eastern deserts, but the climate obliged them somewhat to mitigate their austerities. St Romanus d. *c.* 460, and was buried at La Beaume, where his sister was abbess.

*ROMANUS, ST. May 22. MAY, p. 268

A monk who encouraged and helped St Benedict when he first fled from Rome to Subiaco. d. *c.* 550

†*ROMANUS, ST, mart. August 9. AUG., p. 113

He was a doorkeeper of the Roman church who, together with the priest Severus and the clerics Claudius and Crescentius, was martyred at the same time as St Laurence in 258.

*ROMANUS, ST, bp. October 23. OCT., p. 306

He was bishop of Rouen for ten years and d. in 639. The chapter of Rouen formerly had the privilege of releasing a prisoner condemned to death every year on the feast of the Ascension in honour of this saint.

*ROMANUS and BARULA, SS, marts. November 18. NOV., p. 234

St Romanus was a Palestinian deacon martyred at Antioch in 304. Nothing certain is known of his companion Barula.

ROMANUS THE MELODIST, ST. October 1. OCT., p. 6

Romanus, a Syrian Jew, was one of the clergy of the church of Constantinople, probably during the sixth century, and the greatest of the Greek hymn writers : about a thousand hymns are attributed to him.

*ROMARICUS, ST, ab. December 8. DEC., p. 109

He was a monk of Luxeuil, formerly a Merovingian nobleman, who with St Amatus (September 13) founded the abbey of Remiremont (*Romarici mons*) in the Vosges. Romaricus succeeded Amatus as its abbot. d. 653.

†*ROMUALD, ST, ab. February 7. FEB., p. 97

B. *c.* 951 of the Onesti, dukes of Ravenna. To expiate his part in a duel in which his father had killed his opponent he became a monk and then a hermit. For thirty years he wandered about reforming monasteries and establishing hermitages in northern Italy and southern France, the best known and most lasting of his foundations being that of the Camaldolese hermit monks, which began a revival in the eremitical life of the West. This took place at Camaldoli, near Arezzo, in 1009, and the order still exists as an independent branch of the Benedictines. There seems to have been a tendency both to restlessness and harshness in Romuald's character, but he attracted many during his life. d. June 19, 1027, his feast on February 7 being the anniversary of the translation of his relics. *Romualdus*.

*ROMULA, ST, virg. July 23. JULY, p. 333

Romula in her old age lived with SS Redempta and Herundo near the church of St Mary Major in Rome ; they were all three much respected by St Gregory the Great. Sixth century.

*ROMULUS, ST, bp. and mart. July 6. JULY, p. 59

According to a late tradition the first bishop of Fiesole was Romulus, a convert of St Peter and martyr under Domitian. Nothing is known of him historically, but there is evidence of an early cultus of a St Romulus at Fiesole.

*ROSALIA, ST, virg. September 4. SEPT., p. 49

According to local tradition Rosalia was a girl of good family who passed her life as a recluse in a cave in Sicily. d. 1160 (?). Her alleged relics were found in 1624 and she was acclaimed as the patron saint of Palermo, the cessation of a plague being attributed to her intercession.

†*ROSE OF LIMA, ST, virg. August 30. AUG., p. 381

She was of Spanish birth, at Lima in Peru in 1586. She emulated St Catherine of Siena, leading a life of penitential mortification in the midst of her family and at first much to their annoyance. She joined the third order of St Dominic and for fourteen years lived practically as an ankress, suffering much from spiritual desolation and encouraged with corresponding light. d. 1617. cd. 1671. St Rose is patroness of South America and the Philippines, being the first canonized saint of the New World. *Rosa.*

*ROSE OF VITERBO, ST, virg. September 4. SEPT., p. 50

Reliable accounts of the life of this saint are wanting. She was a Franciscan tertiary of humble birth and preached in the streets of Viterbo against the emperor Frederick II and the Ghibelline garrison. Marvels were attributed to her and she was much revered by the people, but a local convent refused to admit her into its community. d. *c.* 1252. cd. 1457.

ROSELINA, BD, virg. January 17. JAN., p. 222

Roseline de Villeneuve was a Carthusian nun who became prioress at Celle Roubaud in Provence. She had frequent visions, and her dead body remained flexible and incorrupt for at least a century after her death in 1329. c.c. 1851.

ROTRUDIS, ST, virg. June 22. JUNE, p. 295

The relics of this saint were venerated at the abbey of St Bertin at Saint-Omer ; who she was we do not know—nor, apparently, did the monks of St Bertin, though popular tradition called her a niece or daughter of Charlemagne.

RUADAN, ST, ab. April 15. APR., p. 173

He was one of the chief disciples of St Finian of Clonard and founded the monastery of Lothra. d. 584.

RUDESIND, BD, bp. March 1. MAR., p. 8

He belonged to a noble family of Spanish Galicia, where he is known as " San Rosendo." He gave up the episcopal see of Dumium (Mondonedo) to enter the monastery of Cella Nueva of which he became abbot, and carried out extensive monastic reforms. His biography consists principally of miracles attributed to his intercession. d. 977. *Rudesindus.*

RUDOLF ACQUAVIVA, BD, and other marts. *See* Cuncolim, Martyrs of.

*RUFINA and SECUNDA, SS, virgs. and marts. July 10. JULY, p. 130

Except their existence, their martyrdom in 257, and their burial at Santa Rufina on the Aurelian Way, nothing is certainly known of these maidens.

*RUFUS and **ZOSIMUS, SS,** marts. December 18.   DEC., p. 199
    They were laymen who shared in the sufferings of St Ignatius of Antioch
and were martyred under Trajan *c.* 107.

*RUMOLDUS, ST, mart. June 24.   JULY, p. 28
    In French *Rombaut.* The story that Rumoldus was an Irish bishop
who was slain by the heathen while a missionary in Brabant *c.* 775 has
little historical value; his feast is nevertheless observed in Ireland (July 4).
He was a martyr in whose honour the cathedral of Malines is dedicated.

RUMON, ST. August 28.   AUG., p. 367
    This Rumon was a sixth-century monk, said to have come from
Ireland, whose name (in the form of Ruan, and others) is found in several
places in Devon and Cornwall; he may have been a monk of Glastonbury.
Some have identified Rumon with the Breton St Ronan.

RUMWOLD, ST. November 3.   NOV., p. 28
    There was formerly a cultus of Rumwold at Brackley and Buckingham;
the surprising legend about him was that he died at King's Sutton in
Northamptonshire at the age of three days after having pronounced a
profession of faith in a loud voice. This prodigy was dated in the seventh
century. *Rumwoldus.*

*RUPERT, ST, bp. March 27.   MAR., p. 418
    While bishop of Worms he received permission to preach the gospel in
Bavaria, which he did with such fruit that he has been called the apostle
of that country, though there were many Christians there before he and his
fellow missionaries arrived. He was the originator of the church in Salzburg. St Rupert seems to have been French, not Irish, but his feast is
observed throughout Ireland. d. *c.* 710. *Rupertus.*

RUPERT and **BERTHA, SS.** May 15.   MAY, p. 193
    Rupert is said to have been a hermit who lived with his mother Bertha
on the Rupertsberg, near Bingen, during the ninth century. Their cultus
was popularized by St Hildegard three hundred years later.

*RUSTICUS, ST, bp. October 26.   OCT., p. 340
    He was a monk of Lérins and bishop of Narbonne; d. 461.

†***RUSTICUS** and **ELEUTHERIUS, SS,** marts. October 9. OCT., p. 110
    The priest and deacon who are said to have suffered martyrdom with
the bishop St Dionysius at Paris, *c.* 275.

SABAS, ST, bp. January 14. JAN., p. 181

In Slavonic *Sava*. B. 1174, youngest son of the first Serbian sovereign, Stephen I Nemanya. At the age of seventeen he became a monk at Mount Athos and founded the monastery of Khilandari, which still exists. In 1207 he returned to Serbia to help his brother Stephen II. He organized the first Serbian hierarchy of bishops, being himself appointed its metropolitan by the patriarch of Constantinople, and gave new life to religion in his country by establishing small houses of missionary monks. From Pope Honorius III Sava obtained the recognition of Stephen II as king and a crown for his coronation at Zitcha. d. 1237 in Bulgaria and was eventually buried at the Serbian monastery of Milochevo, but his relics were destroyed in 1594 by the Turks. St Sava is one of the principal patrons of Yugoslavia.

*SABAS, ST, mart. April 12. APR., p. 129

Sabas was a Christian Goth in what is now Rumania and belonged to the order of readers. In 372 he was seized by heathen Gothic soldiers and, upon his refusing to eat food that had been sacrificed to idols, was tortured and then drowned in the river Mussovo, near Tirgovist.

†*SABAS, ST, ab. December 5. DEC., p. 66

St Sabas, one of the greatest of the early monks, was b. in Cappadocia in 439. After being a monk and solitary in various places for years he founded a large *laura* or semi-eremitical monastery in a most wild gorge between Jerusalem and the Dead Sea ; in 493 he was appointed superior general over all the monks of Palestine ; and he played an active part in the public ecclesiastical history of his time in the Near East. d. 532. The monastery he founded still exists, called after him Mar Saba, and is one of the two oldest occupied monasteries in the world , its monks belong to the dissident Eastern Orthodox Church.

†*SABINA, ST, mart. August 29. AUG., p. 377

She is the titular saint of the ancient church of St Sabina on the Aventine at Rome, but nothing is certainly known about her. Sabina is named in the canon of the Ambrosian Mass..

*SABINIAN, ST, mart. January 29. JAN., p. 374

He is believed to have been a martyr at Troyes in the early centuries. *Sabinianus*.

SABINUS, ST, bp. January 17. JAN., p. 219

Bishop of Piacenza and a close friend of St Ambrose. When deacon he was sent on a mission to Antioch by Pope St Damasus. d. 420.

*SABINUS, ST, bp. February 9. FEB., p. 143

Bishop of Canosa in Apulia and a friend of St Benedict. He was sent by the Holy See on a mission to Constantinople, and while at Myra in Lycia had a vision of St Nicholas. d. *c.* 566. The body of St Sabinus was eventually translated to Bari, where his relics were lost for a time and found in 1901.

*SABINUS, ST, bp. and mart.   December 30.   DEC., p. 292
  Sabinus, alleged bishop of Assisi, was put to death for Christ with several converts in 303.

*SACERDOS, ST, bp.   May 5.   MAY, p. 73
  Sacerdos (also Serdon, Sardot, Sadroc) was bishop of Limoges during the early sixth century.

SADOC, BD, mart.   June 2.   JUNE, p. 27
  Sadoc was one of the first Dominicans in Hungary, where he preached and then founded a house of his order at Sandomir in Poland. In 1260 the town was ravaged by the Tartars and Sadoc and all his friars were slain while singing *Salve Regina.* c.c. by Pope Pius VII.

*SADOTH, ST, bp. and mart.   February 20.   FEB., p. 283
  He became bishop of Seleucia-Ctesiphon, the primatial see of Persia, during the persecution of Sapor II. He cared for his flock from a place of hiding, and then was arrested with 128 others. All were put to death, St Sadoth and eight others after five months' imprisonment at Beit-Lapat, 345.

SAHAK. *See* Isaac.

*SALABERGA, ST. September 22.   SEPT., p. 289
  She was the mother of St Beauduin and St Anstrudis ; after her second widowhood she became abbess of the monastery of St John which she had founded at Laon. d. *c.* 665.

SALOME, BD. November 17.   NOV., p. 228
  After the death of her husband, Coloman of Hungary, she joined the Poor Clares and died abbess of Zavichost in Poland in 1268. c.c. by Pope Clement X.

SALOME and **JUDITH, SS.** June 29.   JUNE, p. 384
  These two women are said to have been English recluses of royal blood at the monastery of Ober Altaich in Bavaria during the ninth century. The tradition is a late one, but it has been suggested that one of them may have been Eadburga, the rather shocking daughter of Offa of Mercia, who was driven out of England and may have repented in this fashion.

SALVATOR OF ORTA, BD. March 18.   MAR., p. 317
  A Spanish Franciscan lay brother of the Observance, who lived at Orta, Barcelona, Cagliari, and other friaries in the sixteenth century. d. 1567. c.c. by Pope Clement XI.

*SALVIUS, ST, bp. January 11.   JAN., p. 146
  Otherwise *Sauve.* Bishop of Amiens in the seventh century, famous for miracles. d. *c.* 625. A relic of this saint was formerly treasured at Canterbury cathedral.

*SALVIUS, ST, bp. September 10.   SEPT., p. 129
  Salvius became bishop of Albi in 574 ; he showed special devotedness to his flock during an epidemic in the year of his death, 584.

SALVIUS, ST. October 28.   OCT., p. 349
  This Salvius (in French *Saire*) seems to have been a sixth-century hermit at Saint-Saire in Normandy.

*SALVIUS and **SUPERIUS, SS,** marts. June 26.   JUNE, p. 350
  Their legend states that they were a bishop and his disciple who were murdered by an official's son near Valenciennes *c.* 768 for the sake of the bishop's gorgeous and valuable girdle. The story is not well attested— but there is a lesson in it.

SAMOSATA, THE SEVEN MARTYRS OF. December 9.   DEC., p. 112
Hipparchus and Philotheus, two magistrates of Samosata, and their converts James, Paragrus, Abibus, Romanus, and Lollian were crucified *c.* 311 for refusing to sacrifice to the gods during the public games held by the emperor Maximinus after his campaign against the Persians.

*SAMSON, ST, bp.   July 28.   JULY, p. 394
St Samson was one of the most important of the British missionary bishops of the sixth century. He was a monk under St Illtyd at Llantwit Major and for a short time abbot of the monastery on Caldey island. He visited Ireland, and after a sojourn in Cornwall passed over into Brittany, having been consecrated bishop by St Dyfrig. His centre was at Dol, from whence he made missionary journeys in all directions : his name is found in the Scilly and Channel islands and elsewhere. d. *c.* 565. Samson's feast is kept in the diocese of Cardiff and on Caldey island. *Sampson.*

*SAMSON THE HOSPITABLE, ST.   June 27.   JUNE, p. 361
He founded a great hospital for the sick poor in Constantinople, sometime during the fifth century, being himself both physician and priest.

*SANCHO, ST, mart.   June 5.   JUNE, p. 68
B. at Albi in France and carried away to Cordoba by the Moors. He was enrolled in the guards of Abd ur-Rahman II but, fired by the example of St Isaac (June 3), he openly reviled Mohammed. He suffered death by impalement in 851. *Sanctius.*

SANTUCCIA, BD.   March 21.   MAR., p. 363
Santuccia Terrebotti was a devout woman of Gubbio who, in agreement with her husband, became a Benedictine nun. She inaugurated a reformed convent at Rome. d. 1305.

SAPOR and **ISAAC, SS,** bps. and marts.   November 30.   NOV., p. 348
Sapor and Isaac were bishops martyred in Persia in 339, the one dying in prison and the other being stoned to death. There suffered at the same time SS Mahanes, Abraham, and Simeon.

*SATURNINUS, ST, bp. and mart.   November 29.   NOV., p. 339
Saturninus (Sernin) was a missionary from Rome, venerated as the first bishop of Toulouse. It is said that, having refused to sacrifice to the gods, he was tied by the feet to a bull which was then chased through the streets till the bishop's brains were dashed out, *c.* 257.

†*SATURNINUS, ST, mart.   November 29.   NOV., p. 338
He was a Roman priest, said to have been from Carthage, martyred in 309 (?) and buried in the cemetery of Thraso on the Salarian Way.

*SATURNINUS, etc., **SS,** marts.   February 11.   FEB., p. 166
Saturninus, a priest of Albitina in Africa, with his four children, the senator Dativus, and others were arrested at Mass in 304 and sent to Carthage for examination. Several of them were tortured, and the child Hilarion when threatened by the magistrate replied, " Go on then, but anyhow I am a Christian." It appears that they all died in prison.

*SATURNINUS, and comps., **SS,** marts.   May 2.   MAY, p. 27
This Saturninus was a martyr at Alexandria *c.* 304 but of the Neopolus, Germanus, and Celestine mentioned with him by the Roman Martyrology nothing is known.

*SATYRUS, ST.   September 17.   SEPT., p. 224
He was a lawyer and undertook the administration of the temporal affairs of the diocese of Milan for his brother St Ambrose. The integrity

and kindliness of Satyrus were eulogized by St Ambrose in a funeral sermon. d. *c.* 392.

SAVA. *See* Sabas.

SAVIN, ST. October 9. OCT., p. 116

He is venerated as the apostle of the Lavedan district of the Pyrenees and is said to have been a hermit, but even the century (fifth ?, ninth ?) in which he lived is a matter of conjecture. *Savinus.*

SCHENUTE, ST, ab. July 1. JULY, p. 3

One of the formative influences in Egyptian monasticism, who became a monk at Deir al-Abiad in 371. He is said to have ruled over 4000 monks and nuns, and he was the first to institute something in the nature of monastic vows as now understood. His monastery of Deir Amba-Schenute was still peopled by dissident Coptic monks towards the end of the nineteenth century. d. *c.* 460. *Sinuthius.*

†*SCHOLASTICA, ST, virg. February 10. FEB., p. 147

The sister of St Benedict, who ruled a convent at Plombariola, near Monte Cassino, under her brother's direction. St Gregory in his *Dialogues* gives a moving account of St Benedict's last meeting with St Scholastica, three days before her death in 543.

SCILLITAN MARTYRS, THE. *See* Speratus.

*SEBALD, ST. August 19. AUG., p. 224

Sebald is venerated as the patron saint of Nuremberg in Bavaria. He is said to have accompanied St Willibald into Germany from Rome and was a missionary in the Reichswald. Eighth century. *Sebaldus.*

†*SEBASTIAN, ST, mart. January 20. JAN., p. 242

All that can be safely asserted about this famous saint is that he was a Roman martyr, who had some connection with Milan and was venerated there even in the time of St Ambrose, and that he was buried on the Appian Way (in 288 ?). According to the popular story he was shot to death with arrows. *Sebastianus.*

SEBASTIAN MAGGI, BD. December 16. DEC., p. 185

He was a friar of the Order of Preachers and twice vicar of the reformed province of Lombardy, where he worked doggedly for improved discipline. He was for a time confessor of Savonarola, whom he appreciated and admired. d. 1496. c.c. 1760.

SEBASTIAN VALFRÉ, BD. January 30. JAN., p. 388

B. in Piedmont in 1629, and was an Oratorian father at Turin. As a prefect of the Little Oratory and director of souls he was much sought after and took endless trouble with all who came to him, while he sought out sinners in the streets and by-ways and converted them in marvellous fashion. He was especially like St Philip Neri in his cheerfulness, though he suffered grievous spiritual trials. d. 1710. bd. 1834.

SEBASTIAN OF APPARICIO, BD. February 25. FEB., p. 349

He was a valet and farm worker in Spain, then emigrated to Mexico, where he did well as a carrier and road contractor. After marrying and being widowed twice well after middle age, he gave his property to the Poor Clares and at the age of seventy became a Franciscan lay brother at Puebla de los Angeles. He lived this new life for twenty-six years, chiefly engaged in begging for the community, and d. in 1600. bd. 1787.

*SEBBE, ST. August 29. AUG., p. 377

He became king of the East Saxons in 664 and reigned justly for thirty years. He d. in London, clothed in the monastic habit, in 694 and was buried in St Paul's. There seems to have been no cultus of St Sebbe in the past, but his feast is now kept in the diocese of Brentwood on September 1. *Sebbus*.

SECHNALL, ST, bp. November 27.   Nov., p. 324
He was a disciple of St Patrick and was made bishop at Dunshaughlin in Meath. He wrote the earliest known Latin hymn written in Ireland, *Audite, omnes amantes Deum*. d. *c*. 450. *Secundinus*.

*SECUNDUS, ST, mart. June 1.   JUNE, p. 3
An alleged martyr at Amelia in 304 who is the patron of several places in central Italy : but his historical existence is doubtful.

*SECUNDUS and **ALEXANDER, SS,** marts. August 26.   AUG., p. 317
They are said to have been soldiers in the Theban Legion (September 22) put to death at Ventimiglia and near Bergamo respectively. Their extant story is worthless.

SENAN, ST, bp. March 8.   MAR., p. 127
Senan, the most famous of the Irish saints of that name, was trained as a monk at Kilmanagh in Ossory. He is said then to have visited Rome and on his way back to have stayed with St David in Wales (there are also traces of him in Cornwall). He made several religious foundations and finally established a monastery on Inis Cathaig, now called Scattery Island, in the Shannon estuary. Here St Senan d. *c*. 560. He is commemorated to-day throughout Ireland. *Senanus*.

*SENATOR, ST, bp. May 28.   MAY, p. 333
A legate of Pope St Leo I to Constantinople, afterwards bishop of Milan. d. 475.

SENOCH, ST, ab. October 24.   OCT., p. 324
He was a hermit at what is now Saint-Senou in Touraine and d. in 579. His biography was written by St Gregory of Tours, who knew him personally.

SENORINA, ST, virg. April 22.   APR., p. 260
Abbess first at Venaria and then at Basto in Portugal. d. 982.

SEPTEMBER, THE MARTYRS OF. September 2.   SEPT., p. 28
These are 191 of the many people put to death in France on September 2–3, 1792, by the mob, with the approval of the Legislative Assembly, for refusing the oath and constitution of the clergy which had been condemned by the Holy See. Among them were John du Lau, Archbishop of Arles, Francis de la Rochefoucauld, Bishop of Beauvais, and his brother Louis, Bishop of Saintes, Charles de la Calmette, Count of Valfons, and other prelates, priests, and religious. 120 of them perished at the Carmelite Church in the rue des Rennes at Paris. bd. 1926.

*SEQUANUS, ST, ab. September 19.   SEPT., p. 256
Also *Seine, Sigon*. He was a monk of Réomé who founded a monastery at the place now called Saint-Seine near the source of the river of that name. d. *c*. 580.

SERAPHINA, ST, virg. March 12.   MAR., p. 220
St Seraphina is specially venerated, as " Santa Fina," at San Geminiano in Tuscany. She was a young girl who suffered from a complication of painful and repulsive diseases, which she bore with wonderful cheerfulness in God's name. After the death of her parents she had only one friend to look after her properly, and she died in her youth in 1253.

SERAPHINA SFORZA, BD. September 9.   SEPT. p. 104
She received considerable persecution from her husband Alexander Sforza, Lord of Pesaro, and eventually left him and became a Poor Clare. Her prayers brought her husband to repentance before his death. d. 1478. c.c. 1754.

*SERAPHINO, ST. October 12.   OCT., p. 176
His life was of that uneventfulness which one associates with the vocation of a lay brother (in this case of the Capuchins), though he reached spiritual heights and many miracles are recorded of him. He d. at Ascoli-Piceno in Italy in 1604. cd. 1767.

*SERAPION, ST, bp. March 21.   MAR., p. 360
Serapion was bishop of Thmuis in Lower Egypt and played a considerable part in the ecclesiastical affairs of his day. His writings are lost but the *Euchologium* which he edited was discovered and published in the nineteenth century. d. c. 370.

*SERAPION, ST, bp. October 30.   OCT., p. 358
This bishop of Antioch d. c. 212. He is chiefly remembered for his theological writings.

*SERAPION, BD, mart. November 14.   NOV., p. 180
He is said to have been b. in England, to have joined the Mercedarians in Spain, and to have been crucified by the Moors for preaching the gospel while a hostage among them in 1240. c.c. 1728. Another Serapion, martyr at Alexandria c. 250, is mentioned in the Roman Martyrology on November 14.

SERENICUS, ST, ab. May 7.   MAY, p. 88
After being a hermit with his brother St Serenus he was made abbot by a community near Hyesmes on the Sarthe. d. c. 669.

SERENUS, ST, mart. February 23.   FEB., p. 316
Called " the Gardener " because he lived as an anchorite in a garden which he tended at Mitrovicza (Sirmium) in Yugoslavia. Having drawn attention by an alleged insult to the wife of a Roman officer he was arrested and found to be a Christian, and having refused to sacrifice to the gods he was beheaded in 302. But it is not certain to what extent this story is genuine.

SERENUS, ST. May 7.   MAY, p. 88
He was brother to St Serenicus and spent his life as a hermit in various parts of France. d. c. 669

SERF, ST, bp. July 1.   JULY, p. 10
There are several legends about St Serf, connecting him with Scotland and the Orkneys, but they are extravagant and even the century of his life is uncertain. He d. and was buried at Culross. *Servanus.*

*SERGIUS I, ST, pope. September 8.   SEPT., p. 88
Sergius I was pope from 687 till his death in 701 and his life is a part of general ecclesiastical history. His cultus began immediately after his death. He had a number of interesting contacts with England.

†*SERGIUS and BACCHUS, ST, marts. October 7.   OCT., p. 84
They were officers of the Roman army in Syria. On refusing to sacrifice to the gods in 303 St Bacchus was beaten to death and St Sergius was beheaded a week later, at Resapha in Mesopotamia.

SERLO, BD ab. March 3.   MAR., p. 43
A monk of Mont-Saint-Michel in Normandy to whom William the Conqueror confided the abbey of Gloucester : he received the abbatial

blessing from St Wulstan of Worcester. He raised the community from two monks to one hundred and built the abbey church anew (predecessor of Gloucester cathedral). Serlo wrote a letter of warning and rebuke to William Rufus, which the king received an hour or two before he was killed in the New Forest. Serlo died in 1104, and his name is found in two Benedictine martyrologies.

SERNIN, ST. *See* Saturninus (of Toulouse).

*SERVATIUS, ST, bp. May 13. MAY, p. 159
In French *Servais.* An early bishop of Tongres who had a considerable cultus in the Low Countries during the Middle Ages. d. 384.

SERVITE MARTYRS OF PRAGUE, THE. August 31. AUG., p. 396
They were four Servite friars from Tuscany who had been sent into Bohemia to preach against the Hussites. The monastery in which they were staying at Prague was attacked by the heretics and they were burnt to death in the church together with sixty other friars in 1420. c.c. 1918.

*SERVULUS, BD. December 23. DEC., p. 225
Servulus was a cripple who lived by begging at the porch of the church of San Clemente at Rome ; he shared the alms he received with his fellows and was revered by the whole neighbourhood. d. *c.* 590.

SETHRIDA, ST, virg. January 10. JAN., p. 132
Stepdaughter of Anna, King of the East Saxons ; she followed St Fare as abbess of Faremoutier. d. *c.* 660.

SEVEN APOSTLES OF BULGARIA, THE. July 17. JULY, p. 238
SS Cyril and Methodius had a general oversight of the Bulgars and after the death of St Methodius in 885 five of his followers were missionaries among them. The chief of them was St Clement of Okhrida (d. July 17, 916), and the others were St Gorazd, St Nahum, St Sabas, and St Angelarius. They are venerated liturgically in Bulgaria both collectively and separately.

†*SEVEN BROTHERS, THE, marts. July 10. JULY, p. 127
These martyrs suffered at Rome during the course of the second century but there is no evidence, apart from their doubtful *acta*, that they were the sons of St Felicitas, or indeed brothers at all.

†*SEVEN HOLY FOUNDERS, THE. February 12. FEB., p. 177
Between 1225 and 1227 seven young Florentines joined the Confraternity of our Lady : they were Bonfilio Monaldo, Alexis Falconieri, Benedict (Amadeus) dell' Antella, Batholomew (Hugh) Amidei, Ricovero (Sostenes) Uguccione, Gherardino (Manettus) Sostegni, and John Buonagiunta. Together they had a vision of our Lady, as the result of which they withdrew from secular life and formed a community on the deserted slopes of Monte Senario. This was the beginning of the order of Servants of Mary or Servite friars. St Bonfilio was the first superior, St Buonagiunta the second, and St Manettus the fourth. St Amadeus became prior of the monastery at Carfaggio, St Hugh and St Sostenes spread the order in France and Germany respectively. St Alexis, a lay brother, outlived them all and was the only one to see the order fully recognized. He d. 1310. They were all cd. in 1887.

*SEVEN SLEEPERS, THE, marts. July 27. JULY, p. 375
The legend of the Seven Sleepers of Ephesus, who were walled up in a cave by the emperor Decius and awoke alive under Theodosius II 362 years later, is a Christian version of a well-known folk theme. The truth

of the story was questioned by Cardinal Baronius, but he did not remove their entry from the Roman Martyrology.

*SEVERIAN, ST, bp. and mart. February 21.   FEB., p. 292

A bishop of Scythopolis who was murdered for his opposition to the monophysite heretics in 453. *Severianus.*

*SEVERINUS, ST, bp. January 8.   JAN., p. 116

An early bishop of Septempeda, now called after him San Severino, in the marches of Ancona. There has been confusion between him and St Severinus of Noricum.

*SEVERINUS, ST, ab. January 8.   JAN., p. 114

The place of origin of St Severinus is unknown but we first hear of him as a hermit in the East. He then went as a missionary to Noricum, the country which is now Austria, of which he is called the apostle. His first success was in famine-stricken Faviana, where his preaching touched the heart of a wealthy food-hoarder. He founded a number of monasteries, of which the chief was on the Danube near Vienna, and earned the respect of the leaders of the barbarians. Six years after his death in 482 many of his monks were driven out and they took his relics into Italy ; in 910 they were translated to a monastery in Naples.

*SEVERINUS, ST, ab. February 11.   FEB., p. 171

This Severinus was said to have been abbot of Agaunum in the fourth century, but this and other details of his life are not trustworthy. d. *c.* 507.

*SEVERINUS, ST, bp. October 23.   OCT., p. 305

In French *Seurin.* He was bishop of Bordeaux and d. *c.* 420. He has been wrongly identified with St Severinus, bishop of Cologne, who was also commemorated on October 23.

SEVERINUS BOËTHIUS, ST, mart. October 23.

This famous statesman and philosopher, author of *De Consolatione Philosophiæ,* and often referred to as "the Last of the Romans", was accused of plotting against the Ostrogothic king Theodoric, by whose orders Boëthius was imprisoned and executed at Pavia in 525. He is venerated as a martyr in that city and his feast annually observed, as it is in the church of St Mary *in Portico* at Rome. c.c. 1883.

SEXBURGA, ST. July 6.   JULY, p. 63

She was one of the saintly children of King Anna of the East Angles, and after the death of her husband, King Erconbert of Kent, she joined the nuns she had established at Minster in Sheppey. Afterwards she was abbess of Ely in succession to her sister St Etheldreda. d. *c.* 699.

SIBYLLINA BISCOSSI, BD, virg. March 23.   MAR., p. 382

A blind orphan who was adopted by some Dominican tertiaries in her native city of Pavia ; when she was convinced that it was the will of God that she should not recover her sight she became an ankress in a cell adjoining the friars' church and lived thus to the age of eighty. d. 1367. c.c. 1853.

*SIDONIUS APOLLINARIS, ST, bp. August 21.   AUG., p. 261

He was in turn soldier, statesman, country gentleman, and bishop of Clermont in Gaul, and poet and man of letters all the time. His character and abilities were such that he was selected for the see of Clermont while he was still a layman, living with his wife and family on his estate in Auvergne. Sidonius was the last considerable writer of the Gallo-Roman school, but his letters are much more valuable and interesting than his

A DICTIONARY OF SAINTS

verse ; as a bishop he was noted for the simplicity and sincerity of his daily life. d. *c.* 488.

SIGEBERT III, ST. February 1. FEB., p. 16

After the death of his father, Dagobert I, Sigebert governed Austrasia, his brother Clovis ruling in the rest of France. The reign of Sigebert was notably peaceful, and the young man gave himself up to good government and charitable works. Among his monastic foundations were Stavelot and Malmédy. d. 656. *Sigisbertus.*

SIGFRID, ST, bp. February 15. FEB., p. 230

Sigfrid, or Siegfried, is venerated as the apostle of Sweden, but his history is obscure. He seems to have been a priest of York or Glastonbury who went as missionary bishop to Scandinavia. Sigfrid converted King Olav of Sweden and established bishops in East and West Gothland. His own centre was at Wexiow, and when it was plundered and his three nephews murdered by the heathen, he refused to let the culprits be punished or to accept compensation from Olav. d. 1045. Sigfrid is said to have been canonized by the English pope Adrian IV in 1158. *Sigfridus.*

SIGFRID, ST, ab. August 22. AUG., p. 270

He was appointed abbot of Wearmouth, as coadjutor to St Benedict Biscop, in 686, and d. in 689. There is no trace of any liturgical cultus of St Sigfrid.

SIGIRANUS, ST, ab. December 5. DEC., p. 79

Sigiranus (Cyran) was archdeacon of Tours, of which see his father was bishop, but his desire was for the contemplative life. He accordingly founded and directed the abbeys of Meobecq and Lonrey. d. *c.* 655.

SIGISBERT, BD. July 11. JULY, p. 138

A disciple of St Columbanus who was a missionary in Switzerland and founded the monastery of Dissentis. d. *c.* 636. c.c. 1905. *Sigisbertus.*

*SIGISMUND, ST, mart. May 1. MAY, p. 12

Sigismund was a king of Burgundy, of Vandal extraction, and corresponding instincts : he had one of his sons strangled for rebuking his stepmother. At the same time Sigismund was a benefactor of the Church and founded the great monastery of St Maurice at Agaunum in Valais. After he had been defeated in battle by the sons of Clovis, he lived in hiding in a monk's habit near Agaunum, but was found and put to death by King Clodomir in 523. Thereafter he was revered as a martyr. *Sigismundus.*

*SILAS, ST. July 13. JULY, p. 164

Silas (Sylvanus) was a principal companion of St Paul of whom mention is made in the New Testament.

†*SILVERIUS, ST, pope and mart. June 20. JUNE, p. 250

Silverius was the son of Pope St Hormisdas and was chosen pope in 536 while still a subdeacon. He refused to restore the heretical bishop Anthimos to Constantinople at the request of the monophysite empress Theodora ; accordingly a charge of treason was trumped up against him and he was carried away prisoner. He d. of ill-treatment, or was murdered, on an island off Naples *c.* 537.

SILVESTER, BD. June 9. JUNE, p. 122

A wool-carder who in middle age became a Camaldolese lay brother at Florence. He was quite illiterate but so endowed with infused wisdom that he was often consulted by learned men. d. 1348.

†*SILVESTER I, ST, pope. December 31.   DEC., p. 298

Silvester, a Roman, became pope in 314, less than a year after the
emperor Constantine had granted toleration to Christianity. He is remembered rather on account of the events which followed this, including the
Council of Nicæa, than of his personal life and achievements, of which
little is known ; but doubtful and spurious legends are not lacking. It
is not true, for example, that Constantine granted numerous rights to
Silvester and his successors and endowed the Church with the lands of
Italy, or that Silvester baptized the emperor. d. 335.

†*SILVESTER GOZZOLINI, ST, ab. November 26.   NOV., p. 303

He was b. at Osimo in 1177 and deserted first the law and then a secular
canonry to become a hermit. In 1231 he organized his followers into a
congregation under the Rule of St Benedict at Monte Fano, near Fabriano,
which soon had ten houses—the first of the Italian Benedictine reforms.
St Silvester governed his monks with great wisdom and holiness for thirty-
six years, and d. 1267. Equivalently cd. 1598. A few small monasteries
of Sylvestrines ('' Blue Benedictines '') still exist.

*SILVIN, ST, bp. February 17.   FEB., p. 253

A regionary bishop who preached the gospel to the heathen in the
region of Thérouanne. He is said to have lived for forty years on fruit and
vegetables and to have owned nothing except his clothes and a horse. d. c.
720. *Silvinus*.

†*SIMEON, ST, bp. and mart. February 18.   FEB., p. 259

Said to have been a relative of our Lord (Matt. xiii, 55). He succeeded
St James as bishop at Jerusalem and was crucified at a great age, c.
107.

*SIMEON, ST. June 1.   JUNE, p. 7

He was b. at Syracuse in Sicily and became a monk and hermit in
Palestine. He was sent on a mission by the abbot of Sinai to Duke Richard
II in Normandy. After many adventures he reached Rouen and eventually
settled down as a recluse at Trier, where he was venerated by all as a
saint and a wonder-worker. d. 1035. cd. 1042.

*SIMEON, ST. July 26.   JULY, p. 368

He was an Armenian who was a pilgrim in Europe, where he earned a
reputation for miracles and for heroic charity. d. 1016.

*SIMEON, HOLY. October 8.   OCT., p. 97

Holy Simeon, the just and devout man who awaited the consolation of
Israel (Luke ii, 25), is named in the Roman Martyrology and his feast is
observed in certain places.

SIMEON and other abbots, BB. November 16.   NOV., p. 1 /

During the twelfth-thirteenth century the abbey and congregation of
Cava in Italy was governed by a remarkable series of abbots of much
holiness and wisdom. There are particularly venerated the fifth to the
eleventh abbots, Simeon, Falco, Marinus, Benincasa, Peter II, Balsamus,
and Leonard, and the fifteenth, Leo II. This ancient cultus was confirmed
in 1928.

*SIMEON BARSABÆ, ST, bp. and mart. April 21.   APR., p. 249

One of the longest individual entries in the Roman Martyrology is
devoted to St Simeon Barsabæ, bishop of Seleucia-Ctesiphon, and his
companions, martyrs in Persia in 341 during the persecution of King
Sapor II.

*SIMEON SALUS, ST. July 1. JULY, p. 9

He was an Egyptian who lived a solitary life for twenty-nine years in the desert of Sinai ; he then went to Emesa in Syria, where out of humility he allowed himself to pass for a simpleton. Sixth century.

*SIMEON STYLITES, ST. January 5. JAN., p. 70

The best known of the pillar-saints, the son of a Cilician shepherd, who became a monk in a Syrian monastery while still a boy ; later he was dismissed from another monastery for his imprudent austerities. After some years as a hermit people used to throng to him, and it was to avoid them that he first took up his residence on a platform at the top of a pillar. He lived thus for thirty-seven years, gradually increasing the height of the pillar from about ten feet to about sixty, and for some forty years he refrained entirely from food throughout Lent : sometimes he was so weak that he had to tie himself to a pole lest he fall off his pillar. This extraordinary way of life aroused admiration (and imitation) as well as curiosity, and emperors and patriarchs as well as crowds of simple folk came to consult him. St Simeon died on his pillar in his sixty-ninth year in 459.

*SIMEON STYLITES THE YOUNGER, ST. September 3. SEPT., p. 33

B. at Antioch in 521. He joined a community of hermits and while still a boy began to live on a pillar, leading this extraordinary life for over sixty years. Simeon was ordained and celebrated the holy Mysteries on a platform built on the pillar, and people flocked to him from all parts to seek his advice and to benefit from his miraculous powers. He wrote to the emperor Justin II in defence of the veneration of holy images. d. 597.

†*SIMON AND JUDE, SS, aps. October 28. OCT., p. 346

No mention is made of St Simon " the Zealous " in the Bible except that he was one of the twelve apostles. St Jude (Thaddeus) is usually regarded as brother of St James the Less and was the author of the epistle which bears his name. According to the tradition of the West, SS Simon and Jude were martyred together in Persia, but the matter is very uncertain.

SIMON BALLACHI, BD. November 3. NOV., p. 40

A lay brother confessor of the Friars Preachers at Rimini. d. 1319. c.c. 1821.

SIMON FIDATI, BD. February 3. FEB., p. 56

B. c. 1295 at Cascia, joined the Austin friars, when he distinguished himself as a preacher and writer, and was called on to take part in the public life of Perugia, Florence, and Siena. Of late years it has been suggested that certain ascetical works hitherto attributed to the Dominican friar Dominic Cavalca were really written by Bd Simon Fidati ; and it has been alleged that Luther (also an Austin friar) derived some of his teachings from views incautiously expressed by Bd Simon in his *De Gestis Domini Salvatoris*. d. 1348. c.c. 1833.

SIMON DE ROJAS, BD. September 28. SEPT., p. 360

A confessor of the Trinitarian Order, who was a chaplain at the court of Philip III of Spain. d. 1624. bd. 1766.

SIMON STOCK, ST. May 16. MAY, p. 211

Simon Stock, one of the best-known of Carmelite saints, was b. in Kent. He was elected prior general of the order in 1247 and his rule was marked by notable developments : for example, he established Carmelite houses in the four university towns of Oxford, Cambridge, Paris, and

Bologna, and put into effect modifications of the rule enabling the religious to live as mendicant friars rather than as hermits. According to Carmelite tradition our Lady appeared in a vision to St Simon and declared the privilege of the brown Carmelite scapular, in consequence of which its wearing has become so widespread a devotion in the Church. d. 1265. St Simon's feast is kept by the Carmelites and in the dioceses of Birmingham, Northampton, and Southwark, but he has not been formally canonized.

SIMON YEMPO, BD, mart. December 4. DEC., p. 64
A Japanese lay catechist, and ex-Buddhist monk, who was martyred by burning at Tokio in 1623. bd. 1867.

SIMON OF CRESPY, ST. September 30. SEPT., p. 389
He was brought up at the court of William the Conqueror, in Normandy, avoided two royal marriages, and received the monastic habit at Condat in the Jura. He was called to Rome as a counsellor of the Holy See, and d. there c. 1080.

SIMON OF LIPNICZA, BD. July 30. JULY, p. 421
He was a great preacher of the Friars Minor in Poland. d. 1482. bd. 1685.

SIMON OF TODI, BD. April 20. APR., p. 241
Simon Rinalducci was a distinguished preacher of the Austin friars who preferred to keep silence under a false accusation rather than cause dissension and scandal among his brethren. d. 1322. c.c. 1833.

*SIMON OF TRENT, ST, mart. March 24. MAR., p. 388
A child of two and a half years old alleged to have been put to death by a Jewish physician out of hatred of the faith at Trent in 1475. The case is not proved.

*SIMPLICIAN, ST, bp. August 16. AUG., p. 156
He was friend and adviser to St Ambrose and succeeded him in the see of Milan at an advanced age. St Simplician considerably influenced the conversion of St Augustine. d. 400. *Simplicianus.*

*SIMPLICIUS, ST, pope. March 10. MAR., p. 14
Simplicius was pope for sixteen years in very troubled times and he made his influence felt in secular as well as ecclesiastical affairs. He was an energetic opponent of Monophysism and of Constantinopolitan ambition, but of his personal life no details are known. d. 483.

*SIMPLICIUS, ST, bp. June 24. JUNE, p. 323
He was bishop of Autun in the fourth or early fifth century ; nothing is known of him except legends related by St Gregory of Tours.

†*SIMPLICIUS and others, **SS,** marts. July 29. JULY, p. 403
Simplicius, Faustinus, and Beatrice were martyrs in Rome under Diocletian of whom no reliable particulars are known.

*SIRICIUS, ST, pope. November 26. NOV., p. 306
The name of Pope Siricius was added to the Roman Martyrology by Benedict XIV on account of his " learning, piety, and zeal for religion." He ruled for fifteen years and d. in 399.

*SISINNIUS and other marts, **SS.** May 29. MAY, p. 349
Sisinnius, Martyrius, and Alexander are alleged to have been Cappadocians who were commissioned by St Vigilius of Trent to preach the gospel in the Tyrol. Here they were murdered by pagans in 397.

SISOES, ST. July 4. JULY, p. 34
One of the best-known of the hermits of the Egyptian desert after the

death of St Antony. "His zeal against vice was without bitterness."
d. *c.* 429.

*SIXTUS I, ST, pope and mart. April 6.   APR., p. 70

Sixtus I was pope from 117 to 127 ; he was a Roman by birth, but
we have no particulars of his life or alleged martyrdom. The Sixtus named
in the canon of the Mass is probably not this one, but Sixtus II. *Xystus.*

†*SIXTUS II, ST, pope and mart. August 6.   AUG., p. 71

He succeeded Pope St Stephen I in 257 and in the following year was
seized and beheaded while preaching to the Christian assembly. Sixtus II
was the most highly venerated among the popes martyred after St Peter,
and he is named in the canon of the Mass.

*SIXTUS III, ST, pope. August 19.   AUG., p. 221

Sixtus III was pope from 432 till his death in 440. He banished the
heretic Nestorius, built or restored several basilicas, and dedicated a
number of churches, but of his personal life nothing is now known.

*SOCRATES AND STEPHEN, SS, mart. September 17.   SEPT., p. 223

The Roman Martyrology commits itself to the statement that these
martyrs suffered in Britain. Nothing is known of them, but Bithynia
would seem to be the more likely scene of their passion.

SOLA, ST. December 3.   DEC., p. 48

Sola (or Solus) was an English disciple of St Boniface in Germany.
He was a hermit, and on the piece of land given to him by Charlemagne
grew up the abbey of Solnhofen, a dependency of Fulda. d. 794.

SOLANGIA, ST, virg. and mart. May 10.   MAY, p. 122

She is venerated in the French province of Berry as a shepherdess
who was killed by a young nobleman when she resisted his attempts on her
chastity, *c.* 880.

SOLOMON, ST, mart. June 25.   JUNE, p. 339

This Solomon was the ruler of Brittany who successfully defended his
country against both Franks and Northmen ; he did penance for the
crimes of his earlier years and after his assassination in 874 was venerated
as a martyr. There are many Breton legends about this national hero,
who is called Selyf in their speech. *Salomon.*

*SOPHRONIUS, ST, bp. March 11.   MAR., p. 190

He was the patriarch of Jerusalem who convened a synod to condemn
Monothelism, and sent a legate to urge the Holy See to do the same, which
happened at a synod at the Lateran in 649. But before that Sophronius
had been driven from his see when the Saracens took Jerusalem in 638,
and he is thought to have died of grief very soon after. This saint is
generally identified with Sophronius the Sophist, who was fellow-hermit
and pilgrim with John Moschus, author of the *Spiritual Meadow.*

†*SOTER, ST, pope and mart. April 22.   APR., p. 255

Very little is known about this pope and there are no particulars of his
martyrdom ; d. 174.

*SOTERIS, ST, virg. and mart. February 10.   FEB., p. 148

A martyr at Rome, under Diocletian in 304, of whom St Ambrose
speaks.

*SOZON, ST, mart. September 7.   SEPT., p. 75

According to a Greek legend Sozon was a young Cilician shepherd who
smashed an idol with his crook and was accordingly burned, at
Pompeiopolis in 304.

*SPECIOSUS, ST. March 15.   MAR., p. 261

A monk who received the habit from St Benedict himself and died in the monastery at Capua c. 545.

*SPERATUS, ST, mart. July 17.   JULY, p. 226

Speratus and six other men and five women are known as the Scillitan Martyrs from the place of their passion, Scillium in Africa, in 180. Their *acta* are unusually free from later editorial "improvement."

*SPES, ST, ab. March 28.   MAR., p. 426

An abbot of Campi in central Italy who for many years of his life was deprived of sight. d. c. 513.

*SPEUSIPPUS, etc., SS, marts. January 17.   JAN., p. 217

According to a probably fictitious legend Speusippus, Eleusippus, and Meleusippus were three twin brothers who, with their grandmother Leonilla, suffered martyrdom at Langres under Marcus Aurelius.

*SPIRIDION, ST, bp. December 14.   DEC., p. 163

Spiridion, shepherd of sheep and pastor of souls, figures in numerous stories of marvels. He became bishop of Tremithus in Cyprus and was mutilated during the persecution of Galerius; he was present at the Council of Nicæa and is said there to have converted a heathen philosopher. d. c. 348.

†*STANISLAUS, ST, bp. and mart. May 7.   MAY, p. 85

Stanislaus Szczepanovsky was b. in 1030 and appointed bishop of Cracow in 1072. He proved to be an exemplary bishop, to the extent of excommunicating his prince, Boleslaus II the Cruel, for his oppressive rule and evil life. In revenge Boleslaus with his own hand murdered the bishop while he was celebrating Mass on May 8, 1079. Pope Gregory VII laid Poland under an interdict for this crime, and Innocent IV cd. Stanislaus in 1253; but some Polish historians allege that the bishop had plotted to dethrone his sovereign.

*STANISLAUS KOSTKA, ST. November 13.   NOV., p. 165

B. in 1550, son of a Polish senator. He made up his mind to be a Jesuit, and was received into the Society at the age of seventeen in the face of angry opposition from his family. Stanislaus was more than a model novice, but before the year was out he had died, on August 15, 1568. He was indeed "made perfect in a short while and fulfilled many times by the angelic innocence of his life." cd. 1726.

STEPHANA QUINZANI, BD, virg. January 2.   JAN., p. 44

B. in 1457 near Brescia, and was a secular Dominican tertiary until she was enabled to found a convent of that order. A contemporary account (1497) is extant, signed by twenty-one witnesses, describing in detail one of the ecstasies in which Bd Stephana represented in her own person the different stages of the passion of Christ. d. 1530. Cultus confirmed by Pope Benedict XIV.

STEPHEN, ST, bp. and mart. June 2.   JUNE, p. 26

Very little is known of this St Stephen, who is venerated as first bishop of Helsingborg in Sweden. He is said to have been a monk of New Corbie in Saxony and eventually slain by the heathen in 1075 (?) at Upsala or Nora. *Stephanus.*

†*STEPHEN, ST, mart. December 26.   DEC., p. 249

The martyrdom of Stephen, the first deacon and the Church's first martyr for Christ, whom St Luke calls "a man full of faith and of the

Holy Ghost," is narrated in the Acts of the Apostles, caps. vi and vii ; he was stoned to death by order of the Jewish Sanhedrin at Jerusalem, and among those taking part was the future St Paul. Another feast of St Stephen, commemorating the finding of his reputed relics at Kafr Gamala *c.* 415, is kept on August 3 throughout the Western church.

†*STEPHEN I, ST, pope and mart. August 2.   AUG., p. 24

He became pope in 254 and his short reign was notable for the controversy about the rebaptizing of people christened by heretics : St Stephen declared the practice to be opposed to the apostolic tradition of the Church. He d. in 257, it is said put to death by the heathen while sitting at his throne during Mass, but this is doubtful.

STEPHEN BANDELLI, BD. June 12.   JUNE, p. 161

A confessor of the Order of Preachers, who d. at Saluzzo, near Turin, in 1450. c.c. 1856.

STEPHEN BELLESINI, BD. February 3.   FEB., p. 59

B. at Trent 1774 and joined the Augustinians. When his community was dispersed by revolution he devoted himself to the instruction of children and was made inspector of schools for the Trentino by the government. He rejoined his order at Bologna, became master of novices at Rome, and finally parish priest at the shrine of our Lady of Good Counsel at Gennazzano. He caught cholera while attending the sick during an epidemic and d. 1840. bd. 1904.

STEPHEN CUÉNOT, BD, bp. and mart. February 8.   FEB., p. 129

B. 1802, joined the Société des Missions Etrangères in Paris, and was sent to Annam. During the persecution of 1833 he was consecrated bishop at Singapore and returned to Annam, where he made many converts and in fifteen years organized three vicariates in Cochin China. When persecution again broke out in 1861 Bd Stephen was imprisoned and died within a few days, on November 14, just before the order for his execution arrvied. He was bd. with a number of his fellow-martyrs in 1909.

*STEPHEN HARDING, ST, ab. April 17.   APR., p. 200

Stephen Harding, an Englishman by birth and education, was one of the founders of the Cistercian reform of the Benedictines and himself drew up the constitutions of Citeaux. On his way back from a pilgrimage to Rome he became a monk of Molesme and in 1098 migrated with St Robert and the others to Citeaux, where in 1009 he became abbot. He appointed St Bernard abbot of the daughter house at Clairvaux and in 1119 presented the Charter of Charity to the general chapter of the new congregation ; these famous constitutions were approved by Pope Callixtus II and have inspired several later monastic codes. d. 1134, c.c. 1623. His feast is kept in the Plymouth diocese (he was probably born at Sherborne) on March 28.

*STEPHEN THE YOUNGER, ST, mart. November 28.   Nov., p. 332

He was b. at Constantinople in 714 and resigned the government of the hermit-monks of Mount St Auxentius to become a solitary in the same place. Stephen was a firm and influential opponent of Iconoclasm and both cunning and violence were used by the emperor Constantine Copronymus to win him over to the side of the heretics. Stephen was immovable, so he was first banished and then, in 764, killed by a gang at the instigation of the emperor. SS Basil, Peter, Andrew, and over three hundred other monks suffered for the same cause about the same time.

*STEPHEN OF GRANDMONT, ST, ab. February 8.　　　FEB., p. 125

Stephen was a son of the lord of Thiers in the Auvergne, who passed the early part of his life in Italy where he was ordained. In 1077 he founded at Muret, near Limoges, a community of hermit monks on the model of some' he had seen in Calabria. After his death in 1124 the community had to move from Muret to Grandmont, where it developed into the Grandmontine "reform" of the Benedictine Order ; it is now extinct. Stephen was cd. in 1189, at the instance of King Henry II of England.

†*STEPHEN OF HUNGARY, ST. September 2.　　　SEPT., p. 16

He succeeded his father Geza as sovereign prince of the Magyars of Hungary in 997 and was soon engaged in war with those of his people who resented his Christianization ; on the site of his victory he founded the still-existing abbey of Pannonhalma (Martinsberg). St Stephen established the diocesan organization of Hungary and received from the Holy See special powers, whose nature is a matter of dispute. His religious and political policies and his military successes against invaders welded the Magyars into a unity, but his last years, after the death of his heir Bd Emeric, were darkened by violent intrigues for the succession to the throne. d. 1038. His relics were enshrined by order of Pope St Gregory VII in 1083, and his principal feast in Hungary is the anniversary of the translation, August 20.

STEPHEN OF OBASINE, BD. March 8.　　　MAR., p. 138

He was a secular priest in the Limousin who with another, Peter, founded an establishment of hermit monks in the forest of Obasine, and afterwards a large convent nearby. The unwritten rule was very strict, and lest it should become relaxed Bd Stephen aggregated his foundations to the Order of Citeaux in 1142. d. 1154.

*STEPHEN OF RIETI, ST, ab. February 13.　　　FEB., p. 200

St Gregory the Great refers several times to this saint in his writings as one "whose speech was so rough but his life so cultured." He was abbot of a monastery near Rieti and d. c. 560.

STILLA, BD, virg. July 19.　　　JULY, p. 277

A laywoman, foundress of the church of St Peter at Abenberg, near Nuremberg, where she has always been venerated since her death c. 1141. c.c. 1927.

*STURMIUS, ST, ab. December 17.　　　DEC., p. 196

He was a Bavarian disciple of St Boniface, who sent him to preach the gospel in Saxony. To this end Sturmius founded a monastery in 744 which became the great abbey of Fulda ; the missionary labours of the monks were handicapped by the action of the bishop of Mainz, St Lullus, who caused the removal of St Sturmius from the abbacy for a time, and by the wars waged against the Saxons by Pepin and Charlemagne. d. 779. cd. 1139.

*SULPICIUS I, ST, bp. January 29.　　　JAN., p. 379

Bishop of Bourges from 584 till his death in 591. He is sometimes called (probably erroneously) Sulpicius Severus, which has caused confusion between him and the writer of that name.

*SULPICIUS II, ST, bp. January 17.　　　JAN., p. 220

While bishop of Bourges he defended his flock against the tyranny of an official of King Dagobert ; his care for the poor and afflicted caused him to be so beloved that his death in 647 was followed by extraordinary scenes of popular morning. He is the titular saint of the famous Paris seminary of Saint-Sulpice.

SULPICIUS SEVERUS, " ST." January 29.   JAN., p. 375

Sulpicius Severus, author of a famous Life of St Martin and other writings, who lived in Roman Gaul in the fourth–fifth century, was for a time included in the Roman Martyrology through a confusion with St Sulpicius of Bourges. For this reason the title " saint " is still sometimes added to the name of Severus, but there is no authority for it.

SUNNIVA, ST, virg.   July 8.   JULY, p. 99

According to the Norse legend Sunniva was an Irish princess who fled from her country with her brother Alban and others, and the whole company was cast up by the sea on the island of Selje off the coast of Norway ; one version says that they were there slain by people from the mainland. This is supposed to have happened during the tenth century. King Olaf Trygvessön found some bones on Selje and built a church over them in 995.

†*SUSANNA, ST, virg. and mart.   August 11.   AUG., p. 133

This Susanna is commemorated together with St Tiburtius (August 11), but there is no known connection between them. It is said that she was put to death in 295 for refusing, on account of a vow of virginity, to marry the Roman emperor's son, but the details of her story seem to be devoid of foundation.

*SWITHBERT, ST, bp.   March 1.   MAR., p. 6

He was one of the monks who accompanied St Willibrord to Friesland in 690 and worked with great success in south Holland and north Belgium. He was consecrated bishop without fixed see by St Wilfrid of York in 693. His labours on the right bank of the Rhine were ended by Saxon invasion, and St Swithbert spent his last years in a monastery that he founded at what is now Kaiserwerth. d. *c.* 714. *Suitbertus.*

*SWITHIN, ST, bp.   July 15.   JULY, p. 199

He was chaplain and counsellor to King Egbert of the West Saxons and was appointed to the see of Winchester in 852. He was a very worthy bishop and after his death in 862 an unusually large number of miracles was reported at his tomb. The origin of the popular superstition attached to his feast-day is not known. That feast is observed in the dioceses of Southwark and Portsmouth on July 15 and Birmingham on July 3, the first date being the anniversary of the translation of St Swithin's relics in 1093. *Swithunus.*

*SYAGRIUS, ST, bp.   August 27.   AUG., p. 339

He became bishop of Autun *c.* 560, and among the events of his episcopate entertained St Augustine and his monks on their journey from Rome to convert the English. d. 600.

SYLVESTER.   *See* Silvester.

*SYMMACHUS, ST, pope.   July 19.   JULY, p. 273

He became pope in 498 and the personal aspect of his pontificate is a record of persecution and slander which he suffered, especially from the supporters of the antipope Laurence. Symmachus first introduced the hymn *Gloria in Excelsis* into the liturgy, and was the first to bestow the *pallium* outside of the Italian province. d. 514.

†*SYMPHORIAN, ST, mart.   August 22.   AUG., p. 268

He was beheaded at Autun, where he belonged to a distinguished

A DICTIONARY OF SAINTS

family, about the year 180, for spurning an image of the goddess Cybele.
He is commemorated liturgically with St Timothy and St Hippolytus on
August 22. *Symphorianus.*

†*SYMPHOROSA, ST, mart. July 18.   JULY, p. 248
Symphorosa was the widow of the martyr St Getulius and she herself
was put to death for the Faith *c.* 135. The seven male martyrs who are
commemorated with her are called her sons, in accordance with their *acta*,
but this is doubtful.

*SYNCLETICA, ST, virg. January 5.   JAN., p. 76
A wealthy Macedonian lady of Alexandria who distributed her fortune
and lived for the rest of her life as a hermitess in a disused tomb. She
suffered many inward spiritual torments but triumphed over them, only
to be afflicted for four years with cancer, from which she eventually died
at the age of eighty-four *c.* 400.

TANCO, ST, bp. and mart. February 15. FEB., p. 230

Or *Tatto.* According to the legend he was an Irishman who became abbot of Amalbarich in Saxony in succession to one suspiciously named Patto, and followed the same man as bishop of Werda. He was killed by the heathens while exhorting them to behave themselves *c.* 808.

*TARACHUS and comps., SS, marts. October 11. OCT., p. 144

Tarachus, Probus, and Andronicus were slain by the sword near Tarsus in Asia Minor in 304. Tarachus was a veteran of the Roman army, sixty-five years old.

TARASIUS, ST, bp. February 25. FEB., p. 339

Tarasius was a patriarch of Constantinople distinguished for his opposition to the iconoclast heresy. With the Empress Irene he brought about the seventh oecumenical council (Nicæa II), at which the heresy was condemned and holy images ordered to be restored to the churches. He was persecuted by the emperor Constantine VI because he would not countenance his bigamous marriage, and at the same time was opposed by St Theodore and the Studite monks, who thought his attitude to the emperor was too mild. d. 806.

*TARSICIUS, ST, mart. August 15. AUG., p. 183

It is learned from a fourth-century poem by Pope St Damasus that the boy Tarsicius suffered a violent death at the hands of a Roman mob rather than give up to profanation the Blessed Sacrament which he was carrying to some Christians in prison.

TARSITIA, ST, virg. January 15. JAN., p. 194

Little is known of this saint, who is venerated at Rodez ; she seems to have been an ankress in the sixth century.

TATIAN DULAS, ST, mart. June 15. JUNE, p. 184

A martyr tortured and put to death for deriding the gods of heathendom at Zephyrinus in Cilicia *c.* 310 (?). *Tatianus.*

*TATIANA, ST, virg. and mart. January 12. JAN., p. 149

Nothing whatsoever is known with certainty about this martyr ; it is possible that she is the same as St Martina (Jan. 30).

TEILO, ST, bp. February 9. FEB., p. 141

Teilo was born at Penally, near Tenby, and was a great monastic leader in South Wales, his principal monastery being at Llandeilo Fawr in Carmarthenshire. He was a pupil of St Dyfrig and was venerated as his episcopal successor in the neighbourhood of Llandaff, whence his feast is now kept in the archdiocese of Cardiff. Sixth century. *Teliaus.*

TELEMACHUS, ST. *See* Almachius.

†*TELESPHORUS, ST, pope and mart. January 5. JAN., p. 75

He governed the Church for ten years during the persecution of Hadrian, and was himself martyred in 136.

†*TERESA, ST, virg. October 15.   OCT., p. 197

Teresa-of-Jesus, or " of Avila," was one of the greatest, most attractive, and widely appreciated women whom the world has ever known, and the only one to whom the title Doctor of the Church is popularly, though not officially, given. She was b. at Avila in Spain in 1515 and, after a short period of uncertainty, joined the Carmelites. There was another period of lukewarmness and distraction, for the discipline of the order was very much relaxed, but this presented itself as a challenge to Teresa and in 1562 she founded the first convent of nuns of the restored primitive observance. This she followed up with fifteen further foundations all over Spain, as well as, with St John-of-the-Cross, establishing her reform among the friars : all this was in the teeth of the most violent opposition, labouring under ill health, and with no material resources. Teresa was, moreover, one of the greatest of mystical writers (*The Interior Castle*, *The Way of Perfection*, etc., with numerous letters), and received supernatural gifts as lofty as her doctrine. The character displayed in her autobiography and letters, forthright, realist, humorous, kindly, has endeared her to all succeeding generations : " she is great from head to foot, but the influence that radiates from her is immeasurably greater still," wrote the Dominican Bañez. d. 1582. cd. 1622. *Teresia*.

TERESA REDI, BD, virg. March 11.   MAR., p. 200

Teresa Margaret (Anna Maria) Redi was b. in 1747 and became a Carmelite at Florence in 1765. As infirmarian she was always cheerful and imperturbable, when most of the time she was more fit herself to be a patient than a nurse. d. 1770. bd. 1929.

†*TERESA OF LISIEUX, ST, virg. October 3.   OCT., p. 22

The spread and enthusiasm of the culture of the young Carmelite nun, Teresa-of-the-Child-Jesus, not exteriorly distinguished from hundreds of others, is one of the most remarkable religious phenomena of modern times. She was b. of middle-class parents at Alençon in 1873 and, after a certain amount of opposition, became a Carmelite at Lisieux when she was only fifteen years old. During the remaining nine years of her life she remained in the same convent, became in effect novice mistress, and d. on September 30, 1897. Within a few years, under the name of " The Little Flower," she became known throughout the world ; her " little way " of simplicity and perfection in the doing of small things and discharge of daily duties has become a pattern to numberless " ordinary " folk ; her autobiography, written at the command of her superiors, is a famous book ; numerous graces and miracles are attributed to her intercession. cd. 1925. This St Teresa is the patron saint of foreign missions and of all works for Russia, being so named by Pope Pius XI.

TERESA OF PORTUGAL, BD. June 17.   JUNE, p. 223

One of the three holy daughters of Sancho the Great, King of Portugal. She married Alfonso IX of Leon, but after they had had several children the union was pronounced invalid on account of consanguinity. Teresa, therefore, returned to Portugal and founded a convent of Cistercian nuns at Lorvão, where she d. in 1250. c.c. 1705.

TERNAN, ST, bp. June 12.   JUNE, p. 154

He was an early missionary bishop among the Picts, seemingly at Abernethy, but even the century in which he lived is unknown.

TETRICUS, ST, bp. March 20.   MAR., p. 336

Uncle of St Gregory of Tours and bishop of Langres ; d. 572.

TETRICUS, ST, bp. and mart.   April 12.   APR., p. 135
He was bishop of Auxerre and was murdered by his archdeacon in 707 ; the miracles reported at his tomb caused him to be venerated as a martyr.

THADDEUS. *See also* Simon and Jude.

THADDEUS MACHAR, BD, bp   October 25.   OCT., p. 336
Thaddeus (Tadhg) MacCarthy was appointed bishop of Ross in 1482, but he was victim of a conspiracy and in 1488 was driven from his see. He was then nominated by the Holy See to the united dioceses of Cork and Cloyne, but was prevented by certain powerful families from taking up office. So he appealed to Rome for the third time, but d. at Ivrea in Italy while returning home in 1497. He was buried in the cathedral there and his shrine was soon renowned for miracles. c.c. 1895.

THAÏS, ST.   October 8.   OCT., p. 99
The well-known story of Thaïs, a wealthy and beautiful courtesan of Alexandria who was converted by St Paphnutius (or by St Bessarion or St Serapion) and became a recluse in a convent, is probably only a moral tale invented for edification.

THALASSIUS and **LIMNÆUS, SS.**   February 22.   FEB., p. 305
Two fifth-century hermits of whom Theodoret writes from personal knowledge in his *Philotheus*. They lived in Syria, and Limnæus, who was a disciple of St Maro, was famous for his power of healing.

THALELÆUS, ST.   February 27.   FEB., p. 372
A hermit in Cilicia who led a fakir-like life in a sort of open barrel and was nicknamed *Epiklautos*, " weeping much." d. *c.* 450.

*THALELÆUS, ST, mart.   May 20.   MAY, p. 250
He is said to have been a physician who suffered death for Christ at Aegæ in Cilicia in 284 (?).

*THARSILLA and **EMILIANA, SS,** virgs. December 24.   DEC., p. 233
They were aunts of St Gregory the Great and lived a holy life in the house of their father Gordian at Rome. d. *c.* 550.

*THEA and others, **SS,** marts.   July 25.   JULY, p. 364
Thea and Valentina were sisters who were burned to death for Christ at Gaza in 308. Paul was beheaded at the same time for praying aloud for the victims.

†*THEBAN LEGION, THE, marts.   September 22.   SEPT., p. 284
According to the legend the Theban Legion consisted of Christian soldiers recruited in Upper Egypt. While on service in Gaul they refused to sacrifice to the gods (alternatively, they refused to kill innocent Christians in the course of their duty) and, after being twice decimated, were massacred almost to a man. This story had many ramifying legends, in which the principal names are SS Maurice (*primicerius* of the legion), Exuperius, Candidus, Vitalis, Ursus, two Victors, Alexander at Bergamo, Gereon at Cologne. That St Maurice and some companions were martyred *c.* 287 near Agaunum (St Maurice-en-Valais) seems to be a fact of history, but that a whole legion was involved is highly improbable.

†*THECLA, ST, virg. and mart.   September 23.   SEPT., p. 294
Thecla was one of the most revered heroines of the earlier ages of the Church, but it is doubtful if she ever existed, for the widespread account of her depends entirely on a second-century romance called the *Acts of Paul and Thecla*, an extremely extravagant composition, which, moreover, smacks in parts of heresy. According to this she was a convert of St Paul,

underwent "three most cruel torments" (referred to in the *Rituale Romanum* in the recommendation of a departing soul) for refusing marriage, followed the apostle dressed as a boy, was sent to teach the word of God in her native Iconium, and died a solitary at Seleucia.

*THECLA, ST, virg. October 15. OCT., p. 214

This Thecla was one of the nuns sent by St Tetta of Wimborne to help in the mission of St Boniface in Germany by their prayers and influence. She became abbess of Kitzingen. d. *c.* 790.

THEOBALD, ST, bp. May 21. MAY, p. 260

An archbishop of Vienne of whose history little is recorded. d. 1001. c.c. 1903. *Theobaldus.*

*THEOBALD, ST. June 30. JULY, p. 11

In French *Thibaud.* A son of Count Arnoul, b. in Brie in 1017, who left his home with another young nobleman and became a pilgrim and hermit. He finally settled down near Vicenza, where he was ordained priest, and d. there in 1066.

THEOBALD ROGGERI, ST. June 1. JUNE, p. 11

He is said to have belonged to a good family at Vico, near Mondovi, and to have left his home to become a lowly shoemaker at Alba ; after a pilgrimage to Compostella he took up still more humble occupations and shared all he earned with the poor and suffering ; d. 1150. But there is no reliable evidence for all this.

THEOBALD OF MARLY, ST, ab. July 27. JULY, p. 383

He was abbot of the Cistercian house of Vaux-de-Cernay ; d. 1247.

*THEOCTISTE, ST, virg. November 10. Nov., p. 118

The tale of the death of St Theoctiste, a woman solitary on the Greek island of Paros in the ninth century, is a fiction imitated from the last days of St Mary of Egypt. *Theoctistes.*

THEODARDUS, ST, bp. May 1. MAY, p. 16

An archbishop of Narbonne who is described in the Montaubon breviary as "an eye to the blind, feet to the lame, a father of the poor, and a comfort to the afflicted." d. 893.

*THEODARDUS, ST, bp. and mart. September 10. SEPT., p. 130

He succeeded St Remaclus in the see of Maestricht. As he was murdered by robbers, *c.* 670, while on a journey undertaken in defence of the rights of the Church he was venerated as a martyr.

THEODORA, ST. February 11. FEB., p. 175

The Empress Theodora, wife of the Emperor Theophilus, is venerated in the East, but her claim to sanctity is doubtful. While she was regent for her son Michael the Drunkard she put an end to Iconoclasm and introduced the feast of Orthodoxy, i.e. of the restoration of the holy images, for the first Sunday in Lent. She spent the last years of her life in a convent. d. 867.

*THEODORA, ST. September 11. SEPT., p. 142

The story of St Theodora of Alexandria is a romance, belonging to the same class as that of Pelagia of Antioch (October 8), and concerned with a penitent woman who masqueraded as a monk. The Roman Martyrology speaks of her in very restrained terms.

*THEODORE, ST, bp. April 22. APR., p. 259

He was the son of an innkeeper at Sikion in Galatia and founded several monasteries in Asia Minor before he was made bishop of Anastasiopolis. d. 613. *Theodorus.*

*THEODORE and **THEOPHANES, SS.** December 27.   DEC., p. 261

Two monks of Mar Saba, brothers, who were sent to Constantinople to oppose Iconoclasm. They were treated with barbarity by the emperor, who had verses cut in the flesh of their faces, whence they are called *Grapti*, " the Written-on." Theodore died in consequence of his sufferings *c.* 841, and Theophanes, who was a poet, followed him *c.* 845.

*THEODORE STUDITES, ST, ab.   November 11.   Nov., p. 127

This Theodore was one of the most famous monks of the Byzantine church. He was made abbot of the Studium at Constantinople when it was in an advanced state of decay and under his rule it became one of the greatest monasteries of the world ; St Theodore ranks with St Pachomius and St Benedict as a monastic legislator, his regulations spreading to Mount Athos, Russia, Rumania, and Bulgaria, where and elsewhere they still form the basis of Eastern monastic life. He was also a notable witness to the authority of the see of Rome and a spirited defender of and sufferer for the veneration of holy images during the second Iconoclast persecution. For his defence of orthodoxy in this matter he was imprisoned for seven years, though his position concerning images was a notably moderate one, being based solely on theological principles. In his monastery he especially fostered learned studies and the practice of the fine arts, particularly calligraphy. d. 826.

†*THEODORE TYRO, ST, mart.   November 9.   Nov., p. 105

He is venerated, with St George and St Demetrius, as one of the three chief great " warrior-saints " of the East, but it is not certain that he was ever a soldier. He was probably a martyr at Amasea *c.* 306, and his shrine at Euchaïta was a great place of pilgrimage. He is said to have set fire to a temple of Cybele.

*THEODORE OF CANTERBURY, ST, bp.   September 19.   SEPT., p. 258

He was born at Tarsus in Cilicia and was a member of a Greek monastery in Italy. In 668, at the age of sixty-six, he was consecrated bishop and appointed to the see of Canterbury. Theodore proved one of the greatest of its archbishops : he was the first prelate whom the whole English church obeyed, and religion and learning alike flourished under his rule. He made visitations in all parts of the country, dealt with the difficulties between St Wilfrid and St Chad, and held the first national council, at Hertford in 673. St Theodore was himself involved in trouble with St Wilfrid of York about the extent of the northern diocese ; it was at last composed with the help of St Erconwald. St Theodore found the Church in England a rather disorganized missionary body : he left it a properly organized province of the Catholic Church, looking to Canterbruy as its metropolitan see. d. 690. His feast is observed in the dioceses of Westminster, Birmingham, Brentwood, Salford, Southwark, Hexham, and Lancaster.

*THEODORE OF HERACLEA, ST, mart.   February 7.   FEB., p. 104

One of the great " military martyrs " honoured as such in the East. He is said to have been a military governor in Bithynia who suffered at Heraclea in 319. This Theodore was called " Stratelates " to distinguish him from St Theodore Tyro of Amasea, but it is probable that they were the same person.

*THEODORE THE HOLY, ST, ab.   April 27.   DEC., p. 265

He was a disciple of St Pachomius and followed him as abbot of Tabenna and general superior of the whole " congregation " during the difficulties that followed the founder's death. Theodore had previously been "reduced to the ranks" for assuming the second office during the lifetime of Pachomius. One of St Theodore's miracles provides an early example of the use of blessed water as a sacramental. d. *c.* 368.

*THEODORET, ST, mart. October 23.　　　　　　　　Oct., p. 304

He was a priest of the principal church of Antioch and was beheaded in the time of Julian the Apostate for continuing to celebrate the Holy Mysteries at the tombs of the martyrs, in 362. He is called " Theodore " in the Roman Martyrology.

*THEODORIC, ST, ab. July 1.　　　　　　　　　　July, p. 5

In French *Thierry.* He was abbot of Mont d'Or, near Rheims ; d. *c.* 533. *Theodericus.*

*THEODOSIA, ST, virg. and mart. April 2.　　　　　Apr., p. 19

A Tyrian girl who was martyred with great cruelty at Cæsarea *c.* 306.

*THEODOSIA, ST, virg. and mart. May 29.　　　　　May, p. 350

She was a nun of Constantinople who was tortured and killed in 745 for leading a riot of women against the destroyers of sacred images.

*THEODOSIUS THE CENOBIARCH, ST. January 11.　Jan., p. 139

B. in Cappadocia in 423. He learned the elements of the religious life in Jerusalem and was given charge of a church of our Lady on the Bethlehem road. He began to attract numerous disciples and at last established for them a huge monastery not far from the Dead Sea ; it had three churches, for the languages of different nations, and hundreds of monks. Sallust, Patriarch of Jerusalem, gave Theodosius oversight of all the monasteries (as distinct from hermitages—in Palestine—whence his title of " Cenobiarch." The Emperor Anastasius tried to bribe St Theodosius to support the monophysite heresy, and his refusal and public exhortations to orthodoxy led to his banishment until the emperor's death. Theodosius died in 529 at the age of 105, and miracles were recorded at his grave.

*THEODOTA, ST, mart. July 17.　　　　　　　　July, p. 233

She was tortured and beheaded by the Iconoclasts at Constantinople *c.* 735 for hiding three holy *eikons* from the government searchers. Her real name was Theodosia.

*THEODOTA, ST, mart. August 2.　　　　　　　　Aug., p. 27

St Theodota with her three sons was martyred at Nicæa in 304 ; the ancient anniversary of their passion was on September 2.

THEODOTA, ST, mart. September 29.　　　　　　　Sept., p. 366

She is said to have been a martyr at Philippopolis in Thrace *c.* 318, but her *acta* cannot be taken seriously. They state that she was a converted harlot, whom the most violent tortures were unable to kill.

*THEODOTUS, ST, mart. May 18.　　　　　　　　May, p. 226

The story of the passion of SS Theodotus, Thecusa, and their companions at Ancyra under Diocletian is in all probability a pious fiction written for the edification of the faithful.

*THEODULPHUS, ST, bp. June 24.　　　　　　　　June, p. 324

He was abbot of Lobbes in Hainault and missionary bishop for the surrounding country ; d. 776.

*THEODULUS and JULIAN, SS, marts. February 17.　Feb., p. 249

These two suffered at Cæsarea immediately after SS Elias and his companions in 308, but are mentioned separately on February 17 in the Roman Martyrology. Theodulus was an old man, formerly in the household of the governor Firmilian, who without trial sentenced him to be crucified. Julian, a young catechumen, was burnt alive for honouring the bodies of the other martyrs.

*THEOPEMPTUS, ST, bp. and mart.   January 3. JAN., p. 51
Bishop of Nicomedia, and said to have been one of the first victims of the persecution of Diocletian in 284.

THÉOPHANE VÉNARD, BD, mart. February 2. FEB., p. 45
Bd Théophane, a priest of the Missions Etrangères at Paris, was sent to Hong Kong in 1852, and from thence to Western Tonkin where almost at once he was confronted with persecution. He suffered a long and bitter imprisonment and was executed most barbarously in 1861. bd. 1909.

*THEOPHANES, ST, ab. March 12. MAR., p. 216
Leaving his wife, who became a nun, he founded two monasteries and governed one of them, Mount Sigriana, near Cyzicus, as abbot. The emperor Leo the Armenian, recognizing his influence, tried to convert Theophanes to Iconoclasm and when he failed had him beaten and imprisoned. After two years of close confinement he was banished in 817 to the island of Samothrace, where he died seventeen days after his arrival as the result of the cruelty with which he had been treated. Theophanes wrote a short history of the world that is of considerable importance as a Byzantine document.

THEOPHILUS OF CORTE, BD. May 21. MAY, p. 263
He was a Capuchin friar who spent his life preaching and establishing friaries in his native Corsica and various parts of Italy. d. 1740. bd. 1896.

THEOPHILUS THE PENITENT, ST. February 4. FEB., p. 66
Whatever his true history may have been this Theophilus has come down to us as the hero of a religious romance in which, having been treated unjustly by his bishop, he made a pact with the Devil. When he repented he had a vision of our Lady who returned the pact to Theophilus after he had done penance.

*THEOPHYLACT, ST, bp. March 7. MAR., p. 116
He was bishop of Nicomedia and opposed Iconoclasm, prophesying a violent end for the emperor Leo the Armenian. Theophylact was accordingly banished and he died, still in exile, thirty years later in Caria, 845. *Theophylactus.*

THEOTONIUS, ST. February 18. FEB., p. 271
He was archpriest of Viseu in Portugal, but resigned his office to become a simple curate in the same town, where he worked indefatigably for the good of the people, twice publicly rebuking the Queen for setting them a bad example. He became a canon regular at Coimbra, and as prior of the house insisted on the most reverend and unhurried singing of the Divine Office. He d. 1166, and his biography was written by a contemporary who was a canon under him.

THETHMAR, ST. May 17. MAY, p. 222
Also *Theodemar.* He was a missionary among the Wends, and probably a Premonstratensian canon regular. He d. at the abbey of Neumünster in 1152. *Theodemarus.*

THEUDERIUS, ST, ab. October 29. OCT., p. 354
A monk from Lérins who established a monastery near Vienne; here during the last twelve years of his life he lived in an ankerhold in the church. d. *c.* 575. Theuderius is the " Chef " of Saint-Chef-d'Arcisse.

†*THOMAS, ST, ap. December 21.   DEC., p. 213

All that is known of St Thomas the Apostle, called *Didymus, i.e.* " the twin," is what is told in the gospels : his incredulity about our Lord's resurrection has passed into proverbial speech. An old but unverified tradition makes St Thomas the apostle of southern India (where there are Christians of early origin), and it states further that he was martyred near Madras and buried at Mylapore.

THOMAS ABEL, BD, mart. July 30.   JULY, p. 424

He was chaplain to Queen Catherine and was so active in the matter of the validity of her marriage with Henry VIII that he was imprisoned in the Tower and left without trial for six years. Eventually he was attainted for denying the king's spiritual supremacy, and h.d.q. at Smithfield, London, in 1540. bd. 1886.

†*THOMAS AQUINAS, ST, doct. March 7.   MAR., p. 101

B. in the kingdom of Naples *c.* 1226, educated first by the Benedictines of Monte Cassino, and became a Dominican in 1244. St Thomas spent his relatively short life in teaching, writing, and praying, deriving more light and help from the crucifix than from books. His principal works were the *Summa contra Gentiles* and the *Summa Theologica,* which is the classical and practical scientific exposition of theology and summary of philosophy, a work of so vast extent that it has caused the author to be called the Universal Teacher. St Thomas was also a poet and in the proper office for the feast of Corpus Christi he welded poetry, theology and worship into a glorious work of art. St Thomas died while on his way to take part in the fourteenth œcumenical council (Lyons II) in 1274. At his canonization in 1323 Pope John XXII said that St Thomas " has enlightened the Church more than all other teachers, and more profit can be gained from a year's study of his works than from a lifetime given to those of other theologians." He was declared a doctor of the Church in 1567 and patron saint of universities and all other places of learning in 1880.

†*THOMAS BECKET, ST, bp. and mart. December 29.   DEC., p. 270

Thomas Becket was b. in 1118 in London (his mother was not a Saracen, as legend asserts). After studying in Paris he filled certain posts success- fully, received several benefices, and in 1154 was ordained deacon and nominated archdeacon of Canterbury ; in the following year he was lord chancellor—an apparently worldly man, waiting on the king's will : vigorous, hot-tempered, fond of field sports, popular, magnificent, a bosom friend of Henry II. But when he was advanced to the primatial see of Canterbury in 1162 Thomas abandoned his luxury, resigned his secular office, and opposed the encroachments of the king on the liberties of the clergy and the rights of the Church. From being, in his own words, " A proud vain man, a feeder of birds and follower of hounds," he had become " a shepherd of sheep." The disputes went on for seven years, getting ever more violent, and St Thomas spent some time in exile ; he returned to England on December 1, 1170 and at the same time King Henry in a fit of rage let fall imprudent words in the presence of his knights. Four of them came to Canterbury and in the evening of December 29 murdered the archbishop in a side chapel of his cathedral. The people canonized him as a martyr at once and the Holy See did so formally three years later. St Thomas's shrine made Canterbury one of the most important and famous cities in Christendom : her archbishop had made the Church in England safe for 350 years ; and he was the great exemplar of the English martyrs of the sixteenth and seventeenth centuries—St Thomas More resembled him in more than name.

THOMAS CORSINI, BD. June 23.   JUNE, p. 317

A confessor of the Servite Order, in which he was a lay brother. d. 1345.

THOMAS GARNET, BD, mart. June 23.   JUNE, p. 317

First a secular priest and then a Jesuit, h.d.q. for his priesthood at Tyburn in 1607. Bd Thomas, the first martyr from St Omer's College, was a nephew of the famous Father Henry Garnet, S.J. bd. 1929.

THOMAS HÉLYE, BD. October 19.   OCT., p. 268

When a young man at Biville in Normandy this Thomas undertook to teach the children of his village ; later he was ordained and spent some years as a sort of diocesan missionary, and was famous for miracles. d. 1257. c.c. 1859. Bd Thomas's relics were hidden at the revolution and are now again in their shrine at Biville.

*THOMAS MORE, ST, mart. July 9.   JULY, p. 110

B. in Milk Street, Cheapside, London, in 1478. More went to Oxford and was called to the Bar in 1501. His first wife was Jane Colt, and their house was a meeting-place of all the religious and learned men of the day, both from England and abroad. On the death of Jane, More married Alice Middleton ; soon after, in 1516, he published *Utopia* and in the same year his swift advancement by King Henry VIII and Cardinal Wolsey began. In 1529 he succeeded the disgraced Wolsey as lord chancellor. In this office he had to proceed against heretics, which he did with scrupulous fairness and moderation. Having to oppose the king over his " divorce " and other matters, More resigned the chancellorship in 1532. In 1534, with St John of Rochester, he refused the oath in favour of the offspring of Anne Boleyn and was imprisoned in the Tower for fifteen months. He was tried and convicted for opposing the Act of Supremacy (which made the king the head of the Church in England), and was beheaded on Tower Hill in 1535. cd. 1935. It has been justly remarked that even had this remarkable man not met his death for the Faith, he would have been a proper candidate for canonization as a confessor—both in public and private life St Thomas More was an ideal Christian.

THOMAS PERCY, BD, mart. August 26.   AUG., p. 320

Thomas Percy, Earl of Northumberland, was beheaded at York in 1572 at the age of forty-four for his part in the Rising of the North against the religious policy of Elizabeth. Bd Thomas had some scruples about the insurrection, but during nearly three years of imprisonment he resolutely refused to purchase his life and freedom by apostasy. bd. 1896. His feast is observed in the dioceses of Hexham, Leeds, and Middlesbrough.

THOMAS PLUMTREE, BD, mart. February 4.   FEB., p. 75

B. in Lincolnshire, scholar of Corpus Christi, Oxford, and rector of Stubton. At the Rising of the North he was " Preacher to the Rebels " and celebrated Mass in Durham cathedral. He was specially singled out for punishment ; h.d.q. at Durham in 1570 on January 4, but his feast is kept on February 4 in the diocese of Hexham.

THOMAS SHERWOOD, BD, mart. February 7.   FEB., p. 111

Sherwood intended to go to Douay to study for the priesthood, but was denounced as a Catholic and arrested in London. He was racked in the Tower in a vain endeavour to make him disclose where he had assisted at

Mass, was condemned for denying the Queen's supremacy, and was h.d.q. at Tyburn in 1578. bd. 1895.

THOMAS SOMERS, BD, mart. December 10.   DEC., p. 129
   A secular priest from Westmorland who worked in the London district and was h.d.q. for his priesthood at Tyburn in 1610. bd. 1929.

THOMAS TUNSTAL, BD, mart. July 13.   JULY, p. 175
   Thomas Tunstal (*alias* Helmes), secular priest and Benedictine, came on the English mission in 1610 and spent most of the rest of his life in various prisons. H.d.q. for his priesthood at Norwich in 1616. bd. 1929.

THOMAS TZUGI and comps., **BB,** marts. September 6.   DEC., p. 319
   A Japanese Jesuit who, with two lay coadjutors of the Society, was martyred by burning at Nagasaki in 1627. bd. 1867.

THOMAS WHITEBREAD and Comps., **BB,** marts. June 20.   JUNE, p. 266
   Five Jesuits were h.d.q. at Tyburn in 1679 on a bogus charge of conspiring to murder King Charles II, part of the Oates "plot." They were Thomas Whitebread, a native of Essex, William Harcourt (*alias* Waring, *vere* Barrow), from Lancashire, John Fenwick (*vere* Caldwell) of Durham, John Gavan, a Londoner, and Antony Turner, a convert from near Melton Mowbray. bd. 1929.

THOMAS WOODHOUSE, BD, mart. June 19.   JUNE, p. 248
   The first priest to suffer martyrdom under Queen Elizabeth. He was arrested in 1561 and passed twelve years in prison, during which he was admitted by letter into the Society of Jesus. H.d.q. at Tyburn in 1573.

THOMAS OF CORI, BD. January 19.   JAN., p. 239
   He was a shepherd in the Roman Campagna before he became an Observant Franciscan. He spent most of his life in the friary of Civitella, hidden among the mountains around Subiaco. d. 1729. bd. 1785.

THOMAS OF DOVER, ST, mart. August 5.   AUG., p. 68
   Thomas Hales was a Benedictine of Dover Priory who in 1295 was murdered by French raiders for refusing to give up the monastery valuables. Miracles were recorded at his tomb and an altar was dedicated in his honour in the priory church in 1500.

THOMAS OF FLORENCE, BD. October 31.   OCT., p. 380
   Though only a lay brother Thomas Bellacci was made master of the novices of the Observant Friars Minor at Fiesole ; afterwards he opposed the Fraticelli in Tuscany and, when over seventy, preached in Syria and Ethiopia where, to his sorrow, he narrowly escaped martyrdom by the Mohammedans. d. 1447. c.c. 1771.

*THOMAS OF HEREFORD, ST, bp. October 3.   OCT., p. 33
   Thomas Cantelupe was a Norman, b. at Hambledon, near Great Marlow, *c.* 1218. He studied at Oxford and in Paris, was chaplain to Pope Innocent IV, chancellor of Oxford University, and then chancellor of the realm. He found that neither of the last two posts was easy, but was glad to return to Oxford when he was deprived of the great seal by King Henry III. In 1275 St Thomas was elected bishop of Hereford, and his episcopate was largely a struggle with the lords spiritual and temporal who had encroached on his diocese. He was fearless in rebuking sinners in high places and deprived many pluralists of superfluous benefices. His last years were troubled by dissensions with Archbishop Peckham of Canter-

bury. d. August 25, 1282. cd. 1320. St Thomas's feast is observed in the dioceses of Cardiff, Birmingham, Salford, Shrewsbury, and (on October 22) Westminster.

THOMAS OF TOLENTINO, BD, mart. April 9. APR., p. 108

During the fourteenth century he was a Franciscan missionary in Armenia, Persia, and India. On his way to Ceylon for China in 1321 he was seized by Mohammedans and beheaded. c.c. 1894.

†***THOMAS OF VILLANOVA, ST,** bp. September 22. SEPT., p. 276

He was b. near Villanueva in Spain in 1488, the son of a miller, graduated with distinction in the University of Alcalá, and joined the Augustinian friars at Salamanca in 1516. St Thomas filled various offices in his order with great success, and in 1544 was elected to the archbishopric of Valencia. He is particularly remembered for his love and goodness for the poor : they were his constant care both spiritually and temporally, and he was not interested in whether they were " deserving " or not ; he was also notably averse from using the coercive weapons of the Church in upholding her authority and he established a special work on behalf of the Moriscos in order to keep them out of the hands of the Spanish Inquisition. Many examples are recorded of St Thomas's supernatural gifts, such as his power of healing and of multiplying food, and he left a number of theological writings which have been re-edited of recent years. d. September 8, 1555. cd. 1658.

THOMAS OF WALDEN, BD. November 2. NOV., p. 22

Thomas Netter was b. at Saffron Walden *c.* 1375 and became a Carmelite friar. He was a prominent opponent of the Lollards and took part in the Council of Constance. King Henry V, whose confessor he was, died in his arms. Thomas, whose cultus among the Carmelites has never been confirmed, d. at Rouen in 1430 and miracles are said to have taken place at his tomb there.

THOMASIUS, BD. March 25. MAR., p. 401

A Camaldolese monk who went to live as a solitary and was lost sight of altogether until he was accidentally found. d. 1337.

THORLAC, ST, bp. December 23. DEC., p. 228

This great reforming bishop of the Church in Iceland was b. in 1133 and studied in Paris and Lincoln ; he became bishop of Skalholt in 1177. His episcopate was devoted to an uphill struggle against abuses, particularly simony and the disregard of the canons against clerical marriage. d. 1193. He was " canonized " locally in 1198 but the cultus has never been confirmed.

THREE HOLY KINGS, THE. July 23. JAN., p. 89

The men from the East who visited the new-born Christ are variously known as the Three Kings of Cologne, the Three Wise Men, the Magi, Caspar, Melchior, and Balthazar, etc. Their feast is kept on July 23 at Cologne because their alleged relics rest in the cathedral there.

***TIBURTIUS,** etc., **SS,** marts. April 14. APR., p. 158

Tiburtius, Valerius, and Maximus are characters in the *acta* of St Cecilia, according to which document Valerius was her husband and Tiburtius his brother, who suffered martyrdom together with an official named Maximus *c.* 190 (?).

†***TIBURTIUS, ST,** mart. August 11. AUG., p. 128

He was a martyr by beheading at Rome *c.* 288, so far as is known.

TIGERNACH, ST, bp. April 4. APR., p. 48
    The account of St Tigernach (Tierney) written from tradition centuries after his death cannot be considered historically accurate. His memory is associated with the monastery of Clones, which he founded, and he is said to have succeeded St Macartan as bishop at Clogher. d. 549.

*TIGRIUS, ST, mart. January 12. JAN., p. 149
    In the year 404 Tigrius, a priest, was tortured and exiled, and Eutropius, a reader, was put to death, on a false charge of setting fire to the cathedral and senate-house at Constantinople as a protest against the banishment of St John Chrysostom.

TILBERT, ST, bp. October 2. SEPT., p. 77
    He was the eighth bishop of Hexham and d. in 789. No details are known of his life.

TILLO, ST. January 7. JAN., p. 104
    Otherwise *Theau, Tilloine.* A Saxon captive in the Low Countries who became apostle of the district round Courtrai. Having retired to a hermitage at Solignar he d. at a great age *c.* 702.

†*TIMOTHY, ST, bp. and mart. January 24. JAN., p. 291
    The " beloved son in faith " of St Paul and his companion on his missionary journeys. To him on his appointment as bishop in Ephesus while yet young St Paul wrote two pastoral epistles now in the canon of Holy Scripture. St Timothy is believed to have been beaten and stoned to death for opposing the worship of Diana in the year 97, when he was over eighty. *Timotheus.*

†*TIMOTHY, ST, mart. August 22. AUG., p. 268
    A priest of Antioch who was martyred in Rome between 311 and 313. He is commemorated liturgically together with St Hippolytus and St Symphorian on August 22.

*TIMOTHY and other marts., **SS.** August 19. AUG., p. 220
    Timothy, bishop of Gaza, was burnt to death for the Faith at that place in 304. With him are named St Thecla, who was thrown to the beasts at Cæsarea, and St Agapius, who suffered by drowning two years later.

*TIMOTHY and **MAURA, SS,** marts. May 3. MAY, p. 41
    Timothy and Maura were martyred in Upper Egypt three weeks after they had been married, *c.* 286.

TIMOTHY OF MONTECCHIO, BD. August 26. AUG., p. 320
    He was a confessor of the Franciscan Order in Italy. d. 1504. c.c. 1870.

†*TITUS, ST, bp. February 6. JAN., p. 58
    The Gentile disciple of St Paul, who was twice sent on missions to the church of Corinth. He was ordained bishop for the island of Crete, recalled by St Paul, and eventually returned to Crete where he died (at Gortyna, *c.* 96 ?).

TORELLO, BD. March 16. MAR., p. 286
    Being suddenly converted from a dissolute life, Bd Torello became a hermit near his native town of Poppi in the Casentino and lived a life of solitude and austerity for over fifty years. d. 1282. c.c. by Pope Benedict XIV.

TORIBIO, ST. *See* Turibius.

*TORQUATUS, ST, bp. and mart. May 15. MAY, p. 189
    He was, with his six companions, the first evangelizer of Spain in the first century, according to a mediæval legend, but nothing certain is

known about them. St Torquatus is specially venerated at Guadix in Granada.

TRESSAN, ST. February 7.   FEB., p. 106
   An Irishman, called Trésain in France, where he was priest at Mareuil on the Marne under St Remigius. d. *c.* 550.

*TRIPHYLLIUS, ST, bp. June 13.   JUNE, p. 169
   He was the disciple and companion of St Spiridion and was made bishop of Nikosia in Cyprus. St Jerome speaks of him as a most eloquent preacher and writer. d. *c.* 370.

TRIVERIUS, ST. January 16.   JAN., p. 202
   This saint gives his name to the village of Saint-Trivier but there is no trustworthy account of his life. d. 550 (?).

*TROND, ST. November 23.   Nov., p. 284
   He was missionary in Brabant and founded a monastery at the place now called Saint-Trond, near Louvain. d. *c.* 695. *Trudo.*

*TROPHIMUS, ST, bp. December 29.   DEC., p. 283
   He is venerated as the first bishop of Arles, in the third century.

TRUDPERTUS, ST. April 26.   APR., p. 291
   A hermit in the Black Forest of Germany who gave his name to a Benedictine monastery. It is even uncertain in what century he lived.

TRUMWIN, ST, bp. December 2.   DEC., p. 29
   He was made bishop over the southern Picts in 681 by St Theodore of Canterbury, but a few years later was driven by the heathen from his see at Abercorn. He retired to the abbey of Whitby, and d. there *c.* 690.

†*TRYPHON and **RESPICIUS, SS,** marts. November 10.   Nov., p. 114
   Tryphon is said to have been a young herdsman, martyred at Nicaea *c.* 250 ; the name of Respicius is first found joined with his in an eleventh-century *passio*, and nothing is known of him.

TUDWAL, ST, bp. December 1.   DEC., p. 2
   Tudwal was a sixth-century Welsh monk who is venerated in Brittany as the first bishop in the district of Tréguier. His name occurs at three places in the Llŷn peninsula in Caernarvonshire. *Tugdualus.*

*TURIAF, ST, bp. July 13.   JULY, p. 172
   Bishop of Dol in Brittany, about whom there is little reliable information. d. *c.* 750. *Turiavus.*

*TURIBIUS, ST, bp. April 16.   APR., p. 180
   While occupying the see of Astorga in Spain he distinguished himself by his efforts against the Priscillianist heresy. d. *c.* 450.

*TURIBIUS, ST, bp. April 27.   APR., p. 309
   Toribio of Mogrobejo was b. in 1538 in Spain and attracted the notice of King Philip II. After being president of the Inquisition of Granada he was in 1580 appointed archbishop of Lima in Peru, where a reforming prelate was badly needed. For years St Turibius had to contend with the rapacity, arrogance, and general wickedness of the Spanish conquerors, who were the strongest argument of the Peruvians against becoming Christians, and the Spanish clergy themselves were the first people the archbishop had to deal with. He served his flock with the most unremitting care, making visitations that took years to complete, founding churches, seminaries, and hospitals, and fearing no man. d. March 23, 1606. cd. 1726.

TUTILO, ST. March 28.   MAR., p. 428
A monk of Saint Gall and the religious and musical associate of St Notker Balbulus. He was also a poet, painter, and stone-carver, and noted for his aversion from publicity. d. *c.* 915.

†*TWELVE BROTHERS, THE, marts. September 1.   SEPT., p. 6
These young men, also called the "Martyrs of the South," were various early martyrs in Apulia in Italy whom later legend incorporated into one family.

*TYCHON, ST, bp. June 16.   JUNE, p. 197
An early (fifth century ?) bishop of Amathus (Limasol) in Cyprus, greatly venerated there as a wonder-worker and patron of vine-growers.

*TYRANNIO, ST, bp. and mart. February 20.   FEB., p. 281
Bishop of Tyre, who with others was martyred in Phœnicia in 310. On the same day the Roman Martyrology mentions other martyrs who suffered in the same district some six years earlier, as related by Eusebius.

TYSILIO, ST, ab. November 8.   NOV., p. 97
Tysilio (Suliau), son of Brochwel Ysgythrog, prince of Powỳs, was abbot of the church of Meifod in Montgomeryshire and founded several churches in other parts of Wales. After the battle of Chester *c.* 617 he migrated to Brittany and settled at Saint-Suliac, where he d. *c.* 640.

†***UBALDUS, ST,** bp. May 16. MAY, p. 209

Ubaldus Baldassini was b. at Gubbio *c.* 1100 and as dean of the cathedral there introduced community life under a rule among the canons. In 1128 he was appointed bishop of Gubbio and in that office continued to be a type of the lovable Christian produced by regular observance. On one occasion he defied Frederick Barbarossa in defence of the episcopal city and in Umbria his name is a household word for courage and goodness to this day. d. 1160. cd. 1192.

UBALDUS ADIMARI, BD. April 9. APR., p. 107

A young man of Florence, converted from a turbulent and dissolute life by St Philip Benizi who admitted him to the Servite order. d. 1315. c.c. 1821.

UGANDA, THE MARTYRS OF. June 3. JUNE, p. 43

The central African mission of the White Fathers was begun in 1878 and in 1886 King Mwanga resolved to stamp out the beginnings of Christianity in Uganda, to a considerable extent because it interfered with his own vicious habits. About a hundred people were killed with horrible cruelty and twenty-two, the circumstances of whose martyrdom were known, were bd. in 1920. Prominent among them were Charles Lwanga and other royal " pages " and Matthias Marumba, the headman of a district, whose mangled body was left in agony for three days.

ULFRID, ST, bp. and mart. January 18. JAN., p. 227

An English missionary in Germany and Sweden. He was slain for preaching against the worship of Thor *c.* 1029.

ULPHIA, ST, virg. January 31. JAN., p. 400

An ankress at Saint-Acheul in the diocese of Amiens. d. *c.* 750.

ULRIC. *See also* Wulfric.

*****ULRIC, ST,** bp. July 4. JULY, p. 38

Ulric was nominated bishop of Augsburg in 923, when that diocese had been laid waste by the Magyars. He was a model bishop, but after thirty years saw his diocese again devastated by civil war and the Magyars. In his old age he had to meet an unjust charge of nepotism. d. 973. The canonization of St Ulric by Pope John XV in 993 is the first solemn canonization by a pope of which there is record. *Uldaricus.*

ULRIC OF ZELL, ST, ab. July 14. JULY, p. 186

He received the monastic habit at Cluny in 1061 and was prior at Marcigny, Peterlingen, and the Rüggersburg. He founded a new house of his order at Zell in the Black Forest, and wrote down the constitutions and customs of the abbey of Cluny. d. 1093.

ULTAN, ST, ab. May 2. MAY, p. 28

Ultan was brother to St Fursey and St Foillan and was a monk with them at Burghcastle. For a time he taught chant to the nuns at Nivelles and afterwards became abbot of Fosses and Péronne. d. *c.* 675.

ULTAN, ST, bp. September 4. SEPT., p. 47
There are several Irish saints named Ultan ; this one appears to have been bishop in Ardbraccan during the seventh century. He was noted for his fondness for children and is said to have collected the writings of St Brigid.

*URBAN, ST, mart. September 5. SEPT., p. 60
He was a priest of Constantinople who with a number of other clerics of that city was deliberately left to perish in a burning ship because they had appealed to the emperor Valens against Arian persecution. d. 370. *Urbanus.*

*URBAN I, ST, pope and mart. May 25. MAY, p. 300
During his pontificate from 222 to 230 the Church enjoyed peace and Urban I seems to have been venerated as a martyr in error.

*URBAN II, BD, pope. July 29. JULY, p. 409
The pontificate of Bd Urban II (Odo of Lagery) is part of the general history of Europe. He was prior of Cluny and, first as cardinal bishop of Ostia and in 1088 as pope, did much to extend the uncompromising Christianity of that monastic reform to church and people in general. He had to contend with the antipope Guibert of Ravenna, and he inaugurated the First Crusade, in consequence of an appeal for help against the Seljuk Turks from the Eastern emperor Alexius I. It appears that Urban owed much of his policy and tenacity to the counsel of St Bruno, the Carthusian founder, whom the pope at his accession summoned to his side. d. 1099. bd. 1881.

*URBAN V, BD, pope. December 19. DEC., p. 206
William de Grimoard, a Frenchman, was a great canonist and abbot of St Germain d'Auxerre. He was elected pope at Avignon in 1362 and took the papacy back to Rome, but he was forced to retire to France again in 1370 ; he d. in the same year. Urban was a patron of learning and Oxford was among the universities that profited by his help. c.c. 1870.

URSICINUS, ST, ab. December 20. DEC., p. 210
The missionary monk, a disciple of St Columbanus, who gives his name to Saint-Ursanne in Switzerland, where he had a small monastery. d. *c.* 625.

*URSMAR, ST, bp. April 19. APR., p. 226
Abbot and bishop of Lobbes and a zealous missionary in Flanders. d. 713. *Ursmarus.*

†*URSULA and her comps., **SS,** marts. October 21. OCT., p. 285
It may be inferred from an ancient inscribed stone at Cologne that some maidens were martyred there some time before the fourth century when a church was built in their honour. This is all that can be said with reason-able certainty of the martyrs made famous by the great and ramified legend of St Ursula and her Eleven Thousand Virgins. There is no reason to suppose that Ursula's companions numbered more than a few. Her feast is now treated with considerable reserve in the Roman liturgy and it was a project of Pope Benedict XIV to suppress it altogether, as the Benedictines have done.

URSULINA, BD, virg. April 7. APR., p. 88
A young woman of Parma who in consequence, as she alleged, of supernatural enlightenment visited both the Clementine and Urbanist popes and urged them to come to an agreement for the healing of the

schism in the papacy. She narrowly escaped being tried for sorcery.
d. 1410.

*URSUS, ST, bp. April 13.   APR., p. 147
    A bishop of Ravenna about whom little certain is known. d. 398.

*UTICA, THE MARTYRS OF. August 24.   AUG., p. 291
    A number of martyrs of uncertain date who were put to death at
Utica in Africa. The expression " White Mass " used in reference to them
does not arise from their bodies being calcined with lime but from the place
of their execution, Massa Candida.

VALENCIENNES, THE MARTYRS OF. October 17. OCT., p. 247

Eleven Ursuline nuns who were guillotined at Valenciennes in 1794 because, having left the town at the revolution, they had returned and unlawfully reopened their school. bd. 1920.

VALENTINE, ST, bp. January 7. JAN., p. 101

A missionary bishop in Rhætia in the fourth–fifth century of whom practically nothing is known. His relics were translated from the Tyrol to Trent and thence to Passau in the eighth century. *Valentinus.*

†*VALENTINE, ST, mart. February 14. FEB., p. 214

A priest of Rome who probably suffered in the persecution of Claudius the Goth *c.* 269. He was buried on the Flaminian Way and a basilica was built over his tomb in 350. This is the Valentine after whom " valentines " are named.

*VALENTINE, ST, bp. and mart. February 14. FEB., p. 215

There are references to a martyr named Valentine who was said to be bishop of Terni (Interamna), some sixty miles from Rome. He may be the same as the St Valentine just mentioned.

*VALERIAN, ST, mart. September 15. SEPT., p. 43

He was beheaded for the Faith at Tournus, near Autun, *c.* 178. *Valerianus.*

*VALERIAN, ST, bp. and mart. December 15. DEC., p. 175

When over eighty years old he was forced to die from exposure, near his episcopal city of Abbenza in Africa, for refusing to give up the sacred vessels to the Arian king Genseric, in 457.

*VALERIUS, ST, bp. January 29. JAN., p. 374

An early bishop of Trier, probably in the early fourth century.

*VALERIUS and **RUFINUS, SS,** marts. June 14. JUNE, p. 176

Martyrs at or near Soissons towards the end of the third century.

VALÉRY, ST. *See* Walaricus.

*VARUS, ST, mart. October 19. OCT., p. 263

Varus is said to have been a Roman soldier in Upper Egypt who was martyred early in the fourth century for ministering to imprisoned Christians.

*VEDAST, ST, bp. February 6. FEB., p. 90

Otherwise *Vaast.* He was a fellow worker with St Remigius of Rheims and was by him appointed first bishop of Arras, where he laboured for forty years with much fruitfulness. The English version of " Vedast " seems to have been " Foster " : cf. St Vedast's church in Foster Lane, London. d. 539. *Vedastus.*

†*VENANTIUS, ST, mart. May 18. MAY, p. 225

He is said to have been a martyr at Camerino during the third century, but nothing whatsoever is known for certain about him. The honours paid to him in the liturgy of the Western church are due to the personal action of Pope Clement X, who had been bishop of Camerino.

VENANTIUS FORTUNATUS, ST, bp. December 14. DEC., p. 166

Though his feast is observed in several French and Italian dioceses Venantius Fortunatus is better known as a poet than as a saint, probably rightly. He was b. near Treviso *c.* 535 and at the age of thirty settled down at Poitiers where he was ordained priest ;· here he enjoyed the close friendship of St Radegunde and, among numerous other poems, many of them personal panegyrics not free from flattery, wrote the great hymn " Vexilla regis prodeunt." He also compiled biographies of St Martin, St Radegunde, and other saints. Shortly before his death *c.* 605 Venantius was appointed bishop of Poitiers. His letters to the nuns of Holy Cross are of great interest.

*VENERIUS, ST, bp. May 4. MAY, p. 54

He became bishop of Milan in 400 and his cultus was revived by St Charles Borromeo. d. 409.

VENTURA SPELLUCCI, BD, ab. May 3. MAY, p. 44

He built a hospice and monastery for monks of the now extinct order of Cruciferi at Spello, near Assisi, and himself directed them as abbot. Twelfth century.

VEREMUNDUS, ST, ab. March 8. MAR., p. 136

Under the rule of this abbot the monastery of Hyrach became the principal one in Navarre during the eleventh century. During a time of famine he is said by his prayers to have nourished over three thousand foodless people. d. 1092.

*VERENA, ST, virg. September 1. SEPT., p. 4

The cultus of this Swiss maiden has a reasonable antiquity but nothing is known about her : she has been drawn into the legend of the Theban Legion.

*VERIDIANA, ST, virg. February 1. FEB., p. 18

B. in 1432 at Castelfiorentino, where she lived in a hermitage adjoining a chapel of St Antony. Miracles were ascribed to her. She seems to have been associated with the Vallombrosan Order, but the Franciscans claim her as a tertiary. d. 1242. c.c. 1533.

VERONICA, ST. July 12. JULY, p. 154

Veronica is the name traditionally given to the woman who is said to have wiped the face of Jesus when He fell beneath His cross on the road to Calvary, and a number of legends have grown up around her. She is not named in the Roman Martyrology.

*VERONICA GIULIANI, ST, virg. July 9. JULY, p. 124

B. in 1660 and joined the Capuchinesses at Città di Castello in 1667. From the time of her profession she experienced numerous visions and other mystical phenomena, the evidence for which constitutes St Veronica's case as possibly one of the most remarkable known to hagiology. She was at the same time a very level-headed and practical religious, and was novice mistress of her convent for thirty-four years. d. 1727. cd. 1839.

*VERONICA OF BINASCO, BD, virg. January 13. JAN., p. 158

She was a daughter of hard-working peasants at Binasco, near Milan, and became a lay sister in a convent of Augustinian nuns. She was the recipient of many remarkable visions and revelations, some of which seem to have been greatly exaggerated in the course of time. d. 1497. c.c. 1517.

*VICTOR, ST. February 26. FEB., p. 363

He was a hermit at Arcis-sur-Aube in Champagne, of whom St Bernard speaks in two of his sermons and for whose feast at the Benedictine monastery of Montiramey he composed a proper office. d. *c.* 610.

†*VICTOR I, ST, pope and mart. July 28. JULY, p. 389

He was pope from *c.* 189 till *c.* 200. It is not certain that he was a martyr.

*VICTOR III, BD, pope. September 16. SEPT., p. 212

As Desiderius he was the greatest of the abbots of Monte Cassino after St Benedict and in 1086 was elected pope by acclamation, taking the name of Victor. But his pontificate was very like that of St Celestine V. Rome was occupied by the imperial antipope, Guibert of Ravenna, the gentle Victor fled, and soon after d. at Monte Cassino in 1087. c.c. by Pope Leo XIII.

*VICTOR and **CORONA, SS,** marts. May 14. MAY, p. 172

The passion of these martyrs appears to belong to the second century, but time, place, and circumstances are equally doubtful.

*VICTOR MAURUS, ST, mart. May 8. MAY, p. 96

A Mauretanian soldier who was beheaded for confessing the faith of Christ at Milan in 303 ; he is associated by St Ambrose with the martyrs Nabor and Felix.

*VICTOR OF MARSEILLES, ST, mart. July 21. JULY, p. 302

An army officer who suffered for Christ in 304 at Marseilles, where his tomb was a place of pilgrimage at an early date.

*VICTORIA and **ANATOLIA, SS,** virgs. and marts. December 23.
DEC., p. 224

These sisters were martyred in Italy *c.* 250, but the true circumstances are not known. Their valueless *acta* state that they suffered because they refused marriage.

VICTORIAN, ST, ab. January 12. JAN., p. 151

Abbot of Asan in Aragon, whose epitaph by Venantius Fortunatus speaks of his miracles and virtues. d. 558. *Victorianus.*

*VICTORIAN, ST, mart. March 23. MAR., p. 380

With four others Victorian was tortured and executed by the Arian Vandals at Adrumetum in 484.

*VICTORINUS, ST, bp. and mart. November 2. NOV., p. 20

Victorinus, bishop of Pettau in Upper Pannonia, was distinguished as a scriptural exegete. He was martyred *c.* 303.

*VICTORINUS, ST, and other marts. February 25. FEB., p. 336

Victorinus and six other citizens of Corinth after being persecuted in 249 were exiled, or retired, to Egypt. Here in 284 they finished their confession, being put to death in various cruel ways at Diospolis in the Thebaid.

*VICTRICIUS, ST, bp. August 7. AUG., p. 84

With Hilary and Martin he was one of the three very great bishops in Gaul during the fourth century. About 350 he was sentenced to death for resigning from the Roman army on the ground that a Christian should not bear arms, and when next heard of he is bishop of Rouen. He undertook missionary work far beyond the bounds of his diocese and on one occasion visited Britain to settle some local dispute. Victricius may fairly be regarded as the first bishop of Rouen to exercise metropolitan powers. d. *c.* 409.

*VIGILIUS, ST, bp. and mart. June 26.   JUNE, p. 348

Vigilius, made bishop of Trent in 385, practically completed the conversion of the Trentino and the Italian Tyrol to Christianity. He was stoned to death at Rendana in 405 for overturning a statue of Saturn. Pope Benedict XIV stated that St Vigilius was the first martyr to be canonized by the Holy See.

*VIGOR, ST, bp. November 1.   Nov., p. 15

St Vigor was a bishop of Bayeux who d. *c.* 537.

VILLANA DE' BOTTI, BD. February 28.   FEB., p. 385

Villana was the daughter of a Florentine merchant ; she was an abnormally pious child, but after marriage went just as far the other way until she reformed and joined the Dominican tertiaries. Her reform was complete, she made great progress in the spiritual life, and after her husband's death suffered from the evil tongues of some of her fellows. d. 1360. c.c. 1824.

VIMIN, ST, bp. January 21.   JAN., p. 260

Otherwise *Wynnin, Gwynnin.* A sixth-century Scottish saint whose history is very confused. He is said to have founded the monastery of Holywood, called in Latin *Sacrum Boscum,* later famous for many learned men, particularly John a Sacro Bosco.

†*VINCENT, ST, mart. January 22.   JAN., p. 263

A deacon of Saragossa who suffered torture and death in the year 304 at Valencia. His cultus spread throughout the Church at a very early date and his relics were diffused abroad. In some places he is honoured as the patron of vine-dressers. *Vincentius.*

†*VINCENT FERRER, ST. April 5.   APR., p. 55

The life of this great Dominican saint has been considerably overlaid with legend. He was b. at Valencia *c.* 1350 and in troublous times travelled through Spain, France, Switzerland, and Italy preaching penance, working many wonders, and converting thousands. St Vincent's other great work was in the mending of the so-called Great Schism of the West (he was a supporter of the popes of the Clementine obedience) : " But for you," wrote Gerson to him after the resignation of Peter de Luna, " this union could never have been achieved." d. 1418. cd. 1455.

VINCENT MADELGARUS, ST, ab. September 20.   SEPT., p. 267

Before he became a monk in the abbey of Hautmont and took the name of Vincent, Madelgarus was the husband of St Waldetrudis ; their children, Landericus, Madelberta, Aldetrudis, and Dentelinus, are all venerated as saints. He founded the abbey of Soignies and d. there in 677.

VINCENT STRAMBI, BD, bp. September 25.   JAN., p. 137

B. at Civita Vecchia in 1745, the son of a druggist. He entered the Passionist congregation, and from the age of thirty-five filled one office of authority after another in it, at the same time being a much sought-after missioner. Much against his will he had in 1801 to accept the see of Macerata and Tolentino, from which he was expelled seven years later for refusing to take the oath of allegiance to Napoleon. He returned in 1813 and carried on with the renewal of his diocese, only to see it threatened again by the occupation of the troops of Murat. Blessed Vincent himself interviewed both Murat and the general of the pursuing Austrians, and so saved Macerata from being sacked. At the request of Leo XII he resigned his see and went to the Quirinal as the pope's confidential adviser, where he continued to lead a very mortified life. Among his penitents in Rome was Bd Anna Maria Taigi. d. 1824. bd. 1925.

*VINCENT OF AGEN, ST, mart. June 9.   JUNE, p. 119

He is said to have been a Gascon deacon who was martyred at Agen *c.* 300.

*VINCENT OF LÉRINS, ST. May 24.   MAY, p. 288

Vincent, a monk of Lérins, is famous as the author of an early treatise against heresies, called the *Commonitorium*, in which is enunciated for the first known time that for a dogma to be regarded as true it must have been held " always, everywhere, and by all the faithful." He has sometimes been credited with the authorship of the so-called Athanasian Creed. d. *c.* 445.

†*VINCENT DE PAUL, ST. July 19.   JULY, p. 259

St Vincent seems to have been born in 1580 and ordained priest at the age of twenty. He was captured by Moors but escaped and went to Paris, where he was " taken up " by the Oratorian father Bérulle and by Mme de Gondi. The sad state of the French peasantry led to the foundation of the Congregation of the Mission (Vincentians, Lazarists) in 1625 and afterwards, with Bd Louise de Marillac, of the Sisters of Charity. St Vincent was a man of unbounded love for the poor and unfortunate, whether slaves in Barbary, victims of war in France, or crofters in the Hebrides, so that his name is for ever associated with relief of the destitute. His conviction that spiritual starvation is far worse than any bodily affliction or lack of food was not affected by the fact that the sufferers whom he helped did not always share it. d. 1660. cd. 1737. St Vincent is the patron saint of all charitable societies.

VINCENTIAN, ST. January 2.   JAN., p. 37

Venerated in the diocese of Tulle as a seventh-century hermit, but there seems to be no other evidence extant that he ever existed. *Vincentianus.*

▶ VINCENZA GEROSA, BD, virg. June 4.   JUNE, p. 56

B. 1784 and for forty years gave herself to domestic duties and works of charity. Then about 1823 she was brought into intimate contact with Bd Bartolomea Capitanio whom she helped in the founding of the Suore della Carità at Lovere in Italy. After Bartolomea's death in 1833 Bd Vincenza carried on with the work until her own death in 1847. She was a first-rate organizer, yet an extremely humble woman, and the congregation progressed rapidly under her guidance (it now has 550 charitable establishments in Italy and the foreign missions). bd. 1933. *Vincentia.*

VINDICIAN, ST, bp. March 11.   MAR., p. 192

This saint played an important part in the ecclesiastical history of Flanders during the seventh century. He was bishop of Cambrai and is said to have been the messenger of protest from his fellow bishops to King Thierry after the murder of St Leger. He had a special interest in the abbey of St Vaast at Arras. d. 712. *Vindicianus.*

VIRGILIUS, ST, bp. March 5.   MAR., p. 65

He was called from his monastery to be archbishop of Arles, and it appears that he consecrated St Augustine of Canterbury at the request of Pope St Gregory. The same pope rebuked Virgilius for trying to convert Jews by force. d. *c.* 610.

*VIRGILIUS, ST, bp. November 27.   Nov., p. 327

He was an Irish monk (Feargal) who *c.* 747 was made abbot of St

Peter's at Salzburg. Later he became bishop of that city, and among other good works sent missionaries into Carinthia. Virgilius is said to have had difficulties with Pope St Zachary because of his views about the physical universe ; what they were exactly is not clear. d. 784. cd. 1233. His feast is kept throughout Ireland.

*VITALIAN, ST, pope. January 27.   JAN., p. 346

He had a troubled pontificate from 657 till his death in 672. St Vitalian sent Theodore of Tarsus to England as archbishop of Canterbury. *Vitalianus.*

VITALIS, ST. January 11.   JAN., p. 145

An aged monk of Gaza who caused great scandal by his strange methods of trying to recall erring women to virtue ; he was vindicated only after his death, *c.* 625.

†*VITALIS, ST, mart. April 28.

SS Vitalis and Valeria are said to have been the parents of SS Gervase and Protase and to have been likewise martyred, the one at Ravenna, the other at Milan. Their extant story is probably spurious. This Vitalis is named in the canon of the Ambrosian Mass.

VITALIS, BD, ab. September 16.   JAN., p. 108

The chronology of his life is very perplexing, but he was at different times chaplain to Robert of Mortain (half-brother of William the Conqueror), a hermit, and founder of the great abbey of Savigny. Bd Vitalis visited England several times, where on one occasion his sermon is said to have been understood by the common people even though they could understand only English. He died in choir at Savigny on September 16, 1122, but occurs in the *Acta Sanctorum* on January 7.

*VITALIS and AGRICOLA, SS, marts. November 4.   NOV., p. 53

Vitalis was a slave martyred at Bologna *c.* 304, his master Agricola being put to death shortly after.

VITONUS, ST, bp. November 9.   NOV., p. 108

He was bishop of Verdun for over twenty-five years and d. *c.* 525. His name, in its French form, is particularly remembered as that of the eponymous patron of the Benedictine congregation which had its origin at the abbey of Saint-*Vannes* in 1600.

†*VITUS, MODESTUS, and **CRESCENTIA, SS,** marts. June 15.

                                     JUNE, p. 182

The cultus of these three saints goes back to early times and they were certainly martyrs in southern Italy. But nothing is known of their true history and the date of their passion is only a matter of conjecture (300 ?) ; their legends are late and worthless compilations. They may have been Sicilians. St Vitus was invoked against epilepsy and kindred complaints, whence the name St Vitus' Dance.

VIVALDUS, ST. May 11.   MAY, p. 133

Or *Ubald*. A tertiary of St Francis who nursed the leprosy-stricken Bd Bartolo of San Gemignano for twenty years. d. 1300.

VLADIMIR, ST. July 15.   JULY, p. 202

Vladimir, Great Prince of Kiev, was b. in 956 and brought up a pagan. He married Anne, sister of the Greek emperor Basil II, was himself baptized, and Greek clergy began to evangelize the Russians : the conversion of the country is dated from 988. Vladimir's two sons by Anne, Boris and Gleb, who were put to death by their heathen half-brother, are venerated as martyrs under the name of SS Romanus and David. Vladimir d. in 1015.   *Vladimirus.*

VODALUS, ST. February 5.   FEB., p. 85
Or *Voel*. A Scot or Irishman who preached the gospel in Gaul and became a hermit at Soissons. d. *c.* 720.

VOLKER, BD, mart. March 7.   MAR., p. 117
A monk of Sigeburg, near Lubeck. " a brother of great simplicity," who was murdered by heathen raiders in 1132.

*VOLUSIAN, ST, bp. and mart. January 18.   JAN., p. 226
Volusian was a fifth-century bishop of Tours who was afflicted with a very bad-tempered wife. He was driven from his see by the Goths and d. in exile *c.* 496. His martyrdom for the Faith has not been established. *Volusianus.*

VULPHY, ST. June 7.   JUNE, p. 92
First a parish priest at Rue, near Abbeville, and then a solitary. d. *c.* 643. There is little serious evidence for his legend, but he had a strong cultus at Montreuil-sur-Mer, where his relics are still venerated. *Wulflagius.*

WALARICUS, ST, ab.   April 1.   APR., p. 5

Walaricus (Valéry) was a monk under St Columbanus at Luxeuil and then a missionary in northern France, where he became abbot of Leuconaus at the mouth of the Somme, where two towns are named after him. d. *c.* 622. This saint was specially invoked for a favourable wind by William the Conqueror before setting out for England in 1066.

*WALBURGA, ST, virg.   February 25.   FEB., p. 338

She was a nun at Wimborne. When her kinsman St Boniface was evangelizing the Germans she was sent out with other nuns to help him. She became supreme abbess of the double monastery of Heidenheim. founded by her brother St Winebald, whose life she wrote. d. 779. St Walburga is honoured in France, Germany, and the Low Countries under various names, *e.g.* Vaubourg, Walpurgis (*cf.* Walpurgisnacht, May 1, the eve of one of her festivals), and some of the attributes of the earth goddess Walborg seem to have been transferred to her. St Walburga's so-called miraculous oil is a fluid that exudes from the rock on which her shrine rests at Heidenheim.

WALDEBERTUS, ST, ab.   May 2.   MAY, p. 29

He was the best-known of the successors of St Columbanus as abbot of Luxeuil, which under his direction reached the height of its fame ; it was he who introduced the Rule of St Benedict there. Waldebertus died, famous for miracles, *c.* 668. " Walbert " is the French form of his name.

*WALDETRUDIS, ST.   April 9.   APR., p. 104

St Waldetrudis, or Vaudru, came of a family of saints (Walbertus and Bertilia), married a saint, Vincent Madelgarus, and had three holy children, Landericus, Adeltrudis, and Madelberta. After her husband had entered the abbey of Haumont she founded a convent round which the town of Mons grew up. She is greatly venerated in Belgium. d. *c.* 688.

WALFRID, ST, ab.   February 15.   FEB., p. 229

A citizen of Pisa who with his wife and two of his children withdrew from secular life and became religious. Walfrid and some friends established a monastery at Palazzuolo, of which he was appointed abbot. d. *c.* 765. *Gualfredus.*

WALSTAN, ST.   May 30.   MAY, p. 377

He was b. at Bawburgh in Norfolk and spent his days as a farm-labourer at Taverham and Costessey. d. 1016. His cultus seems never to have spread beyond that neighbourhood. There is still a St Walstan's Well at Costessey. *Walstanus.*

WALTER, ST, ab.   May 11.   MAY, p. 131

He was an Augustinian canon and abbot of l'Esterp in the Limousin. He had so great a reputation for the conversion of sinners that Pope Victor II gave him special faculties for dealing with penitents. d. 1070. *Gualterius..*

WALTER OF PONTOISE, ST, ab. April 8.　　　　　APR., p. 96

Against his will he was made abbot of a new Benedictine house at Pontoise and from time to time during his life he tried to resign the office, once fleeing to Cluny and once to Rome ; at length he resigned himself to a life of administration and persecution instead of contemplation, and directed his abbey till he died in 1095.

WALTHEOF, ST, ab. August 3.　　　　　AUG., p. 57

Waltheof (*Walthenus*) was a kinsman of William the Conqueror and a friend of St Aelred at the court of David I of Scotland. He joined a community of Austin canons in Yorkshire and then became a Cistercian at Wardon in Bedfordshire, later being elected abbot of Melrose. Here he was noted for his care of the poor, especially during the famine in 1154. d. 1160.

WALTMANN, BD, ab. April 11.　　　　　APR., p. 127

He accompanied St Norbert to Cambrai to preach against certain heretics there, and in gratitude for his success was appointed abbot of St Michael's in that city. d. 1138. *Gualtmannus.*

*WANDRILLE, ST, ab. July 22.　　　　　JULY, p 318

Wandrille was a distinguished official at the court of King Dagobert I. In 629 both he and his wife retired into religious houses. After many years of varied experience as a monk Wandrille founded the abbey of Fontenelle, which soon became one of the most famous monasteries of western Europe. d. 668. *Wandregisilus.*

WANINGUS, ST. January 9.　　　　　JAN., p. 125

A wealthy lord under Clotaire III, and governor of the Pays de Caux, who in consequence of a vision of St Eulalia of Barcelona reformed his life. He helped St Wandrille by contributing towards his monastic foundations and himself founded a large convent near Fécamp. d. *c.* 683.

†*WENCESLAUS, ST, mart. September 28.　　　　　SEPT., p. 339

After the murder of his grandmother St Ludmila, Wenceslaus (Vaclav) did not undertake the government of Bohemia until he came of age ; he then patiently and firmly opposed the heathen party among his nobles and continued the evangelization of his country, which he acknowledged to be a 'fief of the Holy Roman emperor. Wenceslaus was slain in a political plot by his brother in 929, and was at once acclaimed a martyr by the people. He is the patron-saint of Czechoslovakia ; the occurrence of his name in a modern English carol has no significance.

WERBURG, ST, virg. February 3.　　　　　FEB., p. 51

Daughter of King Wulfhere of Mercia and St Ermenilda. She became a nun of Ely and founded other convents at Hanbury, Weedon, and Trentham. She died at the last named *c.* 699, and her body was enshrined with great solemnity in Chester cathedral. St Werburg is the patron of that city and her feast is kept in the dioceses of Birmingham and Shrewsbury. *Werburga.*

WERNHER, ST, mart. April 19.　　　　　APR., p. 231

Wernher was a small boy venerated at Trier as a victim of Jewish " ritual murder " in 1275. The evidence adduced one hundred and fifty years after the alleged event is extremely unsatisfactory.

WIBORADA, ST, virg. and mart. May 2.　　　　　MAY, p. 30

For some years she worked for Saint-Gall and other monasteries, binding books and so on, and then became a recluse in a cell adjoining the church of St Magnus at Saint-Gall. Here she was murdered by the invading Hungarians in 925. She was the spiritual mother of St Ulric.

*WIGBERT, ST, ab. August 13. AUG., p. 163

He was one of seven missionaries of this name who worked with St Boniface among the Germans, and became abbot of the monasteries of Fritzlar and Ohrdruf. d. *c.* 746. *Wigbertus.*

*WILFRID, ST, bp. October 12. OCT., p. 167

He was a Northumbrian, b. in 634, and after studying at Canterbury, Lyons, and Rome was made abbot of Ripon. Wilfrid worked zealously to substitute Roman for Celtic discipline in various matters, with notable success at the Synod of Whitby, but his enthusiasm led to serious troubles. He was appointed to the see of York, but was so long in taking it over that St Chad was put there in his place ; Wilfrid was put in possession in 669, but he incurred the enmity of King Egfrid, who encouraged St Theodore of Canterbury to divide the huge northern diocese. St Wilfrid made an appeal to Rome (the first recorded in English history) and was successful, but on his return he was banished by Egfrid. He settled down at Selsey and spent five years evangelizing the South Saxons, till in 686 he was recalled to York. But the difficulties continued and Wilfrid had again to go into exile and make a second appeal to Rome. It was not till 706 that he was restored to Ripon and Hexham, St John of Beverley remaining at York ; but he was then seventy-two years old and he d. soon after, in 709. St Wilfrid stands out as a man of unusual force of character, greatly respected by his many opponents, a fruitful missionary, and a notable upholder of the authority of the Roman See ; his feast is kept in the dioceses of Leeds, Portsmouth, Middlesbrough, Hexham, Liverpool, Northampton, Shrewsbury, and Nottingham. *Walfridus, Wilfridus.*

WILFRID THE YOUNGER, ST, bp. April 29. APR., p. 329

He was a disciple of St John of Beverley and succeeded him in the see of York. d. 744.

WILFRIDA, ST. September 9. SEPT., p. 103

St Wilfrida, or Wulfrida, was the mother of St Edith of Wilton by King Edgar (also venerated as a saint) in circumstances that are obscure and apparently not free from scandal. Wilfrida was professed as a nun by St Ethelwold after the birth of Edith. d. *c.* 988.

*WILGEFORTIS, ST, virg. and mart. July 20. JULY, p. 287

Wilgefortis (or *Liberata, Uncumber, Kummernis, Livrade,* etc.) is an entirely mythical personage round whom centres one of the most obviously false and preposterous of the pseudo-pious romances by which simple Christians have been deceived or regaled. She was represented as a girl who grew a beard and moustache so that she would not have to be married.

*WILLEHAD, ST, bp. November 8. NOV., p. 98

He was a Northumbrian who *c.* 765 went to preach the gospel to the Frisians. He worked hard, but with not much success, and in 780 Charlemagne sent him among the Saxons : he was the first missionary to cross the Weser. After the revolt of Witikind, when he had to fly, Willehad was consecrated bishop and fixed his see at Bremen, where he made many converts. d. 789. *Willehadus.*

WILLIAM, ST, ab. January 1. JAN., p. 20

Born at San Giuglio, near Novara, in 962. Became a Cluniac monk and was sent as abbot to revive the monastery of St Benignus at Dijon, which became the headquarters of a reform covering Burgundy, Lorraine, and Italy. At different times St William had to stand up to the Emperor St Henry, to King Robert of France, and to the Holy See. He refounded the abbey of Fécamp, which had importance for the ecclesiastical life of England, and died there in 1031. *Gulielmus.*

*WILLIAM, ST, ab. April 6. APR., p. 78
A canon regular in Paris who was invited to Denmark to help in the reform of the regular clergy there. He was made abbot of Eskilsoë, later at Ebelholt, and laboured at his difficult task for thirty years. d. 1203.

WILLIAM and other marts., **SS.** May 29. MAY, p. 351
William Arnaud and two other Dominicans, Stephen of Narbonne and another Franciscan, two Benedictines, four secular clerics, and a layman, all directly or indirectly connected with the Inquisition set up by the Synod of Toulouse in 1228, were treacherously murdered by Albigensians at Avignonet in 1242. c.c. 1866.

WILLIAM ANDLEBY, BD, and others. *See* York Martyrs.

WILLIAM CUFITELLA, BD. April 7. APR., p. 89
A Franciscan tertiary who lived in solitude for seventy years near Scicli in Sicily. He was a friend of Bd Conrad of Placentia. d. 1411. c.c. 1537.

WILLIAM FILBY and others, **BB.** *See* London Martyrs of 1582.

WILLIAM FIRMATUS, ST. April 24. APR., p. 282
In consequence of a dream warning him against avarice this William became a hermit at Laval and elsewhere in France, and made two pilgrimages to Jerusalem. d. *c.* 1090.

WILLIAM FREEMAN, BD, mart. August 13. AUG., p. 167
A secular priest from Yorkshire who was h.d.q. for his priesthood at Warwick in 1595. bd. 1929.

WILLIAM GNOFFI, BD. April 16. APR., p. 188
William of Polizzi in Sicily was a member of a mendicant community who submitted himself to severe bodily austerities in protection against the temptations to sinful sensuality to which he was subject. d. *c.* 1317.

WILLIAM HART, BD, mart. March 15. MAR., p. 264
B. at Wells, educated at Lincoln College, Oxford, and ordained in Rome in 1581. He worked on the mission in Yorkshire till he was betrayed by an apostate in the house of Bd Margaret Clitherow. Hanged for his priesthood at York in 1583.

WILLIAM HOWARD, BD, mart. December 29. DEC., p. 289
William was the grandson of Bd Philip Howard and was made Viscount Stafford after his marriage to Mary, sister of the last Baron Stafford, in 1637. He was a trusty, if undistinguished, supporter of King Charles I, and somewhat given to litigation. When over sixty he was denounced for complicity in the " Popish plot " invented by Oates and, after two years' imprisonment, was beheaded on Tower Hill in 1680. bd. 1929.

WILLIAM LACEY, BD, mart. August 22. AUG., p. 271
Mr and Mrs Lacey, Yorkshire gentlefolk, suffered persecution as recusants for fourteen years. After his wife's death Mr Lacey became a secular priest and was h.d.q. at York in 1582 for denying the Queen's supremacy in spiritual matters.

WILLIAM MARSDEN, BD, mart. April 25.   APR., p. 288

A secular priest, born in Lancashire, h.d.q. for his priesthood in the Isle of Wight in 1586. bd. 1929.

WILLIAM PINCHON, ST, bp. July 29.   JULY, p. 414

He was bishop of Saint-Brieuc in Brittany and his virtues and miracles were remarkable, but few details are known. d. 1234. cd. 1249.

WILLIAM SAULTEMOUCHE, BD. *See* James Salès.

WILLIAM SCOTT, BD, mart. May 30.   MAY, p. 368

Maurus William Scott, b. at Chigwell, was a Benedictine from the abbey of St Facundo in Spain. He was h.d.q. for his priesthood at Tyburn in 1612. bd. 1929.

WILLIAM TEMPIER, BD, bp. March 27.   MAR., p. 419

This William was chosen bishop of Poiters in 1184 and was a determined opponent of simony. His tomb became a place of pilgrimage because of the miracles reported there. d. 1197.

WILLIAM WARD, BD, mart. July 26.   JULY, p. 369

William Ward (*vere* Webster) was a secular priest from Westmorland. He was a missionary in England for thirty-three years, of which twenty were spent in prison. h.d.q. for his priesthood at Tyburn in 1641.

*WILLIAM OF BOURGES, ST, bp. January 10.   JAN., p. 129

William de Donjeon became a monk in the abbey of Pontigny and was abbot first of Fontaine-Jean and then of Châlis. The see of Bourges desiring to have a Cistercian for its archbishop, William was elected in 1200. He had difficulties with the king, with his chapter, and with Albigensian heretics, all of which he overcame by his patience and firmness. d. 1209.

WILLIAM OF FENOLI, BD. December 19.   DEC., p. 206

A confessor of the Carthusian Order : he was a lay-brother in the charterhouse *Casularum* in Lombardy. d. *c.* 1205. c.c. 1860.

WILLIAM OF GELLONE, ST. May 28.   MAY, p. 336

Duke William of Aquitaine fought against the Saracens and was regarded as the ideal Christian knight. He founded the abbey of Gellone, near Aniane, and in later life himself became a monk there. d. 812.

WILLIAM OF HIRSCHAU, BD, ab. July 4.   JULY, p. 42

He was second abbot of the refounded monastery of Hirschau in Würtemberg, and had to deal both with the depredations of the local count and with the building up of a stable community. His personal reputation attracted many suitable aspirants. He was one of the four chief German supporters of Pope St Gregory VII against the emperor Henry IV. Bd William was a man of very varied accomplishments : he invented a clock and wrote a treatise on music. d. 1091.

*WILLIAM OF MALEVAL, ST, ab. February 10.   FEB., p. 152

Having spent many years in penance and pilgrimages this William was set to reform a monastery near Pisa, but failed and began a community of his own on Monte Pruno. He was no more able to maintain discipline here, and retired to the solitude of Maleval, in the neighbourhood of Siena, in 1155. Here he was joined by a few followers, who afterwards became the congregation of Hermits of St William or Gulielmites ; they were later absorbed by the Hermits of St Augustine. St William d. 1157.

WILLIAM OF NORWICH, ST, mart. March 24.   MAR., p. 389

A twelve-year-old boy alleged to have been put to death by two Jews out of hatred of the faith at Norwich in 1144 ; the body was found hanging from a tree in Mousehold Wood. The case is not proved.

WILLIAM OF ROCHESTER, ST, mart. May 23.   DEC., p. 316

According to tradition William was a pilgrim from Perth who was murdered at Rochester in 1201. Miracles were alleged to have followed, and William's body was enshrined in the cathedral.

WILLIAM OF ROESKILDE, ST, bp. September 2.   SEPT., p. 24

He was an Englishman, chaplain to King Canute, by whom he was made bishop of Roeskilde. He boldly stood up for Christian life against the iniquities of King Sweyn Estridsen and was a zealous missionary among the pagan Danes. d. 1076.

WILLIAM OF TOULOUSE, BD. May 18.   MAY, p. 229

A confessor of the order of Hermit Friars of St Augustine, who d. in 1369. c.c. 1893.

†*WILLIAM OF VERCELLI, ST, ab. June 25.   JUNE, p. 340

Also called " of Monte Vergine." He was b. at Vercelli in 1085 and after living as a pilgrim and hermit came to Monte Virgiliano, now Monte Virgine, in the Apennines. Here he organized his disciples into a community of hermit-monks under a severe rule, and established similar houses, for men and for women, elsewhere. d. 1142. cd. 1160. St William's second successor adopted the Benedictine rule, and Monte Vergine still exists as an abbey *nullius* of the Subiaco congregation.

WILLIAM OF YORK, ST, bp. June 8.   JUNE, p. 109

William Fitzherbert, or " of Thwayt," was appointed to the see of York in 1142 ; the appointment was contested on the ground of simony, but eventually he was consecrated and enthroned with the permission of Pope Innocent II. But his enemies were active, he was negligent of his own interests, and in 1147 he was deposed. For some years he lived a very mortified life in retirement and was then restored to York by the Holy See, where he was joyfully received. d. 1154. cd. *c.* 1226. Among those who brought about the deposition of St William was St Bernard of Clairvaux.

*WILLIBALD, ST, bp. July 7.   JULY, p. 76

He was b. in Wessex. After travelling for six years in the East he became a monk at Monte Cassino and was then sent to join his kinsman St Boniface on the mission in Germany. He was made the first bishop of Eichstätt, where he converted many of the heathen and founded a large monastery at Heidenheim. d. *c.* 786. *Willebaldus.*

*WILLIBRORD, ST, bp. November 7.   NOV., p. 84

B. in Northumbria *c.* 658 and was a monk at Ripon and in Ireland. He set out *c.* 690 with eleven other English monks to preach the gospel to the Frisians and six years later was consecrated bishop in Rome ; he set up his chair at Utrecht. Under the protection of Pepin of Heristal, but with set-backs from the heathen Radbod, Willibrord made converts in all parts of Frisia, but his efforts in Denmark and Heligoland were unsuccesful ; he is venerated as the Apostle of the Frisians, though he was not the only prominent one (*e.g.* St Swithbert). In his old age he retired to the monastery he had founded at Echternach in Luxemburg, where he d. in 739. *Willibrordus.*

WILLIGIS, ST, bp. February 23. FEB., p. 322

Willigis was one of the outstanding ecclesiastical statesmen of the tenth century. Though of humble birth he was made archbishop of Mainz by the emperor Otto II and he played a leading part in the affairs of the empire, which owed much of its influence at this time to him. He spread the Faith in southern Scandinavia and built and restored many churches. Willigis had a serious dispute with the Bishop of Hildesheim, in which he admitted that he was wrong and retired gracefully. " His countenance was always unruffled, and his inward peace was even more remarkable." d. 1011.

WILTRUDIS, ST. January 6. JAN., p. 91

The widow of Berthold, Duke of Bavaria, who became a nun and founded the convent of Bergen bei Neuburg. d. *c.* 986.

WINCHESTER MARTYRS OF 1591, THE. July 7. JULY, p. 81

On July 7, 1591, at Winchester, Roger Dickenson, a secular priest of Lincoln, was h.d.q. for his priesthood, and a Hampshire farm-labourer, Ralph Milner, was hanged for helping him. In the same year and place, but on an unknown date, Laurence Humphrey, a young convert layman, was h.d.q. for speaking disrespectfully of Queen Elizabeth while ill and in delirium. All three bd. in 1929.

WINIBALD, ST, ab. December 18. DEC., p. 201

Winibald, an Englishman, became a missionary under St Boniface and, with his sister St Walburga, founded the double monastery of Heidenheim. His missionary work was hampered by bad health and by the ill will of his heathen neighbours. d. 761. *Winebaldus.*

*WINIFRED, ST, virg. and mart. November 3. Nov., p. 25

The spring of St Winifred (Winefride, Gwenfrewi) at Holywell in North Wales has been a place of pilgrimage and miracle for over a thousand years, but great uncertainty surrounds the saint. The core of her legends is that she was attacked by Caradog of Hawarden because she refused his amorous advances, that her wounds were healed (or she was restored to life) by St Beuno, that a spring gushed out where this happened, that she became a nun and abbess at Gwytherin, and d. *c.* 650. All the information about her is too late to enable any certainties to be established. Her feast is kept in the dioceses of Menevia and Shrewsbury. *Wenefrida.*

*WINOC, ST, ab. November 6. Nov., p. 72

Winoc and three other monks (said to have been British) were sent by St Bertinus to establish a monastery among the Morini at Wormhoult, from whence they evangelized the neighbourhood. d. 717 (?). In 1030 the abbot's relics were translated to a monastery at Berg-Saint-Winoc. *Winocus.*

WINWALOE, ST, ab. March 3. MAR., p. 37

He was a Breton, a disciple of St Budoc on Isle Verte, who founded the monastery of Landevenec by Brest, and is presumably the same Winwaloe whose name is found in varying forms in Cornwall and Wales. d. 532. *Guengaloeus.*

*WIRO, ST. May 8. MAY, p. 100

Wiro, born somewhere in the British Isles, was the companion of the missionaries St Plechelm and St Otger, first in their native land and then in the Netherlands. A monastery was afterwards founded on the site of their church at Odilienberg, near Ruremond. Seventh century.

WISTAN, ST. June 1.   JUNE, p. 6

Grandson of Wiglaf, king of Mercia. He is said to have been murdered in 849 by Bertulph of Mercia who had been preferred to the throne because of Wistan's youth. This led to a popular local cultus in Shropshire and at Evesham, whither Wistan's body was taken from Repton in Derbyshire.

WITHBURGA, ST, virg. July 8.   JULY, p. 95

She was the youngest of the holy daughters of King Anna of the East Angles ; she lived an austere life of solitude at Holkham and at Dereham in Norfolk ; d. March 17, 743.

WITTIKUND, BD. January 7.   JAN., p. 105

Duke of Westphalia and one of Charlemagne's most tenacious opponents until he was converted to Christ when accidentally present at Mass while moving in disguise among the Christian armies. d. c. 804.

*WIVINA, ST, virg. December 17.   DEC., p. 197

She was foundress and abbess of the convent of Bigarden, near Brussels. d. c. 1170.

*WOLFGANG, ST, bp. October 31.   OCT., p. 378

In 956 St Wolfgang became a teacher in the cathedral scho l at Trier ; later he joined the Benedictines and was made head master of the abbey school at Einsiedeln ; from thence he went as a missionary into I annonia, and in 972 was appointed bishop of Ratisbon (Regensburg). He governed the see for twenty-two years, founded the diocese of Prague, restored canonical life among his clergy, and was held in the greatest respect both by the people and at the imperial court : he educated the young prince who was afterwards the emperor St Henry. d. 994. cd. 1052. *Wolfgangus.*

WOLFHELM, BD, ab. April 22.   APR., p. 261

As abbot of Gladbach, Siegburg and then Brauweiler he was a considerable figure in the religious life of his time, but not many details of this career are known. d. 1091.

WOOLLOS, ST. *See* Gundleus.

WULFHILDA, ST, virg. September 9.   SEPT., p. 103

She founded the convent of Horton in Dorsetshire and later became abbess of Barking. d. c. 980.

*WULFRAM, ST, bp. March 20.   MAR., p. 338

An archbishop of Sens who resigned his see in order to be a missionary among the heathen Frisians, many of whom he converted. d. 703 (?). *Wulfrannus.*

WULFRIC, ST. February 20.   FEB., p. 288

Wulfric, born near Bristol, was a " hunting parson " of the Middle Ages who was turned to better ways by a conversation with a beggar. He became a hermit at Haselbury and d. there 1154. His tomb at Haselbury-Plucknett in Somerset used to be a place of pilgrimage.

*WULFSTAN, ST, bp. January 19.   JAN., p. 236

More usually *Wulstan*. B. at Long Itchington in Warwickshire, studied at Evesham and Peterborough, monk of Worcester, and bishop there in 1062. He was an unlearned man but strong, and refused to give up his see at the Norman conquest, so he was allowed to keep it. The suppression of the slave-trade from Bristol was attributed to his opposition. He rebuilt Worcester cathedral and d. 1095 at the age of eighty-seven. cd. 1203. His feast is kept in the dioceses of Birmingham, Clifton, and Northampton. *Wulstanus.*

A DICTIONARY OF SAINTS

*WULMAR, ST, ab.   July 20.   JULY, p. 296

He founded and ruled a monastery on his father's estate at a place in Picardy now called Samer, *i.e.* Saint-Vulmaire.   d. 689.   *Vulmarus.*

WULSIN, ST, bp.   January 8.   JAN., p. 120

He was the monk whom St Dunstan put in charge when he restored the abbey of Westminster ; Wulsin was blessed as abbot in 980 and became bishop of Sherborne in 993.   d. 1005.   *Vulsinus.*

XYSTUS. *See* Sixtus.

YORK MARTYRS OF 1597, THE. July 4. JULY, p. 49
The following martys suffered at York on July 4, 1597 : William Andleby, a secular priest who had worked in Yorkshire for twenty years, was h.d.q. for his priesthood ; Thomas Warcop, gentleman, was hanged for sheltering Mr Andleby ; Edward Fulthrop was h.d.q. for having been reconciled with the Church ; and another layman, Henry Abbot, was hanged for persuading to become a Catholic. All these were beatified in 1929. Other martyrs executed at York will be found herein under their own names.

ZACHARY, ST, pope.   March 15.   MAR., p. 261

He was a Calabrian Greek, elected pope in 741. He induced the Lombards not to attack Ravenna and Rome, sanctioned the assumption of the Frankish crown by Pepin, and was in touch with St Boniface in Germany, whom he greatly helped. In all his works he joined a conciliatory spirit with far-sighted wisdom. d. 752. *Zacharias.*

ZDISLAVA BERKA, BD. January 1.   JAN., p. 23

Venerated as a secular tertiary of the Order of Preachers. She was a noblewoman of Bohemia, whose husband was at first not properly appreciative of the virtues of his wife. She founded a Dominican priory, and d. 1252. c.c. 1907.

*ZENO, ST, bp. April 12.   APR., p. 133

Zeno was made bishop of Verona during the reign of Julian the Apostate and is still greatly honoured in that diocese. There are interesting particulars of him and his flock in some of his homilies that have survived. d. 371.

*ZENO, ST, mart. July 9.   JULY, p. 107

In the Roman Martyrology St Zeno is associated with the slaughter by Diocletian of the Christians who had been working on the building of the baths which bear that emperor's name.

*ZENO and ZENAS, SS, marts. June 23.   JUNE, p. 307

Zeno is said to have been a wealthy Christian at Philadelphia, near the Dead Sea, who was beheaded with his servant Zenas for overturning a pagan altar on which they were invited to sacrifice. *c.* 304.

*ZENOBIUS, ST, bp. May 25.   MAY, p. 301

He was a friend of St Ambrose and bishop of Florence, of which city he is the principal patron ; many stories are told of his miraculous powers. d. *c.* 390 (?).

†*ZEPHYRINUS, ST, pope and mart. August 26.   AUG., p. 316

He was elected pope in 199 and the persecution under Septimius Severus began soon after ; from his sufferings at this time he deserved the title of martyr, though he probably did not die (in 217) by the hand of the executioner.

*ZITA, ST, virg. April 27.   APR., p. 303

Zita, the patroness of domestic workers, was a maidservant in the family of a merchant of Lucca. She was not content with being a good servant, but was a good neighbour too, giving away her own clothes and food (and sometimes her master's) to the needy ; for a time she suffered from the ill will of her fellow-servants, who made mischief about her with the master, but eventually she became the friend and confidant of the whole household. Several miraculous happenings are related of St Zita. She d. in 1278, having served the same family for forty-eight years. *Zita.*

*ZOË, ST, mart. May 2.   MAY, p. 27

According to the Greek legend she was a Christian slave at Attalia in Asia Minor who, with her husband Hesperus, and two children, was roasted to death for refusing to eat food sacrificed to the gods *c.* 135. The name of Hesperus appears in the Roman Martyrology as Exsuperius.

*ZOILUS, ST, mart. June 27. JUNE, p. 361

He suffered with other martyrs at Cordoba during the persecution of Diocletian ; he is said to have been still only a youth.

*ZOZIMUS, ST, bp. March 30. MAR., p. 445

For thirty years he was an obscure monk at Santa Lucia, near Syracuse, and was then in a miraculous way chosen as abbot. Subsequently he became bishop of Syracuse, and d. at a great age there *c.* 660. *Zosimus.*

*ZOZIMUS, ST, ab. April 4. APR., p. 20

Abbot of a monastery near the Jordan, who figures as the confidant of St Mary of Egypt in the fictitious legend that grew up around her.

*ZOZIMUS, ST, pope. December 26. DEC., p. 253

Nothing is known of the personal life of St Zozimus, a Greek. His two years' pontificate was chiefly notable for a condemnation of Pelagianism. d. 418.

AND IN OTHER PLACES MANY
OTHER HOLY MARTYRS AND
CONFESSORS AND MAIDENS:

THANKS BE TO GOD

Printed by Offset in Great Britain by
Billing and Sons Ltd., Guildford and Esher